During the first four months of 1783, when the United States was neither wholly at war nor wholly at peace, a cluster of difficult problems confronted James Madison and his fellow delegates in Congress. Faced with the interlocking issues of finance, demobilization, and foreign affairs, Congress held many contentious sessions early in the year. The sparseness of the official journal enhances the value of the notes on debates, recorded by Madison, for illuminating the discussions.

Madison often doubted whether Congress, after maintaining for nearly eight years a sufficient union of the thirteen states to gain freedom from Great Britain, could harmonize their conflicting interests sufficiently to preserve the Confederation and render it solvent. In this period of transition the old problems of winning independence and replacing war with peace were succeeded by the new problems of devising tighter bonds of interdependence among the states and agreeing upon the revenue-producing measures required to "insure domestic tranquility." To attain these goals was Madison's main objective during the months spanned by the present volume.

THE PAPERS OF

James Madison

SPONSORED BY

The University of Chicago

AND

The University of Virginia

JAMES MADISON

CATHERINE FLOYD

THE PAPERS OF
James Madison

VOLUME 6

1 JANUARY 1783—30 APRIL 1783

EDITED BY

WILLIAM T. HUTCHINSON AND WILLIAM M. E. RACHAL

EDITORIAL STAFF

JEAN SCHNEIDER   ROBERT L. SCRIBNER

THE UNIVERSITY OF CHICAGO PRESS

CHICAGO AND LONDON

Standard Book Number: 226-11560-7
Library of Congress Catalog Card Number: 62-9114

The University of Chicago Press, Chicago 60637
The University of Chicago Press, Ltd., London

ADVISORY BOARD

CONTENTS

1783

CONTENTS

CONTENTS

CONTENTS

ILLUSTRATIONS

INTRODUCTION

During the first four months of 1783, when the United States was neither wholly at war nor wholly at peace, a cluster of difficult problems confronted James Madison and his fellow delegates in Congress. Although hostilities on land had virtually ended with the surrender of Cornwallis' army in October 1781, captures of American merchant ships continued off the Atlantic coast until mid-April 1783, or soon after British military headquarters in New York City received authentic word of the "Cessation of Arms" declared by King George III on 14 February of that year. Four days after issuing a similar proclamation on 11 April, Congress ratified the preliminary articles of peace between Great Britain and the United States. At long last the new nation was rid of armed conflict, but British troops remained on American soil, and the war would not officially end until the ratification of a definitive treaty of peace.

Madison and his congressional colleagues could not fully share in the public rejoicing occasioned by the arrival of the preliminary articles. Although these were generally satisfactory, the dispatches which accompanied them revealed how completely the American commissioners, in spite of a stipulation in the Treaty of Alliance between the United States and France, had neglected to consult with Vergennes during the negotiations. This affront to the court of France was the more serious because Congress, unable to procure adequate funds from the states and beset by importunate military and civilian creditors, had counted upon a large loan of money from King Louis XVI to replenish the empty treasury of the Confederation.

Faced with the interlocking issues of finance, demobilization, and foreign affairs, Congress held many contentious sessions early in 1783. The sparseness of the official journal enhances the value of the notes on debates, recorded by Madison, for illuminating the discussions. He often doubted whether Congress, after maintaining for nearly eight years a sufficient union of the thirteen states to gain freedom from Great Britain, could harmonize their conflicting interests sufficiently to preserve the Confederation and render it solvent. In this period of transition the old problems of winning independence and replacing war with peace were succeeded by the new problems of devising tighter bonds of interdependence among the states and agreeing upon the revenue-producing measures required to "insure domestic tranquility." To attain these goals was Madison's main objective during the months spanned by the present volume. In his words, "the idea of erecting our national independence on the ruins of public faith and national honor" is "horrid to every mind which retained either honesty or pride." He recognized that the unanimity of the delegates in deploring "the idea" did not signify their readiness to concur upon the means of avoiding the catastrophe.

Among the creditors of the Confederation those of the most anxious concern to Congress were the troops of Washington's main army in their cantonments bordering the lower Hudson River. On 6 January 1783 a deputation of their officers submitted a memorial asking Congress for pay long overdue and confirmation of the pledge of 1780 to extend half pay for life to officers who should serve for the duration of the war. Spurred by this petition, by the pressure of many influential civilians for the defaulted interest on their loan-office certificates, by Rhode Island's refusal to approve the proposed 5 per cent impost amendment of the Articles of Confederation, by Virginia's repeal of its ratification of that amendment, and by the warning of Robert Morris, superintendent of finance, that the treasury was empty and he would resign unless means of providing adequate funds were found by 31 May, Congress necessarily merged the issue of appeasing the army with the general problem of raising sufficient dependable revenue to restore public credit.

This problem was extraordinarily complex and baffling. The exact size of the debt was unknown; the amount of annual revenue which would be "adequate" was uncertain; and the income to be expected from each suggested tax was conjectural. The evidences of a considerable portion of this debt were a medley of formal and informal vouchers, or merely of claims based on lost or destroyed vouchers, for money, goods, or services furnished by a state or its citizens on behalf of a continental, rather than a strictly local, war-connected enterprise. Being nebulous and unsystematized, this "unliquidated" debt was rarely referred to by the delegates except as a problem of the future. Central in their attention was the "liquidated" debt. This mainly comprised the army pay and the principal of, and interest on, foreign loans and loan-office certificates. Compared with the unliquidated debt, these obligations totaled a fairly definite sum, even though they had been incurred in continental paper currency and state paper currencies of bewildering

degrees of depreciation, as well as in the specie of France, the Netherlands, and Spain.

From the outset of the debates Madison realized that the principal
of the debt could not be paid quickly. To obtain money enough to pay
the troops their just due, to meet the interest on the foreign and domestic loans, and to cover the day-by-day operational expenses of the government marked the limit of any reasonable expectation. Even these
charges amounted annually to about $3,000,000. Disagreeing with Mor-
ris and Hamilton, Madison opposed a deliberate perpetuation of the
principal of the debt as a prime means of strengthening the Union by
holding to it the allegiance of its major creditors. On this general issue
Madison insisted that good faith required Congress to assume for eventual payment every item of the unliquidated debt which was rightfully
a charge against the Confederation and not to permit a state to assume
for payment any part of the liquidated debt which was owed to its own
citizens. In his view, to honor the small creditors' just claims as scrupulously as those of the large would help equally to preserve the Union.

Within this general context Madison and his fellow delegates sought
in committees during January and February 1783 to prepare a revenue-
producing plan sufficiently impartial in its distribution of tax burdens
and modest in its requests for more congressional power to win quick
acceptance by Congress and thereafter by every state legislature, no
matter in what economic pursuits its constituents were mainly engaged. In his papers Madison accented the following definite questions as important subjects of debate both by committees and Congress:
whether (1) the long-recommended uniform 5 per cent impost should
be supplemented with tariff rates of varying amounts on specific articles; (2) the impractical and never applied land-evaluation base for
allocating financial requisitions, as required by the Articles of Confederation, should be supplanted by a population base; (3) the state-
by-state land values or censuses, whichever came to be the base, should
be frequently reviewed so as to reflect in the quotas the changing distribution of wealth or population; (4) the new quotas should be lessened for states which had recently been "overrun by the enemy" and
should also be made retroactive so as to alter the former quotas still
unpaid; (5) the "reasonable" continental war expenses, incurred by a
state without prior authorization of Congress, should be assumed; (6)
a state, at its option, should be permitted to pay the debts owed to its
own citizens by Congress; (7) first preference in debt payments should
be accorded to a particular group of creditors, such as the army or

the owners of loan-office certificates; (8) a definite source of revenue, such as tariff duties, should be reserved for the sole benefit of one group of creditors; (9) full pay for a specified number of years should be substituted for half pay for life to continental officers serving for the duration of the war; (10) Virginia and the five other states having "ancient" titles to most of the trans-Appalachian territory as far as the Mississippi River should concede that Great Britain's cession of that area in the preliminary articles of peace empowered Congress to raise money by selling the land or using it as security for floating new loans.

Madison ranked among the half-dozen most prominent members of Congress during the deliberations on these specific issues and on those of more general scope. Already well known as a skillful draftsman, he collated into a systematic whole the separate parts of the plan for restoring public credit and, after its adoption in amended form, prepared an "Address to the States," urging them to accept the recommendations. In origin both of these documents were committee reports. For this reason Madison was unable in the report to include several rejected proposals which he had favored or to exclude several others which he had opposed. Congress deleted from the plan, before approving it, two provisions much desired by him and other southern delegates. In later years the "Address" would be misinterpreted as evidence of Madison's warm approval of every proposal in the plan. On the contrary, his advocacy signified his belief that no better compromise could be effected among the sharply conflicting views of the delegates and that, if the states should reject the plan, the Union together with the other "fruits of the Revolution" most probably would be lost.

The maintenance of the Union was to Madison pre-eminently imperative—justifying him in supporting the proposed impost amendment in spite of its rejection by the Virginia legislature, in yielding on matters of detail for the sake of promoting accommodation, and even in ceasing to express his constitutional views after his insistence upon their correctness seemed only to exacerbate the divisions within Congress. During the debates in January and most of February on the extent of congressional control in the area of finance, his nationalism and that of Morris, Hamilton, and Wilson were closely attuned. Madison contended that Congress was not merely an administrative or executive agent of the states but had substantive legislative powers, including implied powers, within the general fields of authority delegated by the Articles of Confederation. Although he adhered to this stand during most of the controversy involving the British flag-of-truce ship "Amazon" and the encroachment of a Pennsylvania law upon the war power of Congress, he commented on 21 February, when the issue was peaceably adjusted, that the outcome proved "mildness" to be "the soundest policy." On the same day Madison spoke at length in support of Congress' broad legislative domain. In the perspective of the next two months, this address was his valedictory on that subject. Beginning in the closing week of February, his main objective became the attainment of compromise on fiscal issues rather than an acceptance of his constitutional views. He recognized that flexibility of means as a mode of reaching surpassingly important ends was of the essence of statesmanship.

Madison tempered his constitutional doctrines with realism. To be effective, a policy of government must not break sharply with the past, disregard the economic life of the present, or benefit only one geographic section of the United States or group in American society. Finding an acceptable "balance" or "equilibrium" was evidence of the highest patriotism. Fifty years later he characterized extremists who threatened to destroy the Constitution of the United States as those who either would "squeeze it to death" or "stretch it to death." If "the Articles of Confederation" is substituted for "the Constitution," this comment will aptly reflect his fear in 1783.

The papers in the present volume illustrate Madison's middle-of-the-road stand on issues other than those directly related to constitutional interpretation or fiscal policy. Congress should not attempt to assume jurisdiction over the trans-Appalachian territory or encourage separate statehood for Kentucky or Vermont without the consent of the seaboard states claiming title to those areas. The payment of private debts owed to British creditors and the return to Loyalists of their confiscated property, as stipulated in the preliminary articles of peace, should be delayed until after the conclusion of the definitive treaty and a release by the British of the slaves their army had harbored. Americans should take full advantage of the fact that they held far more prisoners of war than the British, by delaying a general cartel until the British had evacuated their posts on American soil in the West and had specified an early date of withdrawal from New York City and the Maine coast. In mid-March 1783 Madison was the more impressed with the wisdom of Washington because he peaceably averted a threatened mutiny at Newburgh by assuring the officers and troops that he would urge Congress to redress their just grievances. Madison approved the granting of leaves and furloughs rather than discharges to officers and men commissioned or enlisted for the duration of the war as a means of quieting their ominous impatience to go home and of holding firm to his own position that only the ratification of a definitive peace treaty could end the war.

Representing a state heavily dependent for its economic welfare upon overseas markets for tobacco, Madison naturally favored commercial treaties. At the same time he was restrained by his belief that they should be equally advantageous to all their signatories. How this reciprocity could be provided in a pact between the United States, possessing no colonies, and Great Britain, for example, possessing many colonies and barring most foreign trade with them, was one of the unsolved problems referred by Congress on 4 April to Madison and the other members of a committee instructed to propose "the proper arrangements to be taken in consequence of peace." These "arrangements," collectively known as a "peace establishment," should also include policies applicable to domestic, Indian, and foreign affairs.

During the first four months of 1783 the course of public affairs in Congress rarely gave Madison valid cause for rejoicing. Probably one of his keenest disappointments, although nothing in his writings supports this assumption, was the rejection by Congress on 23 January of his proposal, made on behalf of a committee, to acquire over thirteen hundred volumes and pamphlets for the use of the delegates. Besides reflecting his lifelong belief that men in high public office should be familiar with history, geography, and the art of government and diplomacy, and revealing his choice of books for conveying that knowledge, the bibliography foreshadowed the creation of the Library of Congress nearly twenty years later.

News from Virginia was depressing in its emphasis upon scarcity of money, uncollectable taxes, delinquency in supplying the financial quota owed to the Confederation treasury, and inability to forward more than a little of the pay due to Madison and his fellow delegates in Congress. Edmund Randolph, who wrote weekly when possible, had few other matters of interest to report because the legislature was not in session. He shared Madison's hope that the April elections would return enough "spotless" and "radical whigs" to the General Assembly to assure a willingness, not evident in the October 1782 session, to adopt "a liberal policy with respect to continental revenue" and the "collective interests of the whole" United States. To Madison's and Jefferson's great regret, Randolph decided that the increasing pressure of his own creditors obliged him to continue as attorney general rather than to seek the less remunerative and more exposed position of delegate to the General Assembly.

Although Madison was much disturbed by the somber outlook of public affairs during the winter and spring of 1783, he enjoyed his stay in Mrs. Mary House's boarding house more than ever before. He and Jefferson, who lived there for nearly eleven weeks, discovered a mutual congeniality of no little importance to the future history of Virginia and the United States, as well as to their own careers. Among the lodgers was the family of William Floyd, a delegate in Congress from New York. Floyd's daughter, Catherine, sixteen years of age and familiarly known as "Kitty," apparently was as happy in Madison's company as he was in hers. After they became engaged in April, he informed Jefferson, who had encouraged the courtship, that final arrangements for their marriage would be postponed until autumn. Except for an occasional brief absence because of illness, Madison had shared in every session of Congress for over three years. On 29 April he left Philadelphia with Kitty and her father to accompany them as far as New Brunswick on their homeward journey. This unique episode in Madison's early career, coinciding in time with a momentary calm in the stormy history of Congress during 1783, brings the present volume to an appropriate close.

EDITORIAL NOTE

Of the one hundred and eighty-five papers in this volume, one hundred and one have appeared either in whole or in part, but rarely with any annotation, in earlier editions of the writings of James Madison. One hundred and twenty-five of the documents are altogether or largely in his hand. These include seventy-three notes on debates in Congress covering eighty of its sessions, twelve committee reports or motions, thirty-seven letters, and three memoranda. Madison signed fourteen dispatches prepared by his colleagues in the Virginia delegation to Congress. Incoming mail comprised thirty-one letters addressed to him personally. Twelve letters were directed to the Virginia delegation. Besides these, there are three editorial notes about missing correspondence.

The editors gratefully acknowledge the aid extended by the late Douglass Adair, Julian P. Boyd of the Papers of Thomas Jefferson, the Honorable J. Rives Childs, Jasper E. Crane, Fulmer Mood, Rear Admiral Schuyler N. Pyne, U.S.N. (Ret.), Robert Rosenthal of the University of Chicago Library, Nathaniel N. Shipton of the William L.

Clements Library, University of Michigan, Miss Gayle Thornbrough of the Manuscript Division, Library of Congress, and Miss Anne Freudenberg and the late John Cook Wyllie of the University of Virginia Library. Editing in the University of Chicago office benefited from the successive services of Roderick Brumbaugh, Miss Carole B. Romm, and Miss Cheryl Seaman as project assistants.

EDITORIAL METHOD

ABBREVIATIONS

FC   File copy. Any version of a letter or other document retained by the sender for his own files and differing little if at all from the completed version. A draft, on the other hand, is a preliminary sketch, often incomplete and varying frequently in expression from the finished version.

JM   James Madison.

LC   Library of Congress.

MS   Manuscript. A catchall term describing numerous reports and other papers written by Madison, as well as items sent to him which were not letters.

NA   National Archives.

PCC Papers of the Continental Congress, a collection in the National Archives.

RC   Recipient's copy. The copy of a letter intended to be read by the addressee. If the handwriting is not that of the sender, this fact is mentioned in the headnote.

Tr   Transcript. A copy of a manuscript, or a copy of a copy, customarily handwritten, made considerably later than the date of the manuscript and ordinarily not by its author or by the person to whom the original was addressed. The "Force Transcripts," made under the direction of Peter Force in the mid-nineteenth century, are those most frequently used in the present series.

SHORT TITLES FOR BOOKS

Only those books used very frequently, and a few whose titles are so long as to necessitate an abbreviation, have been given short titles. This list applies only to Volume VI.

Boyd, *Papers of Jefferson.* Julian P. Boyd *et al.*, eds., *The Papers of Thomas Jefferson* (18 vols. to date; Princeton, N.J., 1950——).

Brant, *Madison.* Irving Brant, *James Madison* (6 vols.; Indianapolis and New York, 1941–61).

Burnett, *Letters.* Edmund C. Burnett, ed., *Letters of Members of the Continental Congress* (8 vols.; Washington, 1921–36).

Cal. of Va. State Papers. William P. Palmer *et al.,* eds., *Calendar of Virginia State Papers and Other Manuscripts* (11 vols.; Richmond, 1875–93).

Fitzpatrick, *Writings of Washington.* John C. Fitzpatrick, ed., *The Writings of George Washington, from the Original Sources, 1745–1799* (39 vols.; Washington, 1931–44).

Gwathmey, *Historical Register of Virginians.* John H. Gwathmey, *Historical Register of Virginians in the Revolution: Soldiers, Sailors, Marines, 1775–1783* (Richmond, 1938).

Hansard's Parliamentary Debates. William Cobbett, ed., *The Parliamentary History of England from the Earliest Period to the Year 1803* (36 vols.; London, 1806–20; continued as *Hansard's Parliamentary Debates*).

Heitman, *Historical Register Continental.* F. B. Heitman, *Historical Register of Officers of the Continental Army during the War of the Revolution* (Washington, 1914).

Hening, *Statutes.* William Waller Hening, ed., *The Statutes at Large; Being a Collection of All the Laws of Virginia, from the First Session of the Legislature, in the Year 1619* (13 vols.; Richmond and Philadelphia, 1819–23).

JCC. Worthington Chauncey Ford *et al.,* eds., *Journals of the Continental Congress, 1774–1789* (34 vols.; Washington, 1904–37).

JCSV. H. R. McIlwaine *et al.,* eds., *Journals of the Council of the State of Virginia* (4 vols. to date; Richmond, 1931——).

JHDV. Journal of the House of Delegates of the Commonwealth of Virginia; Begun and Held at the Capitol, in the City of Williamsburg. Beginning in 1780, the portion after the semicolon reads, *Begun and Held in the Town of Richmond. In the County of Henrico.* The journal for each session has its own title page and is individually paginated. The edition used is the one in which the journals for 1777–1786 are brought together in two volumes, with each journal published in Richmond in 1827 or 1828, and often called the "Thomas W. White reprint."

McIlwaine, *Official Letters,* H. R. McIlwaine, ed., *Official Letters of the Governors of the State of Virginia* (3 vols.; Richmond, 1926–29).

Madison, *Letters* (Cong. ed.). [William C. Rives and Philip R. Fendall, eds.], *Letters and Other Writings of James Madison* (published by order of Congress; 4 vols.; Philadelphia, 1865).

Madison, *Papers* (Gilpin ed.). Henry D. Gilpin, ed., *The Papers of James Madison* (3 vols.; Washington, 1840).

Papers of Madison. William T. Hutchinson, William M. E. Rachal, *et al.,* eds., *The Papers of James Madison* (6 vols. to date; Chicago, 1962——).

Pa. Archives. Samuel Hazard *et al.,* eds., *Pennsylvania Archives* (9 ser., 138 vols.; Philadelphia and Harrisburg, 1852–1949).

Swem and Williams, *Register.* Earl G. Swem and John W. Williams, eds., *A Register of the General Assembly of Virginia, 1776–1918, and of the Constitutional Conventions* (Richmond, 1918).

Syrett and Cooke, *Papers of Hamilton.* Harold C. Syrett and Jacob E. Cooke, eds., *The Papers of Alexander Hamilton* (15 vols. to date; New York, 1961——).

Va. Gazette. Virginia Gazette, or, the American Advertiser (Richmond, James Hayes, 1781–86).

Wharton, *Revol. Dipl. Corr.* Francis Wharton, ed., *The Revolutionary Diplomatic Correspondence of the United States* (6 vols.; Washington, 1889).

MADISON CHRONOLOGY

1783

January–April	JM, delegate to Congress, continues to reside in Philadelphia.
2 January	JM moves instructions concerning consular convention with France.
6 January	JM appointed member of grand committee to consider memorial from army.
9 January	JM appointed member of committee to confer with Robert Morris on land evaluation as basis for allocating financial quotas among states.
13 January	JM appointed member of grand committee to consider land-evaluation problems.
17 January	JM appointed member of committee to treat of jurisdictional controversy with Pennsylvania over cargo of ship "Amazon."
20 January	Great Britain concludes preliminary articles of peace with France and Spain.
20 January	In Paris, John Adams and Benjamin Franklin sign "Declaration" suspending hostilities.
ca. 22 January	Theodorick Bland, Jr., a Virginia delegate to Congress, returns to Philadelphia.
22 January	Congress ratifies contract on loans from Louis XVI of France.
23 January	JM's recommended list of works to form library for Congress rejected.
23 January	Congress ratifies treaty of commerce and convention with Netherlands.
24 January	Congress receives reports on army memorial and "Amazon" issue.

24 January	Morris informs Congress that unless provision for adequate revenue is made by 31 May, he will resign as superintendent of finance.
25 January	Congress resolves to seek from states sufficient money and sources of revenue to fund United States debt.
26 January	Thomas Jefferson leaves Philadelphia, intending to embark at Baltimore for France as peace commissioner.
27 January	Arthur Lee, a delegate to Congress from Virginia, returns to Philadelphia.
27 January	Congress learns Virginia has repealed ratification of proposed impost amendment and can pay little of financial quota in 1783.
28 January	JM delivers major speech on need by Congress for general funds.
5 February	News is current in Philadelphia that on 30 November 1782 commissioners of Great Britain and United States signed preliminary articles of peace.
6 February	John Francis Mercer, a delegate from Virginia, enters Congress.
10 February	Congress upholds contracts of its agents with merchants-capitulant of Yorktown against charges by Virginia.
14 February	Congress instructs Jefferson to delay departure for France.
14 February	George III of Great Britain proclaims "Cessation of Arms."
18 February	Congress instructs Morris to submit analysis of Confederation debt.
20 February	JM and five other delegates in Congress informally discuss critical financial situation and unrest in army.
21 February	"Amazon" controversy settled amicably.
21 February	JM delivers major speech on nature and extent of powers of Congress.

21 February	JM appointed to special committee to report plan for restoring public credit.
21 February	British House of Commons censures terms of peace with United States.
24 February	Earl of Shelburne's ministry forced to resign.
26 February	Jefferson returns to Philadelphia.
26 February	JM's motion on outrages by enemy adopted by Congress.
26 February	JM in notes on debates summarizes presumed position of each state on debt and revenue issues.
26–27 February and 3 March	Congress debates partial reports of committee on restoring public credit.
6 March	JM's draft of full report on restoring public credit received, amended, and ordered by Congress to be printed.
10–11 March	Morris submits analysis of Confederation debt, and comments on report on restoring public credit.
10–15 March	George Washington averts threatened mutiny in army.
12 March	Congress is informed that Gustavus III of Sweden solicits treaty of amity and commerce with United States.
12 March	Congress receives official copy of preliminary articles of peace with Great Britain.
12–24 March	Congress frequently debates preliminary articles of peace, especially the "secret" article, and conduct of American negotiators.
18–21 March	Congress further debates and amends report on public credit.
19 March	JM delivers his principal speech on conduct of American peace negotiators.
19 March	Morris declares public credit vanished, new European loans impossible, and money to pay army lacking.
20 March	Virginia delegates reveal instructions to oppose return of confiscated property to Loyalists.

22 March	Congress commutes lifetime half pay promised to continental army officers serving for duration of war into five years of full pay.
24 March	Informed that Great Britain, France, and Spain have signed preliminary articles of peace, Congress moves to end hostilities at sea.
27–28 March	JM offers amendments to report on restoring public credit.
29 March	JM's motion to require superintendent of finance to submit detailed annual report on receipts and expenditures rejected by Congress.
29 March	Congress appoints committee to inquire into proceedings of department of finance.
29 March	JM submits report on funds of secretary for foreign affairs.
29 March	Lacking instructions from London, British commanders in New York City refuse to end hostilities at sea.
1 April	Duke of Portland's coalition ministry assumes office in Great Britain.
1 April	Congress cancels Jefferson's mission to France.
1 April	Lee leaves Philadelphia for Virginia.
4 April	JM appointed to committee to recommend peacetime policies in all areas of congressional jurisdiction.
4 April	Congress is offered site in New York for permanent capital.
4 April	Congress requests states to halt troop recruitment and appoints committee to recommend other means of reducing military expenses.
7 April	Elections to Virginia General Assembly held.
9 April	Congress is informed by British commanders that enemy cruisers off coasts are being recalled.
9 April	JM appointed to committee to investigate title to trans-Appalachian territory.

10 April	Virginia delegates suggest in letter to Governor Benjamin Harrison that state offer Congress site for permanent capital.
11 April	Robert R. Livingston's proposed proclamation ending hostilities amended and adopted by Congress.
12 April	Jefferson leaves Philadelphia to return to Virginia.
12 April	JM appointed chairman of committee to report on general state of instructions regarding commercial treaties.
12 April	JM's recommendation against ratifying preliminary articles of peace is rejected, and Congress ratifies the articles.
17 April	JM's effort to amend report on restoring public credit is unsuccessful.
18 April	Congress adopts the plan for restoring public credit.
18 April	JM appointed chairman of committee to draft address to accompany plan for restoring public credit.
18 April	Congress resumes debate on status of western lands.
21 April	JM and supporters unsuccessful in move to have Congress assume "reasonable" but unauthorized expenses of states overrun by enemy.
21 April	Harrison issues proclamation enjoining Virginians to desist from hostilities with enemy.
22 April	JM reveals his engagement to Catherine Floyd in a letter to Jefferson.
22 April	Washington writes his first letter to JM.
23 April	Congress authorizes Washington to furlough or discharge officers and men engaged for duration of war.
24 April	Congress begins the demobilization of Nathanael Greene's southern army.
24–26 April	JM's draft of "Address to the States, by the United States in Congress Assembled" amended and unanimously adopted.
29 April	JM leaves Philadelphia to accompany Catherine Floyd and family to New Brunswick, N.J.

THE PAPERS OF

James Madison

Notes on Debates

MS (LC: Madison Papers). For a description of the manuscript of Notes on Debates and a discussion of JM's reasons for recording what was said and done in Congress, see *Papers of Madison*, V, 231–34.

Wednesday Jany. 1st. 1783

The decision of the controversy between Connecticut & Penna. was reported.[1]

The communications, made from the Minister of France, concurred with other circumstances in effacing the impressions made by Mr. Jay's letter & Marbois's inclosed.[2] The vote of thanks to Ct. Rochambeau passed with unanimity & cordiality & afforded a fresh proof that the resentment agst. France had greatly subsided.[3]

[1] In his old age JM wrote "Connecticut" above "Cont." without deleting the abbreviation. Although the "decision" is not noted in the printed journal of Congress for 1 January, the record kept by the clerk of the congressional "court of commissioners" sitting at Trenton, N.J., from 12 November until 30 December 1782, when the five commissioners unanimously decided in favor of Pennsylvania, was spread on the journal of 3 January 1783 (*JCC*, XXIV, 6–32). See also *Papers of Madison*, V, 289–90; 291, n. 12; 416; 419, n. 23.

[2] For the dispatch of John Jay and the intercepted letter of the Marquis de Barbé-Marbois, secretary of the French legation and consul of France in Philadelphia, see *ibid.*, V, 436; 438, n. 5; 441; 443, n. 2; 466. On 1 January Congress listened to Robert R. Livingston's written summary of his conversations on 30 and 31 December with the Chevalier de La Luzerne, minister plenipotentiary of King Louis XVI to the United States, and to La Luzerne's letter of 31 December 1782 to Elias Boudinot, president of Congress. These communications stressed "the good faith" of France in the peace negotiations, her determination to prosecute the war "with vigor" to a successful conclusion, and her appreciation of the resolutions of Congress and several of the state governments declaring their firm adherence to the alliance. These assurances evidently allayed the distrust of French policy aroused by the dispatches of Jay and Barbé-Marbois (Wharton, *Revol. Dipl. Corr.*, VI, 177–82, 187–88).

During or shortly after a visit at Montpelier, 19–23 April 1830, Jared Sparks recorded: "In speaking of Mr. Jay's suspicions respecting the policy of the French court at the time of making peace, Mr. Madison observed that 'he had two strong traits of character,—suspicion and religious bigotry'" (*Va. Mag. Hist. and Biog.*, LX [1952], 267). See also JM Notes, 19 March 1783.

[3] For the Comte de Rochambeau, who was about to leave Philadelphia to embark at Annapolis for France, see *Papers of Madison*, V, 344, n. 7; 429, n. 5; 443, n. 3. For the two resolutions of "thanks," see *JCC*, XXIV, 1–2. In a letter of 12 April 1783, Elias Boudinot, president of Congress, asked Lafayette why Rochambeau had left America "without taking the least Notice of" the resolutions, or even acknowledging Boudinot's covering letter (Burnett, *Letters*, VI, 136).

3

To James Madison, Sr.

RC (LC: Madison Papers). Cover addressed by JM to "Col. James Madison Orange County Virginia." Docketed by James Madison, Sr., "Jany 1. 1783." In his old age JM wrote "Madison Jr Jany 1. 1783" on the cover above "Jany. 1: 1783," which also is in his hand.

Jany 1st. 1783

HOND SIR

Mr. Fitzpatrick[1] this moment called on me with notice of his having seen you and b[e]ing desired to let me know that you & the family were well. I had the pleasure of hearing the same by Mr. Jefferson who arrived here a few days ago[2] Mr. F. sets out so quickly that I have but barely time to tell you that I am well & to inclose you a bundle of Newspapers, from which you will be able [to] gather all the late news. The negociations for peace are said to be going on under the late Commission to Mr. Oswald which authorises him to treat with Commisrs. from the *13 United States*.[3] Mr. Jefferson will depart in a little time, in order to give his aid in case it be in season.[4] The insidiousness & instabil-[it]y of the B. cabinet forbid us to be sanguine, especially as the releif of Gibralter was posterior to Oswald's Commission, and the interests to be adjusted among the belligerent parties are extremely complicated.[5]

I am with great affection yr. dutf. son

J MADISON JR.

[1] Probably Thomas Fitzpatrick (d. 1787), a native of Ireland who was brought as a child to Pennsylvania and had settled in Albemarle County, Va., by 1750 (Albemarle County Court Records, Will Book 3, p. 35, and Deed Book 1, p. 229, microfilm in Va. State Library; Reba Fitzpatrick Lea, *The "Belfield" Fitzpatricks and "Elim" Colemans: Their History and Genealogy* [Lynchburg, Va., 1958], p. 12).

[2] Having been reappointed by Congress as a peace commissioner, Thomas Jefferson reached Philadelphia on 27 December. See *Papers of Madison*, V, 232; 473; 474, n. 7.

[3] For the revised commission, dated 21 September 1782, of Richard Oswald from King George III, see *ibid.*, V, 418, n. 17.

[4] On 26 January Jefferson left Philadelphia to go to Baltimore, whence he expected to embark for France (JM to Randolph, 28 Jan. 1783).

[5] See n. 3. A British fleet, commanded by Admiral Lord Howe, had forced the Spanish and French in mid-October 1782 to raise their siege of Gibraltar. See *Papers of Madison*, V, 198, n. 10.

Instructions to Benjamin Franklin *in re* Consuls

MS (NA: PCC, No. 25, II, 177). Undated.

EDITORIAL NOTE

In a dispatch of 23 October 1782, Thomas Barclay, consul of the United States in France, informed Congress that the exequatur issued to him by the court of France barred him from appointing vice consuls and consular agents as long as he was consul rather than consul general. He also pointed out that Article III of the proposed consular convention between the United States and France, adopted by Congress on 25 January 1782, "interdicted" the consular appointees "from all traffick or commerce for their own or another's benefit." In Barclay's judgment this restriction would cause merchants in the ports to decline to serve as consuls, even though they were the persons best qualified for appointment (NA: PCC, No. 91, I, 13–15). See also *Papers of Madison*, III, 201, n. 1; *JCC*, XXII, 48.

On 24 December 1782, upon receiving Barclay's dispatch, Congress referred it to a committee comprising Thomas FitzSimons (Pa.), Alexander Hamilton (N.Y.), and John Lewis Gervais (S.C.) (NA: PCC, No. 185, III, 50; No. 186, fol. 76). This committee recommended on 2 January 1783 that the proposed consular convention be suspended, that Barclay be commissioned as consul general, that he be empowered to appoint as many vice consuls and consular agents in French ports "as he shall deem necessary," and that they be permitted to trade as merchants "till Congress shall otherwise direct" (*JCC*, XXIV, 3). For JM's purpose in offering the present motion, see JM Notes, 6 Jan. 1783.

[2 January 1783]

That the Minister Plenipo: at the Ct. of Versailles[1] be instructed to propose that the plan of the Convention respecting consular powers[2] may be so varied[3] as to leave the parties at liberty to prohibit or permit to their respective Consuls, the privilege of carrying on commerce on their private accts. and also to propose such other variations as may be consequent thereon.[4]

[1] Benjamin Franklin.

[2] See ed. n.

[3] From "Versailles" through "varied," JM originally wrote, "be authorized & instructed so to vary the propos plan of the Convention regulating the consular powers."

[4] The printed journal of Congress leaves the erroneous impression that JM's motion was an addendum to, rather than a proposed substitute for, the report of the FitzSimons committee. See ed. n.; *JCC*, XXIV, 3–4. On 2 January Congress laid over the report and JM's motion for decision at a later date. In his Notes on Debates for 2 January, JM recorded only, "Nothing requiring notice." For the next mention of the subject of consular powers, see JM Notes, 6 Jan. 1783.

Notes on Debates

MS (LC: Madison Papers). For a description of the manuscript of Notes on Debates, see *Papers of Madison*, V, 231–34.

Friday 3d. Jany.

The vote of thanks to the Minister of France which passed yesterday was repealed in consequence of his havg expressed to the President a desire that no notice might be taken of his conduct as to the point in question & of the latter's communicating the same to Congress.[1] The temper of Congress here again manifested the transient nature of their irritation agst. France[2]

The motion of Mr. Howel put on the Secret Journal gave Congress a great deal of vexation. This expedient for baffling his scheme of raising a ferment in his state & exposing the foreign transactions was adopted only in the last resort; it being questioned by some whether the articles of confederation warranted it.[3]

The answer to the note of the French Minister passed unanimously & was a further testimony of the abatement of the effects of Mr. Jay's letter &c.[4]

The proceedings of the Court in the dispute between Cont. & Pa. were after debates as to the meaning of the confederation in directing such proceeding to be lodged among the acts of Congress entered at large on the Journals.[5] It was remarked that the Delegates from Cont. particularly Mr. Dyer were more captious on the occasion than was consistent with a perfect acquiescence in the decree.[6]

---

[1] On 9 December 1782 Robert R. Livingston, secretary for foreign affairs, informed Elias Boudinot, president of Congress, that La Luzerne had sought and received "assurances," presumably from the Comte de Rochambeau and the Marquis de Vaudreuil, of "such a force" of warships to "be detached from the West Indies as would be adequate to the protection of the trade upon this coast during the winter" (Wharton, *Revol. Dipl. Corr.*, VI, 121–22). See also *Papers of Madison*, V, 429, n. 5. For the resolution thanking La Luzerne for this "new proof of his attachment to the welfare of the United States," see *JCC*, XXIV, 3, and n. 1.

In requesting Boudinot to have the resolution with its allusion to the disposition of the French fleet during the winter "repealed," La Luzerne may have been motivated by considerations of military security. Even though the resolution had been entered only in the manuscript secret journal of Congress, the proclivity of David Howell to disclose confidential information afforded a warning much too recent to go unheeded.

[2] The "irritation" had been caused late in December 1782 by John Jay's dispatch questioning the good faith of France toward the United States in the peace negotiations and by the intercepted dispatch of Barbé-Marbois opposing the Ameri-

can claim to share in the Newfoundland fisheries. See *Papers of Madison*, V, 436; 438, nn. 5, 7. Marbois's opposition only reflected that of the Comte de Vergennes on the same issue (Richard B. Morris, *The Peacemakers: The Great Powers and American Independence* [New York, 1965], pp. 325–26).

3 For the case of David Howell (R.I.), see Index to *Papers of Madison*, V, under Howell, David, secret proceedings of Congress. On 27 and 31 December 1782, Howell, and on 3 January 1783, his Rhode Island colleagues, Jonathan Arnold and John Collins, introduced motions in Congress to send Governor William Greene of Rhode Island copies or extracts of dispatches to Robert R. Livingston or Robert Morris from ministers, agents, or other friends of the United States in Europe (*JCC*, XXIII, 832–33, 837; XXIV, 3, 32–34). Although the delegates from Rhode Island asserted that Howell wished to use these documents only to demonstrate the accuracy of his sanguine statements about the credit of the United States abroad, the motions were vexatious. They "frequently interrupted and delayed the important business of Congress," usually included quotations from confidential communications, and the quotations, being out of context, were "liable to misguide." The "expedient" of entering these motions "only in the manuscript Secret (Domestic) Journal, and in Secret Journal, No. 8"—thereby preserving their secret nature by excluding them from the journal to be printed—came as an unpleasant surprise to the Rhode Island delegation and was of doubtful constitutionality (*JCC*, XXIV, 32, n. 2, 36; Burnett, *Letters*, VII, 10). See also Wharton, *Revol. Dipl. Corr.*, VI, 194–97.

Article IX of the Articles of Confederation stipulated that Congress "shall publish the Journal of their proceedings monthly, except such parts thereof relating to treaties, alliances or military operations, as in their judgment require secrecy" (*JCC*, XIX, 220; XX, 588; *Papers of Madison*, III, 148, n. 1; 339 40; 340, n. 1). The motions of the Rhode Island delegates related only indirectly to any of these three exceptions. For this reason, confining a record of the motions to the secret journal denied these delegates their probable constitutional right to submit an official "transcript" of their motions to the legislature of their state and also appeared, in effect, to infringe their guaranteed right of "Freedom of speech and debate in Congress" (*JCC*, XIX, 215, 220–21).

Following what probably was a long debate, Congress decided to postpone further consideration of the issue and to refer to a committee the motions of the Rhode Island delegates and several suggestions for amending the motions or for amending the proposed amendments thereto (*JCC*, XXIV, 32 36). This committee, with John Taylor Gilman (N.H.) as its chairman, reported on 13 January (NA· PCC, No. 186, fol. 77). See also *JCC*, XXIV, 45 46, 46, n. 1.

4 See n. 2. On 3 January a translation of La Luzerne's "note" of 31 December 1782 to Congress was read to the delegates. The French minister conveyed "the satisfaction which the King his master has felt" because Congress not only had refused to negotiate terms of peace with British emissaries in America but was also holding firm in every other respect to the terms of the alliance with France. Although La Luzerne was hopeful "that this just and wise as well as prudent advantageous conduct" would soon bring "a happy termination" of the war, he mentioned recent British naval victories as a warning to Congress not to slacken its "preparations for an ensuing campaign." Congress thereupon directed Livingston to express to La Luzerne the "great pleasure" occasioned by his communication and the "abhorrence" with which all the delegates regarded "every act derogatory to the principles of the alliance" (*JCC*, XXIV, 4–6).

5 For the unanimous decision on 30 December 1782 in favor of Pennsylvania rendered by the commissioners appointed by Congress to adjudicate the boundary dispute between that state and Connecticut, see *Papers of Madison*, V, 419, n. 23. The "debates" on 3 January evidently centered upon the meaning of the provi-

sion of Article IX of the Articles of Confederation which directed that "the judgment or sentence and other proceedings" of a court adjudicating a dispute between states should be "lodged among the acts of congress for the security of the parties concerned" (*JCC*, XIX, 218).

6 For Eliphalet Dyer, see *Papers of Madison*, V, 289; 292, n. 16. As representatives of a state already embarrassed by the adverse decision of the court, he and his Connecticut colleagues may have insisted that to "lodge" the pertinent papers did not entail their being "entered at large on the Journals" for publication.

From Edmund Randolph

RC (LC: Madison Papers). Owing to fading of the ink, considerable portions of the letter are scarcely legible. Cover addressed to "The honble James Madison jr Esqr of congress Philadelphia." Docketed by JM, "Jany. 3d. 1783."

RICHMOND. Jany. 3. 1783.

MY DEAR SIR

The post of yesterday brought your two favors of the 17th. and 24th of decr.[1]

The prospect of softening the states who were at first the most obdurate against the impost of five per cent on imported and captured goods increases the discontent, which the repeal of our law excited in my mind, and which I communicated to you in a former letter.[2] I cannot remember whether I then suggested those reasons, which were said to have accomplished the repeal. But as the enumeration of them is short I will endanger a repetition, by informing you, that the act was considered as a measure but ill concocted, having passed at Stanton, the asylum of the assembly from Tarlton's horses,[3] that the most striking mark of this ill concoction was the consignment of funds to the disposal of congress, not warranted by the confederation, that altho' the objections of a present incapacity to enforce the plan of the confederation for raising a continental revenue was perhaps powerful,[4] yet it was better to submit to this evil, than to encourage congress to persist in[?] that scheme of supplying the treasury of the U S, directed by it;[5] and that a revenue, raised by such a duty would render congress, too remote from the controuling influence of separate states. I cannot learn that any question was made upon the power of Virginia to revoke her grant. On the first reflection, I conceived, that she possessed it not.[6] But as the grant was founded on the condition of the concurrence of the other states, as that concurrence was expected in a reasonable time, as Virginia

8

was not to be constantly bound, until negotiations with the opposing states should convert them,[7] even if her own circumstances might change, it would seem as if the positive refusal of R.I. & M. had absolved her from her part of the Engagement.[8] But alas! whether the power of abrogation remained with the assembly or not, to what tribunal will you appeal, if they persist in asserting it?[9] Will you again deputize? If you do, it may be well to defer the election of the members till about April, as the assembly will not sit before May, and those members should be fitted to the probable temper of the new delegates.[10]

Colo. Bland left my house yesterday morning, on the 12th day from which time you may expect him at Philadelphia. He carries with him a list of the acts of the last session. The acts themselves shall be forwarded, as soon as they are published.[11]

I have heard that it appeared from the report of the financier that congress exceeded the two hundred millions which they prescribed as the limit of the paper emissions before that of March 1781. It came from your brother, who attended the last assembly, and astonishes me, being so repugnant to the declaration of congress, and what I supposed to be the fact.[12]

Oswald's new commission has revived the hope of peace.[13] But on what ground does it rest? On the slippery one of Shelburne's finess,[14] and precarious hold of office, and the jarring pretensions of the various powers, concerned in the war. Has the relief of Gibraltar given no retrograde motion to S's affectation of peace?[15] Has the arrival of the Russ[ian] fleet with naval stores added nothing to his expectations from the navy?[16] Or do the exertions of America furnish him with fresh cau[se] of alarm? For my own part, I view peace at a great distance, and will for ever suffocate in my own mind the belief of its approach, until G.B. shall have gone thro' the quackeries[?] of administration from every faction, and the people themselves refuse further succours.

The rising of the assembly[17] produces a relapse into former barrenness, leaving me nothing to add, than assurances of the warmest friendship.

[1] *Papers of Madison*, V, 414–16; 448–50.

[2] This paragraph recapitulates Randolph's comments about the repeal on 6 and 7 December by the Virginia General Assembly of its ratification of the proposed impost amendment to the Articles of Confederation in his letter of 13 December 1782 to JM (*ibid.*, V, 401).

[3] That is, the cavalry commanded by Lieutenant Colonel Barnastre Tarleton. See *Papers of Madison*, III, 96, n. 6; 159, n. 5; 160, n. 6.

[4] For the impracticality of raising revenue by employing the method stipulated

in Article VIII of the Articles of Confederation, see *ibid.*, IV, 56, n. 5; 122; 431, n. 1; V, 295, n. 10.

5 Following "congress to," Randolph wrote one or two words on top of another one or two words. The outcome being virtually illegible, "persist in" is only a doubtfully accurate decipherment of the jumbled letters. The objection to having the proposed impost collected by appointees of Congress rather than of each state had often been advanced by opponents of the amendment. See *ibid.*, V, 416, n. 3.

6 In his letter of 13 December 1782 to JM, Randolph had questioned the constitutionality of the annulment by the Virginia General Assembly of its ratification of the amendment. See *ibid.*, V, 401; 405, n. 26.

7 On 5 January 1782 the Virginia General Assembly had suspended "the operation of" its ratification act of 23 June 1781 until all other states should agree to the amendment (*JHDV*, May 1781, p. 32; Oct. 1781, p. 74; Hening, *Statutes*, X, 409–10, 451).

8 "M," Massachusetts, had ratified the proposed amendment on 4 May 1782 (*Papers of Madison*, IV, 221, n. 11). Randolph would have been more accurate had he written "G," for Georgia (*ibid.*, V, 291, n. 9; JM Notes, 29 Jan. 1783).

9 The Articles of Confederation included no provision for a tribunal before which a sovereign state could be haled by Congress.

10 For a previous instance when Congress did deputize, see *Papers of Madison*, IV, 270, and n. 2; V, 373–74. For Randolph's comments upon the outcome of the election of delegates in April, see his letter of 26 April 1783 to JM. The Virginia General Assembly was scheduled to convene on 5 May (*JHDV*, May 1783, p. 3).

11 Theodorick Bland, a delegate from Virginia to Congress, arrived in Philadelphia on or just before 22 January (JM to Randolph, 22 Jan. 1783). On 5 February Governor Harrison was informed by the "public printer," James Hayes, Jr., of Richmond, that "utter want of funds with which to procure workmen and material" rendered him unable "to print the Laws" (*Cal. of Va. State Papers*, III, 432). Harrison's letter of 15 May 1783 to the speaker of the House of Delegates reveals that this situation was still unchanged (Executive Letter Book, 1783–1786, p. 125, MS in Va. State Library).

12 Although none of JM's brothers, Francis (1753–1800), Ambrose (1755–1793), or William (1762–1843), was a member of the Virginia General Assembly, one of them may have attended as a spectator. JM's second cousin, Thomas Madison (1746–1798), served as a delegate from Botetourt County during the recent session, and Randolph perhaps concluded that he was JM's brother (Swem and Williams, *Register*, p. 15; Robert Douthat Stoner, *A Seed-Bed of the Republic: A Study of the Pioneers in the Upper (Southern) Valley of Virginia* [Roanoke, Va., 1962], pp. 305–7).

The total emissions of the old continental bills of credit had not much exceeded $200,000,000 face value. On 1 September 1779 Congress resolved that "on no account whatever" would more than that total be issued (*JCC*, XIV, 1013–14). Having emitted that amount, Congress on 18 March 1780, not 1781, apportioned the $200,000,000 by quotas among the states for cancellation at the ratio of 40 to 1 (*JCC*, XVI, 216, 262–67). Contrary to plan, the process of cancellation was far from completed by the close of 1782 and remained a problem for about seven more years. See Index to *Papers of Madison*, V, under Continental Congress, actions on paper money; Madison, James, views of paper currency; Money, continental paper. The "financier" was Robert Morris.

13 JM to James Madison, Sr., 1 Jan. 1783, and n. 3.

14 Finesse. The Earl of Shelburne had been head of the British ministry since 4 July 1782 (*Papers of Madison*, IV, 240, nn. 17, 18).

15 JM to James Madison, Sr., 1 Jan. 1783, n. 6.

16 Randolph may have noted in the *Pennsylvania Packet* of 17 December 1782 a news item of 24 September from London to the effect that the "Baltic Convoy," numbering "near 300 sail" and laden with "a vast supply of naval stores," had arrived at a port in Yorkshire.

17 The Virginia General Assembly had adjourned on 28 December 1782 (*JHDV*, Oct. 1782, p. 91).

From Benjamin Harrison

RC (LC: Madison Papers). Unsigned but in Harrison's hand. Cover missing. Docketed in an unknown hand, "Harrison Ben."

RICHMOND Jany 4th. 1783

DEAR SIR

I have recd. your several favors and am much oblig'd to you for them, but more particularly for that in Cypher,[1] the sentiments are just and perfectly coinside with mine, would to god our countrymen could see things thro' our medium, or rather would give them selves time to think, for I am really of opinion they do not want judgment but that from an indolence of disposition it is painful to them to judge for themselves, and therefore pin their faith on other mens sle[e]ves,[2] many of whom from badness of heart designedly lead them to wrong measures. That we have bad men amongst us is quite clear to me, some late measures added to a chain of foregoing ones prove it beyond a doubt.[3] A certain preamble[4] will point out the cloven footed monster, his actions and those of his connexions tho' cover'd with the thickest covering, may be, and are seen thro' by the discerning eye, and yet being ever on the watch like the great Enemy of mankind, by silken words, or high sounding patriotic speeches he leads to error, even those who think they know and are on their guard against him. There is but one thing now left them that gives the least prospect of obtaining the promis'd honors and riches,[5] and that they are pursuing in as many shapes as Proteus ever took,[6] you will easily find what I mean by what will be sent you thro' another channel,[7] but here I must stop not having leisure to communicate in a way that can not be understood by others, my full thoughts on this interesting subject.

Mr. Nicolson a mercht. of this town will set out soon for Philada. by him you will receive the balance of the money due you.[8] I hear nothing from South Carol[i]na[9] nor indeed from any other quarter but thro' you[.]

I am Dr Sr your most affect. and obedt Servt

[1] Except for "a private letter to the Governor," now missing, which JM enclosed in his letter of 10 December 1782 to Edmund Randolph, no other written communication from JM to Harrison during that month has been identified. JM's letter of the tenth comprised a "more explicit & pointed" description of the critical financial situation of Congress than that in the dispatch of the same date from the Virginia delegates to Harrison (*Papers of Madison*, V, 389–90; 394; 395, n. 8). In view of the chief subject of the present reply, JM probably had addressed the governor even more emphatically on the same matter later that month, after receiving Edmund Pendleton's letter of 9 December mentioning the rescission by the Virginia General Assembly of its ratification of the proposed impost amendment to the Articles of Confederation.

[2] That is, "to depend or rely upon" other men (James A. H. Murray *et al.*, *The Oxford English Dictionary* [12 vols. and a suppl. vol., Oxford, 1919 ptg.], IX, Part I, p. 197).

[3] The longstanding feud between the "James River" Harrisons and the "Northern Neck" Lees strongly suggests that the governor meant to include Richard Henry Lee and Arthur Lee among the "bad men" (Casenove Gardner Lee, Jr., *Lee Chronicle: Studies of the Early Generations of the Lees of Virginia*, ed. by Dorothy Mills Parker [New York, 1957], pp. 177, 184–85, n. 23). Among the "late measures" Harrison assuredly numbered the repeal of the ratification of the impost amendment and the instructions *in re* confiscated property (*Papers of Madison*, V, 409–10; 410, n. 3).

Although Arthur Lee informed JM that he alone of all the delegates in the Virginia General Assembly had opposed the "torrent" for repeal of the ratification of the impost amendment, Randolph believed that the Lees, with typical "affectation of candor" in ostensible opposition to each other's views, probably maneuvered collusively for the purpose of "*piquing*" Robert Morris, the Confederation superintendent of finance (*Papers of Madison*, IV, 355; JM to Randolph, 4 Feb.; Randolph to JM, 7 Feb. 1783). Arthur Lee perhaps revealed his true sentiments respecting the repeal when he advised a Massachusetts correspondent that the Articles of Confederation were "a stumbling block to those who wish to introduce new, and I think arbitrary systems" (Burnett, *Letters*, VII, 51). See also JM Notes, 28 Jan. 1783.

[4] Harrison referred to the preamble of the act of 6–7 December 1782 repealing the statute by which the impost amendment had been ratified. This preamble, drafted by a committee of three delegates of whom Richard Henry Lee was one, declared that "permitting any power, other than the general assembly of this commonwealth, to levy duties or taxes upon the citizens of this state within the same, is injurious to its sovereignty, may prove destructive of the rights and liberty of the people, and so far as congress might exercise the same is contravening the spirit of the confederation in the eighth article thereof" (*JHDV*, Oct. 1782, pp. 49, 52, 55, 58; Hening, *Statutes*, XI, 171). Such a declaration was, in effect, an instruction to the Virginia delegates in Congress not only to oppose an attempted revival of the amendment but to set themselves against any proposal to grant Congress an independent income—a fact that did not escape JM's observation (JM to Randolph, 28 Jan. 1783).

[5] It was Dr. John Berkenhout, a British secret agent, who allegedly had promised the Lees "honors and riches" (*Papers of Madison*, V, 427, n. 7). Both of the Lees were legitimately ambitious for high public office. Arthur Lee hoped to become secretary for foreign affairs in both 1781 and 1783, and he and Richard Henry Lee would have welcomed being appointed as minister to Great Britain or France in 1784. By then, Richard Henry Lee was president of Congress. In the following year Congress elected Arthur Lee to the Treasury Board (William Emmett O'Donnell, *The Chevalier de La Luzerne, French Minister to the United States, 1779–1784*

[Bruges, 1938], p. 169; Burnett, *Letters*, VI, 176 n.; VII, 190, 618, 623, second n. 2, 632–33; VIII, 158, 178; also see JM to Jefferson, 10 June 1783).

⁶ Proteus, "the old man of the sea" in Greek and Roman mythology, was an unwilling seer, who assumed "every possible shape" to avoid having to prophesy. Harrison suggested that the Lees' principles and policies were as flexible as their drive for wealth and position was constant.

⁷ Harrison probably meant the several instructions of the Virginia General Assembly to its delegates in Congress, enclosed with his dispatch of 4 January to them (*q.v.*, and n. 5). It is possible, of course, that "another channel" referred to "Mr. Nicolson," mentioned in the next paragraph, or to Edmund Randolph, who reported Richmond news almost weekly in his letters to JM.

⁸ For George Nicolson and Harrison's debt to JM for books purchased in Philadelphia, see *Papers of Madison*, V, 340; 341, n. 2. When, if ever, Nicolson reached that city has not been determined.

⁹ Harrison no doubt referred particularly to the expected news that the British troops had evacuated Charleston. For the arrival of word that the enemy had left the city on 14 December 1782, see Harrison to Delegates, 11 Jan. 1783, and n. 6.

Benjamin Harrison to Virginia Delegates

FC (Virginia State Library). In the hand of Thomas Lyttleton Savage, assistant clerk of the Council of State. Addressed to "Virginia Delegates in Congress."

IN COUNCIL Januy: 4th. 1783

GENTLEMEN

Your favors of the 17th. & 24th. of last Month¹ came to hand by Post one of them was not franked, and of course Postage was demanded on it² this was as usual but there were two other packets from General Washington and the Secretary of foreign Affairs³ that were both franked, and yet Postage was demanded on them, is this a regulation of Congress? if it is, is it right, that States at such a distance who must necessarily correspond with your public Officers should be at so much greater expence than those that are nearer.⁴ You have herewith several resolutions of the Assembly which relate to you,⁵ one of them respects the Tobacco for which mr. Thomson granted a passport   you will find his Letter to mr. Clark has been laid before the Assembly but that it is by no means satisfactory. they granted the Indulgence of exporting 685 hhds: of Tobacco at the request of Congress with great reluctance and to accomodate the financier who had received the Money for it, but this seems to be a private affair between the Secretary and the Shipper in which the public had no Interest, and therefore requires explanation, and the more so as the Manner in which it was done by the agent here

13

seems to justify a suspition that it would not bear examination. I mean not to reflect on your Secretary   I know him well and have a very high Opinion of him, yet I fear he has been taken in; if such Things are permitted to be done by the Servants of Congress, how shall we be able to put a Stop to the illicit Trade so much complained off.[6] I have the mortification to send you an Act pass'd the last session of Assembly repealing the former one giving Congress a Duty of five per centum on imported Articles &ca. their reasons for doing it I only know from the preamble, having never heard a word of it till the Bill was laid on my Table after the rising of the Assembly[7] I dread the Consequence of the Measure but it being my province to acquiese in it I shall drop the Subject.

Nathan has agreed to an arbitration of his demands against the State. I shall therefore again trouble you with the papers either by this or the next Post and beg the favor of you to have the Business settled in the Manner formerly proposed, that is of submitting it to Gentlemen of the Law.   the Acceptance of the Bills will otherwise be look'd on as binding the State which from what I have heard will not be doing it Justice.[8] I beg the favor of you to send us the Journals of Congress for the Year 1780 which will complete our set.[9]

I am &c.

B. H.

[1] *Papers of Madison,* V, 412–13; 446–47.

[2] On 2 January 1783 Harrison addressed a note to James Hayes, Jr., the postmaster at Richmond, curtly admonishing him not to "withhold the public Letters in your Office till the Postage is paid" (McIlwaine, *Official Letters,* III, 418).

[3] Washington's letter of 11 December was in response to one from Harrison on 23 November 1782 and dealt largely with clothing the troops in the southern army (Fitzpatrick, *Writings of Washington,* XXV, 419). The dispatch from Livingston was his circular letter of 23 December 1782 to the executive of each state, which enclosed a copy of Richard Oswald's "commission to treat with the thirteen United States of America," requested that it be withheld from publication as possibly only "another of those artifices so often practiced to deceive and put us off our guard," and gave assurance that a treaty of commerce between the Netherlands and the United States had been almost certainly signed on 7 October 1782 (Wharton, *Revol. Dipl. Corr.,* VI, 161). See also *Papers of Madison,* IV, 403, n. 3; 410–11; V, 447, and n. 8; JM to James Madison, Sr., 1 Jan., and n. 3; Randolph to JM, 3 Jan.; JM Notes, 17 to 21 Jan. 1783.

[4] The Virginia delegates apparently made no reply to these two questions. Although a deputy postmaster was forbidden by ordinances of Congress of 18 and 28 October to collect postage on a franked letter, he could charge its recipient a commission of "not exceeding twenty per centum" of what the postage fee would have been for the same letter, if unfranked. The recipient of an unfranked letter was obliged to pay an amount of postage proportionate to the weight of the letter and his distance from the place where it had been mailed. The 20 per cent fee was

somewhat modified by a supplementary ordinance of 24 December 1782, but the postmaster at Richmond probably did not know of this change when he asked for his fee from the governor (*JCC,* XXIII, 676, 678, 688–89, 830).

[5] Probably enclosed with the dispatch were several instructions from the Virginia General Assembly. These were instructions *in re* peace negotiations, 17 December; confiscated property, 17 December; financial quota, 28 December; settlement of accounts, 28 December; and possibly, artillery, 25–26 December (*Papers of Madison,* V, 408–10; 451–52; 459–60). See also Harrison to Delegates, 19 Apr. 1783, and n. 5.

[6] *Papers of Madison,* V, 461–63; 464, nn. 2, 3, 7–9.

[7] *Ibid.,* V, 401; 431, n. 3; 442; 445, nn. 16, 17; 449; 472; 474, n. 5; 477–78; also Randolph to JM, 3 Jan. 1783, and n. 2.

[8] For the financial claim of Simon Nathan against Virginia, see Index to *Papers of Madison,* V, under Nathan, Simon; also, Harrison to Delegates, 11 Jan. 1783.

[9] The journal of Congress for 1781 was published in that year, and for 1782 in 1783, but the journal for 1780, which originally was issued only in monthly parts, was not brought together in one volume, and that considerably abridged, until 1786 or 1787 (*JCC,* XVIII, 1237; XXI, 1203; XXV, 991). As early as January 1782 Harrison had in his possession the monthly installments of 1780 through July, but when, if ever, he received those for the last five months of that year is not known. See *Papers of Madison,* IV, 25.

Notes on Debates

MS (LC: Madison Papers). For a description of the manuscript of Notes on Debates, see *Papers of Madison,* V, 231–34.

Monday Jany. 6th.[1]

The Memorial from the army was laid before Congress and referred to a grand Committee.[2] This reference was intended as a mark of the important light in which the memorial was viewed.

Mr. Berkley[3] having represented some inconveniencies incident to the plan of a Consular Convention between France & U. S. particularly the restriction of Consuls from trading & his letter having been committed, a report was made proposing that the Convention should for the present be suspended. To this it had been objected that as the convention might already be concluded such a step was improper; and as the end might be obtained by authorising the Minister at Versailles to propose particular alterations that it was unnecessary. By Mr. Madison[4] it had been moved that the report should be postponed to make place for the consideration of an instruction & authority to the sd. Minister for that purpose; and this motion had in consequence been brought before Congress.[5] On this day the business was revived. The sentiments of the members were various, some wishing to suspend such part of the convention only as excluded Consuls from commerce; others thought this exclusion too important to be even suspended; others again thought the whole ought to be suspended during the war; & others lastly contending that the whole ought to be new modelled; the Consuls having too many privileges in some respects, & too little power in others. It was observable that this diversity of opinions prevailed chiefly among the members who had come in since the Convention had been passed in Congress; the members originally present adhering to the views which then governed them.[6] The subject was finally postponed; 8 States only being represented, & 9 being requisite for such a question.[7] Even to have suspended the convention after it had been proposed to the Court of France & possibly acceded to would have been indecent and dishonorable; and at a juncture when G. B. was courting a commercial intimacy, to the probable uneasiness of France, of very mischevous tendency.[8] But experience constantly teaches that new members of a public body do not feel the necessary respect or responsibility for the acts of their predecessors, and that a change of members & *of circumstances* often proves fatal to consistency and stability of public measures. Some conversation in private by the old members with the most judicious of the new in this instance has abated the fondness of the latter for innovations, and it is even problematical whether they will be again urged.

In the evening of this day the grand Committee met and agreed to meet again the succeeding evening for the purpose of a conference with the Superintendt. of Finance.[9]

[1] The matters recorded by JM in his Notes on Debates for 6 January are not mentioned in the printed journal of Congress for that day (*JCC*, XXIV, 37–38).

[2] For a summary of this memorial, see *Papers of Madison*, V, 473; 474, n. 8. For the report of the grand committee, which included Oliver Wolcott of Connecticut as chairman and JM as the member representing Virginia, see JM Notes, 24 Jan. 1783.

[3] Thomas Barclay, U.S. consul in France.

[4] JM originally indicated his name by "M" only. Many years later he inserted slantwise the other six letters of his surname after the initial.

[5] The paragraph to this point summarizes the debate on, and JM's motion relating to, this issue on 2 January 1783. See Instructions *in re* Consuls, 2 Jan. 1783, and ed. n., and nn. 3, 5.

[6] For the proposed Franco-American consular convention, adopted by Congress on 25 January 1782, see *Papers of Madison*, III, 201, and n. 1; *JCC*, XXII, 46–54.

[7] On 7 January ten states were sufficiently represented in Congress to cast effective votes. On that day Georgia had no delegate in attendance; Maryland and Virginia each had only one; and New Hampshire, Massachusetts, Rhode Island, New York, Delaware, and North Carolina each had only two, or the minimum required to make a state's vote count in determining the outcome of a division upon a motion. A delegate from each of two of the six states last named probably was

absent on 6 January. A consular convention fell under the rubric of "treaties," which was among the general subjects, listed in Article IX of the Articles of Confederation, upon which no effective action could be taken by Congress unless a minimum of nine states was in attendance with two or more delegates (*JCC*, XIX, 220).

8 For examples of efforts by British agents, merchants, or shipowners to renew trade with Americans, see *Papers of Madison*, V, 308; 311, n. 12; 425; 427, n. 12; 461; 469; 471, n. 38.

9 JM's Notes on Debates for 7 January 1783 (*q.v.*, and n. 1) permit little doubt that this grand committee was the one to which the memorial from the army had been referred rather than the one, of which JM was also a member, appointed to recommend ways and means to replenish the empty treasury of Congress, after consulting with Robert Morris. For the latter committee, see *Papers of Madison*, V, 377; 378, nn. 1, 6; 379, n. 7; 380, n. 11; 381, n. 16; 442 43; 416, n. 22.

To Joseph Jones

RC (LC: Madison Papers). JM's note to Jones is on the upper portion of a page on which Jones, writing below the note, penned his reply. Neither writer dated or signed his communication. Many years later JM docketed the page, "Virga Govr. of (Harrison Jany. 7 1783."

EDITORIAL NOTE

On 6 January 1783 JM and Joseph Jones, who was unable to attend Congress because of ill health, were the only Virginia delegates in Philadelphia. Probably on that day, JM had Governor Harrison's dispatch of 28 December 1782 (*Papers of Madison*, V, 465), together with his own note of transmittal, taken to Jones. For the latter's reply, see Jones to JM, 6 Jan. 1783. Since this exchange of notes related to the response which JM would make on behalf of the Virginia delegation to the governor's communication, JM filed them with the draft copy of his letter of 7 January 1783 to Harrison (*q.v.*) and in his old age wrote the docket of that letter on the left margin of the page of notes.

[*ca.* 6 January 1783]

Mr. Jones will please to send back the public letter & Mr. M. will answer it, and the news from Col Monroe if any particularly as to the Impost,[1] also how he[2] finds himself to day

1 A letter from James Monroe, a member of the Virginia Council of State, to his uncle Joseph Jones probably arrived in the same mail which included Governor Harrison's dispatch to the Virginia delegates. Disappointed in his hope that the governor would have explained why the General Assembly had rescinded its ratification of the impost amendment, JM was eager to know whether Monroe had thrown light on that subject. See JM to Randolph, 7 Jan. 1783, and n. 2.

2 Jones.

From Joseph Jones

RC (LC: Madison Papers). See JM to Jones, 6 Jan. 1783, hdn.

[*ca.* 6 January 1783]

Mr. Jones begs to return to Mr. Madison the public letter and thanks him for his offer to answer it.[1] Col. M.'s Letter contains not a word ab. the impost or indeed any thing of consequence—he only mentions Mr. Lee's prevailing on taking the question to recall him[2] and some further observ. respecting the office he formerly wished to be appointed to.[3] My disorder has been much checked since yesterday.[4]

[1] JM to Jones, 6 Jan.; JM to Harrison, 7 Jan. 1783.

[2] *Papers of Madison*, V, 425; 426, n. 5; 427, nn. 6, 7.

[3] The office to which Monroe, who was ineligible for promotion in the continental army, had "formerly" aspired was that of lieutenant colonel commandant of a Virginia state regiment (George Morgan, *The Life of James Monroe* [Boston, 1921], pp. 71–76); but his failure to procure military employment had been compensated by civil preferment (*Papers of Madison*, IV, 152; 154, n. 14; 209, n. 4).

[4] To judge from the tallied polls, Jones had been absent from Congress on Friday, 3 January, and would not be present on Tuesday, 7 January 1783 (*JCC*, XXIV, 36, 40–42). See Delegates to Harrison, 7 Jan.; JM to Randolph, 7 Jan. 1783.

Notes on Debates

MS (LC: Madison Papers). For a description of the manuscript of Notes on Debates, see *Papers of Madison*, V, 231–34.

Teusday Jany. 7th. 1782 [3].

See the Journals[1]

In the evening the grand Committee had the assigned conference with Mr. Morris who informed them explicitly that it was impossible to make any advance of pay in the present State of the finances to the army and imprudent to give any assurances with respect to future pay until certain funds should be previously established.[2] He observed that even if an advance cd. be made it wd. be unhappy that it sd. appear to be the effect of demands from the army; as this precedent[3] could not fail to inspire a distrust of the spontaneous justice of Congress & to produce repetitions of the expedient. He said that he had taken some measures with a view to a payment for the army which depended on events not within our command, tha[t] he had communicated these measures to

Genl Washington under an injunction of secrecy,[4] and that he could not as yet disclose them without endangering their success: that the situation of our affairs within his department was so alarming that he had thoughts of asking Congress to appoint a Confidential Committee to receive communications[5] on that subject and to sanctify by their advice such steps as ought to be taken. Much loose conversation passed on the critical state of things the defect of a permanent revenue, & the consequences to be apprehended from a disappointment of the mission from the army; which ended in the appointment of friday evening next for an audience to General McDougal, Col. Brooks & Col. Ogden[6] the Deputies on the subject of the Memorial, the Superintendt. to be present.[7]

[1] JM misdated these notes by one year. Confining his record for 7 January to the evening meeting of the grand committee to which Congress had referred the memorial of officers in Washington's army, JM suggested by this entry that the printed journal adequately summarized the proceedings of Congress during the day. The delegates devoted most of that session to another unsuccessful effort to agree upon the exchange ratio between specie and depreciated continental paper currency for settling "the accounts of the several states, and of individuals therein, against the United States." The long discussion, interspersed with four indecisive tallied polls, was upon a report of another grand committee, of which JM was also a member. In the polls, JM voted against postponing consideration of the report, against having each state separately determine a ratio which would "render the most substantial justice," and against both a 1-to-40 and a 1-to-75 ratio (*JCC*, XXIV, 38–42). JM may have neglected to summarize the arguments pro and con on each proposal because they largely duplicated those recorded in his Notes on Debates for 7 December 1782, when the same issues were debated (*Papers of Madison*, V, 377-78).

[2] JM Notes, 6 Jan. 1783, and nn. 2, 9. By "certain" Robert Morris (or JM) meant "assured" funds.

[3] JM interlineated the last two syllables of this word and canceled "clamorous," which he originally had written between "of" and "demands." Even though Morris may have used the adjective, JM perhaps decided to delete it because he had found that the "representations" in the memorial reflected "a proper spirit and are full of good sense" (*Papers of Madison*, V, 473).

[4] The "measures" which Morris mentioned but did not reveal to the grand committee were those which, under an injunction of secrecy, he had communicated in cipher to Washington on 16 October 1782. Hoping to sell "bills of exchange to the amount of half a million dollars" in Havana, Morris assured Washington that "a part of the money shall be applied as pay" for the army (LC: Washington Papers). In acting with "the profoundest secrecy," Morris relied for his exoneration by Congress upon its resolution of 3 July 1781, reading: "That the superintendant of finance be and he is hereby empowered to pursue such measures as he may think proper for exporting and importing goods, money and other articles, at the risque and for the account of the United States, at such times and in such manner as he shall deem necessary and useful to the public service" (*JCC*, XX, 721; NA: PCC, No. 137, II, 287).

It was late in November 1782 before John Brown of Philadelphia, as Morris' agent for executing the transaction, was able to sail for Havana in the newly built merchant ship, "Duc de Lauzun," which Morris had purchased and loaded with flour and "Salted Provisions." Although Morris, in his capacity as agent of marine, had bought the vessel for the United States, he and probably Thomas FitzSimons appear to have been the joint owners of the flour. The "salted provisions" were army rations which had deteriorated through being held too long (NA: PCC, No. 137, II, 283–86). Morris directed Brown to sell the cargo and a maximum of $200,000 worth of bills of exchange in Havana. Morris trusted that these bills would be honored in the first instance by a firm of merchants in Cadiz. Upon receipt, they would forward the bills to Paris for acceptance by a banking house, which would be reimbursed by the bankers in Amsterdam who were floating a loan on behalf of the United States (NA: PCC, No. 137, II, 291–320; *Papers of Madison*, V, 450, n. 5). Morris apparently did not know until late in March 1783, when the frigate "Alliance" docked at Philadelphia, that though Brown had sold the flour and "salted provisions" for $72,447, the agent had failed in his principal mission. In Morris' words, "some persons in the Havanna discredited the Bills and finally prevented the sale of them" (NA: PCC, No. 137, II, 279–80). For the many documents occasioned by the planning and execution of this complicated affair, see *ibid.*, No. 137, II, 279–334.

[5] See JM Notes, 9–10 Jan. 1783, for emphasis upon the need for secrecy.

[6] For these officers, see *Papers of Madison*, V, 473; 474, n. 8. The next "friday evening" was that of 10 January 1783.

[7] JM Notes, 9–10 Jan. 1783.

Virginia Delegates to Benjamin Harrison

Draft (LC: Madison Papers). Written and initialed by JM. Addressed by him to "Govr of Virginia." For JM's docket, see JM to Jones, 6 Jan. 1783, hdn. and ed. n. Recipient's copy not found, but it was advertised for sale by George H. Richmond of New York City in his catalogue of November 1902, part 1, p. 28, item 430. JM designated the letter "official." See JM to Randolph, 7 Jan. 1783.

PHILADA. 7 Jy. 1783.

Your Excy's favor of the 28 Ult:[1] was duly recd. by yesterday's mail. The extract from the Journal of Congress herewith inclosed contains the answer to the objections of R. Island agst. the impost recommended by Congress; and which was to have been enforced by a deputation to that State.[2] You have been already informed of the effect which the sudden repeal of the accession of Virga. had on the measure.[3]

Genl. McDougal Col: Brooks of Massachsts. & Col: Ogden of N. Jersey arrived here some days ago, charged with a very solemn representation from the army of the grievances which oppress them. The redress principally urged is an immediate advance of part, & adequate provision for the residue of their arrears.[4] Yr. Excelly will readily conceive the dilemma in which Congress are placed, pressed on one side by justice humanity & the public good to fulfil engagements to which their funds are incompetent, and on [the] other left without even the resource of answering that every thing which could have been done has been done.[5]

The tribunal erected for the controversy between the States of Pa. & Connecticut have unanimously adjudged & reported to Congress that the former has no right to the lands in question, and that the jurisdiction & pre-emption of all the territory lying within the charter boundary of Pena. & claimed by Connecticut, do of right belong to Pennsa.[6]

Another severe relapse has confined Mr. Jones for some days to his room & prevents his being a party to this letter.[7]

J. M.[8]

[1] *Papers of Madison*, V, 465.

[2] JM evidently enclosed a copy of an extract from the printed journal of 16 December 1782 (*JCC*, XXIII, 798–810). See also *Papers of Madison*, V, 373–74; 376, n. 29; 407, and n. 1; 414–15; 416, nn. 3, 6; 445, nn. 16, 18; 449; 472–73.

[3] *Ibid.*, V, 477–78.

[4] *Ibid.*, V, 473; 474, n. 8; JM Notes, 6 Jan. 1783, and n. 9.

[5] That is, if Virginia and the other states had furnished their financial quotas to Congress, the soldiers would not have remained unpaid. In the *Virginia Gazette* of 4 January 1783, George Webb, the continental receiver general, reported that Virginia had furnished only $35,710 during December 1782 for the use of Congress (*Papers of Madison*, V, 454, n. 3). This sum, in fact, was all that the state in 1782 had supplied of its quota of $1,307,594 for the year (NA: PCC, No. 142, II, 234–35). No money whatever was paid in January 1783 (*Va. Gazette*, 8 Feb. 1783).

[6] JM Notes, 3 Jan. 1783, and nn. 5, 6. Instead of "the former," JM obviously should have written "the latter."

[7] JM to Jones, 6 Jan. 1783, and ed. n., and n. 6.

[8] Harrison's dispatch of 31 January 1783 to the Virginia delegates (*q.v.*) makes clear that he received this letter, of which the present copy is only a draft.

To Edmund Randolph

RC (LC: Madison Papers). Unsigned but in JM's hand. Cover franked by "J Madison, Jr." and addressed to "Edmund Randolph Esqr. Richmond." Docketed by Randolph, "Fm J. Madison Jan: 7 1783." At the top of the page of the letter, above the date, JM wrote "Randolph, Edm." Unless otherwise noted, the italicized words are those written by JM in the Randolph code, for which see *Papers of Madison*, V, 307; 309, n. 1; 339, n. 5.

PHILADA. 7 Jany. 1783.

MY DEAR SIR

Your[1] favor of the 27th. ult: disappointed me by its silence as to the 5 Per Ct. The Governor's letter led us to hope that the subject would be resumed and the arrival of yesterday's mail was awaited with a general anxiety on that account. Not a line however in any letter public or private touches on the subject.[2] My last I hope will have led to some explanations on it.[3] The official letter to the Governor will inclose a copy of the answer to the objections of Rhode Island which was to have cooperated with the deput[at]ion to that State,[4] if Virginia had not frustrated the whole plan by her defection.

The deputation from the army which arrived here a few days ago has laid their grievances before Congress. They consist of sundry articles the capital of which are a defect of an immediate payment, and of satisfactory provision for completing the work hereafter. How either of these objects can be accomplished, and what will be the consequence of failure, I must leave to your own surmises. I wish the disquietude excited by the prospect was the exclusive portion of those who impede the measures calculated for redressing complaints against the justice & gratitude of the public.[5]

The Resolution of the House of Delegates against restitution of confiscated effects is subject to the remark you make.[6] The preliminary requisition of an acknowledgment of our Independence in the *most ample manner,*[7] seems to be *still more in*cautious, since it *disaccords* with *the treaty of alliance* which *admits* the *sufficiency of a tacit* acknowledgment.[8]

Mr. J. is still here.[9] I must as I apprehended postpone a copy of my extract from his remarks to the next mail, to which I will add what you wish from C's papers if any thing be in them.[10]

Another severe relapse has undone all his late recovery & his condition is at present as low and as alarming as it has been in any stage of his disorder.[11]

[1] In his old age JM or someone at his bidding placed a bracket in front of "Your" to designate the letter for publication, but Henry D. Gilpin did not print the closing two paragraphs (Madison, *Papers* [Gilpin ed.], I, 497–98).
[2] For Randolph's letter of 27 December and Benjamin Harrison's dispatch of 28 December 1782 to the Virginia delegates, see *Papers of Madison,* V, 453–54; 465. JM received both these letters on 6 January. See JM to Jones, 6 Jan. 1783. For the meaning of "the 5 Per Ct.," see Randolph to JM, 3 Jan. 1783, and n. 2.
[3] JM's "last" letter to Randolph was that of 30 December 1782 (*Papers of Madison,* V, 472–74).

4 Delegates to Harrison, 7 Jan. 1783, and hdn., and n. 2.
5 *Ibid.*, and nn. 4, 5.
6 *Papers of Madison,* V, 409–10; 410, nn. 1, 3, 4; 454; JM Notes, 16 Jan. 1783, and n. 8.
7 These three words were underlined by JM.
8 In encoding "sufficiency" JM omitted 285, signifying "cy." He underlined the ciphers for "tacit." Article VIII of the "Treaty of Alliance, Eventual and Defensive," concluded between the United States and France in 1778, reads: "Neither of the two parties shall conclude either truce or peace with Great Britain, without the formal consent of the other first obtained; and they mutually engage not to lay down their arms until the independence of the United States shall have been formally, or tacitly, assured by the treaty or treaties, that shall terminate the war" (*JCC,* XI, 448, 451, 457).
9 Thomas Jefferson was in Philadelphia from 27 December 1782 until 26 January, when he left for Baltimore, arriving there on 30 January 1783 (*Papers of Madison,* V, 473; 474, n. 6; Jefferson to JM, 31 Jan. 1783; Boyd, *Papers of Jefferson,* VI, 226 n; XV, 608).
10 JM refers to Jefferson's answers to the queries of Barbé-Marbois. See *Papers of Madison,* V, 7–11; 13, n. 24; 282; 287, n. 20; 331; 402; 473; 475, n. 15; JM to Randolph, 28 Jan. 1783, and n. 14. "C's papers" refers to those of Colonel John Cox, mentioned by Randolph in his letter of 27 December 1782 to JM (*Papers of Madison,* V, 454; 457, n. 17).
11 By "his," JM meant Joseph Jones. See JM to Jones, 6 Jan. 1783, and ed. n.

Notes on Debates

MS (LC: Madison Papers). For a description of the manuscript of Notes on Debates, see *Papers of Madison,* V, 231–34.

[9–10 January 1783]

Wednesday Jany. 8—Thursday Jany 9th & Friday Jany 10.[1]

On the report*[2] for valuing the land conformably to the rule laid down in the fœderal articles,[3] the delegates from Connecticut contended for postponing the subject during the war, alledging the impediments arising from the possession of N.Y. &c. by the enemy;[4] but apprehending (as was supposed) that the flourishing state of Connecticut compared with the Southern States, would render a valuation at this crisis unfavorable to the former. Others particularly Mr. Hamilton & Mr. Madison were of opinion that the rule of the confederation was a chimerical one,[5] since if the intervention of the individual states were employed their interests would give a biass to their judgments or that at least suspicions of such biass wd prevail;[6] and without their interven-

---

* this proposed to require the States to value the land and return the valuations to Congress[.] The above to be a marginal note[.]

tion, it could not be executed but at an expence, delay & uncertainty which were inadmissable; that it would perhaps be therefore preferable to represent these difficulties to the States & recommend an exchange of this rule of dividing the public burdens for one more simple easy & equal.[7] The Delegates from S. Carolina generally & particularly Mr. Rutlidge advocated the propriety of the constitutional rule & of an adherence to it, and of the safety of the mode in question arising from the honor of the State.[8] The debates on the subject were interrupted by a letter from the Superintendant of Finance: informing Congress that the situation of his department required that a committee sd. be appointed with power to advise him on the steps proper to be taken; and suggesting an appointmt. of one consisting of a member from each State, with authority to give their advice on the subject. This expedient was objected to as improper, since Congress wd. thereby delegate an incommunicable power, perhaps, and would at any rate lend a sanction to a measure without even knowing what it was; not to mention the distrust which it manifested of their own prudence & fidelity.[9] It was at length proposed & agreed to, that a special committee consisting of Mr. Rutlidge Mr. Osgood[10] & Madison should confer with the Superintendt of Finance on the subject of his letter and make report to Congress. After the adjournment of Congress this Committee conferred with the Superintendt[11] who after being apprized of the difficulties which had arisen in Congress, stated to them that the last acct. of our money affairs in Europe shewed that contrary to his expectation and estimates there was $3\frac{1}{2}$ Million of livres short of the bills actually drawn, that further draughts were indispensable to prevent a stop to the public service; that to make good this deficiency there was only the further success of Mr. Adams' loan, and the friendship of France to depend on, that it was necessary for him to decide on the expediency of his staking the public credit on these contingent funds by further draughts,[12] and that in making this decision he wished for the sanction of a Committee of Congress; that this sanction was preferable to that of Congress itself only as it wd. confide the risk attending bills drawn on such funds to a smaller number, and as secrecy was essential in the operation as well to guard our affairs in general from injury, as the credit of the bills in question from debasement.[13] It was supposed both by the Superntendt & the Committee that there was in fact little danger of bills drawn on France on the credit of the loan of 4 Million of dollars, applied for,[14] being dishonored; since if the negociations on foot were to terminate in peace, France would prefer an advance in our favor to exposing us to the necessity of resorting to G. B. for it; and that if the war sd. continue the necessity of such an aid to its prosecution would prevail. The result was that the Committee should make such report as would bring the matter before Congress under an injunction of secrecy, and produce a resolution authorising the Superintdt. to draw bills as the public service might require on the credit of applications for loans in Europe. The report of the Committee to this effect was the next day accordingly made & adopted unanimously.[15] Mr. Dyer[16] alone at first opposed it, as an unwarrantable & dishonorable presumption on the ability & disposition of France; Being answered however that without such a step, or some other expedt. which neither he nor any other had suggested, our credit would be stabbed abroad and the public service wrecked at home; and that however mortifying it might be to commit our credit, our faith & our honor to the mercy of a foreign nation, it was a mortification wch. cd. not be avoided without endangering our very existence; he acquiesed and the resol: was entered unanimously.[17] The circumstance of unanimity was thought of consequence, as it wd. evince the more the necessity of the succor and induce France the more readily to yield it.   on this occasion several members were struck with the impropriety of the late attempt to withdraw from France the trust confided to her over the terms of peace when we were under the necessity of giving so decisive a proof of our dependance upon her.[18] It was also adverted to in private conversation as a great unhappiness that during negociations for peace, when an appearance of vigor & resource were so desirable, such a proof of our poverty & imbecility[19] could not be avoided.*[20]

The conduct of Mr. Howel &c. had led several & particularly Mr. Peters into an opinion that some further rule & security ought to be provided for concealing matters of a secret nature. On the motion of Mr. Peters a committee composed of himself Mr. Williamson &c. was appointed to make report on the subject.[21] On this day the report was made. It proposed that members of Congress should each subscribe an instrument pledging their faith & honor not to disclose certain enumerated matters.

The enumeration being very indistinct and objectionable, and a written engagement being held insufficient with those who without it wd. violate prudence or honor, as well as marking a general distrust of the prudence & honor of Congress, the report was generally disrelished; and

* See Jany. 13. last page & insert here what is there as of Friday 10th[.]

after some debate in which it was faintly supported by Mr. Williamson, the committee asked & obtained leave to withdraw it.[22]

A discussion of the report on the mode of valuing the lands was revived. It consisted chiefly of a repetition of the former debates.[23]

In the evening according to appt. on teusday last, the grand Committee met, as did the Superintendt. of Finance. The chairman Mr. Wolcot informed the committee that Cols. Ogden & Brooks two of the deputies from the army had given him notice that Genl. McDougal the first of the deputation was so indisposed with a rheumatism[24] as to be unable to attend, and expressed a desire that the Committee would adjourn to his lodging at the Indian queen tavern[25] the deputies being very anxious to finish their business, among other reasons, on acct. of the scarcity of money with them. At first the Committee seemed disposed to comply; but it being suggested that such an adjournmt. by a Committee of a member from each State, would be derogatory from the respect due to themselves, especially as the Mission from the army was not within the ordinary course of duty,[26] the idea was dropped. In lieu of it they adjourned to monday evening next, on the ostensible reasons of the extreme badness of the weather which had prevented the attendance of several members.[27]

1 For evidence that nothing which JM recorded under this caption occurred on "Wednesday Jany. 8," see n. 2.

2 JM wrote the first sentence of his note in the left margin of the page and the second sentence at the bottom of that page. Judging from the handwriting, both sentences postdate his record for 9–10 January, and the second sentence was added in his old age as a direction to the editor of the first edition of his papers. See Madison, *Papers* (Gilpin ed.), I, 249, and n.

On 20 November 1782 Congress appointed a committee of five, with John Rutledge as chairman and JM as one of the members, "to report the best scheme for a valuation" (*Papers of Madison*, V, 294; 295, n. 12). On 6 January 1783, although unnoted in the printed journal or in JM's Notes on Debates for that day, the committee's report, drafted by Rutledge, was submitted to Congress and docketed, "Assigned for Consideration" on "Thursday Jany 9th 1782," a misdating of one year (NA: PCC, No. 24, fols. 79–84). This docket, the silence of the printed journal of 8 January about the report (*JCC*, XXIV, 43), the lack of positive evidence in JM's own record that the report was considered on that day, and the certainty that all else which he mentions occurred on 9 or 10 January, warrant little doubt that his caption "Wednesday Jany. 8" should have been omitted or qualified by an expression such as, "Nothing requiring notice." See also n. 9.

3 Article VIII of the Articles of Confederation stipulated that the expenses incurred by Congress for prosecuting the war and maintaining "the common defence or general welfare" should be defrayed "by the several states in proportion to the value of all land within each state, granted to or surveyed for any Person, as such land and the buildings and improvements thereon shall be estimated accord-

ing to such mode as the united states in congress assembled, shall from time to time direct and appoint" (*JCC*, XIX, 217). For comment on this provision and a summary of the Rutledge committee's recommendations, see JM Notes, 14 Jan. 1783, nn. 6, 7.

4 The delegates from Connecticut were Eliphalet Dyer, Oliver Ellsworth, and Oliver Wolcott (Burnett, *Letters*, VII, lxiii, lxiv). New York City and environs and part of the coastal area of the Maine district of Massachusetts were still occupied by the enemy. The *Pennsylvania Gazette* of 8 January reported that on 4 January Rivington's *Royal Gazette* of New York City had announced the evacuation of Charleston, S.C., by the British. Congress was not officially informed of this event until the arrival on 15 January 1783 of General Nathanael Greene's dispatch of 19 December 1782 (JM Notes, 15 Jan. 1783).

5 JM Notes, 14 Jan. 1783, and n. 4.

6 *Ibid.*, and n. 7.

7 *Ibid.*, nn. 4–7.

8 The delegates from South Carolina were John Lewis Gervais, Ralph Izard, David Ramsay, and John Rutledge (Burnett, *Letters*, VII, lxxv–lxxvi). "The constitutional rule," partially quoted in n. 3, further required that the financial quotas, determined by Congress and requisitioned from the states, should be met by taxes, "laid and levied by the authority and direction of the legislatures of the several states within the time agreed upon by the united states in congress assembled" (*JCC*, XIX, 217). For a repetition by Rutledge of his opinion, see JM Notes, 14 Jan. 1783.

9 Robert Morris' letter is dated 9 January 1783 and was laid before Congress on that day (*JCC*, XXIV, 43). To assure secrecy and dispatch, Morris wanted Congress to vest its authority of ultimate decision in a grand committee, which thereby could empower him to proceed with a course of action for meeting the financial emergency.

10 Samuel Osgood of Massachusetts.

11 This conference was held either in the afternoon or evening of 9 January.

12 In a dispatch of 11 January 1783 to Benjamin Franklin, Morris revealed that he had arrived at the amount of the overdraft by examining the statement of account, "lately received," from Ferdinand Grand, banker for the United States in Paris, and by assuming that the loan of six millions of livres, negotiated by John Adams with Dutch bankers, had not produced "above three millions" (Wharton, *Revol. Dipl. Corr.*, VI, 202 4; *JCC*, XXIII, 741; *Papers of Madison*, V, 128, n. 6; 129, n. 8; 362). Morris was overly sanguine about the outcome of the Dutch loan, for in a letter of 6 November 1782, which Morris had not received by early in January, Adams expressed "fear" that no more than 1,500,000 guilders had actually been made available (*Wharton, Revol. Dipl. Corr.*, V, 858–59; VI, 220). By "contingent funds" Morris meant those which could be drawn upon if the Dutch bankers fulfilled their contract and if Louis XVI of France consented to make a further advance of money from the royal treasury.

13 That is, if it became generally known that Morris was attempting to pay bills with drafts made upon a non-existent fund, they would have little, if any, exchange value.

14 On 14 September 1782 Congress had resolved to seek an additional loan of this amount from France (*Papers of Madison*, V, 129, n. 9). As late as 1 November 1783 Franklin's effort to have King Louis XVI grant this favor had been unsuccessful—not "by want of good will to assist us, as some have unjustly supposed, but by a real want of the means" (Wharton, *Revol. Dipl. Corr.*, VI, 721).

15 The "next day" was 10 January. See Conference with Morris, 10 Jan. 1783, and n. 5.

16 For the "long-winded" Eliphalet Dyer, "whose harangues," according to La Luzerne, "introduced the custom of reading newspapers in Congress" (Brant, *James Madison*, II, 223), see *Papers of Madison*, V, 292, n. 16; 384, n. 6.

17 *JCC*, XXIV, 43–44.

18 JM Notes, 1 Jan., and n. 2; 3 Jan. 1783, and n. 4.

19 JM used this word in the sense of "weakness" or "incapacity."

20 In his note, which immediately follows "avoided" in the manuscript, JM referred to his two paragraphs prefaced by "* see Friday Jany. 10th" at the close of his notes on debates for 13 January. The editors have followed his instructions. These two paragraphs were either an afterthought of JM, or he had included them in a rough draft of the proceedings of 9–10 January but inadvertently overlooked them when making a fair copy of that draft.

21 To this point in the paragraph, JM refers to the motion of Richard Peters of Pennsylvania on 23 December 1782, resulting in his appointment as chairman of a committee, comprising also Hugh Williamson of North Carolina and John Taylor Gilman of New Hampshire, to report the rules of secrecy theretofore adopted by Congress and to recommend "any further regulations which may be necessary to adopt on that subject" (NA: PCC, 186, fol. 76). For the conduct of the Rhode Island delegates, David Howell and Jonathan Arnold, see JM Notes, 3 Jan. 1783, and n. 3.

22 For the committee's report, drafted by Peters, see *JCC*, XXIII, 828–29, n. 1; *Papers of Madison*, V, 421, n. 10. The report is not mentioned in the printed journal of Congress for 10 January 1783 (*JCC*, XXIV, 43–44). The Peters committee apparently never submitted an amended version of the report.

23 See the first paragraph of the present Notes on Debates and nn. 2, 3; also JM Notes, 13 Jan. 1783.

24 JM Notes, 6 Jan., and n. 2; 7 Jan. 1783, and n. 6. For General McDougall's illness, see Fitzpatrick, *Writings of Washington*, XXV, 323.

25 The tavern was situated on Fourth Street between Market and Chestnut streets, about two blocks from the State House, where Congress met, and hardly more than a block from the boarding house at Fifth and Market streets where JM lived (*Pa. Mag. Hist. and Biog.*, XII [1888], 103, 503; *Papers of Madison*, IV, opp. 323).

26 Although this was true, the deputation had Washington's sympathetic support. See *Papers of Madison*, V, 473; 474, n. 8.

27 JM Notes, 13 Jan. 1783.

Report on Conference with Robert Morris

MS (NA: PCC, No. 31, fols. 339–40). In Charles Thomson's hand, except for one passage written by John Rutledge and another by JM. See nn. 4 and 5. On the folio below the report, Charles Thomson recorded and signed an account of the action of Congress upon the report. He docketed the folio, "Report of Mr Rutlidge   Mr Osgood   Mr Madison on the Superintendt letter of 9 Jany 1783 & proceedings thereon Jany 10: 1783 Secret."

Friday Jany 10. 1783

The Comee. consisting of Mr Rutlidge Mr Osgood & Mr Madison to whom was referred a letter of 9 Jany 1783 from the Superintendt of finance to confer with him thereon and report thereon, report that they have conferred with the Superintendt.[1] who communicated to them the[2] Subject referred to in his letter[3] under their Promise of Secrecy[4]—untill Congress shall direct them to communicate the same to them; and request the sense of Congress whether the Committee shall now make such communication[5]

[1] JM Notes, 9–10 Jan. 1783, and nn. 9, 11.
[2] Between "them" and "the" Thomson wrote and canceled "under an injunction of secrecy."
[3] JM Notes, 9–10 Jan. 1783, and nn. 12, 14.
[4] The words from "under" through "Secrecy" are in John Rutledge's hand. For Morris' insistence upon secrecy in his conference with the committee, see *ibid.*, and nn. 9, 13.
[5] The words from "untill" to the close of the report are in JM's hand. Following the submission of the report, Congress ordered the members of the committee to reveal what they had been told by Morris. For a summary of his confidential communication to the committee, see JM Notes, 9–10 Jan. 1783. Upon being apprised of this communication and especially of Morris' inability, unless he drew bills "to an amount beyond the known funds procured in Europe," to maintain the army and fulfill his other contracts, Congress by a unanimous vote authorized Morris to draw, if necessary, up to the total "of the money directed to be borrowed" abroad and ordered "the whole of this matter be kept secret" (*JCC*, XXIV, 43–44; JM Notes, 9–10 Jan. 1783).

Benjamin Harrison to Virginia Delegates

FC (Virginia State Library). In the hand of Thomas L. Savage. Addressed to "Virginia Delegates in Congress."

Council Chamber Januy: 11th. 1783.

Gentlemen

Your favor of the 31th. of last Month is before me the contents of it were in some Measure answer'd by the last post.[1] Why the Bill laying an impost of 5 pCt. on imported Articles was repealed, is left to conjecture, other than is declared by the preamble,[2] the Assembly had your Letter as you suppose and therefore could not be ignorant of the disagreeable Consequences that would flow from a repeal of the Law.[3] You have enclosed such papers as are necessary respecting the Arbitration with mr: Nathan, I have no other directions to give but to request you to persue the same Methods for having the Matter adjusted as were proposed by Gover. Jefferson.[4] I give you Joy on the long expected event of the evacuation of Charles Town's taking place[5]   you will know the particulars before this reaches you from Major Burnett,[6] who is gone on; will not the going of the french Troops more than counterbalance this?[7] I confess I have my fears it will. Will it not be proper to call on mr: Nathan to swear he paid the full sum mentioned in the Bills in Gold and Silver for them.[8]

I am Gentl. &c.

B. H.

[1] *Papers of Madison*, V, 477–78; Harrison to Delegates, 4 Jan. 1783.

[2] Harrison to JM, 4 Jan. 1783, and n. 4.

[3] By "your Letter," Harrison referred to that of the Virginia delegates to him on 10 December 1782 (*Papers of Madison*, V, 389–90; 390, n. 1). See also *ibid.*, V, 430; 431, n. 2; Harrison to JM, 4 Jan. 1783, and n. 1.

[4] *Papers of Madison*, V, 228–29; 229, nn. 2, 3, 5, 6; 344, and n. 10. For the "Methods" agreed upon by Governor Thomas Jefferson in Council in March 1781 for settling Simon Nathan's claim, see *Papers of Madison*, III, 20; 21, n. 1; 22, nn. 3, 4.

[5] Harrison to JM, 4 Jan. 1783, and n. 9. The reoccupation of Charleston on 14 December 1782 by the American army was announced in the *Virginia Gazette* of 11 January 1783.

[6] Major Ichabod Burnet (1756–1783) of Trenton, N.J., was graduated from the College of New Jersey in 1775. He was secretary of the Essex County, N.J., Committee of Safety in 1776, and aide-de-camp to General Nathanael Greene from 9 January 1778 until the close of the war. Arriving in Philadelphia on 15 January 1783 with Greene's dispatch reporting the evacuation of Charleston by the British, Burnet proceeded to Newburgh and on 6 February "popped in unexpectedly" at Washington's headquarters. He died at Charleston, S.C., on 12 September (Irving C. Hanners, *The Society of the Cincinnati in the State of New Jersey* ... [Bethlehem, Pa., 1949], p. 65; Burnett, Letters, VII, 17, 18; Fitzpatrick, *Writings of Washington*, XXVI, 104).

[7] For the departure of Rochambeau's army and the French fleet from Boston on 24 December 1782, see *Papers of Madison*, V, 429, n. 5; 475, n. 10; JM Notes, 3 Jan. 1783, and n. 2.

[8] Whether specie or depreciated currency had been paid by Nathan in becoming a creditor of Virginia was the major issue in delaying a settlement of his claim. See *Papers of Madison*, III, 20; 21, n. 1; 22, nn. 3, 4; 65; 186, n. 9; V, 228; 229, nn. 2, 3, 5, 6; Harrison to Delegates, 28 Jan. 1783, and n. 2.

Notes on Debates

MS (LC: Madison Papers). For a description of the manuscript of Notes on Debates, see *Papers of Madison*, V, 231–34.

Monday Jany. 13.

Report on the valuation of land was referred to a Grand Committee.[1]

A motion was made by Mr. Peters 2ded. by Mr Madison "that a committee be appointed to consider the expediency of making further applications for loans in Europe. & to confer with the Superintdt. of Finance on the subject."[2] In support of this motion Mr. P. observed that notwithstanding the uncertainty of success the risk of appearing unreasonable in our demands on France, and the general objections agst. indebting the U. S. to foreign nations, the crisis of our affairs demanded the experiment; that money must if possible be procured for the army and there was ground to expect that the Ct. of France wd. be influenced by an apprehension that in case of her failure[3] & of a pacification, G. B. might embrace the opportunity of substituting her favours. Mr. Madison added that it was expedient to make the trial because if it failed our situation cd. not be made worse, that it would be prudent in France & therefore it might be expected of her, to afford the U. S. such supplies as would enable them to disband their army in tranquility, lest some internal convulsions might follow external peace, the issue of which ought not to be hazarded, that as the affections & gratitude of this Country as well as its separation from G. B. were her objects in the Revolution, it would also be incumbent on her to let the army be disbanded under the impression of deriving their rewards through her friendship to their Country;[4] since their temper on their dispersion through the several States and being mingled in the public councils, would very much affect the general temper towards France, and that if the pay of the army[5] could be converted into a consolidated debt bearing interest, the requisitions on the States for the principal might be reduced to requisitions for the interest, and by that means a favorable revolution so far introduced into our finances.

The Motion was opposed by Mr. Dyer[6] because it was improper to augment our foreign debts, & would appear extravagant to France. Several others assented to it with reluctance; and several others expressed serious scruples as honest men agst. levying contributions on the friendship or fears[7] of France or others, whilst the unwillingness of the States to invest Congress with permanent funds rendered a repayment so precarious. The motion was agreed to, and the Committee chosen Mr. Ghoram, Mr. Peters, Mr. Izzard.[8]

In the evening according to appointment the Grand Committee gave an audience to the deputies from the army, viz Genl. McDougal & Cols.

Ogden & Brooks.[9] The first introduced the subject by acknowledging the attention manifested to the representations of the army by the appt. of so large a committee.   his observations turned chiefly on the 3. cheif topics of the memorial,[10] namely an immediate advance of pay, adequate provision for the residue and half pay[11]—on the first he insisted on the absolute necessity of the measure to soothe the discontents both of the officers & Soldiers, painted their sufferings & services, their successive hopes & disappointments throughout the whole war,[12] in very high coloured expressions, and signified that if a disappointment were now repeated the most serious consequences were to be apprehended; that nothing less than the actual distresses of the army would have induced at this crisis so solemn an application to their country, but tht. the seeming approach of peace, and the fear of being still more neglected when the necessity of their services should be over, strongly urged the necessity of it. His two colleagues followed him with a recital of various incidents & circumstances tending to evince the actual distresses of the army, the irritable state in which the deputies left them and, the necessity of the consoling influence of an immediate advance of pay. Col: Ogden said he wished not indeed to return to the army if he was to be the messenger of disappointment to them. The deputies were asked 1st. what particular steps they supposed would be taken by the army in case no pay cd. be immediately advanced; to which they answered that it was impossible to say precisely, that altho' the Sergeants & some of the most intelligent privates had been often observed in sequestered consultations, yet it was not known that any premeditated plan had been formed; that there was sufficient reason to dread that at least a mutiny would ensue, and the rather as the temper of the officers, at least those of inferior grades, would with less vigor than heretofore, struggle agst. it.[13] They remarked on this occasion, that the situation of the officers was rendered extremely delicate & had been sorely felt, when called upon to punish in Soldiers a breach of engagements to the public which had been preceeded by uniform & flagrant breaches by the latter of its engagements to the former.[14] General McDougal said that the army were verging to that state which we are told will make a wise man mad, and Col: Brooks said that his apprehensions were drawn from the circumstance that the temper of the army was such that they did not reason or deliberate cooly on consequences, & therefore a disappointment might throw them blindly into extremities. They observed that the irritations of the army had resulted in part from the distinctions made between the Civil & military lists, the former regularly receiving their salaries, and the latter as regularly left unpaid. They mentioned in particular that the members of the Legislatures would never agree to an adjournment without paying themselves fully for their services. In answer to this remark it was observed that the Civil officers on the average did not derive from their appointments more than the means of their subsistance; and that the military altho not furnished with their pay properly so called were in fact furnished with the same necessaries.[15]

On the 2d. point towit "adequate provision for the general arrears due to them." the deputies animadverted with surprize and even indignation on the repugnance of the States, some of them at least, to establish a fœderal revenue for discharging the fœderal engagements.[16] They supposed that the ease not to say affluence with wch. the people at large lived sufficiently indicated resources far beyond the actual exertions, and that if a proper application of these resources was omitted by the Country & the army thereby exposed to unnecessary sufferings, it must naturally be expected that the patience of the latter wd. have its limits. As the deputies were sensible that the general disposition of Congress strongly favoured this object, they were less diffuse on it. Genl. McDougal made a remark wch. may deserve the greater attention as he stepped from the tenor of his discourse to introduce it, and delivered it with peculiar emphasis: He said that the most intelligent & considerate part of the army were deeply affected at the debility and defects in the federal Govt. and the unwillingness of the States to cement & invigorate it; as in case of its dissolution, the benefits expected from the Revolution wd. be greatly impaired, and as in particular, the contests which might ensue amg. the States would be sure to embroil the officers which respectively belonged to them.[17]

On the 3d. point to wit "half pay for life" they expressed equal dissatisfaction at the States which opposed it,[18] observing that it formed a part of the wages stipulated to them by Congress & was but a reasonable provision for the remnant of those lives which had been freely exposed in the defence of their country, and would be incompatible with a return to occupations & professions for which military habits of 7 years standing unfitted them. They complained that this part of their reward had been industriously and artfully stigmatized in many states with the name of pension, altho' it was as reasonable that those who had lent their blood and services to the public sd. receive an annuity thereon, as those who had lent their money;[19] and that the officers whom new arrangements had from time to time excluded, actually laboured

33

under the opprobrium of pensioners,[20] with the additional mortification of not receiving a shilling of the emolumts. They referred however to their Memorial to shew—that they were authorised & ready to commute their half pay for any equivalent & less exceptionable provision.[21]

After the departure of the deputies, the Grand Committee appointed a subcommittee consisting of Mr. Hamilton, Mr. Madison & Mr. Rutlidge to report arrangements in concert with the Superintendt. of Finance for their consideration.[22]

[1] For the report, see *JCC*, XXIV, 113–14, n. 1. For the issue of "the valuation of land," see JM Notes, 9–10 Jan., and nn. 2, 3, 8. For the discussion by the grand committee, see JM Notes, 14 Jan. 1783.

[2] Both here and later in this paragraph JM added his surname long after he wrote these notes. For the context of the motion made by Richard Peters, see JM Notes, 9–10 Jan., and n. 21.

[3] That is, in case France declined to grant the desired loan.

[4] The antecedent of "her" in each instance is "France," while "their" as used twice near the close of this passage refers to the troops of the continental line.

[5] On 15 March 1783 Robert Morris informed Congress that on 1 January of that year the arrears of pay to the army totaled $11,300,000, or about as much as either the foreign debt or the loan-office debt (NA: PCC, No. 137, II, 199).

[6] For Eliphalet Dyer, see JM Notes, 9–10 Jan. 1783, n. 16.

[7] JM interlineated "fears" above a canceled "jealousy."

[8] Nathaniel Gorham of Massachusetts, Richard Peters of Pennsylvania, and Ralph Izard of South Carolina. For the report of the committee, see JM Notes, 17 Jan. 1783.

[9] *Papers of Madison*, V, 473; 474, n. 8; JM Notes, 9–10 Jan. 1783.

[10] For a summary of the contents of the memorial, see *Papers of Madison*, V, 474, n. 8.

[11] The ordinance of Congress, providing that "officers who shall continue in the service to the end of the war" would "be entitled to half pay during life," had been enacted on 21 October 1780 and extended, with modifications, on 17 January 1781 to embrace officers "in the hospital department and medical staff" (*JCC*, XVIII, 958–62, 1100; XIX, 68–69). See also *Papers of Madison*, II, 138, n. 5.

[12] Edmund Cody Burnett, *The Continental Congress* (New York, 1941), pp. 105–8, 231, 310–16, 442–71, *passim*.

[13] Fitzpatrick, *Writings of Washington*, XXV, 226–29, 229 n., 231 n., 268–70, 289; XXVI, 26–27.

[14] That is, although soldiers were obliged to obey the Articles of War and were punished for breaking them, Congress suffered no penalty for failing to provide what it had guaranteed to the troops in pay and rations. See *JCC*, V, 788, 788–807; VII, 264–66.

[15] That is, the average salary of civilian officials of the government barely covered the cost of food, clothing, and housing which the troops were supplied at no expense to themselves. This statement obviously took no account of the comparative quality of these necessities.

[16] *Papers of Madison*, V, 208, n. 5; 282; 457–58; 458, n. 5.

[17] General Alexander McDougall's remark concerning the possible "dissolution" of the Confederation and subsequent strife "among the states" had been expressed nearly a year before by JM. "If our voluminous & entangled accts. be not put into some certain course of settlemt. before a foreign war is off our hands it is easy to see

they must prove an exuberan[t] & formidable source of intestine dissentions" (*Papers of Madison*, IV, 56; 57, n. 7). See also JM Notes, 19 and 21 Feb. 1783.

18 See n. 11. The resolution of Congress on 21 October 1780, guaranteeing officers half pay for life, had been opposed by the delegates from Massachusetts, Connecticut, and New Jersey (*JCC*, XVIII, 959).

19 That is, the owners of interest-bearing bonds or loan-office certificates.

20 The "officers" referred to here were those who had been "deranged," or rendered supernumerary, by the ordinances of Congress reorganizing the continental army. See *Papers of Madison*, IV, 445; V, 237, n. 1; 306, n. 2; JM Notes, 17 Jan. 1783, and n. 6.

21 After commenting that very few civilians questioned the justice of the half-pay-for-life provision but many disliked its duration, the officers' memorial stated: "To prevent, therefore, any altercations and distinctions, which may tend to injure that harmony which we ardently desire may reign, throughout the community, we are willing to commute the half pay pledged, for full pay, for a certain number of years, or for a sum in gross, as shall be agreed to by the committee sent with this address" (NA: PCC, No. 42, VI, 63).

22 For the grand committee's report, drafted by Hamilton, see JM Notes, 24 Jan. 1783.

Notes on Debates

MS (LC: Madison Papers). For a description of the manuscript of Notes on Debates, see *Papers of Madison*, V, 231–34.

No. V

Teusday Jany. [14][1] 15th. 1783.

Congress adjourned for the meeting of The Grand Committee to whom was referred the report concerning the valuation of the lands and who accordingly met.[2]

The Committee were in general strongly impressed with the extreme difficulty & inequality if not impracticability of fulfilling the article of Confederation relative to this point;[3] Mr. Rutlidge however excepted, who altho' he did not think the rule so good a one as a census of inhabitants, thought it less impracticable than the other members. And if the valuation of lands had not been prescribed by the fœderal articles, the Committee wd. certainly have preferred some other rule of apportionment, particularly that of numbers under certain qualifications as to Slaves. As the fœderal Constitution however left no option, & a few* only were disposed to recommend to the States an alteration of it,[4] it was necessary to proceed 1st. to settle its meaning, 2dly. to settle the

* Mr. Hamilton was most strenuous on this point. Mr. Wilson also favd. the idea. Mr. Madison also but restrained in some measure by the declared sense of Virga.: Mr. Ghoram, and several others also, but wishing a previous experience.

least objectionable mode of valuation. On the first point, it was doubted by several members wher. the returns which the report under consideration required from the States would not be final and whether the Arts: of Confn: wd. allow Congress to alter them after they had fixed on this mode:[5] on this point no vote was taken.   a 2d. question afterwards raised in the course of the discussion was how far the Art: required a specific valuation, and how far it gave a latitude as to the mode. on this point also there was a diversity of opinions,[6] but no vote taken.

2dly. As to the mode itself referred to the Gd. Comme., it was strongly objected to by the Delegate from Cont. Mr. Dyer, by Mr. Hamilton, by Mr. Wilson by Mr. Caroll & by Mr. Madison, as leaving the States too much to the bias of interest, as well as too uncertain & tedious in the execution.[7] In favr. of the Rept. was Mr. Rutlidge the father of it, who thought the honor of the States & their mutual confidence a sufficient security agst. frauds & the suspicion of them. Mr. Ghoram favd. the report also, as the least impracticable mode, and as it was necessary to attempt at least some compliance with the fœderal rule before any attempt could be properly made to vary it. An opinion intertained by Massachusts that she was comparatively in advance to the U. S. made her anxious for a speedy settlement of the mode by which a final apportionment of the common burden cd. be effected.[8] The sentiments of the other members of the Committee were not expressed.

Mr. Hamilton proposed in lieu of a referrence of the valuation to the States, to class the lands throughout the States under distinctive descriptions, viz arable, pasture, wood &c. and to annex a uniform rate to the several classes according [to] their different comparative values calling on the States only for a return of the quantities & descriptions. This mode would have been acceptable to the more compact & populous States, but was totally inadmissible to the Southern States.[9]

Mr. Wilson proposed that returns of the quantity of land & of the number of inhabitants in the respective States sd. be obtain'd, and a rule deduced from the combination of these data. This also would have affected the States in a similar manner with the proposition of Mr. Hamilton. On the part of the So. States it was observed that besides its being at variance with the text of the Confederation[10] it would work great injustice, as would every mode which admitted the quantity of lands within the States, into the measure of their comparative wealth & abilities.

Lastly it was proposed by Mr Madison that a valuation sd. be attempted by Congress without the intervention of the States.[11] He observed that as the expence attending the operation would come ultimately from the same pockets, it was not very material whether it was borne in the first instance by Congress or the States, and that it at least deserved consideration whether this mode was not preferable to the proposed reference to the States.

This conversation ended in the appt. of a Subcommittee consisting of Mr. Madison Mr. Carroll & Mr. Wilson who were desired to consider the several modes proposed, to confer with the Superintendt of Finance, & make such report to the Gd. Come. as they sd. judge fit.[12]

[1] Many years later, to amend the erroneous dating of his original caption, JM interlineated the correct day "14" in brackets without canceling "15th." For a probable explanation of the Roman numeral above the date, see *Papers of Madison*, V, 231.

[2] For the appointment of the Rutledge committee on this subject, for the first submission of the report to Congress, and for the "valuation" provision of the Articles of Confederation, see JM Notes, 9–10 Jan., and nn. 2, 3, 8; 13 Jan. 1783. See also n. 7, below. Having on 13 January appointed, and referred the report to, a grand committee comprising the twelve members (Georgia was then unrepresented in Congress), each of whom had been nominated by his state delegation, Congress directed the committee to "meet in the comte room tuesday Jany 14 in the afternoon at six o'clock" (NA: PCC, No. 186, fol. 79). Congress adjourned by that hour, for, in accord with Article 19 of the "Rules for conducting business," every delegate "may attend the debates of a grand committee" (JCC, XX, 479).

[3] JM Notes, 9–10 Jan. 1783, n. 3.

[4] See JM's footnote. Probably only "a few" in Congress shared the more or less "strenuous" wish of Alexander Hamilton, James Wilson (Pa.), JM, and Nathaniel Gorham to have the states agree to a change in the "rule of apportionment" stipulated by the Articles of Confederation, because an amendment to become effective required the ratification of every state legislature. "We are," Hamilton wrote to George Clinton, governor of New York, "tied down by the Confederation" (Syrett and Cooke, *Papers of Hamilton*, III, 241).

"The declared sense of Virga." was a resolution enacted by the General Assembly in its session of May 1782 and laid before Congress by the Virginia delegates on 24 July of that year, stating that "it will not be expedient to authorise Congress to alter the mode appointed by the Confederation, for apportioning the quotas of the respective states, as is proposed in the act of 20 February, 1782" (JCC, XXII, 413; *Papers of Madison*, IV, 55; 57, n. 6). Gorham had first attended Congress on 12 December 1782 (JCC, XXIII, 786).

[5] The "several members" evidently doubted whether Congress, if it adopted the Rutledge report, could change data sent in by a sovereign state so as to make them accord with the stipulations of that report. In other words, would Congress have the constitutional right to devise a single standard whereby to measure and equalize the returns?

[6] Article VIII of the Articles of Confederation delegated to Congress the power to "direct" and "from time to time" to alter the mode to be used by each state for evaluating within its borders the privately owned land, "as such land and the build-

ings and improvements thereon shall be estimated" (*JCC*, XIX, 217). Doubt is warranted whether Congress in prescribing "the mode" could require a separate listing of the value of these three types of property, or whether, if so, a consolidated figure for each type, rather than "a specific valuation" of each type, shown opposite the name of the owner, would be sufficient.

Furthermore, if the grammatical construction of the relevant sentence in Article VIII must be solely depended upon to define its meaning, unimproved land on which there were no buildings might thereby be exempted. Until the issues of the western cessions and their controversial boundaries should be resolved, great quantities of land might be either taxed more than once, or, more likely, not taxed at all for the benefit of the Confederation.

7 See n. 4. "Mr. Caroll" was Daniel Carroll of Maryland. The government of a state would be inclined from "a bias of interest" to underestimate the value of privately owned land within the state in order to keep its financial quota as small as possible.

"Uncertain" and "tedious" reflect the following complicated "mode" recommended by the Rutledge committee: (1) each state legislature, as it might "judge most convenient and proper," would divide the state into districts and appoint in each district "principal" resident "freeholders" to make the valuation; (2) these "commissioners" would return a "schedule" to the executive of the state listing the name of each landowner and the value "in specie dollars" of his land, buildings, and improvements; (3) the executive, on or before 1 January 1784, would "transmit to Congress" a copy of the state's valuation law and the "returns" of the quantity and value of land and of the buildings and improvements thereon in each district; (4) Congress would "examine" the estimates from each state and "proceed," provided the estimates were "approved," "to make such requisitions upon the respective states, as shall be agreeable to the Articles of Confederation." Of this summary, the fourth portion may have been added to the Rutledge report after 15 January 1783 (*JCC*, XXIV, 113, and n.).

8 Although by 31 December 1782 Massachusetts had paid merely 7 per cent of her quota for that year, she was exceeded in this respect only by Connecticut, Rhode Island, New Jersey, and Pennsylvania (NA: PCC, No. 137, II, 757–61).

9 With the exception of New York, where the old "patroonships" of the Hudson River Valley remained in relatively few hands and imposed a barrier to expansion of the population, the ratio of land to inhabitants was measurably higher in the southern states than in those north of Chesapeake Bay. Much land, especially the enormous acreages west of the Appalachians held by Georgia, North Carolina, and Virginia, had not been surveyed, but to tax it, under whatever classification, would have been manifestly unfair to these war-ravaged southern states.

Many years later a son of Hamilton denied that his father made so "impracticable" a recommendation, for it contravened the eighth article of the Articles of Confederation and hence "would certainly have been rejected by the States" (John C. Hamilton, *History of the Republic of the United States of America, as Traced in the Writings of Alexander Hamilton and of his Cotemporaries* [7 vols.: Philadelphia, 1857–64], II, 399 n.). The younger Hamilton so interpreted the eighth article as to limit its application to those lands only upon which there were "buildings and improvements." See n. 6. He did not know, because the information was not to be found in the printed journals of Congress available in his day, that on 6 February 1783 his father unsuccessfully moved in Congress that the states "be required" to form themselves into districts and report to Congress the "quantity of land" therein, including that "unimproved" (Syrett and Cooke, *Papers of Hamilton*, III, 249; *JCC*, XXIV, 114 n.).

John Church Hamilton was convinced that JM often falsified his notes in order to asperse the reputation of Alexander Hamilton (John C. Hamilton, *History of the Republic*, II, 356 n., 358 n., 362 n., 368 n., 374 n., 439 n.; *Papers of Madison*, V, 234; 379, n. 7). JM and Hamilton in 1783 were closely attuned on most ways and means of providing Congress with money. The proposal here at issue accorded with Hamilton's nationalism and his view of the land-valuation dilemma (n. 4, above; JM Notes, 27 Jan., and n. 23; 28 Jan., and nn. 12, 45; 31 Jan. 1783, and n. 17). For evidence of the concord between the two men on financial questions submitted to tallied votes in Congress, see *JCC*, XXIV, 39–42, 94, 115–16, 131–32.

[10] JM Notes, 9–10 Jan. 1783, n. 3; also n. 4, above.

[11] Article VIII of the Articles of Confederation sanctioned JM's nationalistic proposal.

[12] For the conference of this subcommittee with Robert Morris, see JM Notes, 31 Jan. 1783.

Virginia Delegates to Benjamin Harrison

RC (Historical Society of Pennsylvania). In JM's hand, including the signature for "Jos: Jones." Addressed to "His Excy. The Govr. of Virginia." Docketed, apparently by Harrison, "Virginia Delegates in Congress Jany 14. 83." In LC: Madison Papers is JM's file copy of this letter. Except for a few differences in punctuation and abbreviations and only "We have the hon" as the complimentary close, the text of the file copy is identical with that of the recipient's copy.

PHILADA. 14th Jany. 1783.

SIR

The post having brought no mail yesterday from Virginia we have not the pleasure of acknowledging by his return any letter from your Excellency.

Congress have not recd. since the last post any official information from Europe. The gazette inclosed contains such as has come from that quarter through other channels.[1]

The evacuation of Charlestown has at length been published from N. York, and no doubt remains of its reality. But no official report of it from Genl. Greene has yet reached us.[2]

The deputies from the army have been heard by a Committee of Congress on the subject of their memorial.[3] Their explanations on the several topics contained in it are deeply affecting: and demonstrate the necessity of every possible effort for their relief. The result of the deliberations of Congress for that purpose will be the subject of a future letter to your Excellency.[4]

We have the honor to be with great respect yr. Excy's Obt. & hble servts.

Jos: Jones
J. Madison Jr.

[1] Probably the *Pennsylvania Packet* of 14 January 1783, which published European news items ranging from 10 September through 20 November 1782.

[2] Harrison to JM, 4 Jan., n. 9; JM Notes, 9–10 Jan., n. 4; Harrison to Delegates, 11 Jan. 1783, and n. 5.

[3] Delegates to Harrison, 7 Jan., and n. 5; JM Notes, 13 Jan. 1783.

[4] Delegates to Harrison, 11 Feb. 1783.

To Edmund Randolph

RC (LC: Madison Papers). Unsigned but in JM's hand. Cover franked by "J Madison Jr." and addressed to "Edmund Randolph Esqr. Richmond." Docketed by Randolph, "James Madison Jany 14. 1783."

Philada. Jany 14. 1783

My dear Sir

Yesterday's post having arrived without a mail from Virga. I was disappointed of the pleasure of a letter from you.[1]

All the foreign articles which have come to hand are published in the inclosed gazette of this morning.[2] The evacuation of Charleston is at length reduced to certainty by the publications in the N. York paper and we expect every moment an official report of it from Gl Greene.[3]

The deputies from the army are still here. The explanations which they have given to a Committee on the topics of the Memorial are of the most serious nature.[4] I wish they could with propriety be promulged throughout the U.S. They would I am sure, at least put to shame all those who have laboured to throw a fallacious gloss over our public affairs, and counteracted the measures necessary to the real prosperity of them.[5]

The deliberations of Congress have been turned pretty much of late on the valuation of lands prescribed by the articles of confederation. The difficulties which attend that rule of apportionment seem on near inspection to be in a manner insuperable. The work is too vast to be executed without the intervention of the several States, and if their intervention be employed, all confidence in an impartial execution is at end.[6]

I have not been able to find sufficient leisure for taking the copies which you asked & which I promised.[7] I am the less uneasy at the delay as the conveyance by the post is rendered so precarious by the weather

Docr. Shippen desired me to obtain an answer from you on the case of Mr. Cuthburt, and particularly whether you are likely to recover any thing for him.[8]

Mr. Jefferson has not yet taken his departure. We hope the causes which have prevented it will not continue many days longer.[9]

[1] For Randolph's explanation of why he had not written, see his letter of 15 Jan. 1783 to JM.

[2] Delegates to Harrison, 14 Jan. 1783, n. 1.

[3] Harrison to JM, 4 Jan., n. 9; JM Notes, 9–10 Jan., n. 4; Harrison to Delegates, 11 Jan. 1783, and nn. 5, 6.

[4] Delegates to Harrison, 7 Jan., and n. 5; JM Notes, 13 Jan. 1783. Late in his life JM or someone by his direction placed a bracket at the beginning of this paragraph and also at the close of the next paragraph to indicate the portion of the letter which should be published in the first edition of his papers (Madison, *Papers* [Gilpin ed.], I, 498).

[5] The meaning of the last clause would be clearer if JM had written "have counteracted." He no doubt had in mind the repeal by the Virginia General Assembly of its ratification of the impost amendment, the refusal of the Rhode Island House of Representatives to ratify the amendment, the published letter or letters of David Howell denying the existence of a severe financial crisis in "public affairs," and the efforts of Jonathan Arnold and his colleagues from Rhode Island to oblige Congress to make available for publication from confidential communications excerpts which, taken from their context, would tend to support Howell's misrepresentations. On 14 January Congress adopted a committee report, drafted by Alexander Hamilton, refusing to release any confidential letters other than those no longer under an "injunction of secrecy," but agreeing to transmit to the executive of Rhode Island the excerpts from congressional proceedings which the delegates from that state had sought to obtain. These excerpts were to be accompanied "with a request that precautions may be taken to prevent their appearing in the public prints" (*JCC*, XXIV, 32–36, 45–46). See also JM Notes, 3 Jan., and n. 3; 9–10 Jan. 1783, and nn. 21, 22.

[6] JM Notes, 9–10 Jan., and nn. 2, 3, 8; 14 Jan. 1783, and nn. 2, 4–9, 11.

[7] JM to Randolph, 7 Jan., and n. 10.

[8] Dr. William Shippen, Jr. (1736–1808), was director general of the medical department of the continental army from 11 April 1777 to 3 January 1781. In London in 1762, shortly before returning to Philadelphia after being graduated with an M.D. degree by the University of Edinburgh, Shippen married Alice Lee, a sister of Richard Henry and Arthur Lee. Shippen surely would have directed his query to his brother-in-law Arthur Lee, if Lee had been in Philadelphia (Cazenove G. Lee, Jr., *Lee Chronicle*, pp. 195, 242–43, 348–49). The fact that Anthony Cuthbert (1751–1832), who in 1780 served as a captain of the Philadelphia City artillery, manufactured masts suggests that he was plaintiff in a suit to collect a debt owed him by the owner or operator of a vessel (*Lineage Book of the National Society of the Daughters of the American Revolution*, CXXVI [1916], 99; *Heads of Families at the First Census of the United States Taken in the Year 1790: Pennsylvania* [Washington, 1908], p. 234; *Pa. Archives*, 3d ser., XVI, 317). Neither the identity of the

court in Virginia nor of the defendant, except that his surname appears to have
been "Reuors," has been determined. See Randolph to JM, 1 Feb. 1783.
  [9] JM to Randolph, 7 Jan. 1783, and n. 9.

Notes on Debates

MS (LC: Madison Papers). For a description of the manuscript
of Notes on Debates, see *Papers of Madison,* V, 231–34.

Wednesday Jany. 15.

A letter dated 19th. December from Genl Greene was recd. notifying
the evacuation of Charlstown.[1] It was in the first place referred to the
Secy of Congs for publication, excepting the passage which recited the
exchange of prisoners, which being contrary to the Resolution of the
16 of Ocr. agst. partial exchanges, was deemed improper for publication.[2] It was in the next place referred to a come. in order that some
complimentary report might be made in favor of Genl. Greene & the
Southn. army. Docr. Ramsay havg come in after this reference and
being uninformed of it, moved that a Committee might be appointed
to devise a proper mode of expressing to Genl. Greene the high sense
entertained by Congress of his merits & services. In support of his
motion he went into lavish praises of Gl. Greene, and threw out the
idea of making him a Lieutent. General. His motion being opposed as
somewhat singular and unnecessary after the reference of Gl. Greene's
letter, he withdrew it.[3]

A letter was red. from Genl. Washington inclosing a certificate from
Mr. Chittenden of Vermont acknowledging the receipt of the com-
munication which Gl Washington had sent him of the proceedings of
Congress on the   day of   .[4]

  [1] Harrison to Delegates, 11 Jan. 1783, n. 6.
  [2] The extract from Greene's dispatch, as printed in the *Pennsylvania Packet* of
16 January, closes with "Published by order of Congress, CHARLES THOMSON, Secretary." The resolution of 16 October 1782 declared, "That Congress will not go into
any partial exchanges of prisoners of war in future, but will take most effectual
measures in their power, for the safe keeping of all prisoners of war, until a general
cartel on liberal and national principles be agreed to and established" (*JCC,* XXIII,
661). The relevant passage in Greene's dispatch reads, "I had the happiness to negotiate a few Weeks ago a general Exchange of all the Civil and Militia Officers,
as well as privates of every denomination under military paroles, belonging to the
Southern department" (NA: PCC, No. 155, II, 603–6).
  [3] Although the printed journal for 15 January includes the motion which David
Ramsay introduced and later withdrew, it omits the motion adopted by Congress

before his arrival (JCC, XXIV, 46–47, 47, n. 1). John Rutledge, chairman, Thomas Mifflin (Pa.), and Hugh Williamson comprised the committee. On 17 January 1783 Congress adopted by a unanimous vote the committee's report, drafted by Williamson, expressing "the thanks of the United States in Congress assembled" to Greene and "the officers and private soldiers under his command" (JCC, XXIV, 47–48). On 24 January in a letter congratulating Greene, John Rutledge stated that the general's "particular Friends" had "thought it not adviseable to propose" his promotion (Burnett, Letters, VII, 22).

4 Papers of Madison, V, 334–35; 335, nn. 7, 10; 336, nn. 12, 13, 17, 19; 388, and n. 3; 396, and n. 6. On 5 December 1782 Congress adopted resolutions concerning Vermont which had been drafted by Hamilton and introduced by Thomas McKean (Del.) two days before (ibid., V, 367, n. 2; 368, n. 3; JCC, XXIII, 765–66, 769). On 11 December Elias Boudinot, president of Congress, forwarded a copy of these "proceedings" to Washington, who dispatched them on 23 December by a courier to "Governor" Thomas Chittenden at Bennington, Vt. Washington's reply to Boudinot, enclosing Chittenden's acknowledgment of receipt, under a "State of Vermont" superscription, was dated 8 January 1783 (Fitzpatrick, Writings of Washington, XXV, 458; XXVI, 14–15; NA: PCC, No. 152, XI, 53–54, 57).

From Edmund Randolph

RC (LC: Madison Papers). Letter unsigned but in Randolph's hand. Addressed by Randolph to "The Honble Jas. Madison jr. esqr. of congress Philadelphia." Docketed by JM, "Jany. 15. 1782," a misdating by a year.

PETTUS'S[1] Jany 15. 1782[3]

MY DEAR SIR

The extreme badness of the weather prevented me from sending a letter from hence to Richmond for the post of last week.[2]

As I am really uneasy, at a little seeming omission on my part to Mr Jones, I must beg you to mention to him that until friday last, I had supposed that Colo. Monroe had procured a bill for Mr. Henry's money, lodged in my hands for his use from Mr Ross.[3] Having an account much in my favor with Ross, I thought no more of the matter, after Colo. M. had undertaken to procure a draught. You will readily conceive my surprize, when I heard from that Gentleman, that this money had never been remitted. I have given him[4] an order for the money to be sent by the present post, and have desired him to state the matter to Mr. Jones, who will otherwise be surprized at my not availing myself of the opportunity by Colo. Bland.[5]

I shall certainly transmit a state of the constitutional question and argument, as soon as a mass of papers, now before me, is reduced.[6]

The approaching election will probably be marked by some singularities. By the resolutions of the house of delegates, a man to be elected must be a spotless whig.[7] I suspect that so[me] of the candidates will not be able to produce evidence of patriotism of a very early date, and that violent contentions will ensue: And yet it would seem, that the determined spirit of the last assembly ought to satisfy those, who hoped for wicked measures, that nothing but staunch republicanism, and a due attachment to the French alliance will ever be acceptable to Virginia.[8] There is much conversation among those, with whom I mix, concerning the revival of committees. They may, I think, be rendered auxiliary to the resolutions above mentioned, by acting as a censorial power. It is inconceivable, how much mischief is produced by the malignant rumours, which the bad circulate, and which cannot be the subject of punishment by law. But their effect might be counteracted, if committees were at liberty to animadvert on them, not by a corporal or pecuniary penalty, but by exhibiting the offende[rs] to the world, as not well-affected: The jurisdiction of these bodies may be so restrained, as to prevent the repetition of those extravagancies, for which some of them were censureable at the beginning of the war.[9] I confess, that the measure is much favored by me, because I have had experience of the baneful influence of the observations of those, who keep within the law, & yet are sapping the Zeal of our weak citizens by secret whispers. I believe, that I could procure a committee to be elected by the people of this county, and I should certainly attempt it, if such an institution, entered into without the previous assent of the legislature, would not carry the appearance of an opposition to government.[10]

The evacuation of Charlestown has increased the sterility of the south in news. It is said, but I cannot determine with what truth, that considerable purchases have been made of the british goods found there: and that a great quantity of them is destined for Virginia.[11] Great stratagem must be used to accomplish their introduction here, and North Carolina has shewn by a late condemnation of a cargo of british goods that they will not be suffered to pass thro' her territory without arrest.[12]

Ought not the debts of the U.S. to be entered on the secret journal? I ask this question, because I have seen in various hands a particular account of them. In time of peace indeed, or even in time of war, if the states were required to pay a proportion of them, a minute history of these debts ought to be forwarded, that it might be seen, on what principles a requisition of money was made: But at this day, when the mere current expences of the war are demanded, it has the aspect of something more than folly for any *member of congress* to publish them abroad.[13]

I have not got your letter of this week from the office.[14]

[1] For "Pettus's," see *Papers of Madison*, IV, 148, n. 2.

[2] The *Virginia Gazette*, 18 January 1783, announced that, "owing to the different rivers being rendered impassible by the ice," no mail from the north had reached Richmond "this week."

[3] Randolph's "friday last" was 10 January 1783. Joseph Jones, a delegate to Congress from Virginia; James Monroe, Jones's nephew and a member of the Virginia Council of State; James Henry of Accomack County, who had borrowed money from Jones in 1780; and David Ross, a prominent Petersburg merchant and owner of ships, mines, and plantations, who from 27 December 1780 to 24 May 1782 had been the commercial agent of Virginia. See *Papers of Madison*, I, 318 n. 1; II, 89, hdn.; III, 60, n. 8; IV, 154, n. 14; V, 309; 312, n. 21. Probably bearing upon Henry's debt to Jones is the following notation by Jones on an undated memorandum concerning the money owed by Virginia about 1 April 1783 to Jones, JM, and Theodorick Bland, delegates in Congress: "NB. upon going over the aud. list with the Auditors before I left Richmond I discover an omission of 7770 ⅓ dols. adv.[?] on acct of Mr. James Henry when in Congress and applied to his use which by letter from him I find he has accounted for to me   I must therefore be debited with it. J. Jones" (MS in Va. State Library).

[4] James Monroe.

[5] Bland left Farmingdell (Farmingdale), his estate in Prince George County, on 27 December 1782 and, after a leisurely journey, arrived in Philadelphia by 22 January 1783 (MS in Va. Historical Society; JM to Randolph, 22 Jan. 1783).

[6] Randolph referred to his brief as attorney general of Virginia in the Case of the Prisoners (*Caton* v. *Commonwealth*) in October 1782. See *Papers of Madison*, V, 217–18; 218, n. 9; 263; 265, n. 7; 290; 382; 384, n. 4; 474; Randolph to JM, 7 Mar. 1783.

[7] *Papers of Madison*, V, 453; 455, n. 8. An announcement of the elections to be held on 7 April first appeared in the *Virginia Gazette* of 4 January. See also Randolph to JM, 7 Feb. 1783.

[8] Among others to whom Randolph referred may have been Arthur Lee, openly critical of "the French alliance," David Mason, allegedly disloyal, and James Mc-Craw, who had been expelled from the House of Delegates for views "inimical to the U. S." See *Papers of Madison*, V, 400–401; 403, nn. 9, 10; 404, n. 17; 425; 427, n. 7; 454; 456, n. 13.

[9] Randolph referred to the committees of correspondence, the local committees of safety, and the provincial Committee of Safety, which both before and during the period of transition in Virginia from colony to commonwealth had served as the *de facto* governing bodies, concerting resistance against royal officials, exposing Loyalists, and sometimes punishing them harshly without resort to judicial process. See *Papers of Madison*, I, 146–47; 147, n. 1; 161; 162, n. 10; 164, n. 1; 190–91; 192, n. 6.

On 19 December 1782 Harrison had issued a proclamation, requiring "all civil Magistrates, County Lieutenants and other inferior officers of Militia" to search for and arrest "subjects of the King of Great Britain" who illegally "have been suffered to remain" in Virginia and "form a seditious and malignant party in the bowels of the State," and who "by calumny and falsehood alienate the affections of the good citizens from the Government, and retard the execution of the best of Laws" (*Va. Gazette*, 21 and 28 Dec. 1782, and 4 Jan. 1783).

[10] For Randolph, attorney general of Virginia, to favor the creation of an extra-legal "censorial power" for the purpose of detecting and repressing citizens who broke no law but disseminated "secret whispers" reveals his conviction that Virginians "not well-affected" were numerous, influential, or both.

[11] For the evacuation of Charleston, see Harrison to Delegates, 11 Jan. 1783, and n. 6. John Banks of the Richmond firm of Hunter, Banks, and Company had purchased in Charleston, even before its evacuation by the enemy, large quantities of British goods. Although some of the clothing was for the use of General Greene's troops, many of the articles had been bought by Banks as a speculation for his own profit or that of his partners. See *Cal. of Va. State Papers*, III, 428–30; *Va. Gazette*, 25 Jan. 1783; *Papers of Madison*, V, 287, n. 19.

[12] Randolph may be referring again, as he possibly had in his letter of 22 November 1782 to JM, to the "Batchelor," a vessel owned by Hunter, Banks, and Company (*Papers of Madison*, V, 308; 311, n. 14).

[13] Whose were "the various hands" or who was the particular "member of Congress" if any, to whom Randolph referred, has not been determined. If he was suggesting Theodorick Bland or Arthur Lee, neither of these delegates can be shown to have revealed confidential information about finances. The amount of the foreign debt had been spread on the public journal of Congress as early as 24 May 1782. Robert Morris, superintendent of finance, did not know even approximately the total of the non-interest-bearing ("unliquidated") portion of the domestic debt. On the other hand, the fact that loan-office certificates and other debentures paid 6 per cent interest was obviously no secret. Therefore, anyone who noted in the public journal of Congress Morris' estimate of the sum needed annually to meet this obligation could ascertain readily the principal of the interest-bearing, domestic debt. See *JCC*, XXII, 290–93, 295–96, 437; XXIII, 771; *Papers of Madison*, IV, 284; V, 129, n. 13; 156, n. 7; 158, n. 7; 376, n. 27.

On 18 February 1783, Congress adopted Bland's motion directing Morris to submit a detailed analysis of the foreign and domestic debt, as of the first of that year. Although Morris' covering letter, giving about $35,327,770 as the total of the debt, exclusive of the "unliquidated" portion and the "old continental Bills and Arrearages of Half Pay," was entered in the journal of 10 March, his itemization of this total was not printed therein until 29 April, or two weeks after Congress had ratified the preliminary peace treaty (*JCC*, XXIV, 139, 180–81, 241–42, 285–86). See also JM Notes, 26 Feb. and n. 46; 11 Mar. 1783, and n. 9.

[14] Randolph referred to JM's letter of 30 December 1782 (*Papers of Madison*, V, 472–74).

Notes on Debates

MS (LC: Madison Papers). For a description of the manuscript of Notes on Debates, see *Papers of Madison*, V, 231–34.

Thursday Jany. 16.

Mr. Rutlidge informed Congress that there was reason to apprehend that the train of negociations in Europe had been so misrepresented in the State of S. Carolina as to make it probable that an attempt might be made in the Legislature to repeal the confiscation laws of that State,

& even if such attempt sd. fail, the misrepresentations cd. not fail to injure the sale of the property confiscated in that State.[1] In order therefore to frustrate these misrepresentations he moved that the Delegates of S. Carolina might be furnished with an extract from the letter of the 14th. of Ocr. from Docr. Franklin, so far as it informed Congress, "that something had been mentioned to the American Plenipotentiaries relative to the Refugees & to English debts, but not insisted on: it being answered on their part that this was a matter belonging to the individual States and on which Congress cd. enter into no Stipulations."[2] The motion was 2ded. by Mr. Jarvais & supported by Mr. Ramsay.[3] It was opposed by Mr. Elseworth & Mr. Wolcott as improper, since communication of this intelligence, might encourage the States to extend confiscations to British debts, a circumstance which wd. be dishonorable to the U. S. & might embarrass a treaty of peace.[4] Mr. Fitzimmons expressed the same apprehensions. So did Mr. Ghorum. His Colleague Mr. Osgood was in favr. of the motion.[5] By Mr. Madison[6] the motion was so enlarged and varied as "to leave *all* the delegates at liberty to communicate the extract to their Constents. in such form & under such cautions as they sd. judge prudent."[7] The motion so varied was adopted by Mr. Rutlidge & substituted in place of the original one. It was however still opposed by the opponents of the original motion. Mr. Madison observed that as all the States had espoused in some degree the doctrine of confiscations, & as some of them had given instructions to their delegates on the subject,[8] it was the duty of Congress without enquiring into the expediency of Confiscations, to prevent as far as they cd. any measures which might impede that object in negociations for peace, by inducing an opinion that the U. S. were not firm with respect to it; that in this view it was of consequence to prevent the repeal & even the attempt of a repeal of the confiscation law of one of the States,[9] and that if a confidential communication of the extract in question would answer such a purpose, it was improper for Congress to oppose it. on a question the motion was negatived, Congress being much divided thereon. Several of those who were in the negative, were willing that the Delegates of S. Carolina[10] sd. be licenced to transmit to their State what related to the Refugees, omitting what related to British debts[11] and invited Mr. Rutlidge to renew his motion in that qualified form. others suggested the propriety of his contradicting the misrepresations in general with out referring to any official information recd. by Congress. Mr. R. said he wd. think further on the subject, and desired that it might lie over.[12]

1 At least one source of John Rutledge's information was probably supplied by his brother Edward, who in February 1782 had guided through the legislature of South Carolina a bill adding to the rigors of an earlier law providing for the confiscation or heavy amercement of Loyalists' estates (*Papers of Madison*, V, 51, n. 4).

On 10 October commissioners of South Carolina and of the enemy in Charleston effected a compact whereby the British, upon evacuating the city, would restore every refugee and captured slave within their lines in return for a pledge that the state would cease sequestering the property of Loyalists and open her courts to suits by Loyalists for recovery of estates already confiscated. Although the British by no means fully honored this agreement when they left Charleston on 14 December 1782, the legislature inclined toward a policy of leniency, both because a restoration of good feeling was desirable and because many of the most influential families had been Loyalists or at least of doubtful loyalty (*ibid.*, V, 440, n. 4; David Ramsay, *The History of South-Carolina, from its First Settlement in 1670, to the Year 1808* [2 vols.; Charleston, 1809], I, 468, 472–74, 477).

2 The quotation is a paraphrase of a sentence in Franklin's dispatch of 14 October to Robert R. Livingston, secretary for foreign affairs. After "States," Franklin wrote, "the Congress had no authority to repeal those laws, and therefore could give us none to stipulate for such repeal" (Wharton, *Revol. Dipl. Corr.*, V, 811).

3 John Lewis Gervais and David Ramsay, delegates from South Carolina.

4 At the outset of this sentence, JM canceled "The latter observed that." Oliver Ellsworth and Oliver Wolcott were delegates from Connecticut. In the *Virginia Gazette* of 13 November 1782, an unidentified but obviously well-educated author, signing himself "Independent Whig," argued that the legislature, in its "wisdom" and "as the fountain of justice," must recognize how completely the very fact of revolution had extinguished all private debts owed by Virginians to British creditors.

5 Thomas FitzSimons, a delegate from Pennsylvania; Nathaniel Gorham and Samuel Osgood, delegates from Massachusetts.

6 Here and later in these notes JM originally indicated his own name only as "Mr. M" and Rutledge's only as "Mr. R." Later he completed each of these initialed surnames except the "Mr. R." in the last sentence.

7 Neither Rutledge's motion nor JM's enlargement thereof is entered in the printed journal for 16 January 1783 (*JCC*, XXIV, 47). "Constents." is an abbreviation of "Constituents."

8 See the instructions of the Virginia General Assembly, 17 December 1782. Although these instructions were not received by the Virginia delegates until 20 January 1783, JM knew of them as early as 29 December from Randolph's letter to him on 20 December 1782. See *Papers of Madison*, V, 409–10; 410, nn. 1–4; 425; 454; 473; also, JM to Randolph, 7 Jan. 1783.

9 South Carolina.

10 Besides Gervais, Ramsay, and Rutledge, Ralph Izard was also attending Congress as a delegate from South Carolina (*JCC*, XXIV, 42, 94).

11 The "Refugees" were Loyalists who had fled or been banished from their homes.

12 For renewed discussion of the subject, see JM Notes, 9 May 1783; *JCC*, XXV, 964.

From the Reverend James Madison

RC (LC: Madison Papers). Docketed by JM, "Madison Js. Revd Jany. 16. 1783."

Jany. 16th. 1783

DEAR COL.[1]

I recd yesterday your's of the 24th. Ulto.[2] and am much obliged for the part you have taken in both the affairs mentioned. As the Price is so high, I am not very much disappointed at the Want of Ingredients:[3] As to the Seal, we shall take it very kind of you to forward it as soon as convenient. The Money shall be paid by a Bill without Delay. Opportunities to Richmond probably are much more frequent than to this Place, & will answer nearly as well.[4]

It appears, I think now, that the principal Stumbling Block is removed. The Commission you mention, certainly promises a Solicitude on the Part of Britain, at least, for Negotiation, if it has not in Fact; given up the grand Point for wh. we contend.[5] No Country ever stood more in Need of Peace than this. Virginia, wh. ought by Nature, & wh. a Peace will prove it to be, the most flourishing of the Union, is now almost a sapless Trunk. Our Money continually drained from among us, centers elsewhere, we have not eno' for common purposes, & even this little is every Day growing less & less. But, I fear, from a Copy of a late Letter wh. is now generally circulated, that Obstacles to Peace will still arise, wh. the unsuspecting did not foresee. The Authority upon wh. it rests, is that of our public Ministers abroad. It's Contents are now no Secret to the World. They are in the Mouth of every Body, & whether true or not, seem to have excited a general Alarm.[6]

A Question was asked by the Author of the Letter before alluded to, before a Committee of the House, & a large Concourse of Strangers, was asked too of a Member of C. itself, "Do you not know that a *Majority* of C. are under the Influence of the French Minister?"[7] If this really be the Case, perhaps Peace, and even honle. Peace, will in vain hold out the Olive to America herself. I hope however that you are not under this Influence. If you are, the World does you great Injustice, for you are not even suspected.[8] But it was certainly a curious Question, considering from whence it came & to whom it was directed, & withall the Occasion on wh. it was proposed. You know probably the Circumstances wh. called forth all this Matter allud[ed to] in our Assembly. If you do not, I do not feel myself disposed to enter into a Detail, as I am sure, it wd give you little Satisfact[ion.] It may serve however hereafter for the curious Retailer of historical Affairs to make many sage Reflections upon.

I once more take the Liberty to inclose a Letter in yours. I would not omit answering one recd from Dr Coste,[9] & it appeared the best Channel to forward it to him, as you probably have frequen[t] Communication with the F. Army. I shall not however make a practice of this, nor even now shd not impose[?] it, but that I apprehended, it wd. not otherwise get to him.

Many friends here wish you all Happiness & no one more sincerely than

J.M.

If the Doct has left Ama. the Letter may be burnt—[10]

[1] For JM's appointment as a colonel of the militia of Orange County, Va., see *Papers of Madison,* I, 163.

[2] Not found.

[3] What article was priced "so high" has not been identified. Perhaps JM, in his missing letter of 24 December, informed the Reverend James Madison about the cost of making "Cakes for Electrical" experiments, which had interested the clergyman in his letter of 3 October to JM. If this surmise is accurate, the "Ingredients" would correspond with "the other Parts of the Apparatus" mentioned in that letter (*Papers of Madison,* V, 179; 180, n. 5).

[4] Although the College of William and Mary already had a seal, and the faculty minutes omit mention of the need for another, the Reverend James Madison no doubt referred to a second seal being made for the college of which he was the president. See Jones to JM, 25 May, and Receipt of Robert Scot, engraver, 16 June 1783 (LC: Madison Papers). To desire a private carrier to deliver the seal is understandable, for a package weighing only a pound would have cost nearly $15.00, if sent by the continental postal service from Philadelphia to either Richmond or Williamsburg (*JCC,* XXIII, 676–77).

[5] In his missing letter of 24 December 1782 to the Reverend James Madison, JM evidently had included at least most of the information mentioned in the first paragraph of his letter on the same day to Edmund Randolph (*Papers of Madison,* V, 448). Richard Oswald's revised "Commission," by authorizing him as a representative of King George III to treat for peace with the commissioners "of the thirteen United States of America" rather than with thirteen "colonies or plantations," conceded the "grand Point for wh. we contend" and thus removed the "principal Stumbling Block" on the road to peace (Wharton, *Revol. Dipl. Corr.,* V, 613–14, 748–50; *Papers of Madison,* V, 415–16; 418, n. 17).

[6] The "late Letter" almost certainly was that of Arthur Lee to Mann Page, Jr. See *ibid.,* V, 184, and n. 4. The "Contents" of this letter and even its exact date are unknown. The Reverend James Madison probably meant that France, chiefly because of unfulfilled obligations to her ally Spain, was putting "Obstacles" in the way of peace between the United States and Great Britain. Lee's letter to Page had been written in September or October 1782, or before dispatches from John Jay and John Adams, warning against the allegedly devious course of France in the peace negotiations, had reached Congress. On the other hand, friends of Lee in Massachusetts appear to have kept him informed about the anti-French comments of John Adams in his private letters (Richard Henry Lee, *Life of Arthur Lee, LL.D.* [2 vols.; Boston, 1829], II, 277–78). Included in the *Virginia Gazette* of 11

January 1783 is an "Extract of a letter from Paris, October 18" reporting offers by Great Britain to cede territory in North America to France if she would withdraw from her alliance with the United States.

[7] For the inquiry by a committee of the Virginia House of Delegates occasioned by Arthur Lee's letter to Mann Page, see *Papers of Madison*, V, 184, and n. 4; 339, and n. 7; 400; 403, nn. 9–14; 404, nn. 16–19; Randolph to JM, 15 Jan. 1783, n. 13. The "Member" of Congress whom Lee addressed was Theodorick Bland (*Papers of Madison*, V, 341; 401; 404, n. 17). The "French Minister" to the United States was the Chevalier de La Luzerne. For other apparent evidences of his "Influence," see Burnett, *Letters*, VI, 460–61; William E. O'Donnell, *Chevalier de La Luzerne*, pp. 47–50; 62–65, and nn.

[8] This sentence and the expression of "hope" may have been the clergyman's tactfully humorous way of suggesting that a report had reached him of JM's and La Luzerne's friendship. For examples of it, but especially of the cordial relations between JM and Barbé Marbois, secretary of the French legation, see *Papers of Madison*, II, 114–16; 116, n. 1; IV, 288; 326–30; 334; 403–4; V, 102; 103, n. 10; 152.

[9] For Dr. Jean François Coste, see *ibid.*, IV, 338, n. 7; V, 93, n. 13.

[10] Dr. Coste possibly had left the United States either on 24 December 1782, when the French army began its voyage from Boston to the West Indies, but he more likely did so on 7 January 1783, when the Comte de Rochambeau and members of his staff sailed from Annapolis for France. Rochambeau and Dr. Coste were close friends. See *ibid.*, V, 344, n. 7; 429, n. 5; 443, n. 3; Jean-Edmond Weelen, *Rochambeau, Father and Son* (New York, 1936), pp. 122, 186, 270.

Notes on Debates

MS (LC: Madison Papers). For a description of the manuscript of Notes on Debates, see *Papers of Madison*, V, 231–34.

Friday Jany. 17th.

The Committee on the motion of Mr. Peters of the   day of relative to a further application for foreign loans, reported that they had conferred with the superintendt. of Finance[1] & concurred in opinion with him, that the applications already on foot were as great as could be made prudently, until proper funds should be established.[2] The latent view of this report was to strengthen the argt. in favr. of such funds, and the report it was agreed should lie on the table[3] to be considered along with the report which might be made on the memorial from the army, & which wd involve the same subject.[4]

The report thanking Gel. Greene for his Services was agreed to without opposition or observation. Several however thought it badly composed, and that some notice ought to have been taken of Majr. Burnet aid to Gl. G. who was the bearer of the letter announcing the evacuation of Charlestown.[5]

Mr. Webster & Mr. Judd agents for the deranged officers of the

Massachusetts & Cont. lines were heard by the Gd. Committee, in favr. of their constituents. The sum of their representations was that the sd. officers were equally distressed for, entitled to, & in expectation of provision for fulfilling the rewards stipulated to them, as officers retained in Service[6]

1 The blank spaces should be filled with "13th" and "January," respectively. See JM Notes, 13 Jan. 1783, and nn. 2, 8.

2 Delegates to Harrison, 7 Jan. and n. 5; JM Notes, 9–10 Jan. 1783, and nn. 12, 14. By "proper funds" JM meant an assured income from domestic sources such as the proposed impost or payment by many of the states of the long-in-arrears financial requisitions of Congress.

3 *JCC*, XXIV, 48–49. The unexpressed or "latent" tenor of the committee's report was that Congress must establish "proper funds" or else the hope of borrowing more money overseas would not be realized.

4 JM Notes, 6 Jan., and n. 2; 7 Jan., and n. 4; 13 Jan. 1783, and n. 16.

5 Harrison to Delegates, 11 Jan., and nn. 5, 6; JM Notes, 15 Jan., and n. 3; 26 Feb. 1783, and n. 6; JCC, XXIV, 47–48, 48, n. 1.

6 JM Notes, 13 Jan., and n. 20. The memorial, drafted by Pelatiah Webster and William Judd on behalf of deranged officers of the Connecticut line, had been first submitted to Congress late in July 1782. The lengthy consideration accorded the memorial at that time was concluded by a resolution deferring further attention to the matter until 1 January 1783. During the debate in July, Theodorick Bland offered the motion which is erroneously entered in the printed journal for 8 January 1783 (*Papers of Madison*, IV, 444–45; 446, n. 3; 450–51; 451, n. 2; *JCC*, XXIV, 43, and n. 1).

On that date, having been reminded by Webster and Judd of the above memorial and having received from Webster on 7 January a separate petition on behalf of the deranged officers of the Massachusetts line, Congress referred both documents to the grand committee, which had been appointed on 6 January to consider the memorial from the officers of Washington's army (NA: PCC, No. 19, VI, 504–5, 507; JM Notes, 6 Jan. 1783; *JCC*, XXIV, 43, and n. 1). See also JM Notes, 24 Jan.; 25 Jan. 1783; *JCC*, XXIV, 154, n. 1, 169–70, 170, n. 1.

Born in Connecticut, Pelatiah Webster (1725–1795) was graduated by Yale College, served briefly as a pastor in Massachusetts, and thereafter became a merchant in Philadelphia. A staunch patriot, he was imprisoned and lost much property during the occupation of that city by the British. He is principally remembered as the author of essays on trade and finance, and above all, of *A Dissertation on the Political Union and Constitution of the Thirteen United States of North America*, published in 1783.

William Judd (*ca.* 1740–1804) of Farmington, Conn., rose from private to major in the militia, 1757–1776. Commissioned captain in the continental army on 1 January 1777, he served until deranged in grade of major just four years later. He was a member of the General Assembly, 1785–1794, and voted for ratification of the Federal Constitution in the state convention of 1788. Prominent as a Jeffersonian Republican, he was deprived of his commission as justice of the peace by the Federalist-dominated legislature in 1804, because he insisted that the royal charter, under which the state government continued to operate, was not equivalent to a constitution adopted by the people (*Collections of the Connecticut Historical Society*, IX [1903], 223; X [1905], 44, 150, 260, 334; Fitzpatrick, *Writings of Washington*, XV, 319, and n. 3; *JCC*, V, 750; Richard J. Purcell, *Connecticut in Transition, 1775–1818* [Washington, 1918], pp. 254–64).

Notes on Debates

MS (LC: Madison Papers). For a description of the manuscript of Notes on Debates, see *Papers of Madison*, V, 231–34. JM preceded his entry for 21 January with the notation, "From Friday 17 to Tuesday 21. See Journals." See JM Notes, 17 Jan.; *JCC*, XXIV, 47–49.

[21 January 1783]

A letter from Mr. Adams of 8th day of October 1782 containing prophetic observations relitive to the Expedition of Ld. Howe for the relief of Gibralter, & its consequences &c &c excited &c &c.[1]

Another letter from do. relative to the Treaty of Amity & Commerce & the Convention with the States Genl concerning vessels recaptured, copies of which accompanied the letter.[2] These papers were committed to Mr. Madison, Mr. Hamilton & Mr. Elsworth.[3]

[1] Judging from the contrasting color of the ink and style of the handwriting, JM made three additions to his record for this date long after he penned his original notes. These addenda are (1) "of 8th day of October 1782," (2) "with the States Genl" in the second paragraph, and (3) the names of the committee, beginning with "to" in the final sentence. The first of these alterations should have been inserted after "Another letter" at the outset of the second paragraph. In the first paragraph JM referred to John Adams' dispatch from The Hague on 23 September 1782 to Robert R. Livingston, secretary for foreign affairs. Characterizing Gibraltar as only a "trophy of insolence to England and of humiliation to Spain," Adams depreciated the "utility" of "that impenetrable rock" in an era when "freedom of commerce is so much esteemed," and added that he "had no expectation at all" of a successful outcome of the siege by the armed forces of Spain and France (Wharton, *Revol. Dipl. Corr.*, V, 750–51). For the accuracy of Adams' "prophetic observations," see *Papers of Madison*, V, 198, n. 10.

Jared Sparks recorded that he was told by JM at Montpelier on 25 April 1827: "It was customary in the Old Congress for the Secretary to read to the Congress assembled all the letters of our ministers in foreign countries. The letters of John Adams were not interesting to the members in general, because they contained much extraneous matter, discussions and speculations on government, and narratives of events abroad. He had a great deal of leisure, was fond of writing, and thus his letters became voluminous. But Mr. Madison thinks they would be very interesting for the mass of readers at the present day" (Herbert B. Adams, *The Life and Writings of Jared Sparks* [2 vols.; Boston, 1893], II, 33).

[2] With his dispatch of 8 October 1782 to Livingston, Adams enclosed "an authentic copy" of "the treaty of commerce and the convention concerning recaptures," which he had signed on that day as the minister of the United States to the Netherlands (Wharton, *Revol. Dipl. Corr.*, V, 803). For the text of these agreements, see *JCC*, XXIV, 68–82.

[3] The appointment of this committee is not recorded in the printed journal for 21 January 1783 but is noted in NA: PCC, No. 186, fol. 80. See Report on Treaty, 23 Jan. 1783.

Virginia Delegates to Benjamin Harrison

RC (Virginia State Library). In JM's hand, except for Joseph Jones's signature. Docketed by Harrison, "Virginia Delegates Jany 21st 1783."

PHILA: 21st. Janry 1783.

SIR.

The Post which arrived late yesterday evening brought us your Excellencys letters of the 4th. and 11th. with their several inclosures. we shall loose no time in carrying into execution the intentions of the Executive respecting the settlement with Mr. Nathan and communicate the result to your Excellency.[1] the other matters from the Assembly shall also be duly attended to.[2] we hope it will be convenient for the Treasurer in the begining of next month to furnish us with a supply.[3] very respectfully we are

yr Excellencys obed hum: servts:

JAMES MADISON JR.

JOS: JONES

[1] Harrison to Delegates, 4 Jan., and nn. 5, 6; 11 Jan., and n. 4. For further comment upon the claim of Simon Nathan, see Delegates to Harrison, 28 Jan.; 4 Feb.; Harrison to Delegates, 15 Feb. 1783.

[2] For the delegates' attention to the Virginia legislature's instructions *in re* Virginia's financial quota of 1783 and the impost amendment, see JM Notes, 27 Jan.; *in re* the tobacco contract with the merchants-capitulant of Yorktown, see JM Notes, 31 Jan.; *in re* loss of vouchers pertinent to the settlement of Virginia's accounts with Congress, see *JCC*, XXIV, 106, 123; and *in re* Virginia's confiscation of Loyalists' property, see JM Notes, 20 March 1783.

[3] On 1 January 1783 JM's salary as a delegate was in arrears more than £865 Virginia currency. See Jacquelin Ambler, "the Treasurer," to JM, 1 Feb. 1783.

Notes on Debates

MS (LC: Madison Papers). For a description of the manuscript of Notes on Debates, see *Papers of Madison*, V, 231–34.

Wednesday January 22

Congress adjourned to give the Come. on the Treaty & convention time to prepare a report thereon.[1]

[1] JM Notes, 21 Jan., and nn. 2, 3; Report on Treaty, 23 Jan. 1783.

To Edmund Randolph

Printed text (Madison, *Papers* [Gilpin ed.], I, 111–12). The manuscript of the letter, which is missing, probably was lost between 1840 and 1865, the dates of publication of the Gilpin and Congressional editions, respectively. JM inadvertently dated the letter "1782" rather than 1783. The error was his rather than Gilpin's, for JM's own chronological list of his letters to Randolph, prepared *ca.* 1821, shows this letter as of "1782. Jany. 22" (LC: Madison Papers). See also *Papers of Madison*, III, 100, ed. n.; IV, 41, ed. n. The manuscript of this letter may have contained one or more sentences omitted by Henry D. Gilpin. See Randolph to JM, 7 Feb. 1783, and n. 10.

PHILADELPHIA, January 22, 1782[3][1]

DEAR SIR,

The repeal of the impost act by Virginia is still considered as covered with some degree of mystery.[2] Colonel Bland's representations do not remove the veil. Indeed, he seems as much astonished at it, and as unable to penetrate it, as any of us.[3] Many have surmised that the enmity of Doctor Lee against Morris is at the bottom of it. But had that been the case, it can scarcely be supposed that the repeal would have passed so quietly.[4] By this time, I presume, you will be able to furnish me with its true history, and I ask the favor of you to do it.[5] Virginia could never have cut off this source of public relief at a more unlucky crisis than when she is protesting her inability to comply with the continental requisitions.[6] She will, I hope, be yet made sensible of the impropriety of the step she has taken, and make amends by a more liberal grant. Congress cannot abandon the plan as long as there is a spark of hope.[7] Nay, other plans on a like principle must be added. Justice, gratitude, our reputation abroad, and our tranquillity at home, require provision for a debt of not less than fifty millions of dollars,[8] and I pronounce that this provision will not be adequately met by separate acts of the States. If there are not revenue laws which operate at the same time through all the States, and are exempt from the control of each—the mutual jealousies which begin already to appear among them will assuredly defraud both our foreign and domestic creditors of their just claims.[9]

The deputies of the army are still here, urging the objects of their mission. Congress are thoroughly impressed with the justice of them, and are disposed to do every thing which depends on them. But what can a Virginia Delegate say to them, whose constituents declare that they are unable to make the necessary contributions, and unwilling to establish funds for obtaining them elsewhere? The valuation of lands is still under consideration.[10]

[1] See hdn.
[2] Randolph to JM, 3 Jan., and nn. 2, 5; Harrison to JM, 4 Jan.; JM to Randolph, 7 Jan. 1783.
[3] Randolph to JM, 3 Jan. 1783, and n. 11.
[4] Harrison to JM, 4 Jan. 1783, and nn. 3, 4.
[5] Randolph to JM, 7 Feb. 1783.
[6] *Papers of Madison*, V, 457–58; Delegates to Harrison, 21 Jan. 1783, and n. 2.
[7] The "amends" obviously could not be made before the Virginia General Assembly convened in May 1783, unless a special session met earlier. By "the plan," JM meant the proposed impost amendment of the Articles of Confederation.
[8] Considerations of "Justice" and "gratitude" to King Louis XVI of France should impel Congress to pay the overdue interest on loans from the royal treasury and on loans, for which he had stood security, from Dutch bankers. Prolonged default in meeting these interest charges would injure the "reputation" of the United States abroad and thereby bar Congress from negotiating further loans. Similar considerations and also "tranquillity at home" required that the "just claims" of the clamorous civilian creditors and the obviously discontented continental army should be honored. See *Papers of Madison*, V, 424, n. 9; 473; 474, n. 8; Randolph to JM, 3 Jan., and n. 12; 15 Jan., n. 13; JM to Randolph, 7 Jan.; JM Notes, 9–10 Jan., and nn. 12–14; 13 Jan., and nn. 5, 17; 17 Jan., and n. 2; Conference with Morris, 10 Jan. 1783, n. 5.
[9] JM Notes, 7 Jan., and n. 4; 9–10 Jan.; 14 Jan., and nn. 7, 9, 11; 27 Jan.; 28 Jan.; JM to Randolph, 14 Jan. 1783.
[10] JM Notes, 9–10 Jan., and nn. 2, 3; 14 Jan., and nn. 2, 4, 6, 7, 9; JM to Randolph, 14 Jan., and nn. 4, 5; Delegates to Harrison, 21 Jan. 1783, n. 2.

Report on Treaty and Convention
with the Netherlands

MS (NA: PCC, No. 19, I, 29–32). In JM's hand, except as mentioned in n. 16. Docketed by JM, "Report of the Committe[e] on the letter of the 8th. of Ocr. 17[82] from Mr. Adams with the copi[es] of Treaty & Convention accompan[y]ing the same." Below this docket, Charles Thomson added: "Mr. Madison Mr. Hamilton Mr. Elsworth Passed Jany 23d, 1783."

[23 January 1783]

The Committee consisting of Mr. Madison Mr. Hamilton & Mr. Elseworth to whom were referred the letter of the 8th. of Ocr. 1782 from the Minister Plenipo: at the Hague with copies of a Treaty of Amity & Commerce, and of a convention concerning vessels recaptured,[1] Report, That on a comparison of the former with the instructions given to the said Minister Plenipo: on that subject,[2] they find that no variations have taken place which affect the substance of the plan proposed by Congress. Those which the Committee have thought most worthy of being remarked to Congress are

1st. the clause in Art: 4. which imposes some degree of restraint on the exercise of religious worship:[3]

2dly the clause in Art: 5 which restrains the protection to be afforded by Ships of war of one party to vessels of the other party, to cases in which they shall have a common enemy:[4]

3dly. the tenor of Art: 6. which seems more cautiously[5] to exclude any claims by Citizens or subjects of one of the parties, to the privilege of holding real estates within the jurisdiction of the other party:[6]

4thly. the clause in Art: 10. which provides that no examination of papers shall be demandable in cases of vessels convoyed by Ships of war of either of the parties; but that credence shall be given to the word of the officer conducting the convoy.[7]

5thly. the clause in Art: 12. which extends from 2 to 6 months the period after a declared war between one of the parties & another nation, within which effects of the other party on board the vessels of such nation shall be exempt from confiscation:[8]

6thly. the clause in Art: 18th. which extends from 6 to 9 months and in some contingences still farther, the period after a rupture between the parties themselves, which shall be allowed to their Citizens & subjects respectively to retire with their effects:[9]

Art: 22d. which confines the reservation in favor of the Treaty between his M. C. M. & the U. S. to the 9, 10, 17, & 22d: Articles thereof; which reservation will be in like manner confined with respect to his C. M. in case of his accession to the said Treaty.[10]

On the whole the Committee are of opinion that the Treaty ought to be immediately & fully accepted & ratified, & accordingly report an Act for that purpose

With respect to the Convention entered into by the said Minister concerning vessels recaptured, the Committee are of opinion that although no express authority has been delegated by Congress on that subject, at least if the said Convention is to remain in force after the termination of the present war, yet that the same is adapted to the mutual advantage of the parties, and ought also to be forthwith ratified;[11] an Act for which purpose the[y] accordingly add to their report

Acts of Ratification

The United States of America in Congress Assembled to all who shall see these presents, Greeting.

Whereas by our Commission dated at Philada. the   day of John Adams[12] formerly a Delegate from Mass: & &c. was nominated and constituted our Minister with full powers on the part of the U. S. of America, to concert & conclude with persons equally empowered on the part of their High Mightinesses the States Genl. of the United Netherlands, a Treaty of Amity & Commerce, having for its basis the most perfect equality and for its object the mutual advantage of the parties; we promising in good faith to ratify whatever should be transacted by virtue of the said commission: And Whereas our said Minister in pursuance of his full powers, at the Hague on the 8th. day of Octobr. 1782, with Geo. Van Randwyk &c &c plenipotentiaries[13] named for that purpose on the part of their High Mightinesses the States Genrl. of the U. Netherlands did conclude & sign on the part of their said high Mightinesses &c. and of the U. S. of America a Treaty of Amity & Commerce in the words following, to wit.

insert the Treaty[14]

Now Be it Known that we the said U. S. of America in Congress Assembled have accepted & approved, & do by these presents ratify & confirm the said Treaty, and every Article & clause thereof; and we do authorise & direct our Minister Plenipo: at the Hague to deliver this our act of ratification in exchange for the ratification of the said Treaty by their H.M. the States Genl. of the U. Netherlands

Done in Congress at Philada. & &c.

In testimony whereof &c.[15]

Whereas J Adams our Minister Py at the Hague on the 8th. day of Octr 1782,[16] with George Van Randwyck &c &c[17] Ministers Plenipo: of the Lords the States Genl. of the United Netherlands, did conclude & sign on the part of the said Lords &c. the States Genl of the Ud Netherlands and of the U.S. of A. a convention concerning vessels recaptured in the words following to wit,

insert the convention[18]

Now Be it known that we the said U.S. of A. in Congress assemb[led] have accepted & approved & do by these presents ratify & confirm the same; and do authorise & direct the Minister Plenipo: of the U.S. at the Hague, to deliver this our Act of Ratification in exchange for the Ratification of the said Convention by the Lords the States Genl. of the U. Netherlands.

Done in Congress &c &c

In Testimony whereof, &c &c.   X   X[19]

The Committee further report & recommend the following Proclamation

By the U.S. in Congress Assembled

A Proclamation

Whereas in pursuance of a Plentipotentiary Commission given on the 29 day of Decr. 1780 to John Adams Esqr. a Treaty of Amity & commerce between their High Mightinesses the States Genl. of the U. Netherlands & and t[he] U. States of Amer: was on the 8th. day of Ocr. 1782 by the said J.A. concluded with Plentipotentiaries named for that purpose by their s[aid] High Mightinesses the States Genl. of the United Netherlands, & Wher[eas] the said Treaty hath been this day approved & ratified by the U.S. in Congress Assembled, as the same is contained in the words following to wit[20]

insert the Treaty from the American Column only

And Whereas a Convention concerning Vessels recaptured was at the place & on the day abovemend. concluded by the said Minister Plenipo: on the part of these U.S. with the said Plenipotentiaries on the part of the said Lords the States General of the United Netherlands; and the same hath been this day approved & ratified by the U.S. in Congress Assembled, as it is contained in the words following, to wit[21]

insert the Convention from the American Column only

Now therefore to the end that the said Treaty & Convention may with all good faith be performed & observed on the part of these U. States All the Citizens & inhabitants thereof, and more especially all Captains & other officers & seamen belonging to any Vessels of war of these U.S. or any of them, or of any private armed vessels commissioned by Congress, are hereby enjoined & required to govern themselves strictly in all things according to the stipulations above recited, And it is

Done in Congress &c.

In Testimony whereof &c.[22]

¹ For the reference of John Adams' dispatch and enclosures to the committee, see JM Notes, 21 Jan. 1783, and nn. 2, 3.

² For "the instructions" of 29 December 1780 as modified on 16 August 1781, see *JCC*, XVIII, 1206–17; XXI, 877–80; *Papers of Madison*, IV, 391–92; 394, n. 24; 410–11; 412, n. 9. For the treaty and convention, see *JCC*, XXIV, 68–82.

³ Article IV guaranteed "entire and perfect liberty of conscience" to "the subjects and inhabitants of each party," provided that all of them submit "as to the public demonstration of it, to the laws of the country" (*JCC*, XXIV, 69). Article IV of Adams' instructions called for "full and entire liberty to worship in their own way, without any kind of molestation" (*JCC*, XVIII, 1208). For Adams' comment on Article IV of the treaty, see Wharton, *Revol. Dipl. Corr.*, V, 805.

⁴ *JCC*, XXIV, 70. In Article V of the instructions, the expression "in cases when they may have a common enemy" is "omitted," and in its stead appears "upon all occasions" (*JCC*, XVIII, 1208).

⁵ JM interlineated "more cautiously" above a canceled "more explicitly."

⁶ The words "real estates" do not appear in Article VI of either the instructions or the treaty. The matter in question concerned the degree of liberty to be accorded to a citizen or subject of one of the countries to dispose of property owned by him in the other country during his lifetime, or by bequests in his will, or by his heirs or executors after his death. In the instructions, the types of property are particularized as "effects, merchandise, money, debts or goods, moveable or immoveable." In the treaty, the word "effects" alone appears (*JCC*, XVIII, 1209; XXIV, 70–71). Although, as used in law, the word "effects" does not include realty, thus sustaining JM in a position he had assumed but which Congress had refused to endorse, the committee viewed the word "cautiously," because the "extreme incorrectness" of the English version of the treaty warranted doubt whether the Dutch word had been translated accurately (*Papers of Madison*, IV, 410–11; 412, n. 9; JM Notes, 23 Jan. 1783). The treaty also contained stipulations, not found in the instructions, concerning the scope of the freedom with which "guardians, tutors, or curators" could dispose of "effects" bequeathed to minors. For Adams' comment on Article VI of the treaty, see Wharton, *Revol. Dipl. Corr.*, V, 804.

⁷ In the instructions there was no exception under which, in time of war, an "examination of papers" could not be demanded (*JCC*, XVIII, 1211–12; XXIV, 71–72).

⁸ This tripling of the period in which immunity from confiscation was guaranteed probably reflected the concern of the Dutch over their trade in the distant East Indies. See *JCC*, XVIII, 1213–14; XXIV, 72–73.

⁹ Although a six-months' limit had been stipulated in the seventeenth article of the instructions, "Art: 18th" of the treaty extended this limit to nine months. The "contingences still farther" allowed a ship "the time necessary" to complete its voyage and prohibited capture "if the declaration of war was not or could not be known in the last port" which the vessel had entered (*JCC*, XVIII, 1215; XXIV, 74–75).

¹⁰ Taken in sequence, the "9, 10, 17, & 22d: Articles" of the treaty between France and the United States excluded the citizens or subjects of the one country from sharing the inshore fisheries of the other country; excluded the "citizens and inhabitants" of the United States from sharing in "the right" of the French to fish on the "banks of Newfoundland" and "part of the coast of that island," and in the inshore fisheries of St. Pierre and Miquelon; forbade the United States or any state thereof to levy export duties on French merchandise shipped from them—this guarantee in "compensation of the exemption" from export duties on molasses carried by citizens of the United States from the French West Indies; and stipulated that, in the event of war between France and the United States, neither country for

six months after the beginning of hostilities would molest "merchants" of the one country living in the other or prevent them from "selling and transporting their goods and merchandises" (*JCC*, XI, 427–28, 433, 435–36).

"Art: 22d" of the treaty between the Netherlands and the United States stipulated that nothing in the treaty should "be understood in any manner to derogate from" the four articles summarized above or from similar articles in a treaty which might be concluded between the United States and his Catholic Majesty King Charles III of Spain (*JCC*, XXIV, 75–76). For Adams' comment upon Article XXII of the treaty with the Netherlands, see Wharton, *Revol. Dipl. Corr.*, V, 805. See also JM Notes, 29 Jan. 1783, n. 3.

[11] For the text of the "Convention between the Lords the States General of the United Netherlands and the United States of America, concerning vessels recaptured," see *JCC*, XXIV, 80–82. This agreement established "some uniform principles" with regard to prizes captured by the warships of each nation and to "vessels of the subjects of either party, captured by the enemy and re-captured by vessels of war commissioned by either party." Congress had authorized Adams as minister to the Netherlands to conclude "such treaty, conventions and agreements as he shall judge conformable to the ends we have in view." Congress later directed him to propose a Franco-Dutch-American alliance "limited in its duration to, the present war" (*JCC*, XVIII, 1205; XXI, 877). Adams evidently believed that this limitation did not also apply to conventions.

[12] The date of John Adams' commission was 29 December 1780 (*JCC*, XVIII, 1205).

[13] The States-General of the Netherlands required that a treaty to which it was a party be signed by two "deputies" for Holland and one deputy for each of the other six provinces. Although George Van Randwyck and the other seven Dutch signatories are named in *JCC*, XXIV, 67, the spelling of their names does not agree in every instance with that in [David] Hunter Miller, ed., *Treaties and Other International Acts of the United States of America* (8 vols.; Washington, 1931–48), II, 95. See also JM Notes, 23 Jan. 1783, n. 2.

[14] Following "Treaty," "from the American Column only" is canceled. Although the journal of Congress reproduces those documents only as rendered in English, Hunter Miller prints the treaty and the convention in parallel columns of Dutch and English (*JCC*, XXIV, 68–78, 80–82; *Treaties*, II, 59–95). For the agitation in Congress respecting the "extreme incorrectness" of the "American" version and the final decision that the matter be "dropped," see JM Notes, 23 Jan.; 29 Jan. 1783.

[15] The treaty was ratified on 27 December 1782 by "their High Mightinesses, the States General of the United Netherlands" and on 23 January 1783 by "The United States in Congress Assembled." See JM Notes, 29 Jan. 1783, n. 2. The absence from Philadelphia of Robert R. Livingston, secretary for foreign affairs, explains why he delayed signing the treaty until shortly after his return on 11 February 1783 (Burnett, *Letters*, VII, 43, n. 3). The ratifications were exchanged at The Hague on 23 June 1783 (Wharton, *Revol. Dipl. Corr.*, VI, 502). See also *Papers of Madison*, V, 296, n. 2. For the words following "In testimony whereof," see *JCC*, XXIV, 66.

[16] Following "Whereas," JM originally wrote "the said J Adams &c." After canceling "the said" and "&c.," someone other than JM interlineated above "Adams" "our Minister Py at the Hague." Following "on the," JM's "day & at the place aforesaid" was deleted and replaced by "8th. day of Octr 1782," interlineated in an unknown hand (NA: PCC, No. 19, I, 31).

[17] *JCC*, XXIV, 67.

[18] Following "convention," "from the American Column only" is canceled. See n. 14.

19 For the words following "In Testimony whereof," see *JCC*, XXIV, 67.

20 For slight changes in phraseology, word arrangement, and punctuation of this preamble as printed in the official journal, see *JCC*, XXIV, 67–68.

21 The same comment as in n. 20 applies to this preamble. See *JCC*, XXIV, 80.

22 The words "And it is" and "In Testimony whereof &c," are omitted in the printed journal. The "&c" following "Done in Congress" is replaced in the journal by "this twenty-third day of January, in the year of our Lord one thousand seven hundred and eighty-three, and of our sovereignty and independence the seventh" (*JCC*, XXIV, 82). Congress thereby authorized Elias Boudinot, the president, to issue a proclamation calling for an observance of the provisions of the treaty and convention five months before their ratification by the two countries was exchanged. See n. 15, above; Delegates to Harrison, 28 Jan. 1783; *JCC*, XXV, 983.

Report on Books for Congress

MS (LC: Continental Congress Miscellany). Nine undated pages in JM's hand, with the exception of one entry. Docketed by Charles Thomson: "Report of Comee. List of Books to be imported for the use of Congress   Read Jany 24. 1783. Question taken to empower Superint: finance & Secy to import them. Passed in the Negative. Comee. Mr. Madison   Mr. Williamson   Mr. Mifflin." The last ten unnumbered folios of NA: PCC, No. 183 comprise an undated and undocketed copy of the book list, of which a part is in Thomson's hand and the rest in several hands, none JM's. Except for some variations in spelling and capitalization, this copy is identical in contents and in the sequence of items entered in the list written by JM.

In his Notes on Debates for 23 January (*q.v.*), JM stated that the committee "reported" the book list on that day. This may be true in the sense that, under the fourth rule of the rules of procedure adopted on 4 May 1781, the list was "delivered" to Charles Thomson, secretary of Congress; but if that was the case, the same rule, quite in accord with Thomson's docket, provided that the report should be "read" on 24 January (*JCC*, XX, 476). In his manuscript "Committee Book 1781–1785," Thomson's entry, "Report Jany," is obviously not helpful. Further evidence lacking, the report is placed here so that it will precede the account by JM of the debate. It is possible that having stated the committee "reported" on 23 January, JM decided to follow the entry with a summary of the debate as of that date rather than to insert it in broken sequence when taken up on the twenty-fourth. Although Gaillard Hunt, drawing on PCC, incorporated the report as part of the journal for 24 January (*JCC*, XXV, 83–92), Thomson himself made no entry in the manuscript journal, in all likelihood because the report was not adopted.

On 1 July 1782 Theodorick Bland proposed that there be compiled "a list of books to be imported for the use of the United States in Congress Assembled." Following adoption of the motion, Bland, contrary to established usage but probably in accord with his own wish, was not named chairman or even a member of the committee designated to prepare the list. In his stead JM was appointed chairman, with his old mentor John Witherspoon (N.J.) and John Lowell (Mass.) as his colleagues (NA: PCC, No. 186, fol. 39). On 21 November the motion was renewed, presumably by JM, because Witherspoon and Lowell had left Philadelphia earlier that month (Burnett, *Letters*, VI, xlvi, xlviii). This second motion is not recorded in the journal, but Congress on that day reconstituted the committee by replacing these two men with Hugh Williamson (N.C.) and Thomas Mifflin (Del.) (NA: PCC, No. 186, fol. 69). JM alone seems to have prepared the report, although he may have consulted Witherspoon before the learned clergyman returned to his home in Princeton. See William W. Woodward, ed., *The Works of the Rev. John Witherspoon, D.D., LL.D.* . . . (4 vols.; Philadelphia, 1802), III, 232–574, *passim*.

During the latter half of 1782 the primary issues before Congress concerned finance, commerce, prisoners of war, western lands, and international affairs, including the alliance with France, the hoped-for terms of peace, the unsatisfactory relations with Spain, and the treaties with the Netherlands and Sweden. Most of the subject classifications in JM's report reflect the needs of Congress for the guidance of authoritative works on these topics. See JM Notes, 23 Jan. 1783.

Under many of his subheadings and in several of his references to individual authors JM neglected to specify what particular volumes he had in mind. See, for example, the entries numbered 24, 34, 36, 37, 55, 71, 169, 172, 175, 200, 202, 204, 250, 277, 279, 280. For this reason, neither he nor any other delegate in Congress could have known the exact number of titles and volumes in print by 1783 which were included in his list. Those cited below total approximately 550 titles in about 1,300 volumes. In making this estimate, the present editors have excluded from their count the volumes of an individual author's work or in a continuing series which would not be published by the close of 1783; works listed by JM that, although separately available in print, were included in a collection also recommended by him; and whatever number of volumes he may have envisaged under his rubric "All political tracts" (No. 280). Whenever a work on his list had appeared simultaneously in two printings, the editors have selected for tallying the set which comprised the fewer volumes.

JM certainly did not derive the names of authors and the titles of their books from a single source. Besides the modest library of James Madison, Sr., and JM's own growing collection of works, the private libraries of Donald Robertson, the Reverend John Witherspoon, and the Reverend James Madison suggest themselves, as do the institutional libraries of the College of New Jersey, the College of William and Mary, and the Library Company of Philadelphia. For the last of these, see *A Catalogue of the Books*

Belonging to the Library Company of Philadelphia . . . (Philadelphia, 1789). Again JM may have acquired much information by browsing in Philadelphia bookstores and scanning advertisements in the gazettes of that city.

Among the volumes that attracted JM's attention were the "near 4000" that Colonel Isaac Zane, Jr., had purchased from Mary Willing Byrd, the widow of Colonel William Byrd III, and brought in October 1781 to Philadelphia for sale at Robert Bell's bookstore near St. Paul's Church on Third Street (Edwin Wolf, 2nd, "The Dispersal of the Library of William Byrd of Westover," *Proceedings of the American Antiquarian Society*, LXVIII [1957–58], 19–106, and esp. 23–25; *Papers of Madison*, I, 133, n. 1; 185, n. 1; V, 404, n. 18). At least at one of Bell's many auctions during the year beginning on 23 October 1781, JM bought a "few scarce books" from the Byrd collection (*ibid.*, IV, 126–27, nn. 4–5; Edwin Wolf, *op. cit.*, pp. 25–27). William Pritchard, proprietor of another bookstore, who succeeded Bell in October 1782 as Zane's agent, was still selling books from the collection at the time of JM's report to Congress and for several years thereafter (*Papers of Madison*, IV, 126; 127, n. 4; Edwin Wolf, *op. cit.*, pp. 28–29, 31). Although eighty-two of the titles in the Byrd collection were also among those recommended by JM in his report to Congress, at least fifty of the eighty-two were so familiar and so obviously appropriate for inclusion in his list that he most probably jotted them down from memory (John Spencer Bassett, ed., *The Writings of "Colonel William Byrd, of Westover in Virginia, Esqr."* [New York, 1901], pp. 413–43).

During January 1783, when Thomas Jefferson was rooming at JM's boarding house in Philadelphia, the two men surely conversed on the subject of a reference library for Congress. By comparing entries in Jefferson's so-called "1783 catalogue" (microfilm of MS in Mass. Historical Society), especially with JM's report under the caption "America," a kinship between the two lists is made evident. Most striking are the eleven entries between "Wafer's Voyages" (No. 215) and "Ellis's voyage to Hudson's Bay" (No. 225). Except for variations in spelling and capitalization, these entries in the "catalogue" and the report are identical. They embrace a total of thirty-one explorers' accounts, but twenty-four of them were to be found only in printed collections. Of the twenty-four, twenty-one were printed only in Samuel Purchas (No. 239) or Richard Hakluyt (No. 240). Jefferson's "catalogue," which was a record of works he already possessed and of others he desired to acquire, contains on a preliminary page the date "1783, Mar. 6"; but it was an expanding record, and its contents at any given date cannot be known (Boyd, *Papers of Jefferson*, VI, 216). For this reason, it is at least possible that JM derived the sequence of eleven entries from the holdings of the Library Company of Philadelphia or other sources, and that Jefferson thereupon used JM's list to add to his own, rather than vice versa.

In this connection, it probably is relevant to note that the two men were together during only the last four weeks preceding the submission of the report by JM, that during this period JM was much occupied with important financial and other issues before Congress, that the closest parallel between the entries in his book list and those in Jefferson's "1783 catalogue" is under the caption "America," the final section of the list, and that JM, having been a member of the committee since 1 July, and its chairman since 21 November 1782, was not customarily laggard in fulfilling an assignment. About 35 of his definite recommendations were of titles apparently owned by the Library Company of Philadelphia in 1782 but not entered in Jefferson's "catalogue," while about 140 others could have been derived from the holdings of that company as well as from that "catalogue." See also E[mily] Millicent Sowerby, comp., *Catalogue of the Library of Thomas Jefferson* (5 vols.; Washington, 1952–59).

Imperfections undoubtedly remain in the titles cited. The growing number of bibliographical aids prepared by authorities of presumably equal expertness, or at least of high reputation, often disagree concerning the punctuation, capitalization, and occasionally even the spelling or wording of the same edition of a work. To reconcile these differences by scanning the title pages was in numerous instances a manifest impossibility. The editors are confident only that where JM specified a work by naming the author, suggesting the title, or both, they have correctly identified his entry.

In general the format adopted for presentation of the list represents an attempt to establish the "ideal" purchase for all JM's entries, except No. 280. Included are the date of original publication and the date of the latest, or in certain cases of an earlier, superior, edition as of 1783. Omitted, on the other hand, are references to the many editions which, though dated even later than those selected, are incomplete or obviously inferior. Abbreviated titles are used; otherwise the present footnotes would be at least four times longer than they now are. The names of translators, unless specified by JM or known to have importantly enhanced the value of a work by their editing or augmentation of it, are not mentioned. Finally, the nature and length of this report are believed to warrant numbering JM's entries sequentially and placing each footnote immediately after the volume to which it refers rather than grouping all the annotations at the close of the list.

[23 January 1783]

The Committee instructed on the motion of Col. Bland to report a list of books proper for the use of Congress, recommend that Superitendt. of Finance & the Secy. of Congress be empowered to take order for procuring the books enumerated below; the same when procured to be under the care of the said Secy.

[1]   Encyclopédie Méthodique

Charles Joseph Panckoucke (1736–1798) *et al.*, eds., *Encyclopédie méthodique, ou par ordre de matières* . . . (192 vols., Paris and Liège, 1782–1832). For Thomas Jefferson's and JM's interest in this work, see Sidney L. Jackson, "*The Encyclopédie Méthodique*, A Jefferson Addendum," *Virginia Magazine of History and Biography*, LXXIII (1965), 303–11.

[2]   Dictionaire de l'homme d'Etât

Jean Baptiste René Robinet (1735–1820) *et al.*, eds., *Dictionnaire universel des sciences morale, économique, etc., ou bibliothèque de l'homme d'état* . . . (30 vols., London [i.e., Neuchâtel], 1777–1783).

Law of Nature and Nations

General captions, as above, were written by JM in the left margin of his manuscript and have been italicized by the present editors.

[3] Cudworth's Intellectual System

Ralph Cudworth (1617–1688), *The True Intellectual System of the Universe* . . . (London, 1678; 2d ed., 2 vols., London, 1743).

[4] Cumberland's Law of Nature

Richard Cumberland (1632–1718), *A Treatise of the Laws of Nature* . . . (London, 1672; 2d ed., London, 1727).

[5] Wolfius's Law of Nature

Christian (1679–1754), Freiherr von Wolff, *Institutions du droit de la nature et des gens* . . . (Two separate Latin original works: (1) 8 parts, Frankfort, Leipzig, and Magdeburg, 1740–1748, and (2) Magdeburg, 1749; Elie Luzac [1723–1796], tr. and ed., 6 vols.; 2 vols., Leyden, 1772).

[6] Hutchinson's Moral Philosophy

Francis Hutcheson, Sr. (1694–1747), *A System of Moral Philosophy* . . . (Latin original MS; Francis Hutcheson, Jr. [*ca.* 1722–*ca.* 1773], tr. and ed., 2 vols., London and Glasgow, 1755).

[7] Beller's delineation of universal Law

Fettiplace Bellers (1687–1732), *A Delineation of Universal Law* . . . (Posthumous, London, 1740; 3d ed., London, 1754).

[8] Ferguson's analysis of Mor: Philosophy

Adam Ferguson (1723–1816), *Institutes of Moral Philosophy* . . . (Original work, title according with JM's entry, Edinburgh, 1761; rev. and superseded by above title, Edinburgh, 1769; 3d ed., Edinburgh, 1773). Ferguson had served as secretary to the Carlisle peace commission in 1778 (*Papers of Madison*, III, 272, n. 2). See No. 156 for one of Ferguson's works owned by JM.

[9] Rutherforth's institutes of Natural Law

Thomas Rutherforth (1712–1771), *Institutes of Natural Law* . . . (2 vols., Cambridge, 1754–1756). This is a commentary on the work next listed.

[10] Grotius's Law of Nature and Nations

Hugo Grotius (Huig van Groot) (1583–1645), *The Rights of War and Peace; Wherein Are Explained the Law of Nature and Nations* . . . (Latin original ed., Paris, 1625; English ed., 3 vols., London, 1738). For previous references to Grotius, see *Papers of Madison*, IV, 16, n. 23; V, 92; 93, n. 7; 437, n. 2; for other works by the same author in the book list, see Nos. 16 and 94.

[11] Puffendorf's Law of Nature and Nations with notes by Barbeyrac

Samuel (1632–1694), Freiherr von Pufendorf, *The Law of Nature and Nations* . . . (Latin original ed., Lund, 1672; Jean Barbeyrac [1674–1729], tr. and ed., French ed., *Avec des notes,* Amsterdam, 1706; English ed., variant title, London, 1710; 4th ed., above title, London, 1749). For a previous reference to this work, see *Papers of Madison*, V, 437, n. 2. For other works by Pufendorf, see Nos. 12 and 89; for others involving Barbeyrac, Nos. 30 and 34e.

[12] Puffendorf de officio hominis et civis

Samuel, Freiherr von Pufendorf (see No. 11), *The Whole Duty of Man, according to the Law of Nature* . . . (Latin original ed., a résumé of No. 11, Lund, 1673; English ed., London, 1691; 4th ed., London, 1716).

[13] Vattell's Law of Nature and Nations

Emerich de Vattel (1714–1767), *The Law of Nations; or, Principles of the Law of Nature* . . . (French original ed., Neuchâtel and Leyden, 1758; English ed., 2 vols., London, 1759–1760; 2d ed., 2 vols. in 1, London, 1760). For Vattel, see *Papers of Madison*, II, 132–33; 135, n. 12; IV, 16, n. 23; V, 437, n. 2.

[14] Vattell's Questions in Natural Law

Emerich de Vattel (see No. 13), *Questions de droit naturel* . . . (Berne, 1762).

[15] Burlamaqui's Law of Nature & Nations

Jean Jacques Burlamaqui (1694–1748), *The Principles of Natural Law. In Which the True System of Morality and Civil Government Are Established* . . . (French original ed., 2 vols., Geneva, 1747; English ed., 2 vols., London, 1748; 2d ed., 2 vols., London, 1763).

[16] Grotius's Mare liberum

Hugo Grotius (see No. 10), *Mare liberum, sive, de jure quod Batavis competit ad indicana commercia dissertatio* . . . (Leyden, 1609; 2d ed., Leyden, 1663).

[17] Selden's Mare clausum

John Selden (1584–1654), *Mare clausum; The Right and Dominion of the Sea* . . . (Latin original ed., London, 1635; English ed., London, 1663).

[18] Molloy de jure maritimo

Charles Molloy (1646–1690), *De jure maritimo et navali; or, A Treatise of Affairs Maritime and of Commerce* . . . (London, 1676; 10th ed., 2 vols., London, 1778).

[19] Beaux lex mercatoria

Wyndham Beawes (d. *ca.* 1777), *Lex mercatoria rediviva: or, The Merchant's Directory* . . . (London, 1750; Thomas Mortimer [1730–1810], continuator, 4th ed., London, 1783).

[20] Jacob's lex mercatoria

Giles Jacob (1686–1744), *Lex mercatoria: or, The Merchant's Companion* . . . (London, 1718; 2d ed., London, 1729).

[21] Lee on captures

Richard Lee, *A Treatise of Captures in War* . . . (London, 1759). The treatise, which deals exclusively with captures at sea, is chiefly a translation of part of a work by Bynkershoek, for whom see No. 30a.

[22]   Ordinances of Marine of France

Ordonnance de la marine, du mois d'août 1681. Commentée & conferée sur les anciennes ordonnances, le droit romain & les nouveaux règlemens . . . (2d ed., Paris, 1747).

[23]   Admiralty Laws of G. Britain

Laws, Ordinances, and Institutions of the Admiralty of Great Britain . . . (London, 1746; 4th ed.[?], 2 vols., London, 1776).

[24]   do.   of the several others of Europe

Unless this sweeping entry signifies uncertainty, it betrays overconfidence. Innumerable copies of maritime ordinances, orders in council, edicts, and regulations, averaging between four and twelve pages, were constantly being printed, and the flow was accelerated by the fact of war; but the day when each maritime power of Europe would publish these promulgations as a codified whole was still largely in the future. If JM meant to indicate the collecting of admiralty laws as separately published, spatial considerations prohibit making the attempt in the present volume. If he meant that only those laws already codified should be purchased, he can be easily accommodated. There appear to have been available within this meaning in 1783 one useful general work in French; the Dutch code, years in the building; and the Russian code, published, 2 volumes in 1, St. Petersburg, in 1781. This last-named work, however, is not cited below, for it would scarcely have been included in a library of Congress in 1783.

24a. René Josué Valin (1695–1765), *Nouveau commentaire sur l'ordonnance de la marine du mois d'août 1681. Où se trouve la conférence des anciennes ordonnances des us & coutumes de la mer, tant du royaume que des pays étrangers, & nouveaux règlemens concernans la navigation & le commerce maritime* . . . (2 vols., La Rochelle, 1760; 3d ed., 2 vols., La Rochelle, 1776).

24b. *Recüeil van alle de Placaten, Ordonnatien, Resolutien, Instructien, lysten en Waarchouwinger, betreffende de Admiraliteyten, Convoyen, Licenten, en verdere Zee-saarken* . . . (11 vols., The Hague, 1701–1773; *Generale Index* . . . 2 vols., The Hague, 1773–1775).

[25]   Wiquefort's Ambassador

Abraham van Wicquefort (1598–1682), *The Ambassador and His Functions, to Which Is Added, an Historical Discourse concerning the Election of the Emperor* . . . (French original ed. of *L'ambassadeur*, 2 vols., The Hague, 1680–1681; of *Discours historique*, Paris, 1658; works combined, 2 vols., Cologne, 1689–1690; English ed., variant title, 2 vols. in 1, London, 1716; 3d ed., above title, 2 vols., London, 1740).

[26]   El Embaxador, par Antoine de Vera

Juan Antonio Vera Figueroa y Zúñiga (1588–1658), Conde de la Roca, *Le parfait ambassadeur* . . . (Spanish original ed., 2 vols. in 1, Seville, 1620; French ed., 2 vols., Leyden, 1709).

[27]   L'Ambasciatore Politice Christiano, par le prince Charles Marie Carafe

Carlo Maria Caraffa (1646–1695), Prince de la Roccella e di Buteria, *L'ambasciatori politiche-christiane.* . . . This title comprises the second part of Caraffa's *Opere* (3 parts in one vol., Mazzarino, 1692). When *L'ambasciatori* was first published has not been ascertained, but in all probability it was after 1684, when the author was Spanish ambassador to Rome, and it was certainly before the date in 1688 when, translated into Spanish, it was published at Palermo.

[28] De la charge et dignité de l'ambassadeur,
      par Jean Hotman

Jean Hotman (1552–1636), Sieur de Villiers Saint-Paul, *The Ambassador* . . . ("Sieur de Villiers," only attribution, French original ed., title according with JM's entry, Paris, 1602; J. S. [probably James Shaw], tr. and ed., English ed., London, 1603). For a charge against this work, see No. 32.

[29] Le Ministre public dans les cours etrangeres &c,
      par J. de la Sarraz du Franquesnay

Jean, Sieur de La Sarraz du Franquesnay, *Le ministre public dans les cours étrangeres* . . . (Paris and Amsterdam, 1731).

[30] De foro legatorum par Bynkershock traduit en
      Francois par Barbeyrac, sous le titre de traite
      du Juge competent des Ambassadeurs &c. with
      all his other works.

30a. Cornelis van Bynkershoek (1673–1743), *Traité du juge compétent des ambassadeurs, tant pour le civil, que pour le criminel* . . . (Latin original ed., Leyden, 1702; Jean Barbeyrac [see No. 11], tr., French ed., The Hague, 1723; 3d ed., 2 vols., The Hague, 1746).

30b. ———, *Cornelii van Bynkershoek, jurisconsulti . . . opera omnia* . . . (Béat Philippe Vicat [1715–1777], comp. and ed., 2 vols. in 1, Leyden, 1767). JM and his consultants may not have known of the Vicat edition, which included the original Latin version of 30a.

[31] De legationibus par Alberic Gentilis

Alberico Gentili (1522–1608), *De legationibus libri tres* . . . (London, 1585; 2d ed., Hanau, 1607).

[32] Legatus par Charles Paschal

Carlo Pasquale (1547–1625), Visconte di Quente, *Legatus . . . distinctum in capita septem et septuaginta* . . . (Rouen, 1598; 3d ed., Amsterdam and Leyden, 1645). Pasquale charged that the work of Hotman (No. 28) was no more than extracts from the above.

[33] Legatus par Frederick Marsalaer

Fredrik van Marselaer (1584–1670), *Legatus libri duo* . . . (Variant title, Antwerp, 1618; 2d ed., above title, Antwerp, 1626; 4th ed.[?], Antwerp, 1663).

Treaties and Negociations

[34] Corps diplomatique

34a. Jean Le Clerc (1657–1736), *Négociations secrètes touchant la paix de Munster et d'Osnaburg* . . . (Variant subtitle, 4 vols., The Hague, 1724–1726; 2d ed., 4 vols., The Hague, 1725–1726).

34b. [Jean Yvres de Saint-Prest (d. 1720)], *Histoire des traités de paix, et autres négotiations du six-septième siècle . . . Ouvrage . . . qui peut servir d'introduction au corps diplomatique . . .* (Posthumous, 2 vols., Amsterdam, 1725).

34c. Jean Dumont (d. 1726), Baron de Carlscroon, comp. and ed., *Corps universel diplomatique du droit des gens; contenant . . . des traitez . . . faits en Europe depuis le règne de l'empereur Charlemagne jusques à présent . . .* (8 vols., The Hague; 8 vols. in 16, Amsterdam, 1726–1731).

34d. Jean Rousset de Missy (1686–1762), comp. and ed., *Supplément au corps diplomatique . . .* (3 vols., Amsterdam, 1726–1731; 2d ed., 3 vols., Amsterdam, 1739).

34e. Jean Barbeyrac (see No. 11), *L'histoire des anciens traitez . . . de l'antiquité depuis les tems les plus reculez jusques à l'empire de Charlemagne . . .* (2 vols., Amsterdam, 1726–1731; 2d ed., 2 vols., Amsterdam, 1739).

[35] Rymer's foedera

Thomas Rymer (1641–1713) and Robert Sanderson (1660–1741), comps. and eds., *Foedera, conventiones, literae, et cujuscunque generis acta publica, inter reges Angliae et alios quosvis imperatores, reges, pontifices, principes, vel communitates . . . ab anno 1101, ad nostra usque tempora habita aut tractata . . .* (20 vols., London, 1704–1732; George Holmes [1662–1749], comp. and ed., 2d ed., 20 vols., London, 1727–1735; 3d ed., 10 vols., The Hague, 1739–1745).

[36] A complete collection of Treaties

As in the case of admiralty codes (No. 24), even a partial fulfillment of this recommendation would fill scores of pages with the titles of international treaties as separately published. The following six collections, in addition to the work listed next above, appear to have been the best and most nearly complete of those available in 1783.

36a. Jean Rousset de Missy (see No. 34d), comp. and ed., *Recueil historique d'actes, négotiations, mémoires et traitez, depuis la paix d'Utrecht jusqu'à . . . celle d'Aix-la-Chapelle . . .* (21 vols., Amsterdam, Leipzig, and The Hague, 1728–1754; 2d ed., 21 vols., The Hague, 1728–1755).

36b. John Almon (1737–1805), comp. and ed., *A Collection of All the Treaties . . . between Great Britain and Other Powers, from the Revolution in 1688, to the Present Time . . .* (2 vols., London, 1772). For other compilations with which Almon was involved, see Nos. 36c, 120, and 247a.

36c. John Almon (see No. 36b) and John Debrett (d. 1822), comps. and eds., *A Collection of Treaties . . . Being a Supplement to A Collection of Treaties . . . from the Revolution in 1688 . . .* (London, 1781). For another work partly edited by Debrett, see No. 120.

36d. William Harris (d. 1770), comp. and ed., *A Complete Collection of All the Marine Treaties Subsisting between Great Britain and France, Spain . . . Tunis, &c. Commencing in the Year 1546, and Including the Definitive Treaty of 1763 . . .* (London, 1763; 2d ed., London, 1779).

36e. José Antonio de Abreu y Bertodano (1717–1775), comp. and ed., *Colección de los tratados . . . hechos . . . desde antes del establecimiento de la monarchia góthica hasta el feliz reynado del rey N[uestro]. S[oberano]. D[on]. Fernando VI . . .* (12 vols., Madrid, 1740–1752).

36f. Maciej (Matthias) Dogiel (1715–1760), comp. and ed., *Codex diplomaticus Poloniae et magni ducatus Lithuaniae in quo pacta, foedera, tractatus pacis . . . nunc primum ex archivis publicis eruta ac in lucem protracta exhibentur* . . . (Vols. I, IV–V, Vilna, 1758–1764; Vols. II and III never published).

[37]   Abbe Mably's public law of Europe—principles of Negociation—other political works.

37a. Gabriel Bonnot de Mably (1709–1785), *Le droit public de l'Europe; fondé sur les traités* . . . (2 vols., Geneva, 1746; 5th ed., 3 vols., Geneva, 1776). Although JM implied that *Des principes des négotiations* was a separate work, the phrase constituted the beginning words of the main title in earlier versions of the above.

37b. ———, *Concerning Legislation: or the Principles of Laws* . . . (French original ed., 2 vols., Amsterdam, 1776; English ed., 2 vols., Amsterdam, 1777).

37c. ———, *De l'étude de l'histoire* . . . (Paris, 1778; 2d ed., Maestricht, 1778).

37d. ———, *Doutes proposés aux philosophes économistes, sur l'ordre naturel et essentiel des sociétés politiques* . . . (The Hague, 1768).

37e. ———, *Du gouvernement et des loix de la Pologne* . . . (London, 1781). Thomas Jefferson, who while in Europe assisted JM in adding to his personal library, wrote on 2 August 1787, "You have now Mably's works complete except that on Poland" (Boyd, *Papers of Jefferson*, XI, 662). See also *ibid.*, VIII, 463; XI, 666.

37f. ———, *Observations on the History of Greece* . . . (French original ed., Geneva, 1749; English ed., Geneva, 1766).

37g. ———, *Observations on the Romans* . . . (French original ed., Geneva, 1751; English ed., London, 1751).

37h. ———, *Observations sur l'histoire de France* . . . (2 vols., Geneva, 1765).

37i. ———, *Parallèle des romains et des français par rapport au gouvernement* . . . (2 vols., Paris, 1740).

37j. ———, *Phocion's Conversions; or, the Relation between Morality and Politics* . . . (Anon., French original ed., Amsterdam, 1763; William Macbean, tr. and ed., English ed., London, 1769; 2d ed., London, 1770).

37k. ———, *Two Dialogues, concerning the Manner of Writing History* . . . (French original ed., Paris, 1783; English ed., London, 1783).

[38]   De la maniere de negocier avec les souverains &c. par Callier.

François de Callières (1645–1717), *The Art of Negotiating with Sovereign Princes* . . . (French original ed., Paris, 1716; English ed., London, 1716; 3d ed., London, 1738).

[39]   Discours sur l'art de negocier par Pequet

Antoine Pecquet (1704–1762), *De l'art de négocier avec les souverains* . . . (Variant title, according with JM's entry, Paris, 1737; 3d ed., above title, Frankfort and Leipzig, 1764).

[40]   Histoire du traité de Westphalie par le P. Bougeant

(Le Père) Guillaume Hyacinthe Bougeant (1690–1743), (S.J.), *Histoire du traité de Westphalie* . . . (2 vols., Paris, 1744; 3d ed., 3 vols., Paris, 1767).

[41]   Burche's view of negociations between F. & Engld.

Thomas Birch (1705–1766), *An Historical View of the Negotiations between the Courts of England, France, and Brussels, from the Year 1592 to 1617* . . . (London,

1749). For other works involving Birch, see Nos. 57, 119, and 148; for a work that may have been from his pen, 107.

[42] Negociations du P. Jeannin

Pierre Jeannin (1540–1622), *Les négotiations de Monsieur le Président Jeannin* . . . (Nicolas Castille, comp. and ed., 4 vols., Paris, 1656; 3d ed., 4 vols. in 2, Amsterdam, 1695).

[43] du Cardinal D'ossat

Arnaud (1536–1604) Cardinal d'Ossat, *Let[t]res du Cardinal d'Ossat* . . . (Abraham Nicolas Amelot de La Houssaye [1634–1706], comp. and ed., 2 vols., Paris, 1697; 9th ed.[?], 5 vols., Amsterdam, 1732).

[44] du Maral. d'Estrades

Godefroi Louis (1607–1686), Comte d'Estrades et maréchal de France, *Lettres, mémoires et négociations de Monsieur le Comte d'Estrades* . . . (Prosper Marchand [d. 1756], comp. and ed., 9 vols., London [i.e., The Hague], 1743; 2d ed., 9 vols., The Hague, 1763).

[45] de la paix de Westphalie

Adam Adami (1610–1663), *Relatio historica de pacificatione Osnabvrgo-Monasteriensi ex avtographo avctoris restitvta atqve actorvm pacis Vestphalicae* . . . (Anon., variant title, Frankfort on the Main, 1696; Johann Gottfried von Meiern [1692–1745], ed., 2d ed., above title, Leipzig, 1737; 3d ed., Ratisbon, 1739).

[46] du Maral. de Noailles

Adrien Maurice (1678–1766), Duc de Noailles et maréchal de France, comp., *Mémoires politiques et militaires, pour servir á l'histoire de Louis XIV & de Louis XV* . . . (Claude François Xavier Millot [1726–1785], ed., 6 vols., Paris, 1766; 2d ed., 6 vols., Paris, 1777). For a work wholly by Millot, see No. 56.

[47] de la paix d'Utrecht

Casimir Freschot (1640–1720), *The Compleat History of The Treaty of Utrecht* . . . (French original ed., 6 vols. in 12, Utrecht, 1714–1715; English ed., 2 vols., London, 1715).

[48] des autres paix de ce siecle

Friedrich August Wilhelm Wenck (1741–1810), *Codex ivris gentium recentissimi, e tabvlarorivm exemplorvmque fide dignorum monvmentis compositvs* . . . *continens diplomata inde ab A. MDCCXXXV usque ad A. MDCCLXXII* . . . (3 vols., Leipzig, 1781–1795).

[49] Lamborty's Memoirs & negociations

Guillaume de Lamberty (1660–1742), comp. and ed., *Mémoires pour servir à l'histoire du XVIIe siècle, contenant les négociations* . . . (14 vols., Amsterdam and The Hague, 1734–1740).

[50] Cardl. Mazarine's letters

Jules (1602–1661) Cardinal Mazarin, *Lettres du Cardinal Mazarin où l'on voit le secret de la négociation de la paix des Pirénées* . . . (original ed., Amsterdam, 1690; Léonor Jean Christine Soulas d'Allainval [1700–1753], comp. and ed., 2 vols., Amsterdam, 1745).

[51]   De Witt's letters.

Johan de Witt (1625–1672) *et al., Lettres et négociations . . . depuis l'année 1652, jusqu'à l'an 1669, inclus* . . . (Two separate Dutch original works: (1) 3 vols., Amsterdam, 1719, and (2) 6 vols., The Hague, 1723–1725; French ed., 5 vols., Amsterdam, 1725). For another work partially by de Witt, see Nos. 95 and 163.

General History

[52]   Universal History

George Sale (*ca.* 1697–1736) and continuators, *An Universal History, from the Earliest Account of Time* . . . (41 vols., London, 1736–1765; 3d ed., 60 vols., London, 1779–1784).

[53]   Modern History

Thomas Salmon (1679–1767) and continuators, *Modern History: or, The Present State of All Nations* . . . (32 small vols., London, 1725; 3d ed., 3 vols., London, 1744–1746). For another work by Salmon, see No. 67.

[54]   Raleigh's History of the World

Sir Walter Raleigh (*ca.* 1552–1618), *The History of the World* . . . (Anon., London, 1614; 11th ed., 2 vols., London, 1736).

[55]   Voltaire's Historical works

For two of Voltaire's "Historical works" that JM listed separately, see Nos. 103 and 128.

55a. François Marie Arouet de Voltaire (1694–1778), *The Age of Louis XV* . . . (French original ed., 2 vols., Berlin, 1751; English ed., 2 vols., London, 1774).

55b. ———, *Annals of the Empire; from the Reign of Charlemagne* . . . (French original ed., 2 vols., Berlin and The Hague, 1754; English ed., London, 1781).

55c. ———, *An Essay on Universal History, the Manners and Spirit of Nations from the Reign of Charlemaign to the Age of Lewis XIV* . . . (French original ed., 7 vols., Geneva, 1754; English ed., 3 vols., London, 1754–1757; French 2d ed., augmented, 8 vols., Geneva, 1761–1763; English 5th ed., augmented, 4 vols., London, 1782).

55d. ———, *An Essay upon the Civil Wars of France* . . . (French original ed., London, 1727; English ed., London, 1727; 5th ed., Dublin, 1760).

55e. ———, *Histoire du parlement de Paris* . . . ("Abbé Big," pseud., 2 vols., Amsterdam, 1769; 6th ed., 2 vols., n. p. [Paris?], 1771).

55f. ———, *History of Charles XII. King of Sweden* . . . (French original ed., Rouen, 1731; English ed., London, 1734; 4th ed.[?], London, 1760).

55g. ———, *The History of the War of Seventeen Hundred and Forty One* . . . (Anon., French original ed., London, 1756; English ed., London and Dublin, 1756; 3d ed., London, 1756).

55h. ———, *The Philosophy of History* . . . ("*le feu l'abbé Bazin,*" pseud., French original ed., Geneva, 1765; English ed., London, 1766).

[56]   Abbé Millot Histoire generale

Claude François Xavier Millot (see No. 46), *Elements of General History* . . . (French original ed., 9 vols., Paris, 1772–1773; English ed., 5 vols., London, 1778–1779).

[57]   Dictionaire of Bayle

Pierre Bayle (1647–1706), *A General Dictionary, Historical and Critical* . . . (French original ed., 2 vols., Rotterdam, 1696; Thomas Birch [see No. 41] "and Other Hands," trs. and eds., English ed., 10 vols., London, 1734–1741).

[58]   Burnett's History of his own times

Gilbert Burnet (1643–1715), *Bishop Burnet's History of His Own Time* . . . (Sir Thomas Burnet [1694–1753], ed., 2 vols., London, 1724–1734; Roger Flexman [1708–1795], ed., 2d ed., 4 vols., London, 1753–1754; 3d ed., 4 vols., London, 1766).

[59]   Mosheim's Ecclesiastical History

Johann Lorenz von Mosheim (1694–1755), *An Ecclesiastical History, Antient and Modern, from the Birth of Christ, to the Beginning of the Present Century* . . . (Latin original ed., Frankfort, 1726; Archibald MacLaine [1722–1805], tr. and ed., English ed., 3 vols., London, 1765–1768; 6th ed., 6 vols., London, 1782).

[60]   Warner's Eccles: History of England

Ferdinando Warner (1703–1768), *History of England as Relates to Religion and the Church* . . . (Variant title, according with JM's entry, 2 vols., London, 1756–1757; 2d ed., above title, 2 vols., London, 1759).

Chronology

[61]   Lenglet du frenoy tablettes chronologiques
de l'Histoire universelle

Nicolas Lenglet du Fresnoy (1674–1755), *Chronological Tables of Universal History . . . from the Creation of the World . . . to the Death of King George II* . . . (French original ed., 2 vols., Paris, 1729; Thomas Floyd [Flloyd] [d. *ca.* 1763], tr. and continuator, English ed., 2 vols., London, 1762; continued to 1775 in French ed., 2 vols., Paris, 1778).

[62]   Blair's chronological tables

John Blair (d. 1782), *The Chronology and History of the World . . . to the Year of Christ, 1779; Illustrated in LVI. Tables* . . . (Variant subtitle, London, 1754; 4th ed., London, 1779).

Geography

[63]   Bushing's Universal Geography

Anton Friedrich Büsching (1724–1793), *A New System of Geography* . . . (German original ed., 6 vols., Hamburg, 1754–1761; English ed., 6 vols., London, 1762).

[64]   Smith's System of Geography

Atlas geographus, or A Complete System of Geography . . . (Issued serially by the month, London, 1709–1712, by Ralph Smith [d. *ca.* 1713], bookseller; 2d ed., 5 vols., London, 1711–1717).

[65]   Guthrie's Geographical Grammer

William Guthrie (1708–1770), *A New Geographical, Historical, and Commercial Grammar* . . . (Variant title, London, 1770; 6th ed., above title, London, 1779). The work was suspected of being that of Guthrie's fellow Scot John Knox (1720–1790), printer, bookseller, and philanthropist.

[66]   La Martinier, Dictionaire Geographique

Antoine Augustin Bruzen de la Martinière (1662–1746), *Le grand dictionnaire géographique, historique, et critique* . . . (9 vols. in 10, The Hague, 1726–1739; 4th ed., 6 vols., Paris and Venice, 1768).

[67]   Salmon's Gazetteer

Thomas Salmon (see No. 53), *The Modern Gazetteer; or, A Short View of the Several Nations of the World* . . . (London, 1746; 8th ed., London, 1769). See also *Papers of Madison*, I, 37 n.

[68]   Priestly's Historical Chart

Joseph Priestley (1733–1804), *A Description of a New Chart of History Containing a View of the Principal Revolutions of Empire That Have Taken Place in the World* . . . (London, 1760; 5th ed., London, 1781). For another work by Priestley, see No. 69; for a previous reference to him, in his role as a political scientist, *Papers of Madison*, I, 145, and n. 8.

[69]   Biographical Chart

Joseph Priestley (see No. 68), *A Description of a Chart of Biography; with a Catalogue of All the Names Inserted in It, and the Dates Annexed to Them* . . . (Warrington, Eng., 1765; 7th ed., London, 1778).

[70]   Jeffery's Historical & Chronological Chart

Thomas Jefferys (d. 1771), *The Study of Geography Improved* . . . *Being a More Certain and Expeditious Method of Conveying the Knowledge of That Science, and Fixing It in the Memory* . . . (London, 1767). For a previous allusion to Jefferys, see *Papers of Madison*, IV, 9; 15, n. 14; for other works by him, Nos. 71f and 71h.

[71]   Collection of best maps.

71a. Jean Baptiste Bourguignon d'Anneville (1697–1782), *Géographie ancienne abrégée* . . . (3 vols., Paris, 1768; 2d ed., 2 vols., Nuremberg, 1781–1786).

71b. Rigobert Bonne (1727–1794) *et al., Atlas moderne; ou collection de cartes sur toutes les parties du globe terrestre* . . . (3 vols., Paris, 1762–1771).

71c. Thomas Kitchin (d. 1784), *General Atlas, Describing the Whole Universe* . . . (London, 1773). For another work, partially that of Kitchin, see 71e.

71d. César François Cassini de Thury (1714–1784), *Carte de la France, publiée sous la direction de l'Académie des Sciences* . . . (180 sheets, 2 tables of directions, and 1 chart of triangles, Paris, 1744–1787). For Jefferson's attempt to employ Cassini's method of astronomical triangulation for the determination of the size of Virginia in square miles, see *Papers of Madison*, V, 10; 14, n. 30.

71e. Thomas Kitchin (see No. 71c) *et al., The Large English Atlas; or, A New Set of Maps of All the Counties of England and Wales* . . . *With Three General Maps of England, Scotland, and Ireland* . . . (London, 1747; 6th ed., London, n. d. [1777?]).

71f. Thomas Jefferys (see No. 70), *The American Atlas; or, A Geographical Description of the Whole Continent of America* . . . (London, 1775; 3d ed., London, 1778).

71g. Thomas Hutchins (1730–1789), *A Topographical Description of Virginia, Pennsylvania, Maryland and North Carolina, Comprehending the Rivers Ohio, Kenhawa, S[c]ioto, Cherokee, Wabash, Illinois, Missis[s]ippi,* &c. . . . (London, 1778). For other allusions to this work, see *Papers of Madison,* III, 98, n. 1; Harrison to Delegates, 20 Mar. 1783, and n. 4.

71h. Thomas Jefferys (see No. 70), *A Description of the Spanish Islands and Settlements on the Coasts of the West Indies* . . . (London, 1762; 2d ed., London, 1774).

71i. James Rennel (1742–1830), *Memoir of a Map of Hindoostan; or The Mogul's Empire* . . . (London, 1783).

Particular History

JM wrote each of the eighteen subheadings in the left margin.

Greacian

[72]   Goldsmith's History of Greece

Oliver Goldsmith (1728–1774), *The Graecian History, from the Earliest State to the Death of Alexander the Great* . . . (2 vols., London, 1774). For another work by Goldsmith, see No. 77.

[73]   Stanyan's History of Greece

Temple Stanyan (*ca.* 1677–1752), *The Graecian History. From the Original of Greece, to the Death of Philip of Macedon* . . . (2 vols., London, 1707; 6th ed.[?], 2 vols., London, 1781).

[74]   Potter's Grecian Antiquities

John Potter (*ca.* 1674–1747), *Archaeologia graeca: or, The Antiquities of Greece* . . . (2 vols., London, 1697–1698; 9th ed., 2 vols., London, 1775).

Roman

[75]   Coussin Histoire Romaine

Louis Cousin (1627–1707), comp. and tr., *Histoire romaine* . . . *Traduite sur les originaux grecs* . . . (2 vols., Paris, 1678; 2d ed., 2 vols., n. p. [Amsterdam?], 1686).

[76]   Histoire de Constantinople

Louis Cousin, comp. and tr., *Histoire de Constantinople* . . . *Traduite sur les originaux grecs* . . . (8 vols., Paris, 1672–1674; 2d ed., 8 vols., n. p. [Amsterdam?], 1685).

[77]   Goldsmith's Roman History

Oliver Goldsmith (see No. 72), *The Roman History, from the Foundation of the City of Rome, to the Destruction of the Western Empire* . . . (2 vols., London, 1769; 4th ed., 2 vols., London, 1781).

[78]   Hooke's Roman History

Nathaniel (Nathanael) Hooke (d. 1763), *The Roman History; from the Building of Rome to the Ruin of the Commonwealth* . . . (Vols. I–III of 4 vols., London,

1738–1764; [Gilbert Stuart (1742–1786), continuator], Vol. IV, London, 1771; 5th ed., 4 vols., London, 1770–1771).

[79]   Vertot's Revolutions of Rome

René Aubert de Vertot D'Aubeuf (1655–1735), *The History of the Revolutions That Happened in the Government of the Roman Republic* . . . (French original ed., 3 vols., Paris, 1719; English ed., 3 vols., London, 1720; 6th ed., 2 vols., London, 1770). For other works by Vertot, see Nos. 126 and 133; for one questionably attributed to him, No. 125b.

[80]   Gibbon's on the decline of the Rom: Empire

Edward Gibbon (1737–1794), *The History of the Decline and Fall of the Roman Empire* . . . (6 vols., London, 1776–1788). Three volumes had been published by 1783.

[81]   Kennet's Roman Antiquities

Basil Kennett (1674–1715), *Romae antiquae notitia, or, The Antiquities of Rome* . . . (London, 1696; 15th ed., London, 1773; reprint, London, 1776).

[82]   Plutarch's Lives

Plutarch (*ca.* 46–120), *Plutarch's Lives, Translated from the Original Greek with Notes Critical and Historical* . . . (John Langhorne [1735–1779] and William Langhorne [1721–1772], trs. and eds., 6 vols., London, 1770; 3d ed., 6 vols., London, 1778). For previous references to Plutarch, see *Papers of Madison*, I, 5; 27, n. 47; 42, n. 14; 91; 93, n. 4.

Italian

[83]   Guicciardini's History

Francesco Guicciardini (1483–1540), *The History of Italy, from the Year 1490, to 1532* . . . (Posthumous Italian original ed., 20 books, Florence, 1561–1564; English ed., 10 vols., London, 1753–1756; 3d ed., 10 vols., London, 1763).

[84]   Giannini History of Naples

Pietro Giannone (1676–1748), *The Civil History of the Kingdom of Naples* . . . (Italian original ed., 4 vols., Naples, 1723; English ed., 2 vols., London, 1729–1731).

[85]   Nani History of Venice

Giovanni Battista Felice Gasparo Nani (1616–1678), *Histoire de la république de Venice* . . . (Italian original ed., 2 parts: (1) Venice, 1662, and (2) posthumous, Venice, 1679; English ed., London, 1673; French ed., 6 vols., Cologne and Amsterdam, 1682–1702). There was also an Italian edition (2 vols. in 4, Venice) as late as 1720.

[86]   Padre Paolo on the Venetian Republic

Pietro Sarpi (1552–1623) (known to his contemporaries by his assumed religious name, Servite Paolo), *The History of the Qvarrels of Pope Pavl. V. with the State of Venice* . . . (Italian original ed., Venice, 1606; English ed., London, 1626). There was a French edition (Paris) as late as 1759. For another work by Sarpi, see No. 152.

German and Holland

[87] Histoire d'Allemagne par Barre

Joseph Barre (1692–1764), *Histoire générale de l'Allemagne depuis l'an de Rome 648, jusqu'à l'an 1740 de Jésus Christ* . . . (Variant title, 10 vols., Paris, 1748; above title, 10 vols. in 11, Paris, 1748).

[88] Pfeffel Abregé chronolo: de l'hist: d'Allema:

Christian Friedrich Pfeffel von Kriegelstein (1726–1807), *Nouvel abrégé chronologique de l'histoire et du droit public d'Allemagne* . . . (Variant title, Paris, 1754; 2d ed., augmented, 2 vols., Mannheim, 1758; 6th ed., 2 vols., Paris, 1777).

[89] Puffendorf de origine imperii german: notis Titii

Samuel, Freiherr von Pufendorf (see No. 11), *De statu imperii Germanici* . . . ("Severini de Monzambano," pseud., Geneva, 1667; Gottlieb Gerhard Titius [1661–1714], ed., 2d ed., Leipzig, 1708; Christian Thomasius [1655–1728], ed., 3d ed., Magdeburg, 1714).

[90] Robinson's History of Charles V

William Robertson (1721–1793), *The History of the Reign of the Emperor Charles V.* . . . (3 vols., London, 1769; American ed., variant title, 3 vols., by subscription, Philadelphia: Robert Bell [1732–1784], 1770; 3d London ed., 4 vols., 1777). For other works by Robertson, see Nos. 121 and 242.

[91] Bentivoglio History of war in Flanders

Guido (1579–1644) Cardinal Bentivoglio, *The History of the Wars of Flanders* . . . (Italian original ed., 3 vols., Cologne [Leyden?], 1632–1639; English ed., so-called "third" but the only one complete, 2 parts, London, 1678).

[92] Le Clerk's History of the United Provinces

Jean Le Clerc (see No. 34a), *Histoire des Provinces-Unies des Pays Bas* . . . (3 vols., Amsterdam, 1723–1728; 2d ed., 4 vols., Amsterdam, 1728–1737).

[93] Strada

Famiano Strada (1572–1649), *Histoire de la guerre de Flandre* . . . (Latin original ed., 2 vols., Rome, 1632; French ed., 2 vols., Paris, 1644–1649; 6th ed., 4 vols., Brussels, 1739).

[94] Grotius de rebus Belgicis

Hugo Grotius (see No. 10), *De rebus Belgicis; or The Annals and History of the Low-Countrey Warrs* . . . (Posthumous Latin original ed., Amsterdam, 1657; English ed., London, 1665).

[95] De Witt's State of Holland

[Pieter de la Court (1618–1685)] and Johan de Witt (see No. 51), *Mémoires de Jean de Witt, grand pensionnaire de Hollande* . . . (Dutch original ed., The Hague, 1662; 2d ed., revised and augmented, variant title, The Hague, 1667; French ed., The Hague, 1667; 3d ed., Ratisbon, 1709). For JM's entry of the same work in English translation adhering closely to the Dutch original title, see No. 163.

[96]   Watson's History of Philip II

Robert Watson (ca. 1730–1781), *The History of the Reign of Philip the Second, King of Spain* . . . (2 vols., London, 1777; 3d ed., 3 vols., London, 1779).

French

[97]   Histoire de France de l'abbé Veli Villaret,
       Garnier et continuateurs

Paul François Velly (1709–1759), Claude Villaret (1715–1766), and Jean Jacques Garnier (1729–1805), *Histoire de France depuis l'établissement de la monarchie jusqu'au règne de Louis XIV* . . . (48 vols., Paris, 1760–1786). There were no "*continuateurs*" beyond Garnier, who ceased publication after recording events of the year 1564.

[98]   D'avila History of Civil Wars of France

Enrico Caterino Davila (1576–1631), *The History of the Civil Wars of France* . . . (Italian original ed., 15 vols., Venice, 1630; English ed., 2 vols., London, 1758).

[99]   Philip de Comines

Philippe de Comines (1445–1511), Sieur d'Argenton, *Memoirs of Philip de Comines* . . . (Denis Godefroy [1615–1681], ed., French original ed., 3 vols., Paris, 1649; successively augmented; 4th ed., 3 vols., Brussels, 1706; Thomas Uvedale [ca. 1641–1732], tr. and ed., English ed., from 4th French ed., 2 vols., London, 1712; 4th ed.[?], 2 vols., London, 1782).

[100]   Sully's memoirs

Maximilien de Béthune (1559–1641), Duc de Sully, *Memoirs of Maximilien de Bethune, Duke of Sully* . . . (French original ed., 2 vols., Amsterdam [i. e., Chateau de Sully], n. d. [1638]; English ed., 3 vols., London, 1756; 6th ed., 3 vols., Dublin, 1781).

[101]   Prefixe Henry IV

Hardouin de Beaumont de Péréfixe (1605–1670), *The History of Henry IV., King of France and Navarre* . . . (French original ed., Amsterdam, 1661; English ed., London, 1663; 2d ed., London, 1672). A French edition, which was at least the tenth, was published (Paris) in 1776.

[102]   Cardinal de Retz Memoirs

Jean François Paul de Gondi (1614–1679), Cardinal de Retz, *Memoirs of the Cardinal de Retz. Containing the Particulars of His Own Life* . . . (French original ed., 3 vols., Nancy, 1717; 2d ed., augmented, 4 vols., Amsterdam, 1719; Peter Davall [d. 1763], tr. and ed., English ed., 4 vols., London, 1723; 4th ed., 4 vols., London, 1777). For JM's knowledge of this work, see *Papers of Madison*, I, 7–16; 24–27, nn. 1–47; 107, n. 4; III, 225, n. 5.

[103]   Voltaire's Louis XIV

François Marie Arouet de Voltaire (see No. 55), *The Age of Louis XIV* . . . (French original ed., 2 vols., Amsterdam, 1739; English ed., 3 vols., London, 1779–1781).

79

British

[104] Matthew Paris by Watts

Matthew Paris (d. 1259) *et al., Monachi albanensis angli, historia major* . . . (Latin original MSS; W[illiam] Wa[t]ts [*ca.* 1590–1649], comp. and ed., 2 parts, London, 1639–1640; 4th ed., London, 1684).

[105] William of Malmbury

105a. William of Malmesbury (*ca.* 1093–*ca.* 1143). *De gestis regum anglorum* . . . in Sir Henry Savile (1549–1622), comp. and ed., *Rerum anglicarum scriptores post Bedam praecipui* . . . (London, 1596; 2d ed., Frankfort, 1601).

105b. ———, *Vita Sancti Aldhelmi* . . . in Vol. III of [William Fullman (1632–1688)], and Thomas Gale (*ca.* 1635–1702), comps. and eds., *Historiae anglicanae scriptores* (3 vols., Oxford, 1684–1691); or Vol. II of Henry Wharton (1664–1695), comp. and ed., *Anglia sacra, sive collectio historiarum* (2 vols., London, 1691).

[106] Polydore Virgil

Polydorus Virgilius (Polidoro Vergilio) (*ca.* 1470–*ca.* 1555), *Anglicae historiae libri viginti septem* . . . (26 books, Basel, 1534; 27 books, 6th ed., Basel, 1555; 14th ed.[?], Leyden, 1651).

[107] Rappin's History of England

Paul de Rapin (1661–1725), Sieur de Thoyras, *The History of England from the Earliest Period to the Revolution in 1688* . . . (French original ed., 13 vols., The Hague, 1723–1735; Nicholas Tindal [1687–1774], tr., ed., and continuator, English ed., 15 vols., London, 1725–1731; continued *to the Accession of King George II*, 2 vols., 4 vols., London, 1732–1751; 6th ed. of entire work, 21 vols., London, 1757–1763). It was charged that these volumes were really written by Thomas Birch (see No. 41), with the assistance of "persons of political eminence."

[108] Hume's History of England

David Hume (1711–1776), *The History of England, from the Invasion of Julius Caesar to the Revolution in 1688* . . . (6 vols., London and Edinburgh, 1754–1762; 7th ed., 8 vols., London, 1778). See *Papers of Madison*, I, 103; 104, n. 5. For Hume as a political essayist, see No. 168.

[109] Kennett's English History

White Kennett (1660–1728), Vol. III of *A Complete History of England . . . to the Death of His Late Majesty King William III* . . . ([John Hughes (1677–1720), ed.], 3 vols., London, 1706; J. S. [probably John Strype (1653–1737), ed.], 2d ed., 3 vols., London, 1719).

[110] Clarendon's History

110a. Edward Hyde (1609–1674), Earl of Clarendon, *The History of the Rebellion and Civil Wars in England* . . . (Laurence Hyde [1641–1711], Earl of Rochester, ed., 3 vols., Oxford, 1702–1704; 13th ed.[?], 3 vols., Oxford, 1732).

110b. ———, *The Life of Edward Earl of Clarendon . . . A Continuation of His History of the Grand Rebellion* . . . (Original MS; posthumous, 3 vols., Oxford, 1759; 4th ed., 3 vols., Oxford, 1761).

[111]   Ludlow's Memoirs

Edmund Ludlow (*ca.* 1617–1692), *Memoirs of Edmund Ludlow, Esq.* . . . ([Isaac Littlebury (d. 1710), ed.(?)], 3 vols., Vevey, 1698–1699; 4th ed., London, 1771).

[112]   Littleton's History of Henry II

George Lyttleton (1709–1773), Baron Lyttleton, *The History of the Life of Henry the Second* . . . (4 vols., London, 1767–1771; 4th ed., 6 vols., London, 1777–1787).

[113]   Parliamentary History

Thomas Osborne (d. 1767) and William Sandby (*ca.* 1717–1799), comps. and eds., *The Parliamentary or Constitutional History of England* . . . (24 vols., London, 1751–1761; Andrew Millar [d. 1768], comp., ed., and continuator, 2d ed., 24 vols., London, 1761–1762).

[114]   Parliamentary debates

[John Torbuck (d. *ca.* 1755), comp. and ed.], *A Collection of the Parliamentary Debates in England from 1668 to the Present Time* . . . (Slightly variant title, 21 vols., Dublin, 1739–1742; reprint, 21 vols., London, 1741–1742; 2d ed., 24 vols., London, 1749).

[115]   Annual Register

[Edmund Burke (1729–1797)] *et al.*, eds., *The Annual Register; or, A View of the History, Politic(k)s and Literature of the Year [1758 to 1860]* . . . (102 vols., London, 1759–1861). General index, 1758–1780, inclusive (London, 1783).

[116]   History of the Reign of Geo: III

[Robert Macfarlane (1734–1804) *et al.*], *The History of the First Ten Years of the Reign of George the Third* . . . (Variant title according with JM's entry, Vol. I of 4 vols., London, 1770–1796; 4th ed., above title, 4 vols., London, 1783–1796).

[117]   Cabàla

[Hercules Langrish(c)(?)], "A Noble Hand," anonym, comp., *The Prince's Cabala; or, Mysteries of State* . . . *in the Reigns of King Henry the Eighth, Queen Elizabeth* . . . *and King Charles* . . . (Variant title, 2 parts, London, 1654; 4th ed., above title, London, 1715).

[118]   Rushworth's Collection

John Rushworth (*ca.* 1612–1690), comp. and ed., *Historical Collections of Private Passages of State . . . anno 1618 . . . to the Death of King Charles the First 1648* . . . (8 vols., part posthumous, London, 1659–1701).

[119]   Thurloe's State papers

John Thurloe (1616–1668), comp., and Thomas Birch (see No. 41), comp. and ed., *A Collection of the State Papers of John Thurloe Esqr. from the Year 1638 to the Restoration of King Charles II. 1660* . . . (7 vols., London, 1742).

[120]   Parliamentary Register

John Almon (see No. 36b), John Debrett (see No. 36c), and John Stockdale (*ca.* 1749–1814), eds., *The Parliamentary Register; or History of the Proceedings and Debates of the House of Commons (and House of Lords); Containing an Account of the Most Interesting Speeches and Motions* . . . *November, 1774[-July 1813]* . . . (112 vols., London, 1775–1813). For JM's references in Congress to an issue of this periodical, see *Papers of Madison,* V, 140; 143, n. 8; 144; 146, n. 5.

Scotch

[121] Robinson's History of Scotland

William Robertson (see No. 90), *The History of Scotland during the Reigns of Queen Mary and of King James VI. Till His Accession to the Crown of England* . . . (2 vols., London, 1759; 7th ed.[?], 2 vols., London, 1776).

Irish

[122] Leland's History of Ireland

Thomas Leland (1722–1785), *The History of Ireland from the Invasion of Henry II* . . . (3 vols., London, 1773; 4th ed., 3 vols., Cork, 1775).

Spanish & Portuguese

[123] Mariana's History of Spain.

Juan de Mariana (1536–1624), Fernando Carmago y Salcedo (1572–1652), and Basilio Váren de Soto (d. 1673), *The General History of Spain. From the First Peopling of It . . . to the Death of King Philip III . . . To Which Are Added, Two Supplements* . . . (Latin original ed., 2 vols., Toledo, 1592–1601; Spanish ed., 2 vols., Toledo, 1601; Carmago's "Supplement," Madrid, 1650; Váren's, Madrid, 1678; English ed., London, 1699).

[124] Miniana

Juan Manuel de Miñana (1671–1730), *Historia de España, o continuación* . . . (Posthumous Latin original ed., 4 vols. in 2, The Hague, 1733; Spanish ed., Vols. XI and XII of Mariana's *Historia general* [No. 123], 16 vols. in 12, Lyons, 1737–1739; 2d ed., 16 vols. in 12, Lyons, 1751–1756).

[125] Revolutions d'Espagne du P. D'Orleans [et] du Vertot

125a. Pierre Joseph D'Orléans (1644–1698) and continuators, *Histoire des révolutions d'Espagne; depuis de la déstruction de l'empire des goths, jusqu'à . . . réunion . . . en une seule monarchie* . . . (Pierre Julien Rouillé [1681–1740], ed., 3 vols., Paris, 1734; reprint, 12 vols., Paris, 1737).

125b. René Aubert de Vertot D'Aubeuf (see No. 79) (author?), *The History of the Revolutions in Spain, from the Decadence of the Roman Empire . . . to . . . the Accession of Lewis I. to the Crown* . . . (5 vols., London: J. Morgan, 1724). No edition of this work in French has been found. It may be that J. Morgan, who flourished in London between 1724 and 1761, was more than printer and bookseller.

[126] Revolutions of Portugal by Vertot.

René Aubert de Vertot D'Aubeuf (see No. 79), *The Revolutions of Portugal . . . Revised and Considerably Enlarged* . . . (French original ed., Paris, 1689; 4th ed., augmented, The Hague, 1734; English ed., London, 1721; 6th English ed., augmented, Glasgow, 1758).

Prussian

[127]   Memoirs of the House of Brandenburg

[Frederick (1712–1786) II, the Great, King of Prussia], "the Hand of a Master," anonym, *Memoirs of the House of Brandenburg, from the Earliest Accounts* (*to the Death of Frederick William, the Present King's Father*) . . . (French original ed., Berlin, 1748; English ed., London, 1748). For a legal code inspired by Frederick II, see No. 194.

Russian

[128]   History of Peter the Great by Voltaire

François Marie Arouet de Voltaire (see No. 55), *The History of the Russian Empire under Peter the Great* . . . (French original ed., 2 vols., Geneva, 1759–1763; English ed., 2 vols., London, 1763; 3d ed., 2 vols., London, 1780).

Danish

[129]   Molesworth's account of Denmark

Robert Molesworth (1656–1725), Viscount Molesworth, *An Account of Denmark, As It Was in the Year 1692* . . . (London, 1694; 4th ed.[?], London, 1738, long held to be the most "elegant"; 5th ed.[?], Glasgow, 1752).

[130]   History of Denmark by Mallet

Paul Henri Mallet (1730–1807), *Histoire de Dannemarc . . . depuis l'établissement de la monarchie jusques à l'avènement de la maison d'Oldenbourg au throne* . . . (3 vols. in 4, Copenhagen, 1758–1777; 2d ed., 6 vols., Geneva, 1763–1777).

Sweedish

[131]   Dalin's History of Sweeden

Olof von Dalin (1708–1763), *Geschichte des Reiches Schweden* . . . (Swedish original ed., 4 vols., Stockholm, 1747–1762; German ed., 3 parts in 2 vols., Greifswald and Rostock, 1756–1763).

[132]   Mallet's form of govt. in Sweeden

Paul Henri Mallet (see No. 130), *Forme du gouvernement de Suède, avec . . . les lois fondamentales et le droit public de ce royaume* . . . (Danish original ed., Copenhagen, 1756; French ed., Copenhagen and Geneva, 1756).

[133]   Vertot's Revolutions of Sweden

René Aubert de Vertot D'Aubeuf (see No. 79), *The History of the Revolutions in Sweden; Occasioned by the Change of Religion, and Alteration of the Government* . . . (French original ed., Paris, 1695; English ed., London, 1696; 7th ed., London, 1742).

[134]   Sheridan's do. of do.

Charles Francis Sheridan (1750–1806), *A History of the Late Revolution in Sweden* . . . (London, 1778; 2d ed., London, 1783).

Polish

[135] Abbe Coyer's History of J. Sobiesky.

Gabriel François Coyer (1707–1782), *The History of John Sobieski, King of Po-*
land ... (French original ed., 3 vols., Amsterdam and Paris, 1761; English ed., London, 1762).

[136] William's History of the Nortn. Govts.

John Williams (d. 1809?), *The Rise, Progress, and Present State of the Northern*
Governments; viz., The United Provinces, Denmark, Sweden, Russia, and Poland
... (2 vols., London, 1777).

Swiss

[137] Stanyan's History of Switzerland

[Abraham Stanyan (*ca.* 1669–1732)]; Temple Stanyan (see No. 73), by erroneous
attribution, *An Account of Switzerland, Written in the Year 1714* ... (Anon.,
variant title, London, 1714; 2d ed., Edinburgh, 1756). Long after JM's lifetime this
work was still attributed erroneously to Abraham Stanyan's younger brother.

Genevan

[138] Keate's History of Geneva

George Keate (1729–1797), *A Short Account of the Ancient History, Present Gov-*
ernment, and Laws of the Republic of Geneva ... (London, 1761).

Turkes

[139] Mignot's History of the Ottoman Empire

Vincent Mignot (*ca.* 1730–1791), *Histoire de l'empire ottoman, depuis son origine*
jusqu'à la paix de Belgrade en 1740 ... (4 vols., Paris, 1771).

[140] P. Recaut's do.

Richard Knolles (*ca.* 1550–1610), Thomas Nabbes (d. *ca.* 1645), and Sir Paul Rycaut
(Ricaut) (1628–1700), *The Turkish History, from the Original of That Nation to*
the Growth of the Ottoman Empire ... *With a Continuation to the Year*
MDCLXXXVII ... (Knolles, variant title, London, 1603; continued by Nabbes,
London, 1638; continued by Rycaut, 6th ed., above title, 3 vols., London, 1687–
1700).

Chinese

[141] Duhaldes History of China

Jean Baptiste Du Halde (1674–1743), *The General History of China* ... (French
original ed., 4 vols., Paris, 1735; English ed., 4 vols., London, 1736; 3d ed., 4 vols.,
London, 1741).

Politics

[142] Plato's Republic by Spend

Plato (*ca.* 428–*ca.* 348 B.C.), *The Republic of Plato* ... (Harry Spens [*ca.* 1713–
1787], tr. and ed., Glasgow, 1763). See *Papers of Madison*, I, 5; 17; 28, n. 61; 35; 42,
n. 10.

[143]   Aristotle's do.

Aristotle (384–322 B.C.), *A Treatise on Government* . . . (London, 1776; reprint, London, 1778). See *Papers of Madison,* I, 17; 35; 37; 41, n. 2.

[144]   More's Utopia

Sir Thomas More (1478–1535), *Utopia: Containing an Impartial History . . . of That Island* . . . (Latin original ed., London, 1516; English ed., London, 1684; 6th ed.[?], Glasgow, 1762).

[145]   Filmer on Government

145a. Sir Robert Filmer (d. 1653), baronet, *Observations concerning the Original and Various Forms of Government* . . . (Original separate works, London, 1647–1652; collected under above title, London, 1696).

145b. Sir Robert Filmer, *Patriarcha; or the Natural Power of Kings Asserted* . . . (Posthumous, London, 1680; 2d ed., London, 1685).

[146]   Hooker's Ecclesiastical polity

Richard Hooker (*ca.* 1554–1600), *Of the Laws of Ecclesiastical Polity* . . . (London, n. d. [1592]; 2d ed., augmented, London, 1597; John Gauden [1605–1662], comp. and ed., 8th ed., further augmented, London, 1662; 19th ed., London, 1739).

[147]   Hobbe's Works

As a youth JM became acquainted with at least one of Hobbes's works. Probably in 1782 he purchased the copy of *Leviathan* originally owned by William Byrd II of Westover (*Papers of Madison,* I, 16; 27, n. 47; 35; IV, 126; 127, n. 4).

147a. Thomas Hobbes (1588–1679), *The Moral and Political Works of Thomas Hobbes, of Malmesbury* . . . (Separate Latin original publications, some posthumous, London and various continental cities, 1629–1688; 3d Francis Thom[p]son, comp., tr., and ed., above title, London, 1750; 2d ed., London, 1759). The collection did not include 147b.

147b. ———, *Elementa philosophica de cive* . . . (Paris, 1642; 4th ed., Amsterdam, 1669).

[148]   Harrington's works

James Harrington (1611–1677), *The Oceana of James Harrington Esq and His Other Works* . . . (Separate original works, London, 1655–1660; John Toland [1670–1722], comp. and ed., above title, London, 1700; Thomas Birch [see No. 41], comp. and ed., 2d ed., augmented, London, 1737; 4th ed., London, 1771).

[149]   Sidney on Government

Algernon Sidney (Sydney) (1622–1683), *The Works of Algernon Sidney* . . . (Separate posthumous works, London, 1696–1763; Joseph Robertson [1736–1820], comp. and ed., above title, London, 1772).

[150]   Locke on Government

John Locke (1632–1704), *Two Treatises on Government* . . . (London, 1690; Thomas Hollis [1720–1774], ed., 6th ed., superior, London, 1764; 7th ed., London, 1769; American reprint, Boston: Peter Edes [1732–1811] and John Gill [1732–1785], 1773). For "Locke on money," see No. 178. For other works by Locke, see *Papers of Madison,* I, 5; 21; 30, n. 85; 33; 41, n. 4; 42, n. 13; 212, nn. 5, 7; V, 84, n. 3.

[151]   Macchiavelli's works

Niccolò Machiavelli (1469–1527), *The Works of Nicholas Machiavel* . . . (Original Italian works, most posthumous, Venice, Florence, and Rome, 1524–1546; Ellis Farneworth [d. 1763], comp., tr. and ed., above title, 2 vols., London, 1762; 2d ed., 4 vols., London, 1775).

[152]   Father Paul on the Venetian Republic

Paoli Sarpi (see No. 86), *The Maxims of the Government of Venice. In an Advice to the Republic; How It Ought To Govern Itself* . . . (Italian original ed., Venice, 1606; English ed., London, 1707; 2d ed., London, 1738).

[153]   Montagu's rise & fall of antient republics

Edward Wortley Montagu (1713–1776), *Reflections on the Rise and Fall of the Antient Republicks* . . . (London, 1759; 4th ed., London, 1778).

[154]   Montesquieu's works

Charles Louis de Secondat (1689–1755), Baron de la Brède et de Montesquieu, *The Complete Works of Monsieur de Montesquieu* . . . (Separate French original works, Amsterdam, Geneva, and London, 1721–1748; François Richer [1718–1790], comp. and ed., 3 vols., Amsterdam and Leipzig, 1758; rev. ed., augmented, 6 vols., Amsterdam and Leipzig, 1764; English ed., 3 vols., London, 1767; 4 vols., London, 1777). JM regarded Montesquieu highly as a political philosopher (*Papers of Madison*, I, 5; 6; 307 n; 310, n. 4; II, 225; 226, and n. 7).

[155]   Beccaria's works

Cesare Bonesana (1738–1794), Marchese di Beccaria, *Opere diverse di Cesare Beccaria* . . . (Separate Italian original works, Lucca, Brescia, and Milan, 1762–1771; compiled, 3 parts, Naples, 1770–1771).

[156]   Ferguson's History of Civil Society

Adam Ferguson (see No. 8), *An Essay on the History of Civil Society* . . . (Edinburgh, 1767; 5th ed., London, 1782). JM owned a copy of this work (*Papers of Madison*, I, 131; 133, n. 1; 143; 148–49).

[157]   Miller on distinction of Ranks in Society

John Millar (1735–1801), *The Origin of the Distinctions of Ranks in Society* . . . (Variant title, London and Dublin, 1771; 3d ed., above title, London, 1779).

[158]   Steuart's principles of Political œconomy

Sir James Steuart (after 1773, Steuart-Denham) (1712–1780), baronet, *An Inquiry into the Principles of Political Œconomy* . . . (2 vols., London, 1767; 2d ed., 3 vols., Dublin, 1770). For a previous reference to this work, see *Papers of Madison*, V, 308; 310, n. 9.

[159]   Smith on the wealth of Nations

Adam Smith (1723–1790), *An Inquiry into the Nature and Causes of the Wealth of Nations* . . . (2 vols., London, 1776; 2d ed., 2 vols., London, 1778).

[160]   Baron Biefield's political Institutions.

Jacob Friedrich (1717–1770), Freiherr von Bielfeld, *Institutions politiques* . . . (5 vols., Leyden, 1759–1762; augmented, 3 vols., Leyden, 1767–1772; 5th ed., Leyden, 1774).

[161]   Histoire politique du siecle par Mauberti

Jean Henri Maubert De Gouvest (1721–1767), *Histoire politique du siècle* . . . *depuis la paix de Westphalie, jusqu'à la dernière paix d'Aix la Chapelle inclusivement* . . . (2 vols., London [i.e., Lausanne], 1754–1755).

[162]   Richlieu's Political Testament

Armand Jean Du Plessis (1585–1652), Cardinal et Duc de Richelieu, *Maximes d'état, ou, testament politique* . . . (Paul Hay [1620–ca. 1690], Marquis du Châtelet *et al.*, comps. and eds., variant title, 2 parts, Amsterdam, 1688; augmented in successive editions; above title, 10th ed.[?], 2 vols., Paris, 1764; 11th ed.[?], 2 vols., London and The Hague, 1770). See *Papers of Madison*, I, 7; 24, n. 3.

[163]   de Witt's Maxims

[Pieter de la Court] and Johan de Witt (see No. 51), *The True Interest and Political Maxims of the Republic of Holland* . . . [John Campbell (1708–1775)], tr. and ed., variant title, London, 1743; Campbell's name on title page, 2d ed., above title, London, 1746). The title adheres closely to that of the Dutch original edition of 1662, but the work is the same as JM entered under No. 95. For another work, partially by Campbell, and successive references thereto, see Nos. 223 and 224a-b.

[164]   Petty's political Arithmetic

Sir William Petty (1623–1687), *Essays in Political Arithmetic* . . . (Variant title, London, 1687; 4th ed., above title, contents corrected and augmented, London: Daniel Browne [d. 1762], 1755).

[165]   Wallace on the numbers of mankind

R[obert] W[allace] (1697–1771), *A Dissertation on the Numbers of Mankind* . . . (Edinburgh, 1753).

[166]   Davenant's Works

Charles Davenant (1656–1714), *The Political and Commercial Works of . . . Charles D'Avenant* . . . (Separate original works, London, 1695–1712; Sir Charles Whitworth [*ca.* 1714–1778], comp. and ed., above title, 5 vols., London, 1771).

[167]   Temple's works

Sir William Temple (1628–1699), baronet, *The Works of Sir William Temple* . . . (Separate original works, London, 1676–1695, and unpublished MSS; Jonathan Swift [1667–1745], comp. and ed., above title, 7 vols., London, 1700–1709; 9th ed., 4 vols., London, 1770). See JM Notes, 24 March 1783, and n. 17.

[168]   Hume's political essays

David Hume (see No. 108), *Essays and Treatises on Several Subjects* . . . (2 vols., London, 1741–1742; 10th ed., 2 vols., Dublin, 1779). See *Papers of Madison*, I, 303; 306–7 n.; 310, n. 2. For Hume as a philosopher, *ibid.*, I, 73; 74, n. 7; 195–96; 212, n. 5.

[169]   Postlethwayt's works

169a. [Malachy Postlethwayt (*ca.* 1707–1767)], "A British Merchant," anonym, *The African Trade, the Great Pillar and Support of the British Plantation Trade in America* . . . (London, 1745).

169b. Malachy Postlethwayt, *Considerations on the Making of Bar Iron with Pitt or Sea Coal Fire* . . . (London, 1747).

87

169c. ———, *Considerations on the Revival of the Royal-British-Assiento; between His Catholick Majesty, and the Honourable the South Sea Company* . . . (London, 1749).

169d. ———, *Great Britain's Commercial Interest Explained and Improved* . . . (Variant title, 2 vols., London, 1757; 2d ed., above title, 2 vols., London, 1759).

169e. ———, *Great-Britain's True System* . . . *To Which Is Prefixed* . . . *a New Plan of British Politicks, with Respect to Our Foreign Affairs* . . . (London, 1757).

169f. ———, *In Honour of the Administration. The Importance of the African Expedition* . . . *for the peculiar Benefit* . . . *of all British African and West-India Merchants* . . . (London, 1758).

169g. ———, *The Merchant's Public Counting House* . . . *Wherein Is Shewn the Necessity of Young Merchants Being Bred to Trade with Greater Advantages* . . . (London, 1750).

169h. ———, *The National and Private Advantages of the African Trade Considered* . . . (Anon., London, 1746; 2d ed., London, 1772).

169i. ———, *A Short State of the Progress of the French Trade and Navigation* . . . (London, 1756).

169j. ———, *The Universal Dictionary of Trade and Commerce* . . . (Variant title, 2 vols., London, 1751; 4th ed., above title, 2 vols., London, 1774).

[170] Anderson's Dictionary of Commerce

Adam Anderson (*ca.* 1692–1765), *An Historical and Chronological Deduction of the Origin of Commerce, from the Earliest Accounts to the Present Time* . . . (2 vols., London, 1762; 2d ed., 2 vols., London, 1764).

[171] Burgh's political disquisitions

James Burgh (1714–1775), *Political Disquisitions; or, An Enquiry into Public Errors, Defects, and Abuses* . . . (3 vols., London, 1774–1775; American ed., 3 vols., Philadelphia: Robert Bell [see No. 90] and William Woodhouse [d. 1793], 1775).

[172] Price's Political works

172a. Richard Price (1723–1791), *Additional Observations on the Nature and Value of Civil Liberty, and the War with America* . . . (London, 1777; American ed., Philadelphia: William Hall [1752–1834] and William Sellers [*ca.* 1725–1804], 1778). For the "*Observations*" to which the present work is "*Additional*," see No. 172e. For a reference to Price in his role as a student of human-life expectancy, see JM Notes, 25 Jan. 1783, and n. 9.

172b. ———, *An Appeal to the Public on the Subject of the National Debt* . . . (London, 1771; 4th ed., 2 vols., London, 1783).

172c. ———, *A Discourse Addressed to a Congregation at Hackney* . . . *February 21, 1781, Being the Day Appointed for a Public Fast* . . . (London, 1781).

172d. ———, *An Essay on the Population of England* . . . (London, 1780; 2d ed., London, 1780). For another "essay," to which the present work is the sequel, see No. 172j.

172e. ———, *The General Introduction and Supplement to the Two Tracts on Civil Liberty* . . . (London, 1778; 2d ed., London, 1778). For the "Two Tracts"—that is, *Observations* and *Additional Observations*—see Nos. 172f and 172a, respectively.

172f. ———, *Observations on the Nature of Civil Liberty, the Principles of Government, and the Justice and Policy of the War with America* . . . (London, 1776; American reprints, Boston, New York, Philadelphia, and Charleston, 1776; 15th ed.[?], 2 vols., London, 1783). For the *General Introduction* to this work, see No. 172e; for the sequel, No. 172a.

172g. ———, *Observations on Public Loans* . . . (London, 1777).

172h. ———, *Observations on Reversionary Payments; on Schemes for Providing Annuities for Widows, and for Persons in Old Age* . . . *and on the National Debt* . . . (London, 1771; 4th ed., 2 vols., London, 1783).

172i. ———, *The State of the Public Debts and Finances at Signing the Preliminary Articles of Peace in January, 1783* . . . (2d ed., London, 1783).

172j. Richard Price and William Morgan (1750–1833), *An Essay Containing an Account of the Progress from the Revolution and the Present State of Population in England and Wales* . . . (London, 1779). For the sequel to this work, see No. 172d.

172k. Richard Price and J[ohn] Horne Tooke (1736–1812), *Facts Addressed to Landholders . . . and Generally to All the Subjects of Great Britain and Ireland* . . . (London, 1780).

172l. Richard Price et al., *A Collection of Letters* . . . *Addressed to the Volunteers of Ireland, on the Subject of Parliamentary Reform* . . . (London, 1783).

[173]   Gee on trade

Joshua Gee, *The Trade and Navigation of Great-Britain Considered* . . . (London, 1729; 7th ed., Glasgow, 1767).

[174]   Child on trade

Sir Josiah Child (1630–1699), in 1678 created baronet, *A New Discourse of Trade: Wherein Are Recommended Several Weighty Points* . . . (From an expanded essay, variant title, London, 1668; 2d ed., above title, London, 1694; 7th ed., London, 1775).

[175]   Tucker on trade

175a. Josiah Tucker (1712–1799), *Cui Bono? Or, An Inquiry What Benefits Can Arise to the English or the Americans, the French, Spaniards, or Dutch, from the Greatest Victories* . . . *in the Present War* . . . (Gloucester, 1781; 3d ed., London, 1782).

175b. ———, *Dispassionate Thoughts on the American War* . . . (London, 1780).

175c. ———, *The Elements of Commerce, and Theory of Taxes* . . . (Privately printed, Bristol, 1753).

175d. ———, *An Essay on the Advantages and Disadvantages Which Respectively Attend France and Great Britain, with Regard to Trade* . . . (Glasgow and London, 1749; 4th ed., Glasgow, 1756).

175e. ———, *Four Tracts, together with Two Sermons, on Political and Commercial Subjects* . . . (2 parts, Gloucester, 1774, including one "tract" previously published [London] in 1763; 3d ed., title unchanged but a fifth "tract" added, London, 1775; so-called "third" ed., title unchanged but a sixth "tract" added, Gloucester and London, 1776).

175f. ———, *An Humble Address and Earnest Appeal to Those* . . . *Ablest To Judge* . . . *Whether a Connection with, or a Separation from the Continental Colonies of America, Be Most for the National Advantage* . . . (Gloucester, 1775; 3d ed., Gloucester and London, 1776).

175g. ———, *Reflections on the Expediency of Opening the Trade to Turkey* . . . ("A Sincere Well-wisher to the Trade and Prosperity of Great-Britain," anonym, London, 1753; 2d ed., London, 1755).

[176] Law on money & trade

John Law (1671–1729), of Lauriston, *Money and Trade Considered* . . . (Anon., Edinburgh, 1705; 5th ed., Glasgow, 1760; also reprinted in Vol. IV of *A Fourth Collection of Scarce and Valuable Tracts*, 4 vols., London: Francis Cogan [d. *ca.* 1760], 1751–1752).

[177] Arbuthnot on weights and measures

John Arbuthnot (1677–1735), *Tables of Antient Coins, Weights, and Measures, Explained and Exemplified* . . . (Variant title, London, 1705; 2d ed., above title, London, 1727; so-called "second" 5th[?] ed., 2 parts, London, 1754).

[178] Locke on money

John Locke (see No. 150), *Several Papers Relating to Money, Interest and Trade* . . . (Three separate tracts, London, 1692–1695; above title comprises reprints of 2d eds., 3 parts, London, 1695–1696).

[179] Lowndes on do.

179a. W[illiam] L[owndes] (1652–1724), *A Further Essay for the Amendment of Gold and Silver Coins* . . . (London, 1695).

179b. William Lowndes, *A Report Containing an Essay for the Amendment of the Silver Coins, Made to the Right Honourable the Lords Commissioners of His Majesties Treasury* . . . (London, 1695).

[180] Neckar on Finance

Jacques Necker (1732–1804), *State of the Finances of France, Laid before the King* . . . *Printed by Order of His Most Christian Majesty* . . . (French original ed., Paris, 1781; English ed., London, 1781). For comments about "Neckar on Finance," see *Papers of Madison*, II, 223; 225, n. 2; III, 234; JM Notes, 29 Jan. 1783, n. 17.

Law

[181] Justinian's Institutes by Harris

Justinian (Flavius Anicius Iustinianus) I (483–565), Emperor of the East, *Domini Justiniani institutionum libri quatuor. The Four Books of Justinian* . . . (Tribonian [d. *ca.* 545] *et al.*, comps. and eds., promulgations in original Greek and Latin, Byzantium, 528–534; George Harris [1722–1796], tr. and ed., English ed., 4 parts, London, 1756; 2d ed., London 1761).

[182] Codex juris Civilis

Justinian I, Emperor of the East, *Corpus juris civilis reconcinnatum, in tres partes distributum* . . . (Tribonian [see No. 181] *et al.*, comps. and eds., promulgations in original Greek and Latin, Byzantium, 528–565; Eusebius Beger [1721–1788], ed., Latin ed., 3 vols. in 2, Frankfort and Leipzig, 1767–1768). JM's entry is at fault. If he meant to indicate only the "Codex" for separate purchase, by 1783 it had not been republished for nearly 250 years. The "Corpus," on the other hand, included both the "Codex" and the "Institutes." See No. 181.

[183] Taylor's elements of Civil Law

John Taylor (1704–1766), *Elements of the Civil Law* . . . (Cambridge, Eng., 1755; 3d ed., London, 1769).

[184]   Domat's Civil Law

Jean Domat (Daumat) (1625–1696), *The Civil Law in Its Natural Order* . . . (Anon., French original ed., 5 vols. in 4, Paris, 1689; William Strahan [d. 1748], tr. and ed., English ed., 2 vols., London, 1722; 2d ed., 2 vols., London, 1737).

[185]   Coke's Institutes

185a. Sir Edward Coke (1552–1634), *The First Part of the Institutes of the Lawes of England; or, A Commentary upon Littleton* . . . (London, 1628; 12th ed., London, 1738). For a previous reference to this work, see *Papers of Madison*, I, 108; 110, n. 4.

185b. ———, *The Second Part of the Institutes of the Lawes of England, Containing the Exposition of Many Ancient and Other Statutes* . . . (London, 1642; 6th ed., London, 1681).

185c. ———, *The Third Part of the Institutes of the Lawes of England: concerning High Treason, and Other Pleas of the Crown and Criminall Causes* . . . (London, 1644; 6th ed., London, 1680).

185d. ———, *The Fourth Part of the Institutes of the Lawes of England: concerning the Jurisdiction of Courts* . . . (London, 1644; 6th ed., London, 1681).

[186]   Blackstone's Commentaries

Sir William Blackstone (1723–1780), *Commentaries on the Laws of England . . . Continued to the Present Time* . . . (4 vols., Oxford, 1765–1769; Richard Burn [1709–1785], continuator, 9th ed., 4 vols., London, 1783). See *Papers of Madison*, I, 98; 102–3; 103, n. 3; IV, 307, n. 5.

[187]   Cunningham's Law Dictionary

Timothy Cunningham (d. 1789), *A New and Complete Law-Dictionary, or General Abridgment of the Law* . . . (2 vols., London, 1764–1765; 3d ed., 2 vols., London, 1782–1783). For another work by Cunningham, see No. 190.

[188]   Statutes at large by Ruffhead

Owen Ruffhead (1723–1769), comp. and ed., *The Statutes at Large, from Magna Charta, to the End of the Last Parliament* . . . (Partly posthumous, 18 vols., London, 1769–1800).

[189]   Lex Parliamentaria

George Petyt (Pettyt), *Lex parliamentaria; or, A Treatise of the Law and Custom of the Parliaments of England* . . . ("G. P.," London, 1690; 3d ed., London, 1748).

[190]   Cunningham's law of Exchange

Timothy Cunningham (see No. 187), *The Law of Bills of Exchange, Promissory Notes, Bank-Notes, and Insurances* . . . (London, 1760; 6th ed., London, 1778).

[191]   Collection of Laws to prevent frauds in the Customs

191a. Samuel Baldwin, comp. and ed., *A Survey of British Customs . . . as Established by 12 Car. II., cap. 4 . . . to 14 Geo. III. . . .* (Variant title, London, 1770; 2d ed, above title, London, 1774).

191b. Henry Mackay (d. 1783), comp. and ed., *A Complete and Alphabetical Abridgement of All the Excise-Laws or Custom-Laws Therewith Connected, in Force in England and Wales* . . . (Edinburgh, 1779).

191c. *20 Geo. III., cap. 9. An Act for Allowing Ireland To Trade with Foreign Parts* ... (London, 1780).

[192] Book of rates

William Sims and Richard Frewin, comps., *The Rates of Merchandise ... Compiled, by Order of the Commissioners of His Majesty's Customs* ... (London, 1782).

[193] Clarke's practice of Courts of Admiralty

Francis Clerke (Clarke) (d. *ca.* 1605), *The Practice of the Court of Admiralty of England* ... (Posthumous Latin original ed., Dublin, 1666; 3d ed., above title, Latin and English texts on facing pages, London, 1722; 4th ed.[?], augmented, London, 1743).

[194] Fredencian Code

Frederick II, King of Prussia (see No. 127), *The Fredencian Code; or, A Body of Law for the Dominions of the King of Prussia* ... (Samuel von Coccéji [1679–1755], comp. and ed., Latin original ed., 2 vols., Berlin, 1747; French ed., 2 vols., Paris, 1751–1753; English ed., from the French, 2 vols., Edinburgh, 1761; 2d ed., 2 vols., London, 1766).

War

[195] Vauban's Works

Sébastien Le Prestre de Vauban (1633–1707), maréchal de France, *Oeuvres de M. de Vauban* ... (Separate original works, Paris and The Hague, 1685–1707; above title, 2 vols., The Hague, 1737; 2d ed., 2 vols., Amsterdam and Leipzig, 1771).

[196] Bellidore's Works

196a. Bernard Forest de Bélidor (*ca.* 1697–1761), *Oeuvres diverse concernant l'artillerie et le génie* ... (Separate original works, Paris, 1720–1757; above title, Amsterdam, Leipzig, and Paris, 1764).
196b. ———, *Dictionnaire portatif de l'Ingénieur* ... (Paris, 1755; Charles Antoine Jombert [1712–1784], augmenter, 2d ed., Paris, 1768).

[197] Fouquier's Memoirs

Antoine Manassès de Pas (1648–1711), Marquis de Feuquières, *Memoirs of the Late Monsieur de Feuquières, Lieutenant General of the French Army* ... (French original ed., Paris, 1711; English ed., 2 vols., London, 1735–1736; 2d ed., 2 vols., London, 1737; also 4 vols., London, 1740).

Marine

[198] Falconer's Universal Dictionary of Marine

William Falconer (1732–1769), *An Universal Dictionary of the Marine: or, A Copious Explanation of the Technical Terms ... of a Ship* ... (London, 1769; 3d ed., London, 1780).

[199] Burchett's Naval History

Josiah Burchett (*ca.* 1666–1746), *A Complete History of the Most Remarkable Transactions at Sea* ... (London, 1720).

[200]   History of the several Voyages round the Globe

200a. John Hamilton Moore (d. 1807), comp. and ed., *A New and Complete Collection of Voyages and Travels* . . . (2 vols., London, 1778). For another work, partially contained in Moore, see No. 234.

200b. David Henry (1710–1792), comp. and ed., *An Historical Account of All the Voyages round the World, Performed by English Navigators* . . . (4 vols., London, 1773–1774). For another work, partially contained in Henry, see No. 216.

200c. Johann Georg Adam Forster (1754–1794), more commonly known as George Forster, *Voyage round the World, in His Britannic Majesty's Sloop Resolution, Commanded by Captain James Cook, during the Years 1772, 3, 4, and 5* . . . (2 vols., London, 1777).

200d. Pierre François Marie (1748–1793), Vicomte de Pagès, *Voyages autour du monde, et vers les deux pôles, par terre et par mer, pendant les années 1767, 1768, 1769, 1770, 1771, 1773, 1774 & 1776* . . . (2 vols., Paris, 1782).

200e. William Ellis, *An Authentic Narrative of a Voyage Performed by Captain Cook and Captain Clerke, in His Majesty's Ships, Resolution and Discovery, during the Years 1776–1780* . . . (2 vols., London, 1782).

[201]   Murray's Ship Building and navagation

Mungo Murray (d. 1770), *A Treatise on Ship-building and Navigation* . . . (London, 1754; 2d ed., London, 1765).

[202]   Collection of best Charts

202a. Jacques Nicolas Bellin (1703–1772), *Le petit atlas maritime, recueil des cartes et plans des quatre parties du monde* . . . (5 vols., Paris, 1764). For other works by Bellin, see Nos. 202g and 202l.

202b. John Seller (d. *ca.* 1700) *et al.*, comps. and eds., *The English Pilot . . . Describing the Southern Navigation upon the Coasts of England, Scotland, Ireland . . . to the Canary . . . and Western Islands . . . the Whole Mediterranean Sea . . . the Whole Northern Navigation . . . the West-India Navigation, from Hudson's Bay to the River Amazones* . . . (4 vols., London, 1671–1675; 16th ed.[?], 4 vols., London, 1773).

202c. Joseph Frederick Walsh (Wallet) Des Barres (Desbarres) (1722–1824), *The Atlantic Neptune, Published for the Use of the Royal Navy of Great Britain* . . . (2 vols., London, 1777; 3d ed., augmented, 4 vols., London, 1781).

202d. Cyprian Southark (1662–1745), *The New England Coasting Pilot from Sandy Point of New York, unto Cape Canso in Nova Scotia, and Part of Island Breton* . . . (London, n. d. [*ca.* 1720]; 4th ed., London, 1775).

202e. *A New and Accurate Chart of the Bay of Chesapeake . . . Drawn from the Several Draughts Made by the Most Experienced Navigators* . . . (London: Robert Sayer [*ca.* 1724–1794] and James Bennet [d. *ca.* 1830], 1776). For another work published by Sayer and Bennet, see No. 202j.

202f. *A Map of East and West Florida, Georgia, and Louisiana, with the Islands of Cuba, Bahama, and the Countries Surrounding the Gulf of Mexico, with the Tract of the Spanish Galleons, and of Our Fleets thro' the Straits of Florida* . . . (London: John Bew [d. 1793], 1781).

202g. Jacques Nicolas Bellin (see No. 202a), *Remarques sur la carte réduite de l'océan septentrionale compris entre l'Asie et l'Amérique suivant les découvertes qui ont été faites par les Russes* . . . (Paris, 1766).

202h. Alexander Dalrymple (1737–1808), *Memoirs of the Chart of Part of the Coast of China* . . . (London, 1771). For other charts by Dalrymple, see Nos. 202i, 202k, and 202m.

202i. Alexander Dalrymple, *Memoir of a Chart of the Southern Ocean* . . . (London, n. d. [*ca.* 1769]).

202j. Jean Baptiste Nicolas Denis d'Aprè de Mannevillette (1707–1780), *The East-India Pilot, or Oriental Navigator: Containing a Complete Collection of Charts, Maps, Plans, &c.* . . . *Chiefly Composed, from the Last Edition of the Neptune Oriental* . . . (French original ed. of *Neptune oriental*, Paris, 1745; "Last Edition," Paris and Brest, 1775; with *supplément*, Paris and Brest, 1781; English ed., London: "R. Sayer and J. Bennet" [for whom see No. 202e], n. d. [*ca.* 1782]).

202k. Alexander Dalrymple (see No. 202h), *A Collection of Views of Lands in the Indian Navigation* . . . (149 plates, London, 1771–1796).

202l. Jacques Nicolas Bellin (see No. 202a), *Remarques sur la carte de la presqu'île de l'Inde, contenant les côtes de Malabar, Coromandel, etc., depuis le golphe de Cambaye jusqu'aux bouches du Gange* . . . (Paris, 1766).

202m. Alexander Dalrymple (see No. 202h), *Memoir of a Chart of the East Coast of Arabia, from Dofar to the Island of Maziera* . . . (London, 1783).

[203] Fol. £6.6 Naval architecture. By Marmaduke Stalkartt.

This entry is not in JM's hand.
Marmaduke Stalkartt (d. 1782), *Naval Architecture; or, The Rudiments and Rules of Ship Building Exemplified in a Series of Draughts and Plans* . . . (231 pp. "Fol[io]" of text and 14 folding plates, London, 1781, when marketed for £6.6s. sterling).

Languages

[204] Best latin Dictionary with best grammar & dictionary
of each of the modern languages

The present editors have limited their choices to works suitable for use by persons whose native tongue was English. Dictionaries or grammars of American Indian languages are also omitted.

204a. Robert Ainsworth (1660–1743), *Thesaurus linguae latinae compendarius, or A Compendious Dictionary of the Latin Tongue* . . . (3 parts, London, 1736; Thomas Morell [1708–1784], reviser and augmenter, 5th ed., 3 vols., London, 1773; 7th ed., 3 vols., London, 1783).

204b. John Richardson (1741–*ca.* 1811), *A Grammar of the Arabic Language* . . . (London, 1776).

204c. John Richardson, *A Dictionary of Persian, Arabic, and English* . . . (2 vols., Oxford, 1777).

204d. Nathaniel Brassy Halhed (1751–1830), *A Grammar of the Bengal Language* . . . (Hugli, Bengal, 1778).

204e. *A Short Introduction to the Danish Language for the Use of Those Who Choose To Learn It in a Methodical Way* . . . (London: R. Hilton, 1774).

204f. Andreas Berthelson, *An English and Danish Dictionary, Containing the Words of Both Languages* . . . (London, 1754).

204g. Willem Sewel (1654–1720), *A Complete Dictionary, English and Dutch, to Which Is Added a Grammar for Both Languages* . . . (Variant title, 2 vols., Amsterdam, 1691; Egbery Buys [d. 1769], reviser and augmenter, 6th ed., above title, 2 vols., Amsterdam, 1766).

204h. James Wood (ca. 1751–1815), *Grammatical Institutes; or A Practical English Grammar on a New Plan* . . . (London, 1778).

204i. Samuel Johnson (1709–1784), *A Dictionary of the English Language* . . . (2 vols., London, 1755; 4th ed., 2 vols., London, 1775). For a reference to this work, see No. 204o.

204j. Abel Boyer (1667–1729), *The Complete French Master* . . . (London, 1694; 18th ed., London, 1756).

204k. Louis Chambaud (d. 1776), *Nouveau dictionnaire* . . . (*A New Dictionary, English and French, and French and English*) . . . (London, 1761; Jean Perrin [d. post-1800], reviser and augmenter, 2d ed., 2 vols., London, 1778). For another dictionary, partly French, see No. 204o.

204l. William Shaw (1749–1831), *An Analysis of the Galic Language* . . . (London, 1778; 2d ed., Edinburgh, 1778).

204m. William Shaw, *A Galic and English Dictionary* . . . (2 vols., London, 1780).

204n. Gebhard Friedrich August Wendeborn (1742–1811), *Elements of German Grammar* . . . (London, 1774; 2d ed., London, 1775).

204o. Christian Ludwig (1660–1728), *A Dictionary, English, German and French* . . . *Augmented with More Than 12,000 Words Taken out of Samuel Johnson's English Dictionary, and Other's* . . . (Variant subtitle, 2 vols., Leipzig, 1706–1716; John Bartholomew Rogler [1728–1791], augmenter, 3d ed., above subtitle, Leipzig, 1763). For Samuel Johnson's dictionary, see No. 204i.

204p. John Fergusson (d. 1791), *A Dictionary of Hindostan* . . . (London, 1773). The work was rare by 1783 because of loss at sea of the greater part of the stock.

204q. David Francesco Lates (d. 1777), *A New Method of Easily Attaining the Italian Tongue* . . . (London, 1762; 2d ed., London, 1766).

204r. Giuseppe Marc' Antonio Baretti (1719–1789), *A Dictionary of the English and Italian Languages* . . . (2 vols., London, 1760; 2d ed., 2 vols., London, 1771). For another dictionary by Baretti, see No. 204x.

204s. Thomas Bowrey (ca. 1630–1713), *A Dictionary, English and Malayo* . . . *To Which Is Added Some Short Grammar Rules* . . . (London, 1701).

204t. Sir William Jones (1746–1794), *A Grammar of the Persian Language* . . . (London, 1771). For a Persian dictionary, see No. 204c.

204u. Antonio Vieyra (1712–1797), *A New Portuguese Grammar* . . . (Variant title, London, 1768; 2d ed., above title, London, 1778).

204v. Antonio Vieyra, *A Dictionary of the Portuguese and English Language* . . . (2 vols., London, 1773).

204w. Hippolyto San José Giral del Pino, *A New Spanish Grammar, or The Elements of the Spanish Language* . . . (London, 1767; 2d ed., London, 1777).

204x. Giuseppe Marc' Antonio Baretti (see No. 204r), *A Dictionary, Spanish and English* . . . (2 parts, London, 1778; 2d ed., 2 vols., London, 1778).

204y. Jacob Serenius (1700–1776), *English and Swedish Dictionary* . . . (Hamburg, 1734; 2d ed., Harg and Stenbro, 1757).

204z. John Philip Fabricius and John Christian Breihaupt, *Dictionary Malabar and English Wherein the Words and Phrases of the Tamulian Language* . . . *Are Explained* . . . (2 vols., Wepery, India, 1779–1786).

America.

[205]   Les nouvelles descouverts dans l'Amerique
        Septentrionale. Paris 1697

Louis Hennepin (1640–*ca.* 1710), *A Discovery of a Large, Rich, and Plentiful
Country in North America; Extending above 4000 Leagues* . . . (French original
ed., Paris, 1697; English ed., London, 1720). For the sequel to this work, see No.
229; for a third work by Hennepin, No. 287.

[206]   Tonti's account of la Sale's voiage to N. America

Henri, Chevalier de Tonti (*ca.* 1650–1704) (author by attribution), *An Account of
M. de La Salle's Last Expedition and Discoveries in North America* . . . (French
original ed., Paris, 1697; English ed., London, 1698). Tonti denied having any hand
in this work and described the real author as being "*un Aventurier Parisien.*"

[207]   Histoire de l'Amerique Septentrionale par
        Baquiville de la Poterie. Rouen 1722

Claude Charles Le Roy (*ca.* 1668–1738), Sieur de Bacqueville de la Potherie,
Histoire de l'Amérique Septentrionale . . . (4 vols., Paris, 1721–1722; 2d ed., 4 vols.,
Amsterdam, 1723; alleged "new" ed., 4 vols., Paris, 1753, being the 1st ed. with only
a new title page). No evidence has been found of an edition published at Rouen.

[208]   Discription geographique et historique des
        cotes de l'Amerique Septenle. par le Sieur
        Denys

Nicolas Denys (1598–1688), *Description géographique et historique des costes de
l'Amérique Septentrionale* . . . (2 vols., Paris, 1672; 2d ed., 2 vols., Paris, 1688).

[209]   Oldmixon's Brit: Empire in America

John Oldmixon (1673–1742), *The British Empire in America, Containing the History of the Discovery, Settlement, Progress and Present State of All the British
Colonies* . . . (2 vols., London, 1708; 2d ed., 2 vols., London, 1741).

[210]   Kalm's travels through N. America

Pehr Kalm (1715–1779), *Travels into North America; Containing Its Natural History* . . . (Swedish original ed., 3 vols., Stockholm, 1753–1761; English ed., 3 vols.,
Warrington, Eng., 1770–1771; 2d ed., 2 vols., London, 1772).

[211]   Carver's travels through N. America

Jonathan Carver (1732–1780), *Travels through the Interior Parts of North America,
in the Years 1766, 1767, and 1768* . . . (London, 1778; 3d ed., London, 1781).

[212]   Ogilvie's America

John Ogilby (1600–1676), comp., tr., and ed., *America: Being the Latest, and Most
Accurate Description of the New World Collected from the Most Authentic Authors* . . . (London, 1671; 2d ed., London, 1673).

[213]   Novus orbis, autore Joanne de Laet: fol: Basiliac 1555

Johannes de Laet (1593–1649), *L'histoire du nouveau monde ou description des
Indes Occidentales* . . . (Dutch original ed., Leyden, 1625; Latin ed., Leyden, 1633;

French ed., containing new materials, Leyden, 1640). JM's note following the author's name is erroneous.

[214]   Novae novi orbis historiae, i. e. rerum ab
        Hispanis in India occidentali gestarum Calvetonis
        Geneva 1578

Girolamo Benzoni (1519–*ca.* 1570), *Novae novi orbis historiae, id est, rerum ab Hispanis in India Occidentali hactenus gestarum* . . . (Italian original ed., Venice, 1565; Urbain Chauveton, tr., Latin ed., Geneva, 1578; 5th ed.[?], Cologne, 1612).

[215]   Wafer's Voyages

Lionel Wafer (*ca.* 1660–*ca.* 1705), *A New Voyage and Description of the Isthmus of America, Giving an Account of the Author's Abode There* . . . (London, 1699; 2d ed., London, 1703).

[216]   Dampier's Voyages

William Dampier (1652–1715), *The Voyages and Adventures of William Dampier* . . . (Separate original works, London, 1697–1709; above title, 2 vols., London, 1776; 2d ed., 2 vols., London, 1777). Dampier's "Voyages," although combined with much questionable material, could also be found in Vols. I–III of the Knaptons (No. 224c), and in part they were reprinted in Vol. I of Moore (No. 200a) and Vol. I of Henry (No. 200b).

[217]   Chancellor's

217a. Clement Adams (*ca.* 1519–1587), *The Newe Nauigation and Discouerie of the Kingdom of Moscouia, by the Northeast, in the Yeere 1553* . . . *Performed by Richard Chancelor* . . . (Latin original ed., no copy of which is known to be extant, London, 1554; reprinted, with accompanying English text, in Vol. I of Hakluyt [No. 240]).

217b. Richard Chancellor (d. 1556), *A Letter of Richard Chancellor . . . Touching His Discouerie of Moscovia* . . . in Vol. III of Purchas (No. 239).

217c. Clement Adams, *Some Additions for the Better Knowledge of This Voyage . . . from the Mouth of Captaine Chancelor* . . . in Vol. III of Purchas (No. 239).

[218]   Borough's

218a. Stephen Burrough (1525–1584), *The Nauigation and Discouerie toward the Riuer of Ob . . . Passed in the Yeere, 1556* . . . in Vol. I of Hakluyt (No. 240).

218b. ———, *The Voiage . . . an. 1557, from Colmogro to Wardhouse* . . . in Vol. I of Hakluyt (No. 240).

[219]   Forbishers

219a. Christopher Hall, *The First Voyage of Master Martin Frobisher, to the Northwest, for the Search of the Straight or Passage to China . . . in the Yeere . . . 1576* . . . in Vol. III of Hakluyt (No. 240).

219b. Dionyse Settle, *A True Reporte of the Laste Voyage into the West and North-west Regions, &c., 1577, Worthily Atchieved by Captaine Frobisher* . . . (Two separate eds., one incomplete, London, 1577; complete version reprinted in Vol. III of Hakluyt (No. 240).

219c. Thomas Ellis, *The Third and Last Voyage unto Meta Incognita, Made by Master Martin Frobisher, in the Yeere 1578* . . . in Vol. III of Hakluyt (No. 240).

219d. George Best (d. *ca.* 1584), *A Trve Discovrse of the Late Voyages of Discouerie, for the Finding of a Passage to Cathaya by the Northweast, under the Conduct of Martin Frobisher* . . . (London, 1578, very rare; also reprinted in Vol. III of Hakluyt (No. 240).

[220] Hudson's

220a. Henry Hudson (d. 1611) and John Playse, *Divers Voyages and Northerne Discoveries* . . . in Vol. III of Purchas (No. 239).

220b. ———, *A Second Voyage* . . . *for Finding a Passage to the East Indies by the North-east* . . . (Hessel Gerritsz [*ca.* 1581–1632], ed., separate Latin and Dutch eds., Amsterdam, 1612; English version in Vol. III of Purchas [No. 239]).

220c. Robert Juet (d. 1611), *The Third Voyage* . . . *toward Nova Zembla* . . . in Vol. III of Purchas (No. 239).

220d. Henry Hudson, *An Abstract of a Journall* . . . *for the Discoverie of the North-west Passage, Begunne the 17th of Aprill, 1610* . . . in Vol. III of Purchas (No. 239).

220e. Abacuk Prickett, *A Larger Discourse of the Same Voyage, and the Successe Thereof* . . . in Vol. III of Purchas (No. 239).

220f. Thomas Woodhouse (d. 1611), *A Note Found in the Deske of Thomas Wydowse, Student of Mathematicks, Hee Being One of Them Who Was Put into the Shallop* . . . in Vol. III of Purchas (No. 239).

[221] Davis's

221a. John James, *The First Voyage of Master Iohn Dauis, Undertaken in Iune 1585. for the Discouerie of the New Passage* . . . in Vol. III of Hakluyt (No. 240) and Vol. I of Purchas (No. 239).

221b. John Davys (*ca.* 1550–1605) of Sandridge, *The Second Voyage Attempted* . . . *for the Discouerie of the New Passage, in anno 1586* . . . in Vol. III of Hakluyt (No. 240) and Vol. I of Purchas (No. 239).

221c. John James, *The Third Voyage Northward, Made by Iohn Dauis Gentleman* . . . *in the Yeere, 1587* . . . in Vol. III of Hakluyt (No. 240).

221d. John Davys of Sandridge, *A Traverse-Booke* . . . *for the Discouerie of the North-west Passage, anno 1587* . . . in Vol. III of Hakluyt (No. 240).

221e. Henry Morgan, *The Relation of the Course Which* . . . *Two Vessels of the Fleet of M*[aster]. *Iohn Dauis Held After He Had Sent Them from Him To Discouer the Passage between Groenland and Island* . . . in Vol. III of Hakluyt (No. 240).

[222] Baffin's

222a. William Baffin (d. 1622), *The Fourth Voyage of James Hall to Groeneland* . . . *anno 1612* . . . MS; partly printed in Vol. III of Purchas (No. 239). The manuscript was not published in full during JM's lifetime.

222b. ———, *A Journal of the Voyage Made to Greenland* . . . *in the Yeere 1613* . . . in Vol. III of Purchas (No. 239).

222c. John Gatonby, *A Voyage into the North-west Passage* . . . in Vol. V of Awnsham Churchill (d. 1728) and John Churchill (d. *ca.* 1714), comps. and eds., *A Collection of Voyages and Travels* (6 vols., London, 1704–1732; 3d ed., 6 vols., London, 1752).

222d. Robert Fotherby, *A Voyage of Discoverie to Greenland &c. anno 1614* . . . in Vol. III of Purchas (No. 239).

222e. William Baffin, *A True Relation of Such Things as Happened in the Fourth Voyage for the Discoverie of the North-west Passage . . . in the Yeere 1615 . . .* in Vol. III of Purchas (No. 239). Reprinting of the original manuscript after JM's lifetime revealed the gross defects of Purchas' editing.

222f. ———, *A Brief and True Relation or Journall, Contayning Such Accidents as Happened in the Fift[h] Voyage, for the Discoverie of a Passage to the North-west . . . in the Yeere of our Lord 1616 . . .* in Vol. III of Purchas (No. 239). Baffin gave to Purchas a manuscript narrative, journal, and map, none of which has subsequently been found. Purchas printed only the narrative, not the "Journall."

[223] James's

Thomas James (ca. 1593–ca. 1635), *The Strange and Dangerous Voyage of Captain Thomas James in His Intended Discovery of the North-west Passage into the South Sea . . .* (Title archaically spelled, London, 1633; 2d ed., title as above, London, 1740; also printed in Vol. II of the Churchills [No. 222c] and in Vol. II of John Harris [1667–1718], comp. and ed., *Navigantium atque itinerantium biblioteca; or, A Complete Collection of Voyages and Travels,* 2 vols., London, 1705; John Campbell [see No. 163], reviser and augmenter, 2d ed., 2 vols., London, 1744–1748; 3d ed., 2 vols., London, 1764).

[224] Wood's

224a. John Wood, *An Account of a Voyage for the Discoverie of the North-east Passage . . . 1676 . . .* in Vol. II of *An Account of Several Late Voyages and Discoveries,* 2 vols., London: Samuel Smith (d. ca. 1703) and Benjamin Walford (d. ca. 1710), 1694; also in Vol. I of Harris and of Harris and Campbell (No. 223).

224b. ———, *Supplement to His North-east Voyage; Navigation and Observations North-west of Greenland . . .* in Vol. I of Harris and of Harris and Campbell (No. 223).

224c. ———, *A Voyage through the Streights of Magellan . . .* in *A Collection of Original Voyages,* London: W. Hacke, 1699; also in Vol. IV of *A Collection of Voyages,* 4 vols., London: James Knapton (1687–1736) and John Knapton (d. 1770), 1729.

[225] Ellis's voyage to Hudson's Bay

225a. Henry Ellis (1721–1806), *A Voyage to Hudson's Bay, by the Dobbs Galley and California, in the Years 1746 and 1747, for Discovering a North-west Passage . . .* (London, 1748).

225b. [Theodore Swaine Drage, supposed author], "the Clerk of the California," anonym, *Account of a Voyage for the Discovery of a North-west Passage by Hudsons Streights . . . in the Year 1746 and 1747 . . .* (2 vols., London, 1748–1749).

[226] Voyage au-pays des Hurons par Gabl. Sabard Theodat Paris 1632

Gabriel Sagard-Théodat, *Le grand voyage dv pays des Hvrons, situé en l'Amérique vers la mer douce, és derniers confins de nouuelle France, dite Canada . . .* (Paris, 1632).

[227] Moeurs des Sauvages de l'Amerique par Lafitau

Joseph François Lafitau (1681–1746), *Moeurs des sauvages amériquains, comparées aux moeurs des premiers temps . . .* (Two separate eds., variant texts, 2 vols., 4 vols., Paris, 1724; 3d ed., 2 vols., 4 vols., Paris, 1734).

[228]   Adair's History of the American Savages

James Adair (ca. 1709–ca. 1783), *The History of the American Indians; Particular-ly Those Nations Adjoining to the Missisippi, East and West Florida, Georgia, South and North Carolina, and Virginia* . . . (London, 1775).

[229]   Hennepin's Voyages

Louis Hennepin (see No. 205), *Voyage ou nouvelle découverte d'un très-grand pays, dans l'Amérique, entre le Nouveau Mexique & la Mer Glaciale* . . . (Variant title, Utrecht, 1698; above title, Amsterdam, 1711, bound together with a work relating to Caribbean explorations).

[230]   La Hontan's do.

Louis Armand de Lom d'Arce (1666–ca. 1715), Baron de La Hontan, *New Voyages to North-America. Containing an Account of the Several Nations of That Vast Continent* . . . (French original ed., 3 vols., The Hague, 1703; English ed., 2 vols., London, 1703; 2d ed., 2 vols., London, 1735). Portions of the work allegedly were by Nicolas Gueudeville (ca. 1654–ca. 1721).

[231]   Jone's Journal to the Indian nations

David Jones (1736–1820), *A Journal of Two Visits Made to Some Nations of In-dians on the West Side of the River Ohio, in the Years 1772 and 1773* . . . (Bur-lington, N. J., 1774).

[232]   Voyage de la nouvelle France par le Sieur Champlain

Samuel de Champlain (1567–1635), *Les voyages de la nouvelle France occidentale, dicte Canada, faits . . . depuis l'an 1603. iusques en l'an 1629* . . . (Paris, 1632, with-drawn; reissue, with four revised pages, Paris, 1632; reissue, with only new title page, Paris, 1640).

[233]   Histoire de la Nouvelle France par l'Escarbot Paris

Marc Lescarbot (ca. 1590–ca. 1630), *Histoire de la Nouvelle-France . . . depuis cent ans jusques à hui* . . . (2 parts, Paris, 1609; 3d ed., revised and augmented, Paris, 1618; abridged English version in Vol. IV of Purchas [No. 239]).

[234]   Histoire de la Nle. France avec les fastes
          chronologiques du nouveau monde par le pere
          Charlevoix

Pierre François de Charlevoix (1682–1761), *Histoire et description générale de la Nouvelle France, avec le journal historique d'un voyage* . . . (3 vols.; 6 vols., Paris, 1744; a portion available in English, in Vol. II of Moore [No. 200a]). The "fastes chronologiques" were a portion of the contents of Vols. III and V of the Paris printings as respectively listed.

[235]   Memoirs des rois de France & de l'Angleterre
          sur les possessions &c. en Amerique 1755.
          4 Vol: 4°

Étienne de Silhouette (1709–1765) *et al.*, comps. and eds., *Mémoires des commis-saires du roi et de ceux de Sa Majesté Britannique, sur les possessions & les droits respectifs des deux couronnes en Amérique* . . . (4 vols., quarto, Paris, 1755–1757). For a previous reference to this work, see *Papers of Madison*, V, 10; 13, n. 28.

[236]   Relation d'un voyage en Acadie par Dierville.
        Rouen 1708

[?] Diéreville, *Relation du voyage du Port-Royal de l'Acadie, ou de la Nouvelle-France* . . . (Rouen, 1708; 2d ed., Amsterdam, 1710).

[237]   Josselyn's account of New England

John Josselyn, *An Account of Two Voyages to New-England* . . . (London, 1674; 2d ed., London, 1675).

[238]   Thomas's account of Pennsylva. & N. Jersey

Gabriel Thomas, *An Historical and Geographical Account of the Province and Country of Pensilvania; and of West-New-Jersey in America* . . . (London, 1698).

[239]   Purchases Pilgrimage. 5 Vol: fol:

Samuel Purchas (*ca.* 1575–1626), comp. and ed., *Haklytus posthumus or Purchas His Pilgrimes. Contayning a History of the World, in Sea Voyages, and Lande-Travells, by Englishmen and Others* . . . (4 vols., London, 1625). JM's erroneous entry is explicable. He employed a short title for *Purchas His Pilgrimage. Or Relations of the World and the Religions Observed in All Ages and Places* . . . , first published (London) in 1613. This work is unrelated to the *Pilgrimes;* but because of the similarity in titles, and because both works were published in folio and in volumes of the same size, cataloguers for many years listed the augmented fourth edition of the *Pilgrimage* (London, 1626) as being Volume V of the *Pilgrimes.* For other works contained in the *Pilgrimes* in whole or in part, see Nos. 217b-c, 220a-f, 222a-b, 222d-f, 233, and 265. See also *Papers of Madison*, IV, 101; 102, n. 4.

[240]   Hackluyt's Voyages

Richard Hakluyt (*ca.* 1552–1616), comp. and ed., *The Principal Navigations, Voiages, Traffiques and Discoveries of the English Nation, Made by Sea or Ouerland . . . within the Compasse of These 1500 Yeeres* . . . (Variant title, London, 1589; 2d ed., augmented, above title, 3 vols., London, 1598–1600). For other works contained in this collection in whole or in part, see Nos. 217a, 218a-b, 219a-d, 221a-e, 261. For a previous reference to Hakluyt, see *Papers of Madison*, V, 9, 11, nn. 3, 5, 7.

[241]   Abbe Reynal's Hist: Pol: & Philos: of East &
        W. Indies

Guillaume Thomas François Raynal (1713–1796) [and allegedly Denis Diderot (1713–1784) *et al.*], *A Philosophical and Political History of the Settlements and Trade of the Europeans in the East and West Indies* . . . (Anon., French original ed., 6 vols., Amsterdam, 1770; J[ohn] O[badiah] Justamond [d. 1786], tr. and ed., English ed., 6 vols., Edinburgh, 1782; 2d ed., 8 vols., London; 6 vols., Dublin, 1783).

[242]   Robinson's History of America

William Robertson (see No. 90), *The History of America* . . . (Partly posthumous, 3 vols., London and Dublin, 1777–1796; 2d ed., 3 vols., London, 1778–1796).

[243]   Russell's Hist: of do.

William Russell (1741–1793), *The History of America, from Its Discovery* . . . (2 vols., London, 1778).

[244]   Colden's History of the 5 Nations

Cadwallader Colden (1688–1776), *The History of the Five Indian Nations . . . Depending on the Province of New-York . . .* (variant title, New York, 1727, best ed.; 3d ed., 2 vols., London, 1755).

[245]   Burke's account of the Europ: Settlemts. in America

[William Burke (*ca.* 1723–1798)], *An Account of the European Settlements in America . . .* (2 vols., London, 1757; Edmund Burke [see No. 115], reviser, 5th ed., 2 vols., 1766; 6th ed., 2 vols., London and Dublin, 1777).

[246]   Douglas's Summary

William Douglass (*ca.* 1691–1752), *A Summary, Historical and Political . . . of the British Settlements in North-America . . .* ("W. D., M. D." continuing "numbers," Boston, 1747–1751, left uncompleted by death of author; 3d ed., 2 vols., London, 1760). See *Papers of Madison*, I, 184, and n. 1.

[247]   Collection of Charters

247a. John Almon (see No. 36b), comp. and ed., *The Charters of the British Colonies in America . . .* (London, 1774; 2d ed., Dublin, 1776). Although not included in this work, "The Grants, Concessions, and Original Constitution" of New Jersey were a portion of the contents of No. 278z.

247b. Richard Parker (d. *ca.* 1725), comp. and ed., *The Two Charters Granted by King Charles IId. to the Proprietors of Carolina . . .* (London, 1705). See *Papers of Madison*, V, 10; 13, n. 27.

[248]   Neal's History of New England

Daniel Neal (1678–1743), *The History of New-England . . . to the Year of Our Lord, 1700 . . .* (2 vols., London, 1720; 2d ed., 2 vols., London, 1747).

[249]   Prince's Chronological History of N. England

Thomas Prince (1687–1758), *A Chronological History of New-England . . . In the Form of Annals . . .* (2 vols., Vol. II with variant main title, *Annals of New-England*, Boston, 1736–1755).

[250]   Tracts relating to N. England by Cotton Mather

250a. Cotton Mather (1663–1728), *The Bostonian Ebenezer. Some Historical Remarks, on the State of Boston . . .* (Boston, 1698).

250b. [Cotton Mather], *The Declaration of the Gentlemen, Merchants, and Inhabitants of Boston, and the Country Adjacent . . .* (Boston and London, 1689).

250c. Cotton Mather, *Late Memorable Providences relating to Witchcraft and Possessions . . .* (Boston, 1689; 3d ed., Boston and Edinburgh, 1697).

250d. ———, *A Letter on the Character of the Inhabitants of New England . . .* (Boston, 1718).

250e. ———, *The Present State of New-England . . . upon the News of an Invasion by Bloody Indians and French-men . . .* (Boston, 1690).

250f. ———, *The Short History of New England. A Recapitulation of Wonderfull Passages Which Have Occurr'd . . .* (Boston, 1694).

250g. ———, *Some Few Remarks, upon a Scandalous Book, against the Government and Ministry of New-England . . .* (Boston, 1701).

250h. ———, *Souldiers Counselled and Comforted . . . in the Just War of New-England against the Northern & Eastern Indians . . .* (Boston, 1689).

250i. ———, *A True Account of the Tryals, Examinations, Confessions, Condemnations, and Executions of Divers Witches, at Salem, in New-England . . .* (London, 1693).

250j. ———, *The Wonders of the Invisible World: Being an Account of the Tryals of Several Witches, Lately Ex[e]cuted in New England . . .* (Boston and London, 1693).

[251]   Mather's ecclesiastical History of N. England

Cotton Mather (see No. 250), *Magnalia Christi americana; or, The Ecclesiastical History of New England . . . unto the Year of Our Lord, 1698 . . .* (London, 1702).

[252]   Hubbards History of N. England

William Hubbard (*ca.* 1621–1704), *A Narrative of the Indian Wars in New-England, from . . . 1607, to the Year 1677 . . .* (Boston, 1677; imperfect ed., London, 1677; 3d ed.[?], Boston, 1775).

[253]   Morton's New England's Memorial

Nathaniel Morton (1613–1685), *New-England's Memorial: or, A Brief Relation of the Most Memorable and Remarkable Passages of the Providence of God, Manifested to the Planters . . .* (Boston, 1669; 3d ed., Newport, R. I., 1772).

[254]   Hutchinson's History of Massachusetts bay

Thomas Hutchinson (1711–1780), *The History of the Colony of Massachusetts Bay . . .* (3 vols., Vols. I–II, Boston, 1764–1767; John Hutchinson [1793–1865], ed., Vol. III, London, 1828; 2d ed., London, 1760 [for 1765]–1828).

[255]   Collection of papers relating to the History of do.

Thomas Hutchinson, *A Collection of Original Papers relative to the History of the Colony of Massachusetts-Bay . . .* (Boston, 1769).

[256]   Smiths History of N. York.

William Smith (1728–1793), *The History of the Province of New-York, from the First Discovery . . .* (London, 1757; 2d ed., London, 1776).

[257]   Smith's History of N. Jersey

Samuel Smith (1720–1776), *The History of the Colony of Nova-Caesaria, or New-Jersey . . . to the Year 1721. With Some Particulars Since . . .* (Burlington, N.J., 1765).

[258]   Historical review of Pennsa.

[Richard Jackson (d. 1787), Benjamin Franklin (1706–1790), *et al.*], *An Historical Review of the Constitution and Government of Pennsylvania . . .* (London, 1759). After "Pennsa." JM wrote and canceled "by Franklyn," possibly because of uncertainty of attribution.

[259]   Franklin's other works

Benjamin Franklin, *Political, Miscellaneous, and Philosophical Pieces . . .* (Benjamin Vaughan [1751–1835], comp. and ed., London, 1779). For Vaughan, see Comment by Jefferson, 25 Jan. and n. 1; JM Notes, 19 Mar. 1783, n. 9. The "Vaughan" was the only authorized compilation of Franklin's works available in 1783. Even Franklin himself probably could not have assembled all his "other works," including many of concealed authorship, occasional pamphlets, and newspaper ephemerae. That assembling would await twentieth-century scholarship.

[260] Smith's History of Virga.

260a. John Smith (1580–1631), *The Generall Historie of Virginia, New-England, and the Summer Isles . . . ano. 1584 to This Present 1626* . . . (Variant subtitle, London, 1624; so-called "second" ed., London, 1626, and six succeeding so-called eds., pages of all printed in 1624 and subtitle updated, as above; so-called "eighth" ed., London, 1632). For other works by Smith, see Nos. 260b and 280a.

260b. John Smith, *The True Travels, Adventures and Observations of Captaine John Smith . . . Together with a Continuation of His Generall Historie . . . since 1624, to This Present 1629* . . . (London, 1630; 3d ed., London, 1744; also in Vol. II of the Churchills [No. 222c]).

[261] Beverley's do. of do.

[Robert Beverley (*ca.* 1673–1722)], "a Native and Inhabitant of the Place," anonym, *The History and Present State of Virginia* . . . ("R: B: gent:," London, 1705; 2d ed., revised and augmented, London, 1722).

[262] Keith's do. of do.

Sir William Keith (1680–1749), baronet, *The History of the British Plantations in America . . . Part I. Containing the History of Virginia* . . . (London, 1738; no other "Part" was ever published).

[263] Stith's do. of do.

William Stith (1707–1755), *The History of the First Discovery and Settlement of Virginia* . . . (Two separate eds., one superior, the other with type readjusted and on poor paper, Williamsburg, 1747; reissue of each ed. with new title page, London, 1753). For previous references to Stith, see *Papers of Madison*, V, 9; 11, n. 7; 12, nn. 8–9.

[264] De incolis Virginiae ab Anglico Thoma. Heriot

Thomas Harriot (1560–1621), *Admiranda narratio fida tamen, de commodis et incolarvm ritibus Virginiae* . . . (Original English ed., *A Briefe and True Report of the New Found Land of Virginia.* . . . London, 1588, very rare; Latin ed. in Part I of Theodor de Bry [1528–1598] *et al.*, comps., trs., and eds., *Collectiones peregrinationum in Indiam Orientalem et Indiam Occidentalem* [25 parts, Frankfort, 1590–1634]). JM and his consultants either did not know or had forgotten that the English version was reprinted in Vol. III of Hakluyt (No. 240).

[265] Discourses of Virginia

Ralph Hamor, *A Trve Discourse of the Present State of Virginia, and the Successe of the Affaires There till the 18 of June. 1614* . . . (London, 1615; also partly reprinted in Purchas [No. 239]).

[266] Virginia by E. W.

Edward Williams, *Virginia in America: More Especially the South Part Thereof . . . the Fertile Carolana, and No Lesse Excellent Isle of Roanoak* . . . (Variant title, London, 1650; 2d ed., containing an additional chapter, London, 1650; 3d ed., above title, London, 1651).

[267]   Jones's present State of Virginia

Hugh Jones (*ca.* 1670–1760), *The Present State of Virginia. Giving a Particular and Short Account of the Indian, English, and Negroe Inhabitants* . . . (London, 1724).

[268]   A discourse & view of Virga. by Sir Wm. Berkeley
        Govr. 1663

Sir William Berkeley (*ca.* 1608–1677), *A Discourse and View of Virginia* . . . (London, 1662; 2d ed., London, 1663).

[269]   An account of the life & death of Nat: Bacon. 1677.

Strange News from Virginia; Being a Full and True Account of the Life and Death of Nathaniel Bacon . . . (London: William Harris, 1677).

[270]   History of the present State of Virginia

James Blair (1656–1743), Edward Chilton, and Henry Hartwell, *The Present State of Virginia, and the College* . . . (London, 1727).

[271]   A short collection of the most remarkable passages
        from the original to the dissolution of the Virga.
        Company. 1651.

Arthur Wodenoth (Woodnoth) (*ca.* 1590–*ca.* 1650), *A Short Collection of the Most Remarkable Passages from the Originall to the Dissolution of the Virginia Company* . . . (London, 1651).

[272]   Lederer's discoveries in Virginia and Carolina
        in 1669. & 1670. by Sr. Wm. Talbot 1672.

John Lederer (b. *ca.* 1644), *The Discoveries of John Lederer, in Three Several Marches from Virginia, to the West of Carolina, and Other Parts of the Continent: Begun in March 1669, and Ended in September 1670* . . . (Latin original MSS; Sir William Talbot, baronet, tr. and ed., London, 1672).

[273]   Brickell's History of North Carolina

John Brickell (*ca.* 1710–1745), *The Natural History of North-Carolina. With an Account of the Trade, Manners and Customs of the Christian and Indian Inhabitants* . . . (Dublin, 1737, an almost verbatim plagiarism of Lawson [No. 274]; 2d ed., Dublin, 1743).

[274]   Lawson's do. of do.

John Lawson (d. 1712), *The History of Carolina; Containing the Exact Description and Natural History of That Country,* . . . *and a Journal of a Thousand Miles, Travel'd thro' Several Nations of Indians* . . . (Variant title, London, 1709; 3d ed., above title, London, 1718).

On 15 July 1831 the aged Madison, having observed "in a Newspaper paragraph" referring to a fire in Raleigh that "nothing was saved from the Library of the State, particularly 'Lawson's History of it,'" autographed and forwarded a personal copy of the work to Governor Montfort Stokes of North Carolina (LC: Madison Papers). For a plagiarism of the work, see No. 273.

[275] Description of South Carolina with its civil Natural and commercial History 1762.

[James Glen], *A Description of South Carolina; Containing Many Curious and Interesting Particulars relating to the Civil, Natural and Commercial History of That Colony* . . . (London, 1761). If JM's pen did not slip, he was misinformed; there was no edition of 1762.

[276] Huet's History of S. Carolina

Alexander Hewat (*ca.* 1745–1829), *An Historical Account of the Rise and Progress of the Colonies of South Carolina and Georgia* . . . (2 vols., London, 1779).

[277] Collection of papers relative to Georgia

In attempting to cover the deficiencies in the published history of Georgia, JM would have found a "Collection of papers" to contain a surprisingly large number of printed items—that number not sufficing, however, to cover serious gaps in the historical record. A limited but typical selection from the De Renne collection of Georgiana is here presented (Azalea Clizbee, comp., *Catalogue of the Wymberley Jones De Renne Georgia Library at Wormsloe, Isle of Hope near Savannah, Georgia* [3 vols., Wormsloe, 1931], I, 1–226 *passim*).

277a. George Cadogan, *The Spanish Hireling Detected: Being a Refutation of the Several Calumnies and Falshoods in a Late Pamphlet, Entitul'd "An Impartial Account"* . . . (London, 1743). For "An Impartial Account," see No. 277f; for a rejoinder to this "Refutation," No. 277e.

277b. James Johnston, comp. and ed., *Account of the Siege of Savannah, by the French and Rebels, Commanded by Count d'Estaing and General Lincoln* . . . (Savannah, 1780).

277c. [Benjamin Martyn (1699–1763)], *An Account Shewing the Progress of the Colony of Georgia, from Its First Establishment* . . . (London, 1741; reprint, Annapolis, 1742). This work also has been attributed to Lord John Perceval, for whom see No. 277g.

277d. Benjamin Martyn, *Reasons for Establishing the Colony of Georgia . . . With Some Account of the Country and the Design of the Trustees* . . . (Anon., London, 1733; 2d ed., London, 1733).

277e. [James Edward Oglethorpe (1696–1785)], *A Full Reply to Lieut. Cadogan's Spanish Hireling, &c.* . . . (London, 1743). For the work to which this was "A Full Reply," see No. 277a.

277f. [James Edward Oglethorpe], *An Impartial Account of the Late Expedition against St. Augustine under General Oglethorpe* . . . (London, 1742). For an attack on this work, see No. 277a.

277g. [Lord John Perceval (1711–1770), later Earl of Egmont, supposed author], *Faction Detected by the Evidence of Facts. Containing an Impartial View of Parties at Home, and Affairs Abroad* . . . (London, 1742; 5th ed., London, 1743). The work has also been attributed to William Pulteney (1684–1764), later Earl of Bath.

277h. [Lord John Perceval], *Remarks upon a Scandalous Piece, Entitled a Brief Account of the Causes That Have Retarded the Progress of the Colony of Georgia* . . . (London, 1743). For the "Scandalous Piece," see No. 277k.

277i. Georg Philipp Friedrich von Reck (1710–1798) and Johann Martin Bolzius (1703–1765), *An Extract of the Journals of Mr. Commissary von Reck, Who Conducted the First Transport of the Saltzburgers to Georgia; and of the Reverend Mr. Bolzius* . . . (London, 1734).

277j. South Carolina (Colony), *Report of the Committee Appointed To Examine into the Proceedings of the People of Georgia . . . and the Dispute Subsisting between the Two Colonies . . .* (Charleston, 1737).

277k. Thomas Stephens, *A Brief Account of the Causes That Have Retarded the Progress of the Colony of Georgia . . . A Proper Contrast to A State of the Province of Georgia . . .* (London, 1743). For the "State" to which this work was allegedly a "Proper Contrast," see No. 277l, and for a counterblast to the above assertedly "Scandalous Piece," No. 277h.

277l. William Stephens (1671–1753), *A Journal of the Proceedings in Georgia, Beginning October 20, 1737 . . .* (3 vols., London, 1742). The appendix of Vol. II is the author's *A State of the Province of Georgia, Attested upon Oath in the Court of Savannah, November 10, 1740,* also separately published (London) in 1742. Against this "State" was directed the "Brief Account" which purported to be a "Proper Contrast" (No. 277k).

277m. Patrick Sutherland, *An Account of the Late Invasion of Georgia . . .* (London, 1743).

277n. Patrick Tailfer *et al.,* *A True and Historical Narrative of the Colony of Georgia, in America, from the First Settlement Thereof . . .* (Charleston, 1741).

277o. Trustees for Establishing the Colony of Georgia in America, *An Account Shewing the Progress of the Colony of Georgia in America from Its First Establishment . . .* (London, 1741).

277p. John Wesley (1703–1791), *An Extract of the Rev. Mr. John Wesley's Journal, from His Embarking for Georgia to His Return to London . . .* (Bristol, n.d. [1739?]).

277q. George Whitefield (1714–1770), *A Continuation of the Reverend Mr. Whitefield's Journal, After His Arrival in Georgia . . .* (London, 1741).

[278]   Laws of each of the United States

Scores of single acts or ordinances were published separately. For this reason, the citations below are confined to volumes containing the statutes enacted during an entire legislative session or during more than one session.

278a. *Acts and Laws, Passed by the General Court or Assembly of His [Her] Majesties Province of New-Hampshire in New England . . .* (Boston, 1669, 1706, 1716, 1718–1719, 1721–1722, 1726–1728).

278b. *Acts and Laws of His Majesty's Province of New-Hampshire, in New-England . . .* (Portsmouth, 1761–1766).

278c. *Acts and Laws of the Colony of New-Hampshire . . .* (Exeter, 1776).

278d. *Acts and Laws of the State of New-Hampshire . . .* (Exeter, 1780). The text comprises laws enacted from 1776 through 1780.

278e. *The General Laws and Liberties of the Massachusetts Colony in New-England, Revised and Reprinted . . .* (Cambridge, Mass., 1672; reprint, London, 1675).

278f. *Several Laws and Orders Made at the General Court Holden [Held] at Boston . . .* (Cambridge, 1672–1684).

278g. *At the Convention of the Governour and Council, and Representatives of the Massachusetts Colony . . .* (Cambridge, 1689).

278h. *Acts and Laws Passed by the Great and General Court or Assembly of the Province of Massachusetts-Bay in New England, from 1692 to 1719 . . .* (London, 1724).

278i. *Acts and Laws, Passed by the Great and General Court or Assembly of Their [His, Her] Majesties [Majesty's] Province of the Massachusetts-Bay, in New-England, Begun and Held at Boston [Cambridge, Concord, Roxbury, Salem]* . . . (Boston, 1719–1774).

278j. *In the Fifteenth Year of the Reign of George the Third, King &c. Acts and Laws, Passed by the Great and General Court or Assembly of the Colony of Massachusetts-Bay in New-England* . . . (Watertown, 1775).

278k. *In the Year of Our Lord, 1776 [1777]. Acts and Laws, Passed by the Great and General Court or Assembly of the Colony of Massachusetts-Bay in New-England* . . . (Watertown and Boston, 1776–1777).

278l. *Acts and Laws, Passed by the Great and General Court or Assembly of the State of Massachusetts Bay, in New England* . . . (Boston, 1778–1780).

278m. *Acts and Laws, Passed by the Great and General Court or Assembly of the Commonwealth of Massachusetts* . . . (Boston, 1781–1783).

278n. *Acts and Laws of the English Colony of Rhode-Island and Providence-Plantations, in New-England* . . . (Boston, 1719; 4th revision, Newport, 1767).

278o. *Acts and Laws of the English Colony of Rhode-Island and Providence Plantations, in New-England, in America. Made and Passed Since the Revision in June, 1767* . . . (Newport, 1772).

278p. *At a General Assembly of the Governor and Company of the English Colony of Rhode-Island, and Providence Plantations, in New-England* . . . (Newport and Providence, 1773–1776).

278q. *At a General Assembly of the Governor and Company of the State of Rhode-Island and Providence Plantations* . . . (Providence and Attleborough, 1777–1783).

278r. *Acts and Laws of His Majesties Colony of Connecticut in New-England* . . . (New London and Hartford, 1715–1727).

278s. *Acts and Laws Passed by the General Court or Assembly of His Majesty's Colony of Connecticut in New-England* . . . (New London, 1728–1748).

278t. *Acts and Laws Passed by the General Court or Assembly of His Majesty's [English] Colony of Connecticut in New-England* . . . (New London, 1750–1776).

278u. *Acts and Laws, Made and Passed by the General Court or Assembly of the State of Connecticut, in New-England* . . . (New London, 1777–1783).

278v. Peter Van Schaack (1747–1832), ed., *Laws of New-York from the Year 1691 to 1773 Inclusive* . . . (2 vols., New York, 1774).

278w. *Acts of the General Assembly of the Colony of New-York, February–March, 1774* . . . (New York, 1774).

278x. *Laws of the State of New-York, Commencing with the First Session of the Senate and Assembly, After the Declaration of Independence* . . . (Poughkeepsie, 1782).

278y. *Laws of the State of New-York, Passed at Kingston* . . . (Poughkeepsie, 1783).

278z. "Some Gentlemen Employed by the General Assembly," anonym, eds., *The Grants, Concessions, and Original Constitution of the Province of New-Jersey, the Acts Passed During the Proprietary Governments, and Other Material Transactions Before the Surrender Thereof to Queen Anne* . . . (Philadelphia, 1757).

278aa. Samuel Allinson, ed., *Acts of the General Assembly of the Province of New-Jersey, from the Surrender of the Government to Queen Anne, in the Year of Our Lord 1702, to the 14th Day of January 1776* . . . (2d ed., Burlington, 1776).

278ab. *Acts of the General Assembly of the State of New-Jersey* . . . (Burlington and Trenton, 1777–1780).

278ac. *Acts of the Fifth [-Seventh] General Assembly of the State of New-Jersey* . . . (Trenton, 1781–1783).

278ad. [Joseph Galloway (*ca.* 1731–1803), ed.], *The Acts of the Assembly of Pennsylvania . . . And an Appendix, Containing Such Acts and Parts of Acts, relating to the Proprietary, as Are Expired, Altered or Repealed* . . . (Philadelphia, 1775).

278ae. [Thomas McKean (1734–1817), ed.], *The Acts of the General Assembly of Pennsylvania . . . And an Appendix, Containing Laws Now in Force, Passed between the Thirtieth Day of September 1775, and the Revolution* . . . (2 vols., Philadelphia, 1782–1786). Vol. II contains laws passed through the year 1786.

278af. [Caesar Rodney (1728–1784) and Thomas McKean (see No. 278ae), eds.], *Laws of the Government of Newcastle, Kent, and Sussex, upon Delaware* . . . (2 vols., Philadelphia and Wilmington, 1752–1763).

278ag. *Anno regni sexto [-quinto decimo] Georgii III regis. At a General Assembly Begun at New-Castle . . . the Following Acts Were Passed by the Honourable John Penn [Richard Penn], Esquire; Governor* . . . (Wilmington, 1766–1767, 1769–1770, 1772–1773, 1775).

278ah. *Acts of the General Assembly of the Delaware State* . . . (Wilmington, 1779).

278ai. *Anno millesmo septingentesimo octuagesimo [-primo]. At a General Assembly Begun at Dover in the Delaware State . . . the Following Acts Were Passed* . . . (Wilmington, 1780–1781).

278aj. *Acts of the General Assembly of the Delaware State, at a Session Begun at Dover* . . . (Wilmington, 1782–1783).

278ak. Thomas Bacon (*ca.* 1700–1768), ed., *Laws of Maryland at Large . . . Now First Collected into One Compleat Body, and Published from the Original Acts and Records* . . . (Annapolis, 1765).

278al. *Laws . . . of the Dominion of the Right Honourable Frederick [Henry Harford], Absolute Lord and Proprietary of the Provinces of Maryland and Avalon, Lord Baron of Baltimore, &c.* . . . (Annapolis, 1768, 1770–1774).

278am. *Laws of Maryland, Made and Passed at a Session of Assembly, Begun and Held at the City of Annapolis* . . . (Annapolis, 1777–1783).

278an. *The Acts of Assembly, Now in Force, in the Colony of Virginia. With an Exact Table to the Whole* . . . (Williamsburg, 1769).

278ao. *Acts of the General Assembly, 10 [-12] Geo. III. With an Index* . . . (Williamsburg, 1770 1772).

278ap. *At a General Assembly, Begun and Held at the Capitol, in the City of Williamsburg* . . . (Williamsburg, 1773).

278aq. *Ordinances Passed at a Convention Held at the Town of Richmond, in the Colony of Virginia, on Monday the 17th of July, 1775* . . . (Williamsburg, n. d. [1775]).

278ar. *Ordinances Passed at a Convention Held in the City of Williamsburg, in the Colony of Virginia, on Friday the 1st of December, 1775* . . . (Williamsburg, n. d. [1775]).

278as. *Ordinances Passed at a General Convention . . . Held at the Capitol, in the City of Williamsburg, on Monday the 6th of May, anno Dom: 1776* . . . (Williamsburg, n. d. [1776]).

278at. *At a General Assembly, Begun and Held at the Capitol, in the City of Williamsburg* . . . (Williamsburg, 1777–1779).

278au. *Acts Passed at a General Assembly, Begun and Held in the Town of Richmond* . . . (Richmond, n. d. [1780–1781]).

278av. *Acts Passed at a General Assembly of the Commonwealth of Virginia, Begun and Held at the Public Buildings in the Town of Richmond* . . . (Charlottesville and Richmond, n. d. [1781–1783]).

278aw. *A Complete Revisal of All the Acts of Assembly, of the Province of North-Carolina, Now in Force and Use* . . . (New Bern, 1773).

278ax. *Acts Passed by the Assembly, of the Province of North-Carolina* . . . (New Bern, 1774).

278ay. *The Acts of Assembly of the State of North-Carolina* . . . (n.p., New Bern, and Halifax, 1777–1783).

278az. Nicholas Trott (1662–1740), ed., *The Laws of the Province of South-Carolina* . . . (Charleston, 1736).

278ba. *Acts Passed by the General Assembly of South-Carolina at [a] Session[s] Begun and Holden at Charles-Town* . . . (Charleston, 1736–1737, 1760).

278bb. *Anno regni Georgii III. regis Magnae Britanniae, Franciae & Hiberniae quinto [sexto], At a General Assembly Begun and Holden at Charles-Town* . . . (Charleston, 1765–1766).

278bc. *Acts and Ordinances of the General Assembly of the State of South-Carolina* . . . (Charleston, 1776–1778).

278bd. *Acts Passed at a General Assembly Begun and Holden at Jacksonburg, in the State of South-Carolina* . . . (Philadelphia, 1782).

278be. *Acts and Ordinances Passed at a General Assembly of the State of South-Carolina* . . . (Charleston, 1783).

278bf. *Acts Passed by the General Assembly of Georgia from February 17, 1755 to May 10, 1770* . . . (Savannah, 1763–1770).

278bg. *Acts Passed by the General Assembly of Georgia at a Session Begun the 9th Day of December, 1772* . . . (Savannah, 1773).

[279]   All Treaties entered into with the natives of N. America.

This portion of the order could be filled, at least to the point of supplying copies of all treaties known to be in print; of these a limited number are presented below. An indeterminable multiplicity of written agreements "entered into" with various Indian tribes existed only in manuscript form, for examples of which see *Papers of Madison*, III, 249; 250, n. 7; IV, 125–26; 156, n. 9; V, 62, n. 18; 405, n. 29.

279a. *Articles of Peace between the Most Serene and Mighty Prince Charles II. . . . and Several Indian Kings and Queens, &c. Concluded the 29th Day of May, 1677* . . . (London, 1677).

279b. *An Account of the Treaty between His Excellency Benjamin Fletcher, Captain-General and Governour in Chief of the Province of New-York, &c. and the Indians of the Five Nations* . . . (New York, 1694).

279c. *The Particulars of an Indian Treaty at Conestogoe, between His Excellency Sir William Keith, Bart. Governor of Pennsylvania, and the Deputies of the Five Nations, in June, 1722* . . . (Philadelphia, 1722; reprint, London and Dublin, 1723).

279d. *A Treaty of Peace and Friendship Made and Concluded between His Excellency Sir William Keith . . . and the Chiefs of the Indians of the Five Nations, at Albany, in the Month of September 1722* . . . (Philadelphia, 1722).

279e. *Two Indian Treaties the One Held at Conestogoe in May 1728. And the Other at Philadelphia in June Following, between the Honourable Patrick Gordon Esq. Lieut. Governour of the Province of Pennsylvania, and Counties . . . upon Delaware, and the Chiefs of the Conestogoe, Delaware, Shawanese and Canawese Indians* . . . (Philadelphia, 1728).

279f. *A Treaty of Friendship Held with . . . the Six Nations, Philadelphia, September, and October, 1736* . . . (Philadelphia, 1737).

279g. *The Treaty Held with the Indians of the Six Nations at Philadelphia, in July, 1742* . . . (Philadelphia, 1743).

279h. *A Treaty . . . at the Town of Lancaster, in Pennsylvania, by the Honourable the Lieutenant-Governor of the Province, and . . . the Commissioners for the Provinces of Virginia and Maryland, with the Indians of the Six Nations, in June, 1744* . . . (Philadelphia, 1744).

279i. *An Account of the Treaty Held at the City of Albany, in the Province of New-York, by His Excellency the Governor . . . and . . . the Commissioners for the Provinces of Massachusetts, Connecticut, and Pennsylvania, with the Indians of the Six Nations, in October, 1745* . . . (Philadelphia, 1746).

279j. *A Treaty, between His Excellency the Honourable George Clinton, Captain General and Governor in Chief of the Province of New-York . . . and the Six United Indian Nations, and Other Indian Nations . . . Held at Albany in the Months of August and September, 1746* . . . (New York, 1746).

279k. *A Treaty between the President and Council of the Province of Pennsylvania, and the Indians of Ohio, Held at Philadelphia, Nov. 13, 1747* . . . (Philadelphia, 1748).

279l. *A Treaty Held by . . . Members of the Council of the Province of Pennsylvania, at the Town of Lancaster, with Some Chiefs of the Six Nations at Ohio, and Others . . . in the Month of July, 1748* . . . (Philadelphia, 1748).

279m. *A Treaty Held with the Ohio Indians, at Carlisle, in October, 1753* . . . (Philadelphia, 1753).

279n. *Treaty, or, Articles of Peace and Friendship Renewed between His Excellency Peregrine Thomas Hopson, Esq.; Captain General and Governor in Chief, in and over His Majesty's Province of Nova-Scotia or Accadie . . . and Major Jean Baptiste Cope, Chief Sachem of the Chiben Accadie Tribe of Mickmuck Indians* . . . (Halifax, 1753).

279o. *An Account of Conferences Held, and Treaties Made, between Major-General Sir William Johnson, Bart. and the Chief Sachems and Warriours of the . . . Indian Nations in North America, at Their Meeting on Different Occasions at Fort Johnson, in the County of Albany, in the Colony of New-York, in the Years 1755 and 1756* . . . (London, 1756).

279p. *A Treaty between the Government of New-Jersey, and the Indians, Inhabiting the Several Parts of Said Province, Held at Croswicks . . . the Eighth and Ninth Day of January, 1756* . . . (Philadelphia, 1756).

279q. *A Treaty Held with the Catawba and Cherokee Indians, at Catawba-Town and Broad River, in the Months of February and March, 1756. By Virtue of a Commission Granted by the Honorable Robert Dinwiddie, Esquire, His Majesty's Lieutenant-Governor, and Commander in Chief of the Colony and Dominion of Virginia, to the Honorable Peter Randolph and William Byrd, Esquires* . . . (Williamsburg, 1756).

279r. *Proceedings and Treaty with the . . . Indians, Living at Otsiningo, on One of the West Branches of the Susquehanna River. Negotiated at Fort-Johnson . . . New-York; by the Honourable Sir William Johnson, Bart, &c.* . . . (New York and Boston, 1757).

279s. *The Minutes of a Treaty Held at Easton, in Pennsylvania, in October, 1758. By the Lieutenant Governor of Pennsylvania, and the Governor of New-Jersey; with . . . the Mohawks, Nanticokes & Conoys, Oneydos, Chugnuts, Onondagas,*

Delawares, Cayugas, Unamies, Senecas, Mohickons, Tuscaroras, Minisinks, Tuteloes, and Wapings . . . (Woodbridge, N. J., 1758).

279t. Samuel Wharton (1732–1800), *View of the Title to Indiana* . . . *Containing* . . . *the Deed of the Six Nations to the Proprietors of Indiana—the Minutes of the Congress at Fort Stanwix, in October and November, 1768—the Deed of the Indians, Settling the Boundary Line between the English and Indian Lands* . . . (Philadelphia, 1776).

[280]   All the political tracts which have been or may be
published & may be judged of sufficient importance

For "tracts" which had drawn or would draw JM's attention prior to the close of 1783, see *Papers of Madison*, I, 43; 44, n. 4; 115; 117, n. 7; 133, n. 5; II, 79; 80, nn. 1, 2; 147; 148, n. 11; III, 11; 14, n. 17; IV, 143; 144, n. 2; 155; 157, n. 13; 196; 198, n. 12; 228, n. 7; V, 319; 321, n. 13; Address to the States, 25 Apr. 1783, n. 38. Even if the phrase "of sufficient importance" is narrowly interpreted, a list of "All the political tracts" published during a time-span of 175 years would fill a large volume. A list, satisfactory to JM, might begin and end, respectively, with the following entries.

280a. [John Smith (see No. 260a)], "Th. Watson Gent.," pseud., *A Trve Relation of Such Occurrences and Accidents of Noate as Hath Hapned in Virginia since the First Planting of That Collony* . . . (London, 1608).

280b. Ethan Allen (1738–1789), *The Present State of the Controversy between the States of New-York and New-Hampshire, on the One Part and the State of Vermont on the Other* . . . (Hartford, 1782).

[281]   Brown's History of Jamaica

Patrick Browne (*ca.* 1720–1790), *The Civil and Natural History of Jamaica* . . . (London, 1756; 2d ed., lacking the valuable illustrations of the 1st, London, 1769).

[282]   History of Barbadoes

Richard Hall (d. 1786), *The History of Barbadoes, from 1643 to 1762* . . . (London, 1765).

[283]   Garcilasso de la Vega's History of Florida

Garcilaso de la Vega (*ca.* 1540–1616), called *el inca, Histoire de la conquête de la Floride: ou relation de ce qui s'est passé dans découverte de ce païs par Ferdinand de Soto* . . . (Spanish original ed., 2 vols., Lisbon, 1605; French ed., 2 vols., Paris, 1670; 5th ed., 2 vols., Leyden, 1735). For other works by Vega, see Nos. 297 and 298.

[284]   Cox's Account of Florida

Daniel Coxe (1673–1739), *A Description of the English Province of Carolana. By the Spaniards Call'd Florida, and by the French, la Louisiane* . . . (Variant title, London, 1722; 2d ed., above title, London, 1741; 2d reprint, London, 1741).

[285]   Romans's History of Florida

Bernard Romans (*ca.* 1720–*ca.* 1784), *A Concise Natural History of East and West-Florida* . . . (New York, 1775; 2d ed., New York, 1776).

[286]   Memoirs sur la Louisiane par du Pratz

LePage du Pratz (d. 1775), *The History of Louisiana, or of The Western Parts of Virginia and Carolina: Containing a Description of the Countries That Lie on Both*

Sides of the River Missis[s]ippi ... (French original ed., 3 vols., Paris, 1758; English ed., variant title, 2 vols., London, 1763; 2d ed., above title, London, 1774).

[287]   Description de la Louisiane par Hennepin

Louis Hennepin (see No. 205), *Description de la Louisiane, nouvellement découverte au sud'oüest de la Nouvelle France* ... (Paris, 1683; reprint, Paris, 1688).

[288]   Bossu's travels through Louisiane

Jean Bernard Bossu (1720–1792), *Travels through That Part of North-America Formerly Called Louisiana* ... (French original ed., 2 vols., Paris, 1768; Johann Reinhold Forster [1729–1798], tr. and augmenter, 2 vols., London, 1771).

[289]   Venegas's History of California

Miguel Venegas (1680–ca. 1764), *A Natural and Civil History of California* ... (Spanish original ed., 3 vols., Madrid, 1757; English ed., 2 vols., London, 1759).

[290]   Muratori il christianissimo felice

Lodovico Antonio Muratori (1672–1750), *Il cristianisimo felice nelle missioni de' padri della compagnia di Gesù nel Paraguai* ... (2 vols., Venice, 1743–1749). An English edition of 1759 was only of the first volume.

[291]   Voyages et descouverts des Espagnols dans les Indes
         occidentales par Don Bernardo de las casas

Bartolomé de las Casas (1474–1566), *La découverte des Indes Occidentales, par les espagnols et les moyens dont ils se sont servis pour s'en rendre maitres* ... (Spanish original ed., 9 tracts, Seville, 1552–1553; French ed., Paris, 1697; reprint, Paris, 1701; one tract in English, in Vol. IV of Purchas [No. 239]).

[292]   Herrera's History of the Spanish Colonies in America

Antonio de Herrera y Tordesillas (1549–1625), *The General History of the Vast Continent and Islands of America, Commonly Call'd the West-Indies* ... (Spanish original ed., 4 vols., Madrid, 1601–1615; English ed., somewhat abridged, 6 vols., London, 1725–1726).

[293]   de Solis's History of the Conquest of Mexico by F. Cortez

Antonio de Solis y Ribadeneyra (1610–1686), *The History of the Conquest of Mexico by the Spaniards* ... (Spanish original ed., Madrid, 1684; English ed., 3 parts, London, 1724; Nathaniel Hooke [see No. 78], ed., 2d, corrected, ed., 2 vols., London, 1738; 3d ed., 2 vols., London, 1753).

[294]   Voyages de Gage

Thomas Gage (d. 1656), *A New Survey of the West-Indies. Being a Journal of Three Thousand and Three Hundred Miles within the Main Land of America* ... (Variant title, London, 1648; 2d ed., augmented, main title as above, London, 1655; 4th ed., main and subtitle as above, London, 1699; reprint, London, 1711). A new French translation of the work (2 vols., Paris) was published in 1776.

[295]   Houston's Memoirs

James Houstoun (*ca.* 1690–post-1753), *The Works of James Houstoun, M. D., Containing Memoirs of His Life and Travels in Asia, Africa, America, and Most Parts of Europe* . . . (2 separate printings, titles varying from above and from each other, London, 1747; 2d ed., above title, London, 1753).

[296]   Bouguer voyage au Perou.

Pierre Bouguer (1698–1758), *La figure de la terre, déterminée par les observations de MM. Bouguer, & de la Condamine . . . envoyés par ordre du roy au Pérou . . . avec une relation abregée de ce voyage* . . . (Paris, 1749).

[297]   Garcilasso de la Vega's History of the Incas of Perou

Garcilaso de la Vega *el inca* (see No. 283), *Histoire des incas, rois du Pérou* . . . (Part I, Spanish original ed. of *Commentarios reales*, 2 parts, Lisbon and Cordova, 1609–1617; Thomas François Dalibard [1703–1799], tr. and ed., French ed., 2 vols., Paris, 1744).

[298]   Histoires des Guerres civiles des Espagnols dans les
        Indes, de Garcilasso de la Vega

Garcilaso de la Vega *el inca* (see No. 283), *Histoire des gverres civiles des espagnols dans les Indes* . . . (Part II, Spanish original ed. of *Commentarios reales*, 2 parts, Lisbon and Cordova, 1609–1617; French ed., 2 vols., Paris, 1658; 3d ed., 2 vols., Amsterdam, 1706).

[299]   Histoire de l'Orenoque par Gumilla

José Gumilla (1690–1758), *Histoire naturelle, civile et géographique de l'Orénoque; et des principales rivières qui s'y jettent* . . . (Spanish original ed., Madrid, 1741; 2d ed., 2 vols., Madrid, 1745; French ed., from Spanish 2d ed., 3 vols., Avignon, 1758).

[300]   Bancroft's Natural History of Guiana

Edward Bancroft (1744–1821), *An Essay on the Natural History of Guiana, in South America* . . . (London, 1769).

[301]   Les voyages de Coreal. 1722.

Francesco Coreal (*ca.* 1648–1708), *Recueil de voyages dans l'Amérique Méridionale . . . touchant le Pérou, la Guiane, le Brésil, &c.* . . . (Variant title, according closely with JM's entry, 2 vols., Paris; 3 vols., Amsterdam, 1722; 4th ed., above title, 3 vols., Amsterdam, 1738). Although the French version was allegedly a translation *de l'espagnol,* no Spanish original edition is known to exist.

[302]   Falkner's description of Patagonia

Thomas Falkner (1707–1784), *A Description of Patagonia, and the Adjoining Parts of South America* . . . [William Combe (1741–1823), comp. and ed.], (Hereford, Eng., 1774).

[303]   Nouveau voyage aux iles de l'Amerique

Jean Baptiste Labat (1663–1738), *Nouveau voyage aux isles de l'Amérique, contenant l'histoire naturelle de ce pays* . . . (Author's name only at end of dedication, 2 separate printings, 6 vols. each, Paris, 1722; 2d ed., augmented, 6 vols., The Hague, 1724; 3d ed., 8 vols., Paris, 1742).

[304]   Histoire de St. Domingue par Charlevoix

Pierre François Xavier de Charlevoix (see No. 234), *Histoire de l'isle espagnole ou de S. Domingue* . . . (2 vols., Paris, 1730–1731; 2d ed., 4 vols., Amsterdam, 1733).

[305]   Chanvalon's Voyage à la Martinique

Jean Baptiste Thibault de Chanvalon, *Voyage à la Martinique, contenant diverses observations . . . faites en 1751 & dans les années suivantes . . .* (Paris, 1763).

[306]   Acuogna's relation of the river of Amazons

Cristóbal de Acuña (1597–1680), *Voyages and Discoveries in South-America. The First up the River of Amazons to Quito, in Peru, and Back Again to Brazil . . .* (Spanish original ed., Madrid, 1641; English ed., bound with the accounts of two other travelers, London, 1698).

[307]   Techo's History of Paraguay.

Nicolás del Techo (earlier Du Toict) (1611–1685), *Decades virorum illustrium Paraguariae Societatis Jesu ex historia ejusdem provinciae . . . Cum synopsi chronologica historiae Paraguariae . . .* (Liège, 1673; 3 vols. in 2, Frankfurt and Leipzig, 1767–1768; much abridged English version in Vol. IV of the Churchills [No. 222c]).

Notes on Debates

MS (LC: Madison Papers). For a description of the manuscript of Notes on Debates, see *Papers of Madison*, V, 231–34.

Thursday Jany 23.

The Report of the come. last mentioned consisting of a state of the variations in the Treaty of Amity & commerce with the States General from the plan proposed by Congress, of a form of ratification of the sd Treaty & of the Convention, & of a proclamation comprehending both was accepted & passed; the variations excepted wch. were not meant to be entered on the journals.[1] Both the Committee & Congress were exceedingly chagrined at the extreme incorrectness of the American copies of these national acts, and it was privately talked of as necessary to admonish Mr. Adams thereof, & direct him to procure with the concurrence of the other party a more correct & perspicuous copy.[2] The Report of the Come. as agreed to, havg. left a blank in the act of ratification for the insertion of the Treaty & Convention, & these being contained both in the Dutch & American languages, the former column signed by the Dutch Plenpos. only & the latter by Mr. Adams only. The Secy. asked the direction of Congs. whether both columns or the American only ought to be inserted.[3] On this point several observations were made & different opinions expressed. In general the members seemed to disaprove of the mode usd & would have preferred the use of a neutral language.[4] As to the request of the Secy.[,] Mr. Wilson was of opinion that the American Columns only sd. be inserted, Several others concurred in this opinion;[5] supposing that as Mr. Adams had only signed those columns, our ratifications ought to be limited to them. Those who were of a different opinion, considered the two parts as inseperable & as forming one whole, & consequently that both ought to be inserted. The case being a new one to Congress,[6] it was proposed & admitted that the insertion might be suspended till the next day, by which time some authorities might be consulted on the subject.[7]

A come. consisting of Mr. Madison, Mr. Mifflin & Mr. Williamson reported in consequence of a motion of Mr. Bland, a list of books proper for the use of Congress, and proposed that the Secy. sho'd be instructed to procure the same.[8] In favr. of the Rept. it was urged as indispensable that Congress sd. have at all times at command such authors on the law of Nations, treaties Negociations &c as wd. render their proceedings in such cases conformable to propriety; and it was observed that the want of this information was manifest in several important acts of Congress. It was further observed that no time ought to be lost in collecting every book & tract which related to American Antiquities & the affairs of the U.S. since many of the most valuable of these were every day becoming extinct, & they were necessary not only as materials for a Hist: of the U.S. but might be rendered still more so by future pretensions agst. their rights from Spain or other powers which had shared in the discoveries & possessions of the New World.[9] Agst. the Report were urged 1st. the inconveniency of advancing even a few hundred pounds at this crisis; 2dly. the difference of expence between procuring the books during the war & after a peace. These objections prevailed, by a considerable majority. A motion was then made by Mr. Wilson 2ded. by Mr. Madison to confine the purchase for the present to the most essential part of the books. This also was negatived.[10]

[1] JM Notes, 22 Jan., and n. 1. Having pointed out to Congress the chief variations between the instructions to John Adams and the provisions of the treaty, the committee recommended that the latter should be "fully accepted & ratified" in spite of those differences (Report on Treaty, 23 Jan. 1783, and nn. 3, 4, 6, 7–10).

[2] JM interlineated "extreme" as a replacement for one or two words too heavily deleted to be legible and also interlineated "privately talked of" above a canceled "suggested." The copy of the treaty submitted to Congress was not an original copy, for Adams had retained the original through fear it might be lost or captured at sea, but an "authentic copy" which he forwarded in his dispatch of 8 October 1782 (Wharton, *Revol. Dipl. Corr.*, V, 803–5; L[yman] H. Butterfield *et al.*, eds., *Diary and Autobiography of John Adams*. [4 vols.; Cambridge, Mass. 1961], III, 15–16, 16, n. 2, 17–18, 24–25).

Although misspellings were corrected in the English versions of the treaty and convention before publication, JM's other objections remained much in point. Not only did the treaty refer to "subjects" rather than "citizens" of the contracting powers, but it included a baffling provision for a ship's "visitation at land," referred to what presumably was a bond for good behavior as a "caution" against "mal-versations," related conditions under which shippers should "not be obliged to pay neither for the vessels nor the cargoes, any duties of entry in or out," defined a blockaded port as one "surrounded nearly by some of the belligerent powers," and authorized city magistrates to regulate "the affair of refraction" (JCC, XXIV, 72, 73, 75, 76, 78). "Indeed," wrote Irving Brant, "it was a queer paper" (Madison, II, 266). As for the convention, it provided that either government "shall be free" to regulate the conduct of its own privateers (JCC, XXIV, 81).

[3] Report on Treaty, 23 Jan. 1783, n. 13. Charles Thomson was the "Secy."

[4] Probably French, long the established language of diplomacy.

[5] James Wilson of Pennsylvania, who on 2 January 1783 attended Congress for the first time since September 1777 (JCC, VIII, 746; XXIV, 2). JM originally placed a period after "opinion" and began a new sentence, reading "Some however thought the safest and most proper course wd be." He then canceled these words and changed the period after "opinion" to a semicolon.

[6] Although the originals of the treaty and the convention in the Dutch archives disclose that both Dutch and English texts were signed by each of the plenipoten-tiaries, the attested copies forwarded by Adams showed the negotiators as signing only the text written in their respective tongues (Hunter Miller, *Treaties and Other International Acts*, II, 89, 95).

[7] Report on Treaty, 23 Jan., and nn. 14, 18. The delegates apparently found those "authorities" of no help in clarifying the issue, for JM soon solicited the assistance of the attorney general of Virginia (JM Notes, 24 Jan.; JM to Randolph, 28 Jan. 1783). Perhaps the quandary helps in small measure to explain why JM submitted on 23 or 24 January a list of books for a library of Congress. See Report on Books, 23 Jan. 1783.

[8] *Ibid.*, and hdn. and ed. n.

[9] This sentence probably summarizes what JM himself said in support of the committee's report. See *Papers of Madison*, IV, 143; 154-55; 198, n. 7; 228, n. 7; 306, n. 3; 389, n. 19; V, 56; 312, nn. 18, 19; 454; 457, n. 17.

[10] Neither of the two votes is recorded in the printed journal (JCC, XXIV, 92, n. 1). The statute of 24 April 1800, providing for a Library of Congress, awaited the interest of President Thomas Jefferson before becoming effective.

Notes on Debates

MS (LC: Madison Papers). For a description of the manuscript of Notes on Debates, see *Papers of Madison*, V, 231-34.

Friday Jany. 24th.

Some days prior to this sundry papers had been laid before Congress by the war office, shewing that a Cargo of Supplies which had arrived at Wilmi[n]gton for the British & German Prisoners of war under a pass-port from the Commander in cheif and which were thence proceeding by land to their distination, had been siezed by sundry persons in Chester County under a law of Pennsa. wch. required in Such cases a licence from the Executive authority, who exposed to confiscation all articles not *necessary* for the prisoners, & referrd. the question of necessity to the judgment of its own Magistrates.[1] Congress unanimously considered the violation of the passport issued under the authority as an encroachment on their constitutional & essential rights; but being disposed to get over the difficulty as gently as possible appointed a Come. consisting of Mr. Rutlidge, Mr. Wolcot & Mr. Madison to confer with the Executive of Pa. on the subject.[2] In the first conference the Executive represented to the Committee the concern they felt at the incident, their disposition to respect & support the dignity & rights of the fœderal Sovereignty; and the embarrassments in which they were involved by a recent & present law of the State to which they were bound to conform.[3] The Come. observed to them that the power of granting passports for the purpose in question being inseparable from the general power of war delegated, to Congress, & being essential for conducting the war, it could not be expected that Congress wd. acquiesce in any infractions upon it; that as Pa. had concurred in the alienation of this power to Congress, any law whatever contravening this was necessaryly void, and cd. impose no obligation on the Executive.[4] The latter requested further time for a consideration of the case & laid it before the Legislature then sitting; in consequence of which a Come. of their body was appd. jointly with the Executive to confer with the Committee of Congress.[5] In this 2d. conference[6] the first remarks made by the Come. of Congress were repeated. The Come. of the Legislature expressed an unwillingness to intrench on the jurisdiction of Congress, but some of them seemed not to be fully satisfied that the law of the State did so. Mr. Montgomery lately a member of Congress[7] observed that altho' the general power of war was given to Congress yet that the mode of exercising that power might be regulated by the States in any manner which wd. not frustrate the power, & which their policy might require. To this it was answered that if Congress had the power at all, it could not either by the Articles of Confederation or the reason of things admit of such a controuling power in each of the States, & that to admit such a construction wd. be a virtual surrender to the States of the whole federal power relative to war; the most essential of all the powers delegated to Congress.[8] The Come of the Legisre: represented as the great difficulty with them, that even a repeal of the law wd. not remedy the case without a retrospective law which their Constitution wd. not admit of,[9] & expressed an earnest desire that some accomodating plan might be hit upon. They proposed in order to induce the siezors to wave their appeal to the law of the State, that Congress wd. allow them[10] to appt. one of two persons who sd. have authority to examine into the supplies & decide whether they comprehended any articles that were not warranted by the passport. The Come. of Congress answered that whatever obstacles might lie in the way of redress by the Legislature,[11] if no redress proceeded from them, equal difficulties wd. lie on the other side, since Congress in case of a confiscation of the supplies under the law which the omission of some formalities reqd. by it wd. probably produce, would be obliged by honor & good faith to indemnify the Enemy for their loss out of the common Treasury;[12] that the other States wd. probably demand a reimbursemnt. to the U. S. from Pa. & that it was impossible to say to what extremity the affair might be carried. They observed to the Come. of the Legre. and the Executive, that Congress altho' disposed to make all allowances, and particularly in the case of a law passed for a purpose recommended by themselves,[13] yet they cd. not condescend to any expedient which in any manner departed from the respect wch. they owed to themselves & to the articles of Union. The Come. of Congress however suggested that as the only expedient wch. wd. get rid of the clashing of the power of Congress & the Law of the State, wd. be the dissuading the siezors from their appeal to the latter, it was probable that if the Siezors wd. apply to Congress for Redress that such steps wd. [be] taken as wd. be satisfactory. This hint was embraced & both the Executive & the Come. of the Legre. promised to use their influence with the persons of most influence among the siezors for that purpose. In consequence thereof a Memorial from (see Journal) was sent in to Congress, commited to the same Come. of Congress,[14] & their report of this day agreed to in wch. the Presidt. of Pa. is *requested* to appt. one of the referees.[15] It is proper to observe that this business was conducted with great temper & harmony, & that Presidt. Dickenson in particular manifested throughout the course of it, as great a desire to save the rights & dignity of Congress as those of the State over which he presided. As a few of the Siezors only were parties to the Memorial to Congress, it is still uncertain whe[the]r others may not adhere to their claims under the law in wch. case all the embarrassments will be revived.[16]

In a late report which had been drawn up by Mr. Hamilton & made to Congress, in answr. to a Memorial from the Legislatre. of Pa. (see   ) among other things shewing the impossibility Congress had been under of payg. their Credrs. it was observed that the aid afforded by the Ct. of France had been appropriated by that Court at the time to the immediate use of the army. This clause was objected to as unnecessary, & as dishonorable to Congress. The fact also was controverted. Mr. Hamilton & Mr. Fitzimmons justified the expediency of retaing it, in order to justify Congress the more completely in failing in their engagements to the public Creditors. Mr. Wilson & Mr. Madison proposed to strike out the words appropriated by France, & substitute the words applied by Congress to the immediate & necessary support of the army.[17] This proposition wd. have been readily approved had it not appeared on examination that in one or two small instances, & particularly in the paymt. of the balance due to A. Lee Esqr. other applications had been made of the aid in question.[18] The report was finally recommitted.[19]

A letter from the Supernt. of Finance was received & read, acquaintg Congress that as the danger from the Enemy which led him into the Dept. was disappearing & he saw little prospect of provision being made without which injustice wd. take place of which he wd. never be the Minister, he proposed not to serve longer than may next, unless proper provision sd. be made. This letter made a deep & solemn impression on Congress.[20] It was considered as the effect of dispondence in Mr. Morris of seeing justice done to the public Credtrs. or the public finances placed on an honorable establishmt; as a Source of fresh hopes to the enemy when known, as ruinous both to domestic & foreign Credit: & as producing a vacancy which noone knew how to fill & which no fit man wd. venture to accept. Mr. Ghoram[21] after observing that the Administration of Mr. Morris had inspired great confidence and expectation in his State, & expressing his extreme regret at the event, moved that the letter sd. be committed. This was opposed as unnecessary & nugatory by Mr. Wilson since the known firmness of Mr. Morris after deliberately taking a step wd. render all attempts to dissuade him fruitless: and that as the Memorial from the Army had brought the subject of funds before Congress, there was no other object for a Comme.[22] The motion to commit was disagreed to. Mr. Wilson then moved that a day might be assigned for the consideration of the letter. Agst. the propriety of this it was observd. by Mr. Madison that the same reasons which opposed a Commitmt. opposed the assignment of day: Since Congress cd. not however anxious their wishes or alarming their apprehensions might be, condescend to solicit Mr. Morris even if there were a chance of its being successful; & since it wd. be equally improper for Congress, however cogent a motive it might add in the mind of every member, to struggle for substantial funds, to let such a consideration appear in their public acts, on that subject. The motion of Mr. Wilson was not pressed.

Congress supposing that a knowledge of Mr. Morris' intentions wd. anticipate the ills likely to attend his actual resignation, ordered his letter to be kept secret.[23]

Nothing being said to day as to the mode of insertion of the Treaty & Convention with the States General the Secy. proceeded in retaining both columns.[24]

In consequence of the report to the Grand Comme on the memorial from the army, by the Subcomme, the following report was made by the former to Congs. and came under consideration to day.[25]

"*The Grand Comme having considered the Contents of the Meml. presented by the army, find that they comprehend five different articles:[26]

1. present pay

2. a settlemt. of accts. of the arrearages of pay and security for what is due.[27]

3. A commutation of the half pay allowed by differt. resolutions of Congress for an equivalent in gross:[28]

4. A settlemt. of the accts. of deficiencies of rations & compensation.[29]

5. A settlemt. of accts. of deficiencies of cloathing & compensation.[30]

The Comme are of opinion with respt. to the 1st. that the Superintendt. of finance be directed, conformable to the measures already taken for that purpose, as soon as the State of the public finances will permit, to make such payt. & in such manner as he shall think proper till the further order of Congress.[31]

With respect to the 2d. art: so far as relates to the settlemt. of accts, that the several States be called upon to compleat the settlemt., without delay, with their respective lines of the army up to the first day of Aug: 1780: that the Superintendant be also directed to take such measures as shall appear to him most proper & effectual for accomplishing the object in the most equitable & satisfactory manner, havg. regard to former resolutions of Congs. & to the settlemts. made in consequence thereof. and so far as relates to the providing of security for what shall be found due on such settlemt.[32] Resolved that the troops of the United States in common with all the Creditrs. of the same, have an undoubted right to expect such security, and that Congress will make every effort in their power to obtain from the respective States, *general* & substantial funds adequate to the object of funding the whole debt of the U. S.[33] and that Congs. ought to enter upon an immediate & full con-

* drawn by Col: Hamilton

sideration of the nature of such funds & the most likely mode of obtaining them.

With respect to the 3d. Article the Comme. are of opinion that it will be expedient for Congs. to leave it to the option of all officers entitled to half pay, either to preserve their claim to that provision as it now stands by the several resolutions of Congs. upon that subject or to accept   years full pay to be paid to them in one year after the conclusion of the war in money or placed upon good funded security bearing an annual interest of 6 prCt.[34] provided that the allowance to widows & orphans of such officers as have died or been killed or may die or be killed in the service during the war shall remain as established by the resolution of the   day of   [35]

With respect to the 4 & 5 Art: the Come. beg leave to delay their report untill they have obtained more precise information than they now possess on the subject"

The 1st. Clause of this report relative to immediate pay passed without opposition.[36] The Supt. had agreed to make out 1 months' pay. Indeed long before the arrival of the deputies from the army he had made contingent & secret provision for that purpose; and to ensure it now he meant if necessary to draw bills on the late application for loans. The words "conformable to measures already taken" referred to the above secret provisn, and were meant to shew that the payment to the army did not originate in the Memol. but in an antecedent attention to the wants of the army.[37]

In the discussion of the 2d. clause, the epoch of Aug: 1780 was objected to, by the Eastern delegates. Their States havg. settled with their lines down to later periods, they wishd now to obtain the Sanction of Congress to them.[38] After some debate, a compromise was proposed by Mr. Hamilton by substituting the last day of Decr. 1780. This was agreed to without opposition altho several members disliked it.[39] The latter part of the clause beginning with the word Resolved &c. was considered as a very solemn point, and the basis of the plans by which the public engagements were to be fulfilled & the union cemented.[40] A motion was made by Mr. Bland to insert after the words "in their power" the words, "consistent with the Articles of Confederation["]. This amendment as he explained it was not intended to contravene the idea of funds extraneous to the federal articles, but to leave those funds for a consideration subsequent to providing Constitutional ones.[41] Mr. Arnold however eagerly 2ded. it.[42] No question however was taken on it, Congress deeming it proper to postpone the matter till the next day, as of the most solemn nature; and to have as full a representation as possible. With this view & to get rid of Mr. Bland's motion, they adjourned; & ordering all the members not present & in town to be summoned.[43]

1 On 27 November 1782 Washington issued a passport to the British flag-of-truce ship "Amazon," then in New York Harbor, to protect her from capture on her voyage to Wilmington, Del., with a cargo of clothing and other articles for the British and German prisoners of war quartered in Pennsylvania, Maryland, and Virginia (Fitzpatrick, *Writings of Washington*, XXV, 376–77). The wagons, into which the goods were transferred at Wilmington, were stopped at the Pennsylvania line by the sheriff and other officials of Chester County, Pa. (n. 14). Although they permitted some of the heavily laden vehicles to proceed toward their destinations, they impounded "by a due course of law" most of the commodities, claiming that both their nature and volume made clear an intent to sell them illegally rather than to use them for the relief of the approximately 6,100 prisoners of war. In view of the Pennsylvania statute "for the more effectual suppression of all intercourse and commerce with the enemies of the United States of America," the Chester County officers could strongly defend their action (NA: PCC, No. 149, II, 229–30, 233–40, 243, 245–69).

2 On 17 January 1783, after receiving a protest from the British assistant deputy quartermaster general who had accompanied the cargo of the "Amazon," Major William Jackson, the assistant secretary at war, laid the matter before Congress. Before adjourning that day, Congress appointed John Rutledge, chairman, Oliver Wolcott, and JM a committee to confer with President John Dickinson and the Supreme Executive Council of Pennsylvania (NA: PCC, No. 185, III, 52; No. 186, fol. 80). Besides violating the ninth article of the Articles of Confederation, delegating to Congress "the sole and exclusive right and power of determining peace and war" and "of establishing rules for deciding in all cases, what captures on land or water shall be legal," the action of the Chester County officials transgressed the Articles of War and the law of nations, manifested disrespect for Washington's passport, and invited British retaliation against American prisoners of war confined in the noisome jails of New York City or aboard hulks in its harbor. This last was a practical consideration which would appeal strongly to Dickinson and the executive council, for they had been endeavoring since November 1702 to provide Pennsylvania soldiers incarcerated in New York with food, clothing, and blankets (*JCC*, XIX, 217; *Pa. Archives*, 1st ser., IX, 674–75, 677–78, 756–57, 763; *Colonial Records of Pa.* [16 vols.; Harrisburg, 1851–53], XIII, 451, 446, 459, 481, 483).

3 The first conference of the Rutledge committee with Dickinson and the Supreme Executive Council occurred on 17 January (*ibid.*, XIII, 482). For the statute of Pennsylvania, see n. 1, above.

4 See n. 2. Pennsylvania "had concurred in the alienation" by ratifying the Articles of Confederation on 5 March 1778 (*JCC*, XI, 668). The committee in effect contended that the Articles of Confederation in the areas of its delegated powers was the supreme law of the sovereign states, that Congress in an instance of conflict between the Articles and a state statute was the final judge of the scope of authority conferred by the former and of the constitutionality of the latter, and that, if Congress held a state statute to be "void," it no longer was law and hence need not be enforced by the executive of that state. This assertion of power, uttered over four years before the Constitutional Convention of 1787 and at a time when Congress was unable to make its will effective in domestic affairs, is of marked constitutional interest.

5 The House of the Pennsylvania General Assembly convened on 15 January

1783 (*Pa. Packet,* 18 Jan. 1783). President Dickinson's message of 18 January, having been approved by the Supreme Executive Council, was delivered to the legislature two days later. Designating the issue as one of "high importance," Dickinson pointed out that, because he was obliged by his oath of office to enforce a statute which, in the judgment of Congress, violated "the laws of nations or the rights of the United States," he was "not competent" to grant "the solicited redress" (*Colonial Records of Pa.,* XIII, 482). Upon reading the message and the half-dozen documents which accompanied it, the Assembly named a committee of five members to investigate and recommend appropriate action (*Pa. Packet,* 30 Jan. 1783). In an undated letter, probably written before Dickinson drafted his message, William Bradford, Jr., attorney general of Pennsylvania, advised the senior member of the Supreme Executive Council that "any *wanton & improper* infringement" of Washington's passport would be an indictable offense "against the Law of nations" and that the "goods seized," if "necessary for the Prisoners of war," were "not contraband nor liable to condemnation" (*Pa. Archives,* 1st ser., IX, 731).

6 On 22 January Dickinson and the Supreme Executive Council reviewed for the benefit of the legislative committee what had been said at the conference on 17 January. See n. 2. The "2d conference" with the Rutledge committee took place on 23 January (*Colonial Records of Pa.,* XIII, 485–86).

7 Joseph Montgomery had last attended Congress about 1 November 1782 (*Papers of Madison,* V, 301, n. 1).

8 See n. 4.

9 That is, in seizing the goods the Chester County officials had only performed their duty to enforce the act mentioned in n. 1. Although the passage of a "retrospective law" was not specifically prohibited by any provision in the Pennsylvania constitution of 1776, that instrument did not confer the power to enact such legislation. Section 15, furthermore, provided that laws proposed in one session of the General Assembly could not be passed until the next session, "except on occasions of sudden necessity," which in the present instance might not be deemed by the majority of legislators to have occurred (Francis Newton Thorpe, comp. and ed., *The Federal and State Constitutions, Colonial Charters, and Other Organic Laws of the States, Territories, and Colonies Now or Heretofore Forming the United States of America* [7 vols.; Washington, 1909], V, 3086).

10 For the names of some of "the siezors," see n. 14. The word "them" stands for the Pennsylvania legislature.

11 The phrase following "lie" is interlineated above a canceled "against a retrospective law."

12 Most of the prisoners of war interned in Pennsylvania, Maryland, and Virginia were officers and soldiers surrendered by Cornwallis at Yorktown, Va., on 19 October 1781. By Article V of the Articles of Capitulation, the British army headquarters at New York City had been assured that, upon application, passports would be granted to enable the captives to be supplied with "cloathing and other necessaries" (Benjamin Franklin Stevens, comp. and ed., *The Campaign in Virginia, 1781* (2 vols. [London, 1888], II, 200–201).

13 JM refers to the ordinance of Congress of 21 June 1782 (*JCC,* XXII, 340–41). See also *Papers of Madison,* III, 338; 339, n. 3; IV, 351–52; 353, n. 11; V, 311, n. 12.

14 The minutes of the Pennsylvania Supreme Executive Council for 23 January 1783 make clear that "a draft of a representation to Congress" was proposed, but the share, if any, of the Rutledge committee in composing the document is indeterminable. Before the council adjourned, Persifor Frazer, John Hannum, and Joseph Gardner, three of "the siezors," were admitted to the council chamber. They signed the "representation" and may have helped to draft it (*Colonial Records of Pa.,* XIII, 485–86). This document, now missing, was laid before Congress and re-

ferred to the Rutledge committee on 23 January (NA: PCC, No. 185, III, 52). The committee reported the next day (*JCC*, XXIV, 82–83).

Persifor Frazer (1736–1792), merchant and ironmaster, was a member of the Chester County Committee of Safety at the outbreak of the Revolution. Commissioned a captain of the 5th Pennsylvania Battalion, continental line, in January 1776, he subsequently advanced to the grade of lieutenant colonel. During the Brandywine campaign the British plundered his home and captured him and Hannum. He escaped and rejoined the army in March 1778, only to resign in October of the same year. Proffered the office of clothier general of the continental army in July 1779, he declined, but in May 1782 he became brigadier general of the Pennsylvania militia and so remained until the end of the war. He was treasurer of Chester County, 1781; member of the General Assembly, 1781–1782; commissioner to the Wyoming Valley, 1785; and justice of the state Court of Common Pleas and register of wills from 1786 until his death.

Like Frazer, John Hannum (1742–1799) was a large landowner and served in various official capacities in Chester County during most of his adult life. He, too, had attained the rank of lieutenant colonel when he resigned his commission in the Pennsylvania state line. He was a member of the state legislature, 1781–1785, and of the state convention of 1787 to consider the Federal Constitution (*Colonial Records of Pa.*, XII, 477; *Pa. Mag. Hist. and Biog.*, XI [1887], 213–14).

Dr. Joseph Gardner (1752–1794) raised a company of volunteers in 1776 and commanded the 4th Battalion of militia in Chester County. He was a member of the county Committee of Safety, 1776–1777, of the General Assembly, 1776–1778, of the state Supreme Executive Council, 1779, and of the Continental Congress, 1784–1785. He thereafter resumed the practice of medicine in Philadelphia until 1792, and in Elkton, Md., until his death.

15 *JCC*, XXIV, 82–83. The committee's report, in Rutledge's hand, ordered the assistant secretary at war and requested President Dickinson and the Supreme Executive Council to have "proper persons" examine the undelivered cargo of the "Amazon" for the purpose of determining whether the passport of the vessel had been violated. The assistant secretary at war was also directed to submit a report of this survey, of a similar inquiry into the portion of the cargo already delivered, and of the number of "British or German prisoners of war" to whom presumably all "the cloathing and other necessaries imported in the said vessel" had been consigned. Upon receiving from Charles Thomson a copy of these resolutions, President Dickinson in Council immediately complied with the request (*Pa. Archives*, IX, 741–42, *Colonial Records of Pa.*, XIII, 490–91).

16 Although the three "Slezors," identified in n. 14, stated that their memorial to Congress was "in behalf of themselves and others," these "others" soon justified JM's remark that the outcome of the issue was "uncertain." See JM Notes, 13 Feb. 1783.

17 On 4 December 1782 a committee comprising Rutledge, Hamilton, and JM had been appointed to confer with a committee of the legislature of Pennsylvania in an attempt, temporarily successful, to prevent a diversion of the financial quota requisitioned from that state for the Confederation treasury to the payment of overdue debts owed to citizens of Pennsylvania by Congress (*Papers of Madison*, V, 362; 365, n. 9; 366, and nn. 19, 23, 26; 367, n. 29). By referring to the conference and to "subsequent information" warning that the Pennsylvania General Assembly at its next meeting would "resume the plan which they had suspended," JM's notes for 6 December 1782 strongly suggest that the Rutledge committee had reported back to Congress, either orally or in a document now lost, on or about 5 December 1782 (*ibid.*, V, 373). This probability, in turn, virtually eliminates the "late report which had been drawn up by Mr. Hamilton" as the one which was still being debated on 24 January 1783.

The action of the Rutledge committee, which had been appointed only to meet an instant emergency, was not the formal response by Congress to the Pennsylvania legislature's memorials of 28 August and 12 November 1782. That response was intended to be prepared by the committee named on 20 November, with Daniel Carroll as chairman, to draft a reply to the "Memorials of the *Assembly of Pennsylvania* relative to the liquidation of public accounts and payment of interest for debts due to the citizens of the state" (*JCC*, XXIII, 745, n. 2). Probably early in December, Congress appointed Hamilton to this committee in the place of James Duane, a delegate from New York who had returned home.

In his committee book, Charles Thomson noted only that the Carroll committee reported on 30 January 1783 (NA: PCC, No. 186, fol. 68). This report is in the hand of Thomas FitzSimons, rather than in Hamilton's, and contains no statement approximating the words which JM in his notes on 24 January attributed to Hamilton (NA: PCC, No. 20, II, 141–49; *JCC*, XXIV, 99–105; JM Notes, 30 Jan. 1783, and n. 1). Although this attribution by JM and his account of the debate upon the "late report" by Hamilton, followed by its recommittal to the Carroll committee on 24 January, apparently must remain unsupported because confirmatory evidence, including the Hamilton draft, is missing, the entry by JM in his notes for that day cannot be dismissed as merely fictional.

Arguing principally from the incorrect premise that the report of 30 January was written by his father, John Church Hamilton accused Madison of falsifying his notes by having Alexander Hamilton include in that report, or in an earlier version of it, a statement about "the Ct. of France" appropriating its loans to the United States in 1782 "to the immediate use of the army." According to the son, JM thereby charged Alexander Hamilton with "stating an untruth, and justifying it on the score of expediency." The younger Hamilton also stressed that his father's alleged phraseology, having remained unaltered because the Wilson-JM amendment failed of adoption, should appear, but does not, in the report on 30 January (John C. Hamilton, ed., *The Works of Alexander Hamilton* [7 vols.; New York, 1850–51], II, 230–35; John C. Hamilton, *History of the Republic*, II, 361–63 n.). In this John C. Hamilton made another erroneous assumption. Unless specifically instructed by Congress to the contrary, a committee to which a report was recommitted had complete liberty to alter its phraseology in whole or in part before resubmitting it.

18 Clearly JM and James Wilson did not mean to refute Hamilton but only to replace his statement with one which could not be interpreted as undue subservience to France for allocating her loan "to the immediate use of the army" without reference to Congress. Even before King Louis XVI had loaned 6,000,000 livres, Congress had issued drafts upon the hoped-for amount. Furthermore, Lieutenant Colonel John Laurens and his assistant, Major William Jackson, while on their mission to obtain large quantities of military goods for the continental army, had succeeded in France and the Netherlands only because the cost had been assessed against the loan or because King Louis XVI had guaranteed payment if John Adams should be unable to borrow from Dutch bankers (*Papers of Madison*, II, 256–60; 260, n. 9; III, 245, n. 5; 247; 248, n. 2; IV, 407–9; V, 121, n. 3; 200). For the recompense of Arthur Lee from the French loan, see *ibid.*, V, 299, n. 5. For other examples of how this fund was occasionally levied upon for non-military expenditures, see *ibid.*, V, 21, n. 4; *JCC*, XXII, 291–93.

19 See nn. 17 and 18, above; JM Notes, 30 Jan. 1783, and n. 1.

20 Robert Morris no doubt hoped that his letter, by adding to the pressures already exerted by the memorial from the army and by the threat of Pennsylvania and other states to pay their own citizens who were creditors of the United States, would impel Congress and the state legislatures to agree upon and enforce a plan for yielding adequate revenue to the Confederation treasury. The failure to ratify

the 5 per cent impost amendment to the Articles of Confederation, the delinquency
of most of the states in paying their financial quotas, the continuing resort by Congress to drafts upon funds of an uncertain amount in Europe, and the probable
belief of many delegates that the personal credit and skill of Morris, as superintendent of finance, were indispensable, also account for the "deep & solemn impression"
made by his letter. In his view the financial situation was becoming "utterly in-
supportable," at odds with his "Ideas of Integrity," and fast rendering impossible
of attainment "the last essential Work of our glorious Revolution," that is, the
funding of the public debts "on solid Revenues." Unless "effectual Measures" for
this purpose were taken, he would retire on 31 May (NA: PCC, No. 137, II, 115–
16). See also Randolph to JM, 3 Jan., and n. 2; JM Notes, 7 Jan., n. 4; 13 Jan., and
nn. 5, 17; 28 Jan., and n. 40; 4–5 Mar., and nn.; Conference with Morris, 10 Jan.,
n. 5; Randolph to JM, 15 Jan. 1783, n. 13; Clarence L. Ver Steeg, *Robert Morris,*
pp 169–72, 248, nn. 23, 25.

[21] Nathaniel Gorham of Massachusetts.

[22] For the grand committee appointed to consider and report on the memorial
from the army, see JM Notes, 6 Jan., and nn. 2, 9; 7 Jan.; 9–10 Jan.; 13 Jan., and n.
17; 17 Jan. 1783.

[23] The injunction of secrecy explains why Thomson did not enter the subject in
the official journal intended for publication.

[24] Report on Treaty, 23 Jan., and n. 14; JM Notes, 23 Jan. 1783, and nn. 6, 7.

[25] Above "consideration," JM interlineated and canceled "yesterday &." The
subcommittee, comprising Hamilton, chairman, JM, and Rutledge, had been appointed by the grand committee on 13 January, immediately following its meeting
with the deputation from the army (JM Notes, 13 Jan. 1783). Although neither the
entire text of the subcommittee's report nor the date of its presentation to the
grand committee is known, the debate in Congress on the grand committee's report,
which had been submitted on 22 January, opened the next day (NA: PCC, No. 186,
fol. 78; JM Notes, 25 Jan. 1783, n. 9; Burnett, *Letters,* VII, 20, 35 n.). Unlike JM's
notes, the journal of Congress fails to mention the debate on the twenty-third and
twenty-fourth and reproduces the report of the committee on 25 January, when
two "articles," the first, and the second as amended, were adopted (JCC, XXIV,
93–95). The close approximation of JM's account, most of it verbatim, with the
report in Hamilton's hand strongly suggests that JM made a copy from Hamilton's
draft (Syrett and Cooke, *Papers of Hamilton,* III, 243–44). See also n. 26.

[26] *Papers of Madison,* V, 474, n. 8; JM Notes, 13 Jan. 1783, and n. 21. The quotation mark matching the one at the outset of this paragraph is at the close of the
later paragraph beginning, "With respect to the 4 & 5 Art."

[27] See n. 32, below.

[28] JM Notes, 13 Jan. 1783, nn. 11, 18. See also JCC, XVII, 771–73; XVIII, 958–62;
XX, 541; XXIII, 747–48, 748, n. 1, 797–98, 798, n. 1.

[29] Congress had resolved on 24 August 1780 that officers were entitled to subsist-
ence money in lieu of rations withheld, "according to the just cost of such rations"
(JCC, XVII, 726, 771–73). See also JCC, XXI, 1012–13; XXII, 206; XXIII, 737, and
n., 759–60.

[30] The basic ordinances prescribing the clothing or the money in lieu of clothing
to which officers of each rank were entitled, had been enacted on 17 and 18 August
and 25 November 1779 (JCC, XIV, 973, 978; XV, 1304–6).

[31] See n. 20, and especially the citations at its close.

[32] The ordinance of 12 August 1780 prescribed that whatever was due to officers
and soldiers for service prior to 1 August of that year should be paid by their
respective states (or by Congress in case they did not "belong to the quota of any
state") in the old continental or state currency, with appropriate adjustments for

depreciation. The ordinance further stipulated that service on or after 1 August should be paid by the United States with the new 40-for-1 currency emitted in accordance with the resolutions of 18 March of that year (*JCC*, XVII, 725–27). Although no distinction was made in the army memorial between the pre- and post-1 August 1780 medium of payment, the signers stressed that depreciation had rendered almost worthless the "settlements" and "securities" provided by the states in recompense of part of the service performed during the "four years past" (NA: PCC, No. 42, VI, 59–64; *JCC*, XXIV, 291).

33 See n. 20.

34 JM Notes, 25 Jan. 1783.

35 24 August 1780 (NA: PCC, No. 21, fols. 247–50; *JCC*, XVII, 771–73).

36 JM interlienated "without opposition" above a canceled "yesterday." Since this "Clause" was passed on 25 January, it is possible that the interlineation was made as late as 26 January 1783 (JM Notes, 25 Jan. 1783; *JCC*, XXIV, 95, n. 1). See also n. 25, above.

37 JM Notes, 7 Jan., and n. 4; 9–10 Jan., and n. 9; Conference with Morris, 10 Jan. 1783, and n. 5.

38 See n. 32. On 25 January reinstatement of 1 August was opposed by the unanimous vote of New Hampshire, Massachusetts, and Rhode Island (*JCC*, XXIV, 94).

39 John C. Hamilton wrote later that, in view of the stipulation of the ordinance of 12 August 1780 (n. 32, above) and in view of Alexander Hamilton's vote to reinstate 1 August, the "probability is more than questionable" that Madison's ascription of the compromise proposal to Hamilton was accurate (*History of the Republic*, II, 358 n.). Provided that the army would eventually be recompensed in the new currency at 40-to-1, even though the market ratio of the money to specie was far less favorable, a deferment of five months in the time of starting payment in that currency obviously would impose a considerable financial loss upon at least some of the officers and men. Recognizing this fact, John C. Hamilton implied that Madison had deliberately charged Alexander Hamilton, a veteran, with favoring a breach of contract detrimental to his brother officers and the troops. Although Madison, of course, may have erred in his notes, John C. Hamilton should have mentioned that the vote of his father to reinstate 1 August was on 25 January, after he had conferred again with Robert Morris. See JM Notes, 25 Jan. 1783, and n. 3.

40 The resolution, set off in a separate paragraph in the journal of Congress (*JCC*, XXIV, 94–95), is the final sentence of JM's paragraph above, beginning "With respect to the 2d. art."

41 Upon returning from Virginia, Theodorick Bland had resumed his seat in Congress on 22 or 23 January.

42 Jonathan Arnold of Rhode Island.

43 In accordance with custom, President Elias Boudinot probably directed Charles Thomson, the secretary, to dispatch Robert Patton, doorkeeper and "messenger" of Congress, to inform the absentees, "Gentlemen, your attendance is desired in Congress" tomorrow (*JCC*, X, 386–89). Although the number of delegates in attendance on 24 January is unknown, the thirty-one present the next day permitted eleven of the thirteen states to vote effectively (*JCC*, XXIV, 94). Congress was not empowered by the Articles of Confederation either to compel the attendance of a delegate or to expel him for breaking its own rules. As had recently been discovered in the case of David Howell, the only method of controlling a refractory member was to condemn his conduct to the government of his own state or to publish in the official journal a censure of his conduct (*Papers of Madison*, V, 411, and n. 4; 419–20; 420, nn. 4, 6; 421, n. 10; 422, 423; 424, n. 7).

Notes on Debates

MS (LC: Madison Papers). For a description of the manuscript of Notes on Debates, see *Papers of Madison*, V, 231–34.

Saturday. Jany. 25.

The Secy. of Congress havg. suggested to a member that the Contract with the Ct. of France specifying the sums Due from the U. S. altho' extremely generous on the part of the former had been ratifyed without any such acknowledgmts. by the latter, that this was the first instance in which such acknowlegts. had been omitted, & that the omission wd. be singularly improper at a time when we were Soliciting further aids; these observations being made to Congress, the ratification was reconsidered, and the words "impressed with &c. . . inserted.[1]

The rept on the memorial was resumed. By Mr. Hamilton, Mr. Fitzimmons & one or two others who had conversed with Mr. Morris on the change of the last day of Decr. for the   day of Augst.[2] it was suggested that the change entirely contravened the measures pursued by his department;[3] and moved for a reconsideration of it in order to enquire into the subject. Without going into details they urged this as a reason sufficient. The Eastern delegates, altho' they wished for unanimity & system in future proceedings relative to our funds & finances were very stiff in retaining the vote wch. coincided with the steps taken by their Constituents.[4] Of this much complaint was made. Mr. Rutlidge on this occasion alledging that Congress ought not to be led by general suggestions derived from the office of finance joined by Mr. Gervais, voted agst. the reconsideration. The consequence was th[a]t S. Carola. was divided & six votes only in favr. of the Reconsideration.[5] Mr. Hamilton havg. expressed his regret at the negative & explained more exactly the interference of the change of the Epoch with the measures & plans of the Office of Finance wch. had limited all State advances & settlemts. to Aug: 1780; Mr. Rutledge acknowledged the sufficiency of the reasons & at his instance the latter date was reinstated. On this 2d. question Cont. also voted for Augst. .[6]

The   day of August being re-instated before question on the whole paragraph was taken Mr. Ghorum objected to the word "general" before funds as ambiguous, and it was struck out; not however as improper if referring to all the States, & not to all objects of taxation. Without this word the clause passed unanimously, even Rhode Island concurring in it.[7]

Congress proceeded to the 3d. clause, relative to the commutation of half pay.[8] A motion was made by Mr. Hamilton to fill the blank with "Six." this was in conformity to tables of Dr. Price, estimating the officers on the average of good lives.[9] Liberality in the rate was urged by several as necessary to give Satisfaction & prevent a refusal of the offer. For this motion there were 6 ayes 5 noes; the Southern States & N.Y. being in the affirmative the Eastern & N.J. in the negative. Col: Bland proposed 6½. erroneously supposing the negative of 6. to have proceeded from its being too low.[10] It was on the contrary rather doubtful whether the East: States wd. concur in any arrangemt. on this head; so averse were they to what they call pensions. Several having calculated that the annual amount of half-pay was between 4 & 500,000 Drs, and the interest of the gross sum funded at the rate of 6 years, nearly ⅔ of that sum,[11] Congress were struck with the necessity of proceeding with more caution & for that purpose committed the report to a Committee of 5. Mr. Osgood, Mr. Fitzimmons, Mr. Gervais, Mr. Hamilton & Mr. Wilson.[12]

on the motion of Mr. Wilson Monday next was assigned for the consideration of the Resolu: in the 2d. clause of the Rept. on the Memorial from the army. He observed that this was necessary to prevent the resolution from being like many others—vox et preterea nihil.[13]

---

[1] On 22 January 1783 Congress ratified the contract, concluded between Franklin and the Comte de Vergennes on 16 July 1782, "for ascertaining the sums of money advanced on loan by his Majesty to the United States, and settling the terms of payment." As printed in the official journal of 22 January the first sentence of the ratifying statement includes the insertion of 25 January, mentioned by JM: "NOW KNOW YE, That we the said United States in Congress assembled, impressed with a most lively sense of the generosity and affection manifested by his Most Christian Majesty in the above contract, have ratified and confirmed, and by these presents do ratify and confirm the said contract, and every article and clause thereof" (JCC, XXIV, 63–64). Charles Thomson, the "Secy," may have justified his suggestion by citing the "acknowledgmts," among others, of 4 May 1778, 13 June 1781, and 8 February 1782 (JCC, XI, 457–58; XX, 638–39; XXII, 68–70). For JM's recognition of the generosity of King Louis XVI, see Papers of Madison, V, 157, 159. For the need to seek additional loans from him, see ibid., V, 99; JM Notes, 9–10 Jan., and n. 14; 13 Jan. 1783.

[2] JM Notes, 24 Jan. 1783, and nn. 32, 39.

[3] Robert Morris' efforts to effect a financial accounting with each state and his confidential plans to secure money to pay the army were premised, insofar as the debt owed the officers and troops was concerned, upon the resolution of 12 August 1780 (JCC, XVII, 725–26; JM Notes, 7 Jan. 1783, and n. 4). For the general context of Morris' objection to the change of date, see Clarence L. Ver Steeg, Robert Morris, pp. 165–66.

[4] JM Notes, 24 Jan. 1783, n. 38.

[5] The official journal of Congress for 25 January records no tally.

[6] *JCC*, XXIV, 94. See also n. 3, above. Following the dots, JM wrote, "*Insert the note with this mark here, from last page." The editors have followed his directions and also omitted the asterisk with which he began the paragraph on the "last page" of his notes for 25 January.

[7] In the official journal "the whole paragraph" is broken into two paragraphs, both bearing upon the second article of the army memorial relating to "A settlement of accounts of the arrearages of pay and security for what is due." The first of the two paragraphs centered upon "the arrearages" and contained the date which had been at issue. The second paragraph, after agreeing that all the creditors of the United States had "an undoubted right to expect" security for their repayment, pledged that Congress would "make every effort in their power" to obtain "substantial funds, adequate to the object of funding the whole debt" and would "enter upon an immediate and full consideration of the nature of such funds, and the most likely mode of obtaining them" (*JCC*, XXIV, 93–95). In his notes of 24 January 1783 (*q.v.*), JM combined the paragraphs.

Unlike the text printed in the official journal, the much corrected manuscript of the report, in Hamilton's hand, shows a deleted "general and" before "substantial funds" (NA: PCC, No. 21, fols. 319–22). The objection of Nathaniel Gorham to the inclusion of the adjective "general" may have resulted from concern lest other delegates subsequently point to the word as a pledge justifying a revival of the 5 per cent impost amendment with its provisions unchanged. See JM Notes, 29 Jan. 1783. The vote of the Rhode Island delegates especially impressed JM in view of their recent insistence that foreign loans would supply sufficient income and in view of the refusal of their state to ratify the proposed 5 per cent impost amendment to the Articles of Confederation. See *Papers of Madison*, V, 372; 374, n. 12; 407, n. 1.

[8] The committee proposed that any officer entitled to half pay for life after the war should be allowed to choose whether he preferred this guarantee or one of full pay for an unspecified number of years, to begin one year following the termination of the struggle (*JCC*, XXIV, 95).

[9] A pamphlet entitled *Observations on the Expectations of Lives, the increase of mankind, the influence of great towns on population, and particularly the state of London, with respect to healthfulness and number of inhabitants* . . . written by Richard Price (1723–1791) and published in 1769 in London. Price, a moral and political philosopher, dissenting clergyman in London, and opponent of British policies toward America before the Revolution, was a close friend of Benjamin Franklin and wrote this essay in the form of a letter to him. By "good lives," JM meant those who were likely to live at least to the term assigned as the average expectation at their ages (*Oxford English Dictionary* [1933 ed.], VI, 261). According to Major General Henry Knox, the subcommittee reported to the grand committee "that twelve years was a mean life of the ages of the officers of the Army, and that six whole years' pay was equal, to the country and the army, to the half-pay for life" (JM Notes, 24 Jan. 1783, n. 25; Burnett, *Letters*, VII, 35 n.).

[10] Hamilton's motion, its defeat, and Bland's proposal are not mentioned in the official journal.

[11] The committee proposed an interest rate of 6 per cent annually on "good funded security" (*JCC*, XXIV, 95). If the annual "gross sum" of full pay is taken to be $800,000, the interest on this sum for six years would be $288,000 or slightly over two-thirds of the annual half-pay estimated at $400,000.

[12] Lacking enough "precise information," the grand committee requested more time before making recommendations on the army memorial's fourth and fifth articles asking, respectively, for "A settlement of the accounts of deficiencies of rations and compensation" and "A settlement of the accounts of deficiencies of cloth-

ing and compensation" (*JCC*, XXIV, 93–95). The matter referred to Samuel Osgood's committee was the unresolved issue of the commutation of half pay for life
into full pay for a controversial number of years (JM Notes, 4 Feb. 1783). After
"Mr. Wilson," JM wrote, "⊙ Insert here the note with this mark." The editors accordingly have inserted after "Mr. Wilson" the paragraph which JM prefaced with
"this mark" at the close of his notes for 25 January.

13 "A voice and nothing more." Upon James Wilson's motion, Congress agreed to
consider on 27 January "the means of obtaining from the several states substantial
funds, for funding the whole debt of the United States" (n. 7, above; *JCC*, XXIV,
95; JM Notes, 27 Jan. 1783).

Memorandum on Comment by Thomas Jefferson

LC (Madison Papers). Written by JM on verso of Dr. Benjamin Rush's note of "Jany. 24. 1783 Thursday Evening" to "Mr
Jefferson."

PHILADA. Jany. 25th. 1783

Mr. Jefferson informed me when he put this into my hands that he
should not deliver the letter to Mr. B. Vaughan untill a peace shall be
finally concluded; as he understood that he is a Secy to one of the
British Ministers.[1]

J. MADISON JR.

[1] Dr. Rush's note of 24 January, covering a "letter to Mr. B. Vaughan," probably
reached Jefferson the next day, on the eve of his departure from Philadelphia in the
expectation of embarking at Baltimore for France (JM to Randolph, 7 Jan. 1783,
and n. 9). Being too much occupied to acknowledge Rush's note, Jefferson left it
with JM and perhaps asked him to explain to Rush why delivery of the letter to
Vaughan might be delayed. Whether JM did so is unknown, but Jefferson was
again in Philadelphia for over six weeks, beginning on 26 February, and hence
could have orally thanked Rush for his courtesy (Boyd, *Papers of Jefferson*, VI,
253 n., 261).

In the covering note, besides wishing Jefferson "a safe voyage" and a beneficial
role as a peace commissioner, Rush remarked that his letter would introduce Jefferson, "fellow-worshipper in the temple of Science," to Vaughan, "a gentleman of
knowledge & taste, in Science," who "possesses a most extensive acquaintance
among the literati in London" (*ibid.*, VI, 223). The letter of introduction is now
missing and may have been given back to Rush by Jefferson upon his return to
Philadelphia. When Jefferson was in London in the spring of 1786, he seems to have
met Vaughan for the first time (*ibid.*, IX, 363 n.).

In the autumn of 1782 Benjamin Vaughan (1751–1835) was in Paris, commenting
upon the course of the peace negotiations in confidential dispatches to the Earl of
Shelburne. Believing that the Comte de Vergennes was outwardly supporting the
American peace commissioners but covertly opposing their demands, especially
with regard to boundaries, navigation of the Mississippi River, and the use of
Newfoundland fisheries, John Jay easily persuaded Vaughan, "strongly attached to
the American cause," to return to England on 11 September and let Shelburne

know that he could "cut the cords which tied us to France" by an immediate acknowledgment of the independence of the United States and by yielding to her
stand on those three issues (Wharton, *Revol. Dipl. Corr.*, VI, 29–32; Richard B.
Morris, *The Peacemakers*, pp. 291–93, 333–34, 337–39). Characteristic of Vaughan's
long career was his support of revolutionists, whether in the thirteen colonies, Ireland, or France, and his interest in applied science. Migrating to the United States
in 1796, he settled at Hallowell in the Maine district of Massachusetts. There he
engaged in agricultural experimentation and continued to correspond on political
and scientific topics with prominent Americans, including JM. Vaughan left portions of his large library to Harvard and Bowdoin colleges.

Notes on Debates

MS (LC: Madison Papers). For a description of the manuscript
of Notes on Debates, see *Papers of Madison*, V, 231–34.

No. VI[1]

Monday 27 Jany. 1783.

A letter of Jany 20 from Genl. Washington was rcd. notifying the
death of Lord Sterling[2] & inclosing a report of the Officer sent to apprehend Knowlton & Wells. (See   ).[3]

The following is an extract from the report "he (one Israel Smith)
further sd. that Knowlton & Wells had recd. a lettr. from Jonathan
Arnold Esqr. at Congress part of which was made public, which informed them that affairs in Congress were unfavorable to them & wd.
have them look out for themselves. What other information this letter
contained he cd. not say—I found in my March thro' the State that the
last mentioned gentleman was much in favor with all the principal men
in that State I had any conversation with"[4]

Mr. Arnold being present at the reading informed Congress that he
was surprized how such a notion should have prevailed with respect to
him; that he had never held any correspondence with either Knowlton
or Wells; and requested that he might be furnished with the extract
above. In this he was indulged without opposition. But it was generally
considered, notwithstanding his denial of the correspondence, that he
had at least at second hand, conveyed the intelligence to Vermont.[5]

A long petition was read signed as alledged by near two thousand inhabitants (but all in the same hand writing) of the territory lately in
controversy between Pa. & Va. complaining of the greivances to which
their distance from public authority exposed them & particularly of the
late law of Pena. interdicting even consultations about a new State

within its limits; and praying that Congress wd. give a sanction to their independence & admit them into the Union. The Petition lay on the table without a single motion or remark relative to it.[6] The order of the day was called for, towit the Resolution of saturday last in favor of adequate & substantial funds.[7]

This subject was introduced by Mr. Wilson with some judicious remarks on its importance & the necessity of a thorough & serious discussion of it. He observed that the U States had in the course of the revolution displayed both an unexampled activity in resisting the enemy, and an unexampled patience under the losses & calamities occasioned by the war. In one point only he said they had appeared to be deficient & that was a cheerful payment of taxes.[8] In other free Govts. it had been seen that taxation had been carried farther & more patiently borne than in States where the people were excluded from the Govts., the people considering themselves as the sovereign as well as the subject; & as receiving with one hand what they paid with the other. The peculiar repugnance of the people of the U S. to taxes he supposed proceeded first from the odious light in which they had been under the old Govt. in the habit of regarding them; 2dely. from the direct manner in wch. taxes in this Country had been laid; whereas in all other countries taxes were paid in a way that was little felt at the time.[9] That it cd. not proceed altogether from inability he said must be obvious: Nay that the ability of the U. S. was equal to the public burden might be demonstrated. According to the calculations of the best writers the inhabitants of G. B. paid before the present war at the annual rate of at least 25s. Sterlg per head. According to like calculations the inhabitants of the U. S. before the revolution paid indirectly & insensibly at the rate of at least 10s. Sterlg per head[10] According to the computed depreciation of the paper emissions, the burden insensibly borne by the inhabitants of the U. S. had amounted during the first three or four years of the war to not less than twenty Million of dollars per annum, a burden too which was the more oppressive as it fell very unequally on the people.[11] An inability therefore could not be urged as a plea for the extreme deficiency of the revenue contributed by the States, which did not amount during the past year to $\frac{1}{2}$ a million of dollars, that is to $\frac{1}{6}$ of a dollar per head.[12] Some more effectual mode of drawing forth the resources of the Country was necessary. That in particular it was necessary that such funds should be established as would enable Congress to fulfill those engagements which they had been enabled to enter into.[13] It was essential he contended that those to whom were delegated the power of making war & peace should in some way or other have the means of effectuating these objects; that as Congress had been under the necessity of contracting a large debt justice required that such funds should be placed in their hands as would discharge it; that such funds were also necessary for carrying on the war; and as Congress found themselves in their present situation destitute both of the faculty of paying debts already contracted, and of providing for future exigences, it was their duty to lay that situation before their constituents; and at least to come to an eclaircissement on the subject; he remarked that the establisht. of certain funds for payg wd. set afloat the public paper;[14] adding that a public debt resting on general funds would operate as a cement to the confederacy, and might contribute to prolong its existence, after the foreign danger ceased to counteract its tendency to dissolution[15] He concluded with moving that it be Resold.

"That it is the opinion of Congress that complete justice cannot be done to the Creditors of the United States, nor the restoration of public credit be effected, nor the future exigences of the war provided for, but by the establishment of *general* funds to be collected by Congress."[16]

This motion was seconded by Mr. Fitzimmons[.] Mr. Bland desired that Congress wd. before the discussion proceeded farther, receive a communication of sundry papers transmitted to the Virga. Delegates by the Executive of that State; two of which had relation to the question before Congress. These were 1st. a Resolution of the Genl. Assembly declaring its inability to pay more than £50,000 Va. currency towards complying with the demand of Congress. 2dly. the Act repealing the Act granting the impost of 5 PerCt. These papers were received and read.[17]

Mr. Wolcot expressed some astonishment at the inconsistency of the two acts of Va.; supposed that they had an unfavorable aspect on the business before Congress; & proposed that the latter sd. be postponed for the present.[18] He was not seconded.

Mr. Ghorum favored the general idea of the motion, animadverting on the refusal of Virga. to contribute the necessary sums & at the same moment repealing her concurrence in the only scheme that promised to supply a deficiency of contributions.[19] He thought the motion however inaccurately expressed, since the word "general" might be understood to refer to every possible object of taxation as well as to the operation of a particular tax throughout the States:[20] he observed that the nonpayment of the 1,200,000 Drs. demanded by Congress for paying the interest of the debts for the year[21]   demonstrated that the constitutional mode of annual requisitions was defective; he intimated that lands were already sufficiently taxed; & that polls & commerce were the most proper objects. At his instance the latter part of the motion was so amended as to run "establishment of permanent & adequate funds to operate generally throughout the U. States."[22]

Mr. Hamilton went extensively into the subject the sum of it was as follows: he observed that funds considered as permanent sources of revenue were of two kinds 1st. such as wd extend generally & uniformly throughout the U. S. & wd. be collected under the authority of Congs. 2dly. such as might be established separately within each State, & might consist of any objects which were chosen by the States, and which might be collected either under the authority of the States or of Congs. Funds of the 1st. kind he contended were preferable; as being 1st. more simple. the difficulties attending the mode of fixing the quotas laid down in the confederation rendering it extremely complicated & in a manner insuperable:[23] 2d as being more certain; since the States according to the secd. plan wd. probably retain the collection of the revenue and a vicious system of collection prevailed generally through the U. S. a system by which the collectors were chosen by the people & made their offices more subservient to their popularity than to the public revenue[24]—3d. & as being more œconomical, since the collection would be effected with fewer officers under the management of Congress, than under that of the States.

Mr. Ghorum observed that Mr. Hamilton was mistaken in the representation he had given of the collection of taxes in several of the States; particularly in that of Massachussetts, where the collection was on a footing which rendered it sufficiently certain.[25] Mr. Wilson having risen to explain somethings which had fallen from him; threw out the suggestion that several branches of Revenue if yielded by all the States, would perhaps be more just & satisfactory than any single one; for example an impost on trade combined with a land tax.

Mr. Dyer expressed a strong dislike to a collection by officers appointed under Congress & supposed the States would never be brought to consent to it.[26]

Mr. Ramsay was decidedly in favor of the proposition. Justice he said entitled those who had lent their money & services to the U. S. to look to them for payment; that if general & certain revenues were not provided, the consequence wd. be that the army & public Creditors would have soon to look to their respective States only for satisfaction; that the burden in this case wd. fall unequally on the States;[27]

that rivalships relative to trade wd. impede a regular impost & wd. produce confusions amg. the States; that some of the States would never make of themselves provision for half pay[28] and that the army wd. be so far defrauded of the rewards stipulated to them by Congress; that altho' it might be uncertain whether the States wd. accede to plans founded on the proposition before the house, yet as Congress was convinced of its truth & importance it was their duty to make the experiment

Mr. Bland thought that the ideas of the states on the subject were so averse to a general revenue in the hands of Congs. that if such a revenue were proper it was unattainable; that as the deficiency of the contributions from the States proceeded not from* complaints of their inability but of the inequality of the apportionments, it would be a wiser course to pursue the rule of the confederation, towit to ground the requisition on an actual valuation of lands; that Congress wd. then stand on firm ground & try a practicable mode.

---

* The paper just read from Virga. complained of her inability without mentioning an inequality. This was deemed a strange assertion.[29]

1 For a probable explanation of this Roman numeral, see *Papers of Madison*, V, 231.

2 Washingon's letter from "Head Quarters, Newburgh" was to the president of Congress (Fitzpatrick, *Writings of Washington*, XXVI, 52, 53). At the time of his death on 14 January, Major General William Alexander (1726–1783), "Lord Stirling," commanded the "Continental and State Troops at and above Albany on the Hudson and Mohawk rivers" (*ibid.*, XXV, 86, 89, 100, 326). Prior to the Revolution Stirling gained military experience in the British army in North America, resided in Great Britain from 1755 to 1761 while unsuccessfully prosecuting his claim to the earldom of Sterling, and served as surveyor general and member of the governor's council of his native province of New York. The Continental Congress commissioned him a colonel on 7 November 1775, a brigadier general on 1 March 1776, and a major general on 19 February 1777 (*JCC*, III, 335; IV, 181; VII, 133). His participation in the battles of Long Island, Brandywine, Germantown, and Monmouth was especially noteworthy, even though not uniformly distinguishedl by success. On 28 January 1783 a resolution of Congress testified to his "early and meritorious exertions . . . in the common cause" and his "bravery, perseverance and military talents" (*JCC*, XXIV, 96).

3 Within these parentheses, JM intended to insert a reference to his notes of 25 and 27 November 1782 (*Papers of Madison*, V, 315–16; 317, n. 3; 334; 336, n. 17). Upon receiving instructions from Congress to apprehend Judge Luke Knoulton and Colonel Samuel Wells of Vermont for alleged traitorous intercourse with the British, Washington directed Lord Stirling to handle the "delicate affair." Stirling, in his turn, entrusted the execution of the mission to a detachment of forty-eight Rhode Island troops who, with the exception of their leader, Captain Ebenezer Macomber (Macumber), understood that their objective was to capture deserters (Fitzpatrick, *Writings of Washington*, XXV, 407–8). Macomber (d. 1829) had been an officer of the Rhode Island state line since 1776. He was commissioned

captain on 17 March 1782 and served in that grade for exactly one year before returning to civilian life (Heitman, *Historical Register Continental*, p. 376).

⁴ Captain Macomber and his men had left Saratoga on 25 December 1782 and returned there on 6 January 1783. In accounting to General Stirling on 7 January for the failure of the mission, Macomber reported that he had been told by Israel Smith at Brattleboro, Vt., of the departure of Judge Knoulton from that town and of Colonel Wells from Newfane for an unknown destination, about six days before Macomber's detachment arrived, and soon after each of the fugitives had received letters "from the southward." Among these letters was allegedly one from Jonathan Arnold, a delegate from Rhode Island. Except that JM omitted "very" before "unfavorable," he quoted Macomber's report with approximate accuracy. See Burnett, *Letters*, VII, 37–38.

Macomber believed that Smith, who was known favorably by Governor George Clinton of New York, was a "man of veracity" (NA: PCC, No. 152, XI, 63–66). Israel Smith (1759–1810) was graduated by Yale College in 1781 and admitted to the bar of Vermont in 1783. He was a representative in the Vermont state legislature, 1785, 1788–1791; a representative in Congress, 1791–1797, 1801–1803; chief justice of the Supreme Court of Vermont, 1797–1798; a United States senator, 1803–1807; and governor, 1807–1808.

⁵ Arnold the next day wrote to Washington, hotly denying involvement in "this at present dark and mysterious affair"; but he had laid himself open to suspicion by opposing measures advocated in Congress for coercing the *de facto* government of Vermont, to which "state" he would remove in 1787. See *Papers of Madison*, V, 336, n. 13; 354, n. 25; 389, n. 8; Burnett, *Letters*, VII, 23.

⁶ *Papers of Madison*, IV, 184, n. 2; 215, n. 2; 287, n. 27; V, 276–77; 277, nn. 5, 9; 440. Although President John Dickinson of Pennsylvania in his message of 24 January 1783 to the General Assembly mentioned that he had "sent a large number of copies" of the statute "to prevent the erecting any new and independent State within the limits of this Commonwealth" for distribution "among the inhabitants" of the three westernmost counties, he showed no awareness of the unrest of which the present petition, unnoted in the official journal of Congress, was an expression (*Colonial Records of Pa.*, XIII, 489; *JCC*, XXIV, 96).

The petition, bearing approximately 1800 signatures, all written in the same hand, purported to be from settlers "on the west side of Laurel Hill and Western Waters." After setting forth the usual grievances of frontiersmen—unjust taxes, insecure land titles, lack of protection against marauding Indians, and a too distant government which treated them "more like Slaves than freemen"—the memorialists affirmed that they, as much as easterners, had served the "common cause of liberty and independence" by guarding the western flanks of Pennsylvania, Maryland, and Virginia. Having thus earned the "Rights, Privileges and Immunities of free Citizens of America" and living in an isolated region which "God and Nature seem to have designed" for a separate government, the petitioners asked that Congress erect their area as a "New State," confirm their claims to land, maintain the garrison at Fort Pitt, and, if possible, establish other military posts in the neighborhood (NA: PCC, No. 48, fol. 251).

⁷ JM Notes, 25 Jan. 1783, and n. 13; *JCC*, XXIV, 94–95.

⁸ *Papers of Madison*, IV, 330.

⁹ That is, indirect taxes such as imposts and excises as compared with direct taxes on polls and real estate.

¹⁰ Certainly one of "the best writers" was Dr. Samuel Johnson. To him has been attributed an anonymous pamphlet in which the writer proved, at least to his own satisfaction, that even in times of peace Britons paid four times the taxes paid by American colonials; and in times of war, fought largely on behalf of those colonials, the ratio widened to ten-to-one (*The Right of the British Legislature To Tax*

the American Colonies Vindicated: and the Means of Asserting That Right Proposed [London, 1774], pp. 32 n., 33). Lord North, on the other hand, remarked in the House of Commons on 2 February 1775 that he estimated the taxes paid annually by "every inhabitant" of Great Britain to be "at least 25 shillings" as compared with the "no more than sixpence" for which "an inhabitant of America" was liable (*Hansard's Parliamentary Debates*, XVIII [1774–1777], col. 222). Being subject to so many variables, the "sixpence" is especially vulnerable, but so too is the "10s. Sterlg per head." Members of the House of Lords or House of Commons who were friendly to the colonists in 1775 and early in 1776 frequently insisted either that the Americans indirectly paid heavy taxes because of the duties levied on their exports and imports, or that British subjects living in the mother country would have had to bear a much heavier load of taxation, except for the revenue which accrued to the treasury from this profitable trade (*ibid.*, XVIII, cols. 262, 452, 485–90, 517–19, 521, 534, 1047, 1225). A circular letter, unanimously adopted by Congress on 13 September 1779, and addressed to "Friends and Fellow-Citizens," states that before the Revolution the colonists had "paid an annual tax to Britain of 3,000,-000 sterling in the way of trade" (*JCC*, XV, 1051–62, and esp. 1057).

11 Between 1775 and 1779 the Continental Congress emitted a total of $226,200,000 in paper currency. The amount issued annually during this period rose from $6,000,000 in 1775 to $124,800,000 in 1779. Although the worth of this currency in terms of gold varied from state to state, merchants in Philadelphia were applying a depreciation ratio of 1.25 to 1 by the close of 1776 and of about 42 to 1 three years later. Thereafter the gold value of these "continentals" declined at an increasingly rapid pace. Writing of the situation early in 1781, one authority states: "Approximately $226,000,000 in currency, from which Congress derived a real income of over $40,000,000 in specie, had shrunk to almost nothing. The loss was carried by the people of the nation as money depreciated in their hands—a process sometimes considered as a form of taxation in rough proportion to ability to pay" (E[lmer] James Ferguson, *The Power of the Purse* [Chapel Hill, N.C., 1961], pp. 29–32, 67). James Wilson evidently did not agree that this "form of taxation" had been equitable in its impact.

12 Taking this sentence in conjunction with the sentence immediately preceding it, Wilson seems to have contended, although not altogether persuasively, that because the "inhabitants" had "insensibly borne" from 1775 to 1780 an "oppressive" weight of at least $20,000,000 annually, they should have been able, with comparative ease, to furnish $8,000,000 in taxes during 1782 so as to enable the state governments to meet the requisitions of Congress totaling that amount. Of the $8,000,000, Delaware, North Carolina, South Carolina, and Georgia had paid nothing before 1 January 1783, and the other nine states had supplied only $422,161.44 (NA: PCC, No. 137, II, 757–61). Therefore, to arrive at "⅛ of a dollar per head," Wilson must have estimated the total population, excluding Indians, at about 2,814,125. This figure may be fairly accurate, for a scholarly analysis of primary data, mainly from 1774 to 1776, resulted in an estimate of 2,507,180 (Stella H. Sutherland, *Population Distribution in Colonial America* [New York, 1936], p. xii).

13 That is, the financial obligations incurred by Congress in exercising its constitutional powers sanctioned by the states both before and after the inauguration of the government under the Articles of Confederation on 1 March 1781. According to a report to Congress by Robert Morris, superintendent of finance, the total "Public debt" of the United States on 1 January 1783 could not be stated "with any tolerable precision," but five of the main "engagements" were (1) owed in Europe, $11,925,925; (2) owed to the troops, $11,300,000; (3) owed to holders of loan-office certificates, $11,400,485.64 ⅛; (4) the "liquidated" or funded debt, $638,042.25; and (5) owed to winners in the four lotteries, $63,316.64. These totaled $35,327,769.53 ⅛. To this should be added, as Morris pointed out, the very large but unknown sums

which would be required to cancel "the old continental Bills," to meet the "arrearages of Half Pay" owed to retired or deranged officers, and to discharge the so-called "unliquidated Debt being the monies due to the several states, and to individuals in the several states" (NA: PCC, No. 137, II, 195–207; JM Notes, 13 Jan., and n. 20; 17 Jan., and n. 6; Randolph to JM, 15 Jan. 1783, n. 13). The "unliquidated debt" comprised, for example, the disproportionately large advances of money and supplies by the southern states in 1780–1782 to General Nathanael Greene's army and the written promises to pay given by commissary agents and other military officers upon impressing grain, cattle, horses, etc., from civilians.

[14] By providing dependable and adequate sources of revenue, Congress should be able once more to float domestic loans, and the exchange value of the depreciated paper currency should rise.

[15] *Papers of Madison*, IV, xviii–xix; V, xvii; xviii–xix.

[16] JM no doubt underlined "general" to reflect Wilson's stress upon according the same treatment to every classification of at least the precisely known debt, and funding all of it in the same manner. See n. 13. Wilson's proposal that Congress should collect the funds also deserved emphasis because similar recommendations had been and would be a principal matter of controversy (*ibid.*, II, 304, and n. 3; III, 128, and n. 5; IV, 387; V, 414–15; 416, n. 3; Randolph to JM, 3 Jan., n. 5; JM Notes, 13 Jan., and n. 17; 24 Jan., n. 40; 25 Jan. 1783). See also JM's summary of speeches on this issue, later in his notes for this day.

[17] *Papers of Madison*, V, 385, n. 12; 442; 445, n. 16; 457–58; 458, n. 5; 474, n. 5; 477; 478, n. 2; *JCC*, XXIV, 96; Delegates to Harrison, 28 Jan. 1783, and n. 2.

[18] Oliver Wolcott was chairman of the grand committee appointed on 6 January to consider the memorial from the army. This committee's report on 24 January occasioned a discussion of general financial problems which were still "the business before Congress" three days later (JM Notes, 6 Jan., and n. 2; 9–10 Jan.; 13 Jan.; 24 Jan., and nn. 20, 25, 40; 25 Jan. 1783, and n. 13).

JM was painfully aware of his awkward situation. He had supported an amendment that the Virginia General Assembly repudiated. He was urging the states to fulfill overdue obligations to Congress which that Assembly confessed itself able to help discharge only by a minute contribution, and he was favoring nationalistic measures at a time when the growing emphasis of Richmond appeared to be toward state sovereignty (*Papers of Madison*, V, 372; 374, n. 12; 419–20; 449; 472; 477–78; Delegates to Harrison, 7 Jan., n. 5; JM to Randolph, 7 Jan.; 14 Jan., and n. 5; 22 Jan.; 28 Jan.; JM Notes, 9–10 Jan.; 25 Jan. 1783, and n. 7).

[19] The opening remarks of Nathaniel Gorham were evidently of the same tenor as those of Wolcott.

[20] See n. 16; and JM Notes, 25 Jan. 1783, and n. 7.

[21] *Papers of Madison*, V, 127; 129, n. 13; 209; 211, n. 10.

[22] See James Wilson's motion, and n. 16, above.

[23] Alexander Hamilton referred to "the Mode" of determining financial quotas prescribed by the first paragraph of Article VIII of the Articles of Confederation. For comment upon its "complicated" provisions, see Randolph to JM, 3 Jan., and n. 4; JM Notes, 9–10 Jan., and nn. 3, 8; 14 Jan. 1783, and nn. 4, 6, 7.

[24] For Hamilton's own description of the method of tax assessment and collection in New York, see Syrett and Cooke, *Papers of Hamilton*, III, 135–37, 154, 181. In Virginia the tax collectors were traditionally the sheriffs. Nominated by the justices of peace of their respective counties, appointed by the executive, directed by legislation of the General Assembly, chargeable in any delinquencies by the solicitor general, and subject to judgments of the General Court, they were little amenable to direct popular influence (Hening, *Statutes*, IX, 117, 169–70; XI, 168; *Papers of Madison*, V, 182, n. 1).

[25] In Massachusetts the collectors of the excise were appointed by the General Court (legislature). Other taxes were levied upon the towns by the General Court in proportion to the "valuation of estates within the commonwealth"—a valuation which had to be "taken anew" at least every ten years. The local assessors and the constables who collected these taxes were elected by the town meetings. The sheriffs of the counties, who were appointed by the governor "with the advice and consent of the council," supervised the constables in the performance of their duty in this regard. It was provided that "any or all officers of the commonwealth" should be removed upon impeachment by the House of Representatives and conviction by the Senate (Francis N. Thorpe, ed., *Federal and State Constitutions*, III, 1894, 1897, 1899, 1902; Albert Bushnell Hart, ed., *Commonwealth History of Massachusetts* [5 vols.; New York, 1927–30], III, 347–53). See also JM Notes, 29 Jan. 1783, n. 20.

[26] Eliphalet Dyer. See n. 16.

[27] Except that some of the civilian and military creditors of the Confederation had looked already "to their respective States only for satisfaction" and had been reimbursed, David Ramsay's statement was accurate (*Papers of Madison*, V, 174–75; 293–94; 362–64; 366, nn. 19, 23, 26; JM Notes, 24 Jan. 1783, and nn. 17, 20, 40; E. James Ferguson, *Power of the Purse*, pp. 69, n. 41, 143–45, 180–81). The distribution of the war's "burden," whether viewed in terms of the number of troops recruited, the amount of money or supplies furnished, or the destruction of property incurred, obviously had not been in proportion to the comparative wealth or population of the thirteen states.

[28] JM Notes, 13 Jan. 1783, and n. 18.

[29] The "assertion" to which JM referred was that of his colleague Theodorick Bland. For the "paper just read," see above, and *Papers of Madison*, V, 457–58; JM Notes, 31 Jan. 1783. There had been many "complaints" about "the inequality of the apportionments," even though "the paper just read" did not mention them. See *Papers of Madison*, III, 301, n. 2; 328–29; 329, n. 6; 336; IV, 72, n. 3; 122–23; 123, n. 3; 124, nn. 6, 7; V, 127; 129, n. 13; 169; 423, and n. 2. JM's abrupt close of his notes for 27 January 1783 probably signifies that, having come "to no resolution" on "the order of the day," Congress adjourned (*JCC*, XXIV, 96).

Notes on Debates

MS (LC: Madison Papers). For a description of the manuscript of Notes on Debates, see *Papers of Madison*, V, 231–34.

Tuesday Jany. 28th. 1783

The subject yesterday under discussion was resumed. A division of the question was called for by Mr. Wolcott so as to have a distinct question on the "words to be collected by Congress" wch. he did not like.[1]

Mr. Wilson considered this mode of collection as essential to the idea of a general revenue, since without it the proceeds of the revenue wd. depend entirely on the punctuality energy & unanimity of the States, the want of which led to the present consideration.

Mr. Hamilton was strenuously of the same opinion.

Mr. Fitzimmons informed Congress that the Legislature of Penna. had at their last meeting been dissuaded from appropriating their revenue to the payment of their own Citizens Creditors of the U. S. instead of remitting it to the continental treasury; merely by the urgent representations of a Committee of Congress & by the hope that some general system in favr. of all the public creditors would be adopted; that the Legislature were now again assembled; and altho sensible of the tendency of such an example, thought it their duty & meant in case the prospect of such a system vanished to proceed immediately to the separate appropriations formerly in contemplation.[2]

On the motion of Mr. Madison the whole proposition was new-modelled as follows;

"That it is the opinion of Congress that the establishment of permanent & adequate funds to operate generally throughout the U. States is indispensibly necessary for doing complete justice to the Creditors of the U. S., for restoring public credit, & for providing for the future exigencies of the war." The words "to be collected under the authority of Congress["] were as a seperate question left to be added afterwards.[3]

Mr. Rutlidge objected to the term "generally", as implying a degree of uniformity in the tax which would render it unequal. He had in view particularly a land tax according to quantity as had been proposed by the office of finance. He thought the prejudices of the people opposed to the idea of a general tax & seemed on the whole to be disinclined to it himself, at least if extended beyond an impost on trade; urging the necessity of pursuing a valuation of land, and requisitions grounded thereon.[4]

Mr. Lee 2ded. the opposition to the term "general." he contended that the States wd. never consent to a uniform tax because it wd. be unequal; that it was moreover repugnant to the articles of confederation; and by placing the purse in the same hands with the sword, was subversive of the fundamental principles of liberty.[5] He mentioned the repeal of the impost by Virga. himself alone opposing it & that too on the inexpediency in point of time, as proof of the aversion to a general revenue.[6] He reasoned upon the subject finally as if it was proposed that Congress sd. assume & exercise a power immediately & without the previous Sanction of the States, of levying money on them.[7] In consequence.

Mr. Wilson rose & explained the import of the motion to be that Congress should recommend to the States the investing them with

142

power. He observed that the confederation was so far from precluding, that it expressly provided for future alterations; that the power given to Congress by that Act[8] was too little not too formidable, that there was more of a centrifugal than centripetal force in the States & that the funding of a common debt in the manner proposed would produce a salutary invigoration & cement of the Union.[9]

Mr. Elseworth acknowledged himself to be undecided in his opinion: that on the one side he felt the necessity of continental funds for making good the continental engagements but on the other desponded of a unanimous concurrence of the States in such an establishment. He observed that it was a question of great importance how far the federal govt. can or ought to exert coercion against delinquent members of the confederacy; & that without such coercion no certainty could attend the constitutional mode which referred every thing to the unanimous punctuality of thirteen different councils.[10] Considering therefore a continental revenue as unattainable, and periodical requisitions from Congress as inadequate, he was inclined to make trial of the middle mode of permanent State funds, to be provided at the recommendation of Congs. and appropriated to the discharge of the common debt.[11]

Mr. Hamilton in reply to Mr. Elseworth dwelt long on the inefficacy of State funds, He supposed too that greater obstacles would arise to the execution of the plan than to that of a general revenue. As an additional reason for the latter to be collected by officers under the appointment of Congress, he signified that as the energy of the federal Govt. was evidently short of the degree necessary for pervading & uniting the States it was expedient to introduce the influence of officers deriving their emoluments from & consequently interested in supporting the power of, Congress.*[12]

Mr. Williamson was of opinion that continental funds altho' desirable, were unattainable at least to the full amount of the public exigences. He thought if they could be obtained for the foreign debt, it would be as much as could be expected, and that they would also be less essential for the domestic debt.[13]

Mr. Madison observed that it was needless to go into proofs of the necessity of payg. the public debts; that the idea of erecting our national

* This remark was imprudent & injurious to the cause wch. it was meant to serve. This influence was the very source of jealousy which rendered the States averse to a revenue under the collection as well as appropriation of Congress. All the members of Congress who concurred in any degree with the States in this jealousy smiled at the disclosure. Mr. Bland & still more Mr. L. who were of this number took notice in private conversation that Mr. Hamilton had let out the secret.

independence on the ruins of public faith and national honor must be horrid to every mind which retained either honesty or pride; that the motion before Congress contained a simple proposition with respect to the truth of which every member was called upon to give his opinion.[14] That this opinion must necessarily be in the affirmative, unless the several objects; of doing justice to the public Creditors, &c &c. could be compassed by some other plan than the one proposed, that the 2 last objects depended essentially on the first; since the doing justice to the Creditors alone wd. restore publi[c] credit, & the restoration of this alone could provide for the future exigencies of the war. Is then a continl revenue indispensibly necessary for doing complete justice &? This is the question. To answer it the other plans proposed must first be reviewed.

In order to do complete justice to the public Creditors, either the principal must be paid off, or the interest paid punctually. The 1st. is admitted to be impossible on any plan. The only plans opposed to the continl one for the latter purpose; are 1st. periodical requisitions according to the fœderal articles: 2dly. permanent funds established by each State within itself & the proceeds consigned to the discharge of public debts.[15]

Will the 1st. be adequate to the object? The contrary seems to be maintained by no one. If reason did not sufficiently premonish, experience has sufficiently demonstrated that a punctual & unfailing compliance by 13 separate & independent Govts. with periodical demands of money from Congress, can never be reckoned upon with the certainty requisite to satisfy our present creditors, or to tempt others to become our creditors in future.[16]

2dly. Will funds separately established within each State & the amount submitted to the appropriation of Congress be adequate to the object? The only advantage which is thought to recommend this plan, is that the States will be with less difficulty prevailed upon to adopt it. Its imperfections are 1st. that it must be preceded by a final & satisfactory adjustment of all accts. between the U. S. and individual States;[17] and by an apportionment founded on a valuation of all the lands throughout each of the States in pursuance of the law of the confederation:[18] for although the States do not as yet insist on these prerequisites in the case of annual demands on them with wch. they very little comply & that only in the way of an open acct.;[19] yet these conditions wd. certainly be exacted in case of a permanent cession of revenue; and the difficulties & delays to say the least incident to these conditions, can escape no one.

2dly. the produce of the funds being always in the first instance in the hands & under the controul of the States separately, might at any time & on various pretences, be diverted to State-objects.[20] 3dly. That jealousy which is as natural to the States as to individuals & of which so many proofs have appeared, that *others* will not fulfil their respective portions of the common obligations, will be continually & mutually suspending remittances to the common treasury, until it finally stops them altogether. These imperfections are too radical to be admitted into any plan intended for the purposes in question.

It remains to examine the merits of the plan of a general revenue operating throughout the U. S. under the superintendence of Congress.

One obvious advantage is suggested by the last objection to separate revenues in the different States; that is, it will exclude all jealousy among them on that head, since each will know whilst it is submitting to the tax, that all the others are necessaryly at the same instant bearing their respective portions of the burden.[21]

Again it will take from the States the opportunity as well as the temptation to divert their incomes from the general to internal purposes since these incomes will pass *directly* into the treasury of the U S.

Another advantage attending a general revenue is that in case of the concurrence of the States in establishing it, it would become soonest productive; and would consequently soonest obtain the objects in view. Nay so assured a prospect would give instantaneous confidence & content to the public creditors at home & abroad, and place our affairs in the most happy train.

The consequences with respect to the Union, of omitting such a provision for the debts of the Union also claims particular attention. The tenor of the memorial from Penna. and of the information just given on the floor by one of its delegates (Mr Fitzimmons) renders it extremely probable that that State would as soon as it sd. be known that Congress had declined such provision or the States rejected it, appropriate the revenue required by Congress, to the payment of its own Citizens & troops, creditors of the U. S.[22] The irregular conduct of other States on this subject enforced by such an example could not fail to spread the evil throughout the whole continent. What then wd become of the confederation? What wd. be the authority of Congress? wt. the tie by which the States cd. be held together? what the source by which the army could be subsisted & cloathed? What the mode of dividing & discharging our foreign debts? What the rule of settling the internal accts? What the tribunal by which controversies amg the States could be adjudicated?[23]

145

It ought to be carefully remembered that this subject was brought before Congress by a very solemn appeal from the army to the justice & gratitude of their Country. Besides immediate pay, they ask for permanent security for arrears. Is not this request a reasonable one? will it be just or politic to pass over the only adequate security that can be devised, & instead of fulfilling the stipulations of the U. S. to them, to leave them to seek their rewards separately from the States to which they respectively belong? The patience of the army has been equal to their bravery, but that patience must have its limits; and the result of despair can not be foreseen, nor ought it to be risked.[24]

It has been objected agst. a general revenue that it contravenes the articles of confederation.[25] These Articles as has been observed have presupposed the necessity of alterations in the fœderal system & have left a door open for them:[26] They moreover authorize Congress to borrow money. Now in order to borrow money permanent & certain provision is necessary, & if this provision cannot be made in any other way as has been shewn, a general revenue is within the spirit of the confederation.[27]

It has been objected that such a revenue is subversive of the soverignty & liberty of the States. If it were to be assumed without the free gift of the States this objection might be of force, but no assumption is proposed. In fact Congress are already invested by the States with the constitutional authority over the purse as well as the sword. A general revenue would only give this authority a more certain & equal efficacy. They have a right to fix the *quantum* of money necessary for the common purposes. The right of the States is limited to the *mode* of supply. A requisition of Congress on the States for money is as much a law to them; as their revenue acts when passed are laws to their respective Citizens. If for want of the faculty or means of enforcing a requisition, the law of Congress proves inefficient; does it not follow that in order to fullfil the views of the fœderal constitution, such a change sd. be made as will render it efficient? Without such efficiency the end of this Constitution which is to preserve order & justice among the members of the Union, must fail; as without a like efficiency would the end of State constitutions wch. is to preserve like order & justice among its members.[28]

It has been objected that the States have manifested such aversion to the impost on trade as renders any recommendations of a general revenue hopeless & imprudent. It must be admitted that the conduct of the States on that subject is less encouraging than were to be wished. A review of it however does not excite despondence. The impost was adopted immediately & in its utmost latitude by several of the States. Several also which complied partially with it at first, have since complied more liberally. One of them after long refusal has complied substantially.[29] Two States only have failed altogether & as to one of them it is not known that its failure has proceeded from a decided opposition to it.[30] On the whole it appears that the necessity & reasonableness of the scheme have been gaining ground among the States. He was aware that one exception ought to be made to this inference: an exception too wch peculiarly concerned him to advert to. The State of Virga as appears by an Act yesterday laid before Congress, has withdrawn its assent once given to the scheme.[31] This circumstance cd. not but produce some embarrassment in a representative of that State advocating the scheme[;] one too whose principles were extremely unfavorable to a disregd. of the sense of Constitnts. But it ought not to deter him from listening to considerations which in the present case ought to prevail over it. One of these considerations was that altho' the delegates who compose Congress, more immediately represented & were amenable to the States from which they respectively come, yet in another view they owed a fidelity to the collective interests of the whole. 2dly. Altho' not only the express instructions, but even the declared sense of constituents as in the present case, were to be a law in general to these representatives, still there were occasions on which the latter ought to hazard personal consequences[32] from a respect to what his clear conviction determines to be the true interest of the former; and the present he conceived to fall under this exception. Lastly the part he took on the present occasion was the more fully justified to his own mind by his thorough persuasion, that with the same knowledge of public affairs which his station commanded,[33] the Legislature of Va would not have repealed the law in favor of the impost & would even now rescind the repeal.

The result of these observations was that it was the duty of Congress under whose authority the public debts had been contracted to aim at a general revenue as the only means of discharging them; & that this dictate of justice & gratitude was enforced by a regard to the preservation of the confederacy, to our reputation abroad & to our internal tranquility.[34]

Mr. Rutledge complained that those who so strenuously urged the necessity & competency of a general revenue operating*[35] throughout all

* he was apprehensive that a tax on land according to its quantity not value as had been recomd. by Mr. Morris was in contemplation.

the States at the same time, declined specifying any general objects from which such a revenue could be drawn He was thought to insinuate that these objects were kept back intentionally untill the general principle cd. be irrevocably fixed when Congs. wd. be bound at all events to go on with the project, whereupon Mr. Fitzimmons expressed some concern at the turn wch. the discussion seemed to be taking. He said that unless mutual confidence prevailed no progress could be made towards the attainment of those ends wch. all in some way or other aimed at. It was a mistake to suppose that any specific plan had been preconcerted among the patrons of a general revenue.[36]

Mr. Wilson with whom the motion originated[37] gave his assurances that it was neither the effect of preconcert with others, nor of any determinate plan matured by himself, that he had been led into it, by the declaration on Saturday last by Congs. that substantial funds ought to be provided; by the memor[i]al of the army from which that declaration had resulted[,][38] by the memorials from the State of Pa. holding out the idea of separate appropriations of her revenue unless provision were made for the public creditors,[39] by the deplorable & dishonorable situation of public affairs which had compelled Congress to draw bills on the unpromised & contingent bounty of their ally, and which was likely to banish the Superintdt. of Finance whose place cd not be supplied, from his department.[40] He observed that he had not introduced details into the debate because he thought them premature, until a general principle should be fixed;[41] and that as soon as the pri[n]ciple sd. be fixed he would altho' not furnished with any digested plan, contribute all in his power to the forming such a one.

Mr. Rutlidge moved that the proposition might be committed in order that some practicable plan might be reported, before Congress sd. declare that it ought to be adopted.

Mr. Izard 2ded. the motion from a conciliating view.

Mr. Madison thought the commitment unnecessary: and would have the appearance of delay; that too much delay had already taken place, that the deputation of the army had a right to expect an answer to their memorial as soon as it could be decided by Congress. He differed from Mr. Wilson in thinking that a specification of the objects of a general revenue would be improper, and thought that those who doubted of its practicability had a right to expect proof of it from details before they cd. be expected to assent to the general principle; but he differed also from Mr. Rutledge who thought a commitment necessary for the purpose; since his views would be answered by leaving the motion before the house and giving the debate a greater latitude. He suggested as practicable objects of a general revenue. 1st an impost on trade 2dly. a poll tax under certain qualifications 3dly. a land tax under do.*[42]

Mr. Hamilton suggested a house & window tax.[43] he was in favor of the mode of conducting the discussion urged by Mr. Madison

On the motion for the commt. 6 States were in favor of it, & five agst. it. so it was lost—in this vote the merits of the main proposition very little entered.[44]

Mr. Lee said that it was a waste of time to be forming resolutions & settling principles on this subject. He asked whether these wd. ever bring any money into the public treasury. His opinion was that Congress ought in order to guard agst. the inconveniency of meetings of the different Legislatures at different & even distant periods, to call upon the Executives to convoke them all at one period, & to lay before them a full state of our public affairs. He said the States would never agree to those plans which tended to aggrandize Congress; that they were jealous of the power of Congress; & that he acknowledged himself to be one of those who thought this jealousy not an unreasonable one; that no one who had ever opened a page or read a line on the subject of liberty, could be insensible to the danger of surrendering the purse into the same hand which held the sword.[45]

The debate was suspended by an adjournment.

* a poll tax to be qualified by rating blacks some what lower than whites, a land tax by considering the value of land in each State to be in an inverse proportion of its quantity to the no. of people; and apportioning on the aggregate quantity in each State accordingly, leaving the State at liberty to make a distributive apportionmt on its several districts, on a like or any other equalizing principle.

1 JM Notes, 27 Jan. 1783, and nn. 7, 16, 29.

2 *Papers of Madison*, V, 362–64; 366, nn. 19, 23, 26; 373; 389–90; 394; JM Notes, 24 Jan. 1783, and nn. 5, 17, 18, 19.

3 This paragraph, omitting the final sentence, is a verbatim copy of JM's manuscript draft of the motion, as originally written, except that after the first "U.S." he bracketed "and to be collected under the authority of the U.S. in Congress Assembled" (NA: PCC, No. 36, II, 99). Before introducing the motion JM evidently decided that the bracketed passage constituted a "separate question" and should be reserved for later consideration. Several other alterations by him in the manuscript draft will be mentioned in connection with his notes of 29 January, for those changes embody some of the amendments then made to his motion (JM Notes, 29 Jan. 1783, nn. 8, 11–13).

The "whole proposition," mentioned by JM, was James Wilson's motion of 27 January (JM Notes, 27 Jan. 1783, and n. 16). Although JM referred solely to that motion, he was accused about seventy-five years later by Alexander Hamilton's son, John C. Hamilton, of trying to take the credit for a "new-modelled" suggestion which was only a slightly altered version of a report written by Alexander Hamilton and submitted to Congress on 16 December 1782 (John C. Hamilton, *History of the Republic*, II, 398 n.). A few words or phrases in that report and more of them in Hamilton's report of 24 January, unmentioned by John C. Hamilton, somewhat resemble the phraseology of JM's motion (JM Notes, 24 Jan. 1783; *JCC*, XXIV, 94–95). The distant sources of that motion, however, were Robert Morris' letters of 27 February and 29 July 1782, and its immediate prototype, as JM himself stated later in his notes for 28 January, was James Wilson's motion of 27 January 1783 (NA: PCC, No. 137, I, 347–50; *JCC*, XXII, 115, n. 2, 429–47; XXIII, 798–810; JM Notes, 27 Jan. 1783, and n. 16). John C. Hamilton implied that Wilson's motion had been invented by JM to mask his indebtedness to Hamilton's report of 16 December 1782 (John C. Hamilton, *History of the Republic*, II, 399 n.).

In his motion Wilson embodied two principles: that Congress should have general funds derived from sources uncontrolled by the state governments and that agents of Congress should collect these funds. Both the objective and the method of attaining it were highly controversial. For this reason JM focused his "new-modelled" motion upon the goal, hoping that isolating the motion from methods of attainment would increase its chances of being accepted. By rearranging the phraseology of Wilson's proposal, JM also sought to enhance the attractiveness of his own motion by stressing that the use of funds would be for the general benefit of all the states. See JM Notes, 14 Jan. 1783, and n. 9.

[4] Robert Morris had recommended a "general" tax on land in his letters to Congress of 27 February and 29 July 1782. See n. 3. Morris had suggested that "one dollar for every hundred acres" should be levied uniformly throughout the Union, without regard to the value of the land. See JM Notes, 14 Jan. 1783, and n. 7.

[5] A land tax would be "repugnant to" the eighth article of the Articles of Confederation unless it was assessed upon "the several states in proportion to the value of all land within each state, granted to or surveyed for any Person, as such land and the buildings and improvements thereon shall be estimated" (*JCC*, XIX, 217). Arthur Lee, who had attended Congress on 27 January for the first time since 4 October 1782, was reaffirming a position which, as a member of a committee on much the same problem, he had taken on 5 August 1782 (*JCC*, XXII, 447; XXIII, 639; XXIV, 96).

By approximately quoting the aphorism, "a union of the purse and the sword is tyranny," Lee perhaps reflected a knowledge of Montesquieu's advocacy of the separation of governmental powers (J. V. Prichard, ed., *The Spirit of Laws, by M. de Secondat, Baron de Montesquieu, with d'Alembert's Analysis of the Work, translated from the French by Thomas Nugent, LL.D.* [2 vols.; London, 1878], I, 163). English constitutional doctrine, in which Lee almost certainly was versed, furnished considerable support to the same conclusion. For example, the statute known as the Bill of Rights, enacted by Parliament in 1689, declared as contrary to "ancient rights and liberties" and hence "illegal," "levying money for or to the use of the crown by pretence of prerogative without grant of parliament, for longer time or in other manner than the same is or shall be granted" (Carl Stephenson and Frederick George Marcham, eds., *Sources of English Constitutional History: A Selection of Documents from A.D. 600 to the Present* [New York, 1937], p. 601). For a reply on 21 February to this contention by Lee and other delegates, see JM Notes, 21 Feb. 1783, and n. 10.

[6] Harrison to JM, 4 Jan. 1783, n. 3; also n. 45, below.

[7] See JM's comments later in his notes for this day, and nn. 27 and 28, below.

[8] For the amending provision of "that Act," the Articles of Confederation, see Article XIII (*JCC*, XIX, 221).

[9] In his letter of 29 July 1782 to Congress, Robert Morris wrote, "It is however an advantage peculiar to domestic loans, that they give stability to Government by combining together the interests of moneyed men for its support, and consequently in this Country a domestic debt would greatly contribute to that Union, which

seems not to have been sufficiently attended to, or provided for, in forming the national compact" (*JCC*, XXII, 432). See also *Papers of Madison*, V, 322; 324, n. 14; 363; 366, n. 23.

10 For JM's proposal of 12 March 1781, which would have enabled Congress to coerce a "State or States," see *Papers of Madison*, III, 17–19. See also *ibid.*, III, 71–72; IV, 34; 35, n. 15.

11 By "permanent State funds" Ellsworth meant the proceeds derived from taxes or other revenue-producing sources designated by the legislatures for the sole use of Congress. See JM to Randolph, 22 Jan. 1783, and JM's discussion of this proposal later in his notes for the present day.

12 In his footnote (*q.v.*) commenting upon Hamilton's "remark," JM's "Mr. L." was Arthur Lee. Hamilton was "imprudent" only in affirming in Congress a view he had emphatically expressed elsewhere. In his "The Continentalist No. VI," printed in the *New-York Packet. And the American Advertiser*, 4 July 1782, he had stated, "The reason of allowing Congress to appoint its own officers of the customs, collectors of taxes, and military officers of every rank, is to create in the interior of each state a mass of influence in favour of the Fœderal Government" (Syrett and Cooke, *Papers of Hamilton*, III, 105). In his suggested reply of 16 December 1782 to the speaker of the Rhode Island Assembly on the subject of the impost amendment, Hamilton had strongly implied what he made explicit in his speech of 28 January 1783 (*JCC*, XXIII, 801–3).

13 JM Notes, 27 Jan. 1783, n. 13.

14 See n. 3. Following "Mr. Madison" JM interlineated the passage ending with "pride."

15 See nn. 10 and 11.

16 *Papers of Madison*, V, 389–90.

17 *Ibid.*, IV, 55; 56, n. 6; 91–92; 332; 333, n. 2.

18 JM Notes, 9–10 Jan., and nn. 2, 3; 14 Jan. 1783, and nn. 4, 6, 7, 9.

19 That is, until an evaluation of land and buildings could be determined in the manner prescribed by the Articles of Confederation, and until the total amount of cash and the monetary value of goods and services advanced by the states to Congress and by Congress to the states could be known, each state was maintaining an "open acct" of its expenses on behalf of the Confederation. When a definitive reckoning of these financial costs, state by state, should become possible, adjustments would be made between states which had paid more and those which had paid less than their proportionate share of the total.

20 *Papers of Madison*, V, 282; 287, n. 17; 465; 466, n. 5.

21 The present editors have conformed with JM's direction, interlineated after "burden," to "*transpose this & the following ¶." By "this" he meant the next paragraph; by "the following ¶," the one beginning, "Again it will take." The editors have omitted the asterisks with which he began and closed this latter paragraph.

22 See n. 2.

23 JM's implied answer to each of his rhetorical questions depends upon his premise that if Pennsylvania should violate an important provision of the Articles of Confederation, every state would follow her example by disregarding whatever provision appeared to be inconvenient. Thus the entire document, including the second and third paragraphs of the ninth article designating Congress as "the last resort on appeal" for adjudicating "all disputes and differences" between the states, would become a nullity (*JCC*, XIX, 217–19). See also *Papers of Madison*, V, 242–43; 246, n. 8; JM Notes, 13 Jan. 1783, n. 17.

24 JM Notes, 6 Jan.; 7 Jan., and n. 3; 13 Jan.; 24 Jan., and n. 39; 25 Jan., and nn. 7, 12, 13; Delegates to Harrison, 7 Jan.; 14 Jan.; JM to Randolph, 14 Jan. 1783.

25 Harrison to JM, 4 Jan. 1783, n. 4, and the remarks by Lee made earlier in this debate.

26 See Wilson's remarks and n. 8, above.

27 The ninth article of the Articles of Confederation empowered Congress, provided that at least nine state delegations agreed, to "borrow money" without stated limit, "on the credit of the united states" (*JCC*, XIX, 219). JM contended that the existence of "credit" being essential to the effective exercise of the constitutional right to "borrow," the "spirit of the Confederation" justified Congress in employing whatever means were necessary for establishing credit.

28 In this paragraph, as in the one immediately preceding it, JM took a broadly nationalistic position. In his view, even though Congress regrettably had no power to compel a compliance with an action taken in accordance with the authority delegated by the Articles of Confederation, the states should acknowledge that action to be a law and hence obey it. Furthermore, the spirit of the "fœderal constitution" warranted an amendment conferring upon Congress "a means of enforcing a requisition."

29 Congress adopted the impost amendment on 3 February 1781 and resolved four days later that it would be in provisional effect as soon as all state legislatures not prevented by the enemy from convening had sanctioned it (*JCC*, XIX, 112–13, 124–25; *Papers of Madison*, II, 303–4; 304, n. 3). The legislature of Pennsylvania in April, of New Jersey in June, and of Virginia on the twenty-third of the same month in 1781, ratified the amendment in its "utmost latitude" (*Pa. Packet*, 1 May 1781; NA: PCC, No. 68, fols. 573–75; *Papers of Madison*, III, 349, n. 7). The Virginia General Assembly on 5 January 1782 suspended its statute of approval until the governor should ascertain that all the other states had ratified (*ibid.*, IV, 221, n. 11). This same qualification, except as modified in some instances by including the contents of the resolution of Congress of 7 February 1781, noted above, characterized the acts of ratification of Connecticut, New Hampshire, New York, North Carolina, South Carolina, and Maryland (NA: PCC, No. 72, fols. 554–57; No. 74, fols. 9–12; No. 75, fols. 73–76, 158–63, 320–21; No. 76, fols. 91–93).

No example has been found to support JM's statement that "several" states (or even one state) "which complied partially," later "complied more liberally." Although Maryland withheld her ratification until June 1782, JM probably referred to Massachusetts as the state which "after long refusal" had "complied substantially" in May of that year. Massachusetts accompanied her act of acquiescence with more provisos than any other ratifying state (NA: PCC, No. 74, fols. 193–96; No. 75, fols. 320–21). Although Congress had not asked to be empowered to appoint and supervise the collectors of the impost, the legislatures of Massachusetts, Connecticut, New York, New Jersey, Delaware, Maryland, North Carolina, and South Carolina explicitly conferred this authority but in most instances warned that the regulation must not violate the state's constitution or laws. For Delaware's act of ratification, see NA: PCC, No. 70, fols. 775–78. See also JM Notes, 29 Jan., n. 25; 4 Feb. 1783, n. 10.

30 Unlike Rhode Island, Georgia had not informed Congress why she had not ratified the proposed amendment. See *Papers of Madison*, IV, 387; V, 289; 291, n. 9; 478, n. 2; *JCC*, XXIII, 643.

31 See n. 29. The Virginia General Assembly had rescinded its ratification of the impost amendment on 6 and 7 December 1782 (*Papers of Madison*, V, 385, n. 12; 401). See also JM Notes, 27 Jan. 1783, and n. 17.

32 That is, in his own case, a recall by the Virginia General Assembly, which had appointed him and hence naturally expected him to defend its repeal of the impost amendment. See JM to Randolph, 28 Jan. 1783. The issue of the obligation of a member of Congress to obey instructions from his constituents was of interest to JM even during the last months of his life. He closed a discussion of the matter by writing in his draft of a long letter on 19(?) March 1836 to an unidentified corre-

spondent, "In a case necessarily appealing to the conscience of the Representative its paramount dictates must of course be his guide" (LC: Madison Papers).

33 Following this word JM wrote and canceled "but which could not have been disclosed to the Legislature." JM assumed that if the members of the Virginia General Assembly had known the full extent of Congress' financial plight—a plight so desperate that, if made public, it would have encouraged the enemy—they would not have repealed their act of ratification. See *Papers of Madison*, IV, 175, n. 2; 255, n. 3; V, 331; 363; 373–74; JM to Randolph, 28 Jan. 1783.

34 By alloting in his notes so much space to this speech, JM perhaps meant to signify that it was both longer and more important than any other one hitherto delivered by him in Congress—at least since 4 November 1782, when he began to record its proceedings.

35 N. 4, above, supports JM's footnote. Robert Morris also had recommended "a Poll Tax of one dollar on all freemen, and all male slaves between 16 and 60 (excepting such as are in the federal army, and such as are by wounds or otherwise rendered unfit for service) and an excise of one eighth of dollar per gallon, on all distilled spirituous liquors." In his view, a variety of taxes would serve to distribute their weight among people of different economic pursuits and to assure "particular States" that their citizens would not have to provide most of the congressional funds (*JCC*, XXII, 439, 442).

36 To accept Thomas FitzSimons' statement as accurate is not to deny the probability that "the patrons of a general revenue" had looked to Robert Morris or his reports for guidance. See JM Notes, 25 Jan. 1783.

37 JM Notes, 27 Jan. 1783, and n. 16; also n. 3, above.

38 JM Notes, 25 Jan. 1783, and n. 7.

39 See the fourth paragraph of JM's notes for this day and the citations in n. 2, above.

40 Conference with Morris, 10 Jan., and n. 5; JM Notes, 9–10 Jan., and nn. 12, 13; 13 Jan. 1783. Wilson evidently believed that the resolve of Robert Morris to resign as superintendent of finance largely reflected his unwillingness to "draw bills on the unpromised & contingent bounty" of France. See JM Notes, 24 Jan., and n. 20; 4–5 Mar. 1783, n. 8; also Wharton, *Revol. Dipl. Corr.*, VI, 228–29.

41 The "principle" to "be fixed" was that Congress should have independent sources of revenue. The "details" would be a definition of these sources and, probably also, of the revenue collecting methods.

42 Besides omitting mention of an excise tax on liquor, this paragraph together with the footnote reveals that JM and Robert Morris differed about the "rating" of slaves in levying a poll tax, and especially about the methods of apportioning and collecting a tax on land. See nn. 4 and 37. JM reflects, of course, in his position on these issues his concern lest Virginians and other southerners be overtaxed, as they would be if Morris' proposal to disregard the proportionate value of the land in the several states was accepted by Congress. See JM Notes, 14 Jan. 1783, and nn. 9, 11. In suggesting what a state should be left "at liberty" to do, JM may have had in mind the equalizing land-tax laws enacted on 28 December 1782 by the Virginia General Assembly (*Papers of Madison*, V, 310, n. 10; 350, n. 20; 425–26).

43 In LC: Madison Papers are undated notes by Hamilton on "a Plan for Providing for the Debts of the United States." In this analysis of the debt and of the possible kinds of taxes whereby it could be paid, Hamilton wrote, "For every house half a dollar & for every window above six to Eighteen the additional sum of $\frac{1}{4}$ of a dollar per Window & for every window above Eighteen to thirty $\frac{1}{2}$ of a dollar, for every window above Thirty $\frac{1}{4}$ of a dollar per window" (Syrett and Cooke, *Papers of Hamilton*, III, 248–49; John C. Hamilton, *History of the Republic*, II, 520 n.).

[44] The official journal does not record the tally by which the Rutledge-Izard motion was defeated. The journal limits its notice of this prolonged discussion to the sentence, "Congress proceeded in the consideration of the subject under debate yesterday, agreeably to the order of the day, but came to no resolution thereon" (*JCC*, XXIV, 97).

[45] In a letter to Samuel Adams on 29 January 1783, Arthur Lee wrote: "Every Engine is at work here to obtain permanent taxes and the appointment of Collectors by Congress, in the States. The terror of a mutinying Army is playd off with considerable efficacy. It is certainly a great misfortune to any Country, that their Army should be discontended, and the more so when they have reason on their side, as in the present case. But to remedy temporary evils by permanent Ones is neither wise nor safe" (Burnett, *Letters*, VII, 27–28).

Virginia Delegates to Benjamin Harrison

RC (Virginia State Library). In the hand of Arthur Lee, except for JM's signature. Addressed to "His Excellency The Governor of Virginia." Docketed by Harrison, "Lr. fm our Delegates in Congress Jany 28 '83." Below this, "Jany 28 1783" is written in an unknown hand.

PHILADELPHIA Jany. 28th. 1783

SIR,

Your Excellency's favors of the 4th. & 11th. are before us.[1] We have laid before Congress the Enclosures which were intended for them; & shall acquaint your Excellency of their determinations upon them, as soon as they are made.[2] Mr. Nathan's affair is a matter of some difficulty in the arrangement. We do not see how either Party can be bound by an award, that is not founded on a rule of Court of Law, in a cause depending before it; nor have we any document to show, that the State will be bound in consequence of some legislative Act authorising the Executive to submit the question to Arbitrators. But we shall advise on what is best to be done, & acquaint your Excellency with the result. It woud be a matter of some doubt & delicacy to tempt Mr. Nathan by submitting so large a Sum to his Oath.[3]

We concur most cordially with your Excellency in rejoiceing on the great event of the evacuation of Charles-town.[4] A little time, we hope, will bring us decisive information, whether war or peace will be the issue of the present negociations at Paris; & we shall lose no time in making the communication to your Excellency.[5]

We have the honor to be with the profoundest respect, Yr. Excellency's most obedt. & devotd Servts.

J. MADISON JR.
A. LEE[6]

Congress recd. a few days ago a letter from Mr. Adams of the 8th. of Oct. accompanied by copies of a Treaty of Amity & Commerce & of a Convention concerning recaptures, with the States Genl. Both of them have been ratified and will be published as soon as the length of them will admit.[7]

A Lee

[1] Qq.v.

[2] The "enclosures" which Theodorick Bland presented to Congress on 27 January were the following papers from the General Assembly of Virginia, forwarded to the Virginia delegates in Governor Harrison's letter of 4 January (q.v.): (1) a copy of the act repealing the act ratifying the proposed impost amendment; (2) a copy of a resolution concerning the state's financial quota of 1782; (3) a copy of a resolution in regard to the loss of vouchers for money expended by the state on behalf of the Confederation; (4) a copy of a resolution and other documents about the contract with the merchants-capitulant of Yorktown; and possibly (5) a copy of a resolution respecting the exchange of cannon with the continental army. On 31 January Congress referred the second item to a committee which was discharged on 6 May without making a report, and the third and fourth to another committee which reported on 6 February 1783 (Papers of Madison, V, 452, and n. 1; 457–58; 459–60; 461–63; NA: PCC, No. 185, III, 53; No. 186, fol. 81; JCC, XXIV, 96, 106, 121–23; JM Notes, 27 Jan.; 31 Jan.; 10 Feb. 1783).

[3] Harrison to Delegates, 4 Jan., and n. 8; 11 Jan., and n. 8; Delegates to Harrison, 4 Feb. 1783.

[4] Harrison to Delegates, 11 Jan., and n. 6; Delegates to Harrison, 14 Jan.; JM Notes, 15 Jan. 1783.

[5] Delegates to Harrison, 11 Feb. 1783.

[6] Why Theodorick Bland and Joseph Jones did not sign this letter is unknown. Although Jones had been in Congress on 25 January, his precarious health may have prevented his attendance three days later (JCC, XXIV, 94; JM to Randolph, 28 Jan. 1783; Worthington C. Ford, ed., Letters of Joseph Jones of Virginia, 1777–1787 [Washington, 1889], p. 97). Bland had shared in the debate in Congress on 28 January (JM Notes, 28 Jan. 1783).

[7] JM Notes, 21 Jan., and n. 2; 23 Jan., and n. 1; 24 Jan.; Report on Treaty, 23 Jan. 1783, and nn. 15, 22.

To Edmund Randolph

RC (LC: Madison Papers). Unsigned, and cover missing. Docketed by Randolph, "Mr. Madison. 28th. Jan: 83." To this docket is added in an unknown hand, "in part JO." For a possible explanation of this phrase, see n. 3.

Philada. 28th. Jany. 1783.

My dear Sir,

Notwithstanding the precariousness of the passage over the Susquehanna your favor of the 15th. inst. was duly recd. yesterday.[1] I will mention to Mr. J. your apology for the failure of the remittance, but if I mistake not it will be very little necessary, he having settled the affair of Mr. H. in a way that does not require the payment in question.[2]

The[3] revival of Committees could be a ticklish experiment, and I concieve not admissible but in the last necessity. Would not the circulation of a free & well informed gazette sufficiently counteract the malignant rumours wch. require some antidote? The preparation & circulation of such a paper wd. be a much more easy & œconomical task, than the services which the other expedient would impose if extended throughout the Country, besides that it would produce other useful effects & be liable to no objections. The state of darkness in which the people are left in Va. by the want of a diffusion of intelligence is I find a subject of complaint.[4]

Yesterday was imployed in agitating the expediency of a proposition declaring it to be the "opinion of Congress that the establishment of *genl* funds is essential for doing complete justice to the Creditors of the U.S. for restoring public credit, & for providing for the exigences of the war." The subject was brought on by the Memorial from the army.[5] Such of the Virga. Delegates as concur in this opinion are put in a delicate situation by the preamble to the late repeal of the impost. Persuaded as I am however of the truth of the proposition, & believing as I do that with the same knowledge of facts which my station commands, my Constituents would never have passed that act, and would now rescind it, my assent will be hazarded.[6] For many reasons which I have not time to explain in cypher it is my decided opinion that unless such funds be established, the foundations of our Independence will be laid in injustice & dishonor, and that the advantages of the Revolution dependent on the fœderal compact will be of short duration.[7]

We yesterday laid before Congress sundry papers transmitted by the Govr. The light in which the protest of inability to pay the annual requisition, compared with the repeal of the Impost law placed Virga. did not you may be sure escape observation.[8]

Penna. continues to be visited by the consequences of her patronage of Vermont. A Petition from the inhabitants of territory lately in dispute between her & Virga. was yesterday read in Congs. complaining among other grievances of the interdict agst. even consultations on the subject of a new State within the limits of the former; and praying for the sanction of Congress to their independence, & for an admission into the Union.[9]

Mr. J—on left us on Sunday morning for Baltimore where he is to embark on a French frigate.[10] Col: Bland had arrived at the date of my last. Mr. Lee arrived on Sunday.[11] We hear nothing of Mr. Mercer more than that he may be soon expected.[12]

The only despaches recd. since my last from abroad, are those from Mr. Adams containing copies of the Treaty of Amity & commerce with the U. Provinces & a convention relative to recaptures. They are expressed in two columns one Dutch & the other American, the former signed by the Dutch Plenipos. & the latter by Mr. Adams. The language of the American column is obscure, abounding in foreign idioms & new coined words, with bad grammar & mispellings. They have been ratified & will as soon as possible be proclaimed. It became a question in Congress on which intelligent members were divided whether both columns or the American only ought to be inserted in the act of ratification. The former mode will be pursued.[13] If yr. Library or your recollection can decide the point, favor me with the information.[14]

[1] Randolph to JM, 15 Jan., and n. 2; Jefferson to JM, 31 Jan. 1783, and n. 3.

[2] For James Henry's debt to Joseph Jones, see Randolph to JM, 15 Jan. 1783, and n. 3.

[3] Many years later JM or someone by his direction placed a bracket at the beginning of this paragraph and another at the close of the fifth paragraph to signify the portion of the letter which should be published. See Madison, *Papers* (Gilpin ed.), I, 499–500. Probably it was the clerk of Henry D. Gilpin who at his bidding wrote "in part JO." beside Randolph's docket of the letter. If the phrase was a reminder to cite the journal of Congress in a footnote, Gilpin changed his mind after discovering that JM's notes for 27 January would be much more helpful to readers of the letter than the journal for that date (*ibid.*, I, 500; III, xlvii, n. 103; JM Notes, 27 Jan. 1783; *JCC*, XXIV, 96).

[4] Randolph to JM, 15 Jan. 1783, and nn. 9 and 10. Comments by Joseph Jones and Arthur Lee, who recently had returned from Virginia, may have strengthened JM's own impression of the "darkness in which" her citizens were left by reading the two gazettes of Richmond and the fragmentary journal of Congress, often belatedly published. JM probably was the more sensitive to "malignant rumours," for early in the summer of 1782 he had been wrongfully accused of impugning the loyalty of the people of Williamsburg (*Papers of Madison*, IV, 379, and nn. 1, 3; 403–4; 428–29).

[5] JM Notes, 27 Jan.; 28 Jan. 1783, and nn. 3, 24.

[6] Of JM's fellow delegates from Virginia, Joseph Jones presumably concurred with him, but Theodorick Bland and Arthur Lee opposed. See JM Notes, 27 Jan.; 28 Jan. 1783, and nn. 5, 32, 33, 45.

[7] JM's phraseology of this sentence and of other passages in the letter resembles those in his notes of 28 January (*q.v.*), summarizing his speech in Congress on that day. Which of the two documents he wrote first is not known.

[8] JM Notes, 27 Jan., and nn. 17, 18; Delegates to Harrison, 28 Jan. 1783, and n. 2.

[9] JM Notes, 27 Jan. 1783, and n. 6. The delegates from Pennsylvania were embarrassed to discover that their support of the movement in Vermont for independence from New Hampshire and New York had encouraged a secession movement in the western counties of their own state. See *Papers of Madison*, IV, 130–31; 200–202; 421, n. 22; V, 21; 23, n. 15; 276–77; 277, nn. 5, 9; 352.

10 JM to Randolph, 7 Jan. 1783, n. 9.

11 Randolph to JM, 3 Jan., n. 11; JM Notes, 28 Jan. 1783, n. 6.

12 John Francis Mercer, elected a delegate to Congress by the Virginia General Assembly on 18 December 1782, had been ill but presented his credentials to Congress on 6 February 1783 (*Papers of Madison*, V, 425; 426, n. 3; *JCC*, XXIV, 110–11).

13 JM Notes, 21 Jan., and n. 2; 23 Jan., and nn. 3, 5; 24 Jan.; 29 Jan.; Report on Treaty, 23 Jan. 1783, and nn. 15, 22.

14 Randolph omitted comment on this "point" in his letter of 15 February 1783 (*q.v.*). The explanation may be that, with the General Assembly adjourned and the courts closed, he had become absorbed in completing his vindication of Virginia's land claims west of the Appalachian Mountains. See *Papers of Madison*, IV, 305; 306, n. 3; V, 308–9; 312, n. 18; 457, n. 7; Randolph to JM, 15 Feb. 1783, and nn. 5–7.

Notes on Debates

MS (LC: Madison Papers). For a description of the manuscript of Notes on Debates, see *Papers of Madison*, V, 231–34.

No. VII[1]

Wednesday Jany. 29th. 1783.

Mr. Fitzimmons reminded Congress of the numerous inaccuracies & errors in the American column of the Treaty with Holland and proposed that a revision of it as ratified should take place in order that some steps might be taken for redressing this evil. he added that an accurate comparison of it with the Treaty with France ought also to be made[2] for the purpose of seeing whether it consisted in all its parts with the latter.*[3] He desired the Committe who had prepared the ratification to give some explanation on this subject to Congress.

Mr. Madison as first on that committee[4] informed Congress, that the inaccuracies & errors consisting of mispelling, foreign idioms, & foreign words, obscurity of the sense &c were attended to by the Committee & verbally noted to Congress when their report was under consideration; that the Committee did not report them in writing, as the task was disagreeable, and the faults were not conceived to be of sufficient weight to affect the ratification. He thought it wd. be improper to reconsider

---

* Mr. Hamilton told Mr. Madison privately that Mr. de Marbois speaking of the treaty asked him emphatically whether there were not some articles which required animadversion. Mr. H. did not at the time know what was alluded to. He now supposed the allusion to be to some article supposed to be inconsistent with the Treaty with France; particularly the article referring to the select articles of the latter instead of the whole; which art: Mr. Adams informed Congress had been satisfactory to the D. de Vauguyon.

the act as had been suggested, for the purpose of suspending it on that or any other acct. but had no objection if Congress were disposed to instruct Mr. Adams to substitute with the consent of the other party a more correct counterpart in the American language.[5] The subject was dropped, no body seeming inclined to urge it.

On the motion of Mr. Rutlidge & for the purpose of extending the discussion to particular objects of General Revenue[6] Congress resolved itself into a Committee of the whole to consider of the most effectual means of restoring public credit; and the proposition relative to general revenue was referred to the Committee: Mr. Carroll was elected into the chair, & the proposition taken up.[7]

Mr. Bland proposed to alter the words of the proposition so as to make it read establisht. of funds "on taxes or duties, to operate generally &c" This was agreed to as a more correct phraseology.[8] Mr. Hamilton objected to it at first, supposing thro' mistake that it might exclude the back lands which was a fund in contemplation of some gentlemen.

Mr. Madison having adverted to the jealousy of Mr. Rutlidge of a latent scheme to fix a tax on land according to its quantity, moved that between the words "generally" & "to operate" might be inserted the words "and in just proportion"[9]

Mr. Wilson said he had no objection to this amendmt. but that it might be referred to the taxes individually, & unnecessarily fetter Congress; since if the taxes collectively sd. operate in just proportion it wd. be sufficient. He instanced a land tax & an impost on trade, the former of which might press hardest on the Sourhn. & the latter on the Eastn. but both together might distribute the burden pretty uniformly.[10] From this consideration he moved that the words "on the whole" might be prefixed to the words "in just proportion." This amendt. to the amendment of Mr. Madison was 2ded. by Mr. Boudinot & agreed to without opposition as was afterwards the whole amendmt.[11]

Mr. Wilson in order to leave the scheme open for the back lands as a fund for paying the public debts, moved that the proposition might be further altered so as to read "indispensably necessary *towards* doing complete justice &c" The motion was 2ded. by Mr. Boudinot & passed without opposition[12]

The main proposition of Mr Wilson as thus amended then passed without opposition; in the words following. "That it is the opinion of Congress that the establishment of permanent & adequate funds on taxes or duties which shall operate generally & on the whole in just proportion throughout the U. S. are indispensably necessary towards doing compleat justice to the public Creditors, for restoring public Credit, & for providing for the future exigences of the War."[13]

Mr. Bland proposed as the only expedient that cd. produce immediate relief to the publc Creditors, that Congress sd. by a fixed resolution appropriate to payment of the interest, *all* the monies which should arise from the requisitions on the States. He thought this would not only give immediate relief to the Creditors, but by throwing into circulation the stagnant securities, enliven the whole business of taxation.[14] This proposition was not 2ded.

Mr. Wilson proceeded to detail to Congress his ideas on the subject of continental revenue. He stated the internal debt liquidated and unliquidated at 21. Million of Dollrs. the foreign debt at 8 Million, the actual deficiency of 1782. at 4 Million, the probable deficiency of 83. at 4.Million. Making in the whole 37.Million; which in round numbers & probably without exceeding the reallity may be called 40 Million. The interest of this debt at 6 per Ct. is 2,400,000 Drs, to which it will be prudent to add 600,000, which if the war continues will be needed, and in case of peace may be applied to a navy.[15] An annual revenue of 3 Million of Drs. then is the sum to be aimed at, and which ought to be under the management of Congs. One of the objects already mentioned from wch. this revenue was to be sought, was a poll tax. This he thought a very proper one, but unfortunately the Constitution of Maryland which forbids this tax is an insuperable obstacle.[16] Salt he thought a fit article to be taxed, as it is consumed in a small degree by all and in great quantities by none. It had been found so convenient a subject of taxation, that among all nations which have a system of revenue, it is made a material branch. In England a considerable sum is raised from it. In France it is swelled to the sum of 54,000,000 of livres.[17] He thought it would be improper to levy this tax during the war whilst the price wd. continue so high, but the necessary fall of price at the conclusion of it wd. render the tax less sensible to the people. The suspension of this particular tax during the war would not be inconvenient as it might be set apart for the debt due to France on which the interest would not be called for during the war. He computed the quantity of salt imported into the U. S. annually at 3 Million of Bushels, & proposed a duty of $\frac{1}{3}$ of a Dollar per bushel which wd. yield 1,000,000 of Drs.[18] This duty he observed wd. press hardest on the Eastern States on acct. of the extraordinary consumption in the fisheries.

The next tax which he suggested was on land. 1 Dollar on every 100 Acres according to the computation of the Superintendt of finance

ELIPHALET DYER

OLIVER ELLSWORTH

JAMES WILSON

would produce 500,000 Dollrs. This computation he was persuaded might be doubled; since their could not be less than 100 Million of Acres comprehended within the titles of individuals which at 1 Dr. per 100 Acres would yields 1,000,000, of Dollars. This tax cd. not be deemed too high & would bear heaviest not on the industrious farmer, but on the great land-holder.[19] As the tax on Salt would fall with most weight on the Eastern States, the equilibrium would be restored by this which would be most felt by the Middle and Southern States.

The impost on trade was another source of revenue which, altho' it might be proper to vary it somewhat in order to remove particular objections, ought to be again & again urged upon the States by Congress. The office of Finance has rated this at 500,000 Dollars. He thought a peace would double it in which case the sum of 3,000,000 Drs. would be made up.[20] If these computations however should be found to be too high there will still be other objects which would bear taxation. An Excise he said had been mentioned. In general this species of taxation was tyrannical & justly obnoxious, but in certain forms had been found consistent with the policy of the freeest States. In Massachussets a State remarkably jealous of its liberty, an Excise was not only admitted before but continued since the revolution. The same was the case with Penna. also remarkable for its freedom.[21] An Excise if so modified as not to offend the spirit of liberty may be considered as an object of easy & equal revenue. Wine & imported spirits had borne a heavy Excise in other Countries, and might be adopted in ours. Coffee is another object which might be included. The amount of these three objects is uncertain but materials for a satisfactory computation might be procured. These hints & remarks he acknowledged to be extremely imperfect & that he had been led to make them solely by a desire to contribute his mite towards such a system as would place the finances of the U. S. on an honorable & prosperous footing.

Mr. Ghorum observed that the proposition of Mr. Bland, however salutary its tendency might be in the respects suggested, could never be admitted because it would leave our army to starve and all our affairs to stagnate during its immediate operation.[22] He objected to a duty on salt as not only bearing too heavy on the Eastn. States, but as giving a dangerous advantage to Rivals in the fisheries. Salt he sd exported from England for the fisheries is exempted particularly from duties.[23] He thought it would be best to confine our attention for the present to the impost on trade which had been carryed so far towards an accomplishment, and to remove the objections which had retarded it, by limiting the term of its continuance, leaving to the States the nomination of the collectors, and by making the appropriation of it more specific.

Mr. Rutlidge was also for confining our attention to the Impost, & to get that before any further attempts were made. In order to succeed in getting it however he thought it ought to be asked in a new form. Few of the States had complied with the recommendation of Congs. literally. Georgia had not yet complied. Rhode Island had absolutely refused to comply at all. Virga. which at first complied but partially has since rescinded even that partial compliance. After enumerating the several objections urged by the States agst. the scheme,[24] he proposed in order to remove them the following resolution: viz.

"that it be earnestly recommended to the several States to impose & levy a duty of 5 PrCt. ad valorem at the time & place of importation, on all goods, wares & merchandizes of foreign growth & manufactures wch. may be imported into the said States respectively, except goods of the U. S. or any of them, and a like duty on all prizes & prize goods condemned in the Court of admiralty of said States; that the money arising from such dutys be paid into the continental Treasury, to be appropriated & applied to the payment of the interest and to sink the principal of the money which the U. S. have borrowed in Europe & of what they may borrow, for discharging the arrears due to the army & for the future support of the war & to no other use or purpose whatsoever: that the said duties be continued for 25 years, unless the debts abovemd. be discharged in the meantime, in which case they shall cease & determine, that the money arising from the said duties & paid by any State, be passed to the credit of such State on account of its quota of the debt of the U. States."[25] The motion was seconded by Mr. Lee.

Mr. Woolcot opposed the motion as unjust towards those States which having few or no ports receive their merchandize through the ports of others; repeating the observation that it is the consumer & not the importer who pays the duty. He again animadverted on the conduct of Virga. in first giving & afterwards withdrawing her assent to the Impost recommended by Congress.[26]

Mr. Elseworth thought it wrong to couple any other objects with the Impost: that the States would give this if any thing; and that if a land tax or an excise were combined with it the whole scheme would fail.[27] He thought however that some modification of the plan recommended by Congs. would be necessary. He supposed when the benefits of this continl. revenue should be experienced it would incline the States to concur in making additions to it. He abetted the opposition of Mr.

Wolcot to the motion of Mr. Rutlidge which proposed that each State should be credited for the duties collected within its ports; dwelt on the injustice of it, said that Connecticut before the revolution did not import 1/50 perhaps not 1/100 part of the foreign merchandise consumed within it, and pronounced that such a plan wd. never be agreed to.[28] He concurred in the expediency of new-modelling the scheme of the impost by defining the period of its continuance; by leaving to the States the nomination, & to Congress the appointment of Collectors or vice versa; and by a more determinate appropriation of the revenue.[29] The first object to which it ought to be applied was he thought the foreign debt. This object claimed a preference as well from the hope of facilitating further aids from the quarter,[30] as from the disputes into wch. a failure may embroil the U. S. The prejudices agst. making a provision for foreign debts which sd. not include the domestic ones was he thought unjust & might be satisfied by immediately requiring a tax in discharge of which loan office certificates should be receivable.[31] State funds for the domestic debts would be proper for subsequent consideration. He added as a further objection against crediting the States for the duties on trade respectively collected by them, that a mutual jealousy of injuring their trade by being foremost in imposing such a duty would prevent any from making a beginning.[32]

Mr. Williamson said that Mr. Rutledge's motion at the same time that it removed some objections, introduced such as would be much more fatal to the measure. He was sensible of the necessity of some alterations, particularly in its duration & the appointment of the Collectors. But the crediting the States severally for the amount of their collections was so palpably unjust & injurious that he thought candor required that it should not be persisted in. He was of opinion that the interest of the States, which trade for others, also required it, since such an abuse of the advantage possessed by them would compel the States for which they trade, to overcome the obstacles of nature & provide supplies for themselves. N. Carolina he said would probably be supplied pretty much thro' Virga. if the latter forebore to levy a tax on the former, but in case she did not forbear, the ports of N. C. which are nearly as deep as those of Holland, might & probably wd. be substituted.[33] The profits drawn by the more commercial States from the business they carry on for the others, were of themselves sufficient & ought to satisfy them.

Mr. Ramsay differed entirely from his colleage (Mr Rutlidge). He thought that as the consumer pays the tax, the crediting the States collecting the impost, unjust. N. Carolina, Maryland, N. Jersey & Connecticut would suffer by such a regulation and would never agree to it.[34]

Mr. Bland was equally agst. the regulation, he thought it replete with injustice & repugnant to every idea of finance. he observed tht. this point had been fully canvassed at the time when the impost was originally recommended by Congress, & finally exploded.[35] He was indeed he said opposed to the whole motion (of Mr. Rutlidge) Nothing would be a secure pledge to Creditors that was not placed out of the Controul of the grantors. As long as it was in the power of the States to repeal their grants in this respect, suspicions would prevail, & wd. prevent loans. Money ought to be appropriated by the States as it is by the Parliament of G. B. He proposed that the revenue to be solicited from the States should be irrevocable by them without the consent of Congress, or of nine of the States.[36] He disapproved of any determinate limitation to the continuance of the revenue, because the continuance of the debt could not be fixed and that was the only rule that could be proper or satisfactory. He said he should adhere to these ideas in the face of the act of Virga. repealing her assent to the impost; that it was trifling with Congs. to enable them to contract debts, & to withold from them the means of fulfilling their contracts.[37]

Mr. Lee said he seconded the motion of Mr. Rutlidge because he thought it most likely to succed; that he was persuaded the States would not concur in the impost on trade without a limitation of time affixed to it. With such a limitation and the right of collection, he thought Virga. R. Island & the other States probably wd. concur. The objection of his Colleague (Mr. Bland) he conceived to be unfounded; No act of the States could be irrevocable, because if so called it might notwithstanding be repealed.[38] But he thought there wd. be no danger of a repeal, observing that the national faith was all the security that was given in other countries, or that could be given. He was sensible that some thing was of necessity to be done in the present alarming crisis; and was willing to strike out the clause crediting the States for their respective collections of the revenue on trade, as it was supposed that it wd. impede the measure.[39]

Mr. Hamilton disliked every plan that made but partial provision for the public debts; as an inconsistent & dishonorable departure from the declaration made by Congs. on that subject.[40] He said the domestic Creditors would take the alarm at any distinctions unfavorable to their claims; that they would withhold their influence from any such measures recommended by Congress; and that it must be principally from their influence on their respective legislatures that success could be expected to any applications from Congs. for a general revenue.[41]

¹ For a probable explanation of this Roman numeral, see *Papers of Madison*, V, 231.

² Report on Treaty, 23 Jan., and nn. 9, 10, 15, 22; JM Notes, 23 Jan., n. 6; JM to Randolph, 28 Jan. 1783.

³ Regarding the comment written by JM in his footnote, Article XXII of the treaty referred to "select articles" of the Treaty of Amity and Commerce between the United States and France (Report on Treaty, 23 Jan., and n. 10). These articles related in part to the North American offshore fisheries—a resource of France from which Marbois was eager to bar the United States. See *Papers of Madison*, V, 436–37; 438, n. 5; 441; 443, n. 2; Report on Treaty, 23 Jan. 1783, n. 10. In his dispatch from The Hague on 8 October 1782, forwarding the treaty and convention to Livingston, John Adams wrote: "The rights of France and Spain are sufficiently secured by the twenty-second article; although it is not in the very words of the project transmitted me by Congress, it is the same in substance and effect. The Duc de la Vauguyon was very well contented with it" (Wharton, *Revol. Dipl. Corr.*, V, 805). For La Vauguyon, ambassador from the court of Versailles to the States-General of the United Provinces of the Netherlands, see *Papers of Madison*, IV, 291, n. 19; V, 207, n. 2. For Barbé-Marbois, see JM Notes, 1 Jan. 1783.

Whether the French had the "right" or only a "liberty," granted to them by Great Britain in the Treaty of Utrecht (1714) and confirmed in the Treaty of Paris (1763), to fish off the northern coast of Newfoundland and to dry their catch on that coast during the fishing season was an issue which interested JM. By the tenth article of the Treaty of Amity and Commerce of 30 January 1778, the United States had pledged that neither the Americans nor their government would ever "disturb" the French in the exercise of those "rights" (*JCC*, XI, 428).

Bearing upon this subject are nine pages in JM's hand, comprising his copies of an undated "Letter from Sr. Stanier Porteen Secretary to Lord Weymouth to the latter" and of an "Extract above referred to of a letter from the Earl of Egremont to his grace the Duke of Bedford dated Whitehall March 1st. 1763." JM's docket of these copies reads, "Mr. R. Izard copy of paper obtained by him from the Secretary of Lord Weymouth thro' a member of the B. Parliam." On the cover page of these transcriptions, JM wrote, "The annexed letters were obtained for Mr. R. Izzard at his request by Mr. Dempster member of Parliament, from the Secretary of Lord Weymouth." Stressing the untenability of the claim by France to the "rights" mentioned above, the Porten and Egremont documents implicitly denied that France could extend the privilege granted her by Great Britain to the United States or any other country.

Sir Stanier Porten (d. 1789), an uncle of Edward Gibbon, historian, had been knighted in 1772 and became the keeper of state papers at Whitehall two years later. Thomas Thynne (1734–1796), third Viscount Weymouth and later first Marquis of Bath, was secretary of state of the southern department, 1768–1770, 1775–1779. Charles Wyndham (1710–1763), second Earl of Egremont, was secretary of state for the southern department, 1761–1763. John Russell (1710–1771), fourth Duke of Bedford, was then in Paris as ambassador extraordinary to conclude a peace with France. George Dempster (1732–1818) served in the House of Commons from 1761 to 1790 as the member for the boroughs of Forfar and Fife, Scotland.

When JM copied the Porten and Egremont documents is unknown, but it probably was not before 7 June 1782, when Ralph Izard presented his credentials to Congress as a delegate from South Carolina, and not after 23 March 1783, when a copy of the provisional Articles of Peace reached Philadelphia (*JCC*, XXII, 320; JM Notes, 24 Mar. 1783). When Izard secured copies of the documents is also unknown. Without mentioning the documents, he had written separate letters in September 1778 from Paris to Henry Laurens and John Adams about the conflict in interpretation between France and Great Britain over the articles in the Treaty of Utrecht and Treaty of Paris relating to the Newfoundland fisheries (Wharton, *Revol. Dipl. Corr.*, II, 713–14, 740–49). See also *ibid.*, VI, 82–83.

⁴ For the members of the committee and its appointment by Congress, see JM Notes, 21 Jan.; Report on Treaty, 23 Jan. 1783, hdn.

⁵ JM Notes, 23 Jan., and n. 2; JM to Randolph, 28 Jan. 1783. Omitting any mention of these criticisms, Livingston in his dispatch of 13 February 1783 congratulated Adams "most sincerely upon having surmounted all the obstacles that opposed themselves to the completion of our important connexion" with the Netherlands. "It has, I think, given the last blow to the pride of Britain" (Wharton, *Revol. Dipl. Corr.*, VI, 250).

⁶ In his old age, JM interlineated "General Revenue" over a canceled "gel reve."

⁷ John Rutledge's motion was seconded by Theodorick Bland. Judging from the official journal, a vote on this motion was suspended until, upon the suggestion of Samuel Osgood, Congress had "*Resolved*, That whenever the house is resolved into a Committee of the whole, the chairman of the committee be elected by ballot" (*JCC*, XXIV, 97–98, 98, n. 2). After the Rutledge motion carried, the committee of the whole chose Daniel Carroll to preside. See JM Notes, 4 Feb., and n. 20; 21 Feb. 1783, and n. 28. The "proposition relative to general revenue" was James Wilson's motion of 27 January 1783, as "new-modelled" by JM the next day (JM Notes, 27 Jan., and n. 16; 28 Jan. 1783, and n. 3).

⁸ Bland's amendment was confined to the words "on taxes and duties." JM noted the adoption of this amendment by altering the opening portion of the manuscript draft of his "new-modelled" proposition of 28 January to read, "That it is the opinion of Congress that the establishment of permanent & adequate funds on taxes or Duties which shall operate generally throughout the U.S." He also underlined the words following "Duties." See JM Notes, 28 Jan. 1783, and n. 3.

⁹ JM misstated where he intended this phrase to go. Grammatically it must follow rather than precede "generally," and so it was located in the resolution after being "prefixed" by Wilson's "amendt. to the amendment." See the next paragraph of the text and n. 11.

¹⁰ *Papers of Madison*, V, 375, n. 15; JM Notes, 14 Jan. 1783, and n. 9.

¹¹ See nn. 8 and 9. Upon the adoption of his amendment and Wilson's amendment thereto, JM inserted a caret immediately after "generally" in the manuscript text of his original motion, repeated the same mark on the page below the motion, and wrote "on the whole in just proportions." See JM Notes, 28 Jan. 1783, and n. 3.

¹² This proposal by Wilson consisted only of changing the "for" after "necessary" in JM's original motion to "towards." JM duly canceled "for" in his manuscript but inadvertently interlineated "twoards." See JM Notes, 28 Jan. 1783, and n. 3.

¹³ JM wrote "passd" below the draft of his original motion, altered by him to reflect the particulars in which it had been amended. The motion as passed by the committee of the whole was spread on the official journal of Congress the same day but not adopted until 12 February (*JCC*, XXIV, 97–98); JM Notes, 12 Feb. 1783, and n. 1).

¹⁴ The interest on the "securities," of which the loan-office certificates were a prime example, had been long in default, thus rendering them largely unacceptable ("stagnant") as payment for commodities, as security for private loans, or as capital

for investment. Apparently overlooking the military creditors of the United States altogether (see Nathaniel Gorham's subsequent remarks), Bland defended his proposal with an argument which recalls the following statement by Robert Morris in his report of 29 July 1782: "many persons by being Creditors of the Public, are deprived of those funds which are necessary to the full exercise of their skill and industry, consequently the community are deprived of the benefits which would result from that exercise, whereas if these debts, which are in a manner dead, were brought back to existence, monied men would purchase them up (tho' perhaps at a considerable discount) and thereby restore to the public many useful members, who are now entirely lost, and extend the operations of many more to considerable advantage. For altho' not one additional shilling would be by this means brought in, yet by distributing property into those hands which could render it most productive, the Revenue would be increased while the original stock continued the same" (*JCC*, XXII, 436).

15 Randolph to JM, 15 Jan., n. 13; JM Notes, 27 Jan., and nn. 11, 13. In an undated memorandum, to which reference already has been made, Alexander Hamilton estimated the annual interest on a total debt of $40,000,000 to be $2,280,000. Differing with Wilson, Hamilton calculated the sum owed abroad as $6,000,000 at 4 per cent interest, and the sum owed in the United States as $34,000,000 at 6 per cent interest (JM Notes, 28 Jan. 1783, n. 43).

16 Article XIII of the "Declaration of Rights" of the Constitution of Maryland, adopted in 1776, stated in part, "That the levying taxes by the poll is grievous and oppressive, and ought to be abolished" (Francis N. Thorpe, ed., *Federal and State Constitutions*, III, 1687).

17 Except between 1730 and 1732, Parliament had levied an import duty on salt for many years. The rate was five shillings a bushel in 1783. Taxes were also assessed upon home-manufactured salt (Sir John Sinclair, *The History of the Public Revenue of the British Empire* [3d ed.; 3 vols.; London, 1803–4], II, 20–27, 374–78; Stephen Dowell, *A History of Taxation and Taxes in England from the Earliest Times to the Present Day* [4 vols.; London, 1884], IV, 3–4).

Salt in France was a royal monopoly. The hated gabelle, or salt tax, was collected by agents of the farmers-general, who pocketed each year all money collected in excess of the sum they had contracted to pay to the government. The rate of the tax varied among the provinces, and a few of them were wholly exempted from the assessment. In his *Compte Rendu au Roi*, submitted in January 1781, after six years as director general of the Royal Treasury, Jacques Necker reported that the gabelle yielded 54,000,000 livres annually and hence could not be abolished. On the other hand, he scathingly indicted the administration of the levy for its inequities, cruelties, corruption, and promotion of smuggling among the provinces ([Auguste Louis,] Baron de Staël [-Holstein], comp., *Oeuvres Complètes de M. Necker* [15 vols.; Paris, 1820–21], II, 109–18, 150–51). See also *Papers of Madison*, II, 225, n. 2.

18 During the Revolution the extreme scarcity of salt, especially in states south of New York, is reflected in measures exempting importers from the payment of duties on this vital commodity and promising bounties to domestic producers. See, for example, *JCC*, II, 235, 464–65; IV, 398; VI, 135; VIII, 461–62; IX, 829–30; XV, 1291; XXI, 872–73, 951; *Papers of Madison*, I–IV, index of each volume under military supplies or its subheading, provisions, salt. Estimating the annual consumption of salt in the United States at 1,000,000 bushels and favoring a "Salt duty at $\frac{1}{8}$ of a dollar per bushel," Alexander Hamilton foresaw that this impost would yield only $125,000 (Syrett and Cooke, *Papers of Hamilton*, III, 248).

19 Wilson's argument as well as his figures were taken from Robert Morris' report of 29 July 1782 to Congress. Advocating a land tax, Morris commented, "a large proportion of America is the property of great landholders, they monopolize

it without cultivation, they are (for the most part) at no expence either of money or personal service to defend it, and keeping the price higher by monopoly than otherwise it would be they impede the settlement and culture of the Country. A Land Tax, therefore, would have the salutary operation of an agrarian law without the iniquity" (*JCC*, XXII, 439–40). Alexander Hamilton estimated the proceeds from a "Land tax on Mr. Morris' plan" at only $480,000 (Syrett and Cooke, *Papers of Hamilton*, III, 248).

20 Although Morris in his report on 29 July 1782 had estimated the yearly revenue from a 5 per cent tax on imports and prizes during the war at $600,000, he deducted one sixth of this total to cover "the cost of collection" and "the various defalcations, which will necessarily happen" (*JCC*, XXII, 439).

21 JM Notes, 27 Jan. 1783, n. 25. Under authority of the state constitution of 1780, the General Court, or legislature, of Massachusetts in 1781 continued the excise by statute amended on 7 March 1782 "for the Purposes of Paying the Interest on Government Securities," and further amended on 3 July. On 8 November 1782 the amended statute was superseded by "An Act respecting Excise" (*The Laws of the Commonwealth of Massachusetts, Passed from the Year 1780, to the End of the Year 1800* . . . [3 vols.; Boston, 1801–7], I, 66, 73, 88).

On 6 April 1781 the legislature of Pennsylvania extended for another decade the ten-year excise law of 1 March 1772, and amended that law by stipulating that after 30 May 1781 the tax on "Wine, Rum, Brandy and other Spirits" would be doubled to a rate of 8 *d.* a gallon, payable in specie or its equivalent (*Pa. Packet*, 14 Apr. 1781). In Wilson's view, Pennsylvania and Massachusetts were "remarkable" for their "freedom," because their constitutions provided for more self-government than the people enjoyed in most of the eleven other states (Andrew C. McLaughlin, *A Constitutional History of the United States* [New York, 1935], pp. 110–12; 113, n. 17).

22 See n. 14.

23 JM wrote and canceled at the outset of this sentence, "Before the revolution he said." See n. 17. Gorham may have had in mind that the salt was shipped free of export duty from England to her colonies of Newfoundland and Nova Scotia, which were rivals of New England in the fisheries.

24 JM Notes, 28 Jan. 1783, nn. 29–31.

25 To become effective, the original recommendations of Congress of 3 and 7 February 1781, being in the nature of an amendment to the then pending Articles of Confederation, had to be ratified by every state (JM Notes, 28 Jan. 1783, n. 29). Evidently recognizing the impossibility of attaining that degree of unanimity, in view of the repeated refusal of Rhode Island, the inaction of Georgia, and the recent repeal by Virginia of her act of ratification, Rutledge proposed to avoid the impracticability of an amendment and to quiet the opposition of the ardent state-sovereignty delegates by having Congress request each state to levy and collect a 5 per cent impost for no longer than twenty-five years, with the understanding that the money so raised by each state would be deducted from its portion of the Confederation debt, past and future. Maryland was the only state which had limited to a maximum of twenty-five years the effectiveness of its act ratifying the 5 per cent impost amendment (NA: PCC, No. 75, fols. 320–21).

26 JM Notes, 27 Jan. 1783, and nn. 17, 18.

27 JM Notes, 28 Jan. 1783, and nn. 4, 5, 42, 43. See also nn. 16–19, 21, 23, above.

28 In 1774 the governor of Connecticut informed the Board of Trade that although direct imports from Great Britain were "few," inhabitants of the colony received annually from the mother country, by way of Boston, Rhode Island ports, and New York City, commodities valued at about £200,000 sterling (J. Hammond Trumbull or Charles J. Hoadly, eds., *The Public Records of the Colony of Connecticut* [15 vols.; Hartford, 1850–90], XIV, 344–45 n., 498; Oscar Zeichner, *Con-*

necticut's Years of Controversy, 1750–1776 [Chapel Hill, N.C., 1949], pp. 131–32, 278, n. 25, 307, n. 20). Oliver Ellsworth's fractions are approximately verified by the 1771–1772 statistics of Connecticut's imports and exports in Stella H. Sutherland, *Population Distribution in Colonial America*, pp. 276–330, *passim*.

29 In his motion, as quoted by JM, Rutledge omitted mention of the manner whereby the collectors should be nominated and appointed.

30 *Papers of Madison*, V, 99; 424, n. 9; JM Notes, 9–10 Jan. 1783, and nn. 12–14; 13 Jan. 1783.

31 JM Notes, 30 Jan. 1783, n. 4.

32 JM Notes, 28 Jan. 1783, n. 29.

33 Of North Carolina's five ports of entry, the busiest on the eve of the Revolution were Port Brunswick, Port Roanoke (Edenton), and Port Beaufort (Beaufort and New Bern). At that time, although her direct trade with British and foreign ports was increasing, about two-thirds of her exports and imports, not including her coastal trade, passed through ports in Virginia and South Carolina (Charles Christopher Crittenden, *The Commerce of North Carolina, 1763–1789* [New Haven, Conn., 1936], pp. 41–42 n., 71–72, 75–76, 78, 83, and n. 7, 84; Harry Roy Merrens, *Colonial North Carolina in the Eighteenth Century: A Study in Historical Geography* [Chapel Hill, N.C., 1964], pp. 85–172, *passim*). See also the tables in Stella H. Sutherland, *Population Distribution in Colonial America*.

34 See n. 27; JM Notes, 28 Jan. 1783, n. 29. For the direct foreign trade of Maryland, centered principally at Oxford, Annapolis, and Baltimore, and her heavy dependence upon the port of New Castle, Del., and ports of Virginia, such as Alexandria, see Charles Albro Barker, *The Background of the Revolution in Maryland* (New Haven, Conn., 1940), pp. 110–16. A little of the trade of New Jersey with Great Britain and foreign countries passed through the ports of Perth Amboy, Burlington, and Salem, but most of it focused at Chester, Philadelphia, and New York City (Richard P. McCormick, *Experiment in Independence: New Jersey in the Critical Period* [New Brunswick, N.J., 1950], p. 104).

35 JM Notes, 28 Jan. 1783, n. 29.

36 In opposing Rutledge's proposal, Bland insisted that individuals or companies would not lend money to the government so long as Congress had no constitutional means of compelling state legislatures to provide the money for paying the interest on, or the principal of, these loans. The state legislatures, continued Bland, having refused to follow the example of the British Parliament by making long-term appropriations for specific purposes, must be prevented from exercising, wholly at their option and without the approval of Congress, the power "to repeal their grants" of revenue to the Confederation. See JM Notes, 21 Feb. 1783, and n. 11.

37 JM Notes, 28 Jan. 1783, nn. 31–33. For Bland, a strong proponent of state sovereignty, to speak in support of enhancing congressional power is evidence of how concerned he had become to give Congress the means of discharging its "contracts."

38 See n. 35. Considerations of state sovereignty had been stressed by the Rhode Island legislature in refusing to ratify, and by the Virginia legislature in rescinding its ratification of, the impost amendment (*JCC*, XXIII, 788–89; *Papers of Madison*, V, 407, n. 1; Harrison to JM, 4 Jan. 1783, n. 4). By having each state levy and supervise the collection of the impost, and by limiting its duration, the Rutledge proposal seemed to Arthur Lee to pay sufficient deference to state sovereignty.

39 See n. 25.

40 Hamilton referred to the resolution adopted by Congress on 25 January (JM Notes, 25 Jan. 1783, and n. 7).

41 Hamilton's argument resembles that of Robert Morris in his letter of 29 July 1782 to the president of Congress (JM Notes, 28 Jan. 1783, n. 9).

Notes on Debates

MS (LC: Madison Papers). For a description of the manuscript of Notes on Debates, see *Papers of Madison*, V, 231–34.

Thursday 30 Jany.

The answer to the Memorials from the Legislature of Penna. was agreed to as it stands on the Journal; N. Jersey alone dissenting.[1]

In the course of its discussion several expressions were struck out which seemed to reprehend the States for the deficiency of their contributions. In favor of these expressions it was urged that they were true and ought to be held forth as the cause of the public difficulties in justification of Congress.[2] On the other side it was urged tht. Congress had in many respects been faulty as well as the States, particularly in letting their finances become so disordered before they began to apply any remedy; and that if this were not the case, it would be more prudent to address to the States a picture of the public distresses & danger, than a Satire on their faults; since the latter would only irritate them; whereas the former wd. tend to lead them into the measures supposed by Congress to be essential to the public interest.

The propriety of mentioning to the Legislature of Penna. the expedt. into which Congress had been driven of drawing bills on Spain & Holland without previous warrant; the disappt. attending it, and the deductions ultimately ensuing from the aids destined to the U. S. by the Ct. of France, was also a subject of discussion. On one side it was represented as a fact which being dishonorable to Congress ought not to be proclaimed by them & that in the present case it cd. answer no purpose. On the other side it was contended that it was already known to all the world, that as a glaring proof of the public embarrassmts. it would impress the Legislature with the danger of making those separate appropriations which wd. increase the embarrassments;[3] and particularly would explain in some degree the cause of the discontinuance of the French interest due on the loan office certificates.[4]

Mr. Rutlidge & some other members having expressed less solicitude about satisfying or soothing the Creditors within Pa. through the legislature than others thought ought be[5] felt by every one, Mr. Wilson adverting to it with some warmth, declared that if such indifference should prevail, he was little anxious what became of the answer to the Memorials. Pena. he was persuaded would take her own measures without regard to those of Congress, and that she ought to do so. She was willing he said to sink or swim according to the common fate, but that she would not suffer herself with a millstone of *6,000,000 of the continl. debt about her neck to go to the bottom alone.[6]

* he supposed that sum due by the U. S. to Citizens of Penna. for loans.

[1] The official journal for 30 January is confined wholly to the report, drafted by Thomas FitzSimons, of the committee with Daniel Carroll, chairman (JCC, XXIV, 99–105, 105, n. 1). For the memorials of the Pennsylvania legislature and the appointment of the Carroll committee, see Papers of Madison, V, 293–94; 294, n. 1; 362–64; 366, nn. 19, 23; 373; 389–90; 394; JM Notes, 24 Jan. 1783, and nn. 17, 19, 20. The tone of the present answer is much more conciliatory than that of 1 October 1782 to the legislature of New Jersey on behalf of her unpaid troops (Papers of Madison, V, 173–75; 175, nn. 8, 11), a contrast which may account for the negative vote of the New Jersey delegation.

[2] The inability of Congress to fulfill its pledge to purchasers of loan-office certificates was attributed in the report to the delinquency of the states in furnishing their financial quotas for 1782, to the refusal of three states to empower Congress to levy a duty on imports, and to the delay of every state with trans-Appalachian lands, except New York, to cede them to the Confederation on equitable terms. For the "several expressions" deleted from the report before it was adopted by Congress, see JCC, XXIV, 100, 101–2.

[3] Papers of Madison, V, 20; 21, n. 4; 424, n. 9; 450, n. 5; 451, n. 14; JM Notes, 9–10 Jan., and nn. 12–14; Conference with Morris, 10 Jan., n. 5; JM to Randolph, 22 Jan. 1783, and n. 8.

[4] Most of the latest loans and gifts from King Louis XVI of France necessarily had been used by Congress to buy military matériel overseas rather than to pay the interest due on loan-office certificates owned by residents of the United States. See JM Notes, 24 Jan. 1783, and n. 18. On 3 October 1776 Congress had decided to establish in each state an office for soliciting funds from individuals and business firms. In exchange, they received loan-office certificates, yielding 6 per cent interest annually, and varying in their denominations from $300 (later $200) to $1,000 (later $10,000). On 23 December of that year Congress authorized its commissioners "at the Court of France" to borrow £2,000,000 sterling, to be used in part for the payment of interest on these certificates (JCC, V, 845–46; VI, 955, 1036–37, VII, 143, XV, 1225–26; XVII, 565). Beginning soon thereafter and continuing until 1782, bills of exchange for that purpose were drawn as a matter of routine on the commissioners in Paris, with the expectation that the bills would be honored by the royal treasury (JCC, VIII, 730–31, XII, 1243; XVII, 689; XIX, 161–62, 164, 167–68).

In his report of 29 July 1782, rendered about a month after a congressional committee had proposed overconfidently to use the expected proceeds from the impost to pay the interest on the loan certificates, the superintendent of finance emphasized that there were no French funds for discharging that obligation and that "the idea which many entertain of soliciting Loans abroad to pay the Interest of domestic Debts, is a measure pregnant with its own destruction" (JCC, XXII, 352, 438). Robert Morris also characterized the prevalent belief "that Foreigners will trust us with millions, while our own citizens will not trust us with a shilling" as "among the many extraordinary conceptions which have been produced during the present Revolution" (JCC, XXII, 433). Of necessity, Congress on 9 September 1782 ordered him to instruct the loan officers to stop issuing bills of exchange for the interest due, or to come due, on certificates since 1 March of that year (JCC, XXIII, 555). The next day Congress requisitioned the states for an extra $1,200,000 "as absolutely and immediately necessary for payment of the interest of the public debt" (JCC,

XXIII, 545, 564, 571; *Papers of Madison*, V, 127; 129, n. 13). Thus, with the financial backing of France seemingly at an end, with the proposed impost amendment
unratified, and with most of the states far in arrears in meeting their monetary
quotas, the interest on the loan-office certificates was almost a year in default by
the time of the present debate.

[5] JM obviously omitted "to" between "ought" and "be."

[6] The exact amount owed on 30 January probably cannot be known. By 1
January 1783 the total loan-certificate debt was estimated to be $11,400,485.64 1/8
specie by Morris. Although of this total the loan office for Pennsylvania had issued
certificates worth $3,948,904.14 4/8 specie, citizens of that state had also bought a
large number of certificates from residents of other states (NA: PCC, No. 137, II,
205). James Wilson evidently estimated these outside purchases at over $2,000,000.

In view of the alarming decline in value of paper money, Congress on 28 June
1780 had established "a progressive rate of depreciation" providing that a forty-to-
one ratio, in terms of Spanish milled dollars, should apply after 18 March of that
year to continental currency offered for the loan certificates and to the interest
paid to their owners (*JCC*, XVII, 455–57, 567–69). See also JM Notes, 20 Feb. 1783,
and nn. 6, 7.

Notes on Debates

MS (LC: Madison Papers). For a description of the manuscript
of Notes on Debates, see *Papers of Madison*, V, 231–34.

Friday Jany. 31.

The instructions to the Va. delegates from that State relative to tobo.
exported to N. Y. under passport from Secy of Congress was referred
to a Committee.[1] Mr Fitzimmons moved that the information recd.
from sd. State of its inability to contribute more than   towards the
requisitions of Congress sd. be also committed.[2] Mr. Bland saw no
reason for such committment. Mr. Ghorum was in favr. of it. He
thought such a resolution from Va. was of the most serious import;
especially if compared with her withdrawal of her assent to the Impost:[3]
He said with much earnestness, that if one State should be connived at
in such defaults others would think themselves entitled to a like indulgence. Massts: he was sure had a better title to it than Virga. He said
the former had expended immense sums in recruiting her line, which
composed almost the whole Northn. Army; that 1,200,000 £ (dollar at
6/. had been laid out: & that without this sum, the army would have
been disbanded.[4]

Mr. Fitzimmons abetting the animadversion on Virga. took notice
that of   Dollars reqd. by Congress from her for the year 1782, she

had paid the paltry sum only of 35,000 Drs. and was notwithstanding endeavoring to play off from further contributions.[5] The commitment took place without opposition[6]

The subcommittee consisting of Mr. Madison Carroll & Mr. Wilson had this morning a conference with the Superintendt. of Finance on the best mode of estimating the value of land through the U. S.[7] The Superntendt was no less puzzled on the subject than the Committee had been. He thought some essay ought to be made for executing the confederation if it sd. be practicable, & if not to let the impracticability appear to the States. He concurred with the subcommittee also in opinion that it would be improper to refer the valuation to the States, as mutual suspicions of partiality, if not a real partiality, would render the result a source of discontent; and that even if Congs. shd expressly reserve to themselves a right of revising & rejecting it, such a right could not be exercised without giving extreme offence to the suspected party.[8] To guard agst. these difficulties it was finally agreed, & the sub-committee accordingly reported to the G. Committee,

"That it is expedient to require of the several States a return of all surveyed & granted land within each of them; and that in such returns the land be distinguished into occupied & unoccupied.

That it also was expedient to appoint one Commissr. for each State who should be empowered to proceed without loss of time into the several States; & to estimate the value of the lands therein according to the returns abovementioned, & to such instructions as should from time to time be given him for that purpose."[9]

This report was hurried into the Grand Committee for two reasons: 1st. it was found that Mr. Rutledge, Mr. Bland & several others relied so much on a valuation of land, and connected it so essentially with measures for restoring public credit that an extreme backwardness on their part affected all these measures, whilst the valuation of land was left out.[10] a 2d. reason was that the subcommittee were afraid that suspicions might arise of intentional delay, in order to confine the attention of Congs. to general funds as affording the only prospect of relief.[11]

The Grand Committee for like reasons were equally impatient to make a report to Congress; and accordingly after a short consultation the question was taken whether the above report of the Subcome. or the report (see   ) referred to them sd. be preferred.[12] In favor of the 1st. were Mr. Wilson, Mr. Carroll, Mr. Madison, Mr. Elmore,[13] Mr. Hamilton. In favor of the 2d. were Mr. Arnold, Mr. Dyer, Mr. Hawkins,[14] Mr. Ghorum, Mr. Rutledge & Mr. Gilman: So the latter was immediately handed in to Congress, & referred to the Committee of the whole into which they immediately resolved themselves.[15]

A motion was made by Mr. Bland 2ded. by Mr. Madison that this report sd. be taken up in preference to the subject of general funds. Mr. Wilson opposed it as irregular & inconvenient to break in an unfinished subject; and supposed that as some further experiment must be intended than merely a discussion of the subject in Congress, before the subject of Genl. funds would be seriously resumed, he thought it unadvisable to interrupt the latter.[16]

Mr. Madison answered that the object was not to retard the latter business but to remove an obstacle to it, that as the two subjects were in some degree connected as means of restoring public credit, & inseparably connected in the minds of many members, it was but reasonable to admit one as well as the other to a share of attention: that if a valuation of land sd. be found on mature deliberation to be as efficacious a remedy as was by some supposed, it wd. be proper at least to combine it with the other expedient, or perhaps to substitute it altogether: if the contrary should become apparent, its patrons wd. join the more cordially in the object of a general revenue. Mr. Hamilton concurred in these ideas & wished the valuation of land to be taken up in order that its impracticabil[it]y & futility might become manifest.[17] The motion passed in the affirmative, & the report was taken up.

The phraseology was made more correct in several instances.

A motion was made by Mr. Boudinot 2ded. by Mr. Elseworth to strike out the clause requiring a return of the *"names of the owners,"* as well as the quantity of land. Mr. Elseworth also contended for a less specific return of the parcels of land. The objection agst. the clause were that it would be extremely troublesome & equally useless.[18] Mr. Bland thought these specific returns wd. be a check on frauds & the suspicion of them. Mr. Williamson was of the same opinion, as were also Mr. Lee, Mr. Ghorum, & Mr. Ramsay.* The motion was withdrawn by Mr. Boudinot.[19]

---

* Mr. Dyer ludicrously proposed as a proviso to the scheme of referring the valuation to the States, "that each of the States should cheat equally"

[1] *Papers of Madison*, V, 461–63; 464, nn. 3, 8, 9. The committee comprised Thomas FitzSimons, chairman, Oliver Ellsworth, John Lewis Gervais, Nathaniel Gorham, and Alexander Hamilton (*JCC*, XXIV, 106, and n. 3). See Delegates to Harrison, 11 Feb. 1783.

[2] The blank should be filled with "£50,000 Va. currency." The financial quota of Virginia for 1782 was $1,307,594 (*Papers of Madison*, IV, 104, n. 1; V, 457; JM Notes, 27 Jan. 1783).

3 Randolph to JM, 3 Jan., and n. 2; Harrison to JM, 4 Jan., n. 4; JM to Randolph, 22 Jan.; JM Notes, 27 Jan. 1783, and n. 18.

4 JM Notes, 14 Jan. 1783, and n. 3. Of the 8,761 enlisted men, who had served in Washington's "grand army" throughout, or for a shorter time, in 1782, 4,423 were from Massachusetts (Fitzpatrick, *Writings of Washington*, XXV, 85, 160–61; *American State Papers: Documents, Legislative and Executive, of the Congress of the United States . . . Class V, Military Affairs*, I [Washington 1832], 19). Gorham's estimate of the cost of recruiting was probably about accurate, the outlay for that purpose in 1781 and 1782 alone having been £477,906 or, in Massachusetts currency, approximately $1,593,000 (*Acts and Laws of the Commonwealth of Massachusetts* [1786] [Boston, 1786; reprinted, 1893], pp. 149–50). A dollar was six shillings in that currency.

5 See n. 2. See also Delegates to Harrison, 7 Jan. 1783, n. 5.

6 The "information recd from" Virginia was referred to the committee named in n. 1, above. See also n. 2.

7 For the appointment of this subcommittee of the grand committee, see JM Notes, 14 Jan. 1783.

8 JM Notes, 9–10 Jan., and nn. 4, 8; 14 Jan., and nn. 7, 9; JM to Randolph, 14 Jan. 1783.

9 JM Notes, 9–10 Jan., and n. 3; 14 Jan. 1783, and nn. 6, 9, 11.

10 Among the "several others," whom JM in the next paragraph mentioned in the sentence beginning "In favor of the 2d," Nathaniel Gorham had been especially prominent (JM Notes, 9–10 Jan., and n. 8; 14 Jan.; 27 Jan., and n. 29; 28 Jan., and nn. 4, 5, 29; 29 Jan. 1783).

11 Rutledge had already voiced, if not "suspicions," at least irritation at "delay" (JM Notes, 28 Jan. and nn. 12, 45; 29 Jan. 1783). Judging from JM's notes and the official journal, the land-evaluation issue had been quiescent in Congress since 14 January. During the week immediately preceding 31 January, the debate focused upon methods of taxation, including an impost, whereby "general funds" should accrue to the Confederation. JM and several other members of the subcommittee of the grand committee believed the need was too pressing to wait for money which the "constitutional mode" could supply only after an evaluation of land in each state had been completed. See JM Notes, 28 Jan. 1783, and n. 42.

12 For "the report" of the Rutledge committee of five members, see JM Notes, 9–10 Jan., nn. 2, 8; 14 Jan. 1783, and n. 7; JCC, XXIV, 113–14, 114, n. 1.

13 Jonathan Elmer of New Jersey.

14 Benjamin Hawkins of North Carolina.

15 Daniel Carroll presided over the meeting of the committee of the whole (JCC, XXIV, 105).

16 See n. 11.

17 John C. Hamilton, a son of Alexander Hamilton, charged that his father's position on "the valuation of land" was misrepresented by JM in this entry (John C. Hamilton, *History of the Republic*, II, 374 n.). JM's terse entry almost certainly reflected Hamilton's viewpoint. Both in the grand committee and now in Congress the two men spoke and voted against John Rutledge's recommendation to have each state evaluate its own lands—thus making "the interested party judge of his own cause." In a letter to Governor Clinton of New York on 24 and 27 February, Hamilton enclosed extracts from the journal of Congress for 6, 14, and 17 February 1783 and justified in detail his persistent opposition to state control of land evaluation. He and JM stood together in each of six recorded votes on this issue (Syrett and Cooke, *Papers of Hamilton*, III, 268–74; Hugh Hastings and J. A. Holden, eds., *Public Papers of George Clinton, First Governor of New York . . .* [10 vols.; Albany and New York, 1899–1914], VIII, 66–72; JCC, XXIV, 112–17, 129–32, 133–37).

18 JM Notes, 14 Jan. 1783, n. 7.

[19] The official journal notes that, after deliberating "some time," the committee of the whole reported that it had "made some progress, but not having come to a conclusion, desire leave to sit again on Monday," 3 February. Congress thereupon "*Ordered*, That leave be granted" (*JCC*, XXIV, 105–6).

Benjamin Harrison to Virginia Delegates

FC (Virginia State Library). In the hand of Thomas Meriwether, "third clerk of the Council of State" (*JCSV*, III, 194). Addressed to "The Virginia Delegates in Congress."

RICHMOND January 31th. 1783.

GENTLEMEN

My being absent from this Place attending a beloved and dying Sister[1] occasion'd your receiving no Letter from me by the two last Posts, tho' it was of very little Consequence as nothing worthy your Notice has occured since I wrote last. Your favors of the 7th. and 14th. Instant[2] came safe but I have no Letter by the last post which appears strange as I observed Col: Munroe had one from Mr. Jones.[3] if you wrote which I suppose was the Case it may not be amiss to enquire whether it was sent from the Philadelphia Office or not. a Practice seems to be creeping into the post Office of peeping into public Letters for News,[4] which I think originates with the Speculators there is an alarm of Peace amongst our Merchants and it is not improbable that your Letter has been taken out to see what the advices of Congress are on the Subject.[5] The Memorial of the Officers and the deputing Men of such hight rank in our Army to deliver it will I fear be attended with very serious consequences both here and beyond the water.[6] I know their sufferings are great and I feel very sensibly for them, but as their Situation is not worse than it has been it would have immortalized their Name to have struggled on to the end of the war, when it would have been in the power of the United States to have done them ample and compleat Justice. at present it is absolutely out of our Power. I speak for this State in particular which is so drained of Money, that tho' Tobacco is very scarce no Quantity of it can be sold at any Price for Cash.[7] the Merchants have it not nor can they procure it and the Planters are so totally without it that the Sheriffs from many Counties have declared it impossible to make their Collections.[8]

I am with great respect Gentlemen Your's &c.

B. H.

1 Elizabeth Harrison (Mrs. Peyton) Randolph of Williamsburg. See *Papers of Madison*, IV, 162, n. 8; V, index under her name; Randolph to JM, 1 Feb. 1783.

2 *Qq.v.*

3 Harrison received the delegates' letters of 21 and 28 January in the same post (Harrison to Delegates, 7 Feb. 1783).

4 *Papers of Madison*, V, 359, n. 22.

5 *Ibid.*, III, 43; 44, n. 7; 63–64; V, 71, n. 15; 79, n. 10; 114.

6 *Papers of Madison*, V, 473; 474, n. 8; JM Notes, 13 Jan. and n. 21; Delegates to Harrison, 14 Jan. 1783.

7 Early in January 1783 the treasury of Virginia contained only £5,000 worth of tobacco; the credit of the state was so low that the Board of Auditors could not buy "a single quire" of much-needed paper without paying cash; the official printer, suffering an "utter want of funds," was unable to print the statutes enacted during the October 1782 session of the Virginia Assembly and, according to Jacquelin Ambler, the treasurer, "there is scarce a man in the city of Richmond who can lay down the sum of £175" (*Cal. of Va. State Papers*, III, 415, 416, 417, 432; McIlwaine, *Official Letters*, III, 424). See also Harrison to Delegates, 7 Feb. 1783.

8 *Papers of Madison*, V, 182, n. 1; 259, n. 9.

From Thomas Jefferson

RC (LC: Madison Papers). Docketed by JM, "Jany. 31, 1783," and further docketed, in an unknown hand, "Ths. Jefferson 31. Jan. 1783." The italicized words are those written by Jefferson in cipher.

EDITORIAL NOTE

The present letter makes clear that Jefferson, before leaving Philadelphia for Baltimore, had "concerted" with JM in preparing a code for the greater security of confidential portions of their correspondence. This code, as is further shown by Jefferson's three manuscript pages of instructions now in the University of Virginia Library, was based upon Thomas Nugent, *A New Pocket Dictionary of the French and English Languages* (2d ed.; London· Edward and Charles Dilly, 1774). While writing the present letter, Jefferson obviously used this dictionary but apparently did not have at hand the manuscript instructions for employing the code. Consequently, he simplified the procedures previously "concerted."

What neither he nor Madison could be expected to encipher, except by using the manuscript instructions, were symbols therein arbitrarily assigned without regard to the contents and arrangement of the dictionary. For example, in those instructions the number 1063 stands for "Antilles," and columns of numbers alter the sequence of the 40 lines on each page of the dictionary. Thus, in the column "for writing," line 1 becomes 6, 15 becomes 39, and 33 becomes 20; conversely in the column "for reading," 6 is rendered as 1, 39 as 15, and 20 as 33.

Jefferson's statement in the present letter that words numerically symbolized were to be deciphered by "using the paginal numbers in order" is misleading unless he and JM may have contrived an accessory paginal code, of which no evidence has been found. Almost certainly, then, Jefferson would have been clearer had he written that deciphering was to be accomplished by "using the line numbers in order." With this understanding, page 33, line 19, or 33.19., would locate in the dictionary the noun "anecdote," and in fact Jefferson so encoded the word and JM so interlineated that decipherment.

Much else that is in the manuscript instructions the correspondents could be expected to remember. "Nouns," Jefferson wrote, "are pluralized or genetived" by placing an apostrophe "over them," so that 33.19.' signified "anecdotes" or "anecdote's." Infinitives were to be formed by writing 825.1. followed by the cipher for the verb desired. For example, 825.1. 1.6. denotes "to abandon." The letter "a following a verb denotes it's participle active, p it's participle passive, thus 132.39.a is buying, 132.39.p. is bought. the part. pass. may be used for the indic. imperf. the person will be known by the pronoun prefixed e.g. 402.5. 132.39. is he buys, 402.5. 132.39.p. is he bought."

In Jefferson's present letter and that of 14 February (q.v.) JM interlineated most of the words symbolized, and he did the same in his own letters of 11 and 18 February to Jefferson (qq.v.), after retrieving them. Thanks to this decipherment, the present editors were enabled in large part to reconstruct the code. Clearly, however, each man occasionally erred in his encoding, and JM, in decoding, sometimes used the wrong line or even the wrong page of the dictionary. Furthermore, in a few instances he neglected to interlineate. For these reasons, access to the edition of the dictionary used by Jefferson and JM was almost indispensable.

The popularity of Thomas Nugent's dictionary was exceptionally longlasting. Of its twenty-nine editions, the first was published in London in 1767, the last in the same city in 1878, and a reprint was published in London and New York in 1916. The second edition, as well as several of the other early editions, was revised and augmented. Thus many of the page and line symbols used by Jefferson and Madison will be meaningless unless the second edition of that dictionary is employed in decoding them. Although no copy of that edition appears to exist in the United States, a copy is in the Bibliothèque Nationale in Paris. By a happy circumstance, a friend of the present editors, the Honorable J. Rives Childs, now retired after an eminent career as an American diplomat, was resident during much of 1967 in France. Having been chief of the Bureau of Enemy Ciphers, General Headquarters, American Expeditionary Force, in World War I, he was "much interested" in decoding the four letters mentioned above. For this great courtesy, the editors are much indebted to Mr. Childs.

The second edition of the Nugent dictionary is without pagination. Therefore, Jefferson's comment about "paginal numbers," in addition to the construction placed upon it in paragraph three, above, probably signifies that he and Madison had numbered the pages of their personal copies. This inference becomes virtually a certainty upon observing within this imposed pagination what might be called a built-in slip code. This means that, of all the words enciphered in the correspondence at issue, those from page 1 through page 64 run in normal, unbroken sequence. Beginning with the word "basket," however, a break occurs. In strict sequence "basket" should appear on page

65, line 15, and be rendered 65.15. Instead, the page number is raised by 15 and the symbol rendered as 80.15. "Benevolence," 72.7., is raised by 23 pages, to 95.7. The column of words in the dictionary, headed "BY," beginning on page 103, line 1, is raised by 29, to 132.1. Thus the page numbers are progressively graduated until the section assigned to proper names is reached. There "Romulus," 903.28., is raised by 125 pages and becomes 1028.28. For this reason, even though a third person possessing the requisite edition of Nugent's dictionary should break the code through the first 64 pages, he would transcribe nonsense in deciphering words on and following page 65.

BALTIMORE Jan. 31. 1783.

DEAR SIR

A gentleman returning from this place to Philadelphia gives me an opportunity of sending you a line.[1] we reached Newport the evening of the day on which we left you.[2] there we were misled by an asurance that the lower ferry could not be crossed. we therefore directed our course for the Bald friar's: & thence to another ferry 6 miles above. between these two we lost two days, in the most execrable situation in point of accomodation & society, which can be conceived.[3] in short braving all weather & plunging thro' thick and thin we arrived here last night being the fifth from Philadelphia. I saw Monsr. de Ville-brun last night & augur him to be agreeable enough.[4] I learnt (not from him but others) that to embark their sick &c will keep us three days. having nothing particular to communicate I will give you an *anecdote*[5] which possibly you may not have heard & which is related to me by *Major F . . .*[6] who had it from *Doctr. Frank*[7] *Line* himself. I use the only cypher I can now get at, using the paginal numbers in order, & not as concerted.[8] *Mr. Z.*[9] *while at Paris had often pressed the Dr to communicate to him his*[10] *several negociations with the Ct. of France wch. the Docr. avoided as decently as he* could.[11] *at length he recd. from Mr. Z a*[12] *very intemperate*[13] *lettr.*[14] *he foulded*[15] *it up*[16] *and put it into a pigeon hole. a 2d 3d & so*[17] *on to a fifth or sixth he recd & disposed of in the same way finding no answer could be obtained by*[18] *letter Mr. Z paid him*[19] *a personal visit & gave*[20] *a loose to all the warmth of which he is*[21] *suscepble the Dr. replied I can no more answer this conversation*[22] *of yours than the*[23] *several impatient letters*[24] *you have written me (taking*[25] *them down from the pigeon hole) call on me when you are cool & goodly humoured & I will justify myself to you.* they never saw each other afterwards.[26] as I find no A. in the book erase the B in the first A. B. so that 1.1. may denote A. instead of AB.[27]

I met here the inclosed paper which be so good as to return with my compliments to miss Kitty. I apprehend she had not got a copy of it, and I retain it in my memory.[28] be pleased to present me very affectionately to the ladies & gentlemen whose pleasing society I lately had, at mrs House's[29] and believe me to be

Your assured friend,

TH: JEFFERSON

[1] The "gentleman" was a "Mr. Thomson," otherwise unidentified (JM to Jefferson, 11 Feb. 1783).

[2] Jefferson left Philadelphia on 26 January (JM to James Madison, Sr., 1 Jan., and n. 4; JM to Randolph, 28 Jan. 1783). Newport is on the Christina River, Del., about five miles southeast of Wilmington.

[3] In 1783 the country between the Susquehanna Lower Ferry, which crossed to the present site of Havre de Grace, and the Susquehanna Upper Ferry, which crossed from the present site of Port Deposit, was heavily wooded and sparsely settled. Between these two ferries was Bald Friar's ferry, which originally had been operated by one Fry, who was bald (Fitzpatrick, *Writings of Washington*, XXIII, 104, 106; George Johnston, *History of Cecil County, Maryland* [Elkton, Md., 1881], pp. 238–39, 301, 345; Writers' Program, Maryland, comp., *Maryland, a Guide to the Old Line State* [New York, 1940], p. 323).

[4] Jacques-Aimé le Saige, Chevalier de la Villebrune (La Villèsbrunne), had been senior captain of the men-of-war "Romulus," "L'Hermione," and "Diligente," in Chesapeake Bay ever since the rest of the French fleet, commanded by Admiral de Grasse, left the Bay for the West Indies on 4 November 1781 (Baron Ludovic de Contenson, *La Société des Cincinnati de France et la Guerre d'Amérique, 1778–1783* [Paris, 1934], p. 211). Jefferson expected to sail for France on the "Romulus" (*Papers of Madison*, V, 344, n. 7). See also *ibid.*, II, 159, n. 4; III, 4, n. 6; IV, 43, n. 4; 44, n. 5.

[5] For a discussion of the code, see ed. n.

[6] Instead of the symbol 314.4., which stands for "frank," Jefferson wrote 352.4., meaning "figurative." JM probably understood, by the time he finished the sentence, that "Major Figurative" was David Salisbury Franks, who expected to accompany Jefferson to France as his secretary (*Papers of Madision*, IV, 450, n. 14).

[7] The error mentioned in n. 6, above, was here repeated.

[8] For the probable meaning of "paginal numbers," see paragraph 3 of the ed. n.

[9] "Mr. Z." was conjectured to be either Arthur Lee or John Adams until Irving Brant demonstrated that Jefferson was referring to Ralph Izard (Madison, *Letters* [Cong. ed.], I, 62 n.; Burnett, *Letters*, VII, 40, n. 2; Brant, *Madison*, II, 266–67). The word "mister" does not appear in the dictionary. In every instance where JM interlineated "Mr." in his letters to or from Jefferson, employing the present code, he deciphered the abbreviation from symbols indicating entries in the dictionary, beginning with "master." These symbols were 503.10., used by Jefferson in the present instance, 503.11., and 503.12.

[10] The pronoun "his," not occurring in the dictionary, was suggested by 408.36., the symbol for "hiss."

[11] Since "could," "shall," "should," and "would" are not in Nugent's dictionary, and Jefferson did not have at hand the manuscript instructions in which they were assigned separate symbols, he necessarily spelled out "could" or any other of these words.

12 For Jefferson's amendment of the code in regard to the indefinite article "a," see his closing sentence in the first paragraph of the present letter.

13 The symbol for "intemperate," 456.6., occurs in the section of the dictionary where, in conformance with Latin usage, words beginning with "i" or "j" were both included.

14 For "letter" Jefferson incorrectly wrote 480.1. instead of 480.2.

15 For the preterit of the verb "fold," Jefferson should have written 361.3.p. rather than 365.3.p., denoting the same tense of the verb "foul." This accounts for the strangeness of the decoded spelling.

16 The symbol for "up," 915.1., affords the first instance in this encoded passage of a word that, in accordance with Latin usage, as with "i" and "j" (n. 13, above), would be found among words beginning either with "u" or "v."

17 Instead of 760.33., symbolizing the adverb "so," as written by Jefferson in his second letter of 14 February 1783 to JM, he used in the present instance the symbol 760.1., representing "SO"—a catchword at the head of a column in Nugent's dictionary.

18 Jefferson wrote 132.1., again indicating the catchword of a column, in this instance "BY."

19 JM correctly interlineated "him," for the symbol 408.15., but he did so only after canceling a now unidentifiable word.

20 Jefferson wrote 385.34.p., which JM correctly surmised was intended to be 381.34.p., "gave."

21 Since the symbol 29.1. could be decoded "am," "are," or "is," JM first interlineated "am," before writing "is" over it, as the only form of that verb which would make sense.

22 JM correctly surmised that Jefferson, although he wrote 196.14., the symbol for "conundrum," must have intended to write 195.14., the symbol for "conversation."

23 Jefferson no doubt desired to encode "the," but he wrote 816.26. instead of 816.27.

24 Jefferson missed the correct line by one, writing 480.1.', whereas 480.2.' was the correct symbol for "letters." Instead of "impatient," symbolized by 433.14., JM interlineated a meaningless "imputent."

25 Jefferson wrote 808.8., "take," instead of 808.8.a., "taking." So many were the idiomatic listings of the verb "take" in the dictionary that any line from 807.40. to 808.8., both inclusive, might have been indicated.

26 If Jefferson intended to encode "goodly," as interlineated by JM, he should have used the cipher 386.6. rather than 390.4., signifying "good."

When Ralph Izard was in Paris early in October 1777, word reached him of his appointment by Congress on 7 May of that year as commissioner of the United States "for the court of Tuscany" (*JCC*, VII, 334; Wharton, *Revol. Dipl. Corr.*, II, 403–4). Thereafter he remained in that city for nearly two years, because the grand duke of Tuscany was "prevented" by "the political state of Europe" from receiving him in his official capacity (*ibid.*, III, 33–34). Even before his commission reached him, Izard had become involved on the side of Arthur Lee in Lee's increasingly bitter disagreements with Franklin and Silas Deane (*Papers of Madison*, II, 165; 167, n. 4). Although Izard was not a commissioner of the United States to the court of Versailles, he insisted he should be kept informed and even be consulted by Franklin about the negotiations with Vergennes, because their course and outcome would much affect the course and outcome of the mission to Tuscany.

The six letters mentioned in the "*anecdote*" were probably among the seven of Izard to Franklin on 28 January, 30 January, 29 March, 30 March, 4 April, 25 April, and 17 June 1778 (Wharton, *Revol. Dipl. Corr.*, II, 477–81, 522–23, 529, 537, 558, 618–26). During that winter and spring Izard also wrote lengthy dispatches to his friend Henry Laurens, then president of Congress, criticizing Franklin and commending Arthur Lee (NA: PCC, No. 89, I, 85–87; Wharton, *Revol. Dipl. Corr.*, II, 497–501, 531–32, 547–49).

[27] Each page of Nugent's dictionary, edition of 1774, is divided into columns of words, and each column is headed by a catchword, usually comprising either two or three capital letters. As Jefferson noted, the single letter "A" appears neither as a caption nor as an indefinite article in the first column.

[28] Catherine Floyd (1767–1832), a daughter of William Floyd (1734–1821), a delegate in Congress from New York State. Mr. Floyd and his three children, of whom Catherine was the youngest, were among the lodgers in Mrs. Mary House's boarding house. As Jefferson well knew, JM was manifesting much more than a casual interest in "miss Kitty" (Brant, *Madison*, II, 17, 33, 283). See Report on Books, 23 Jan., ed. n.; JM to Jefferson, 11 Feb. 1783. The nature of "the inclosed paper," perhaps containing verse, is not known, but evidently she had given it to Jefferson while he was in Philadelphia.

[29] Besides the Floyds, Daniel Carroll, and Ralph Izard, others known to have been living with Mrs. House were her daughter and son-in-law, Mr. and Mrs. Nicholas Trist.

From Jacquelin Ambler

RC (LC: Madison Papers). Docketed by JM, "Feby. 1. 1783."
Cover missing.

1. Feb. 1783

DEAR SIR

The Auditors continue to be so thronged with business that I have not been able to obtain from them Answers to any of the other Queries,[1] nor will they undertake to liquidate your Account themselves. I shall therefore as soon as I have a leizure moment get the scale of depreciation left by Colo. Bland, & reduce the Sums myself;[2] and, as it will make no very material difference whether the Account is finally adjusted now or a month or two hence, I will transmit you a Copy of the Account before I make a settlement with the Auditors in order that you may point out any errors or omissions.[3] The Attorney took out a warrt. on your Account some time since. I think the sum was some where about £40. I mention this because I had myself applied for warrants to the amount of the £500. remitted you—& no more.[4] We have not received £20. specie in the Treasury since the rising of the Assembly[5]

I am unhappy in not being able to make some remittance to the Gentlemen of the Delegation, & hearing yesterday there is between £400 & £500 in the hands of the Sheriff of Northampton on the Eastern Shore for Taxes I have written to him pressingly to remit the whole to Mr. Jones or any other Member as soon as possible & to advise by Letter immediately that you may be informed of the Measures he is about to take in the Business—his name is William Sachell.[6] Whatever monies may be received in this way the Gentlemen will please to inform me of immediately & to empower me to take out Warrants for the proportion of each.[7] Is it to be Peace or War?

Yrs.

J.A.

[1] *Papers of Madison*, V, 345–48; 349, n. 10. Ambler was the treasurer of Virginia. The auditors were Bolling Stark, John Boush, and Harrison Randolph (*ibid.*, IV, 367, n. 9).

[2] Using the Philadelphia merchants' table of depreciation, which Robert Morris had sent to Theodorick Bland on 11 November 1782, Ambler intended to "reduce" to their specie equivalents the amounts of old continental or Pennsylvania currency paid by Virginia to JM from time to time during his tenure as a delegate. To comply with the Virginia statute of 1 July 1782, the money still owed JM by the state also had to be converted into its specie value (*ibid.*, V, 19, n. 4; 191; 192, n. 3; Delegates to Harrison, 21 Jan. 1783, and n. 3). The stipulation in the law for allowing each delegate in Congress the equivalent of eight dollars specie (a half johannes) per diem had been interpreted by the auditors to apply "to all times past, as well as future" (*Papers of Madison*, V, 29). Until May 1781, when continental currency ceased to circulate in Philadelphia, JM had been paid with those rapidly depreciating bills. Thereafter the small installments sent to him by Virginia were in Pennsylvania paper money or its equivalent (*ibid.*, III, 162, n. 4; V, 76, n. 4).

[3] Ambler to JM, 8 Feb. 1783.

[4] For the £40 and the £500, see *Papers of Madison*, V, 266, n. 1. These sums appear to have been debited against JM's account in November 1782. "The Attorney" was Edmund Randolph, attorney general of Virginia.

[5] Harrison to Delegates, 31 Jan. 1783, and n. 7.

[6] William Satchell, Sr. (*ca.* 1735–1794), was a master carpenter-planter who owned many acres and over forty slaves in Northampton and Accomack counties. Appointed undersheriff of Northampton County on 15 May 1782, he was on the date of the present letter acting sheriff and served until 12 November 1783, when a new sheriff posted his bond with the county court (Northampton County Court Records, Will Book 29, pp. 282–86; Minute Book, 1777–1783, p. 358; Order Book 30, p. 51, all on microfilm in Va. State Library; *JCSV*, III, 285; Augusta B. Fothergill and John Mark Naugle, comps., *Virginia Tax Payers, 1782–1787, Other than Those Published by the United States Census Bureau* [n.p., 1940], p. 110).

[7] Ambler was disappointed in his expectation that the financial embarrassment of "the Gentlemen" of the Virginia delegation would soon be relieved with tax money collected by Satchell (Ambler to JM, 8 Feb. 1783; 22 Mar.; Delegates to Auditors, 27 Mar. 1783).

From Edmund Randolph

RC (LC: Madison Papers). Letter unsigned but in Randolph's hand. Cover addressed to "The honble James Madison jr. esq of congress Philadelphia. To go by the post." Docketed by JM on the right margin of the cover, "Richmond Feby. 1st. 83," and on the left margin, "Feby. 1. 1783."

PETTUS's[1] NEAR RICHMOND Feby. 1. 1783.

MY DEAR FRIEND

The death of my aunt[2] unfortunately furnishes me with an apology for the late omissions in my correspondence. At this moment I am just returned from Wmsburg, and from the hurry of the post and the labour of getting a letter sent from hence to the mail thro' a snow-storm, I can barely acknowledge the receipt of your great favors of the 7. 14. & 22. Ulto.[3]

So deeply am I impressed with the dismal effects of refusing the five per cent,[4] that if I could accommodate some violent altercations, in which I am involved by the falling of my uncle's estate into my hands and I supposed that incessant efforts would accomplish its revival, I would go into the assembly. But a curious incident has happened to me; my father, who is an alien, having an interest for life in the estate before it of right belongs to me, and his creditors, numerous and greedy, are pressing hard upon me for a delivery of the property to their use. Now if the laws were to justify me in the most exclusive appropriation of those funds to my own use, I would not so apply them: but I cannot bear the separation of negro-families. I have therefore taken a middle mode, to offer the creditors the neat profits during my father's life. These deductions added to the certain necessity and obligation of supporting his family, will incumber me immensely. However if I can make a fortunate compromise, I may afford to resign my office and will go into the legislature.[5]

Our court of admiralty continues in its abhorrence of british goods. A flag vessel was fitted out from this state for carrying Colo. Simmons's tobacco to New-York and on her return took in a few, very few trifles, But their insignificance did not protect them. No law exists for the condemnation of the vessel, and therefore she was acquitted.[6]

I wish, that our state would recollect the importance of providing for continental as well [as] local pay of officers. A large number of horses are to be sold and the warrants of the military officers of the state are to be received in payment, as I am informed. There is certainly much justice in this: but the grant of the 5 pr.ct. would render the public conduct one consistent plan of justice.[7]

In a conversation with McClurg, I mentioned the late arrangement, which was on the point of taking place, and prevented only by a critical retender of Mr. L's services. Modesty would not suffer him to be direct; but it is clear, that he would be inlisted into public service.[8] This winter will probably give a turn to his studies into the channel of politicks.

Be so good as to inform Dr. Shippen, that the death of Reuors put a stop to the suit of Cuthbert for a little time but that it is now going on with the fullest vigor, and shall in no manner be neglected. He has left property, I believe, sufficient for the debt.[9]

---

[1] *Papers of Madison*, IV, 148, n. 2.

[2] Harrison to Delegates, 31 Jan. 1783, and n. 1.

[3] *Qq.v.*

[4] Randolph to JM, 3 Jan., and nn. 2, 6, 7; JM to Randolph, 22 Jan. 1783.

[5] JM to Jefferson, 11 Feb., and n. 12; to Randolph, 11 Feb. 1783. The income from the estate of Randolph's aunt, Elizabeth Harrison Randolph, was to be for the use of his father, John Randolph, a Loyalist living in England with his two daughters, Ariana and Susanna. Edmund Randolph necessarily had to assume, on behalf of his father and sisters, the administration of the estate and the task of paying the debts owed by his father when he left Virginia in 1775 (*Papers of Madison*, IV, 162, n. 8).

In the issues of the *Virginia Gazette* of 1, 8, and 15 February 1783, Edmund Randolph published this notice: "The Creditors of my father, John Randolph, Esq; are requested to meet me, in person or by their Agents, in this City, on the first Monday in March next. It is my intention to propose to them a Mode of adjusting their several claims." In the same issues of the *Gazette*, "The Executors" announced that in Williamsburg on 19 February, property of "the late Mrs. Betty Randolph," including an eight-room house "on the great square," furnishings, stables large enough for twelve horses and two carriages, and "several acres of pasture," would be sold to the highest bidder. No slave in Mrs. Randolph's estate was advertised for sale. See also Randolph to JM, 7 Mar.; 22 Mar. 1783; Moncure Daniel Conway, *Omitted Chapters of History Disclosed in the Life and Papers of Edmund Randolph* (New York, 1888), pp. 48–50.

[6] Colonel Maurice Simons was commercial agent for Virginia in Charleston, S.C., from 15 November 1777 until the fall of the town to the British on 12 May 1780, whereafter he became commissioner for attending the needs of Virginia prisoners of war in that city (*Papers of Madison*, I, 227–28, 229, n. 2; *JCSV*, II, 29, 38, 122–23). On 23 December 1781, then in Richmond, he requested authority to transport Virginia tobacco either to New York City or to Charleston "to discharge the debts contracted by the American Prisoners" (*Cal. of Va. State Papers*, II, 669; *JCSV*, III, 11, 33). On 2 April 1782 Governor Harrison issued a proclamation stating that the Virginia-owned brig "Mentor" would sail to Charleston as a flag with 357 hogsheads of tobacco "for the proper account of Maurice Simmons" (McIlwaine, *Official Letters*, III, 189, 190 n.). This transaction appears to have been completed satisfactorily; but in January 1783 the "Mentor" returned from New York City

with "Goods" consigned, seemingly without Simons' knowledge, to a citizen of Elizabeth City County who was suspected of being an "Enemy of his Country" (*ibid.*, III, 433; *Cal. of Va. State Papers*, III, 287–89). Although the illicit portion of the cargo was condemned, there was, of course, "No law" by which Virginia could confiscate her own craft.

⁷ Randolph referred to the privilege granted "military officers" to buy with their pay warrants the surplus horses, especially those of Colonel Charles Dabney's state "Legion" stationed at Yorktown. Lack of food threatened these animals with starvation (*Papers of Madison*, IV, 406, n. 1; *Cal. of Va. State Papers*, III, 417, 420, 423, 450; McIlwaine, *Official Letters*, III, 398, 399, 417, 427–28, 435). On 28 December 1782 the Virginia General Assembly empowered "the governor, with the advice of council" to sell the horses "in case the said legion be reduced by enlisting into the continental or other service" (*JHDV*, Oct. 1782, p. 91; Hening, *Statutes*, XI, 170). In the *Virginia Gazette* of 25 January and 1 February, Captain Henry Young, quartermaster general of Virginia, announced that he would sell at auction on 7 February 1783 in Richmond "Upwards of One Hundred likely Horses" for specie, tobacco, or several types of Virginia warrants, including "warrants for interest due on military certificates." See Randolph to JM, 7 Feb. 1783.

⁸ Dr. James McClurg, a member of the faculty of the College of William and Mary, had been mentioned by JM and Randolph as a possible successor to Robert R. Livingston as secretary for foreign affairs. See *Papers of Madison*, I, 296, n. 3; V, 201, n. 5; 343; 344, n. 5; 357–58; 402; 406, n. 34; Randolph to JM, 22 Feb. 1783.

⁹ JM to Randolph, 14 Jan. 1783, and n. 8.

Notes on Debates

MS (LC: Madison Papers). For a description of the manuscript of Notes on Debates, see *Papers of Madison*, V, 231–34. Immediately above his entry for this day, JM wrote, "Saturday & Monday No Congress."

Teusday Feby. 4.

An indecent & tart remonstrance was rcd. from Vermont agst. the interposition of Congs. in favor of the persons who had been banished & whose effects had been confiscated.¹ A motion was made by Mr. Hamilton 2ded. by Mr. Dyer to commit it. Mr. Wolcot who had always patronized the case of Vermont wished to know the views of a committment.² Mr. Hamilton said his view was to fulfill the resolution of Congress³ wch. bound them to enforce the measure. Mr. Dyer sd. his was that so dishonorable a menace might be as quickly as possible renounced. He said Genl. Washington was in favor of Vermont,⁴ that the principal people of N. England were all supporters of them, and that Congress ought to rectify the error into which they had been led, without longer exposing themselves to reproach on this subject. It was committed without dissent.⁵

Mr. Wilson informed Congress that the Legislature of Pena. having found the Ordinance of Congs. erecting a Court for piracies so obscure in some points that they were at a loss to adapt thr laws to it, had appointed a Come. to confer with a Come. of Congress. He accordingly moved in behalf of the Pa. delegation that a Come. might be appd. for that purpose. After some objections by Mr. Madison agst. the impropriety of holding a communication with Pa. through Committees when the purpose might be as well answered by a Memorial, or an instruction to its Delegates, a Come. was appd. consisting of Mr. Rutlidge, Mr. Madison & Mr. Wilson.[6]

The Report proposing a commutation for the half pay due to the army, was taken up.[7] On a motion to allow $5\frac{1}{2}$ years whole pay in gross to be funded & bear interest, this being the rate taken from Dr. Price's calculation of annuities,[8] N. H. was no, R. I. no Cont. no, N. J. no, Virginia ay [Mr. Lee no].—other States ay So the question was lost. 5 years was then proposed, on which N. H. was no, R. I. no, Ct. no N. J. no, so there were but 6 ays & the proposition was lost.[9] Mr. Williamson proposed $5\frac{1}{4}$ & called for the yeas & nays. Messrs. Wolcot & Dyer observed tht they were bound by instructions on this subject. Mr. Arnold said the case was the same with him.[10] They also queried the validity of the act of Congs. which had stipulated half pay to the army, as it had passed before the Confederation, and by a vote of less than seven States.[11] Mr. Madison sd. that he wished if the yeas & nays were called it might be on the true calculation, and not on an arbitrary principle of compromise, as the latter standing singly on the journal wd. not express the true ideas of the yeas, and might even subject them to contrary interpretations. He sd. that the act was valid because it was decided according to the rule then in force,[12] & that as the officers had served under the faith of it, justice fully corroborated it; & that he was astonished to hear these principles controverted. He was also astonished to hear objections agst. a commutation come from States in compliance with whose objections agst. the half pay itself, this expedt. had been substituted.[13] Mr. Wilson expressed his surprise also that instructions sd. be given which militated agst. the most peremtory & lawful engagements of Congs. and said that if such a doctrine prevailed the authority of the Confederacy was at an end. Mr. Arnold said that he wished the report might not be decided on at this time, that the assembly of R. I. was in session, & he hoped to receive their further advice.[14] Mr. Bland enforced the ideas of Mr. Madison & Mr. Wilson, Mr. Gilman thought it wd. be best to refer the subject of ½ pay to the several States to be settled between them & their respective lines.[15] By general consent the Report lay over.

Mr. Lee communicated to Congress a letter he had received from Mr. Samuel Adams dated Boston Decr. 22, 1782, introducing Mr.   from Canada, as a person capable of giving intelligence relative to affairs in Canada & the practicability of uniting that province with the Confederated States. The letter was committed.[16]

In Come. of the whole on the Report concerning a valuation of the lands of the U States—[17] A motion was made by Mr. Rutlidge wch. took the sense of Congs. on this question whether the rule of apportionment to be grounded on the proposed valuation sd. continue in force untill revoked by Congs. or a period be now fixed beyond which it sd. not continue in force.[18] The importance of the distinction lay in the necessity of having seven votes in every act of Congs. The Eastern States were generally for the latter, supposing that the Southern States being impoverished by the recent havoc of the enemy would be underrated in the first valuation. The Southern States were for the same reason interested in favor of the former:[19] on the question there were 6 ays only, which produced a dispute whether in a committee of the whole a majority wd. decide, or whether 7 votes were necessary.

In favor of the first rule it was contended by Mr. Ghorum & others, that in Committees of Congress, the rule always is that a majority decides.

In favr. of the latter it was contended that if the rule of other committees applies to a come. of the whole the vote sd. be individual per capita as well as by a majority. that in other deliberative assemblies, the rules of *voting* &c were not varied in Committees of the whole, and that it wd. be inconvenient in practice to report to Congs as the sense of the body a measure approved by 4 or 5 States, since there could be no reason to hope that in the same body in a different form, 7 States wd. approve it, and consequently a waste of time would be the result.[20]

Come. rose[21] & Cons Adjourned.

[1] Governor Thomas Chittenden's twenty-two page letter of 9 January 1783 from Bennington to President Elias Boudinot of Congress remonstrated against the resolutions of 5 December 1782 requiring the authorities of Vermont to permit banished settlers to return and resume possession of their confiscated estates (NA: PCC, No. 40, II, 351–61; *Papers of Madison*, V, 274, nn. 1, 3; 351–52; 367, n. 2; 368, n. 3; 368–69; 388, n. 3; JM Notes, 15 Jan. 1783, and n. 4). Although Chittenden stated that the legislature of Vermont, when it convened on 13 February, would no doubt reply to the resolutions, he amply responded by accusing Congress of imitating Parliament before 1775 by trying unconstitutionally "to controul the internal

Police and Government of this State"; of breaking its pledges of 7 and 21 August 1781 to admit Vermont to the Union if she would fulfill certain conditions, which since then she had fulfilled; and of endeavoring to force Vermont to tolerate within her borders such persons as Charles Phelps, "a notorious cheat and nuisance to Mankind." Somewhat inconsistently, Chittenden closed his "tart" protest by "earnestly soliciting a Federal union with the United States, agreeable to the before recited preliminary agreement." For this "agreement," as embodied in the resolutions of 7 and 21 August 1781, see *JCC*, XXI, 836–39, 892–93; *Papers of James Madison*, III, 224; 225, n. 11; 226, n. 13; V, 371, n. 15. For Charles Phelps, see *ibid.*, V, 353, n. 15.

2 Burnett, *Letters*, VI, 285, 287, 308–9.

3 See n. 1.

4 In his remonstrance, Chittenden had included passages from Washington's letter to him of 1 January 1782 as evidence that the commander-in-chief favored the independence of Vermont and her admittance into the Confederation (Fitzpatrick, *Writings of Washington*, XXIII, 419–22). After reading a printed copy of the remonstrance, Washington on 11 February 1783 sent a copy of his letter of 1 January 1782 to Congress to show that he had been quoted out of context by Chittenden (*ibid.*, XXVI, 119–20).

5 The committee comprised Daniel Carroll, chairman, Nathaniel Gorham, Arthur Lee, John Taylor Gilman, and Oliver Wolcott (*JCC*, XXIV, 108, n. 2). For the report of the committee, see *JCC*, XXIV, 367, and n. 1.

6 On 1 February 1783 the Pennsylvania General Assembly appointed a committee to seek from Congress a clarification of the ordinance of 5 April 1781 for "establishing courts for the trial of piracies and felonies committed on the high seas" (*JCC*, XIX, 354 56). Following a conference between the two committees, Rutledge reported on 5 February 1783 that the question to which the Pennsylvania legislature requested an answer was whether the bench at the trial of an alleged offender against the ordinance must always include "a Judge of the Court of Admiralty" of the state having jurisdiction, or whether the bench could comprise only two or more "judges of the Court of Common Law in such State." Congress on the same day returned this report to the committee with a directive "to report what is proper to be done" (*JCC*, XXIV, 109–10, 110, n. 1). On 4 March 1783 Congress adopted an amendatory ordinance, drafted by Rutledge, stipulating that the bench should include two or more judges, of whom at least one must be a judge of the Court of Admiralty, "provided that nothing herein contained shall extend to prosecutions already commenced, which shall be determined in the same manner as if this ordinance had never been made" (*JCC*, XXIV, 160, 164, and n. 1; *Pa. Packet*, 22 and 25 Mar. 1783).

7 This paragraph and the rest of the notes for this day, with the exception of the entry about the Adams-Lee letter, records a debate in the committee of the whole (*JCC*, XXIV, 108). Prior to 4 February, Congress had last discussed the memorial from the army on 25 January. On that day a committee, with Samuel Osgood as chairman, had been appointed to recommend what should be done about the half-pay commutation issue (JM Notes, 24 Jan.; 25 Jan. 1783, and nn. 8–12). "The Report," which had been submitted on 3 February, was that of the Osgood committee (NA: PCC, No. 186, fol. 80).

8 JM Notes, 25 Jan. 1783, n. 9.

9 These votes which were taken in the committee of the whole are not recorded in the official journal. JM inserted the brackets around "Mr. Lee no."

10 In its session of October 1782 the Rhode Island General Assembly had directed its delegates in Congress "to exert themselves against half pay to retiring officers, or to officers who shall continue in service during the war" (William R. Staples,

Rhode Island in the Continental Congress, with the Journal of the Convention That Adopted the Constitution, 1765-1790 [Providence, 1870], p. 378). In a letter of 4 February 1783 to Governor William Greene, John Collins and Jonathan Arnold remarked that, although they were "extremely mortified to be told" that their predecessor, Ezekiel Cornell, had "fully and absolutely" committed Rhode Island "in favor of Half Pay," they would obey their instructions, "and as the proposed commutation is a change in form and in name, rather than in nature and substance we shall oppose it" (Burnett, *Letters*, VII, 29-30). The stand of Cornell on the half-pay resolution, when it was adopted by Congress on 21 October 1780, had been ambiguous, but nearly two years later he sought evidence to demonstrate that he had opposed it (*JCC*, XVIII, 958-59, 1100; Burnett, *Letters*, V, 425-26; VI, 405-9, 495, and its first n. 2).

In the spring of 1778 Eliphalet Dyer and Oliver Wolcott, together with the other delegates from Connecticut, had strenuously fought against a half-pay proposal—"the most painfull and disagreable question that hath ever been agitated in Congress" (*ibid.*, III, 255-56; *JCC*, XII, 1308, index under "Half pay to officers"). In February 1778 the Connecticut General Assembly instructed its delegates in Congress to move as an amendment to the proposed Articles of Confederation that "no land army shall be kept up by the United States in time of peace, nor any officers or pensioners kept in pay by them who are not in actual service, except such as are or may be rendered unable to support themselves by wounds received in battle in the service of the said States" (Charles J. Hoadly *et al.*, eds., *The Public Records of the State of Connecticut* [11 vols. to date; Hartford, 1894——], I, 532-33). The Connecticut delegates apparently deemed themselves still bound by this instruction, for the General Assembly had not withdrawn it, even though Congress had rejected the suggested amendment on 23 June 1778 (*JCC*, XI, 640; Burnett, *Letters*, V, 429-30). This legislature at its session of May 1782 ratified the 5 per cent impost amendment with the proviso that none of the proceeds be spent "upon the half-pay-establishment" (*ibid.*, VI, 371-72, 399). As late as 1 November 1783 the same General Assembly characterized the recompense of half pay for life or full pay for five years to officers of the continental line who had served for the duration of the war as "incompatible" with the "principles of Liberty" and "Justice" and as a "stretch of power" unwarranted by the Articles of Confederation (NA: PCC, No. 66, II, 248-55). See also JM Notes, 13 Jan. 1783, and nn. 11, 18.

11 On 21 October 1780, although the half-pay proposal was separately adopted by a vote of seven states to three, only six sanctioned the complete set of resolutions of which that proposal formed a part (*JCC*, XVIII, 958-62).

12 On 26 August 1777 Congress resolved that questions coming to a vote should "be determined by the majority of states, as the majority of votes in each shall make appear" (*JCC*, VIII, 676-77). On 1 March 1781 this procedural rule was annulled by the ratification of the Articles of Confederation. Article IX thereof, besides designating important matters which could only be decided by the concurrence of at least nine states, stipulated that all other questions, "except for adjourning from day to day," could be answered "by the votes of a majority of the united states in congress assembled" (*JCC*, XIX, 220).

13 See n. 10. JM's statement reflected the long and acrimonious history of the proposal in Congress of half pay for life. This recommendation, opposed during an extended debate in April and May 1778 by the delegates from New England and New Jersey, was replaced by a compromise resolution, unanimously adopted, which guaranteed after the war one-half pay for seven years, with "certain Provisoes and Limitations," to most continental officers who would serve for the duration of the conflict (*JCC*, XI, 502-3; XIV, 946). Although the advocates of half pay for life finally won their way on 21 October 1780, the issue arose again and again, both

before and after this victory, with New England and New Jersey standing firmly and vehemently in opposition (*JCC*, XIV, 638–40, 908–9, 948–49, 974–78; XV, 1335–38; Burnett, *Letters*, VI, 405–8, 432; *Papers of Madison*, IV, 450–51; 451, n. 2).

[14] See n. 10. In its session of February 1783, the Rhode Island General Assembly highly commended its delegates in Congress for "their strenuous exertions to defeat the operation of measures, which the State considered dangerous to the public liberty" (William R. Staples, *Rhode Island in the Continental Congress*, p. 427).

[15] Samuel Osgood, the chairman of the committee which had rendered the report (n. 7), shared Gilman's view. In a letter of 4 December 1782 to General Henry Knox, Osgood wrote, "I have endeavored to convince the Members of Congress that it would be best to recommend to the States individually, to Satisfy their Officers on Acct. of half Pay" (Burnett, *Letters*, VI, 553). As early as 17 August 1779 Congress temporarily had favored this solution of the issue (*JCC*, XIV, 974–76).

[16] See n. 7. The letter from Adams to Arthur Lee appears with the perhaps erroneous date "Dec. 2d, 1782" in Richard Henry Lee, *Life of Arthur Lee*, II, 231–32. The memorial of Thomas Wiggans and the letter of Adams were submitted to Congress on 4 February 1783 (*JCC*, XXIV, 108, n. 2). Prior to 1770, when Wiggans, a fur-trader, "Settled at the Miami's Town near Detroit," he had lived at Montreal. Before being incarcerated in 1779 for about three years by the British and having all his property confiscated or destroyed by them, Wiggans claimed that he had supplied Illinois troops in the Northwest Territory with munitions and "Dry Goods" and influenced several Indian tribes there to remain neutral in the war. Escaping from prison on 25 August 1782, he finally reached Boston completely destitute. He offered his services to the United States "on any Expedition, or at any post, on the Frontiers, having the Knowledge of the French, and several Indian Languages."

In his letter of introduction, Adams mentioned that Wiggans "will inform you of the state and circumstances of British affairs" in Canada, "and will tell you it is an easy thing to unite that province with these states." On 18 March, Hamilton recommended, on behalf of the committee to which the letter and memorial had been referred, that Wiggans should be directed for employment to the quartermaster general (NA: PCC, No. 41, X, 597–600). A second petition from Wiggans, "praying for relief," was apparently tabled by Congress on 14 April 1783 (NA: PCC, No. 78, XXIV, 359, 362).

[17] JM Notes, 28 Jan., and nn. 4, 42; 29 Jan., and n. 19; 31 Jan., and nn. 11, 17; JM to Randolph, 4 Feb. 1783.

[18] JM Notes, 9–10 Jan., and nn. 2, 3; 14 Jan. 1783, and nn. 4–7, 9.

[19] See n. 12, above; JM Notes, 9–10 Jan.; 14 Jan., and n. 9; 28 Jan., and nn. 19, 12; 29 Jan.; 31 Jan. 1783, and n. 11.

[20] Although the "Rules for conducting business in the United States in Congress assembled," adopted on 4 May 1781, specified how "a grand committee" and "small committees" should be selected, they neither defined the method of voting within committees nor even mentioned a committee of the whole. The nineteenth of these twenty-eight rules, as drafted by a committee, banned Congress from ever employing the device of a committee of the whole, but the prohibition was deleted before Congress adopted the code. Although a committee of the whole, arranged for by Congress on 18 January 1781, had met occasionally until 9 April 1781, the committee of the whole of 29 January 1783 appears to have been the first such committee to postdate the ratification of the Articles of Confederation on 4 March 1781. Perhaps for this reason there was no convincing precedent to cite in regard to voting therein (*JCC*, XIX, 71–367 *passim*). Judging from JM's notes, the committee of the whole voted for the first time on 4 February—thus precipitating the issue. See JM Notes, 29 Jan.; 5–6 Feb.; 8 Feb. 1783, and n. 4.

[21] See n. 7.

Virginia Delegates to Benjamin Harrison

RC (Virginia State Library). In the hand of Theodorick Bland, except for the signatures of the other three delegates. Cover addressed to "His Excellency The Governor of Virginia" Docketed in an unknown hand, "Lr. from the Delegates in Congress. February 4th. 1783."

PHILADELPHIA Feby. 4th: 1783

SIR,

Neither this post nor the preceding one brought us any letter from your Excellency[1]

The affair with Nathan is now under arbitration. There is a reference in the case sent us of a Certificate from Clarke & Todd that the Bills were negociated at the current depretiation. But we find no such Certificate among the Papers transmitted to us, which is likely to turn the arbitration against the State.[2]

Congress have under their Consideration the Papers we were directed to lay before them.[3]

We have not receivd any material Intelligence since our last.

We have the honor to be with the greatest respect Yr. Excellencys most obedt. & most Huml. Servts.

JOS: JONES.
THEOK. BLAND JR.
J. MADISON JR.
A. LEE

[1] Harrison to Delegates, 31 Jan. 1783.

[2] Harrison to Delegates, 4 Jan., and n. 8; 11 Jan., and nn. 4, 8; Delegates to Harrison, 21 Jan. 1783. For the "Certificate" from George Rogers Clark and John Todd, see *Papers of Madison*, III, 21, n. 1. See also the indexes of *ibid.*, III and V, under Nathan, Simon, for further details about his complicated and long-pressed claim against the state of Virginia. For the dispatch of the certificate, see *JCSV*, III, 219; Harrison to Delegates, 15 Feb. 1783.

[3] Harrison to Delegates, 4 Jan., and n. 5; Delegates to Harrison, 21 Jan., and n. 2; JM Notes, 27 Jan., and nn. 17, 18; 31 Jan. 1783, and n. 1.

BARBÉ-MARBOIS.

FRANÇOIS, MARQUIS DE BARBÉ-MARBOIS

CHARLES THOMSON

To Edmund Randolph

RC (LC: Madison Papers). Docketed by Randolph, "Madison. Febr 4. 1783." Except where otherwise noted, the italicized words are those enciphered by JM in the Randolph code. For this code, see JM to Randolph, 7 Jan. 1783, and hdn.

PHILADA. Feby. 4th. 1783

MY DEAR SIR

By a letter recd. from Col: Monroe by Mr. Jones[1] I find that my conjectures as to the cause of your silence by the last post were but too true. To the same cause probably I am to impute your silence by yesterday's mail.[2]

The subject which my last left under the consideration of Congress has employed the chief part of the week.[3] The generality of the members are convinced of the necessity of a continental revenue for an honorable discharge of the continental engagements, & for making future provision for the war.[4] The extent of the plan however compared with the prepossessions of their constituents produces *despondence* & *timidity*. It appears that the *annual* revenue which prudence calls for the objects abovementioned, amounts to the *enormous sum of three million of dollars*.[5] You will ask perhaps from what sources this revenue could be drawn if the States were willing to establish it? Congress have done nothing as yet from which the answer they wd. dictate can be inferred. By individuals on the floor, the *impost, a land tax, poll tax, a tax on salt a &c* have been suggested, and some computation of their productiveness has made them competent to the object.[6] The valuation of the land accordg to the Articles of Confederation is also before Congress & by some considered as a great step towards obtaining the necessary revenue. If you ask by what operation? I shall be the more incapable of answering it than the preceding question.[7]

The repeal of the impost by Virga. is still *unriddled. Dr. Lee says* that *he was* the *only man who opposed* the *torrent* from which it is the more suspected that there has been *some manœuuvre in the transaction*.[8] Mr. *Jones quotes* the instance of *your last election to Congress*.[9]

I find a great check to secret communications from the defects of your cypher. It in the first place is so scanty as to be extremely tedious, and in the next both the letters & figures are in so ambiguous a character that great caution is necessary to avoid errors. I wish we could somehow or other substitute a more convenient one.[10]

I recd. a letter yesterday from Mr. Jefferson at Baltimore. It is dated the 31st. of Jany.[11] and he calculated on sailing in about three days. The industry of the British Ships on the coast may notwithstanding render it necessary to wait longer.

There is not a syllable of news from any quarter. I take it for granted you will have seen a letter purporting to be written by Secy. Townsend, as it came hither from Baltimore. If it be genuine, it is altho' an equivocal, yet a favorable presage on the whole.[12]

Adieu,

J.M.

[1] James Monroe's letter to Joseph Jones has not been found. For references to other correspondence of Monroe with Jones, see JM to Jones, 6 Jan.; Jones to JM, 6 Jan.; and Randolph to JM, 15 Jan. 1783, and nn. 3–4.

[2] Harrison to Delegates, 31 Jan., and n. 1; Randolph to JM, 1 Feb. 1783, and n. 5.

[3] JM to Randolph, 28 Jan., and n. 7; JM Notes, 29 Jan., and nn. 31, 32; 4 Feb. 1783.

[4] JM Notes, 24 Jan.; 25 Jan., and n. 7; 27 Jan., and n. 16; 28 Jan., and n. 3; 29 Jan. 1783, and nn. 8, 9, 13.

[5] Randolph to JM, 15 Jan., n. 13; JM Notes, 29 Jan. 1783, and n. 15. JM underlined but did not encode "*annual.*"

[6] JM Notes, 28 Jan., and nn. 4, 29, 35, 42, 43; 29 Jan. 1783, and nn. 16–21.

[7] JM Notes, 9–10 Jan., and nn. 2, 3, 8; 14 Jan., and nn. 2, 4–7, 9; 28 Jan., and nn. 4, 42; 29 Jan., and n. 19; 31 Jan., and nn. 11, 17; 4 Feb.; 5–6 Feb. 1783, and nn. 7, 9, 13.

[8] JM both encoded and underlined "*only.*" See *Papers of Madison,* V, 401; 472–73; Randolph to JM, 3 Jan., and nn. 2, 5, 7; Harrison to JM, 4 Jan., and nn. 1, 3–6; Harrison to Delegates, 4 Jan.; 11 Jan.; JM to Jones, 6 Jan., and n. 1; JM to Randolph, 7 Jan.; 22 Jan. 1783.

[9] *Papers of Madison,* IV, 336; 355; 358, n. 5.

[10] *Papers of Madison,* V, 339, n. 5; Randolph to JM, 15 Feb. 1783. JM's remarks were well justified. The code comprises most numerals from 1 to 660, many standing for one letter only, others for two letters or syllables, others for complete words, and a few signifying several combinations of letters, such as "idge, ige" or "ic, ick, ik" (MS in University of Virginia Library).

[11] *Q.v.*; Jefferson to JM, 7 Feb. 1783.

[12] For Thomas Townshend, secretary of state for the home department, see *Papers of Madison,* V, 211, n. 19. Townshend's letter of 22 November 1782, written in the name of "His Majesty's Ministers" to the governor and directors of the Bank of England, appears in the *Pennsylvania Packet,* 30 January, and in the *Virginia Gazette,* 1 February 1783. See also Burnett, *Letters,* VII, 32, n. 5. Townshend stated that Parliament would be prorogued on 26 November, and "that the negociations now carrying on at Paris, are thought so near a crisis, as to promise a decisive conclusion, either for peace or war before the meeting of Parliament" on 5 December. The preliminary Articles of Peace between Great Britain and the United States had been signed by their commissioners in Paris on 30 November 1782 (Wharton, *Revol. Dipl. Corr.,* VI, 90–91, 93, 96–100).

Notes on Debates

MS (LC: Madison Papers). For a description of the manuscript of Notes on Debates, see *Papers of Madison*, V, 231–34. For JM's notes which probably relate to 5 February, as distinct from those summarizing the next day's proceedings, see n. 10.

No. VIII

Wednesday Feby. 5. & Thursday Feby 6 1783.

In order to decide the rule of voting in a Come. of the whole,[1] before Congss. should go into the said Come. Mr. Bland moved that the rule sd. be to vote by States. & *the majority of States in Come. to decide.*[2] Mr. Wilson moved to postpone Mr. B's motion in order to resolve that the rule be, to vote by States and according to the same rules which govern Congress; as this genl question was connected in the minds of members with the particular question to which it was to be immediately applied,[3] the motion for postponing was negatived, Chiefly by the Eastern States. A division of the question on Mr. Bland's motion was then called for & the first part was agreed to as on the Journal. The latter clause, to wit, a majority to decide, was negatived; so nothing as to the main point was determined.[4] In this uncertainty Mr. Osgood proposed that Congs. sd. resolve itself into a Come. of the whole. Mr. Carrol as chairman[5] observed that as the same difficulty would occur, he wished Congs. would previously direct him how to proceed. Mr. Hamilton proposed that the latter clause of Mr. Bland's motion shd. be reconsidered and agreed to wrong as it was, rather than have no rule at all. In opposition to which it was sd. that there was no more reason why one & that not the minor side sd. wholly yield to the inflexility of the other thn. vice, versa, and that if they sd. be willing to yield on the present occasion, it wd. be better to do it tacitly, than to saddle themselves with an express & perpetual rule which they judged improper. This expedient was assented to, and Congress accordingly went into

A Committee of the whole

The points arising on the several amendts. proposed were 1st. the period beyond wch. the rule of the first valuation sd. not be in force.[6] on this point Mr. Collins proposed 5 years, Mr. Bland 10 years, Mr. Boudinot 7 years N. Jersey havg instructed her Delegates thereon,[7] The Cont. delegates proposed 3 years,—on the question for 3 years, N. H. no, Mas: no. R. I. ay Cont. ay. all the other States no.—on the question for 5 years, all the States ay except Cont.[8]

The 2d. point was whether & how far the rule sd. be retrospective. on this point the same views operated as on the preceeding. Some were agst. any retrospection, others, for extending it to the whole debt, and others, for extendg it so far as was necessary for liquidating and closing the accounts between the United States and each individual State.[9] The several motions expressive of these different ideas were at length withdrawn, with a view that the point might be better digested, & more accurately brought before Congress. So the rept. was agreed to in the Come. & made to Congress.[10] When the question was about to be put Mr Madison observed that the report lay in a great degree of confusion, that several points had been decided in a way too vague & indirect to ascertain the real sense of Congs. that other points involved in the subject had not recd. any decision; and proposed the sense of Congs. shd. be distinctly & successively taken on all of them & the result referred to a special Come. to be digested &c.[11] The question was however put & negatived, the votes being as they appear on the Journal.[12] The reasons on which Mr. Hamiltons motion was grounded appear from its preamble[13]

[1] JM Notes, 4 Feb. 1783, and n. 20. For a probable explanation of the Roman numeral above the date, see *Papers of Madison*, V, 231.

[2] The italicized words were underlined by JM. Three sentences later in his notes, he probably revealed why he underlined the passage.

[3] That is, with the rule of apportionment to be grounded on the proposed valuation" of land as a basis for requisitioning money from the states by Congress. See JM Notes, 4 Feb. 1783.

[4] Neither Wilson's motion nor the three tallies of votes are shown in the official journal (*JCC*, XXIV, 109). See n. 2.

[5] Daniel Carroll was still chairman of the committee of the whole, which had convened on 29, 31 January, and 4 February 1783. See JM Notes for those days; also for 8 Feb., n. 4; 10 Feb. 1783, n. 15.

[6] See the motion by John Rutledge as recorded in JM Notes, 4 Feb. 1783.

[7] Boudinot erred but was probably corrected by a fellow delegate from New Jersey. On 25 June 1778 there had been read in Congress a "representation" of the New Jersey General Assembly declaring that land valuations, as stipulated in the proposed Articles of Confederation, should be "struck once at least every five years," because the "quantity or value of real property in some states may encrease much more rapidly than in others, and therefore the quota, which is at one time just, will at another be disproportionate" (*JCC*, XI, 649). These implicit instructions to the delegates from New Jersey remained unchanged (Votes and Proceedings of the General Assembly of New Jersey, 1776–1786, microfilm in Princeton University Library). For this reason they voted "ay" on "the question for 5 years."

[8] No delegates from Delaware and Georgia were present in Congress. Rhode Island and Maryland were each represented by only one delegate, but JM apparently counted their votes as effective, even though they would not have been so counted in polls taken during a formal session.

[9] *Papers of Madison*, IV, 56, n. 6; 67–68; 69, n. 7; 71; 72, nn. 1, 2; V, 58, n. 4; 293

and n. 2; 322; 323, n. 5; 357. Immediately following this sentence, JM wrote and canceled: "This was generally satisfactory except to Mr. Dyer & Mr. Mercer who supposed that if as in that case the requisitions of Congs. would be the sum apportioned it would operate too much in favr of the States which wd be underrated in the first valuation." JM's mention of John Francis Mercer, who presented his credentials as a delegate from Virginia on 6 February, almost conclusively demonstrates that the debate on the "2d. point" occurred in the committee of the whole on that day rather than 5 February (*Papers of Madison*, IV, 154, n. 14; JCC, XXIV, 110–11). Therefore, JM's last preceding paragraph summarizes a discussion and vote in the committee on 5 February. See also JM Notes, 7 Feb., and n. 14; 17 Feb. 1783, and n. 1.

The report of the committee of the whole was drafted by Rutledge, with the exception of a small portion in the hand of Boudinot. The five-year time limit of "the rule of the first valuation," agreed upon by the committee of the whole, was not included in the report, but was "filed with" it on a separate sheet of paper.

Although the "2d. point," concerning "how far the rule sd. be retrospective," was not settled by the committee, its report recommended that "the rule of the first valuation" apply "for defraying all the charges of war and other expences which have or shall be incurred for the common defence or general welfare, and allowed by Congress," thus leaving the issue to be determined in formal session. The committee's report embodied that of the Rutledge committee debated on 14 January by a grand committee and debated and amended by the committee of the whole on 31 January, and 4 to 6 February 1783 (JM Notes, 13 Jan.; 14 Jan., and n. 7; 28 Jan., and n. 19; 31 Jan.; 4 Feb. 1783; JCC, XXIV, 112–13, 113, n. 1).

[10] On 5 February, upon receiving the "resolutions" comprising the report, Congress decided to take them "into consideration to-morrow" (JCC, XXIV, 109). The remainder of JM's notes refer to proceedings on 6 February.

[11] Many years after writing his notes, JM inserted his surname. His proposal may not have been in the form of a motion, for it is unmentioned in the official journal. For a partial satisfaction of his desire for clarification, see JM Notes, 7 Feb. 1783.

[12] Only five states voted to adopt the resolution recommended by the committee of the whole. JM voted in the negative (JCC, XXIV, 116). See also JM Notes, 7 Feb. 1783.

[13] Prior to the rejection of the committee's recommendation, a motion by Hamilton, seconded by FitzSimons, to postpone a vote on that recommendation until an equitable method had been devised to evaluate land and apportion tax quotas, state by state, "with such accuracy as the importance of the subject demands," was supported by only four states. Of the five Virginia delegates, Lee did not vote, Bland opposed the motion, and the rest favored it (JCC, XXIV, 114–16). See also John C. Hamilton, *History of the Republic*, II, 399; JM Notes, 17 Feb. 1783, and n. 4.

Notes on Debates

MS (LC: Madison Papers). For a description of the manuscript of Notes on Debates, see *Papers of Madison*, V, 231–34.

Friday Feby. 7.

On motion of Mr. Lee who had been absent when the Report was yesterday negatived, the matter was reconsidered.[1] The plan of takg the sense of Congs. on the several points as yesterday proposed by Mr. Madison was generally admitted as proper.[2]

The first question propd. in Come. of whole by Mr M——n[3] was; Q: Shall a valuation of land within the U. S. as directed by the articles of confederation be immediately attempted!—8 ays—N. Y. only no. The States present, N. H. Mas: Cont. N. Y. N. J. Pa. Va. N. C. S. C. R. I. 1 member, Maryd. 1 do.[4]

By Mr. Wilson[5]

Q: Shall each State be called on to return to the U. S. in Congs. assd. the no. of acres granted to or surveyed for any person, and also the no. of buildings within it? 8 ayes—N. C. no—supposing this not to accord with the plan of referring the valuation to the States, which was patronized by that delegation, a supplement to this question was suggested as follows.[6]

Q: Shall the male inhabitants be also returned, the blacks & whites being therein distinguished? ay. N. C. no for same reason as above. Cont. divided.[7]

By Mr. Madison

Q: Shall the States be called on to return to Congs. an estimate of the value of its lands with the buildings & improvements within each respectively?[8] After some discussion on this point in wch the inequalities which wd. result from such estimates were set forth at large; and effects of such an experiments in Virga. had been described by Mr. Mercer,[9] and a comparison of an average valuation in Pa. & Va. which amounted in the latter to 50 PCt. more than in the former, altho' the real value of land in the former was confessedly thrice that of the latter had been quoted by Mr. Madison[10] the apprehensions from a referrence of any thing more to the States than a report of simple facts increased, and on the vote the States were as follows, N.H. Mas: N.J. Pa. Va. no: Mr. Bland ay. Mr. Lee silent: Cont. N.C. S.C. ay. N.Y. divd. So it passed in the negative[11]

Q: by Mr. Madison   shall a period be now fixed beyond which the rule to be eventually estabd. by Congs. shall not be in force? ay, unanimously.[12]

by Mr. Madison Q: What shall that period be? Cont. was again for 3. years, which being negd. 5 yrs passed unanimously.[13]

Q: by Mr. Madison   shall the rule so to be estabd. have retrospective operation so far as may be necessary for liquidating & closing the accts. between the U.S. & each particular State? Ay—Cont. no. Mr. Dyer & Mr. Mercer understood this as making the amt. of the several requisitions of Congs and not of the paymts. by the states the standard by which the accts. were to be liquidated and thought the latter the just quantum for retrospective apportionment. Their reasoning however was not fully comprehended.[14]

1 JM Notes, 5–6 Feb. 1783, and n. 12; *JCC*, XXIV, 117. "Mr. Lee" was Arthur Lee of Virginia.

2 JM Notes, 5–6 Feb. 1783, and n. 11. In his old age JM inserted his surname, or its last four or five letters, wherever he referred to himself in his notes of 7 February.

3 After adopting Lee's motion, "Congress was then resolved into a committee of the whole" (*JCC*, XXIV, 118). JM's "first question" was seconded by Elias Boudinot (NA: PCC, No. 36, III, 448).

4 The manuscript motion in JM's hand reads, "1. Shall the valuation of the land within the U.S. as directed by the Articles of Confederation be immediately attempted?" Canceled below this is the following, also in JM's hand, "Shall the sd valuation be referred to the several States?" (NA: PCC, No. 36, III, 469; *JCC*, XXIV, 118).

5 James Wilson's motion, seconded by William Floyd, is in Wilson's hand (NA: PCC, No. 36, III, 467). For Charles Thomson's copy of the motion, see *ibid.*, No. 36, III, 448. See also *JCC*, XXIV, 119, and n. 2.

6 At the outset of the debate on land valuation, the North Carolina delegates were William Blount, Benjamin Hawkins, Abner Nash, and Hugh Williamson. They evidently agreed on how the problem should be solved (Burnett, *Letters*, VI, 462–63, 517–18). Blount unquestionably and Nash probably had left Congress by 7 February (*ibid.*, VII, lxxii; Jefferson to JM, 15 Feb. 1783). Nash was a member of the Rutledge committee, which on 6 January had rendered a report on land valuation. Hawkins served on the grand committee to which the Rutledge report was referred on 13 January (JM Notes, 9–10 Jan., and n. 2; 13 Jan.; 31 Jan. 1783; *JCC*, XXIV, 113, and n.).

7 The question is in the hand of Daniel Carroll, and Thomson, although making a copy of the motion, recorded the vote on Carroll's manuscript (NA: PCC, No. 36, III, 448, 467; *JCC*, XXIV, 119, and n. 2). On the issue of slaves in relation to valuation, see JM Notes, 14 Jan.; 28 Jan. 1783, and n. 42.

8 This motion, with several inconsequential differences in phraseology, is in Thomson's hand with interlineations by JM (NA: PCC, No. 36, fol. 461; *JCC*, XXIV, 118, and n. 2).

9 For earlier references to "the inequalities" which would result from an evaluation by each state "of its lands with the buildings & improvements," see JM Notes, 9–10 Jan.; 14 Jan., and nn. 7, 9; 31 Jan.; JM to Randolph, 14 Jan. 1783. John Francis Mercer referred to the "experiments in Virga.," authorized by statutes of 5 and 28 January 1782, to apportion the total revenue to be levied by a tax on land among the counties or districts comprising several counties in accord with the "average price per acre" in each county or district. The evaluations made by the local commissioners were obviously so inconsistent that the returns had to be "equalized" at Richmond (*Papers of Madison*, V, 311, n. 10; 347–48; 350, and nn. 18, 20; JM Notes, 14 Jan., and n. 7; 28 Jan. 1783, and n. 42).

10 In their dispatch of 24 March 1783 to Governor Alexander Martin, the North Carolina delegates in Congress remarked that, for purposes of levying state taxes, Virginia had rated the value of her lands one-third higher than Pennsylvania had rated hers; but, in truth, the average value of land in Pennsylvania was one-third higher than in Virginia (Burnett, *Letters*, VII, 98). Although the source of JM's information is unknown, he may have derived his estimate of the value of Vir-

ginia's land from a recent conversation with Jefferson in Philadelphia (JM to James Madison, Sr., 1 Jan. 1783, nn. 2, 4). See also *Papers of Madison*, V, 345, hdn.; 348; 350, n. 18.

11 *JCC*, XXIV, 118. JM and Mercer evidently voted "no." JM's tally accords with that of Thomson (NA: PCC, No. 36, III, 461; *JCC*, XXIV, 118, and n. 2).

12 Thomson's version reads, "Shall any period be fixed beyond which the rule which shall be eventually established b[y] Congress shall not be in force" (NA: PCC, No. 36, III, 448; *JCC*, XXIV, 118). Jottings in four different hands on an undated page include the following by JM, "Shall any period be fixed beyond which Rule shall be eventually established by Congress, shall not be in force?" Instead of "beyond which," he at first wrote, "at this time for the duration of the" (NA: PCC, No. 24, fol. 69).

13 JM Notes, 5–6 Feb. 1783. Thomson did not note that Connecticut's three-year proposal was rejected, writing only, "Answered unanimously: Not exceeding five years and &c." (NA: PCC, No. 36, III, 448; *JCC*, XXIV, 118, and n. 1).

14 The manuscript of this question, slightly altered in phraseology, is in JM's hand (NA: PCC, No. 36, III, 475; *JCC*, XXIV, 119, and n. 1). JM implied that the question received an affirmative reply, but Thomson copied and canceled this query in his own record (NA: PCC, No. 36, III, 448; *JCC*, XXIV, 119). Evidently the committee of the whole decided to adjourn and resume at its next meeting a consideration of the Dyer-Mercer interpretation of "retrospective operation." See JM Notes, 5–6 Feb., and n. 9; 8 Feb. 1783; *JCC*, XXIV, 119–20.

Benjamin Harrison to Virginia Delegates

FC (Virginia State Library). In the hand of Thomas Meriwether. Addressed to "The Virginia Delegates in Congress."

IN COUNCIL February 7th. 1783.

GENTLEMEN

Your favors of the 21th. and 28th. of last Month[1] came together by Post. we had some reason to expect from advices received here you would have been able to have inform'd us with certainty whether we were to have Peace or War for the next year, the Ultamatum of Great Britain has been gone over so long to France that I think the next Packet from England will put the Matter beyond a doubt, tho' I confess I have no expectations of Peace till Lord Shelburne has seen the Temper of the Parliament and tried his Strength in it.[2] A late Letter from General Muhlenburg informs me that the Financier has discontinued his Contracts for the support of the Post at Winchester and that he has now no means of subsisting the recruits that are daily going there but from this State.[3] This Conduct appears altogether strange to me as the Financier well knows we are restricted by him from furnishing any Necessaries to Troops or Post of the Continent, or what amounts to the same Thing he has declared he will not give us credit for a Shilling so expended, out of the Quota demanded by Congress; the Matter standing thus is it not surprising that he either has not continued his Contracts or taken of[f] the restriction and suffered us to support them out of the Money called for,[4] surely it can not be expected that we should not only find Troops but that we should support them also,[5] if it is[,] more is expected than will be comply'd with. Muhlenburg tells me he understands the States who pay in their Money fastest are to be first attended to and eased from Burthens of this kind, which might be just if all had been alike circumstanced,[6] but this is not the Case, every State to the Eastward of us has been free from Invasions for several years, been in perfect security and carrying on an extensive and lucrative Trade by which Money flowed into them from every Quarter, the very reverse of which has been the Situation of the Southern States, what little Money they had has been carried away to those happier Climes for the Necessaries of Life,[7] nothing proves this plainer than our present Situation, for tho' the last Crop of Tobacco was the shortest ever know[n][8] Money is so extremely scarce that not a Hhd. even of the best kind can be sold for cash; but I will give you no more Trouble on this disagreeable Subject as you have been fully possessed of it long ago. The above digression has led me a little out of my Subject which I trust you will pardon, and that you will excuse me for adding a request that you either lay the subject before Congress or the Financier[9] as shall appear to you most proper, and that you endeavour if possible to obtain an order for the support of the Post at Winchester in the usual mode, or if that can not be done that you obtain an explicit Declaration that we shall receive Credit for what we shall expend in the Support of it, without which the recruiting Service will very soon be at an end, for Men will not enlist when they see those that have done it starving[;] a Consequence which will certainly flow from the rejection of the Propositions.[10]

We have directed General Muhlenburg to contract for the next Month for the feeding such recruits as may be sent him provided they are forwarded on to Fredrick Town so often as their Number amounts to thirty, further than this we can not go, and therefore wish for the determination of Congress as soon as possible.[11]

I am with respect Gentlemen Yours &c.

B. H.

[1] Qq.v. See also Harrison to Delegates, 31 Jan. 1783, and n. 3.
[2] JM to Randolph, 4 Feb. 1783, and n. 12.
[3] Brigadier General John Peter Gabriel Muhlenberg, commander and chief re-

cruiting officer of the continental-line troops in Virginia, wrote to Governor Harrison on 28 January 1783, but the letter has not been found (*Papers of Madison*, II, 149, n. 2; V, 307, n. 6; McIlwaine, *Official Letters*, III, 442, and n. 173). The urgent need to economize in order to have money to pay the troops in the main army, the small number of continental troops in Virginia, and the unsatisfactory terms asked by potential suppliers of food were Robert Morris' reasons for not providing rations in 1783 to "the posts in Virginia" (Clarence L. Ver Steeg, *Robert Morris*, pp. 161, 165). Winchester was the place of "General rendezvous" in Virginia for continental recruits (*Papers of Madison*, IV, 149, n. 2; *JCSV*, III, 203, 215).

4 Harrison's suggestion was the more reasonable because Morris recently had consented to accept tobacco in satisfaction of some of the requisition on Virginia for 1782 (*Papers of Madison*, V, 258; 259, n. 9; 324; 332, n. 2; 381, and n. 2).

5 The governor's concern about food for the soldiers had supplanted his earlier grievance because of Morris' slowness in providing them with clothing (*ibid.*, V, 258; 313).

6 Virginia's delinquency in paying her financial quota had made JM hesitate to request money from the continental treasury for the relief of Virginia prisoners of war released by the British (*ibid.*, V, 325; 326, n. 11; 328).

7 *Ibid.*, V, 169; 322; 323, n. 8; 341, and n. 7.

8 *Ibid.*, V, 110; 341; Harrison to Delegates, 31 Jan. 1783, and n. 7.

9 Robert Morris.

10 Upon receiving the present letter, Arthur Lee evidently succeeded in inducing Morris to "avoid trouble and criticism" by arranging "to supply the troops at Winchester" (Clarence L. Ver Steeg, *Robert Morris*, pp. 161, 245, n. 5).

11 In his letter of 5 February 1783 to General Muhlenberg, Governor Harrison requested him to contract for rations at a maximum daily cost of 8½ pence for each recruit. While being trained in Winchester and in Frederick, Md., recruits helped to guard British prisoners of war (McIlwaine, *Official Letters*, III, 442–43; Fitzpatrick, *Writings of Washington*, XXVI, 340–41). See also *ibid.*, XXVI, 98, 100.

From Thomas Jefferson

RC (LC: Madison Papers). Docketed by JM, "Feby. 7. 1783," and further docketed in an unknown hand, "Ths. Jefferson 7. Feb. 1783." The italicized words are those written by Jefferson in cipher and decoded interlinearly by JM. For the nature of the cipher, see Jefferson to JM, 31 Jan. 1783, ed. n.

BALTIMORE Feb. 7. 1783.

DEAR SIR

I write by this post to the Minister of foreign affairs,[1] but will repeat to you the facts mentioned to him & some others improper for a public letter, & some reflections on them which can only be hazarded to the ear of friendship. the cold weather having set in the evening of the 30th.

Ult. (being the same in which I arrived here) the Chevalr. de Ville-brun was obliged to fall down with his ship & the Guardaloupe to about twelve miles below this;[2] & the ice has since cut off all correspondence with him till yesterday, when I got a boat and attempted a passage. there having passed a small boat before us we got about half way with tolerable ease, but the influx of the tide then happening the ice closed on us on every side & became impenetrable to our little vessel, so that we could get neither backwards nor forwards. we were finally relieved from this situation by a sloop which forced it's way down & put us on board the Romulus, where we were obliged to remain all night. the Chevalr. de Ville-brun communicated to me several letters of intelligence which deserves weight; by which we are informed that the enemy, having no other employment at New York, have made our little fleet their sole object for some time, and have now cruizing for us nothing less than

1.	ship of 64. guns
4.	50.
2.	40.
18.	frigates from 24 to 30. guns, a most amazing force for such an
25.	

object.[3] the merchants who intended to have sent their vessels out with us, have so far declined it, that two vessels only go with us, but they are unfortunately the greatest sluggards in the world.[4] the Minister has given Ville-brun leave to remain if he thinks it expedient till the *Middle of March* but politely & kindly offered the Guardaloupe for my passage if I chose to run the risk.[5] I find that having laid ten months under water she got perfectly sobbed,[6] insomuch that she sweats almost continually on the inside. in consequence of which her commander & several of the crew are now laid up with rheumatisms: but this I should have disregarded had it not appeared that it was giving to the enemy the ship & crew of a friend, & delaying myself in fact by endeavoring at too much haste. I therefore have not made use of the liberty given me by the minister.[7] Ville-brun seems certain he shall not sail till the *first of March* and I confess to you I see no reason to suppose that when that time arrives the same causes will not place our departure as distant as it now seems.[8] What then is to be done? I will mention the several propositions which occur with some reflections on each.

1. to go to Boston & embark thence. would to God I had done this at

first. I might now have been half-way across the Ocean, but it seems very late to undertake a journey of such length, thro' such roads, & such weather: & when I should get there some delay would still necessarily intervene. yet I am ready to undertake it if this shall be thought best.

2. to stay here with patience till our enemies shall think proper to clear our coast. there is no certain termination to this object. it may not be till the end of the war.

3. to fall down to York or Hampton[9] & there wait those favourable circumstances of winds & storms which the winter season sometimes presents. this would be speedier than the 2d. but perhaps it may not be approved of by the commander for reasons which may be good tho' unknown to me. Should this however be adopted we ought to be furnished by the Marine department[10] with, or authorised to employ one or more swift sailing boats to go out of the capes occasionally & bring us intelligence to York or Hampton wherever we should be.

4. to ask a flag for me from the enemy & charter a vessel here. this would be both quickest, & most certain, but perhaps it may be thought injurious to the dignity of the states, or perhaps be thought such a favour as Congress might not chuse to expose themselves to the refusal of. with respect to the last, nothing can be said: as to the first, I suppose, were history sought, many precedents might be found where one of the belligerent powers has received from the other, passports for their plenipotentiaries;[11] & I suppose that Fitzgerald & Oswald got to Paris now under protection of a flag & passport.[12] however these are tender points & I would not wish the sensibility of Congress to be tried on my account, if it would be probably disagreeable.

5. to await a truce. this cannot take place till after preliminaries signed, if then:[13] & tho' these are not definitive, yet it must be evident that new instructions & new or perhaps inconsistent matter would be introduced with difficulty & discredit.

There is an idle report here of peace being actually concluded. this comes by the way of the W. Indies, and must probably be founded on the settlement of preliminaries, if it has any foundation at all.[14]

Should you think that the interference of Congress might expedite my departure in any of the above ways or any other I have suggested these hasty reflections in hopes that you would do in it whatever you think right. I shall acquiesce in any thing, & if nothing further comes to me I shall endeavor to push the third proposition with the Commander,[15] & if I fail in that shall pursue the 2d. I wish to hear from you as often as you have any thing new. I fear I shall be here long enough to receive many letters from you. my situation is not an agreeable one, and the less so as I contrast it with the more pleasing one I left so unnecessarily. Be so good as to present my esteem to the good ladies & gentlemen of your fireside[16] & to accept yourself the warmest assurances of friendship from Dr. Sir

Your friend & servt

TH: JEFFERSON

Feb. 8. the preceding was written the last night. before I close my letter I will ask the favor of you to write me by the return of post and to let me have your own sentiments (whether any thing be, or be not determined authoritatively) which will have great weight with me.[17] I confess that after another night's reflection the 4th. is the plan which appears to me best on the whole, and that the demand from New York is nothing more than what is made at the close of almost every war, where the one or the other power must have a passport: it is no more than asking a flag to New-York. should this however be disapproved, the 3d seems the only remaining plan which promises any degree of expedition. perhaps the minister may have a repugnance to venture the Romulus at York or Hampton, in which case if I could receive his approbation I should be willing to fall down there with the Guardaloupe alone, & be in readiness to avail ourselves of a Northwesterly snowstorm or other favourable circumstance.

[1] Robert R. Livingston. For the letter, see Boyd, *Papers of Jefferson*, VI, 228–29.

[2] La Villebrune was aboard the "Romulus" (Jefferson to JM, 31 Jan. 1783, n. 4). A few days before Cornwallis surrendered at Yorktown on 19 October 1781, the 28-gun British frigate "Guadeloupe" was scuttled by her crew to avoid capture (French Ensor Chadwick, ed., *The Graves Papers and Other Documents Relating to the Naval Operations of the Yorktown Campaign, July to October, 1781* [New York, 1916], p. 151). Probably late the next summer the "Guadeloupe" was raised and added to La Villebrune's command (*Cal. of Va. State Papers*, III, 350).

[3] Among the enemy craft cruising off, and sometimes within, the Virginia capes during the winter of 1782–1783 were the ships of the line "Lion" (64 guns) and "Diomede" (54); the frigates "Centurion" (50), "Amphion" (32), "Cerberus" (28), "Cyclops" (28), "Hussar" (28), "Tartar" (28), "Pandora" (24), and "Harrier" (18); and the privateers "Active," "Admiral Digby," "Kidnapper," and "Prince William Henry" (W[illia]m Laird Clowes, *The Royal Navy: A History From the Earliest Times to the Present* [7 vols.; Boston, 1897–1903], IV, 93; W[illia]m M. James, *The British Navy in Adversity: A Study of the War of American Independence* [London, 1926], pp. 434, 436, 441; *Cal. of Va. State Papers*, III, 435, 436, 452, 458, 469; *Va. Gazette*, 8, 15 Feb.; 1, 15 Mar. 1783).

4 "French transports loaded with Virginia products," noted an enemy observer, "are vainly riding at anchor along the Chesapeake shore" (Bernhard A. Uhlendorf, trans. and ed., *Revolution in America: Confidential Letters and Journals 1776–1784 of Adjutant General Major Baurmeister of the Hessian Forces* [New Brunswick, N.J., 1957], p. 547).

5 La Villebrune, having been instructed by the "Minister," La Luzerne, to make this offer, extended it to Jefferson on 6 February 1783 (Boyd, *Papers of Jefferson*, VI, 227–28).

6 That is, "water-soaked." See n. 2.

7 Jefferson's letter of 7 February 1783 to La Luzerne, declining his invitation, is cited in n. 5.

8 It was April 1783 before the British ships cruising off the Virginia capes were ordered to return to New York Harbor (*Cal. of Va. State Papers*, III, 469).

9 Both Yorktown, eight miles above the headlands of the York River, and especially Hampton, fronting on Hampton Roads, are near the Virginia capes.

10 Robert Morris was agent of marine.

11 Hugo Grotius cited "many precedents" from Greek and Roman history of the "right of safe-conduct" accorded to the truce or peace envoys of a belligerent power by the government of their enemy (Hugo Grotius, *De jure belli ac pacis* [2 vols.; London, 1913–25], II [Francis W. Kelsey *et al.*, trans.], 438, 449, 832, 839–41).

12 Jefferson refers to Alleyne Fitzherbert and Richard Oswald. See *Papers of Madison*, IV, 179, n. 5; Index of Vol. V under their respective names; JM to James Madison, Sr., 1 Jan.; Harrison to Delegates, 4 Jan. 1783, and n. 3. During the negotiations beginning in the summer of 1782, official agents or peace commissioners, including Oswald, often traveled back and forth between Paris and London, protected by passports which usually obliged them to go by way of Ostend (Wharton, *Revol. Dipl. Corr.*, V, 563, 566, 603). The passport issued in 1782 to Henry Laurens, assuring him of immunity from capture by the British during his trip from London to the Netherlands, afforded no precedent, for Laurens, free on parole and Richard Oswald's bond, regarded himself as being only "a prisoner upon parade" (Richard B. Morris, *The Peacemakers*, pp. 265–68; Wharton, *Revol. Dipl. Corr.*, VI, 121; *Papers of Madison*, V, 143–45).

13 Although Great Britain and the United States maintained on the whole a *de facto* truce during 1782 in land warfare, and the signing of preliminary terms of peace concluded by their commissioners in Paris on 30 November of that year was known in America by early in February 1783, hostilities off the Atlantic coast continued until April, when the naval commanders were informed that on 3 and 9 February Great Britain, France, and Spain also had agreed upon the preliminary terms of peace concluded by their commissioners on 20 January. The proclamation of King George III, "declaring the cessation of arms, as well by sea as land," was issued on 14 February (JM Notes, 13 Feb., and 31 Mar. 1783; Wharton, *Revol. Dipl. Corr.*, VI, 223–25, 251–52).

14 JM to Randolph, 4 Feb., and n. 12; Delegates to Harrison, 11 Feb. 1783, and n. 4.

15 La Villebrune.

16 Jefferson to JM, 31 Jan. 1783, and n. 28.

17 On 11 February Congress referred Jefferson's letter of 7 February to Livingston (n. 1, above) to a committee, with Joseph Jones as chairman. For the committee's report, see *JCC*, XXIV, 132; JM Notes, 14 Feb.; JM to Jefferson, 11 Feb., n. 6; 12 Feb.; 15 Feb. 1783.

From Edmund Randolph

RC (LC: Madison Papers). Unsigned but in Randolph's hand. Cover addressed to "The honble James Madison jr. esq of congress Philadelphia." Docketed by JM, "Feby—7–1783." Words or parts of words enciphered in the Randolph code are italicized. See JM to Randolph, 7 Jan., and hdn.; 4 Feb. 1783, and n. 10.

RICHMOND feby. 7. 1783.

MY DEAR FRIEND

The fatal repeal[1] is wrapt up in more than common mystery; the motives being various, as assigned by different persons. Some said, that congress ought not to raise a revenue by other means, than those, prescribed in the confederation;[2] that the sufferance of a deviation from that mode will ultimately lead to an assessment of the quota of Virginia, according to the poll, that a fund, thus independent of her annual grant, will capacitate the U.S. to execute schemes of territorial injury against her.[3] Others affected to penetrate into the most baneful consequences to trade; and rendered their wisdom eminent indeed by foreseeing great superiority, to be obtained by the other states over ours.[4] In what proportion these abominable ideas operated upon the assembly, I cannot particularly learn. But the opinion of an attentive observer of legislative movements is, that the situation of America was not duly reflected on, and thereby an opportunity was presented *to the L——s of piquing Morris*[5] The tenor of *their daily language* justifies the suspicion. *Their character for malice* confirms it. But I rejoice that *they will not* retain *their fangs*, to be able to destroy the U. S, *if the next assembly* be *composed of sound Whigs.*[6]

The Executive have contrived means to appease the murmurs of our state officers on the subject of pay. A large number of horses belonging to the country, were yesterday sold; and the warrants of these gentlemen were admitted as cash.[7] Would god, that similar success could be obtained by you.[8]

The scarcity of cash is here is greater than ever. The cause is supposed to be found in the late draught for raising money for enlistment; not a shilling of which scarcely has been as yet restored to circulation, being still in the hands of the county lieutenants,[9] as I am informed.

Your favor by yesterday's post would increase my importunity for a transcript of your extract from Mr. J——s remarks, if I could assign a better apology for not sending you a state of the great question, than you can for not sending the transcript.[10] But circumstanced, as we are in the bosom of urgent business, we must do these works at leisure.

Notwithstanding the recommendation of the assembly to the electors to choose only radical whigs,[11] I am told, that Mr. Wormeley will be a candidate at the next general election.[12]

[1] Randolph to JM, 3 Jan., and n. 2; JM to Randolph, 7 Jan.; 22 Jan.; 28 Jan.; 4 Feb.; Harrison to Delegates, 11 Jan. 1783.

[2] That is, by Article VIII of the Articles of Confederation (*JCC*, XIX, 217).

[3] If a levy should be apportioned among the states on the basis of a census, Virginia would have the largest quota, especially if a slave were weighted as one person in the count. Even amid the economically depressed conditions of 1783, Virginians might have been unpleasantly surprised by the outcome if Congress had used the comparative value of real and personal property in the thirteen states as a basis for gauging tax quotas. According to the federal census of 1790, the per capita wealth of the free population in the southern states was $217.07, in the middle states $145.41, and in New England $137.98 (U.S. Bureau of the Census, *A Century of Population Growth: From the First Census of the United States to the Twelfth, 1790–1900* [Washington, 1909], p. 144).

[4] Randolph's personal view is disclosed by his irony.

[5] For the hostility of the Lees toward Robert Morris, see Harrison to JM, 4 Jan. 1783, and nn. 3, 4. Certainly in a position to be an "attentive observer" was John Beckley, clerk of the House of Delegates, who was living in the same house with Charles Hay, Randolph's law clerk (*Papers of Madison*, V, 340, n. 14; 426, n. 3).

[6] Randolph to JM, 3 Jan., and n. 10; 15 Jan., and nn. 7, 8; JM to Randolph, 22 Jan. 1783, and n. 7.

[7] Randolph to JM, 1 Feb. 1783, and n. 7.

[8] Delegates to Harrison, 21 Jan.; Ambler to JM, 1 Feb. 1783, and n. 7.

[9] That is, the funds entrusted to the county lieutenants for paying the recruits money bonuses and the recruiting officers' fees, as stipulated in the statute of 2 July 1782 (Minute Book, House of Delegates, May 1782, p. 86, MS in Va. State Library; Hening, *Statutes*, XI, 14–20; *Papers of Madison*, IV, 362, n. 48; V, 92; 93, n. 9).

[10] The latter portion of the sentence refers to a promise by Randolph to send a copy of his argument in the "Case of the Prisoners" (*Caton* v. *Commonwealth*) to JM. See *Papers of Madison*, V, 217–18; 218, n. 9; 263; 265, n. 7; 290; 382; 384, n. 4; 474.

[11] *Ibid.*, V, 455, n. 8; Randolph to JM, 3 Jan., and n. 10; 15 Jan., and nn. 7, 8; JM to Randolph, 22 Jan. 1783, and n. 7.

[12] Randolph probably had in mind Ralph Wormeley, Jr. (1744–1806). After several years of study at Eton College and Cambridge University, Ralph, Jr., returned to Rosegill, his father's plantation fronting the Rappahannock River in Middlesex County. In 1775, having served for four years in the Governor's Council and being critical of both the Loyalists and their opponents, Ralph, Jr., was haled before the Virginia Convention of May 1776. This assemblage, after noting that he had manifested "great contrition for his unworthy conduct," ordered him to stay within the bounds of his family's estates in Berkeley and Frederick counties (*The Proceedings of the Convention of Delegates Held at the Capitol, in the City of Williamsburg, in the Colony of Virginia, on Monday, the 6th of May, 1776* [Richmond, 1816], pp. 7, 13, 15; H[amilton] J[ames] Eckenrode, *The Revolution in Virginia* [Boston, 1916], pp. 144–47). During his "exile" there, he believed his "Life endangered" by "sundry Persons" who acted "in a riotous and tumultuous manner" (McIlwaine, *Official Letters*, I, 91–92). Pleading for "Justice" rather than an "act of grace," he assured his brother-in-law, Mann Page, Jr., in a letter of 11 May

1778, that he had never "levied war against any of these States, or adhered to, aided or abetted the enemy" (*Cal. of Va. State Papers*, I, 300–301). It was probably Page, a member of the House of Delegates, who persuaded the Virginia General Assembly on 30 May of that year to "discharge" Wormeley "from his present confinement" and permit him to reside again at Rosegill (*JHDV*, May 1778, pp. 29, 33).

On 4–5 June 1781 the crew of a Loyalist privateer plundered that plantation and carried off thirty-six slaves and much other property (*Va. Mag. Hist. and Biog.*, XVIII [1910], 373–77; *Cal. of Va. State Papers*, II, 404–5). For seeking through correspondence with the British commander at Portsmouth, Va., to recover their slaves, Ralph, Jr., and his father were arrested by Governor Thomas Nelson's order for "Conduct which manifests Disaffection to this Government & the Interest of the United States" (McIlwaine, *Official Letters*, III, 50, 55–56; *Cal. of Va. State Papers*, II, 171–72, 549). They appear to have been incarcerated only briefly, if at all, but they were embarrassed again in November 1782 by the premature attempt of Ralph, Jr.'s brother John, a captain in the British army, to return to Rosegill (*Papers of Madison*, V, 281–82; 286, n. 14). Ralph, Jr.'s letters of this period evidence no desire to participate in politics (Letter Book of Ralph Wormeley, of Rosegill, Va., 16 February 1782–23 January 1802, MS transcript, 434 pp., in Va. Historical Society), but he was a member of the House of Delegates in 1787, 1789, and 1790, and of the Virginia Convention of 1788 which ratified the Federal Constitution (Swem and Williams, *Register*, pp. 28, 31, 33; *Cal. of Va. State Papers*, VII, 456–57).

Notes on Debates

MS (LC: Madison Papers). For a description of the manuscript of Notes on Debates, see *Papers of Madison*, V, 231–34.

Saturday Feby. 8.

Come. of the whole.[1]

Mr. Mercer revived the subject of retrospective operation;[2] and after it had been much discussed & the difference elucidated wch. might happen between apportiong. according to the first valuation which sd. be made, merely the sums paid on the requisitions of Congs. & apportiong the whole requisitions, consisting of the sums paid & the deficiencies, which might not be pd. until some distant day, when a different rule formed under different circumstances of the States sd. be in force, the assent to the last question put yesterday was reversed, & there was added to the preceding question, after "5 Years."—"and shall operate as a rule for apportioning the sums necessary to be raised for supporting the public credit & other contingent expences & for adjusting all accounts between the U. States & each particular State for monies paid or articles furnished by them & for no other purpose whatsoever."[3] On this question there were 6 ays, so it became a vote of the Come. of the whole.[4]

[1] JM Notes, 5–6 Feb. 1783, n. 5.
[2] JM Notes, 7 Feb. 1783, and n. 14.

³ The chief matter at issue was the basis on which "retrospective operation," or reapportionment, of the indebtedness of the Confederation should be made according to the first valuation of lands. John Francis Mercer was concerned lest the debt be reapportioned without regard to contributions previously made in money or kind by individual states. Clearly such reapportionment would be disadvantageous to Virginia and other states which, having contributed heavily in kind, would now be called upon to bear a proportionate share of the deficiencies created by states which had contributed slightly. Mercer evidently believed, as did Governor Harrison, that despite appearances of delinquency in discharging past quotas, Virginia's contributions would, with a final settlement of accounts, be found considerable (McIlwaine, *Official Letters*, III, 145).

The reason why Eliphalet Dyer shared this view, as expressed on 7 February, is equally clear (JM Notes, 7 Feb., and n. 14). In 1782, for example, Connecticut had paid over 76 per cent of her financial quota and was owed large sums by Congress for provisions and munitions forwarded to the continental army (NA: PCC, No. 142, II, 191; Fitzpatrick, *Writings of Washington*, XXIII, 86–87, 278; XXIV, 232, n. 13, 368–69).

⁴ Charles Thomson recorded the vote as being seven states "ay." The delegates from New Hampshire, Massachusetts, Connecticut (including Dyer), New York, New Jersey, and Pennsylvania were unanimously in the affirmative, and three (including Rutledge) of the four delegates from South Carolina also supported the amendment. Mercer joined Arthur Lee in voting "no," thus offsetting the "ay" of JM and Joseph Jones and rendering the vote of Virginia ineffective. The votes of Rhode Island and North Carolina were lost by similar deadlocks, and Maryland was represented only by Daniel Carroll (NA: PCC, No. 36, III, 450; JCC, XXIV, 120–21). See also JM Notes, 17 Feb. 1783, and n. 1.

Although the duration to which quotas under the first valuation should be operative was limited to five years, the manuscript motion shows that the phrase "within these years," as affecting the period of time to which the "rule" would be effective, was struck out, probably in debate (NA: PCC, No. 36, III, 463; JCC, XXIV, 120 and n. 1). Mercer, who on 12 February vigorously opposed "the principle of general revenue" for Congress, may have feared that deletion of the phrase would be an invitation to loose construction by a future Congress. On 17 February he joined Dyer in successfully moving a reconsideration of the whole subject of land-valuation quotas so as to have a proposal phrased in a manner acceptable to them (JM Notes, 12 Feb.; 17 Feb.; JM to Randolph, 18 Feb. 1783; JCC, XXIV, 135–37).

From Jacquelin Ambler

RC (LC: Madison Papers). Unsigned but in Ambler's hand. Cover addressed to "The Honobl. James Madison of Congress Philadelphia." Docketed by JM, "Feby. 8. 1783." On the lower half of the second page of the letter are a few computations by JM, evidently relating to the money owed him by Virginia.

RICHMOND VIRGA. 8. Feby. 83.

DEAR SIR

Being very much engaged myself I obtained Mr. Webb's Assistance to procure answers to the other Queries, which he has done & I believe as fully as they can be at this time.[1] I enclose also a State of your Accot. against the Commonwealth, for your Inspection. You will please to make such additions & corrections as you may find necessary.[2]

I have endeavoured by taking the mean of depreciation, according to the Scales left here by Colo. Bland, to do both the State & you justice. minute fractions were not attended to.[3]

I informed you by the last mail that I had written to a Mr. William Satchell Shff of Northampton County (on the Eastern Shore) to remit to Mr. Jones, or any other Gentleman of the Delegation, what Specie he has in his hands payable for Taxes, which I understood from a letter he wrote Mr. Webb was not much Short of £500. provided he could do it on certainty, and in a reasonable time.[4] I was induced to press this matter earnestly on Mr. Satchell on two accounts—in the first place I was apprehensiv[e] you stood much in need of a remittance, & there was little probability of making one from the Treasury until late in March & in the next place the risk that would attend bringing the Money over the Bay while the Enemies Barges are cruizing.[5] Unfortunately the Person who is to carry the Letter to Mr. Satchell is still detained here: I hardly know what to advise as the best meens for obtaining this Money in time. it is too inconsiderable a sum to hire an Express at Philadel. to go for it—especially as there is a *possibility* that Mr. Satchell may either bring or send the money here before my Letter reaches him.[6]

I send you another letter, however, for him[7] in case any favorable opportunity should offer from Phil to that part of the Country.

[1] For the "Queries" and the share of Foster Webb, Jr., commissioner of the Virginia state treasury, in answering them, see *Papers of Madison*, V, 345–40, Ambler to JM, 1 Feb. 1783.

[2] The missing enclosure probably recorded only the auditors' estimate of the money owed by Virginia to JM for his services as a delegate in Congress prior to 1 January 1783 (Ambler to JM, 1 Feb. 1783, and n. 2). For the adjustment of the account, see Ambler to JM, 22 Mar. 1783.

[3] Virginia's debt to JM, as of 31 December 1782, consisted of three items: namely, (1) "12 days travelling to, and 1017 days constant attendance at Philadelphia," (2) $175 in continental currency paid on 15 June 1780 for "an Express returning to Virginia" (*Papers of Madison*, II, 97), (3) $2,760 in continental currency on 6 December 1780 for "Cash advanced to Robt. Jewel Keeper of the New-Goal Phila. for cloathing food & Medicine for 6. Sailors belonging to Virga. returning sick from captivity in New York" (*ibid.*, II, 252; 254, n. 15; Auditors' Ledger, MS in Va. State Library). To change the sums expended by JM listed in No. 2 and No. 3 to their equivalent in specie, Ambler applied the scale of depreciation forwarded by Robert Morris to Theodorick Bland on 11 November 1782 (*Papers of Madison*, V, 192, n. 3). The table indicates that the Philadelphia depreciation rate nearest to 15 June was 62, and to 6 December 1780 was about 100 to 1. Thus for No. 2, disregarding "minute fractions," $175 divided by 3.33 equals £52.5. Multiplying £52.5 by 20

results in 1,050 shillings. Dividing the shillings by 62 converts them into about 16s. specie. In like manner for No. 3, but substituting 100 for 62, the result is £8 6s. specie (Auditors' Ledger, MS in Va. State Library). In regard to item No. 1, the result of multiplying 1,029 days by $8.00 specie, the per diem allowance stipulated in the Virginia statute of 1 July 1782, is $8,232.00 (*Papers of Madison*, IV, 377, n. 12). Although the outcome of dividing these dollars by 3.33, in order to convert them into pounds, is £2472 1s. 5d., the auditors entered £2469 12s. on their ledger. This discrepancy appears to be the only evidence that the auditors may have disallowed one of JM's claims.

  [4] Ambler to JM, 1 Feb. 1783, and n. 6.

  [5] Jefferson to JM, 7 Feb. 1783, and n. 4; *Papers of Madison*, V, 279, n. 3; McIlwaine, *Official Letters*, III, 427, 428, 448–49, 452–53; *Cal. of Va. State Papers*, III, 405, 417, 435.

  [6] Ambler to JM, 1 Feb. 1783, n. 7.

  [7] Not found.

Notes on Debates

MS (LC: Madison Papers). For a description of the manuscript of Notes on Debates, see *Papers of Madison*, V, 231–34.

Monday Feby. 10.

For The Report of the Committee on the Resolutions of Va.[1] concerning the contract Under which Tobo. was to be exported to N. Y. and the admission of circumstancial proof of accts agst. U. S. when legal vouchers had been destroyed by the enemy, see the Journal of this date.[2]

Mr. Mercer informed Congress that this matter had made much noise in Va.[3] that she had assented to the export of the first quantity, merely out of respect to Congs. and under an idea that her rights of Sovereignty; had been encroached upon;[4] and that as a *further quantity* had been exported *without the licence of the State*,[5] the question was unavoidable, whether the authority of Congs. extended to the act. He wished therefore that Congress wd. proceed to decide this question

Mr. Fitzimmons in behalf of the Committee observed that they went no farther than to examine whether the proceedings of the officers of Congs. were conformable to the Resoln: of Congs. & not whether the latter were within the power of Congs.[6]

Mr. Lee. sd. the Rept. did not touch the point that, the additional quantity had been exported without application to the State, altho' the first quantity was licenced by the State with great reluctance, in consequence of the request of Congs. and of assurances agst. a repetition, and that the Superintendt & Secy of Congs. ought at any rate to have made application to the Executive before they proceeded to further exportations.[7]

Mr Rutlidge sd. the Rept. went to the very point, that Va. suspected the Resols: of Congs. had been abused by the Officers of Congs. & the Rept. shewed that no such abuse had taken place;[8] that if this information was not satisfactory, and the State sd. contest the right of Congs. in the case, it wd. then be proper to answer it on that point,[9] but not before; He sd. if the Gentleman (Mr. Lee) meant that the Come. authorised by Congs. on the   day of   to[10] make explanations on this subject to the Legislature of Va. had given the assurances he mentioned, he must be mistaken: for none such had been given. He had he sd. formed notes of his remarks to the Legl. but accordg to his practice had destroyed them after the occasion was over, and therefore cd. only assert this from memory. that nevertheless his memory enabled him to do it with certainty.

Mr. Lee, in explanation sd. he did not mean the Come.[;] that the abuse complained of was not that the Resolun. of Congs. had been exceeded, but that the export had been undertaken without the Sanction of the State.[11] If the acts were repeated, he said, great offence wd. be given to Va.[12]

The report was agd. to as far as the Tobo. was concerned without a dissenting voice.[13] Mr. Lee uttering a no, but not loud enough to be heard by Congress or the chair. The part relating to the loss of Vouchers, was unanimously agd. to.[14]

Come. of the Whole.[15]

The Rept. for valuation of land amended by insertion of "distinguishing dwelling houses from others."[16]

The Come. adjourned & the report was made to Congs.[17]

Mr. Lee & Mr. Jarvais moved that the report might be postponed to adopt another plan to wit "to call on the States to return a valuation: and to provide that in case any return sd. be not satisfactory to all parties, persons sd. be appd. by Congs. & others by the States respectively to adjust the case finally.["] On this question N. H. was divd. Mas: no. R. I. ay. Cont. no. N. Y. divd. N. J. no: Pa. no. Va. no. Mr Madison & Jones no, Mr Lee & Bland ay. N. C. ay, S. C. ay, so the motion failed.[18]

[1] Adopted on 28 December 1782 by the Virginia General Assembly, submitted on 27 January 1783 to Congress by the delegates from that state, and referred four days later to a committee with Thomas FitzSimons as chairman (*Papers of Madison*, V, 459–60; 461–63; *JCC*, XXIV, 96, 106; Delegates to Harrison, 28 Jan. 1783, and n. 2). The committee had rendered its report on 6 February (*JCC*, XXIV, 106, n. 3).

[2] *JCC,* XXIV, 121–23. See also nn. 6 and 14, below.

[3] That is, the contract between agents of the United States and the merchants-capitulant at Yorktown, concluded in accordance with a provision of the Articles of Capitulation of 19 October 1781 and, as amended, ratified by Congress on 11 February 1782. For the "noise" caused in Virginia by "this matter," see *JCC,* XXII, 70–71; *Papers of Madison,* IV, 163, n. 4; 245, n. 7; 267, n. 8; V, 342, and n. 2; 412; 413, n. 5; 461–63; 464 nn.

[4] Governor Benjamin Harrison, together with other prominent Virginians, had regarded the contract (n. 3), as lacking in "propriety" and as setting a "dangerous precedent," especially since the Virginia General Assembly at the session of October 1776 had banned trade in tobacco with the enemy (Hening, *Statutes,* IX, 162; *Papers of Madison,* IV, 244; 245, n. 7; 263–64; 266, nn. 3, 6; 297–98; 299, nn. 10, 11; 323–24). With great reluctance, in the summer of 1782 Harrison and a majority of the House of Delegates consented to facilitate the execution of the contract, even though they doubted whether the Articles of Confederation conferred upon Congress power of sufficient latitude under either the war or the commerce clauses to traverse a state law and to sanction "a dangerous intercourse" between Virginians and the enemy (*JCC,* XIX, 217; McIlwaine, *Official Letters,* III, 223; *JCSV,* III, 41, 86, 106; *Papers of Madison,* IV, 253–54; 254, n. 4; 425, n. 7). See also n. 7, below.

[5] *Papers of Madison,* V, 461–63; 464, n. 8.

[6] By the resolution of 11 February 1782, Charles Thomson, the secretary of Congress, was "empowered to grant letters of passport and safe conduct for the exportation" of the tobacco to New York, "on the conditions and under the limitations which shall," to him and to Robert Morris, "appear most proper and beneficial to the said states, being consistent with the said capitulation: provided always, that permission be not given for the exporting of tobacco, beyond the amount of the produce of the sales of the said goods belonging to the capitulants" (*JCC,* XXII, 71). Having been informed by a representative of the merchants-capitulant that their sales amounted to 44,037 ⅔ Spanish milled dollars, Thomson requested Daniel Clark, the agent of Robert Morris in Virginia, to limit the cargoes of the flag-of-truce vessels strictly to a quantity of tobacco equivalent in value to that sum (*Papers of Madison,* V, 462–63).

For the misunderstanding of Governor Harrison and the General Assembly concerning the amount of money and tobacco involved, see *ibid.,* V, 461; 462–63; 464, nn. 3, 8; also n. 12, below. The FitzSimons committee, knowing of the several agreements made by Thomson and Morris with the agent of the merchants-capitulant, and not instructed to consider whether those agreements encroached upon the sovereignty of Virginia, reported to Congress that the merchants-capitulant had been entitled to even more than 989,588 pounds of tobacco and that the conduct of Morris and Thomson "was in all respects conformable to the resolution of this house" on 11 February 1782 (*JCC,* XXIV, 122–23).

[7] On 14 and 15 June 1782, after being urged by John Rutledge and George Clymer of Pennsylvania, who comprised a deputation from Congress, to co-operate in making the contracts with the merchants-capitulant effective, the Virginia General Assembly reluctantly adopted a resolution acquiescing to the loading of 685 hogsheads of tobacco (*JCC,* XXII, 289–90, 353; *Papers of Madison,* IV, 340, and n. 3).

[8] See n. 6.

[9] See nn. 4 and 12.

[10] On 22 May 1782 (*JCC,* XXII, 289–90).

[11] See nn. 6 and 7.

[12] *Papers of Madison,* IV, 253–54.

[13] *JCC,* XXIV, 123.

14 See n. 1. Congress adopted the recommendation of the FitzSimons committee by directing Robert Morris "to instruct the commissioner appointed to settle the accounts of the State of Virginia, with the United States, to receive such proofs as shall be exhibited to him instead of the vouchers which have been lost or destroyed, in consequence of the invasion of the said State; and that he shall transmit to the Superintendant [Morris] a special report upon all such charges, which report shall be submitted to Congress to be finally decided on" (JCC, XXIV, 123). For the commissioners to settle the accounts of the states with Congress, see JM Notes, 5–6 Feb. 1783, and n. 9, especially the citations listed at the beginning of that note.

15 Ever since the committee of the whole convened for the first time on 29 January 1783, Daniel Carroll had been the chairman (JM Notes, 5–6 Feb., n. 5; 7 Feb. 1783, n. 3).

16 For the report, submitted to Congress on 5 February, negatived the next day, and recommitted on 7 February for further consideration by the committee of the whole, see JM Notes, 5–6 February, and nn. 9, 10, 12; 7 Feb. 1783, and nn. The amendment, offered by an unidentified member of the committee, was inserted immediately after the phrase "the number of buildings within it," in the third paragraph of the committee's report as recorded by Thomson (NA: PCC, No. 36, III, 451–53; JCC, XXIV, 124).

17 Congress granted Daniel Carroll's request, made on behalf of the committee, to permit it "to sit again" because it had not "come to a conclusion" about "sundry resolutions" (JCC, XXIV, 123). See JM Notes, 11 Feb. 1783.

18 JM added the last four words of this paragraph in his old age. Although unrecorded by JM, Mercer's vote also must have been "no."

Notes on Debates

MS (LC: Madison Papers). For a description of the manuscript of Notes on Debates, see *Papers of Madison*, V, 231–34.

Teusday. Feby. 11.

The Rept. made by the Come. of the whole[1] havg. decided that the mode to be grounded on the return of facts called for from the States, ought now to be ascertained.[2]

Mr. Rutlidge proposed 2d by Mr. Gilman, that the States sd. be required to name Comrs. each of them one, who or any nine of them sd. be appd. & empowerd. by Congs. to settle the valuation.[3] Mr. Ghorum was agst. it as parting with a power which might be turned by the States agst. Congs. Mr. Wolcot agst. it; declares his opinion that the confederation ought to be amended by substituting numbers of inhabitants as the rule; admits the difference between freemen & blacks; and suggests a compromise by including in the numeration such blacks only as were within 16 & 60. years of age.[4] Mr. Wilson was agst. relinquishing such a power to the States; proposes that the commissioners be appd. by Congs. and their proceedings subject to the ratification of Congs. Mr. Mercer was for submitting them to the revision of Congs. & this amendment was recd.[5] Mr. Peters agst. the whole scheme of valuation, as holding out false lights & hopes to the public.[6] Mr. Rutlidge thinks Comrs. appd. by the States may be trusted as well as Comrs. appd. by Congs. or as Congs themselves.[7] Mr Wilson observes that if appd. by the States they will bring with them the spirit of agents for their respective States, if appd. by Congs. will consider themselves as servants of U. S. at large & be more impartial.[8]

Mr. Ghorum 2ded. by Mr. Wilson, proposes to postpone in order to require the States to appt. Comrs. to give Congs. information for a basis for a valuation. on the question N.H. no, Mas: ay. R.I. ay. Cont. ay. N.Y. ay[.] N.J. ay. Pa. ay. Va. no, N.C. no, S.C. no. So it was decided in the negative[9]

To make the resolution more clear, "after the words "or any nine of them." the words "concurring therein" were added. Mr. Rutledge says that subjecting the acts of the Comrs. to the revision of Congs. had so varied his plan that he sd. be agst it[10]—on the main question N.H. ay. Mas: ay[.] R.I. ay. Cont. ay. N.Y. no, N.J. no. Pa. ay. Va. ay. [Mr. Madison no], N.C. ay. S.C. ay. So it was agreed to & the resolution declaring that a mode sd. now be fixed struck out as executed.[11] The whole report was then committed to a special Come. consisting of Mr. Rutlidge Mr. Gorham & Mr. Gilman to be formed into a proper act.[12]

[1] The report was that made to Congress on the preceding day (JM Notes, 10 Feb. 1783, and n. 17).

[2] The committee of the whole summarized in four numbered paragraphs what its members had been able to agree upon during their frequent meetings beginning on 29 January, viz., (1) that the valuation of lands, buildings, and improvements within the United States should "be immediately attempted" as directed by the Articles of Confederation; (2) that on or before 1 January 1784 each state should inform Congress of the total acreage privately owned in that state, also the number of dwelling houses, other buildings, whites, and Negroes; (3) that Congress, before calling upon the states for the data mentioned in No. 2, should "now" decide upon the "mode" whereby "the quotas of the several States" would be determined after the data were received; (4) that this "mode" should be "in force" for no more than five years, and during that "term" should be applied only for allocating among the states the sums required for "*supporting the public credit and other* contingent expences, and for adjusting all accounts between the United States and each particular State for monies paid or articles furnished by the several States" (*JCC*, XXIV, 124). If these proposals were agreed to, their enforcement obviously would not allay the immediate financial crisis, characterized by an empty Confederation

treasury and importunate military and civilian creditors of the United States. See JM Notes, 7 Jan.; 13 Jan.; 24 Jan. 1783, and n. 17.

[3] The Rutledge-Gilman motion, as amended during the debate on this day, stipulated that after 2 January 1784 Congress would name an evaluation commissioner for every state which by then had not nominated a commissioner. The thirteen commissioners, having been appointed by Congress, would make the evaluation on the basis of the data submitted in accord with No. 2 of the report of the committee of the whole (n. 2, above). Before becoming effective, this evaluation must be concurred in by at least nine of the commissioners and thereafter subjected to the revision and approval of Congress (JCC, XXIV, 125, and n. 1).

[4] Oliver Wolcott's suggested amendment to the Articles of Confederation was plainly intended to be a sectional compromise.

[5] The Wilson-Mercer view that the proceedings of the commissioners should be submitted to the review of Congress was adopted by Congress and added in President Elias Boudinot's handwriting to the close of the manuscript text of the Rutledge-Gilman motion. See n. 3; and JCC, XXIV, 125, n. 1.

[6] JM and Alexander Hamilton, among other members of Congress, probably concurred with Richard Peters' opinion. See JM Notes, 9–10 Jan.; 14 Jan.; 27 Jan.; 28 Jan.; 31 Jan. 1783, and n. 17.

[7] See JM Notes, 14 Jan. 1783, for a comment of similar tenor by John Rutledge. See also JM Notes, 31 Jan. 1783, and n. 10.

[8] James Wilson apparently made this observation, which resembled Hamilton's supposedly "imprudent & injurious" remark of 28 January, in support of his motion to have a grand committee of Congress, rather than special commissioners, "settle the relative value and adjust the quotas of each State," by using the returns from the states as provided for by the second recommendation in the report of the committee of the whole (JM Notes, 28 Jan. 1783, and n. 12). The allocations agreed upon by the grand committee, comprising a member from each state, were not to become effective until Congress had accepted them. Needing the affirmative votes of at least seven states, Wilson's motion drew the support of only six, including Virginia, and hence failed of adoption. See n. 2; and JCC, XXIV, 125.

[9] See n. 4. The Gorham-Wilson proposal, by having a commissioner from each state come to Philadelphia solely for the purpose of supplying "information" about "the value of lands and buildings" in his state, would have left Congress with the entire authority "to adjust the proportion of the several States upon the principles of Justice and equity." Varying from JM's list of the vote, Gorham's record on the manuscript of his motion shows Rhode Island as being "div," and South Carolina as being "ay" (NA: PCC, No. 36, III, 459; JCC, XXIV, 125–26, 126, n. 1).

[10] As written by Rutledge, the amendment was to add "concurring," not "concurring therein," after "or any nine of them" (NA: PCC, No. 36, III, 457; JCC, XXIV, 125, n. 1). JM should have omitted his first quotation mark. The adoption of the amendment mentioned in n. 5, above, "varied" the "plan" of Rutledge fundamentally by transferring control of the evaluation from the state commissioners to Congress. On this issue he consistently had taken a states'-rights position. See JM Notes, 9–10 Jan., and n. 8; 14 Jan., and n. 7; 29 Jan. 1783 and n. 25.

[11] Thus, by a vote of 8 ayes and 2 noes, recorded neither in the journal nor on the manuscript of Rutledge's motion, the amended motion was adopted and thereafter inserted in the stead of the third recommendation of the committee of the whole. See n. 2; and JCC, XXIV, 124. Reaching a decision about where the determination of the "mode" should be lodged was far from having Congress agree upon what the "mode" should be. See JM to Jefferson, 11 Feb. 1783, and to Randolph on the same day.

[12] JCC, XXIV, 124. See also JM Notes, 14 Feb. 1783, and n. 7.

To Benjamin Harrison

RC (Jasper E. Crane, Wilmington, Del., 1963). Cover addressed to "His Excellency Benjamin Harrison Esqr Richmond." Docketed by Harrison, "Lr. from the Hon. James Madison February 11th. 83."

PHILADA. Feby. 11th. 1783.

SIR

Your Excellency will receive this from the hand of Mr. Dunlap who will represent the advantages which his press at Richmond will derive from a payment of the allowance made for his losses in establishing it. Being sensible of your Excellency's disposition to attend to every application as far as its merits may require, and may depend on yourself, especially when the public interest may be in any manner included, I should have forborne to trouble you on the present occasion, had not my agency in the original contract with Mr Dunlap given him a claim to at least a line introducing his case to your Excellency.[1]

I am Sir wth great respect Yr Excellency's obt & hble servt.

J. MADISON JR

[1] In the autumn of 1780 JM and the other Virginia delegates in Congress had acted as Governor Thomas Jefferson's agents in concluding an agreement with John Dunlap, printer and publisher of the *Pennsylvania Packet*, whereby Dunlap's business associate, James Hayes, Jr., would become the official printer for the government of Virginia and issue a weekly Virginia gazette in Richmond. The ship "Bachelor," laden with Dunlap's printing press and other equipment for Hayes's use, was "driven on shore by stress of weather" near Hampton, Va., in Chesapeake Bay and captured by the British (*Papers of Madison*, II, 22, n. 2; 69; 70, n. 3; 159).

In reply to a petition of Dunlap and Hayes submitted by Joseph Jones, the Virginia General Assembly on 14 and 16 December 1780 passed a resolution authorizing the remuneration of the printers from the state treasury for the "amount of their loss" (*ibid.*, II, 199; *JHDV*, Oct. 1780, pp. 28, 49–50, 53). On 2 July 1782, in response to a petition received on 4 June, a committee of the House of Delegates reported that the claimants were owed £1,200 for their losses and stated that coverage for "the same is included in the Estimate of Debt due by the Commercial Agent, and provided for with the other Debts of that Department by the Law for appropriating the Public Revenue" (Minute Book, House of Delegates, May 1782, p. 61, MS in Va. State Library; Hening, *Statutes*, XI, 12–14). On 5 February 1783 Hayes reminded Governor Harrison that the sum "so generously" voted had not been paid, and as late as 23 March 1788 Dunlap was importuning a new governor, Edmund Randolph, to honor, with interest, the resolution "long since passed" (MSS in Va. State Library; *Cal. of Va. State Papers*, IV, 413–14).

218

Virginia Delegates to Benjamin Harrison

RC (Historical Society of Pennsylvania). In the hand of Joseph Jones, except for the signatures of JM, John Francis Mercer, Arthur Lee, and Theodorick Bland, Jr. Addressed to "His Excellency the Governor of Virginia." Docketed by Harrison, "Lr: from the Delegates in Congress February 11th. 1783."

PHILADELPHIA Feby. 11th. 1783

SIR,

We had the honor of receiving your Excellency's favor, of the 31st. of Jany.; & sympathize very sincerely in the distress you must have felt for a Sister so worthy of being belovd & honord.[1]

The miscarriage of our Letter of the 22d ult. was probably owing to the cause your Excellency supposes. We shall desire the Post-master general to make due enquiry into it, that if any mal-practice can be discovered it may be punishd.[2] The demands of the Officers tho' just, are distressing; & we wish their sentiments had been such, as your Excellency mentions. But we have no reason to apprehend, that they will forget they are Citizens as well as Soldiers; or be dissatisfyd with the best provision that can be made for them, during the distress of the war.[3]

The enclosed hand-bill, which receives some corroboration from the report of a Captain just arrivd from St. Thomas's, is all we know of the issue of the negociations for Peace.[4]

Congress have passd Resolutions, relative to the Tobacco shipt by Mr. Clarke;[5] & the settlement of the State-accounts;[6] copies of which we shall transmit by the next post.[7] The dispute with Mr. Nathan is not yet arbitrated.[8]

We have the honor to be with the highest respect, your Excellency's most obedient & most humbl Servants

> J MADISON JR.
> JOHN F. MERCER
> JOS: JONES.
> A. LEE
> THEOK: BLAND JR

[1] Harrison to Delegates, 31 Jan. 1783, and n. 1.

[2] The delegates had written to Harrison on 21 January (*q.v.*) rather than on "the 22d ult." See Harrison to Delegates, 31 Jan., and n. 3; 18 Feb. 1783. The postmaster general was Ebenezer Hazard.

[3] JM Notes, 13 Jan., and n. 21; 24 Jan.; 28 Jan.; 4 Feb.; JM to Randolph, 22 Jan.; Harrison to Delegates, 31 Jan. 1783.

219

4 The missing enclosure was a handbill issued at Baltimore on 5 February, stating that Captain White of the "Harlequin" had brought a letter of 15 January from St. Kitts giving assurance on the strength of news from Dominica and Guadeloupe that a preliminary peace treaty had been signed (*Pa. Packet,* 11 Feb. 1783). The same issue of the *Packet* reported that a schooner had informed the "Iris," while at sea on her voyage from the West Indies to Annapolis, of the "confirmation of peace" given by Captain John Barry of the "Alliance" during his brief stay in the harbor of St. Thomas. Before receiving the present letter, Governor Harrison certainly had read these reports in the *Virginia Gazette* or in the *Virginia Gazette, and Weekly Advertiser* (Richmond, Nicolson and Prentis) of 15 February. See also JM to Randolph, 11 Feb. 1783.

5 JM Notes, 10 Feb. 1783, and nn. 1, 3, 4, 6, 7, 12. On that day Congress unanimously adopted the report of the FitzSimons committee which, after summarizing the facts "relative to the Tobacco shipt," concluded that Robert Morris and Charles Thomson had acted "in all respects conformable" with the directive of Congress of 11 February 1782 (*JCC,* XXIV, 121–23).

6 JM Notes, 10 Feb. 1783, and n. 14.

7 Delegates to Harrison, 18 Feb. 1783.

8 Harrison to Delegates, 4 Jan., and n. 8; 11 Jan., and n. 8; 15 Feb.; Delegates to Harrison, 21 Jan.; 28 Jan.; 4 Feb. 1783.

To Thomas Jefferson

RC (LC: Madison Papers). Addressed to "Thos. Jefferson Esq." Docketed by Jefferson, "Madison Jas. Feby. 11. 1783." The words italicized in the third paragraph are those written by JM in the cipher described in Jefferson to JM, 31 Jan. 1783, ed. n. Also in LC: Madison Papers is JM's draft of the letter.

PHILADA. Feby. 11th. 1783

DEAR SIR

Your favor of the 31 of Jany.[1] was safely brought by Mr. Thomson. That of the 7. inst:[2] came by yesterday's mail. The anecdote related in the first was new to me; and if there were no other key, would sufficiently decypher the implacability of the party triumphed over.[3] In answer to the second I can only say at this time that I feel deeply for your situation: that I approve of the choice you have made among its difficulties,[4] and that every aid which can depend on me shall be exerted to relieve you from them. Before I can take any step with propriety however it will be expedient to feel the sentiments of Congress, and to advise with some of my friends.[5] The first point may possibly be brought about by your letter to the Secy. of F. A. which I suppose came too late yesterday to be laid before Congress, but which will no doubt be handed in this morning.[6]

The time of Congress since you left us[7] has been almost exclusively spent on projects for a valuation of the land, as the fœderal articles require, and yet I do not find that we have got an inch forward towards the object. The mode of referring the task to the States which had at first the warmest & most numerous support seems to be in a manner abandoned; and nothing determinate is yet offered on the mode of effecting it without their intervention. The greatest misfortune perhaps attending the case is that a plan of some kind is made an indispensable preliminary to any other essay for the public relief. I much question whether a sufficient number of States will be found in favor of any plan that can be devised,[8] as I am sure that in the present temper of Congs. a sufficient number cannot who will agree to tell their Constituents that the law of the Confederation cannot be executed, and to propose an amendment of it.[9]

Congress yesterday received from *Mr. Adams*[10] *several letters dated September* not remarkable for any thing unless it be a[11] *display of his vanity, his prejudice against* the *French Court* & *his venom against Doctr. Franklin.*[12] Other preparations for the post[13] do not allow me to use more cypher at present.

I have a letter from Randolph dated Feby. 1. confirming the death of his aunt. You are acquainted no doubt with the course the estate is to take. He seems disposed in case he can make a tolerable compromise with his Father's creditors to resign his appt. under the State & go into the Legislature. His zeal for some continental arrangemt. as essential for the public honor & saftety forms at least one of his motives, & I have added all the fuel to it in my power.[14]

My neglect to write to you heretofore has proceeded from a hope that a letter wd. nor find you at Baltimore; and no subject has occurred for one of sufft. importance to follow you. You shall henceforward hear from me as often as an occasion presents, until your departure forbids it. The Ladies & Gentlemen to whom I communicated your respects, return them with equal sincerity[15] & the former as well as myself very affectionately include Miss Patsy in the object of them.[16]

I am Dr. Sir Yr. Sincere friend[17]

J. MADISON JR.

[1] *Q.v.*, and n. 1.
[2] *Q.v.*
[3] Jefferson to JM, 31 Jan. 1783, and n. 9.
[4] Jefferson to JM, 7–8 Feb. 1783, and nn. 12, 15. The words "at this time" are not in JM's draft copy of this letter.
[5] The words "of my friends" were a substitution for "individual members" in the

draft copy. Perhaps the change of expression reflects the decision of JM also to consult La Luzerne and Barbé-Marbois, or one of them.

[6] In the draft copy JM wrote "I suppose" immediately after the second rather than the first "which" in the sentence and omitted "no doubt." For Jefferson's letter of 7 February 1783 to Robert R. Livingston, secretary for foreign affairs, see Boyd, *Papers of Jefferson*, VI, 228–29. On 11 February, upon receiving this letter, Congress referred it to a committee with Joseph Jones as chairman (NA: PCC, No. 185, III, 54). Three days later Congress adopted the committee's report recommending that "considering the advices lately received in America, and the probable situation of affairs in Europe," Jefferson "do not proceed on his intended voyage until he shall receive" further instructions from Congress. Livingston at once sent a copy of this resolution to Jefferson (*JCC*, XXIV, 132; Boyd, *Papers of Jefferson*, VI, 239–40). See also JM Notes, 14 Feb. 1783.

[7] That is, on 26 January. See JM to Randolph, 28 Jan. 1783. JM or someone at his bidding placed one bracket at the beginning and another at the end of this paragraph, thus designating it for publication in the first comprehensive edition of his works. See Madison, *Papers* (Gilpin ed.), I, 503.

[8] JM Notes, 27 Jan.; 28 Jan., and nn. 3, 11; 29 Jan.; 31 Jan., and nn. 11, 17; 4 Feb.; 5–6 Feb., and nn. 9, 13; 7 Feb., and n. 9; 8 Feb., and n. 3; 10 Feb.; 11 Feb. 1783, and nn. 2, 3, 5, 8–11.

[9] JM Notes, 27 Jan., and n. 16; 28 Jan., and nn. 12, 27, 28, 41, 45; 29 Jan., and nn. 25, 37, 38; 30 Jan., and nn. 2, 4; 11 Feb. 1783, and n. 4. In the draft of this letter, JM omitted "that in the present temper of Congs." and wrote "is impracticable" instead of "cannot be executed."

[10] JM's "13.1." deciphers only as "Ad.," rather than "Adams." For a clearer symbol signifying the name, see Jefferson to Madison, 14 Feb. 1783 (2d letter), n. 3.

[11] In both the draft and the recipient's copies, JM at this point wrote and canceled "full." It was probably years later that in the draft copy he interlineated "fresh" above the deleted word. John Adams' four dispatches, two of which were dated at The Hague on 6 and 7 September, respectively, and two on 17 September, were addressed to Robert R. Livingston and read in Congress on 10 February 1783. Congress referred the dispatch of 7 September, relating to financial accounts, to a committee with Nathaniel Gorham as chairman (NA: PCC, No. 185, III, 54; No. 186, fol. 83; Wharton, *Revol. Dipl. Corr.*, V, 703–9, 733–38).

Especially in his dispatch of 6 September, Adams revealed pride in his achievements in the Netherlands, conviction that Vergennes was determined to have France control the relations of the United States with other European powers, and distrust of Franklin as Vergennes' puppet who neglected to inform Adams of the progress of peace negotiations. For a highly favorable opinion of Adams' dispatches, see Livingston's acknowledgment of them on 13 February 1783 (Wharton, *Revol. Dipl. Corr.*, VI, 250). See also JM Notes, 21 Jan. 1783, n. 1.

[12] In attempting to indicate the symbol for "French" (368.7.), JM strayed by one page and wrote 367.7. The combined symbols used by him for "Doctr. Franklin" decipher only as "Doctor Frank."

[13] JM to Harrison, 11 Feb. 1783, and to Randolph, the same day.

[14] Randolph to JM, 1 Feb. 1783, and n. 5. The letter of 11 February to Randolph in which JM "added all the fuel" evidently was completed before JM wrote the present letter to Jefferson. Randolph did not become a member of the House of Delegates of the Virginia General Assembly until 1788 (Swem and Williams, *Register*, pp. 28–29).

[15] Jefferson to JM, 31 Jan., and nn. 28, 29; 7–8 Feb. 1783.

[16] Martha (Patsy) Jefferson, age eleven years, was with her father in Baltimore (Boyd, *Papers of Jefferson*, VI, 218, 227). See also *Papers of Madison*, V, 151, n. 5.

[17] JM omitted this complimentary close in his retained draft of the letter.

To Edmund Randolph

RC (LC: Madison Papers). Unsigned but in JM's hand. Docketed by Randolph, "James Madison Feby. 11 1783."

PHILADA. Feby. 11. 1783

MY DEAR FRIEND

I am particularly indebted to you for your favor of the 1st. inst. which you were obliged to forward through so many obstacles.[1] Your idea of going into the legislative councils gives me peculiar satisfaction, & I anxiously wish the arrangements on which it depends may not miscarry.[2] Indeed I think it is a duty to which you owe some sacrifices, greater than I sd. suppose the difference between the profits of your office, & those from which it excludes you, can amount to.[3] of this difference you are the best judge; but in my position I undertake to say, your view of our affairs would furnish still more cogent motives than those you now feel. The valuation of the lands of the U.S. as directed by the articles of Union has employed & puzzled Congress for the past week; and after all the projects & discussions which have taken place, we seem only to have gone round in a circle to the point at which we set out. The only point on which Congress are generally agreed is that something ought to be attempted, but what that something ought to be, is a theorem not solved alike by scarcely any two members: and yet a solution of it seems to be made an indispensible preliminary to other essays for the public relief.[4] The Deputation from the army is waiting the upshot of all these delays and dilemmas.[5]

When I mentioned to you the subject of your conversation with Dr. McC[l]urg, I ought to have added that one reason which influenced the resignation of Mr. Livingston was an expence experienced of 3 thousand dollrs. beyond the salary. I wish this circumstance not to be withheld as it must be material in the case, and it would be a real affliction to me to be accessary to a disappointment.[6] For the same reason it is incumbent on me to observe that I hold it to be very uncertain whether the place in question will be within the option of our friend, as I hold indeed the continuance of the place itself to be a little precarious.[7]

Mr. J. is detained at Baltimore by the danger which besets the capes. This situation he writes me is far from being a pleasant one and yet I fear the avidity and vigilance of the Enemy will prevent his being quickly relieved from it.[8] Mr. Mercer filled up the remaining blank in the Delegation on Wednesday last.[9]

This City is full of reports concerning peace, but they all come by the way of the W.I. and are the more uncertain as they come too thro' mercantile channels.[10] The fall of goods which is taking place augurs well however.[11]

[1] For the "obstacles," see the first paragraph of Randolph to JM, 1 Feb. 1783.

[2] Randolph to JM, 1 Feb., and n. 5; JM to Jefferson, 11 Feb. 1783, and n. 14.

[3] As attorney general, Randolph's salary was £300 specie a year, but he supplemented this income with fees of a growing but unknown amount from private clients (Hening, *Statutes*, X, 493; *Papers of Madison*, IV, 162, n. 8; V, 50, n. 1; 308). Members of the Virginia legislature were compensated with the value in money, as determined by "the grand jury at each and every of the four annual sessions of the general court," of "fifty pounds of neat tobacco by the day for attendance on assembly, two pounds of the like tobacco for every mile they must necessarily travel going to or from the same together with their ferriages" (Hening, *Statutes*, X, 104, 229). If a hundredweight of tobacco was worth an average of 20s. specie, the per diem salary of a member of the House of Delegates was about 10s., or £75 for the approximate 150 days during which the legislature was in session annually (*Cal. of Va. State Papers*, III, 150–51, 168–69).

JM appears to mean that, although the increased fees from private clients which Randolph could anticipate if he resigned as attorney general and entered the House of Delegates probably would not make up the difference between £75 and whatever total the £300 and his income as a practicing lawyer amounted to annually, he should count the monetary "sacrifices" as more than overbalanced by the opportunities he would have as a delegate to render conspicuous public service to both Virginia and the United States. See *Papers of Madison*, V, 30; JM to Jefferson, 11 Feb. 1783, and n. 14.

[4] JM to Jefferson, 11 Feb. 1783, and the citations in its nn. 8 and 9.

[5] JM Notes, 7 Jan., and n. 6; 4 Feb., and nn. 7, 13–15; 18 Feb. 1783, and n. 3. Of the "Deputation," Colonel John Brooks left Philadelphia about 8 February to return to Washington's army. Colonel Matthias Ogden also went to New Jersey at about the same time but never returned to active duty. Continuing to press Congress for a favorable answer to the memorial of the army, General Alexander McDougall remained in Philadelphia until late in May 1783 (Burnett, *Letters*, VII, 35–36 n., 50, n. 3, 72–73 n., 150–51 n., 175, n. 3; Fitzpatrick, *Writings of Washington*, XXVI, 169, 274, 340).

[6] *Papers of Madison*, V, 338, n. 4; Randolph to JM, 1 Feb. 1783, and n. 8.

[7] Both on grounds of economy and as an evidence of the determination of the United States to isolate itself from overseas politics, an increasing number of delegates in Congress believed that, following the conclusion of peace, the foreign service should be reduced at least to a few consuls and chargés d'affaires in the principal ports and capitals of western Europe, respectively. By so doing, the office of secretary for foreign affairs also could be abolished. After the resignation of Robert R. Livingston became effective on 5 June 1783, that office remained vacant until his successor, John Jay, arrived on 21 December 1784. During the interim, committees of Congress handled important matters of diplomacy while the routine duties were performed by Henry Remsen, Jr., a clerk until Congress on 2 March 1784 appointed him undersecretary in charge of "the papers belonging to the Office for foreign affairs" (*Papers of Madison*, V, 428, n. 5; JCC, XXIV, 524 and n. 1; Burnett, *Letters*, VII, 118, 146, 154, 184, 186). See also JM to Randolph, 12 Mar. 1783, n. 13.

[8] Jefferson to JM, 7 Feb. 1783, and nn. 3, 4.

[9] JM to Randolph, 28 Jan. 1783, n. 12.
[10] Delegates to Harrison, 11 Feb. 1783, and n. 4.
[11] In the Philadelphia newspapers during the first two weeks of February, the increasing number of advertisements by merchants who had foreign wares to sell at "cheap" or "reasonable" prices probably reflected their expectation that official word of peace, followed closely by large importations of goods from Europe, would soon arrive. See JM Notes, 13 Feb. 1783.

Notes on Debates

MS (LC: Madison Papers). For a description of the manuscript of Notes on Debates, see *Papers of Madison*, V, 231–34.

Wednesday Feby. 12.

The declaration of Congs. as to Genl. Funds passed o[n] Jany 29 appears on the Journals;[1] and Congress resolved itself into a Come. of the whole[2] in order to consider the funds to be adopted & recommended to the States.

On motion of Mr. Mifflin the impost of 5 PerCt. was taken into consideration. As it seemed to be the general opinion that some variations from the form in which it had been first recommended, wd. be necessary for reconciling the objecting States to it,[3] it was proposed that the sense of the Come. should be taken on that head. The following questions were accordingly propounded:

Qu: 1. Is it expedient to alter the impost as recomme[n]ded on the day   of 1781?[4]

Mr. Lee said the States particularly Virga. wd. never concur in the measure unless the term of years were limited, the collection left to the States, & the appropriation annually laid before them.[5]

Mr. Wolcot thought the revenue ought to be commensurate in point of time as well as amount to the debt; that there was no danger in trusting Congs. considering the responsible mode of its appt.[6] and that to alter the plan wd. be a mere condescension to the prejudices of the States.

Mr. Ghorum favored the alteration for the same reason as Mr. Lee, He said private letters informed him that the opposition to the impost law was gaining ground in Massts. and the repeal of Virga. would be very likely to give that opposition an ascendance.[7] He said our measures must be accomodated to the sentiments of the States whether just or unreasonable.

Mr. Hamilton dissented from the particular alterations suggested, but did not mean to negative the question.[8]

Mr. Bland was for conforming to the ideas of the States as far as wd. in any manner consist with the object.[9]

On the Question the affirmative was unanimous excepting the voice of Mr. Wolcot.[10]

Qu: 2d. Shall the term of duration be limited to 25 years?[11]

Mr. Mercer professed a decided opposition to the principle of general revenue, observed that the liberties of Engd. had been preserved by a separation of the purse from the sword; that untill the debts sd. be liquidated & apportioned he never wd. assent in Congs. or elsewhere to the scheme of the Impost,[12]

Mr. Bland proposed an alternative of 25 years, or until the requisitions of Congs. according to the Articles of Confedn. shall be found adequate.[13] On this proposition The votes were of N. H. divd. R. I. no. Cont. no. N. Y. no N. J no. Pa. no. Virga. ay. N. C. divd. S. C. ay. so the proposition was not agreed.

On the main question for 25 years, it was voted in the affirmative.[14]

Q: 3. Shall the appointment of Collectors be left to the States, they to be amenable to & under the Controul of Congs.? Ay, several States as N. Y. & Pa. dissenting.[15]

[1] The "declaration" adopted by Congress on 12 February was James Wilson's motion of 27 January as "new-modelled" by JM on 28 January, and as amended, reported by the committee of the whole to Congress, and spread on its journal the next day (JM Notes, 27 Jan., and n. 16; 28 Jan., and n. 3; 29 Jan. 1783, and nn. 8, 11–13). The motion was adopted by a vote of seven states. The delegations of Rhode Island, Virginia, and North Carolina deadlocked in the tally. Maryland was represented by only one delegate (JCC, XXIV, 126–27).

[2] JM Notes, 10 Feb. 1783, n. 15.

[3] For the adoption by Congress on 3 February 1781 of the proposed impost amendment to the Articles of Confederation, see JM Notes, 28 Jan. 1783, n. 29. For the reservations by states which had ratified the amendment, the reasons why it had not been ratified by Rhode Island and Georgia, and why Virginia had rescinded her act of ratification, see *Papers of Madison*, V, 289; 291, nn. 9, 11; 374, n. 12; 375, n. 15; 414–15; 416, n. 3; 478, n. 2; Randolph to JM, 3 Jan.; Harrison to JM, 4 Jan., and nn. 3, 4; JM Notes, 28 Jan., nn. 29–31; 29 Jan., n. 25; 4 Feb. 1783, n. 10.

[4] See n. 3.

[5] See n. 7. By stating that Virginia would not ratify the amendment unless its duration was limited, Arthur Lee went beyond the reasons given in the preamble of the rescinding act of her General Assembly on 6 and 7 December 1782 (Randolph to JM, 3 Jan., n. 2; Harrison to JM, 4 Jan. 1783, n. 4; Hening, *Statutes*, XI, 171). Lee meant by the last of his three provisos that Congress, if authorized to levy an impost, must inform the states annually of the amount of money thereby supplied to the treasury of the Confederation. Massachusetts had included the same proviso

in her act of ratification of 3–4 May 1782 (NA: PCC, No. 74, fols. 193–96). See also JM Notes, 19 Feb. 1783, and n. 15.

⁶ Oliver Wolcott's remarks about the proper duration of the impost or other source of revenue only emphasized what had been made explicit in the resolutions of Congress submitting the amendment to the states for ratification (*JCC*, XIX, 112–13). Although the "mode" whereby the customs collectors should be appointed and controlled had been left ambiguous in those resolutions, Wolcott evidently believed that Congress, comprised of delegates serving at the will of state legislatures, could be trusted to administer the impost equitably and deferentially (JM Notes, 28 Jan. 1783).

⁷ Arthur Lee's remarks apparently echoed those expressed by Nathaniel Gorham on 29 January (JM Notes, 29 Jan. 1783). Gorham, a recent arrival in Congress from Massachusetts, was prone to align himself with the Lee-Adams faction, which often had manifested its solidarity on domestic and especially on foreign issues (*Papers of Madison*, V, 4; 15, n. 3; 403, n. 10; 469, n. 2). The Massachusetts General Court had long delayed its ratification of the impost amendment and had qualified its consent with many provisos (JM Notes, 14 Jan., n. 4; 28 Jan. 1783, n. 29).

⁸ Alexander Hamilton frequently and vigorously had advocated the proposed impost amendment, together with the appointment of the customs officers by Congress, both as an almost indispensable financial and nationalizing reform (Syrett and Cooke, *Papers of Hamilton*, III, 78–80, 213–23; *Papers of Madison*, V, 376, n. 27; JM Notes, 27 Jan.; 28 Jan. 1783, and n. 12).

⁹ For Theodorick Bland's earlier comments upon the impost amendment, see JM Notes, 29 Jan. 1783, and nn. 36, 37.

¹⁰ See n. 6.

¹¹ JM Notes, 29 January 1783, and n. 25.

¹² Although the Lees and the Mercers were long-time rivals in Virginia politics, John Francis Mercer here adopted the argument of "purse and sword," which Arthur Lee had used against a "general revenue" in the debate on 28 January (*Papers of Madison*, V, 283, n. 3; 427, n. 7; 455, n. 5; JM Notes, 28 Jan. 1783, and n. 5). For JM's comment on the issue, see JM Notes, 28 Jan., and n. 28; 21 Feb. 1783, and n. 10.

¹³ JM Notes, 29 Jan. 1783, and nn. 25, 36; JM to Jefferson, 11 Feb. 1783, and citations in nn. 8 and 9.

¹⁴ By accepting the "25 years" but rejecting the alternative in Bland's proposal, the committee of the whole may have sought to preclude a contention by state legislatures that if Congress should deem the income from requisitions to be inadequate, it probably would interpret the "alternative" as a justification for disregarding the stipulated time-span of "25 years." See JM Notes, 19 Feb. 1783, and n. 3.

¹⁵ In view of the insistence by Alexander Hamilton of New York and James Wilson of Pennsylvania that the collectors should be appointed by Congress, the adverse vote of the delegations from those states is not surprising. See JM Notes, 27 Jan., and n. 16; 28 Jan., and n. 12; 11 Feb. 1783, and n. 8. The outcome of this poll may reflect the increasing emphasis upon state sovereignty by some of the state delegations in Congress, or at least the readiness of some delegates, who would have preferred the collectors to be appointed by Congress, to defer to the delegates who were uncompromisingly opposed to that mode. In this connection it should be recalled that only eight state legislatures which ratified the proposed impost amendment had been willing for Congress to appoint and supervise the collectors (JM Notes, 28 Jan. 1783, n. 29). Following the vote on this issue, the committee of the whole adjourned and made its recommendations to Congress the next day (JM Notes, 13 Feb.; 18 Feb. 1783; *JCC*, XXIV, 128).

To Thomas Jefferson

RC (LC: George B. McClellan Papers, Vol. I). Cover missing, but docketed by Jefferson, "Madison Jas Feby. 12. 1783."

PHILADA. Feby. 12th. 1783.

MY DEAR SIR

I acknowledged yesterday by the post your two favors of the 30th. ult: & 7th. inst:[1] I add this by Col: Jameson[2] just to inform you that your letter to the Secy. of F. A. has been referred to a Committee consisting of Mr. Jones, Mr. Rutlidge & Mr. Wilson, who are to confer with Mr. Morris as Agent of Marine, and report to Congs. whether any and what remedy can be applied to your embarrassments. I made the first acquainted with the ideas suggested in your last letter, and he will take care to lead the attention of his Colleagues and of Mr. M. to them as far as may be requisite & proper. Mr. Livingston was not here when your letter to him came to hand: but he is now returned. I will take occasion to speak with him before the next post, and will give you the result as well as of the commitment of your letter, if any thing shall have come of it.[3] In the mean time accept of my unfeigned regards.

J. MADISON JR

[1] JM to Jefferson, 11 Feb. 1783. JM should have written "31st," rather than "30th."
[2] Lieutenant Colonel John Jameson, who had been granted leave by Washington on 8 January, was evidently returning, via Baltimore, to his home in Culpeper County, Va. (Fitzpatrick, *Writings of Washington*, XXVI, 15; *Papers of Madison*, II, 201, n. 1; V, 158, n. 2).
[3] JM to Jefferson, 11 Feb., and n. 6; 15 Feb. 1783. Robert R. Livingston, the secretary for foreign affairs, spent from about 11 January to 11 February in New York, performing his duties as chancellor of that state (*Papers of Madison*, V, 428, n. 3). Jefferson's "last letter" to JM was that of 7–8 Feb. 1783 (*q.v.*).

To James Madison, Sr.

RC (LC: Madison Papers). Docketed by JM, "Madison, Js. Feby. 12. 1783."

PHILADA. Feby. 12th. 1783.

HON'D SIR

Col: Jameson[1] affords me an opportunity of writing which I cannot omit, although I have little more to say to you than that I hope you &

the family[2] may be as well as I am myself. I readily suppose from the reports prevalent here that some information on the subject of peace will be expected, & I wish it were in my power to gratify you. The truth is we are in nearly as great uncertainty here as you can be. Every day almost brings forth some fresh rumour, but it is so mingled with mercantile speculations that little faith is excited. The most favorable evidence on the side of peace seems to be a material fall in the price of imported goods, which considering the sagacity and good intelligence of merchants is a circumstance by no means to be despised.[3] A little time will probably decide in the case, when I shall follow this with something more satisfactory. In the meantime I remain Yr. affectionate Son

J. Madison Jr.

Col: Zane lately sent an order on me for the books which I had drawn on you for, and for which you had the money ready.[4] If an oppy. offers I wish you to transmit him the payment.

[1] JM to Jefferson, 12 Feb. 1783, and n. 2.
[2] According to the usages of his day, JM included in "the family" the more than eighty slaves at Montpelier, as well as his parents and other relatives (*Papers of Madison*, I, 190; 191, n. 2; opp. 213; W[illiam] W[allace] Scott, *A History of Orange County Virginia* [Richmond, 1907], p. 236).
[3] Delegates to Harrison, 11 Feb., and n. 4; JM to Randolph, 11 Feb. 1783.
[4] For Colonel Isaac Zane, Jr., see *Papers of Madison*, I, 185, n. 1; IV, 126–27; 127, n. 4; Report on Books, 23 Jan. 1783, ed. n.

Notes on Debates

MS (LC. Madison Papers). For a description of the manuscript of Notes on Debates, see *Papers of Madison*, V, 231–34.

Thursday Feby. 13th.

The Committee report to Congs. the alterations yesterday agreed on with respect to the 5 PerCt. Impost.[1]

The deputy Secy. at War[2] reported to Congress the result of the enquiry directed by them on the   day of   [3] into the siesure of goods destined for the British Prisoners of war under passport from Genl Washington. From this report it appeared that some of the Siezors had pursued their claim under the law of the State & that in consequence the goods had been condemned & ordered for sale. The papers were referred to a Come consisting of Mr. Rutledge, Mr. Ghorum & Mr. Lee, who after havg. retired for a few moments reported, that the Secy at War should be authorised & directed to cause the goods to be taken from the places where they had been deposited,[4] to employ such force as wd. be sufficient, and that the Duke de Lauzun whose Legion was in the neighborhood,[5] should be requested to give the Secy. such aid as he might apply for.

This report was generally regarded by Congs. as intemperate, and the proposed recourse to the French Legion as flagrantly imprudent. Mr. Hamilton said that if the object had been to embroil this Country wth. their allies the expedient would have been well conceived.[*6] He added that the exertion of force would not under these circumstances meet the sense of the people at large. Mr. Ghorum sd. he denied this with respect to the people of Massachusetts.[7]

Mr. Lee on the part of the Come. said that the D. de Lauzun had been recurred to as being in the neighbourhood & having Cavalry under his Command which would best answer the occasion; and that the report was founded on wise & proper considerations.

Mr. Mercer, Mr. Williamson Mr. Ramsay & Mr. Wilson & Mr Madison strenuously opposed the Report, as improper altogether as far it related to the French Legion, and in other respects so until the State of Pa. sd. on a summons refuse to restore the articles seized.[8]

Mr. Rutledge with equal warmth contends for the expediency of the measures reported.

Mr. Mercer & Mr. Madison at length proposed that Congress sd. assert the right on this subject & summon the State of Pena. to redress the wrong immediately. The Report was recommitted, with this proposition & Mr. Wilson & Mr. Mercer added to the Com[e.][9]

The Speech of the K. of G. B. on the 5th Dcr. 1782. arrived & produced great joy in general except among the Merchts. who had great quantities of merchandise in Store the price of which immediately & materially fell.[10] The most judicious members of Congs. however suffered a great diminution of their joy from the impossibility of discharging the arrears & claims of the army & their apprehension of new difficulties from that quarter.[11]

*This was an oblique allusion to Mr. Lee whose enmity to the French was suspected by him &c.

[1] JM Notes, 12 Feb. 1783, and n. 15. The undated report of the committee of the whole is in NA: PCC, No. 36, II, 79. See also JCC, XXIV, 128, and n. 1. No journal was kept of the session of 13 February.

² Major William Jackson. For the issue to which JM refers in this paragraph and the next five paragraphs, see JM Notes, 24 Jan. 1783, and nn. 1–16.

³ On 24 January 1783. See JM Notes, 24 Jan., and nn. 14, 15. With his report, Major Jackson enclosed a printed notice of 10 February by John Gardner, the sheriff of Chester County, Pa., proclaiming an auction on 3 March 1783 of the supplies seized and condemned from the cargo of the flag-of-truce ship "Amazon" (NA: PCC, No. 149, II, 229–68, and esp. 229–30, 243, 245).

⁴ For the committee's report, written by Nathaniel Gorham, see *JCC*, XXIV, 128 n. Most of the "goods" were at "Mr. Ezekiel Webb's Tavern" and Caleb Taylor's home in Birmingham township, Chester County, Pa. (NA: PCC, No. 149, II, 233–40, 243). The secretary at war was Major General Benjamin Lincoln.

⁵ For the Duc de Lauzun and his legion, see *Papers of Madison*, III, 277, n. 4. He and his command were quartered at Burlington, N.J., on the eastern shore of the Delaware River about forty miles from Chester, Pa. (Fitzpatrick, *Writings of Washington*, XXV, 433).

⁶ For evidence of Arthur Lee's opposition to the French, mentioned in JM's footnote, see Randolph to JM, 15 Jan. 1783, and n. 8.

⁷ For Gorham's usual political alignment with Arthur Lee in Congress, see JM Notes, 12 Feb. 1783, and n. 7.

⁸ Intervention by foreign soldiers obviously would exasperate the government of Pennsylvania beyond need, even granting that the Duc de Lauzun should consent to have his legion employed except against the British. Lee's recommendation sharply contrasts with his usual opposition to any encroachment upon the sovereignty of a state.

⁹ JM Notes, 20 Feb. 1783.

¹⁰ An unofficial copy of the speech of King George III, announcing to Parliament the signing on 30 November 1782 of a preliminary peace treaty between the United States and Great Britain, had reached Philadelphia from New York City on 12 February 1783. As quoted by the *Pennsylvania Packet* of 15 February, King George had stated: "I did not hesitate to go the full length of the powers vested in me, and offer to declare them FREE and INDEPENDENT STATES, by an article to be inserted in the Treaty of Peace. Provisional articles are agreed upon to take effect whenever terms of peace shall be finally settled with the Court of France." See also *Pa. Journal*, 15 Feb. 1783. For the effect of the news of peace upon the price of merchandise, see Delegates to Harrison, 11 Feb., and n. 4; JM to Randolph, 11 Feb. 1783, and n. 11. See also *Papers of Madison*, V, 111, n. 8.

¹¹ JM Notes, 13 Jan., and nn. 17, 21; 25 Jan., and nn. 7–12; 4 Feb., and nn. 7, 10, 13–15; JM to Randolph, 11 Feb. 1783, and n. 5; Clarence L. Ver Steeg, *Robert Morris*, pp. 166–68.

To Thomas Jefferson

RC (LC: Madison Papers). Docketed by JM, "Madison Jas. Feby. 13. 1783."

PHILADA. Feby. 13th. 1783.

DEAR SIR

The Chevr. de la Luzerne having just given me notice that he shall send an Express to the Romulus in ½ an hour I sieze the opportunity of inclosing a copy of the British Kings Speech which presages a speedy establishment of peace.[1] What effect this circumstance may have on your mission[2] is at present uncertain. For myself I cannot think that any thing short of a final & authentic ratification ought to be listened to in that view. But I am told that it is the opinion of Mr. Morris that no vessel will sail from any American port whilst the critical uncertainty continues.[3] Whether any & what changes may be produced in the orders to the Romulus will be known from the Commander.[4]

Adieu

J. Madison Jr

[1] For the "Romulus," see Jefferson to JM, 31 Jan., and n. 4. For the speech of King George III to a joint session of Parliament, see JM Notes, 13 Feb. 1783, and n. 10.

[2] That is, to Paris as one of the peace commissioners of the United States.

[3] British men-of-war and privateers were still hovering off the coast of the United States for the purpose of capturing French or American frigates and merchant ships (Jefferson to JM, 7–8 Feb. 1783, and nn. 3, 4, 8). A letter of 12 February from Elizabethtown, N.J., published in the *Pennsylvania Packet* of 18 February 1783, emphasized that knowledge of the signing of the preliminary articles of peace was not deterring "British cruisers" from capturing American vessels in the waters near New York City.

[4] Chevalier de La Villebrune (Jefferson to JM, 31 Jan. 1783, and n. 4).

To Edmund Randolph

RC (LC: Madison Papers). Docketed by Randolph, "J. Madison   Feb: 13. 1783." The italicized words are those enciphered by JM in the Randolph code.

PHILADA. Feby. 13th. 1783

My dear Sir

I[1] heartily congratulate you on the dawn of peace presented in the inclosed paper.[2] Apprehending that the commercial sagacity of this & intervening places, may sieze the crisis to speculate on the Staple of Virga., we have judged it prudent to despatch a messenger with the intelligence to the Government.[3] private letters will also scatter it along the road.

I will not damp your joy by dwelling on prospects which have that tendency; but it will not be improper to hint to you, that there is much reason to believe that the *cloud which has been some time lowering on* the *North Ri*[ver][4] *will not be dispeled by the rays of peace* The opinion seems to be *wel*[l] *founded that the arms which have* secured the *liberties of* [this][5] *country will not* be *laid down until justice* is

232

secured to those who have wielded them and that dangerous convulsions would be *hazarded by orders* for that purpose.[6] I have not time to add more at present:

Farewell

J.M.

[1] Many years later, after recovering this letter, JM or someone at his direction signified by placing a bracket before "I" and another bracket before "Farewell" that the two paragraphs should be included in the first comprehensive edition of his writings. See Madison, *Papers* (Gilpin ed.), I, 504.

[2] For the "paper," see JM Notes, 13 Feb. 1783, n. 10.

[3] The "messenger," whose name was entered in the journals of the Council of State as "Francis Simons," may have been Francis Simmons (d. *ca.* 1786) of Prince Edward County (*JCSV*, III, 223; Prince Edward County Records, Land-Tax Books, 1784–1786, microfilm in Va. State Library). For the probable dispatch which he carried and which Governor Harrison acknowledged in his letter of 24 February to the delegates (*q.v.*), see JM Notes, 13 Feb. 1783, and n. 10. The news that peace was virtually assured should cause a brisk demand for tobacco to export, attended by a rise in its price. Hence if speculators could reach Virginia in advance of that news, they probably would reap a large profit by purchasing the staple. See Harrison to Delegates, 31 Jan., and n. 5; Pendleton to JM, 17 and 24 Feb. 1783, n. 3.

[4] That is, in Washington's main army stationed at Newburgh and its environs along the Hudson (or North) River. The letters within the brackets were erroneously encoded by JM.

[5] JM certainly intended to write 318, the cipher for "this," rather than 218 standing for "Russia."

[6] JM Notes, 13 Feb. 1783. JM's recent source of news, warning that orders to disband the troops without their long overdue pay might cause "*dangerous convulsions,*" is unknown, but rumors to that effect, involving Gouverneur Morris and other prominent civil or military leaders, were current (Louis Clinton Hatch, *The Administration of the American Revolutionary Army* [New York, 1904], pp. 162–67). Letters to Washington from Hamilton on 13 February and from Joseph Jones two weeks later are of a tenor similar to JM's (Syrett and Cooke, *Papers of Hamilton*, III, 254; Worthington C. Ford, ed., *Letters of Joseph Jones*, pp. 97–103).

Notes on Debates

MS (LC: Madison Papers). For a description of the manuscript of Notes on Debates, see *Papers of Madison*, V, 231–34.

Friday Feby. 14.

Mr. Jones Mr. Rutlidge & Mr. Wilson to whom had been referr'd on Teusday last a letter from Mr. Jefferson stating the obstacles to his voyage,[1] reported that they had conferred with the Agent of Marine[2] who sd. there was a fit vessel already for sea in this port but was of opinion the arrival of the British King's Speech[3] would put a stop to the sailing of any vessels from the ports of America untill something definitive should take place; and that if Congress judged fit that Mr. Jefferson sd. proceed immediately to Europe it would be best to apply to the French Minister[4] for one of the Frigates in the Chesapeake.[5] The general opinion of Congs. seemed to be that under present circumstances he sd. suspend his voyage untill the further orders of Congs: and on motion of Mr. Ghorum seconded by Mr. Wolcot the Secy. of For. Affrs. was accordingly without opposition directed to make this known to Mr. Jefferson.[6]

The Report of the Come. for obtaining a valuation of land was made & considered. See the Journal of this date.[7]

[1] Jefferson's letter of 7 February to Robert R. Livingston, secretary for foreign affairs, was referred by Livingston to Congress four days later. Congress then named the committee to recommend a reply.

[2] Robert Morris.

[3] JM Notes, 13 Feb., and n. 10; JM to Jefferson, 13 Feb. 1783.

[4] Chevalier de La Luzerne.

[5] Jefferson to JM, 31 Jan., and n. 4; 7–8 Feb. 1783, and n. 2.

[6] JCC, XXIV, 132. Livingston enclosed a copy of the resolution in his letter of 14 February to Jefferson (Boyd, Papers of Jefferson, VI, 239–40). See also JM to Jefferson, 15 Feb. 1783.

[7] For the appointment of the Rutledge committee to prepare "a proper act" embodying the will of Congress concerning the mode of evaluating privately owned land and the buildings thereon, see JM Notes, 11 Feb. 1783. Judging from the official journal of 14 February, the debate of that day centered upon Arthur Lee's proposal to have any dispute arising from a state's valuation of land referred to "a court of commissioners" comprising a member from each state, appointed by that state rather than by Congress. The judgment of this "court" would be "final." Only nine of the twenty-nine delegates present in Congress voted for the Lee amendment. Among its supporters two were from North Carolina and two from Rhode Island. The four Virginia colleagues of Lee voted with the majority (JCC, XXIV, 129, 130–32). See JM Notes, 17 Feb. 1783.

From Thomas Jefferson

RC (LC: Madison Papers). Undocketed and cover missing, but undoubtedly written to JM.

BALTIMORE Feb. 14. 1783

DEAR SIR

Patsy putting the inclosed into my hands, obliges me to make a separate letter of it, that while I give it the protection of your address I may yet pay it's postage.[1] I suspect by the superscription (which I saw before

Majr Franks amended it) and by what I know of Patsy's hierogliphical writing that miss Polly[2] must get an interpreter from Egypt. be so good as to remind the ladies & gentlemen of the house of my affection for them. I am particularly obliged to Mr. Carrol for an introduction to his relation near this,[3] with whom I have been able to pass agreeably some of my heavy hours. I shall write to E. Randolph on the subject of his going into the legislature and use my interest to promote it. I hope you will be there too when you can no longer be in any more important place.[4] I am with sincere esteem Dr. Sir Your friend & servt

TH: JEFFERSON

[1] For Jefferson's daughter, Martha (Patsy), see JM to Jefferson, 11 Feb. 1783, and n. 16. Her letter obviously could not be franked.

[2] "Polly" was the nickname of Catherine Floyd's older sister, Maria (1764–1805). Jefferson's eldest daughter, Maria, also was known as "Polly" (Benjamin F. Thompson, *History of Long Island from Its Discovery and Settlement to the Present Time* [3d ed.; 3 vols.; New York, 1918], III, 363, 367). For David Salisbury Franks, Jefferson's secretary, see *Papers of Madison*, IV, 450, n. 14; Jefferson to JM, 31 Jan., and n. 6; 14 Feb. 1783 (2d letter).

[3] Most probably Daniel Carroll's cousin Charles Carroll (1723–1783) of "Mount Clare," near Baltimore.

[4] In his letter of 15 February to Randolph, Jefferson urged him to qualify "for a seat in the legislature" and expressed the hope that he would be joined there "e'er long" by JM (Boyd, *Papers of Jefferson*, VI, 247). See JM to Jefferson, 11 Feb. 1783.

From Thomas Jefferson

RC (LC: Madison Papers). At the bottom of the first of four pages Jefferson wrote "Honble James Madison." Docketed by JM, "Ths. Jefferson. 14 Feb. 1783." Also on the docket appears, in an unknown hand, "See passage relating to Mr. Adams." The words italicized are those written by Jefferson in the cipher described in Jefferson to JM, 31 Jan. 1783, ed. n. Unless otherwise noted, the decoding reproduces that which JM interlineated in the document.

BALTIMORE Feb. 14. 1783

DEAR SIR

Yours of the 11th.[1] came to hand last night. *from what you mention in yr.*[2] *letter I suppose the newspapers must be wrong when they say that Mr. Adams*[3] *had taken up his*[4] *abode with*[5] *Dr. Fr——.*[6] *I am nearly at a loss to judge how he will act in the nego——n He hates Fr—— he hates Jay he hates the French he hates the English*[7] *to whom will he ad-*

235

here? his vanity is a liniament in his character wch. had entirely[8] *escaped me   his want of taste I had observed   notwithstandg all this he has a sound head on substantial points and I think he has integrity. I am glad therefore that he is of the commission & expect he will be useful in it. his dislike of all parties, and all men, by balancing his prejudices, may give the same fair play to his reason as* would[9] *a general benevolence of temper   at any rate honesty may be extracted even from poisonous weeds*[10]

My[11] *stay here has given me opportunities of making some experiments on my ama[nu]ensis F—s,*[12]*perhaps better than I may have in France   he appears to have a good eno' heart an understang somewhat better than common but too little guard over his lips, I have marked him particularly*[13] *in the company of women*[14] *where he loses all power over himself and becomes*[15] *almost [a] fright*[16] *his temperature* would *not be proof agst. their alluremts,*[17] *were*[18] *such to be employed as engines agst. him   This is in some measure the vice of his age but it seems to be increased also by his peculiar constitution*[19]

I wrote to the Chevalier de VilleBrun[20] proposing his falling down to York or Hampton which was one of the measures I suggested in my letter to you, & was the most eligible except that of the flag,[21] in my own opinion. his answer, dated Feb. 12. is in these words. 'Je serois bien de l'avis proposé a votre Excellence d'aller mouiller a York ou Hampton pour etre a portee de profiter des premiers vents de Nord Ouest qui me mettroient loin de la côte dans la nuit, surtout si je n'avois pas de convoy a conserver. mais des batiments entrès aujourd'hui raportent avoir eté chassés par quatre fregates jusque sur la Cap Charles et avoir vu au mouillage de Linhaven bay un vaisseau et un fregate qui ont appareillés et pris un Brig qui navigoit avec eux. de plus York et Hampton n'ont pas un canon monté, si l'ennemi, tres superieur, entreprenoit de venir nous y forcer, il y auroit peu de sureté.

Peut etre conviendroit-il autant d'attendre, comme le propose M. de la Luzerne, jusqu'au Mois prochain, des nouvelles d'Europe, ou l'arrivée d'une division des Antilles promise par M. de Vaudreuil, ou bien encore quel'ennemi fatigué ne fut obligé de rentrer a New-York.'[22] *The last basket is relish*[23] *and furnishes matter*[24] *for doubt how far the departure of the Romulus*[25] *is a decided measure   it seems not unlucky*[26] *so for a purpose wherein time is the most*[27] *pressing circumstance The idea of going*[28] *in her is to be abandoned.*[29] to go to *Boston* would be the most œconomical plan. but it would be *five weeks* from my leaving this place before I could expect to sail from thence.[30] of course I may from here be *in France* by the time I should be sailing from *Boston   five weeks,* in a crisis of *negotiation*[31] may be much. should I accept of the *Guade-loupe*[32] and she should be lost, it would under present circumstances draw censure. moreover in this or the former case, besides losing the vessel, what will be my situation? that of a prisoner certainly. from what has been done in Laurence's case they would not release me; in expectation of a high exchange; or if they did, it would only be on parole, in which case I could neither act nor communicate.[33] This plan would have in it's favour œconomy and a possibility (a bare one) of dispatch. that of the flag still appears best.[34] it is favoured by the circumstances of dispatch, safety, & the preservation of my papers, but when I think of the expence I feel myself annihilated in comparison with it.[35] A vessel may be got here, but I question if for less than *a thousand* or *two thousand* pounds.[36]   besides can a passport be obtained from New York without naming the vessel, the crew &c? if not it would take long to furnish these circumstances from hence. the Delaware would be more eligible in that case. otherwise this place is.[37] if this should be adopted, what would be the extent of the protection of the flag to the papers I should carry? these, so far as this question would affect them, would be of three descriptions. 1. my own commission, instructions & other documents relative to my mission. 2. public letters to the Consuls, ministers & others on other business. 3. private letters. I have no means of satisfying myself on these points here. if therefore this measure should be adopted I should thank you for your opinion on them, as you can, where you are doubtful, make enquiry of others.[38] I am exceedingly fatigued with this place, as indeed I should with any other where I had neither occupation nor amusement. I am very particularly indebted here to the politeness & hospitality of Genl. La Vallette[39] who obliges me to take refuge in his quarters from the tedium of my own, the latter half of every day. you are indebted to him too as I should make my long letters much longer & plague you with more cypher were I confined at home all day. I beg you to be assured of my warmest wishes for your happiness.

Th: Jefferson

Feb. 15. 9 o'clock P.M. after sealing up this letter I received yours of yesterday inclosing the King's speech,[40] for which I thank you much. the essential information conveyed to us by that is that the preliminary for our independence (which we before knew to have been agreed between the plenipos) has been provisionally ratified by him. I have thought it my duty to write the inclosed letter[41] which after reading you will be so good as to stick a wafer in & deliver. I wish no supposed inclination of mine to stand in the way of a free change of measure if Congress should think the public interest required it. the argument of œconomy is much strengthened by the impossibility (now certain) of going but in an express vessel. the principal matters confided to me were. 1. the new instruction; which perhaps may have been sent by Count Rochambeau, or may yet be sent.[42] 2. the details of the financier's department which mr Morri[s] not chusing to trust to paper had communicated verbally. these in the event of peace or truce may safely go in paper.[43] 3. the topics which supp[ort] our right to the fisheries, to the Western country, & the navigation of the Mis[sis]sipi.[44] the first of these is probably settled: the two latter should only come into discussion in the Spanish negociation, and therefore would on[ly] have been the subject of private conversation with mr Jay,[45] whose good sense & knolege of the subject will hardly need any suggestions.

I forgot to mention to you in my letter that mr Nash arrived her[e] the day before yesterday on his way to N. Carolina, and that mr Blunt is not yet arrived,[46] but is weekly expected. I am yours affectionately,

Th: Jefferson.

1 *Q.v.*

2 Jefferson erroneously encoded "your" as 94.12., but JM, having started to write a word beginning with "b," canceled it and correctly surmised that the cipher intended was 945.12.

3 In writing the symbol 949.12.', Jefferson turned to the section of the Nugent dictionary of 1774 reserved for proper names and pluralized "Adam." For a more cryptic reference to John Adams, see JM to Jefferson, 11 Feb. 1783, n. 10.

4 Here and in seven other instances in the present letter, Jefferson was ten lines off in indicating "his," 408.36., or "hiss." See Jefferson to JM, 31 Jan. 1783, n. 10. The symbol here employed, 408.26., signified "hint."

5 In seeking to symbolize "with," Jefferson's eye again strayed by ten lines, and he wrote 935.28. instead of the correct symbol, 935.38.

6 Although the two ciphers used by Jefferson stood, respectively, for "frank" and "line," JM interlineated only the abbreviation. For Jefferson's earlier attempt to indicate Benjamin Franklin, see Jefferson to JM, 31 Jan. 1783, and nn. 6, 7. Jefferson may have gleaned the misinformation concerning Adams from an item dated Paris, 3 November 1782, and reprinted in the *Pennsylvania Packet* of 6 February 1783. From 26 October 1782, when he arrived in Paris, until the end of that month, John Adams lodged at the Hôtel de Valois, Rue de Richelieu. Thereafter for nearly a year he occupied an "expensive and noisy" apartment in the Hôtel du Roi, in the "Place du Carrousel, between the Palais Royal and the Quai du Louvre" (L. H. Butterfield *et al.*, eds., *Diary and Autobiography of John Adams*, III, 37, 38, 39, n. 4). Benjamin Franklin resided in Passy (*Papers of Madison*, V, 165, n. 6).

7 The succession of four "hates" is inserted by the present editors. In each instance, JM interlineated a meaningless "has," even though Jefferson wrote 401.25., the symbol of "to hate."

In his diary on 27 October 1782, Adams characterized both Franklin and John Jay as "subtle Spirits"—the former "malicious, the other I think honest." "I shall have," continued Adams, "a delicate, a nice, a critical Part to Act. F's cunning will be to divide Us. To this End he will provoke, he will insinuate, he will intrigue, he will maneuvre. My Curiosity will at least be employed, in observing his Intervention and his Artifice. J. declares roundly, that he will never set his hand to a bad Peace" (L. H. Butterfield *et al.*, eds., *Diary and Autobiography of John Adams*, III, 38–39). See also *ibid.*, III, 51–52, 93; IV, 62–63, 149–50, 157–58; JM to Jefferson, 11 Feb. 1783, and n. 11.

8 The word, symbolized as 459.11., is in the "I(J)" section of the dictionary, where it is spelled "intirely."

9 For Jefferson's reason for not coding "would," see Jefferson to JM, 31 Jan. 1783, n. 11.

10 Jefferson wrote only 926.39., the singular for "weed."

11 Here and in his next intended use of "my" in the same sentence, Jefferson wrote 530.1., instead of the correct symbol, 531.1.

12 JM, in his letter of 18 Feb. to Jefferson (*q.v.*), had correctly encoded "amanuensis" by simply writing 29.18. Jefferson, perhaps being more security-minded than JM, laboriously contrived the word by writing 301.1. ("e"), 32.1. ("an"), 843.31. ("u"), 304.1. ("em"), 1070.4. ("Sis")—"eanuemsis." The last syllable was taken from the section of Nugent's dictionary devoted to proper names. Sis was the name of the present-day Kozan, Turkey. "F—s." or "Franks," was David Salisbury Franks (Jefferson to JM, 31 Jan. 1783, and n. 6).

13 Jefferson wrote 583.5., denoting "particular."

14 Jefferson wrote 936.30., standing for "woman."

15 The present editors have rendered the symbol 91.18. as Jefferson intended; JM interlineated only "become."

16 The editors assume that JM's failure to interlineate "fright," symbolized by 369.9., reflected Jefferson's omission of 1.1., standing for "a." By "fright" Jefferson probably meant "grotesque" or "ridiculous" (*Oxford English Dictionary*, IV, [1933 ed.], 549).

17 Jefferson's cipher 27.8. decodes as "allures" rather than as JM rendered it.

18 Again Jefferson combined ciphers to form a word—in this instance an intended pronoun with an intended column heading. He wrote 925.1., which should have been 926.1. ("we"), and 671.1., which should have been 661.1. ("RE").

19 Jefferson was forty years of age and Franks was approximately two years older. Franks's "peculiar constitution" is unknown to the present editors.

20 Jefferson to JM, 31 Jan. 1783, and n. 4; Boyd, *Papers of Jefferson*, VI, 236 n.

21 Jefferson to JM, 7–8 Feb. 1783, and nn. 9, 11, 12.

22 Except for variations in spelling, capitalization, punctuation, and accent marks, this extract from the Chevalier de La Villebrune's letter of 12 February 1783 is accurate (Boyd, *Papers of Jefferson*, VI, 236). "Indeed I would adopt your Excellency's suggestion to proceed to an anchorage at York or Hampton where I could avail myself of the first northwest winds to take me at night far off the coast, especially if I would not have to protect a convoy. But several vessels arriving today report that they were pursued by four frigates even within Cape Charles and that a Brig in their company was captured by a vessel and frigate which had left and returned to their anchorage in Linhaven bay. Moreover, without a serviceable cannon at York or Hampton, we would have little security there, if the very much stronger enemy should try to approach and board us.

"Perhaps, as M. de La Luzerne advised, it would be better to wait until next month for news from Europe, or for the arrival from the West Indies of the fleet promised by M. de Vaudreuil, or, better still, for the wearied enemy to be obliged to return to New York." For La Luzerne, see JM Notes, 1 Jan. 1783, and n. 2; for

Vice Admiral the Marquis de Vaudreuil, see *Papers of Madison*, IV, 347, n. 4; JM Notes, 3 Jan. 1783, n. 1. Lynnhaven Bay, in Princess Anne County, Va., is an anchorage a few miles southwest of Cape Henry. See also Jefferson to JM, 7–8 Feb. 1783, and nn. 3, 4, 8.

[23] JM did not interlineate "basket," which is symbolized by 80.15. With that noun supplied, Jefferson's metaphor becomes clear: La Villebrune's final suggestion was a condiment designed to conceal unpalatable facts.

[24] To indicate "matter," Jefferson wrote 503.30. but should have written 504.30.

[25] Jefferson to JM, 31 Jan. 1783, n. 4.

[26] JM did not interlineate "unlucky," which is symbolized by 895.17. By using a double negative, Jefferson meant that "her departure seems left to chance."

[27] Jefferson wrote 524.34. to symbolize "most" but should have written 525.34.

[28] Jefferson should have appended an "a" to his symbol 385.36., so as to signify "going" rather than "go."

[29] The meaning of the interlineation by JM would have been clearer if he had written, "It seems not unlucky, so for a purpose wherein time is the most pressing circumstance, the idea of going in her is to be abandoned."

[30] Jefferson to JM, 7–8 Feb. 1783.

[31] JM did not interlineate "negotiation," which was symbolized by 535.17.

[32] The editors have supplied the name of the ship. JM did not interlineate a decipherment of the mystifying symbols 394.19. and especially 928.9. In his letter to JM on 7–8 February (*q.v.*), Jefferson had twice misspelled "Guadeloupe" as "Guardaloupe." The 394.19., signifying "guaranty," suggests the first syllable of this name as he spelled it, but 928.9., meaning "searcher," is unintelligible.

[33] For Henry Laurens, his capture by the British, imprisonment in the Tower of London, and eventual liberation in exchange for the release of Earl Cornwallis from his parole as a prisoner of war, see *Papers of Madison*, III, 232–33; 233, n. 1; V, index under Laurens, Henry, British release and exchange of; Jefferson to JM, 7–8 Feb. 1783, n. 12.

[34] *Ibid.*, and n. 11.

[35] Jefferson probably meant that he doubted whether his value as a peace commissioner would offset the huge cost of chartering a flag-of-truce ship to take him to France.

[36] JM interlineated none of the words symbolized, respectively, by 1.1. ("a"), 819.36. ("thousand"), 843.10. ("two"), and 819.36. again. Instead, he placed a matching asterisk in the left column and there wrote "see Dictionary F & English."

[37] That is, a passport from the British would have to be sought from their military headquarters in New York City.

[38] For the resolution of Congress which largely solved Jefferson's dilemma and relieved JM from making the "enquiry," see JM Notes, 14 Feb., and n. 6; JM to Jefferson, 15 Feb.; 18 Feb. 1783.

[39] For General de La Valette, see *Papers of Madison*, V, 6, n. 2.

[40] The fact that Jefferson acknowledged the receipt of JM's letter of 13 February (*q.v.*) makes clear that he should have dated this postscript "Feb. 14" rather than "15." Jefferson probably had also seen the "Baltimore hand Bill'" in regard to "Peace," mentioned by Governor Harrison in his dispatch of 15 February to the Virginia delegates (*q.v.*, and n. 2).

[41] Jefferson's letter of 14 February 1783 to Robert R. Livingston, secretary for foreign affairs (Boyd, *Papers of Jefferson*, VI, 238–39 and n.).

[42] The Comte de Rochambeau, who sailed early in January 1783 for France by way of Cadiz, Spain, probably carried a copy of the instructions with regard to commerce directed to the American peace commissioners and adopted by Congress on 31 December 1782 (*Papers of Madison*, V, 344, n. 7; 430, n. 5; 476, and nn. 2, 3; 477, and nn. 4, 5; Wharton, *Revol. Dipl. Corr.*, VI, 192–93). Rochambeau was in

Paris by 8 March 1783 (L. H. Butterfield *et al.*, eds., *Diary and Autobiography of John Adams*, III, 110).

[43] The "details" which Robert Morris, superintendent of finance, "communicated verbally" probably included those mentioned in his letters of February and March 1783 to Elias Boudinot, president of Congress, and to Washington (Wharton, *Revol. Dipl. Corr.*, VI, 266–67, 277–82, 308–11).

[44] For these subjects, see *Papers of Madison*, V, index under Fisheries; Jay, John, dispatches and instructions to; Mississippi River.

[45] John Jay, a peace commissioner of the United States who had been minister plenipotentiary-designate at the court of Madrid since 27 September 1779 (*JCC*, XV, 1113).

[46] For the departure of Abner Nash and William Blount from Congress, see JM Notes, 7 Feb. 1783, n. 6.

Benjamin Harrison to Virginia Delegates

FC (Virginia State Library). In the hand of Thomas Meriwether. Addressed to "Virginia Delegates in Congress."

IN COUNCIL February 15th. 1783.

GENTLEMEN

You will receive herewith an Authenticated Copy of the Certificate of Gen: Clarke and Col: Todd which was omitted by a Mistake of the Clerk when Nathans other Papers were forwarded to you. I hope they will get in Time to prevent his obtaining an Award in his favor which appears to me manifestly unjust. surely the Arbitrators will never proceed to a final Settlement without a Paper of such Consequence which they are assured is in being and will soon be sent them.[1] A Baltimore hand Bill gives some people an Expectation that Peace is certainly proclaimed in Europe. I am not so sanguine, tho' I wish it as much as they do, but think the whole report originates from Townsends Letter to the directors of the Bank.[2]

You were formerly so obliging as to favor me with the News Paper,[3] if it is not inconvenient I wish a renewal of the favor, and that you would frank your Letters.[4]

I am Gentlemen Yours &c.   B. H.

[1] Harrison to Delegates, 4 Jan., and n. 8; 11 Jan., and n. 4; Delegates to Harrison, 21 Jan.; 28 Jan.; 4 Feb., and n. 2. The "Clerk" was Thomas L. Savage. See Harrison to Delegates, 11 Jan. 1783, hdn. The "Authenticated Copy" has not been found.

[2] JM to Randolph, 4 Feb. 1783, and n. 12. The "Baltimore hand Bill" printed an extract of a letter of 15 January from St. Kitts which began: "I CONGRATULATE you on the news of peace; indeed I may venture to assure you that it has already taken place in Europe" (*Va. Gazette*, 15 Feb. 1783).

³ Probably the *Pennsylvania Gazette,* the *Pennsylvania Journal,* or the *Pennsylvania Packet.*

⁴ For Harrison's annoyance because of unfranked letters, see Harrison to Delegates, 4 Jan. 1783, and nn. 2, 4. By an ordinance of 18 October 1782, "letters, packets, and despatches to and from the members" of Congress, "while actually attending Congress," were to "be carried free of postage" (*JCC,* XXIII, 678).

To Thomas Jefferson

RC (LC: Madison Papers). Docketed by Jefferson, "Madison Jas."

DEAR SIR   PHILADA. Feby. 15th. 1783.

The[1] Committee, to whom was referred your letter to Secretary Livingston, reported to Congress yesterday that they had conferred with Mr. Morris who was of opinion that no vessel would sail from american ports after the arrival of the British King's speech until the suspence produced by it should be removed, and that if your immediate embarkation was still wished by Congress it would be proper to obtain for that purpose a Frigate from the Chevr. de la Luzerne. He informed the Committee that there was a fit vessel in this river which wd. have sailed for France but for the prospect of peace afforded by the Speech; and which I suppose will still proceed if that prospect should fail. The effect of this information to Congress and of a request from the Committee to be instructed on the subject was, a resolution directing the Secy. of F. A. to acquaint you that it was the pleasure of Congress, considering the present situation of things, that you should suspend your voyage until their further instruction.[2] This resolution will I suppose be forwarded by the post which conveys this.[3] I do not undertake to give any advice as to the steps which may now be proper for you;[4] but I indulge with much pleasure the hope that a return to this place for the present may be the result of your own deliberations.[5]

I am Dear Sir with sincerity Yr friend & servt.

J. MADISON JR.

[1] Many years later JM or someone at his bidding designated by the use of brackets that all of this letter except the complimentary close and signature should be published in the first comprehensive edition of his papers. See Madison, *Papers,* (Gilpin ed.), I, 505–6.

[2] JM Notes, 14 Feb. 1783, and nn. 1, 6. Robert R. Livingston was secretary for foreign affairs.

[3] Boyd, *Papers of Jefferson,* VI, 239–40.

4 Jefferson to JM, 7 Feb., and nn. 11–13; 14 Feb. (2d letter) 1783, and nn. 35, 37, 38, 41.

5 Jefferson reached Philadelphia on 26 February 1783 (Boyd, *Papers of Jefferson*, VI, 253 n.).

From Mark Lynch

RC (LC: Madison Papers). Addressed to "Honble. James Maddison Esqr   Virginia."

SIR   NANTES 15. february 1783

I had the honor to write you the 20. January 1781 under the Sanction of our mutual friend Philip Mazzei Esqr.[1] and to make you a tender of my best Service here. I have not Since been favord with any of yours. As we are now thank God Blessed with the return of a happy & general peace, and that by it we Shall have in future an open & free trade between America & this Country,[2] it is in Consequence that I take the liberty of reiterating to you my offers of Service, for the Execution of whatever commands you may happen to have this way. if a Sincere resolution to fulfill them with equal punctuality & integrity, be a Sufficient title to deserve the prefference of your Business, I beg leave to assure you that no one has a better right to put in for it. I Sincerely wish for frequent occasions to Convince you thereof,

Tobacco, which before the peace, sold here to good advantage, is at present without any Current price. this article must now nec[e]ssarily look down a good deal in Europe.[3] But you may depend it will at all times Sell at least as well here, as at any other Market of this Kingdome, or perhaps of Europe, and the order that prevails in the Commerce of this place, makes it known to be one of the Safest in Europe for the Solidity of the Buyers.[4] Besides, every article necessary in America, can be procured & Shipped here on reasonable terms, which I dare Say you will Experience here after. In Expectation of being favord with your Commands, I have the honor to remain very Respectfully

Sir, Your most Obt. humble Servt.

                                                        M: LYNCH
P.S.

Mr. Mazzei is now at Paris, and intends coming here in the next or following month to Embark for America.[5]

1 Mark Lynch, a merchant of Nantes, had forwarded letters and loaned money to Philip Mazzei, commercial agent of Virginia in Tuscany from 8 January 1778 until 30 November 1782. See *Papers of Madison*, II, 216, and n. 11; IV, 100, n. 21. Lynch's earlier letter to JM has not been found.

[2] Lynch reflected in this statement his knowledge of the signing of preliminary articles of peace on 20 January 1783 by Great Britain, France, and Spain, of an armistice concluded between Great Britain and the United States on that day, and of the "open & free trade" provisions of the Treaty of Amity and Commerce between France and the United States (Wharton, *Revol. Dipl. Corr.*, VII, 226–27; *JCC*, XI, 419–44).

[3] Lynch professed to foresee that tobacco, piled high in Virginia warehouses, would glut the postwar market in Europe and hence sell at a low price. His prediction was to prove erroneous.

[4] Lynch perhaps liked to believe that the mercantile firms of Nantes had gained "Solidity" by the recent elimination through bankruptcy of their competitor, Penet, d'Acosta Frères et Cie (*Papers of Madison*, V, 195, n. 1; 344, n. 10; Livingston to Delegates, 15 Mar. 1783, and n. 1). He would be disappointed in his expectation of French ports becoming important markets for Virginia's exports (Alan Schaffer, "Virginia's 'Critical Period,' " in Darrett B. Rutman, ed., *The Old Dominion: Essays for Thomas Perkins Abernethy* [Charlottesville, 1964], pp. 152–70, and esp. pp. 158–61, 164–68).

[5] Mazzei disembarked at Hampton, Va., on 23 November 1783 (Boyd, *Papers of Jefferson*, VI, 318 n.).

From Edmund Randolph

RC (LC: Madison Papers). Unsigned and without complimentary close but in Randolph's hand. Cover addressed by him to "The honble James Madison jr. Esq. of congress   Philadelphia." The date line and many words in the first six and last six lines of the text are so blotted as to be illegible or doubtfully legible.

RICHMOND Feby. 15. 1783

MY DEAR SIR

I had resolved before the receipt of your favor of the 2d. instant to change our cypher [to] a form less abstruse and more comprehensive.[1]

A hand bill from Baltimore has revived [and encouraged][2] expectation of peace. It has, no doubt, reached you, and will appear to want every mark of authenticity. Yet I cannot persuade those, with whom I converse, that peace is too much intangled by opposite pretentions and hopes, to be adjusted in a short time, even after the European congress shall have entered seriously into the business.[3]

Speculation itself is at rest, and not a breath moves the political surface. So that news is of all things, except specie, the most scarce.[4]

Among the records of 1710, I find an instruction from Queen Anne to her governor here to grant lands according *to the charter*. This extension plainly alludes, from the context to that of 1609, not of 1676.[5]

The acts of assembly in 1753 & 1754, concerning settlements on the Mississippi afford no mean argument in support of our title: they having been confirmed by the king. And a standing instruction to the governors farther shews, that every act was sent over for the royal inspection.[6] Therefore every act referring to similar points with these may be considered, as having equal force.

I perceive, that the boundaries between Penn & Lord Baltimore have been discussed before the british chancellor. The argument is to be found in Vezey's reports 1. Vol. p. [444] and contains much in support of my idea of our charter, and as much against it.[7] Do borrow the book, read the case, and suggest your thoughts.[8]

[1] Randolph almost certainly meant to refer to JM's letter of 4 Feb. 1783 (*q.v.*, and n. 10).

[2] Harrison to Delegates, 15 Feb. 1783, and n. 2. The bracketed words are a doubtful rendition of those so blotted that only a few letters can be discerned.

[3] Randolph was assuming that peace could come only after a "congress" of commissioners from Great Britain, France, Spain, the Netherlands, and the United States had succeeded in reaching agreement despite conflicting "pretentions and hopes" of the nations they represented.

[4] Harrison to Delegates, 31 Jan., and n. 7; 7 Feb., and n. 4; Ambler to JM, 1 Feb. 1783.

[5] On 1 June 1782 the Virginia General Assembly appointed a committee of five, including Randolph, "to collect all Documents and Proofs necessary for establishing the Right of this State to it's Western Territory" (*Papers of Madison*, IV, 91, n. 4; 198, n. 7; 305). A variety of circumstances had obliged Randolph, with almost no help from his colleagues, to perform this unexpectedly difficult task (*ibid.*, IV, 306, n. 3; 395; V, 30; 308–9; 312, n. 18). From its outset, in defending Virginia's title to the territory west and northwest of the Appalachian Mountains, Randolph had stressed that the westward boundaries of Virginia, as stipulated in the charter of 1609 granted by King James I to the London Company, remained unaltered even though that charter had been annulled in 1624 (*ibid.*, IV, 228, n. 7). For the charter of 10 October 1676, granted by King Charles II "to his subjects of Virginia," see *ibid.*, V, 10; Hening, *Statutes*, III, 315–16.

In response to a plea of 19 October 1708 by the Council of Virginia that a current "restraint & prohibition on the takeing up of Land be removed," Queen Anne in Council on 23 February 1710 rescinded the restrictions and permitted the resumption of land grants "as by the charter" theretofore allowed. Because she took no exception to the colonial Council's protestation that Virginia land tenures were too "interwoven" in grants based upon provisions of the charters of 1609 and 1676 to be altered without "the greatest Confusion," she could be said to have tacitly recognized the continuing legality of the charter of 1609 and hence of the boundaries therein stipulated (H. R. McIlwaine *et al.*, eds., *Executive Journals of the Council of Colonial Virginia* [6 vols.; Richmond, 1925–66], III, 194–95, 247; Leonard Woods Labaree, ed., *Royal Instructions to British Colonial Governors, 1670–1776* [2 vols.; New York, 1935], II, 590, 808).

[6] The general instructions of a governor of a royal province required him to

forward to the sovereign in Privy Council for review and possible disallowance every act of the legislature except one designed to meet a temporary emergency. Randolph referred to "An Act for further encouraging persons to settle on the waters of the Mississippi," assented to by the governor of Virginia on 19 December 1753, and "An Act for the encouragement and protection of the settlers upon the waters of the Mississippi," similarly assented to on 23 February 1754 (H. R. Mc-Ilwaine, ed., *Journals of the House of Burgesses of Virginia, 1752–1755, 1756–1758* [Richmond, 1909], pp. 115–16, 127, 130, 132, 170, 181, 183–84, 185; Hening, *Statutes*, VI, 355–56, 417–20). By not disallowing these measures, the King in Council acknowledged at least tacitly the right of the government of Virginia to include all the territory directly west and northwest of the Appalachian Mountains in Augusta County, mentioned in the statute of 1753, and to foster and control settlements along "the waters of the Mississippi."

7 This page number, completely illegible in the text, is what Randolph probably wrote (Francis Vesey, Senior, comp., *Reports of Cases Argued and Determined in the High Court of Chancery, in the time of Lord Chancellor Hardwicke, from the year 1746–7, to 1755* . . . [2 vols.; Dublin, 1771], I, 444–55, and esp. 454). The suit of *Penn* v. *Lord Baltimore*, involving a controversy concerning the rightful boundary between the provinces of Pennsylvania and Maryland, was argued in 1745 and 1750 before the High Court of Chancery. In his opinion, delivered on 15 May 1750, the lord high chancellor declared that, although a suit involving a disputed boundary in America was outside the original jurisdiction of his tribunal, he still could hear the arguments of the parties to the case and issue a decree, subject to appeal to the King in Council, because a royal court of equity could take cognizance of any issue where the litigants had agreed "on *articles* executed in *England* under seal for mutual consideration." This assumption of jurisdiction obviously ran counter to Randolph's insistence that in domestic affairs a committee of Congress, and hence Congress itself, could not exercise the unconstitutional authority to decide among the charter claims of Virginia and other states to overlapping territory north and west of the Ohio River (*Papers of Madison*, III, 284–86; 286, nn. 1, 5; IV, 32–33; 35, n. 10). On the other hand, both Randolph and JM had granted, for the sake of obtaining congressional unanimity in forming international policies, that the crown lands had "devolved," as a result of the Revolution, "upon the United States, collectively taken" (*ibid.*, V, 56–57).

Although Randolph could not welcome the lord high chancellor's decree in favor of the Penn family, even though its charter postdated that of Lord Baltimore by about fifty years, this judgment was based mainly on the fact that many more citizens of Pennsylvania than of Maryland had settled in the disputed area. Randolph therefore could quote with approval the lord high chancellor's statement: "But now in cases of this kind, of two great territories held of the crown, I will say once for all, that long possession and enjoyment, peopling and cultivating countries, is one of the best evidence of title to lands, or district of lands in *America*, that can be; and so have I thought in all cases since I have served the crown; for the great beneficial advantages, arising to the crown from settling, &c. is, that the navigation and the commerce of this country is thereby improved. Those persons, therefore, who make these settlements, ought to be protected in the possession, as far as law and equity can."

Philip Yorke (1690–1764), first Earl of Hardwicke, was lord high chancellor from 1737 until 1756, after serving successively as solicitor general, attorney general, and chief justice.

8 There seems to be no evidence that JM followed Randolph's suggestion or that Randolph adverted later to the matter.

Notes on Debates

MS (LC: Madison Papers). For a description of the manuscript of Notes on Debates, see *Papers of Madison*, V, 231–34.

Monday Feby. 17.

The report respecting a valuation of land being lost as appears from the Journal, it was revived by the motion of Mr. Dyer seconded by Mr. Mercer as it stands, the appointment of Commissrs. by Congress for adjusting the quotas, being changed for a grand Committee consisting of a delegate present from each State for that purpose.[1]

A motion was made to strike out the clause requiring the concurrence of nine voices in the report to Congress; and on the question shall the words stand? the States being equally divided the clause was expunged. It was thereafter reconsidered & reinserted.[2]

The whole report was agreed to with great reluctance by almost all, by many from a spirit of accomodation only, & the necessity of doing something on the subject. Some of those who were in the negative particularly Mr. Madison thought the plan not within the spirit of the Confederation, that it would be ineffectual, and that the States would be dissatisfied with it.[3]

A motion was made by Mr Hamilton 2ded. by Mr Fitzimmons to renew the recommendation of   Feby 1782 for vesting Congress with power to make abatements in favor of States part of which had been in possession of the Enemy. It was referred to a committee.[4]

[1] For the report of the committee of the whole on "valuation," the amendment of that report by Congress on 11 February, the referral of the amended report to the Rutledge committee, and the report of that committee, see JM Notes, 11 Feb., and nn. 1–5, 8, 10, 11; 14 Feb. 1783, and n. 7. On 17 February only six states, rather than the requisite minimum of seven, voted in favor of the committee's recommendation. Among the six was Virginia, with Jones, Bland, and Mercer voting "ay" and Madison and Lee "no" (*JCC*, XXIV, 133–35).

For Mercer's position on the issue, see JM Notes, 8 Feb., and nn. 3, 4; JM to Randolph, 18 Feb. 1783, and nn. 2, 3. The following recommendation in the committee report on 17 February enlisted his, but not JM's support: "the said estimate [of the value of privately owned land and buildings in each state], when approved by Congress, shall be a rule for adjusting all accounts between the United States and the individual states: that is, that each State shall be debited for its just quota or proportion, on the principle aforesaid, of the money theretofore advanced or paid, and of the amount in value of the supplies furnished by all the states for the service of the United States, and credited for the money advanced, and the amount in value of the supplies furnished by such State for the service of the United States: that the said estimate shall operate for a term not exceeding five years, as a rule for apportioning on the several states the sums which Congress shall, from time to time, deem necessary and require to be raised for supporting the public credit and contingent expences" (*JCC*, XXIV, 134–35).

The Dyer-Mercer substitute proposal differed from the committee report in replacing 1 January with 1 March and the commission to adjust quotas with a grand committee of Congress. Nine states, rather than the six which had supported the committee's report, voted in favor of the new recommendation. New York alone opposed. Daniel Carroll, Maryland's sole representative, cast an ineffective negative vote. The division among the Virginia delegates remained unaltered (*JCC*, XXIV, 135–37).

² The proceedings mentioned in this paragraph are not recorded in the official journal.

³ Judging from the feeble handwriting, JM inserted "Mr. Madison" many years later. In a letter of 17 February, Hugh Williamson, after referring to the adopted resolution as one "which the Southern States have carried with great difficulty," continued: "it is not so good as we wished, but the best we could get, for valuing the lands and their improvements, according to the Confederation. I believe we failed in twenty different plans before we fixed on one" (Burnett, *Letters*, VII, 46). JM probably viewed the mode "fixed on" as violating "the spirit" of Article VIII of the Articles of Confederation, for that article omitted any mention of the population of a state as relevant to estimating the value of land therein (*JCC*, XIX, 217).

⁴ On 6 February the Hamilton-FitzSimons motion to postpone the expensive and lengthy operation of evaluating land and to extend, in settling accounts between the United States and each state when the evaluation should be completed, "equitable abatements to such States as have been more immediate sufferers by the war" had been lost by a vote of four states to three (JM Notes, 5–6 Feb. 1783, and n. 13). In view of the adoption of the Dyer-Mercer proposal, the renewed Hamilton-FitzSimons motion, referred to Lee, Dyer, and Samuel Holten of Massachusetts, proposed that the states authorize Congress to make desirable adjustments, according to "the particular circumstances of the several States" at "different periods" during the war (*JCC*, XXIV, 138). See also JM Notes, 26 Feb. 1783.

From Edmund Pendleton

Letters not found (LC: Force Transcripts, fol. 8729).

EDITORIAL NOTE

17 and 24 February 1783. About 1850 a clerk of Peter Force, engaged in copying letters of Edmund Pendleton, wrote:

"MSS. McGuire's.¹   Edmund Pendleton⎫ Edmundsbury,² Feby 17. 1783
                            to James Madison ⎬

"(This letter is much stained, & some of it illegible)

"Another letter dated 'E[d]mundsbury Feb. 24, 1783,' is in the same condition.

"There does not seem to be anything of much public importance in either of the above letters."³

¹ *Papers of Madison*, I, xxii, xxiii. See n. 3, below.
² Pendleton's estate in Caroline County.
³ Although Stan. V. Henkels, a manuscript dealer of Philadelphia, advertised in

his Catalogue No. 694 (1892) much of the Pendleton correspondence which had been among the manuscripts owned by Frederick B. McGuire of Washington, these two letters apparently were not offered at the auction. See *Papers of Madison*, II, 65–66. JM's letters to Pendleton between 5 November 1782 and 30 November 1786, and Pendleton's letters to JM between 23 December 1782 and 15 March 1783, have not been found, with the exception of JM to Pendleton, 8 September 1783.

In a letter of 24 February 1783 to Washington, Pendleton remarked, as he also may have done in substance in his letter of the same date to JM: "The prospect of Peace, and an opinion that our staple commodity [tobacco] will become a very considerable Article in the Commercial Scale, will turn our Application much into its culture, as well as induce Us to hold up what we have for a good price; We were full of Speculators from the Northward to purchase, but the Pig of peace had squeaked from the bag, and retarded their progress, when a Messenger dispatched from our Delegates in Congress to the Executive, and many private letters dropped on the road with the King's Speech, I beleive has stopped it" (David John Mays, ed., *The Letters and Papers of Edmund Pendleton, 1734–1803* [2 vols.; Charlottesville, 1967], II, 438). See JM to Randolph, 13 Feb. 1783, and n. 3.

Notes on Debates

MS (LC: Madison Papers). For a description of the manuscript of Notes on Debates, see *Papers of Madison*, V, 231–34.

Teusday. Feby. 18.

Come. of the whole on the subject of genl. funds.[1] Mr. Rutlidge & Mr. Mercer proposed that the Impost of 5 PerCt. as altered & to be recommended to the States,[2] should be appropriated exclusively, first to the interest of the debt to the army & then in case of surplus to the principal. Mr. Rutlidge urged in support of this motion that it would be best to appropriate this fund to the army as the most likely to be obtained as their merits were superior to those of all other Creditors, and as it was the only thing that promised what policy absolutely required some satisfaction to them.[3]

Mr. Wilson replied that he was so sensible of the merits of the army that if any discrimination were to be made among the public creditors, he should not deny them perhaps a preference, but that no such discrimination was necessary, that the ability of the public was equal to its whole debt, and that before it be split into different descriptions, the most vigorous efforts ought to be made to provide for it entire. That we ought first at least to see what funds could be provided, to see how far they would be deficient, and then in the last necessity only to admit discriminations.[4]

Mr. Ghorum agreed with Mr. Wilson. He said an exclusive appropriation to the army would in some places be unpopular and would prevent a compliance of those States whose Citizens were the greatest Creditors of the United States; since without the influence of the public creditors the measure could never be carried through the States, and these if excluded from the appropriation would be even interested in frustrating the measure, & keeping by that means their cause a common one with the army.[5]

Mr. Mercer applauded the wisdom of the confederation in leaving the provision of money to the States,[6] said that when this plan was deviated from by Congress, their objects should be such as were best known & most approved; that the States were jealous of one another, & wd. not comply unless they were fully acquainted with & approved the purpose to which their money was to be applied, that nothing less than such a preference of the army would conciliate them, that no Civil creditor would dare to put his claim on a levil with those of the army, and insinuated that the speculations which had taken place in loan office certificates might lead to a revision of that subject on principles of equity.[7] that if too much were asked from the States they would grant nothing. He said that it had been alledged that the large public debt if funded under Congress would be a cement of the confederacy. He thought on the contrary it would hasten its dissolution;[8] as the people would feel its weight in the most obnoxious of all forms that of taxation.

on the question the States were all no except. S. Carolina which was ay[x][9]

A motion was made by Mr. Rutlidge 2ded. by Mr. Bland to change the plan of the impost in such a manner as that a tariff might be formed for all articles that would admit of it, and that a duty advalorem sd. be collected only on such articles as would not admit of it.[10]

In support of such an alteration it was urged that it would lessen the opportunity of collusion between collector & importer, & would be more equal among the States.[11] on the other side it was alledged that the States had not objected to that part of the plan, and a change might produce objections that the nature & variety of imports would require necessarily the collection to be advalorem on the greater part of them, that the forming of a book of rates wd. be attended with great difficultes & delays,[12] and that it would be in the power of Congress by raising the rate of the article to augment the duty beyond the limitation of 5 PerCt. and that this consideration would excite objections on the part of the States. The motion was negatived.[13]

[x] Virga. Mr. Jones, Mr. Madison. Mr. Bland no. Mr. Lee Mr. Mercer ay.

A motion was made by Mr. Hamilton 2ded. by Mr. Wilson; that whereas Congress were desirous that the motives & views of their measures sd. be known to their Constituents in all cases where the public safety wd. admit, that when the subject of finances was under debate the doors of Congs. sd. be open. Congs. adjourned it being the usual hour & the motion being generally disrelished.[14] The Pa. delegates[15] said privately that they had brought themselves into a critical situation by dissuading their Constituents from Separate provision for Creditors of U.S. within Pena. hoping that Congr. wd. adopt a general provision, and they wished their Constituents to see the prospect themselves & to witness the conduct of their Delegates.[16] Perhaps the true reason was, that it was expected the presence of public creditors numerous & weighty in Philada.[17] wd. have an influence & that it wd. be well for the public to come more fully to the knowledge of the public finances.

Letter red. from Wm. Lee at Ghent notifying the desire of the Emperor to form a commercial treaty with U. S. & to have a residt. from them.[18] Comd. to Mr. Izard, Ghorum & Wilso[n.][19]

[1] JM Notes, 10 Feb., and n. 15; 12 Feb. 1783, and n. 1.

[2] JM Notes, 12 Feb. 1783, and nn. 3, 5, 13, 14. For the manuscript of the proposal, see NA: PCC, No. 36, II, 21.

[3] For the long overdue pay of the officers and rank and file of Washington's main army as a principal cause of their discontent, see JM Notes, 13 Jan., and nn. 5, 17; 24 Jan., and n. 32; 28 Jan., and citations in n. 24; 4 Feb., and nn. 7, 10–15; 13 Feb.; JM to Randolph, 11 Feb., and n. 5; 13 Feb. 1783, and n. 6. For the unrest, especially in Pennsylvania and Massachusetts, of civilians who were owed money by Congress, see *Papers of Madison*, V, 321–22; 323, nn. 3, 5, 7, 8; 356–57; JM Notes, 24 Jan., and nn. 17, 20; 28 Jan., and nn. 9, 23; 30 Jan. 1783, and nn. 1, 6.

[4] James Wilson's remarks were consistent with those made earlier by him about the necessity of providing Congress with adequate general funds. See JM Notes, 14 Jan., n. 4; 25 Jan., and n. 13; 27 Jan., and nn. 12, 16; 28 Jan., n. 3; 29 Jan.; 31 Jan., n. 11; 12 Feb. 1783, and n. 1.

[5] Nathaniel Gorham's stand reflected both the demands of the many civilian creditors of Congress in Massachusetts and the continuing opposition of that state to the half-pay-for-life guarantee to officers retiring from the continental army upon becoming supernumerary or after serving for the duration of the war. See n. 3, above; JM Notes, 25 Jan.; 4 Feb., and nn. 7, 11, 13, 15. See also JM Notes, 19 Feb. 1783.

[6] That is, as stipulated by Article VIII of the Articles of Confederation (*JCC*, XIX, 217).

[7] JM to Randolph, 15 Jan., n. 13; JM Notes, 29 Jan., n. 14; 30 Jan. 1783, and nn. 2, 4, 6. Compared with paper currency and other evidences of Congress' debt, the loan-office certificates "were not the main object of large-scale speculation" (E. James Ferguson, *Power of the Purse*, p. 252). See JM Notes, 19 Feb. 1783, for further remarks by Mercer on this subject.

[8] James Wilson had been credited with stating that "a public debt resting on general funds would operate as a cement to the confederacy, and might contribute

to prolong its existence, after the foreign danger ceased to counteract its tendency to dissolution" (JM Notes, 27 Jan. 1783). This view had been also expressed by Morris and Hamilton (*Papers of Madison*, V, 322; JM Notes, 28 Jan., and n. 9; 29 Jan. 1783, and n. 41).

[9] Having been introduced, debated, and rejected in the committee of the whole, the Rutledge-Mercer motion is not mentioned in the official journal of Congress for 18 February. At the bottom of the half-page on which Rutledge penned the motion, Daniel Carroll wrote, "negatived."

[10] For the motion, see NA: PCC, No. 36, II, 25; *JCC*, XXIV, 140–41.

[11] That is, if Congress agreed upon the specific duty to be collected on a unit (yard, pound, or gallon, etc.) of each article customarily imported, the opportunities "of collusion" afforded by levying ad valorem duties would virtually disappear.

[12] The length of a compilation of all imported wares would be greatly extended by the need to subdivide most of the individual items into qualitative classifications with a differing ad valorem duty on each class. A British "book of rates" would assist in preparing a schedule of articles but would help little toward deciding what the amount of the duty in each instance in the ports of the United States should be. See Report on Books, 23 Jan. 1783, n. 192.

[13] For further discussion of the impost, see JM Notes, 19 Feb. 1783.

[14] The manuscript of the motion is endorsed, "Mr. Hamilton and Wilson's motion negatived on motion to postpone to take it up, February 18, 1783" (*JCC*, XXIV, 140, and n. 3). See also JM Notes, 19 Feb. 1783. The customary hour of convening the morning session of Congress continued to be ten o'clock, but the time of adjournment in the afternoon was more flexible, even though four o'clock appears to have been the latest hour (*JCC*, VIII, 756, 844, 846; IX, 1031; XXI, 893, 940, 1045; XXIV, 442). "It was necessary for the old Congress to sit with closed doors," JM informed Jared Sparks in 1830, "because it was the executive as well as legislative body; names of persons and characters came perpetually before them; and much business was constantly on hand which would have been embarrassed if it had gone to the public before it was finished" (Herbert B. Adams, *Life and Writings of Jared Sparks*, I, 560).

[15] Thomas FitzSimons, Thomas Mifflin, Joseph Montgomery, and James Wilson.

[16] JM Notes, 24 Jan., and nn. 17, 20; 28 Jan., and nn. 2, 3; 30 Jan. 1783, and n. 1.

[17] JM Notes, 30 Jan. 1783, and n. 6.

[18] In his dispatch of 31 March 1782 from Brussels, Austrian Netherlands, to Robert R. Livingston, secretary for foreign affairs, William Lee, "formerly a commissioner of Congress at the court of Vienna," stated that he had been unofficially informed that "his Imperial and Apostolic majesty, Joseph the Second, Emperor of Germany, King of the Romans, of Hungary, Bohemia, &c., &c., &c.," was "disposed to enter into a commercial treaty with America, and afterwards that a minister or resident from Congress should reside at the court here [Brussels], this being the principal commercial country belonging to his majesty" (Wharton, *Revol. Dipl. Corr.*, V, 291–92). In referring to Congress so much of Lee's letter as bore upon this subject, Livingston commented that Lee's suggestion "merits attention, though in the present state of our affairs Congress may not think it advisable to pass any resolutions thereon, till they are more perfectly acquainted with the actual state of our affairs in Europe, and what alterations may be occasioned by a peace" (*ibid.*, VI, 254).

[19] Charles Thomson's entry in his "Dispatch Book" makes clear that Nathaniel Gorham rather than Ralph Izard was chairman of this committee (NA: PCC, No. 185, III, 54). On 23 July the committee was reconstituted with Ralph Izard as chairman, and Stephen Higginson of Massachusetts, and Richard Peters as the other members. The committee was discharged on 29 September 1783 without having submitted a report (NA: PCC, No. 186, fols. 84, 113).

Virginia Delegates to Benjamin Harrison

RC (Virginia State Library). In the hand of Arthur Lee, except for the signatures of the other four delegates. Docketed, "Lr. from the Delegates in Congress—February 18th. 83."

PHILADELPHIA Feby. 18th. 1783

SIR,

We had the honor of receiving your Excellency's letter of the 7th. & shall communicate what it contains relative to the supply of the Post at Winchester to the Financier, & transmit you his answer. We have reason to believe that he intends renewing the Contract.[1]

On the 14th. we dispatchd a messenger, with the King's Speech, to your Excellency.[2] This is the only authentic information that has yet reachd us relative to Peace. The reports from N. York are, that the Preliminaries were signd the 13th. of Decr. between the American & british Commissioners; but not by those of France & Spain. It can hardly be long, before we are better informed on this subject.[3]

We enclose the Resolutions of Congress on the Tobacco shippd in the Flags, & on the Settlement of the State Accounts.[4]

With sentiments [of] respect & consideration we have the honor to be yr Excellency's Servts.

J. MADISON JR.

JOS. JONES   A. LEE

JOHN F. MERCER

THEOK. BLAND JR.

---

[1] Harrison to Delegates, 7 Feb. 1783, and nn. 3–5, 11. Although Robert Morris seems to have renewed "the Contract," he apparently did not transmit his answer through the delegates or write directly to the governor to that effect (*ibid.*, n. 10).
[2] JM Notes, 13 Feb., n. 10; JM to Randolph, 13 Feb. 1783.
[3] The preliminary articles of peace had been signed by the commissioners of Great Britain and the United States on 30 November. On 10 December 1782, Thomas Townshend, British secretary of state for the home department, issued a passport to the U.S. Ship "Washington," commanded by Captain Joshua Barney, to carry the treaty to Congress. For Barney's arrival at Philadelphia, see JM Notes, 12–15 Mar. 1783. Preliminary articles of peace between Great Britain, France, and Spain were concluded on 20 January (Wharton, *Revol. Dipl. Corr.*, VI, 96–100, 137, n., 226). See also JM to Jefferson, 18 Feb. 1783, and n. 2. Why, both in the present letter and in that of Governor Harrison to the Virginia delegates on 24 February 1783 (*q.v.*), the date of 13 December became associated with the peace treaty is unknown.
[4] JM Notes, 10 Feb. 1783, and nn. 6, 14. Filed with the present letter are a clerk's

copy, signed by "Geo Bond Depy Secy," of the committee's report adopted by Congress, in regard to the "Tobacco," and a clerk's copy, signed by "Chas Thomson secy," of the resolution of Congress concerning the "Accounts" of Virginia. These enclosures are docketed, "The Honble. A Lee Esqr. Resolutions of congress Feby 10th. Feb 1783."

To Thomas Jefferson

RC (LC: Madison Papers). Addressed to "The honble T. Jefferson." Unless otherwise noted, the words italicized are those that were written by JM in the cipher described in Jefferson to JM, 31 Jan. 1783, ed. n. After recovering the present letter from Jefferson, JM wrote "Madison Jas." above the date line. In his old age he or someone at his direction placed a bracket at the close of both the second and fourth paragraphs to indicate that they should be printed in the first comprehensive edition of his writings. Henry D. Gilpin, the editor of that compilation, included only the second paragraph (Madison, *Papers* [Gilpin ed.], I, 508).

PHILADA. Feby. 18th. 1783.

DEAR SIR

Your two favors of the 14th. one of them inclosing a letter to Miss Floyd[1] were recd. by yesterday's mail.

The last paper from N.Y. as the inclosed will shew you has brought us another token of the approach of peace. It is somewhat mysterious nevertheless that the preliminaries with America should be represented by Secy. Townsend as *actually signed* and those with France as *to be signed,* as also that the signing of the latter would constitute a general peace.[2] I have never been without my apprehensions that some tricks would be tried by the British Court notwithstanding their exterior fairness, of late, and these apprehensions have been rendered much more serious by the *tenor of some letters* which *you have*[3] *seen* and particularly by the *intimation of minister of France to Mister Livingston.*[4] These considerations have made me peculiarly solicitous that your mission[5] should be pursued as long as a possibility remained of *your sharing in* the *object of it.*

Your *portrait of your amanuensis*[6] is I conceive drawn to *the life.*[7] For all un*confidential*[8] *services he is a convenient instrument.* For any thing farther ne *sutor ultra* cre*pidam.*[9]

The turn which your case has for the present taken makes it unnecessary to answer particularly the parts of your letter which relate to the expediency of a flag—and the extent of its protection. on the first point, I am inclined to think that the greatest objection with Congress would have been drawn from the risk of a denial. on the second I have no precise knowledge, but the principle would seem to extend to every thing appertaining to the mission as well as to the person of the Minister. Nor can I conceive a motive to the latter indulgence which would admit of a refusal of the former.[10]

I am impatient to hear of the plan which is to dispose of you during the suspense in which you are placed. If Philada. as I flatter myself, is to be your abode, your former quarters will await you.[11]

I am Dear Sir Yr. Affecte. friend,

J. MADISON JR.

An answer to Miss Patsy's letter is in the same mail with this.[12]

[1] *Qq.v.* Martha (Patsy) Jefferson's letter to Maria Floyd was enclosed in Jefferson's earlier letter of 14 February to JM.

[2] JM, who probably enclosed a copy of the *Pennsylvania Packet* of 18 February 1783, underlined rather than encoded the italicized words. His comments appear to reflect two items in this issue of the *Packet:* (1) a copy of the letter of 5 December 1782 from Thomas Townshend, British secretary for the home department, to the lord mayor of London, informing him of the signing of the preliminary articles of peace with the United States, and adding, "it now only remains to sign the same articles between Great Britain and France, to constitute a general peace"; and (2) an extract from an anonymous letter of 12 February 1783 from Elizabethtown, N.J., in which the author, after mentioning a rumor from New York City concerning the signing of a preliminary peace with the United States on 30 November 1782, labeled the report as "too absurd and inconsistent to be credited; because all the powers at war must have signed at one and the same time." Townshend's observation, quoted above, naturally made JM wonder why Spain and the Netherlands had not been mentioned.

[3] JM symbolized "have" as 400.29. rather than as 401.29.

[4] JM's combined symbols for "Livingston," 485.37.a. and 763.31., deciphered respectively as "living" and "son." For examples of JM's "apprehensions," see *Papers of Madison*, V, 159; 171; 172, n. 13; 187; 196–97; 390; 448; JM to James Madison, Sr., 1 Jan.; JM Notes, 13 Jan. 1783. For the "letters" which Jefferson probably saw during his stay in Philadelphia from 27 December 1782 to 26 January 1783, see *Papers of Madison*, V, 438, n. 9; 441; 443, n. 2; JM Notes, 1 Jan., n. 2; JM to Randolph, 7 Jan. 1783, n. 9.

[5] That is, as a member of the American peace commission.

[6] JM correctly encoded "amanuensis" as 29.18. For Jefferson's labored encipherment of the word, see Jefferson to JM, 14 Feb. 1783 (2d letter), n. 12.

[7] For Jefferson's "portrait" of David Salisbury Franks, see Jefferson to JM, 14 Feb. 1783 (2d letter), and n. 19.

[8] JM achieved "confidential" by combining 183.21. ("confident"), 425.31. ("I"), and 24.1., which begins the "AL" column in Nugent's dictionary.

[9] *Ne supra crepidam sutor indicaret*—"let the cobbler stick to his last," from Plinius Secundus Major, *Historia Naturalis* (H[arris] Rackham, trans., *Pliny Nat-*

ural History, with an English Translation . . . [10 vols.; Cambridge, Mass., 1938–63], IX, 324). JM contrived his incorrect and abbreviated rendition of the quotation by writing, "ne 796.6. ['suitor'], 843.31. ['u'], 470.31. ['l'], 830.1. ['TR' column], a cre 603.1. ['pi'], 226.22. ['dam']."

10 Jefferson to JM, 7–8 Feb., and nn. 11, 12; 14 Feb. (2d letter), and nn. 35, 37; JM Notes, 14 Feb., and nn. 1, 6; JM to Jefferson, 15 Feb. 1783.

11 JM to Jefferson, 15 Feb. 1783, and n. 5. Jefferson's "former quarters" had been in Mrs. Mary House's boarding house in Philadelphia (Jefferson to JM, 31 Jan. 1783, and nn. 28, 29).

12 The letter "in the same mail" evidently was Maria Floyd's reply to the letter mentioned in n. 1, above.

To Edmund Randolph

RC (LC: Madison Papers). Unsigned but in JM's hand. Cover franked by "J. Madison Jr." and addressed by him to "Edmund Randolph Esqr. Richmond." Docketed by Randolph, "James Madison Feby 18. 1783." In the first paragraph, the words are italicized which JM enciphered in the Randolph code.

PHILADA. Feby. 18th. 1783.

MY DEAR FRIEND

I am glad to find by your favor of the 7th. instant that the necessity of a readoption of the impost presses so strongly on your mind. To give it a fair experiment with the ensuing assembly it will be indispensable that you should be its advocate on the floor. Those who effected its repeal will never inactively suffer it to be reinstated in our Code.[1] *Mercer* from *what motive God knows says* that *he will crawl to R—d on his bare knees to prevt it.* Having already *changed his opinion on the* subject *he fears perhaps* the *charge of unsteaddiness.*[2] Perhaps too *his zeal* against *a general revenue may be cooled by* the accomplishment in *congress of a plan* for a valuation of land, *on the ruins of* which *he among others* suspected the former was to be *established.*[3] This plan passed Congress yesterday. It proposes that the States shall return to Congs. before Jany next their respective quantities of land the number of houses thereon distinguishing dwelling houses from others, and the no. of Inhabitants distinguishing whites from blacks. These data are to be referred to a Grand Come. by whom a report in which nine voices must unite, is to be made to Congress which report is to settle the proportions of each State, & to be ratified or rejected by Congs. without alteration. Who could have supposed that such a measure could ever have been the offspring of a zealous and scrupulous respect for the Confederation?[4]

The residue of my extract from Mr. J——s remarks is I am persuaded less interesting to your present purposes than you infer from the specimen you have received. The labor of gratifying you however I can assure you will bear no proportion to the pleasure of it, and you may calculate on being shortly furnished with it. I understand from Mr. J. that he has materials for enlarging the whole plan. My expectation of getting from him some day or other a full copy, reduced my extract to parts of immediate use to me, or such as consisting of reflections, not of facts might not be obtained otherwise.[5]

To the Speech of the B. King of which I sent you copy by the Express, I now add in the inclosed gazette a further token of approaching peace. It seems a little mysterious nevertheless that Mr. Secy. Townsend should speak of the preliminaries with the United States as *signed* & those with France as *to be signed*. The former being only provisional may in some measure explain it, but in that case it would seem to be without real use.[6]

In consequence of this prospect the departure of —— has been suspended untill the further orders of Congress. I had a letter from him yesterday but he had not then been apprized of this resolution. He had seen the Speech & had I doubt not anticipated it.[7] What course he will take during the suspense—I can not say. My wish is that he may return to this place where he will be able at least to pass away the time with less tedium.[8]

[1] In his letter of 7 February (q.v.), Randolph had predicted that if the April elections in Virginia returned enough "*sound Whigs*" to the General Assembly, it would reverse the "fatal repeal" of Virginia's ratification of the proposed impost amendment. JM adroitly used this forecast to designate as "indispensable" what he had called "a duty" in his letter of 11 February to Randolph (q.v., and n. 4), namely, for him to become a member of the House of Delegates. Jefferson, although for different reasons, willingly joined JM in urging Randolph to qualify "for a seat in the legislature" (JM to Jefferson, 11 Feb., and n. 14; Jefferson to JM, 14 Feb. (1st letter), and n. 4; Boyd, *Papers of Jefferson*, VI, 246–49). See also Randolph to JM, 3 Jan., and n. 10; 15 Jan., and n. 7; 1 Feb. 1783.

[2] "R——d" stands for Richmond. On 12 February 1783 Mercer spoke in Congress against submitting an altered version of the amendment to the states before the debts of Congress had been "liquidated & apportioned." Failing to have his way in this particular, he appeared willing six days later to support the amendment, provided that the revenue produced by the impost should be allocated first of all to pay the "interest of the debt to the army" (*Papers of Madison*, V, 283, n. 3; 427, n. 7; 455, n. 5; Harrison to JM, 4 Jan., n. 3; JM Notes, 12 Feb., and nn. 1, 12; 18 Feb. 1783; JCC, XXIV, 126–27). Judging from JM's letters of 25 February and 4 March 1783 to Randolph (qq.v.), Mercer soon "changed" again in his stand on the impost and "*a general revenue.*"

[3] See n. 2. JM placed a caret after the comma, interlineated an asterisk, and fol-

lowed it with the ciphers for "on the ruins of." The meaning of the sentence will be largely clarified by JM Notes, 7 Feb., and n. 14; 8 Feb., and nn. 3, 4; 17 Feb., and nn. 1, 3, 4. Even as early as 6 February, before most of the revisions were made, JM had noted that the report of the committee of the whole "lay in a great degree of confusion" (JM Notes, 9–10 Jan., and n. 2; 13 Jan., and n. 1; 14 Jan., and nn. 4–7; 29 Jan., and nn. 7–9, 11, 13; 31 Jan., and nn. 11, 17; 4 Feb., and n. 20; 5–6 Feb., and nn. 9–11, 13; 7 Feb. 1783, and nn. 3, 11). The report of a committee, instructed by Congress on 11 February to assemble these disparate motions and recommendations "into a proper act," was debated three days later and rejected on 17 February. The "accomplishment in *congress*" on that date was the acceptance of the Dyer-Mercer substitute proposal (JM Notes, 17 Feb. 1783, and n. 1; *JCC*, XXIV, 124, 129–37).

4 In his comments about Mercer, JM reflects his scorn of the worth of the "accomplishment" and his unshaken conviction that Congress, both for its own sake and that of the union of states, must be provided with "*a general revenue*" (JM Notes, 9–10 Jan.; 14 Jan.; 28 Jan., and nn. 5, 19; 17 Feb.; JM to Randolph, 14 Jan.; 28 Jan.; 4 Feb. 1783). See also *JCC*, XXIV, 135–37.

5 JM to Randolph, 28 Jan., hdn., and n. 3. JM was fulfilling a promise made on 30 Dec. 1782 (*Papers of Madison*, V, 473). How large a "specimen" of his notes on Jefferson's memorandum for Barbé-Marbois JM had forwarded is unknown, but "the residue" of the extract was enclosed in his letter of 25 February 1783 to Randolph (*q.v.*).

6 Delegates to Harrison, 18 Feb., and n. 3; JM to Jefferson, 18 Feb. 1783, and n. 2.

7 Jefferson to JM, 14 Feb. (2d letter), and nn. 39, 41. JM assumed that Randolph would know that Jefferson was meant. For "this resolution," see JM Notes, 14 Feb., and n. 6; JM to Jefferson, 15 Feb. 1783.

8 *Ibid.*, and n. 5.

Notes on Debates

MS (LC: Madison Papers). For a description of the manuscript of Notes on Debates, see *Papers of Madison*, V, 231–34. All the brackets and the words contained within them in this item are JM's own entries.

No. IX

Wednesday February 19.[1]

The motion made yesterday by Mr. Hamilton for opening the doors of Congress when the subject of finances should be under debate was negatived, Penna. alone being ay.[2]

A motion was made by Mr. Hamilton seconded by Mr. Bland to postpone the clause of the report made by Come. of the whole for altering the Impost, viz, the clause limiting its duration to 25 years,[3] in order to substitute a proposition declaring it to be inexpedient to limit the period of its duration: first because it ought to be commensurate to the duration of the debt. 2dly. because it was improper in the present stage of the business, and all the limitation of which it wd. admit had been defined in the Resolutions of   1782.[4]

Mr. Hamilton said in support of his motion that it was in vain to attempt to gain the concurrence of the States by removing the objections publickly assigned by them against the Impost, that these were the ostensible & not the true objections: that the true objection on the part of R. I. was the interference of the impost with the opportunity afforded by their situation of levying contributions on Cont. &c which rcd. foreign supplies through the ports of R. I:[5] that the true objection on the part of Va. was her having little share in the debts due from the U. S. to which the impost would be applied;[6] that a removal of the avowed objections would not therefore, remove the obstructions whilst it would admit on the part of Congs. that their first recommendation went beyond the absolute exigences of the public; that Congs. having taken a proper ground at first, ought to maintain it till time should convince the States of the propriety of the measure.

Mr. Bland said that as the debt had been contracted by Congress with the concurrence of the States, and Congs was looked to for payment by the public creditors, it was justifiable & requisite in them to pursue such means as would be adequate to the discharge of the debt: & that the means would not be adequate if limited in duration to a period within which no calculations had shewn that the debt wd. be discharged.[7]

on the motion the States were N. Hamshire divided—Masts. no. R. Island ay Cont. divd. N. York. ay. N. Jersey ay. Pena. ay. Virga. no [Mr. Bland ay] N. Carolina ay. S. Carolina ay.[8] Mr. Rutlidge said he voted for postponing not in order to agree to Mr. Hamiltons motion but to move & he accordingly renewed the motion, made in the Come. of the whole; viz that the Impost should be appropriated exclusively to the army. This motion was seconded by Mr. Lee[9]

Mr. Hamilton opposed the motion strenuously, declared that as a friend to the army[10] as well as to the other Creditors & to the public at large he could never assent to such a partial dispensation of Justice; that the different States being differently attached to different branches of the public debt would never concur in establishg a fund wch. was not extended to every branch; that it was impolitic to divide the interests of the civil & military Creditors, whose joint efforts in the States would be necessary to prevail on them to adopt a general revenue.[11]

Mr. Mercer favored the measure as necessary to satisfy the army & to avert the consequences which would result from their disappointment on this subject: he pronounced that the Army would not disband until satisfactory provision should be made, & that this was the only attainable provision;[12] But he reprobated the doctrine of a permanent debt supported by a general & permanent revenue & said that it would be good policy to separate instead of cementing the interest of the Army & the other public creditors, insinuating that the claims of the latter were not supported by justice & that the loan office certificates ought to be revised.[13]

Mr. Fitzimmons observed that it was unnecessary to make a separate appropriation of the Impost to one particular debt, since if other funds sd. be superadded, there would be more simplicity & equal propriety in an aggregate fund for the aggregate debt funded: and that if no other funds should be superadded it wd. be unjust & impolitic: that the States whose Citizens were the chief creditors of the U. S. wd. never concur in such measure; that the mercantile interest which comprehended the chief Creditors of Pena. had by their influence obtained the prompt & full concurrence of that State in the Impost; and if that influence were excluded the State wd. repeal its law: He concurred with those who hoped the army wd. not disband unless provision sd. be made for doing them justice[14]

Mr. Lee contended that as eve[r]ybody felt and acknowledged the force of the demands of the army, an appropriation of the Impost to them wd. recommend it to all the States: that distinct & specific appropriations of distinct revenues was the only true System of finance, and was the practice of all other nations who were enlightened on this subject; that the army had not only more merit than the mercantile creditors; but that the latter would be more able on a return of peace to return to the business which would support them.[15]

Mr Madison said that if other funds were to be superadded as the gentleman [Mr. Rutledge] who made the motion admitted, it was at least premature to make the appropriation in question;[16] that it wd. be best to wait till all the funds were agreed upon & then appropriate them respectively to those debts to which they sd. be best fitted; that it was probable the impost would be judged best adapted to the foreign debt;[17] as the foreign Creditors could not like the domestic ever recur to particular States for separate payments, and that as this wd. be a revenue little felt, it would be prudent to assign it to those for whom the States wd. care least, leaving more obnoxious revenues for those Creditors who wd. excite the sympathy of their Countrymen and cd stimulate them to do justice.[18]

Mr. Williamson was agst. the motion; said he did not wish the army to disband untill proper provision should be made for them; that if force sd. be necessary to excite justice, the sooner force were applied the better.[19]

Mr. Wilson was against the motion of Mr. Rutlidge, observed that no instance occured in the British history of finance in which distinct appropriations had been made to distinct debts *already* contracted; that a consolidation of funds had been the result of experience; that an aggregate fund was more simple & would be most convenient: that the interest of the whole funded debt ought to be paid before the principal of any part of it; and therefore in case of surplus of the impost beyond the interest of the army debt, it ought at any rate to be applied to the interest of the other debts, and not, as the motion proposed, to the principal of the army debt. He was fully of opinion that such a motion wd. defeat itself, that by dividing the interest of the civil from that of the military Creditors provision for the latter would be frustrated.[20]

on the question on Mr. Rutledge's motion the States were N.H. no Mas: no. Cont. no. N.J. no. Virga. no. [Mr. Lee & Mr. Mercer ay]. N.C. no. S. Carolina ay[21]

On the clause reported by the Come: of the whole in favor of limiting the impost to 25. years the States were N.H. ay Mas: ay Cont. divd.* N.Y. no. N.J. no. Pa. ay† Va. ay [Mr. Bland no] N. Carolina ay. S. Carolina ay. So the question was lost[22]

On the question whether the appointment of Collectors of the Impost shall be left to the States, the Collectors to be under the controul of & amenable to Congs. there were 7 ays—N.Y. & Pena. being no & N.J. divided.[23]

* Cont. [Mr. Dyer ay, Mr. Wolcot no].

† Pa. [Mr. Wilson & Fitzsimmons no.]

[1] The printed journal omits mention of a session of Congress on this day. For a probable explanation of the Roman numeral, see *Papers of Madison*, V, 231.

[2] JM Notes, 18 Feb. 1783, and n. 14.

[3] On 13 February the committee of the whole laid before Congress a revised version of the impost amendment which two years earlier had been submitted to the states for ratification. Among the revisions was the "25 years" limitation (*JCC*, XIX, 112–13, 124–25; JM Notes, 12 Feb., and n. 15; 13 Feb. 1783). See also *Papers of Madison*, III, 140; 142, n. 2.

During the debates in the committee of the whole and occasionally in Congress upon altering the impost amendment and relating it to the solution of the larger problem of providing Congress with an adequate "general revenue," Hamilton had manifested far more interest in assuring that Congress should appoint the collectors of the tariff than in preventing its limitation in time. Bland, who moved from a states'-rights to a mildly nationalistic position during this prolonged discussion, apparently wished above all to help reconcile opposing views, thus enabling Congress to adopt a revenue-producing ordinance which all the states might accept. Eager to effect a compromise, Bland was willing to be inconsistent on matters of detail. Thus on 29 January he was against a "25 years" limitation; on 12 February he supported it; on 19 February he joined Hamilton in an effort to eliminate the proviso from the recommendation of the committee of the whole (JM Notes, 24 Jan.; 27 Jan.; 28 Jan., and nn. 12, 45; 29 Jan., and nn. 8, 14, 40, 41; 31 Jan.; 12 Feb. 1783, and nn. 8, 9, 13–15).

[4] Hamilton almost surely referred to resolutions with which he, as chairman of a committee, had closed its long report in rebuttal of the reasons advanced by the Rhode Island General Assembly to justify its refusal to ratify the proposed impost amendment to the Articles of Confederation. Congress adopted the report and the resolutions on 16 December 1782 (JCC, XXIII, 798–810). For a summary of the limitations "defined in the Resolutions," see Papers of Madison, V, 407, and n. 1.

[5] In support of Hamilton's statement about the dependence of Connecticut ("Cont.") upon Rhode Island for goods of foreign origin, see Papers of Madison, V, 375, n. 15; 414–15; JM Notes, 29 Jan. 1783, and n. 28.

[6] Governor Benjamin Harrison probably would have challenged the accuracy of this statement. Although Virginia was greatly delinquent in paying the financial requisitions of Congress and although, as compared with citizens of Pennsylvania, Massachusetts, and several other states, Virginians owned small amounts of loan-office certificates and continental currency, they and the government of their state were creditors of Congress for many provisions and supplies furnished to the continental army (Papers of Madison, V, 58, and n. 4; 169, and n. 2; 279, n. 4; 282; 287, n. 17; 291, n. 11; 328; 347; 349, and nn. 4–6, 10; 351, n. 23; 431, n. 4; 454, n. 3, 457–58; 458, n. 5; 459–60; Harrison to JM, 4 Jan., n. 4; 31 Jan., and n. 7; 7 Feb., and n. 4; Randolph to JM, 15 Jan., n. 13; Rev. James Madison to JM, 16 Jan.; JM Notes, 28 Jan., n. 19; 8 Feb. 1783, and n. 3).

[7] See n. 3. Even the most sanguine members of Congress, including JM, who shared in the debates in the committee of the whole apparently doubted whether any financial plan acceptable to all the states would provide in the near future much more "general revenue" than enough to pay the day-by-day expenses of Congress and the annual interest on the foreign and domestic debt and on the money owed to civilian and military creditors (JM Notes, 28 Jan.; 29 Jan., and nn. 14, 15, 20; 18 Feb. 1783, and nn. 3, 5).

[8] For the Hamilton-Bland motion, see the second paragraph of JM's notes for this day. The motion would have carried if it had been favored by a majority of the delegates from one more state. Consistent with his position on 12 February, JM evidently voted against the motion (JM Notes, 12 Feb. 1783, and n. 13).

[9] JM Notes, 18 Feb. 1783, and nn. 2–9.

[10] By November 1781, when Lieutenant Colonel Alexander Hamilton returned to civilian life, he had served over five years as an officer in the continental army, including over four (1 March 1777 to 30 April 1781) as Washington's military secretary and aide-de-camp.

[11] Papers of Madison, V, 322; 324, nn. 10, 14; 366, n. 23; 376, n. 27; JM Notes, 27 Jan.; 28 Jan., and n. 12; 29 Jan., and nn. 40, 41; 12 Feb. 1783, and n. 8. In line with his opposition to the Rutledge-Lee motion and his concern lest civilian creditors not receive their just due, Hamilton tried without success to have the "doors of Congress" opened whenever "the subject of finances" should be discussed. See JM Notes, 18 Feb. 1783. In a confidential letter written on or about 17 February to Washington, Hamilton "lamented" because there was "much ground" for the opinion widely held in Philadelphia that if the troops laid "down their arms" and scattered to their homes, they thereby would surrender their sole "means" of securing "justice" from Congress (Syrett and Cooke, Papers of Hamilton, III, 253–55).

[12] John Francis Mercer probably considered himself to be as warm "a friend to the army" as did Hamilton. See *Papers of Madison*, IV, 154, n. 14. See also *ibid.*, V, 474, n. 8; JM Notes, 13 Jan., and nn. 5, 17; 13 Feb.; 20 Feb. 1783. On 27 February Joseph Jones wrote to Washington from Philadelphia: "Reports are freely circulated here that there are dangerous combinations in the Army, and within a few days past it has been said, they are about to declare, they will not disband until their demands are complied with" (Fitzpatrick, *Writings of Washington*, XXV, 431–32, n. 42). See also JM Notes, 20 Feb. 1783, n. 18.

[13] JM Notes, 18 Feb. 1783, and the references cited in its nn. 7, 8.

[14] As a prominent banker and merchant of Philadelphia, Thomas FitzSimons could speak authoritatively about how largely the influence of businessmen had accounted for the ratification of the impost amendment by the Pennsylvania General Assembly on 5 April 1781. See *Papers of Madison*, III, 128, n. 5. By "Creditors of Pena.," JM meant creditors of Congress in that state. See JM Notes, 24 Jan., and nn. 17, 20; 28 Jan., nn. 2, 29; 30 Jan. 1783, and nn. 1, 2, 6.

[15] On 29 January Arthur Lee had seconded the motion of Rutledge to use the revenue from the proposed impost for three types of debt, including the arrears due to the army," and on 12 February he prophesied that the states would never ratify the amendment unless it required Congress to inform each state annually how the money accruing from the tariff had been spent (JM Notes, 29 Jan.; 12 Feb. 1783, and n. 5). Although Lee's statement about the "practice" of the legislatures of "enlightened" nations in this regard was accurate, he apparently did not add that the "practice" had been employed as a salutary financial check on the executive branch of the government. The Articles of Confederation provided only for a central Congress and, unlike the case of the sovereign British Parliament, restricted the powers of Congress to those specifically delegated by the sovereign states. See JM Notes, 21 Feb. 1783, and n. 10.

[16] JM Notes, 18 Feb. 1783, and nn. 2–9. The "question" at issue was whether the revenue derived from levying an impost should be devoted "exclusively to the army."

[17] On 29 January Oliver Ellsworth of Connecticut had argued that paying the interest on and principal of the foreign debt was the "first object" to which the revenue accruing from the impost should be applied (JM Notes, 29 Jan. 1783).

[18] Among "those Creditors" were the war veterans or their widows and children, farmers whose property had been taken or destroyed by the continental army, and citizens of little wealth who held depreciated continental currency, loan-office certificates, or other paper evidences of debts owed by Congress. For examples of the "more obnoxious revenues," see JM Notes, 27 Jan.; 28 Jan., and nn. 35, 42, 43; 29 Jan. 1783, and nn. 16–21.

[19] JM Notes, 28 Jan. 1783. On 17 February 1783, Hugh Williamson wrote to James Iredell of North Carolina: "The cloud of public creditors, including the army, are gathering about us; the prospect thickens. Believe me, that I would rather take the field in the hardest military service I ever saw, than face the difficulties that await us in Congress within a few months" (Burnett, *Letters*, VII, 46–47). See also *ibid.*, VII, 97–98.

[20] See n. 7; also JM Notes, 21 Feb. 1783, and n. 10. Although James Wilson and Hamilton were probably the most influential of the ardent nationalists in Congress, Wilson, as a citizen of Pennsylvania, may have been even more determined than was Hamilton to gratify the large number of civilian creditors in his home state. See n. 11, above; JM Notes, 30 Jan., n. 6; 18 Feb. 1783, and n. 4.

[21] That is, for appropriating the impost revenue "exclusively to the army."

[22] This entire paragraph after "On the" was interlineated by JM as a revision in arrangement of a deleted but equivalent analysis by him of the same tally. In

making the revision he appended the footnotes at the bottom of his page. For a renewal of the issue of a twenty-five-year limitation, see JM Notes, 20 Feb. 1783.

[23] The outcome of this tally confirmed the vote in the committee of the whole on 12 February, and thus again rebuffed not only the New York and Pennsylvania delegations but also a few other prominent members of Congress, including JM and Bland of Virginia and David Ramsay of South Carolina (JM Notes, 28 Jan.; 29 Jan.; 12 Feb. 1783, and n. 15). In a letter of 24 February to Governor George Clinton of New York, Hamilton remarked that he had been "left in a small minority" (Syrett and Cooke, *Papers of Hamilton*, III, 268).

Notes on Debates

MS (LC: Madison Papers). For a description of the manuscript of Notes on Debates, see *Papers of Madison*, V, 231–34.

Thursday Feby. 20. 1783

The motion for limiting the impost to 25 years having been yesterday lost, and some of the gentlemen who were in the negative desponding of an indefinite grant of it from the States the motion was reconsidered.[1]

Mr. Wolcot & Mr. Hamilton repeat the inadequacy of a definite term. Mr. Ramsay & Mr. Williamson repeat the improbability of an indefinite term being acceded to by the States, & the expediency of preferring a limited impost to a failure of it altogether.[2]

Mr. Mercer was against the impost altogether but would confine his opposition within Congress: He was in favor of the limitation as an alleviation of the evil.[3]

Mr. Fitzimmons animadverted on Mr. Mercers insinuation yesterday touching the loan-office Creditors, & the policy of dividing them from the military Creditors, reprobated every measure which contravened the principles of justice & public faith; and asked whether it were likely that Mas: & Pa. to whose Citizens $\frac{1}{2}$ the loan office debt was owing would concur with Virga. whose Citizens had lent but little more than three hundred thousand dollars, in any plan that did not provide for that in common with other debts of the U. S.[4] He was against a limitation to 25. years.[5]

Mr. Lee wished to know whether by Loan office Creditors were meant the original subscribers or the present holders of the certificates, as the force of their demands may be affected by this consideration.[6]

Mr. Fitzimmons saw the scope of the question, and said that if another scale of depreciation was seriously in view he wished it to come out, that every one might know the course proper to be taken.[7]

Mr. Ghorum followed the Sentiments of the gentleman who last spoke, expressed his astonishment that a gentleman (Mr. Lee) who had enjoyed such opportunities of observing the nature of public credit, should advance such doctrines as were fatal to it.[8] He said it was time that this point sd. be explained, that if the former scale for the loan office certificates was to be revised and reduced as one member from Virga. (Mr. Mercer) contended, or a further scale to be made out for subsequent depreciation of Certificates, as seemed to be the idea of the other member (Mr Lee), the restoration of public credit was not only visionary but the concurrence of the States in any arrangemts. whatever was not to be expected. He was in favor of the limitation as necessary to overcome the objections of the States.

Mr. Mercer professed his attachment to the principles of justice but declared that he thought the scale by which the loans had been valued unjust to the public & that it ought to be revised & reduced.

On the question for the period of 25 years it was decided in the affirmative seven States being in favor of it. N. Jersey & N. York only being no.[9]

Mr. Mercer called the attention of Congress to the case of the goods siezed under a law of Pena. on which the Come. had not yet reported, and wished that Congs. would come to some resolution declaratory of their rights & which would lead to an effectual interposition on the part of the Legislature of Pena.[10] After much conversation on the subject in which the members were somewhat divided as to the degree of peremptoriness with which the State of Pa. should be called on, the Resolution on the Journal was finally adopted; having been drawn up by the Secy. & put into the hands of a member.[x][11]

The Resolution passed without any dissent.[12]

[The evening of this day was spent at Mr. Fitzimmons by Mr. Ghorum, Mr. Hamilton, Mr. Peters, Mr. Carroll & Mr Madison.[13] The conversation turned on the subject of revenue under the consideration of Congress, and on the situation of the army. The conversation on the first subject ended in a general concurrence (Mr. Hamilton excepted) in the impossibility of adding to the impost on trade any taxes that wd. operate equally throughout the States, or be adopted by them.[14] On the

---

[x] The result proved that mildness was the soundest policy. The Legislature in consequence having declared the law under which the goods were siezed to be void as contradictory to the federal constitution. Some of the members in Conversation sd. that if Congress had declared the law to be void, the displeasure of the legislature might possibly have produced a different issue.

second subject Mr. Hamilton & Mr. Peters who had the best knowledge of the temper, transactions & views of the army,[15] informed the company that it was certain that the army had secretly determined not to lay down their arms until due provision & a satisfactory prospect should be afforded on the subject of their pay;[16] that there was reason to expect that a public declaration to this effect would soon be made; that plans had been agitated if not formed for subsisting themselves after such declaration;[17] that as a proof of their earnestness on this subject the Commander was already become extremely unpopular among almost all ranks from his known dislike to every unlawful proceeding, that this unpopularity was daily increasing & industriously promoted by many leading characters;[18] that his choice of unfit & indiscreet persons into his family was the pretext and with some a real motive;[19] but the substantial one a desire to displace him from the respect & confidence of the army in order to substitute Genl.   as the conductor of their efforts to obtain justice.[20] Mr. Hamilton said that he knew Genl. Washington intimately & perfectly, that his extreme reserve, mixed sometimes with a degree of asperity of temper both of which were said to have increased of late, had contributed to the decline of his popularity; but that his virtue his patriotism & his firmness would it might be depended upon never yield to any dishonorable or disloyal plans into which he might be called; that he would sooner suffer himself to be cut into pieces; that he [Mr Hamilton] knowing this to be his true character wished him to be the conductor of the army in their plans for redress, in order that they might be moderated & directed to proper objects, & exclude some other leader who might foment & misguide their councils; that with this view he had taken the liberty to write to the Genl. on this subject and to recommend such a policy to him.]

[1] JM Notes, 19 Feb. 1783, and n. 8.

[2] *Ibid.*, and n. 3.

[3] JM Notes, 12 Feb., and n. 12; JM to Randolph, 18 Feb. 1783, and n. 2.

[4] JM Notes, 27 Jan., and nn. 13, 16; 29 Jan., and n. 14; 30 Jan., and nn. 2, 6; 18 Feb., and n. 7; 19 Feb. 1783, and nn. 11–14. For the estimated specie value of the loan-office certificates originally purchased by citizens of each state, see JM Notes, 26 Feb. 1783, and n. 46.

[5] That is, of the duration of the proposed impost (JM Notes, 19 Feb. 1783, and n. 8).

[6] Opposing Thomas FitzSimons by using his own emphasis upon "principles of justice," Arthur Lee queried whether they did not oblige a distinction to be made in redeeming loan-office certificates, or even in paying the overdue interest on them, between owners who had originally subscribed for those bonds and speculators who had bought them from the first purchasers at a discount. Lee thus raised questions which JM himself asked when Alexander Hamilton, as secretary of the

treasury, sought to fund the federal debt in 1789–1790. The owners of the certificates always had been preferred creditors of Congress. These certificates, being kept wholly within the control of Congress, being unaffected by the forty-for-one ordinance of 18 March 1780, and being always regarded primarily as an investment rather than currency, had declined far less in real value than the paper money which most Americans had been obliged to take for their goods or services.

The 6 per cent interest on certificates purchased between the opening of the first loan offices in 1777 and 1 March 1778 was paid in specie or its equivalent, thus providing the owners, who had purchased the certificates with depreciated paper money, with a much larger real interest than Congress had guaranteed. Although the many certificates emitted between 1 March 1778 and 1781, when their issuance ceased, returned interest only in paper money, they were mostly taken by merchants in lieu of cash for goods sold to Congress (*Papers of Madison*, II, 49, n. 2; *JCC*, V, 845–46; VII, 158; VIII, 730; XII, 1242–43; XVII, 547–48; XVIII, 1025–26; E. James Ferguson, *Power of the Purse*, pp. 35–40, and nn.).

[7] The depreciation scale for loan-office certificates, established by Congress on 28 June 1780 (*JCC*, XVIII, 567–69), greatly favored their owners. That is, the scale enabled purchasers to buy bonds of a much larger face value than the market value of the depreciated paper currency used to pay for them. Furthermore, the interest was paid on the face value of the bond rather than on its lesser market value resulting from its depreciation in terms of specie. Perhaps partly to spur the wealthy owners of these bonds to bring pressure upon the legislatures of the northern states, and hence upon Congress, to provide the Confederation with a "permanent" source of "general revenue," Robert Morris, superintendent of finance, had suspended the payment of interest on the bonds in October 1781.

In FitzSimons' statement may be read the implication that, if Congress should modify the depreciation scale so as to cause financial loss to the certificate owners, the Pennsylvania General Assembly would assume the payment of interest and perhaps also of the principal of the certificates—an action which had been narrowly averted several times by Congress in the recent past (*Papers of Madison*, IV, 388, n. 13; V, 293–94; 294, n. 1; JM Notes, 24 Jan., and n. 17 including citations, n. 20; 28 Jan., and n. 9; 30 Jan. 1783, and nn. 1, 2, 6; *JCC*, XXIII, 553–55; Clarence L. Ver Steeg, *Robert Morris*, pp. 44, 99).

[8] Nathaniel Gorham apparently reminded Lee of the importance of "public credit" in securing the loans and gifts of money from the treasury of King Louis XVI used by Congress to compensate Lee for his years of service in France as a commissioner of the United States (*Papers of Madison*, V, 300, n. 5).

[9] JM Notes, 19 Feb. 1783, and n. 22. The motion and tally were not recorded in the official journal (*JCC*, XXIV, 141). In LC: Madison Papers are two resolutions written by Theodorick Bland and docketed by Charles Thomson, "Motion of Mr. Bland Feby 20, 1783." Bland wished Congress to accompany its future requisitions upon the states with a report of "the debt funded and unfunded" prior to March 1781, "reduced to Specie value as far as such debts are liquidated—together with the mode in which the monies have been supplied, and the Manner in which they have been appropriated." He further proposed that the report show the "exact state of the debt" incurred from 1 March 1781 to 1 January 1783, noting "all Loans, donations and State Contributions, actually obtained by Congress," how they had been spent, and how much of the debt "contracted within the said Period" remained unpaid. See Burnett, *Letters*, VII, 51; JM Notes, 21 Feb. 1783, and n. 14.

[10] JM Notes, 24 Jan., and nn. 1–6, 9, 12, 14–16; 13 Feb., and nn. 2–8. The "Come." comprised John Rutledge, chairman, Nathaniel Gorham, Arthur Lee, James Wilson, and John F. Mercer (JM Notes, 13 Feb. 1783). Mercer's request led to the submission of reports on the "Amazon" issue by the committee and William Jackson, assistant secretary at war (*JCC*, XXIV, 141).

11 The "Secy." was Charles Thomson; the unidentified "member" probably was either JM or Rutledge. JM could not have written the footnote on 20 February, because it was on 21 February that the Pennsylvania General Assembly repealed, as violating the ninth article of the Articles of Confederation, the provision of the state law which the sheriff of Chester County had enforced by seizing a portion of the "Amazon's" cargo (Pa. Archives, 1st ser., IX, 756–57; Colonial Records of Pa., XIII, 511–13; NA: PCC, No. 69, fols. 421–24; No. 186, III, 54). In his footnote JM is not clear whether the "conversation" was by members of Congress or of the Pennsylvania legislature, or between members of both. Although ambiguous, JM's comment is of constitutional interest, both because the possibility of Congress voiding the Pennsylvania law was envisaged by some of the members and because the legislature of a sovereign state, on the recommendation of its executive and to avoid conflict, had repealed a statute which encroached upon a field of power granted exclusively to Congress by the Articles of Confederation.

The issue of the "Amazon's" cargo troubled public officials of Pennsylvania for at least two more months. The ship itself, supplied with passports both by Congress and the executive of Pennsylvania, cleared early in March from Philadelphia for Charleston with "divers" refugees from South Carolina as her passengers (Papers of Madison, IV, 315; 317, n. 35; V, 332, n. 7; JCC, XXIV, 144–45; Colonial Records of Pa., XIII, 521). Captain William Armstrong, a British quartermaster who had sailed on the "Amazon" from New York City to supervise the delivery of her cargo to the prisoners of war, remained in Philadelphia to press for the release of the goods seized by the sheriff of Chester County (NA: PCC, No. 78, I. 429; JCC, XXIV, 145, n. 1). The sheriff, under orders of President John Dickinson to assemble and deliver those articles to an agent of Benjamin Lincoln, secretary at war, discovered that a considerable part of them, valued at £5527 5s. 1d. Pennsylvania currency, had been "embezzled" and could not be found (Colonial Records of Pa., XIII, 525–26, 538–39). On 24 March Dickinson and the Supreme Executive Council directed the sheriff to search again for the lost goods and report within ten days (ibid., XIII, 540). The outcome is not mentioned in the Council's printed records. They note only that on 19 April 1783 a statement of costs incurred by the Pennsylvania authorities in connection with the "Amazon" issue was approved (ibid., XIII, 563; Pa. Archives, 1st ser., X, 6–7, 12–13). The news of the signing of the preliminary treaty of peace, soon followed by negotiations for the release of all prisoners of war, may explain why the issue of the "embezzled" goods was not pressed (Pa. Packet, 18, 25, 27 Mar.; 10, 12, 15 Apr. 1783).

12 The first paragraph of the "Resolution" declared that the cargo of the British flag-of-truce ship "Amazon" had not violated "the passport granted by" Washington, and the second stated that all of the cargo "ought to be sent" by the Pennsylvania authorities "with all expedition, and without any let or hindrance, to the prisoners for whose use" the "Cloathing and other necessaries" had been "designed" (JCC, XXIV, 141–42).

13 Probably to signify that the rest of his notes for 20 February were not on the proceedings of Congress, JM placed one bracket at the beginning and another at the close of this paragraph. FitzSimons' residence was in the "North Part" of the Philadelphia Dock Ward, which bordered on the south line of the Middle Ward, where JM lived (Pa. Archives, 3d ser., XVI, 773, 803; John F. Watson, Annals of Philadelphia and Pennsylvania in the Olden Time . . . revised by Willis P. Hazard [3 vols.; Philadelphia, 1927], III, 235; Penn Mutual Life Insurance Company, The Independence Square Neighborhood [Philadelphia, 1926], map opp. p. 15).

14 Among the taxes suggested by one or another member of Congress to supplement the proposed impost had been a tax on buildings and improved land, adjusted to their value or quantity or a combination of both, a poll tax, salt tax, window

tax, and excise taxes on various commodities. Although every one of these had been opposed because it would fall more heavily on one state or section than on the others, Hamilton contended that for this very reason, several varieties of taxes could be selected which would equitably counterbalance each other in their incidence upon the diverse economic pursuits within the United States (Syrett and Cooke, *Papers of Hamilton,* III, 269). No doubt he upheld this view the more insistently because of his tenacious advocacy of a permanent, general, and sufficient revenue for Congress' use.

Gorham, on the other hand, had recommended that Congress concentrate solely upon having the states ratify a revised impost amendment to the Articles of Confederation. Thus, although he shared in the "general concurrence" mentioned by JM, Gorham must have recognized that his own state of Massachusetts, as well as Rhode Island, would be deprived of one of its main sources of public revenue if Congress should receive the proceeds from an impost. Hence, if additional taxes should be recommended, he probably would support only those which would bear less heavily upon New England than upon the South (JM Notes, 27 Jan.; 28 Jan.; 29 Jan.; 12 Feb.; 18 Feb.; 19 Feb., and n. 17; JM to Randolph, 4 Feb. 1783).

15 Hamilton was a veteran of long service in the army and also a correspondent of Washington (JM Notes, 19 Feb. 1783, and n. 10). Richard Peters had been secretary of the Board of War from 13 June 1776 to 27 November 1777, and a member of the board thereafter until 29 November 1781 (*JCC,* V, 438; IX, 971; XXI, 1087, 1173).

16 JM Notes, 19 Feb. 1783, and nn. 11, 12, 19.

17 This expectation would be substantially fulfilled about three weeks later. See JM Notes, 17 Mar. 1783, and nn. 1, 2.

18 In a letter probably written on 13 February, Hamilton hinted to Washington that he was losing "the confidence of the army" because he was not "espousing its interests with sufficient warmth" (Syrett and Cooke, *Papers of Hamilton,* III, 254). In a letter of 27 February, Joseph Jones, after warning Washington against officers who appeared to be "determined to blow the coals of discord," continued, "I have lately heard there are those who are abandoned enough to use these arts to lessen your popularity in the army in hopes ultimately the weight of your opposition will prove no obstacle to their ambitious designs" (Worthington C. Ford, ed., *Letters of Joseph Jones,* pp. 99–100). See also JM Notes, 19 Feb. 1783, n. 12.

10 At this time Washington's aides-de-camp were Lieutenant Colonels David Cobb of Massachusetts, David Humphreys and Jonathan Trumbull, Jr., of Connecticut, Richard Varick and Benjamin Walker of New York, and Major Hodijah Baylies of Massachusetts (John C. Fitzpatrick, *The Spirit of the Revolution* [Boston, 1924], pp. 75–76). Of these Richard Varick, a friend of Hamilton and formerly an aide-de-camp of Benedict Arnold, was probably one of the members of Washington's family who was rumored to be "unfit & indiscreet," even though he had been exonerated of complicity in Arnold's treason. As Washington's "recording Secretary," Varick transcribed all the headquarters' papers. Washington had complete confidence in Varick's discretion and loyalty (Fitzpatrick, *Writings of Washington,* XXII, 112, 113–15; XXIV, 40; XXVII, 289–90; Syrett and Cooke, *Papers of Hamilton,* III, 478–79, 594–95, 659).

20 After "Genl," JM heavily deleted several words. To suggest that they may have been "Gates' expert hand" is to construct the first two words from only two or three still discernible letters. Certainly JM interlineated "the" above a canceled "hand." If "Gates' expert" is what he originally wrote, the "as" which is written close to the margin of the page must have been added by JM after he deleted the two dubious words.

Major General Horatio Gates, second in command of the main army, was a friend of Colonel Walter Stewart of Philadelphia. By 12 March 1783, if not before, Washington believed that Stewart served as a liaison between those men making the "plans" in Philadelphia and those circulating "anonymous papers" at Newburgh (JCC, XXVI, 214, n. 2; Papers of Madison, II, 279; 281, n. 4; Syrett and Cooke, Papers of Hamilton, III, 288, n. 1). For those "papers" and Major John Armstrong, Jr., aide-de-camp of Gates and a son of Major General John Armstrong of the Pennsylvania state line, see JM Notes, 17 Mar. 1783, and nn. 1, 2.

Notes on Debates

MS (LC: Madison Papers). For a description of the manuscript of Notes on Debates, see Papers of Madison, V, 231–34.

Friday Feby. 21.

Mr. Mercer made some remarks tending to a reconsideration of the act declaring general funds to be necessary, which revived the discussion of that subject.[1]

Mr Madison said that he had observed throughout the proceedings of Congress relative to the establishment of such funds that the power delegated to Congress by the confederation had been very differently construed by different members & that this difference of construction had materially affected their reasonings & opinions on the several propositions which had been made;[2] that in particular it had been represented by sundry members that Congress was merely an Executive body; and therefore that it was inconsistent with the principles of liberty & the spirit of the Constitution, to submit to them a permanent revenue which wd. be placing the purse & the sword in the same hands;[3] that he wished the true doctrine of the confederation to be ascertained as it might perhaps remove some embarrassments; and towards that end would offer his ideas on the subject.

He said that he did not conceive in the first place that the opinion was sound that the power of Congress in cases of revenue was in no respect Legislative, but merely Executive: and in the second place that admitting the power to be Executive a permanent revenue collected & dispensed by them in the discharge of the debts to wch. it sd. be appropriated, would be inconsistent with the nature of an Executive body, or dangerous to the liberties of the republic.[4]

As to the first opinion he observed that by the articles of Confederation Congs. had clearly & expressly the right to fix the quantum of revenue necessary for the public exigences, & to require the same from the States respectively in proportion to the value of their land; that the requisitions thus made were a law to the States, as much as the acts of the latter for complying with them were a law to their individual members:[5] that the fœderal constitution[6] was as sacred & obligatory as the internal constitutions of the several States; and that nothing could justify the States in disobeying acts warranted by it, but some previous abuse or infraction on the part of Congs.; that as a proof that the power of fixing the quantum & making requisitions of money, was considered as a legislative power over the purse, he would appeal to the proposition made by the British Minister of giving this power to the B. Parliamt. & leaving to the American assemblies the privilege of complying in their own modes; & to the reasonings of Congress & the several States on that proposition.[7] He observed further that by the articles of Confederation was delegated to Congs. a right to borrow money indefinitely, and emit bills of Credit which was a species of borrowing, for repayment & redemption of which the faith of the States was pledged & their legislatures constitutionally bound.[8] He asked whether these powers were reconcileable with the idea that Congress was a body merely Executive? He asked what would be thought in G. B. from whose constitution our Political reasonings were so much drawn, of an attempt to prove that a power of making requisitions of money on the Parliament, & of borrowing money for discharge of which the Parlt sd. be bound, might be annexed to the Crown without changing its quality of an Executive branch; and that the leaving to the Parliamt. the mode only of complying with the requisitions of the Crown, would be leaving to it its supreme & exclusive power of Legislation?[9]

As to the second point he referred again to the British Constitution & the mode in which provision was made for the public debts; observing that although the Executive had no authority to contract a debt; yet that when a debt had been authorized or admitted by the parliament a permanent & irrevocable revenue was granted by the Legislature, to be collected & dispensed by the Executive; and that this practice had never been deemed a subversion of the Constitution or a dangerous association of a power over the purse with the power of the Sword.[10]

If these observations were just as he concieved them to be, the establishment of a permanent revenue not by any assumed authority of Congress, but by the authority of the States at the recommendation of Congs: to be collected & applied by the latter to the discharge of the public debts, could not be deemed inconsistent with the spirit of the fœderal constitution, or subversive of the principles of liberty; and that all objections drawn from such a supposition ought [to] be withdrawn. Whether other objections of sufficient weight might not lie agst. such an establishmt. was another question. For his part altho' for various reasons* he had wished for such a plan as most eligible,[11] he had never been sanguine that it was practicable & the discussions which had taken place had finally satisfied him that it would be necessary to limit the call for a general revenue to duties on commerce & to call for the deficiency in the most permanent way that could be reconciled with a revenue established within each State separately & appropriated to the Common Treasury. He said the rule which he had laid down to himself in this business was to concur in every arrangemt. that sd. appear necessary for an honorable & just fulfilment of the public engagements; & in no measure tending to augment the power of Congress which sd appear to be unnecessary; and particularly disclaimed the idea of perpetuating a public debt.[16]

Mr. Lee in answer to Mr. Madison said the doctrine maintained by him was pregnant with dangerous consequences to the liberties of the confederated States; that notwithstanding the specious arguments that had been employed it was an established truth that the purse ought not to be put into the same hands with the Sword;[17] that like arguments had been used in favor of Ship money in the reign of Charles I it being then represented as essential to the support of the Govt., that the Executive should be assured of the means of fulfilling its engagements for the pub-

---

* Among other reasons privately weighing with him, he had observed that many of the most respectable people of America supposed the preservation of the Confederacy, essential to secure the blessings of the revolution; and permant funds for discharging debts essential to the preservation of Union.[12] A disappointmt to this class wd. certainly abate their ardor & in a critical emergence might incline them to prefer some political connection with G. B. as a necessary cure for our internal instability, again Without permanent & general funds he did not concieve that the danger of convulsions from the army could be effectually obviated, lastly he did not think that any thing wd. be so likely to prevent disputes among the States with the calamities consequent on them.[13] The States were jealous of each other, each supposing itself to be on the whole a creditor to the others: The Eastern States in particular thought themselves so with regard to the S. States (see Mr. Ghorum in the debates of this day). If general funds were not introduced it was not likely the balances wd. be ever be discharged, even if they sd. be liquidated.[14] The consequence wd. be a rupture of the confederacy. The E. States wd. at sea be powerful & rapacious, the S. opulent & weak. This wd. be a temptation. the demands on the S. Sts would be an occasion. Reprisals wd. be instituted. Foreign aid would be called in by first the weaker, then the stronger side; & finally both be made subservient to the wars & politics of Europe.[15]

lic service:[18] He said it had been urged by several in behalf of such an establishment for public credit that without it Congress was nothing more than a rope of sand. on this head he would be explicit; he had rather see Congress a rope of sand than a rod of Iron.[19] He urged finally as a reason why some States would not & ought not to concur in granting to Congress a permanent revenue, that some States as Virga, would receive back a small part by paymt. from the U. S. to its Citizens; whilst others as Pena. wd. receive a vast surplus; & consequently be enriched by draining the former of its wealth.[20]

Mr. Mercer said if he conceived the fœderal compact to be such as it had been represented he would immediately withdraw from Congress & do every thing in his power to destroy its existence: that if Congs. had a right to borrow money as they pleased and to make requisitions on the States that wd. be binding on them, the liberties of the States were ideal;[21] that requisitions ought to be consonant to the Spirit of liberty; that they should go frequently & accompanied with full information. that the States must be left to judge of the nature of them, of their abilities to comply with them & to regulate their compliance accordingly; he laid great stress on the omission of Congs. to transmit half yearly to the States an acct. of the monies borrowed by them &c. and even insinuated that this omission had absolved the States in some degree from the engagements.[22] He repeated his remarks on the injustice of the rule by which loan office certificates had been settled, & his opinion that some defalcations would be necessary.[23]

Mr. Holten was opposed to all permanent funds, and to every arrangement not within the limits of the Confederation.[24]

Mr. Hamilton enlarged on the general utility of permanent funds to the fœderal interests of this Country, & pointed out the difference between the nature of the Constitution of the British Executive, & that of the U. S. in answer to Mr. Lee's reasoning from the case of Ship money.[25]

Mr. Ghorum adverted with some warmth to the doctrines advanced by Mr. Lee & Mercer concerning the loan office Creditors. He said the Union could never be maintained on any other ground than that of Justice; that some States had suffered greatly from the deficiencies of others already; that if Justice was not to be obtained through the fœderal system & this system was to fail as would necessarily follow, it was time this should be known that some of the States might be forming other confederacies adequate to the purposes of their safety.[26]

This debate was succeeded by a discharge of the Committee from the business of devising the means requisite for restoring public credit &c &c,[27] and the business referred to a Come. consisting of Mr. Ghorum Mr. Hamilton, Mr. Madison, Mr. Fitzimmons & Mr. Rutlidge.[28]

[1] For "the act," see JM Notes, 29 Jan., and n. 13. For the "discussion" preceding the adoption of "the act," see also JM Notes, 24 Jan.; 27 Jan.; 28 Jan. 1783. The nature of John Francis Mercer's "remarks" probably can be inferred from what he said later in the debate on this day and what he had said, as summarized by JM in his notes for 5–6 Feb., n. 9; 12 Feb., and n. 12; 17 Feb., and n. 1; 18 Feb.; 19 Feb. 1783. See also JM to Randolph, 18 Feb. 1783, and n. 3.

[2] JM Notes, 13 Jan., and n. 17; 14 Jan., and nn. 4–6, 9; 24 Jan., and nn. 2, 4; 27 Jan.; 28 Jan. 1783, and nn. 10, 11, 45; JM to Randolph, 14 Jan.; 11 Feb. 1783.

[3] For the oft-used warning that a union of "the purse & the sword in the same hands" would permit their possessor to be a tyrant, see remarks by Arthur Lee and Mercer as summarized by JM (JM Notes, 28 Jan., and n. 5; 12 Feb. 1783, and n. 12).

[4] The sharp disagreements between leaders both in and out of Congress concerning the intention of the framers of the Articles of Confederation suggest that JM was idealistic in hoping for his fellow delegates and the members of state legislatures to accept a single "true doctrine" about the scope and nature of the powers of Congress. The issue was more than academic, for if Congress was altogether an "executive," as the term was used in the debate, it was confined to the passive role of executing the will of state legislatures, or at least of nine of them, conveyed in letters to their delegates or to the president of Congress. "Legislative," however, connoted both initiatory and discretionary power exercised within the broad fields of power conferred upon Congress by the Articles of Confederation. Although its framers neglected to describe those fields or Congress as either "executive" or "legislative," they seem to have viewed "the United States, in Congress Assembled" as a permanent body, fluctuating in membership and essentially international in character, which should embody in its "acts," "resolves," "reports," and "ordinances" the concerted will of the Confederation on important domestic and foreign problems requiring a united front to be handled effectively (JCC, V, 546–54, 674–89; XIX, 214–23). Congress obviously had created "the executive departments" of foreign affairs, war, and finance, but many of its other proceedings, in conformance with the powers delegated in the Articles of Confederation, were as obviously "legislative" or "legislative-executive" in nature. See, for example, JCC, VII, 329; XX, 469–71; XXI, 894–96; JM Notes, 18 Feb. 1783, n. 14.

By insisting that a power should be labeled in accordance with its nature, JM skillfully refuted the arguments of Arthur Lee, David Howell, and other delegates. They, by disregarding the vast differences in origin and structure between the governments of the United States and Great Britain, held that the congressional powers "of determining on peace and war," "sending and receiving ambassadors," and "entering into treaties and alliances" must be "executive" in nature, because in Great Britain they were exclusively, except for treaties alienating portions of the imperial domain, the prerogatives of the Crown rather than of Parliament (JCC, XIX, 217; Papers of Madison, IV, 241; 242, n. 3; William Bennett Munro, The Governments of Europe [New York, 1925], pp. 38, 48–49). Even granting the "executive" quality of those powers would not warrant the inference of Lee and his supporters that congressional authority "in cases of revenue" must be of the same nature.

[5] JM's reference was to articles VIII and XIII of the Articles of Confederation (JCC, XIX, 217, 221). His statement is also supported by "the form" of ratification, adopted by Congress on 26 June 1778, and by the acts of ratification by several state

legislatures (*JCC*, XI, 657–58, 663–64, 666–67; XII, 1161–63; XIII, 187; XIV, 618; XV, 1058–59).

⁶ After originally writing "constitution," JM canceled it and wrote "compact" above it. He then deleted "compact" and rewrote "constitution." On 10 July 1778 Congress had designated the Articles of Confederation as "the glorious compact" (*JCC*, XI, 681). See also JM Notes, 14 Jan., and n. 6; 28 Jan. 1783, and nn. 9, 27–29.

⁷ JM referred to the "conciliatory motion" of Lord North, offered in the House of Commons on 20 February 1775 and adopted a week later (*Hansard's Parliamentary Debates*, XVIII, cols. 319–20, 338, 358; XIX, cols. 763–64, 806, 815, 817). The motion invited the legislature of each British colony in America to submit a plan for making sufficient revenue "disposable by Parliament" to help pay for "the common defence" and to support the colony's "civil government" and "administration of justice." If the King and Parliament should approve the plan, Parliament would "for bear" to "levy any duty, tax, or assessment" on that colony, "except only such duties as it may be expedient to continue to levy or to impose for the regulation of commerce" and would credit "the account of" that colony with "the nett produce of the duties last mentioned."

Both the address of the Virginia House of Burgesses on 12 June and of the Second Continental Congress on 31 July 1775 rejecting the offer in the "conciliatory motion" were drafted almost entirely by Thomas Jefferson (Boyd, *Papers of Jefferson*, I, 170–74, 230–33; *JCC*, II, 224–34). Among the reasons stated in each of these documents for refusing to accept the proposal were that (1) it did not surrender the "pretended right" of Parliament to tax the colonies but only extended a conditional offer to suspend the exercise of the power; and (2) it unjustly maintained that Parliament rather than a colony should prescribe how the revenue derived from taxing its own citizens should be spent.

⁸ JM referred to Articles IX, XII, and XIII of the Articles of Confederation (*JCC*, XIX, 219–20, 221; JM Notes, 28 Jan., and n. 27). For the extent to which each of the thirteen sovereign states could be "constitutionally bound," see the last clause of Article II of the Articles of Confederation (*JCC*, XIX, 214; JM Notes, 28 Jan., and nn. 23, 28; 19 Feb. 1783, n. 5).

⁹ By "the Crown," JM apparently meant "the King" or "the King in Privy Council."

¹⁰ See n. 3, above; also JM Notes, 24 Jan., and n. 4; 19 Feb. 1783, and n. 15. Upon the accession of each new sovereign in the eighteenth century, Parliament allocated definite sources of revenue, known as the "civil list revenues," for his support and that of his household, and to be "collected & dispensed" by him within the terms of the "settlement." In 1761 George III surrendered entirely his interest in the hereditary revenues of the Crown in England for the grant of a civil list of £800,000 a year, from which he paid the salaries of judges and ambassadors and certain pensions. Although he retained hereditary revenues in Scotland, possessed separate civil lists in Ireland and the duchies of Cornwall and Lancaster, and was entitled to some admiralty and other dues, the whole totaling nearly an additional million pounds per annum, he successfully appealed to Parliament in 1780 for the payment of debts beyond his ability to discharge (F[rederic] W[illiam] Maitland, *The Constitutional History of England* [Cambridge, England, 1919], pp. 373, 433–36, 440–41; William Hunt, *The History of England from the Accession of George III, to the Close of Pitt's First Administration (1760–1801)* [London, 1905], p. 13).

¹¹ JM Notes, 24 Jan., and n. 20; 25 Jan., and nn. 7, 13; 27 Jan., and nn. 13, 14, 16; 28 Jan., and nn. 3, 11, 27, 28, 41, 45; 29 Jan., and nn. 8, 14, 36; 31 Jan., and n. 11; 12 Feb., and n. 1; 18 Feb., and nn. 4, 8; 19 Feb., and nn. 3, 7, 17; 20 Feb., and n. 14; JM to Randolph, 28 Jan.; 4 Feb.; 11 Feb.; 18 Feb. 1783, n. 3. For the passage by JM to which footnotes No. 12, 13, 14, and 15 refer, see his own footnote at the bottom of page 272.

¹² Among "the most respectable people," JM probably included Thomas Fitz-Simons, Alexander Hamilton, Robert Morris, David Ramsay, George Washington, and James Wilson (JM Notes, 13 Jan.; 24 Jan., and n. 20; 27 Jan., and n. 12; 28 Jan., and n. 34; 29 Jan., and nn. 14, 41; 12 Feb., and n. 8; 18 Feb.; 19 Feb., and n. 23; 20 Feb., and n. 14; JM to Randolph, 28 Jan.; 18 Feb. 1783, and n. 3; Fitzpatrick, *Writings of Washington*, XXVI, 17–18, 82–86, 103–4, 183–88; Clarence L. Ver Steeg, *Robert Morris*, pp. 128–29).

¹³ JM Notes, 13 Jan., and nn. 17, 21; 28 Jan., and n. 23; 8 Feb., n. 3; 11 Feb., and n. 2; 12 Feb., and n. 15; 18 Feb.; 19 Feb., and nn. 11, 12, 19; 20 Feb., and nn. 17, 18; JM to Randolph, 14 Jan.; 22 Jan., and n. 8; 11 Feb.; 25 Feb. 1783; Fitzpatrick, *Writings of Washington*, XXV, 226–29, 430–31; Clarence L. Ver Steeg, *Robert Morris*, pp. 139, 153–54, 166–72, 182–83; Burnett, *Letters*, VII, 34, n. 3; 50, n. 3.

¹⁴ JM Notes, 27 Jan., and nn. 13, 27; 29 Jan.; 30 Jan., and n. 6; 31 Jan., and n. 11; 19 Feb., and n. 6; 20 Feb., nn. 7, 9, 14; JM to Randolph, 4 Feb. JM also could have referred appropriately to his summary of Nathaniel Gorham's remarks on 20 February (JM Notes, 20 Feb. 1783, and n. 8). JM's reference to "Mr. Ghorum" demonstrates that he wrote the footnote after completing the text of his notes for this day.

¹⁵ In his letter of 25 February to Randolph (*q.v.*), JM repeated the substance of the footnote to this point.

¹⁶ The contrast between JM's position as revealed in the last two sentences of this paragraph and his nationalistic view of the powers of Congress expressed in his speech of 28 January (JM Notes, 28 Jan. 1783, and nn. 27, 28) makes clear how much he had become willing, without a surrender of principle, to concede in order to avoid the dismal future he described earlier in the paragraph. Judging from Joseph Jones's letter of 27 February to Washington, Jones and JM were closely attuned in their outlook upon the issue (Burnett, *Letters*, VII, 60–63). Although the long-extended debates had not tempered Hamilton's nationalism, including his belief in the efficacy of "perpetuating a public debt," he, too, for the sake of staving off disunion, expressed the hope that his state of New York would "chearfully comply" with the plan of evaluation which Congress had adopted, even though he had voted against it as "founded on false principles" (Syrett and Cooke, *Papers of Hamilton*, III, 268–74). See also JM Notes, 28 Jan., and n. 9; 19 Feb. 1783, and nn. 3, 7, 13, 20; Clarence L. Ver Steeg, *Robert Morris*, p. 175.

¹⁷ For Arthur Lee's and John F. Mercer's earlier insistence upon this "established truth," see n. 3, above. By 27 February, not without some sacrifice of principle, Mercer would change his position on the general issue (JM Notes, 27 Feb. 1783, and n. 12).

¹⁸ "Ship money," narrowly defined, was a levy imposed by the king of England upon ports, maritime towns, and counties in a time of emergency for the support of the navy. Although King Charles I in 1628 had accepted the statute known as the "Petition of Right," with its denial to him of the power of taking "any gift, loan, benevolence or such like charge" without the consent of Parliament, he had refused to construe this prohibition to include ship money. In the "Ship Money Case" of 1637, a royal court sustained the king by ruling that "a statute derogatory from the prerogative does not bind the king and the king may dispense with any law in cases of necessity." Parliament in 1641 declared this judgment void, and the king assented on 7 August of that year (F. W. Maitland, *Constitutional History of England*, pp. 298–300, 307–8).

¹⁹ The "rope of sand" metaphor, dating in Greek literature from at least as early as the second century A.D., was used frequently by Americans during the Revolution (Samuel Jebb, ed., *Aelius Aristides . . . opera omnia graece & latine* [2 vols.; Oxford, 1722–30], II, 309; Burnett, *Letters*, III, 322, VI, 58). For "rod of Iron," see Psalms 2:9; Revelation 12:5.

[20] *Papers of Madison*, V, 459–60; JM Notes, 8 Feb., and n. 3; 19 Feb., and nn. 6, 18; 20 Feb. 1783, and nn. 4, 6, 9.

[21] That is, "visionary." See nn. 1–9, above; JM Notes, 12 Feb., and n. 12; JM to Randolph, 18 Feb., and nn. 2, 3; 25 Feb. 1783.

[22] JM Notes, 12 Feb., and n. 5; 19 Feb. 1783, and n. 15.

[23] JM Notes, 18 Feb., and nn. 5, 7; 19 Feb., and nn. 14, 18, 20; 20 Feb. 1783, and nn. 4, 6–8.

[24] Samuel Holten, who from 1778 to 1780 had been a delegate from Massachusetts in Congress, submitted his second-term credentials on 4 February (*JCC*, XXIV, 107). See also JM Notes, 27 Feb. 1783.

[25] JM Notes, 19 Feb. 1783, and n. 15.

[26] JM Notes, 12 Feb., and n. 7; 18 Feb., and n. 5; 19 Feb.; 20 Feb., and n. 6; JM to Randolph, 25 Feb. 1783.

[27] Congress accepted the recommendation of the committee of the whole that it "be discharged" from the instructions of 29 January "to consider further the means of restoring and supporting public credit, and of obtaining from the states substantial funds for funding the whole debt of the United States," and that this "business" be "referred to a special committee" (JM Notes, 29 Jan. 1783, and n. 7; *JCC*, XXIV, 97, 144).

[28] In their outlook upon "the business," Hamilton and FitzSimons were nationalistic, Rutledge stressed states' rights, and Gorham and JM, although differing on particular issues, probably would co-operate in seeking a compromise between the two extremes (JM Notes, 27 Jan.; 28 Jan.; 29 Jan.; 12 Feb.; 18 Feb.; 19 Feb., and n. 20; 20 Feb. 1783, and nn. 7, 14; n. 16, above). For the first report of this committee, see JM Notes, 27 Feb. 1783, and n. 8.

Benjamin Harrison to Virginia Delegates

FC (Virginia State Library). In the hand of Thomas Meriwether. Addressed to "The Virginia Delegates in Congress."

RICHMOND February 21th. 1783.

GENTLEMEN

Your favor of the 11th. Instant[1] came to Hand by the Post, as did the missing Letter by the Post before which makes it probable that the delay proceeded from it's not geting to the Post master before the Mail was closed.[2] I enclose you a Paper sent to me by the Commissioners of our Navy at Portsmouth which they received by a Flag from the Lyon Man of War then in Linhaven Bay.[3] the Captain of the Lyon obtain'd it from a french Brig from France which he took within the Capes going to Baltimore. I think you may depend on it's being the Substance of the King of Great Britains Speach tho' it has suffered greatly in the translations both by the french man who turned it into french and by the translator on board the Lyon, the Letter to Townsend bears evident Marks of authenticity.[4] I am led to give more Credit to them from a report which was circulated here some Days ago that the Speach was actually in North Carolina brought by a Vessel from Nantes that left it the 26 of December and that it contain'd in Substance what you may collect from this.[5] I can not help congratulating you on the Occasion tho' I have some trifling fears that I may be a little premature. The necessary Certificate for the Settlement of Nathans Accounts was forwarded you by the last Post and hope will get to hand in Time to save the State from the payment of a sum of Money it does not owe and that Nathan never paid.[6]

I am Gentlemen &c.

B.H.

[1] Q.v.

[2] The "missing Letter" was that of the delegates on 21 January to Harrison (q.v.). See also Harrison to Delegates, 31 Jan.; 7 Feb.; Delegates to Harrison, 11 Feb. 1783. There appears to have been at that time no one with the official title of "Post Master" of Philadelphia, but Harrison probably had in mind Ebenezer Hazard, postmaster general, or his "assistant or clerk," James Bryson (1744–1813). Congress had appointed Bryson to this position, which apparently was equivalent to being Hazard's "deputy" or the assistant postmaster general, on 28 January 1782, following about five years of service by him as "surveyor" of the post offices in "the middle district," comprising the area from Philadelphia to Edenton, N.C. (NA: PCC, No. 61, fols. 495, 499; JCC, IX, 860; XV, 1203; XVII, 553; XXII, 60, 66, n. 1).

Although Congress on 18 October 1782 had empowered the postmaster general to appoint as many postmasters "as he shall think proper," Bryson continued to call himself "assistant" rather than postmaster of Philadelphia (JCC, XXIII, 670; Pa. Packet, 26 Oct., 29 Oct., 16 Nov. 1782). On the date of the present letter, he was making an extended trip "to the southward to settle the posts," and was not expected to return to Philadelphia "before June" (Belknap Papers, Collections of the Massachusetts Historical Society, 5th ser., Vols. II and III [Boston, 1877], II, 199, 203). Sometime later Hazard evidently named Bryson "postmaster of Philadelphia," for that is his title on a "Civil List" which appears to have been prepared in 1787 (NA: PCC, No. 61, fol. 587). There is no doubt that Bryson's tenure ended about 1 October 1789, when Hazard was succeeded as postmaster general by Samuel Osgood (Journal of the Executive Proceedings of the Senate of the United States of America [Washington, 1828——], I, 33; Belknap Papers, III, 192–93, 198, 201). Thereafter the career of Bryson is obscure. He is said to have been in Newport, Ky., at the time of his death. Unless he was then on a trip to the West, he had probably moved there after 1800, for no "James Bryson" is listed among the taxpayers of Kentucky either in that year or in 1790 (Charles Brunk Heineman and Gaius Marcus Brumbaugh, comps., "First Census" of Kentucky, 1790 [Washington, 1940], p. 16; G. Glenn Clift, comp., "Second Census" of Kentucky, 1800 [Frankfort, 1954], p. 38; Lineage Book of the National Society of the Daughters of the American Revolution, CXIV [1915], 153–54).

[3] The unidentified French brig had sailed from Lorient (Va. Gazette, 22 Feb. 1783). For the sixty-four-gun frigate "Lion" and Lynnhaven Bay, see Jefferson to JM, 7–8 Feb., n. 3; 14 Feb. 1783 (2d letter), n. 22. The enclosure is missing, but its probable contents are summarized in n. 4 (q.v.). The "Paper" had been forwarded to Harrison in a letter of 15 February 1783 from Colonel Thomas Newton, Jr. (1742–1807), one of the three commissioners of the Virginia navy (MS in Va. State

Library; *Cal. of Va. State Papers*, III, 436). The other commissioners were Thomas Brown (d. 1803) and Captain Paul Loyall (*ca.* 1721–1807) (*Norfolk Herald*, 15 Oct. 1803; *Norfolk Gazette and Publick Ledger*, 2 Feb. 1807).

Newton, an officer in, and by 1781 commander of, the Norfolk County militia, was a member of the House of Burgesses, 1765–1775, of the Virginia conventions of 1775 and 1776, of the House of Delegates, 1779–1783, 1794–1797, and of the Senate, 1798–1805. He also served four terms as mayor of Norfolk between 1780 and 1794. On 8 March 1794 Newton became one of the seven federal inspectors of the surveys and ports of Virginia. On 23 December 1805 he was appointed federal collector for the district of Norfolk and Portsmouth, a position which he continued to hold until his death (Swem and Williams, *Register*, pp. 9–66 *passim*; *Journal of the Executive Proceedings of the Senate of the United States*, I, 102, 111; II, 8, 10; *Papers of Madison*, II, 296, n. 6; IV, 360, nn. 22, 23; 431, n. 1; V, 90, n. 2; *Va. Mag. Hist. and Biog.*, XX [1912], 365; XXX [1922], 87–88).

⁴ The "Paper" mentioned in the second sentence of this letter probably summarized in garbled form the announcement by King George III on 5 December 1782 to Parliament of the signing of preliminary articles of peace between Great Britain and the United States, and the letter of (not "to") Thomas Townshend on the same day informing the lord mayor of London that a copy of the preliminary treaty had been received (*Va. Gazette*, 22 Feb. 1783). A corrected copy of the king's statement appeared in the *Virginia Gazette* on 1 March. The Virginia delegates, who on 12 February first heard of the king's announcement, sent a copy of it two days later by special messenger to Governor Harrison (JM Notes, 13 Feb., n. 10; Delegates to Harrison, 18 Feb., and n. 3; JM to Jefferson, 18 Feb., n. 2; to Randolph, 18 Feb.; Harrison to Delegates, 24 Feb. 1783).

⁵ The "Vessel" has not been identified, but it probably brought to David Ross the letter mentioned by Governor Harrison in his letter of 24 February to the Virginia delegates (*q.v.*).

⁶ *Papers of Madison*, V, 202–3, and nn. 1, 3, 4; 228–29, and n. 6; 344, and n. 10; Harrison to Delegates, 15 Feb. 1783 and citations in n. 1.

From Edmund Randolph

RC (LC: Madison Papers). Unsigned but in Randolph's hand. Parts of the manuscript are hard to read. Besides revising a few words by writing over rather than above them, he used a porous paper. This caused the ink to spread, thereby blotting several adjacent letters together. He posted the letter on 1 March. See Randolph to JM, 1 Mar. 1783.

Pettus's¹ Feby. 22. 1783.

My dear sir

I easily conceive the difficulty if not impracticability of devising some middle mode, in which the various opinions of the states concerning the assessment of lands can be brought to coincide.² The evil of miscarrying in the attempt, tho' it may perhaps ultimately affect Virginia, may be remedied with respect to the American interest in general, by satisfying the different legislatures, that a new scheme for adjusting the united fund must be adopted.[3] But so earnest will our countrymen be in the retention of the old form, that, I fear, nothing less than a full and clear state[4] from congress or yourselves, of the many obstacles, which occur, will convert them to the adoption of a new plan, and a cession of the 5. percent.[5]

The reports, which have circulated for a few days past, of the appearance of a british fleet in the bay, were founded on the ship or two, which have hitherto obstructed Mr. J's departure.[6]

I am informed, that the executive are now employed in the appropriation of the recruiting money: but cannot assign a reason for the delay until this time.[7]

As a farmer, I have much to complain of violent and excessive rains, which have fallen throughout this winter. The necessary preparations for the early crops have not, I believe been made any where, and a scanty harvest this year will amount to almost a famine next in our neighbourhood. At this time one snow would create greater havock among the cattle of Henrico than the enemy so scarce is provender.[8]

The terrors, which led   to resign, are too powerful for McCl—g to incounter: and the precariousness of the office increases the impediments in a compound rate. He shall be apprized of them, according to th[e] request, contained in your favor of the 7. inst.[9]

[1] *Papers of Madison*, IV, 148, n. 2. See also n. 8, below.

[2] JM to Jefferson, 11 Feb. and the citations in nn. 8 and 9; to Randolph, 11 Feb. 1783. For the "various opinions" in regard to "the assessment of lands," see JM Notes, 12 Feb., and nn. 1, 13; 14 Feb., and n. 7; 17 Feb., and nn. 1, 3, 4; 18 Feb., and nn. 4, 8; 19 Feb., and nn. 6, 7, 11, 18–20; 20 Feb., and nn. 6, 7, 9; 21 Feb., and n. 16; JM to Randolph, 18 Feb. 1783, and n. 3.

[3] Viewing the matter as a nationalist, Randolph was convinced that equitably providing for "the united fund," or in the phrase of Article VIII of the Articles of Confederation, the "common treasury" (*JCC*, XIX, 217), could be attained only by amending the Articles.

[4] That is, "statement." In this connection JM was the principal author of the "Address to the States, by the United States in Congress Assembled," adopted by Congress on 26 April 1783 (*q.v.*). See also JM Notes, 18 March 1783.

[5] JM Notes, 12 Feb., nn. 3, 5, 6, 9, 12–15; 13 Feb., and n. 1; 18 Feb., and nn. 10–12; 19 Feb., and nn. 3, 4, 14–17, 21, 22; 20 Feb., n. 14; 21 Feb., and nn. 4, 16, 27, 28; JM to Randolph, 18 Feb., and nn. 1, 2; 25 Feb. 1783.

[6] Jefferson to JM, 7 Feb., and nn. 3, 4, 8; 14 Feb. (2d letter), and n. 22; JM to Jefferson, 13 Feb. 1783, and n. 3.

[7] For a summary of the contents of a statute enacted by the Virginia General Assembly on 2 July 1782 for recruiting Virginia continental troops, see *Papers of Madison*, V, 93, n. 9; 313, and n. 3. For examples of the allocation of money for the payment of bounties to recruits and fees to the county lieutenants and other officials in charge of recruitment, see *JCSV*, III, 165, 168, 214, 223; McIlwaine, *Official Let-*

ters, III, 419–20; 438, 441, 442–43, 452, 456. For at least a partial explanation of "the delay until this time," see *Papers of Madison*, V, 259, n. 7; Harrison to Delegates, 7 Feb., and nn. 4, 5; Randolph to JM, 7 Feb. 1783, and n. 9. See also Randolph to JM, 1 Mar. 1783. At the same time, embarrassed for cash, the executive had been diverting recruitment money to the payment of pressing demands, with the expectation of replacing those outlays from accruals to the contingent fund (*JCSV*, III, 204, 211).

8 Randolph no doubt referred especially to "Henrico," because the house of Dabney Pettus, in which Randolph and his family resided, was in that county.

9 JM to Randolph, 1 Feb. 1783. Robert R. Livingston, secretary for foreign affairs, should be inserted in the blank. For his resignation on 2 December 1782 and his consent given later that month to continue in the office throughout the winter, see *Papers of Madison*, V, 337; 338, nn. 2, 4; 342–43; 353, n. 3; 428, and n. 1; 449. One of the "terrors," which had prompted Livingston's resignation and probably would have been more frightening to Dr. James McClurg, was the heavy financial cost of the office in excess of the $4,000 salary. Other "impediments" were the uncertainty of appointment by Congress, even though McClurg should be nominated, and "the precariousness" of tenure, even though he should become Livingston's successor (*ibid.*, V, 344, n. 5; 358; 402; 406, n. 34; Randolph to JM, 1 Feb. 1783, and n. 8).

Benjamin Harrison to Virginia Delegates

FC (Virginia State Library). In the hand of Thomas L. Savage. Addressed to "The Virginia Delegates in Congress."

RICHMOND Februy. 24th. 1783.

GENTLEMEN

I am much obliged to you for your favor by Express, part of the Speach had reached us before yours came to hand but it was so incorrect that it did not generally obtain Credit.[1] Mr. Ross has a Letter from his Partner Mr. Edwards at Nantes of the 18th. of December advising him that the Treaty of Peace was signed the 13th. of that Month, and that the Notice was given to the Merchants by an Express; as the Writer is a Man of Credit and reputation I have no doubt of the truth of the Account, tho' it is a little misterious your not having it officially.[2] I have paid the Express ten pounds this currency and taken his receipt. If you get official Notice of the Peace you'l please to send me advice of it by Express   an early Knowledge of it will save a very great Expence to the State.[3]

I am Gentlemen &c.

B.H.

1 The delegates probably had sent the "favor" on 14 February. See JM to Randolph, 13 Feb., and n. 3; Harrison to Delegates, 21 Feb. 1783, and n. 4.

2 For David Ross, see *Papers of Madison*, III, 60, n. 8. See also Delegates to Harri-

son, 18 Feb. 1783, n. 3. "Mr. Edwards" may have been William Edwards who, prior to the declaration of war by Great Britain on the Netherlands, had supplied French markets with British goods routed through Dutch ports (William Lee Letter Book Manuscript Copies, pp. 8, 20, in Va. Historical Society).

[3] For the delegates' compliance with this request, see their letter of 12 March 1783, sent to Harrison "by Express." By receiving news of the "official Notice" at the earliest possible moment, "the State" would save money by immediately stopping military preparations, including the payment of bounties to recruits for the Virginia continental line, and by holding government-owned tobacco for the higher price anticipated as a result of increased demand for the commodity overseas. Assurance that the war had ended might also favorably affect the exchange values of the various kinds of paper currency in relation to specie. See Harrison to Delegates, 31 Jan., and n. 5; JM to Randolph, 13 Feb., and n. 3; Randolph to JM, 22 Feb. 1783, and n. 7.

Notes on Debates

MS (LC: Madison Papers). For a description of the manuscript of Notes on Debates, see *Papers of Madison*, V, 231–34.

No Congress till Teusday 25.

In favor of the motion of Mr. Gilman [see Journal of this date][1] to refer the officers of the army for their *half pay* to their respective States[2] it was urged that this plan alone would secure to the officers any advantage from that engagement: since Congress had no independent fund out of which it could be fulfilled, and the States of Cont. & R. I. in particular would not comply with any recommendation of Cong. nor even requisition for that purpose.[3] It was also said that it would be satisfactory to the officers; and that it would apportion on the States that part of the public burden with sufficient equality. Mr. Dyer said that the original promise of Congress on that subject was considered by some of the States as a fetch upon them, and not within the spirit of the authority delegated to Congress.[4] Mr. Wolcot said the States wd. give Congs. nothing whatever unless they were gratified in this particular. Mr. Collins said R. I. had expressly instructed her delegates to oppose every measure tending to an execution of the promise, out of monies under the disposition of Congress.[5]

On the other side it was urged that the half pay was a debt as solemnly contracted as any other debt; and was consequently as binding under the 12th article of Confederation on the States,[6] & that they could not refuse a requisition made for that purpose; that it would be improper to countenance a spirit of that sort by yielding to it; that such concessions on the part of Congs. wd. produce compliances on the part of the States, in other instances, clogged with favorite conditions; that a reference of the officers to the particular States to whose lines they belong, would not be satisfactory to the officers of those States who objected to half pay,[7] and would increase the present irritation of the army; that to do it without their unanimous consent would be a breach of the contract by which the U. S. collectively were bound to them; and above all that the proposed plan, which discharged any particular State which should settle with its officers on this subject, altho' other States might reject the plan, from its proportion of that part of the public burden, was a direct and palpable departure from the law of the Confederation. According to this instrument the whole public burden of debt must be apportioned according to a valuation of land, nor cd. any thing but a unanimous concurrence of the States dispense with this law.[8] According to the plan proposed so much of the public burden as the $\frac{1}{2}$ pay sd. amount to, was to be apportioned according to the number of officers belonging to each line; the plan to take effect as to all those States which should adopt it, without waiting for the unanimous adoption of the States,[9] and that if Congress had authority to make the number of officers the rule of apportioning one part of the public debt on the States, they might extend the rule to any other part or the whole, or might[10] substitute any other arbitrary rule which they should think fit. The motion of Mr. Gilman was negatived   see the ays & noes on the Journal[11]

[1] Brackets inserted by JM. On 25 January Congress appointed a committee, Samuel Osgood chairman, to consider the offer included in the memorial from the army to have full pay for an unspecified number of years substituted in the stead of the half pay for life promised by Congress to army officers who should serve for the duration of the war (JM Notes, 13 Jan., and nn. 11, 21; 25 Jan. 1783, and n. 12). The report of the committee, first submitted on 3 February, was debated inconclusively the next day in the committee of the whole (JM Notes, 4 Feb. 1783, and n. 15). For three weeks thereafter the unfulfilled financial pledges to the ominously discontented army were mentioned frequently in JM's notes and in the letters of the delegates, but the Osgood committee's report apparently did not again become the focus of discussion until 25 February.

This report proposed that the duration-of-war officers in the continental line of each state should decide collectively for themselves and for the supernumerary officers of their line whether to accept full pay for an unspecified number of years or the half pay for life stipulated in the ordinance of Congress of 21 October 1780. The same option should be exercised collectively by officers similarly entitled to half pay for life but who were in the continental corps not associated with any state. General officers should be privileged to decide individually. Half pay for life should be paid "to the widows of such officers as shall die in the service, during their continuance as widows" (JCC, XXIV, 146).

The same page of the journal records that a motion by John Taylor Gilman, seconded by Silas Condict of New Jersey, requested that further debate on the Osgood committee's report be delayed in order to give consideration to a substitute proposal.

2 JM summarized only the first of the two chief recommendations embodied in the Gilman-Condict motion. The second of these proposed that all states which should compensate the qualified officers of their respective continental lines with half pay for life or with an acceptable "commutation for such sum, in gross," should be "fully and finally discharged from their respective proportions of all taxes and all other payments of monies whatsoever, on account of half-pay," provided that they agree to pay "their just proportion" of the money required to assure half pay for life to continental officers who were not members of the continental line of any state. Benjamin Lincoln, secretary at war, should be instructed to report the "names and rank" of the second group of officers to Congress (*JCC*, XXIV, 146–47). The provisions of the ordinance of 17 August 1779, which was superseded by the ordinance of 21 October 1780, closely resembled the recommendations of the Gilman-Condict motion (*JCC*, XIV, 974–76).

3 The arguments noted in this sentence and in the remainder of the paragraph repeated for the most part those voiced in the debate on 4 February (JM Notes, 4 Feb. 1783, and nn. 10, 11, 13, 14).

4 The word "fetch" is used as a noun meaning "stratagem" or "trick." Dyer perhaps had some warrant for his reference to "a fetch." In a long letter of 11 October 1780, commenting upon Congress' plan to "reform" the continental army by merging some of the regiments and thereby rendering some of the officers supernumerary, Washington urged that all officers, including those moved to the inactive list, should be assured of half pay for life, or at least full pay for seven years, following their retirement.

The report of the committee, Samuel Adams, chairman, to which Washington's letter was referred, recommended in this regard only that some of the supernumerary officers be allowed half pay for an unspecified number of years. On 20 October 1780 John Mathews of South Carolina, seconded by JM, moved that the blank be filled with the words "for life." Congress adopted this motion over the opposition of two members of the committee (Adams and Ezekiel Cornell) and, in fact, of all the delegates from the four New England states and New Jersey. The next day, over the unanimous dissent of the delegates from Massachusetts, Connecticut, and New Jersey, Congress further amended the committee's report by adopting the motion of James Duane to guarantee "half pay during life" to all continental officers "who shall continue in the service to the end of the war." The entire report, as amended, was then adopted though the delegates of Massachusetts, Rhode Island, Connecticut, and New Jersey voted in the negative unanimously (Fitzpatrick, *Writings of Washington*, XX, 157–67, and esp. 157–60; *JCC*, XVIII, 786, 931, 956–57, 958–62; *Papers of Madison*, II, 137; 138, n. 5; JM Notes, 4 Feb. 1783, and nn. 10, 11).

5 JM Notes, 4 Feb. 1783, and nn. 10, 14.

6 Article XII of the Articles of Confederation "solemnly pledged" that the United States in Congress assembled, following the ratification of the Articles, would assume the payment of all "bills of credit emitted, monies borrowed and debts contracted by, or under the authority of congress" before the Articles became effective (*JCC*, XIX, 221).

7 See n. 4.

8 The speaker had in mind articles VIII, XII (n. 6, above), and XIII, limiting amendments to those approved by Congress and every state legislature (*JCC*, XIX, 217, 221–22). For Article VIII, see JM Notes, 14 Jan., n. 6; 28 Jan. 1783, n. 5.

9 See n. 2.

10 JM inadvertently wrote this word twice.

11 JM added this sentence in his old age. Six states opposed the motion; two (New Hampshire and Connecticut) favored it. The two delegates of New Jersey were unable to concert their vote, and Massachusetts and Rhode Island were each represented by only one delegate. The five Virginians, who comprised the largest delegation then in Congress, all voted "no," except John Francis Mercer. Following the tally, Congress decided to postpone further consideration of the Osgood committee's report (n. 1, above) until the next day (*JCC*, XXIV, 148).

To Edmund Randolph

RC (LC: Madison Papers). In JM's hand but lacks signature, cover, and docket. The contents of the letter and the handwriting of the interlineated decoding permit no doubt that Randolph was the recipient. Words italicized in the text are those enciphered by JM in Randolph's code. For this code, see *Papers of Madison*, V, 307; 309, n. 1.

PHILADA. Feby. 25th. 1783.

MY DEAR SIR

Congress are still engaged on the subject of providing adequate revenues for the public debts, particularly that due to the army.[1] The recommendation of the Impost will be renewed with perhaps some little variation, to which will be superadded probably a duty on a few enumerated art[i]cles.[2] *Master Mercer altho' he* continues to *be adverse to* the *measure declares now that he will not carry his opposition out of Congress.*[3] Whether any other general revenues will be recommended is very uncertain. A poll tax seems to be the only one sufficiently simple & equal for the purpose, and besides other objections to which even that is liable, the Constitution of Maryland which interdicts such a tax is an insuperable bar.[4] The plan talked of by some for supplying the deficiency is to call on the States to provide each its proportion of a permanent revenue within itself, and, to appropriate it to the continental debt. The objections against this plan are that as the execution of it will depend on a unanimous & continued punctuality in the 13 States; it is a precarious basis for public credit[5]—that the precariousness will be increased by mutual jealousies among the States that others may be sparing themselves exertions which they are submitting to; and that these jealousies will be still more increased by the mutual opinion which prevails that they are comparatively in advance to the U. States; an opinion which cannot be corrected without closing the accounts between all of them & the U. States; prerequisites to which are a valuation of the land,

and a final discrimination of such parts of the separate expenditures of the States as ought to be transferred to the common mass, from such parts as ought in justice to fall on the particular States themselves.[6] Some States also will contend and it would seem neither agst. the principles of justice nor the spirit of the Confederation, for a retrospective abatement of their share of the past debt according to their respective disabilities from year to year throughout the war.[7] What will be the end of this complication of embarrassments time only can disclose. But a greater embarrassment than any is s[t]ill behind. The *discontents and designs of* the *army are every day takeing a more solemn form* It is *now whis-pered* that *they have not only resolved not to lay down their arms* ti[l]l *justice shall be done them* [but] that *to prev[en]t surprize a public declaration will be made to that effect*[8] It is *added and I fear with too much* certainty, *that the influence of General* [Washington] is *rapidly decreaseing in the army insomuch that* it is *even in contemplation to sub-stitute some less scrupulous guardian of their interests*[9]

There are a variety of rumours concerning peace but none of them of sufficient authority to be particularized. The Speech of the King of G B. to his parliament and the letter to the Lord Mayor of London from Secy. Townsend as it is stated are the only respectable evidence yet recd. There are also rumours on the adverse side which have still less the com-plection of authenticity.[10]

A quantity of cloathing on its passage through this State to the British prisoners of war under a passport of Genl Washington was lately siezed and condemned under a law of this State agst. the importation of British goods. After several fruitless experiments to prevail on the siezors to relinquish their appeal to the law, the Legislature have I am told cut the business short by declaring the law as far as it interfered with the au-thority of the passport to be unconstitutional & void ab initio.[11]

You will suffer me to renew my exhortations to an exchange of your office under the State for a seat in the Legislature. It depends much in my opinion on the measures which may be pursued by Congress & the several States within the ensuing period of 6 months whether prosperity & tranquility, *or confusion and disunion* are to be the fruits of the Revo-lution.[12] The seeds of the latter are so thickly sown that nothing but the most enlightened and liberal policy will be able to stifle them. The *easetern*[13] *states* particularly *Massachussetts conceiv*[e] that *compared with* the *Southern* they are greatly in *advance in* the *general account*[14] A respectable *delegate from Massachussetts* a few days ago being a little *chafed* by some *expressions of Masters Lee and Mercer* unfavorable *to*

loan office creditors said that if *justice* was not to be *obtained thro* the
general confederacy, *the sooner* it *was known the better* [so] that some
states might be *forming other confederacys adequate to the purpose*[,]
adding that *some had suffered* immensely *from the* want *of a* propor-
tional compliance with deman[ds] for men & mon[ey] *by others*[15]
However erroneous these ideas may be, do they not *merit serious atten-
ttion?* Unless some amicable & adequate arrangements be speedily taken
for adjusting all the subsisting accounts and discharging the public engagements, a *dissolution of the union* will be *inevitable*   Will not in that
event the S[outhern] S[tates] *which at sea* will be *opulent and* weak, be
an *easey prey to the easetern* which *will be powerful and rapacious? and*
particularly if supposed *c*[l]*aims of justice* are *on the side of the latter*
will they not be a *ready prete*[x]*t for reprisals?*[16]   The consequence of
such a situation would probably be that *at alliances* would be *soug*[h]*t*
first *by the weaker and then by the stronger party and* this *country* be
made subservi[ent] *to the wars and politics of Europe*[17]

I inclose you the residue of the Extract from Mr. J——s remarks, according to my promise.[18] I could have wished for another conveyance
than the post, but preferred the latter to the uncertainty of finding such
an one. The badness of the roads or something else has prevented the
arrival of the post as yet, so that I must suspend acknowledgmt. of your
favor by him till the next week.[19]

Adieu

[1] JM Notes, 29 Jan., and n. 13; 4 Feb., and nn. 7, 10, 11, 13–15; 12 Feb.; 21 Feb.,
and nn. 27, 28; 25 Feb. 1783, and nn. 1–4, 11.
[2] JM Notes, 18 Feb., and nn. 11, 12; 19 Feb., and n. 17; 20 Feb. 1783, and nn. 9, 11.
[3] JM Notes, 12 Feb., and nn. 5, 12; 18 Feb., and n. 3; 21 Feb.; 27 Feb.; JM to
Randolph, 18 Feb. 1783, and nn. 2, 3.
[4] JM Notes, 28 Jan., and nn. 35, 42, 43; 29 Jan. 1783, and n. 16.
[5] JM Notes, 28 Jan., and nn. 11, 23, 45; 29 Jan. 1783, and n. 25.
[6] JM Notes, 28 Jan., and nn. 19, 23; 5–6 Feb., and n. 9; 7 Feb.; 8 Feb., and n. 3; 11
Feb., and n. 2; 19 Feb., and n. 6; 21 Feb. 1783, and n. 14.
[7] JM Notes, 14 Jan., and n. 9; 27 Jan., and nn. 13, 27; 4 Feb.; 17 Feb., and nn. 1,
3, 4; 19 Feb. 1783, and n. 6.
[8] JM to Randolph, 13 Feb., and n. 6; JM Notes, 19 Feb., and nn. 11, 12, 19; 20
Feb. 1783, and nn. 18–20. Instead of using the cipher 156 meaning "but," JM wrote
136 standing for "bar."
[9] JM Notes, 20 Feb. 1783, and nn. 18, 19. Although JM should have encoded
"Washington" as 491, he wrote 490, meaning "way."
[10] JM Notes, 13 Feb., and n. 10; JM to Jefferson, 18 Feb., and n. 2; Harrison to
Delegates, 21 Feb. 1783, and n. 4. An extract from a letter written on 9 December
1782 in Nantes stated that the renewed peace negotiations in Paris "promise either
a speedy termination of hostilities, or an obstinate continuance of them" (*Pa.
Packet,* 25 Feb. 1783).
[11] JM Notes, 13 Feb., and nn. 6, 8; 20 Feb. 1783, and nn. 10–12.

12 Randolph to JM, 1 Feb., and n. 5; JM to Jefferson, 11 Feb., and n. 14; to Randolph, 11 Feb., and n. 3; Jefferson to JM, 14 Feb. (1st letter), and n. 4. The contents of the present letter from this point to the end of the paragraph much resemble what JM wrote in the footnote to his notes for 21 Feb. (*q.v.*).

13 Here and twice again in this paragraph JM used the cipher for "ease," probably because Randolph's code lacked a cipher for "eas."

14 JM Notes, 19 Feb. 1783, and n. 6.

15 The "respectable *delegate*" was Nathaniel Gorham (JM Notes, 21 Feb. and the citations in n. 23). See also JM Notes, 28 Jan., and n. 45; 30 Jan. 1783, and nn. 2, 4, 6.

16 JM's premise was that the opulence of the southern states depended upon the overseas market for their agricultural staples. Those states were vulnerable because, unlike New England, they lacked sea power and relied largely upon ships of that region to transport their exports and to bring them return cargoes from Europe and slaves from Africa. In 1786 Jefferson estimated that tobacco, rice, and indigo, from the standpoint of their value, constituted 36.4 per cent of all American exports (Boyd, *Papers of Jefferson*, X, 146–47).

17 JM's meaning would have been clearer if he had not written, perhaps inadvertently, the cipher 557, meaning "at," before the ciphers for "alliances." The second syllable of "*subservi*[ent]" is doubtfully decoded from two ink-blotted ciphers which seem to have been 219 and 380, together standing for "ser." The 380 is plainly followed by 474 meaning "vi," but a 378 standing for "ent" has to be interpolated if it is assumed that the intended word was "subservient."

18 JM to Randolph, 18 Feb. 1783, and n. 5. "J——s" was "Jefferson's."

19 JM used "him" to refer to the postrider. JM probably referred to Randolph's letter of 15 February (*q.v.*), although he did not acknowledge its receipt in his letter of 4 March to Randolph.

Motion on Outrages by Enemy

MS (NA: PCC, No. 36, II, 35). In JM's hand. Docketed by Benjamin Bankson, Jr., a clerk in the office of the secretary of Congress: "Motion of Mr. Madison Passed Feby 26. 1783."

Wednesday   Feby 26. 1783.

Resolved[1] That it be recommendd. to the Executives of the several States, whenever any outrages, unauthorised by the laws of war shall be committed on the persons or properties of their respective Citizens by any persons in the service of the Enemy, to transmit immediate information thereof to the Commander in chief or the Commanding officer of a separate army,[2] in order that the measures may be pursued which are pointed out in the Resolution of the   day 1782.[3]

1 Above "Resolved," JM wrote "Mr Madison Mr. Mercer" to signify that he made the motion and John Francis Mercer seconded it. For the immediate context of this motion, see the first paragraph of JM Notes, 26 Feb. 1783, and nn. 1–4.

2 George Washington or Nathanael Greene.

³ Thomas McKean's amended motion, which in its contents resembled the present motion, had been supported by JM and adopted by Congress on 8 November 1782 (*JCC*, XXIII, 719–20; *Papers of Madison*, V, 254–55; 256, nn. 12–15; 257, n. 17). The vote whereby the present motion was agreed to by Congress, perhaps because it was unanimous, was not entered in the journal (*JCC*, XXIV, 149).

Notes on Debates

MS (LC: Madison Papers). For a description of the manuscript of Notes on Debates, see *Papers of Madison*, V, 231–34.

Wednesday Feby. 26.

Mr. Lee observed to Congress that it appeared from the Newspapers of the day that sundry enormities had been committed by the Refugees within the State of Delaware,¹ as it was known that like enormities had been committed on the shores of the Chesapeak, notwithstanding the pacific professions of the Enemy;² that it was probable however that if complaint were to be made to the British commander at N. York³ the practice would be restrained, He accordingly moved that a Committee might be appointed to take into consideration the means of restraining such practices. The motion was 2ded. by Mr. Peters. By Mr. Fitzimmons the motion was viewed as tending to a request of favors from Sr. Guy Carlton. It was apprehended by others that as Genl Washington & the Commanders of separate armies had been explicitly informed of the sense of Congress on this point, any fresh measures thereon might appear to be a censure on them; and that Congress cd. not ground any measure on the case in question; having no official information relative to it. The motion of Mr. Lee was negatived.⁴ But it appearing from the vote to be the desire of many members that some step might be taken by Congress, The motion of Mr. Madison & Mr. Mercer as it stands on the Journal was proposed and agreed to, as free from all objections.⁵

A motion was made by Mr. Hamilton to give a brevet Comm[issi]on to Majr. Burnet aid to Genl. Greene & messenger of the evacuation of Charleston, of L. Colonel: There being six ays only the motion was lost. N. H. no. Mr. Lee & Mercer no.⁶

No. X

1783. Feby. 26. Wednesday—(continued)—⁷

The Committee consisting of Mr. Lee &c. to whom had been referred a motion of Mr. Hamilton recommending to the States to authorize Con-

gress to make abatements in the retrospective apportionment by a valuation of land, in favor of States whose ability from year to year had been
most impaired by the war:[8] reported that it was inexpedient to agree to
such motion because one State (Virga.) having disagreed to such a
measure on a former recommendation of Congress,[9] it was not probable
that another recommendation would produce any effect; and because
the difficulties of making such abatements were greater than the advantages expected from them.[10]

Mr. Lee argued in favor of the report & the reasons on which it was
grounded. The Eastern delegates were for leaving the matter open for
future determination when an apportionment should be in question.[11]

Mr. Madison said he thought that the principle of the motion was conformable to justice & within the spirit of the Confederation: according
to which apportionmts ought [to] have been made from time to time
throughout the war according to the existing wealth of each State. But
that it would be improper to take up this case separately from other
claims of equity which would be put in by other States: that the most
likely mode of obtaining the concurrence of the States in any plan wd.
be to comprehend in it the equitable interests of all of them; a comprehensive plan of that sort would be the only one that would cut off all
sources of future controversy among the States: That as soon as the plan
of revenue sd. be prepared[12] for recommendation to the States it would
be proper for Congs. to take into consideration & combine with it every
*object which might facilitate its progress, & form a complete provision
for the tranquility of the U. States. The Question on Mr. Hamilton's
motion was postponed.[13]

The letter from Mr. Morris requesting that the injunction of secresy
might be withdrawn from his preceding letter signifying to Congress his
purpose of resigning was committed to.[14]

---

* He[15] had in view the followg. objects—1. the abatements proposed by Mr.
Hamilton.[16] 2. a transfer into the common mass of expences of all the separate expences incurred by the States in their particular defence.[17] 3. an acquisition to the
U. States of the vacant territory.[18] The plan thus extended would affect the interest
of the States as follows. viz.; N. Hamshipire would approve the establishment of a
General revenue, as tending to support the confederacy, to remove causes of future
contention, and to secure her trade against separate taxation from the States thro
which it is carried on.[19] She would also approve of a share in the vacant territory.[20]
Having never been much invaded by the Enemy her interest would be opposed to
abatements, & throwing all the separate expenditures into the common mass. The
discharge of the public debts from a common treasury would not be required by
her interest, the loans of her citizens being under her proportion. See the Statement
of them.[21]

Massachussetts is deeply interested in the discharge of the public debts. The expedition to Penobscot alone interests her, she supposes, in making a common mass of expences: her interest is opposed to abatements. The other objects wd. not peculiarly affect her.[22]

Rhode Island as a weak State is interested in a general revenue as tending to support the confederacy and prevent future contentions, but against it as tending to deprive Her of the advantage afforded by her situation of taxing the commerce of the contiguous States. as tending to discharge with certainty the public debts, her proportion of loans interest her rather against it.[23] Having been the seat of the war for a considerable time, she might not perhaps be opposed to abatements on that account. The exertions for her defence having been *previously* sanctioned, it is presumed in most instances, she would be opposed to making a common mass of expences. In the acquisition of vacant territory she is deeply and anxiously interested.[24]

Connecticut is interested in a general revenue as tending to protect her commerce from separate taxation by N. York & Rhode Island: and somewhat as providing for loan office creditors. Her interest is opposed to abatements, and to a common mass of expences.[25] Since the condemnation of her title to her Western claims,[26] she may perhaps consider herself interested in the acquisition of the vacant lands.[27] In other respects she wd not be peculiarly affected.

N. York is exceedingly attached to a general revenue as tending to support the confederacy and prevent future contests among the States. Although her citizens are not lenders beyond the proportion of the State, yet individuals of great weight are deeply interested in provision for public debts. In abatements N. York is also deeply interested.[28] In makg. a common mass also interested, and since the acceptance of her cession, interested in those of other States.[29]

N. Jersey Is interested as a smaller State in a general revenue as tendg to support the confederacy, and to prevent future contests and to guard her commerce agst. the separate taxation of Pensylvania & N.Y. The loans of her Citizens are not materially disproportio[n]ate.[30] Although this State has been much the theatre of the war, she wd. not perhaps be interested in abatements. Having had a previous sanction for particular expenditures, her interest wd. be opposed to a common mass.[31] In the vacant territory, she is deeply and anxiously interested.[32]

Penna. is deeply interested in a general revenue, the loans of her Citizens amounting to more than $\frac{1}{4}$ of that branch of the public debt.[33] As far as a general impost on trade would restrain her from taxing the trade of N. Jersey it would be against her interest.[34] She is interested against abatements; and against a common mass, her expenditures having been always previously sanctioned.[35] In the vacant territory she is also interested.[36]

Delaware is interested by her weakness in a general revenue as tending to support the confederacy & future tranquility of the States; but not materially by the credits of her Citizens: Her interest is opposed to abatements & to a common mass. To the vacant territory she is firmly attached.[37]

Maryland. Having never been the Seat of war & her Citizens being creditors below her proportion, her interest lies agst. a general revenue, otherwise than as she is interested in common with others in the support of the Confederacy & tranquility of the U. S. but against abatements, and against a common mass. The vacant lands are a favorite object to her.[38]

Virga. in common with the Southern States as likely to enjoy an opulent and defenceless trade is interested in a general revenue, as tending to secure her the protection of the Confederacy agst. the maritime superiority of the E. States; but agst it as tending to discharge loan office debts and to deprive her of the occasion of taxing the commerce of N. Carolina.[39] She is interested in abatements, and essentially so in a common mass, not only her excentric expenditures being enormous; but many of her necessary ones havg. rcd. no previous or subsequent sanction. Her cession of territory would be considered as a sacrifice.[40]

N. Carolina. interested in a general revenue as tending to ensure the protection of the Confederacy agst. the maritime superiority of the E. States and to guard her trade from separate taxation by Virginia and S. Carolina. The loans of her Citizens are inconsiderable. In abatements and in a common mass she is essentially interested. In the article of territory, she would have to make a sacrifice.[41]

South Carolina is interested as a weak & exposed State in a general revenue as tending to secure to her the protection of the confederacy agst. enemies of *every* kind, and as providing for the public creditors, her citizens being not only loan offices creditors beyond her proportion, but having immense unliquidated demands agst. U. States. As restraining her power over the commerce of N. Carolina, a general revenue is opposed by her interests. She is also materially interested in abatements, and in a common mass. In the article of territory her sacrifice wd. be inconsiderable.[42]

Georgia as a feeble, an opulent, & frontier State is peculiarly interested in a general revenue, as tending to support the confederacy. She is also interested in it somewhat by the credits of her Citizens. In abatements She is also interested, and in a common mass, essentially so. In the article of territory She would make an important sacrifice.[43]

To make this plan still more complete for the purpose of removing all present complaints, and all occasions of future contests, it may be proper to include in it a recommendation to the States to rescind the rule of apportioning pecuniary burdens according to the value of land, & to substitute that of numbers, reckoning two slaves as equal to one free man.[44]

For a state of the loan office debt turn over.[45]

	Specie dollars
N. H.	336.579,58,7
Mas:	2.361.866.66.5
R. Island	699.725.37.4
Cont.	1.270.115.30
N. York	949.729.57.5
N. Jersey	658.883.69.
Pena.	3.948.904.14.4.
Delaware	65.820.13.7
Maryland	410.218.30.
Virga.	313.741.82.3.
N. Carolina	113.341.11.1
S. Carolina	90.442.10.1
Total[46]	11.437.410.80

This it is to be observed is only the list of loan office debts. The unliquidated debts and liquidated debts of other denominations due to individuals will vary inexpressibly the relative quantum of credits of the several States. It is to be further observed that this only shews the original credits, transfers having been constant. . heretofore they have flowed into Pa. Other States may hereafter have an influx.[47]

[1] According to the *Pennsylvania Packet* of 25 February, a schooner from Grenada exchanged shots in Delaware Bay with "three refugee boats." Two days later an item in the same newspaper told of looting, burning, and physical violence to residents by one band of "refugees" led by British officers from New York City, and another band of "pirates" in mid-February at Thoroughfare Point on Duck Creek, Bombay Hook, and elsewhere along the coast of New Castle County, Del. The anonymous author of the account stated that citizens of the state "lament the want of protection by water" because the raiders "threaten to lay our farms and stores in ashes."

[2] The *Virginia Gazette* of 1 March 1783 published the letter of an unnamed correspondent stating that during the last two weeks of February "eleven bay and

river crafts have been captured, and many of the people on shore plundered and the rest kept in perpetual dread. We pay chearfully every tax laid upon us, and think it cruel that we cannot be protected from the insults and ravages of a handful of refugees, in a small sloop and a few whale boats." The writer wished to know what had become of the Virginia ship of war "Liberty," which had been ordered to cruise in Chesapeake Bay "for the protection of the trade and inhabitants on the shores and rivers thereof." See also McIlwaine, *Official Letters*, III, 448–49; *Cal. of Va. State Papers*, III, 435; *Papers of Madison*, V, 384, n. 5.

3 General Sir Guy Carleton.

4 The vote which "negatived" the Lee-Peters motion was not entered in the official journal (*JCC*, XXIV, 152, and n. 2).

5 Motion on Outrages by Enemy, 26 Feb. 1783, and nn. 1, 3.

6 Harrison to Delegates, 11 Jan., and n. 6; JM Notes, 17 Jan. 1783. Neither the Hamilton motion nor the vote by which it "was lost" appears in the official journal.

7 For the probable explanation of the Roman numeral and JM's repetition of the date, see *Papers of Madison*, VI, 231, ed. n.

8 For Hamilton's motion and its reference by Congress on 17 February to Arthur Lee, Eliphalet Dyer, and Samuel Holten, see *JCC*, XXIV, 138, and n. 1; JM Notes, 17 Feb. 1783, and nn. 3, 4.

9 The reference was to the resolutions of the Virginia General Assembly on 28 May–7 June, which the Virginia delegates had laid before Congress on 24 July 1782 (*Papers of Madison*, IV, 430; 431, n. 1; V, 348; 351, n. 23; *JCC*, XXII, 413; JM Notes, 14 Jan. 1783, and n. 4).

10 JM Notes, 27 Jan., n. 27; JM to Randolph, 25 Feb. 1783 and citations in n. 7; *JCC*, XXIV, 152, and n. 3.

11 That is, on the next occasion when Congress should have to allocate a financial requisition proportionately among the states. See JM Notes, 4 Apr. 1783.

12 See Report on Restoring Public Credit, 6 Mar. 1783.

13 For Hamilton's view of the issue discussed by JM in this paragraph, see Syrett and Cooke, *Papers of Hamilton*, III, 268–74, and esp. 271–72 and 273–74. See also JM Notes, 4–5 Mar. 1783.

14 For a summary of Robert Morris' "preceding letter" of 24 January, see JM Notes, 24 Jan., and nn. 20, 23. In his letter of 26 February, Morris emphasized that the creditors with whom he had "contracted engagements" as superintendent of finance were entitled to know of his intention to resign on 31 May. Besides complying immediately with his request, Congress referred both of his letters to a committee, John Rutledge, chairman (NA: PCC, No. 186, fol. 85; *JCC*, XXIV, 151, 284–85; JM Notes, 27 Feb; 4–5 Mar; JM to Randolph, 4 Mar. 1783; E. James Ferguson, *Power of the Purse*, p. 169).

15 JM wrote this long footnote in spaces of varying sizes in the lower portions of nine pages of the manuscript of his notes on debates. The upper portion of the first of these pages was devoted to the main text of his notes for 26 February, of the second page to the rest of that text and also to the beginning of that for the next day, and of the other pages to the balance of his notes for 27 February 1783.

This summary, besides recalling JM's résumé of 1 May 1782 about the perplexing Vermont issue, is a source of his memorandum on a revenue plan, *ca.* 6 March 1783 (*q.v.*). See also *Papers of Madison*, IV, 200–202. To clarify his thoughts about a complex matter, to be of service to his successor in Congress, and to have a record of value in the event that he should prepare a history of the Revolution, were probably among the reasons why JM wrote the footnote. See *Papers of Madison*, V, 232–34.

In this summary JM stressed three of the four chief points embodied in his report on restoring public credit, 6 March (*q.v.*). Within a week after writing his footnote, JM concluded that he had misjudged the viewpoint of several of the state delegations toward one or more of the principal recommendations of the plan. See Memo. on a Revenue Plan, 6 Mar. JM's report, as adopted in modified form on 18 April, was the last important attempt by Congress to persuade the states to endow the Confederation with sufficient economic power to survive (JM Notes, 18 Apr. 1783, and n. 7).

[16] JM to Randolph, 25 Feb. 1783 and citations in n. 7.

[17] *Papers of Madison*, V, 363; 366, n. 23. For examples of these "expences," see JM Notes, 31 Jan., and n. 4; JM to Randolph, 25 Feb. 1783 and citations in n. 6. JM appears to have originated the proposal to have Congress assume most of the war-connected debts of the states, even though in 1790 he would oppose a similar recommendation by Hamilton. By then, however, the situation had much changed. See Clarence L. Ver Steeg, *Robert Morris*, pp. 175, 249, n. 32.

[18] JM Notes, 14 Jan., n. 9; 29 Jan. 1783.

[19] That is, if Congress were granted the exclusive authority to levy an impost duty, the trade of New Hampshire to the extent that it did not center at Portsmouth would be spared the imposts levied by Massachusetts and other states. New Hampshire had been among the first, and Massachusetts among the last, of the thirteen states to ratify the impost amendment proposed by Congress on 3 February 1781 (Burnett, *Letters*, VI, 372, n. 4).

[20] New Hampshire, having no claim to territory west of the Appalachian Mountains, naturally would benefit from sharing in the possession of that area if it should be ceded to Congress by the states with "sea to sea" charters.

[21] The "Statement" is at the close of JM's present footnote. Although New Hampshire or her citizens held few loan-office certificates, they owned a considerable amount of continental paper currency (*Papers of Madison*, V, 323, n. 8).

[22] For the large debt, including many loan-office certificates, owed by Congress to Massachusetts or her citizens, see the table closing this footnote of JM's; also *Papers of Madison*, V, 323, nn. 3, 8; JM Notes, 17 Feb., n. 1; JM to Randolph, 25 Feb. 1783. A detachment of the British army, which had established a post at the mouth of the Penobscot River in the summer of 1778, was still there. In July and August 1779 an expedition of Massachusetts militia and ships against the British stronghold along the Penobscot River in the district of Maine had been a most costly "Catastrophe." In his letters of 2 and 21 September 1779 to John Jay, president of Congress, Jeremiah Powell, president of the council of Massachusetts, emphasized that the treasury of the Confederation should reimburse the state for the expense of the operation, totaling some $7,000,000, since it had been undertaken with the hope "of great good accruing to the United States" (NA: PCC, No. 65, I, 404, 412; II, 27, 35, 53). During the next decade Massachusetts often, but unsuccessfully, with the exception of a warrant for $2,000,000 issued to her by Congress on 8 April 1780, sought to have this claim satisfied (*JCC*, XVI, 341–42). For these reasons, it was to Massachusetts' financial "interest" to oppose "abatements."

[23] See the table at close of JM's present footnote. Between "loans" and "interest" JM canceled "does not materially." Partly because Rhode Island derived so much income from "taxing the commerce" of Connecticut, she had refused to ratify the proposed impost amendment to the Articles of Confederation (*Papers of Madison*, V, 289; 291, n. 9; JM Notes, 29 Jan., and n. 28; 12 Feb., n. 6; 19 Feb., and n. 5; 20 Feb. 1783, and n. 14). See also Memo. on Revenue Plan, 6 Mar. 1783, ed. n.

[24] Although for the following reason, JM seemed warranted in assuming that "in most instances" Rhode Island would oppose "making a common mass of expences," he soon decided that this conclusion needed to be modified. See Memo. on Revenue Plan, 6 Mar. 1783, ed. n. In the autumn of 1777 and late in the summer of the next year, the British armed forces, which occupied Newport and the rest of the island of Rhode Island from December 1776 to October 1779, repulsed attempts to dislodge them. In contrast with the Penobscot expedition of Massachusetts, these fias-

coes primarily involved continental troops, although Rhode Island militia participated. For this reason, Congress unhesitatingly assumed the cost (*JCC*, VII, 124; VIII, 661–62; IX, 975–76; X, 46–47, 290; XI, 645–47, 758–61). The delegates in Congress from Rhode Island were among the most insistent that states with claims to trans-Appalachian territory should cede it to the United States (*Papers of Madison*, III, 74–75; IV, 35, n. 9; 201; 221, n. 11; V, 200; 201, n. 8; 246, n. 10; 375, n. 15).

25 JM Notes, 29 Jan., and n. 28; 8 Feb., n. 3; 25 Feb. 1783, and nn. 1, 2, 11. JM evidently believed that, although Connecticut had suffered severely from British raids, she would be little helped by "abatements," for she had not been a main theater of war (*Papers of Madison*, III, 258; 260, n. 3; 271; 272, n. 1). JM soon discovered that he had overlooked a circumstance which influenced the Connecticut delegation to favor a "common mass of expences." See Memo. on Revenue Plan, 6 Mar. 1783, ed. n.

26 *Papers of Madison*, V, 419, n. 23; JM Notes, 1 Jan. 1783, and n. 1.

27 *Papers of Madison*, III, 281–82; 284; IV, 32–33; 35, n. 8; 201; 203, n. 11; 390, n. 22; V, 246, n. 11; 247, n. 16.

28 *Ibid.*, V, 366, n. 26; 407, n. 1; JM Notes, 27 Jan.; 28 Jan., and nn. 12, 43; 29 Jan., and n. 41; 31 Jan., and n. 11; 12 Feb., nn. 8, 15; 17 Feb., and n. 4; 18 Feb.; 19 Feb., and nn. 11, 20; 20 Feb., n. 14; 21 Feb., and n. 28. Having suffered severely during the Revolution both from frequent invasions of her "upstate" by the enemy and its Indian allies and from the British occupation of New York City and its environs ever since August 1776, New York naturally would be "deeply interested" in abatements. For loan-office certificates owned by her citizens, see the table concluding JM's present footnote.

29 For the cession by New York of her claims to territory in the Old Northwest, see *Papers of Madison*, V, 242–43; 245, nn. 3–5; 246, nn. 6, 10; 247, n. 14.

30 JM Notes, 29 Jan. 1783, and n. 34. See table at close of JM's present footnote.

31 Being the land-bridge between New York City and Philadelphia, New Jersey had been crossed, recrossed, and fought over frequently by the contending armies between 1775 and 1781. Congress, on the other hand, had guaranteed "particular" military expenditures of the state on numerous occasions during those years. See, for example, *JCC*, III, 345; IV, 150–51, VI, 874–75, 1013; VII, 181; VIII, 600, 659, 712, 750–51; IX, 1036, 1051, 1070; X, 89, 208, 329; XI, 680; XV, 1438.

32 *Papers of Madison*, II, 74–75; III, 210, n. 4; 283, n. 6; IV, 32–33; 201; V, 200; 201, n. 8; 246, n. 10.

33 JM Notes, 27 Jan., and nn. 12, 16; 28 Jan., and nn. 3, 9, 36; 29 Jan., and nn. 14, 19; 18 Feb., and n. 4; 19 Feb., and nn. 14, 20, 23; 20 Feb. 1783, and n. 7.

34 JM Notes, 29 Jan. 1783, and n. 34.

35 For examples of Pennsylvania's "previously sanctioned" expenses, see *JCC*, II, 237; III, 463; IV, 130, 156, 239, 255, 271, 276, 322; V, 819–20, 834; VII, 113, 184, 240, 314; VIII, 475–76, 557, 592, 741; X, 242–43; XI, 642; XII, 722; XV, 1438–39; XVIII, 1223. For Pennsylvania's willingness to assume the debts owed to her citizens by Congress, see JM Notes, 28 Jan., and nn. 2, 23; 30 Jan., and n. 6; 19 Feb. 1783. By 6 March JM had somewhat changed his estimate of Pennsylvania's stand on these issues. See Memo. on Revenue Plan, 6 Mar. 1793, ed. n.

36 *Papers of Madison*, II, 74–75; III, 14, n. 17; 138, n. 7; IV, 200–201; 203, n. 11; V, 201, n. 8; 246, n. 10; 276–77, and nn. 5, 8, 9; 352.

37 See table at close of this long footnote by JM. In 1787, Delaware was not only the first state to ratify the Constitution of the United States but also one of the three states (New Jersey and Georgia, the other two) to ratify it unanimously. "The only battle of the American Revolution on Delaware soil" was a "spirited little affair" on 5 September 1777 at Cooch's Bridge "on the upper waters of the Christina" River (Christopher L. Ward, *The Delaware Continentals, 1776–1783* [Wilmington, Del., 1941], pp. 190–92, 499–501). Because her war-caused property

loss had been small, Delaware naturally opposed "abatements." For her wish to share in "the vacant territory" west of the Appalachian Mountains, see *Papers of Madison*, II, 74–75; IV, 200–201; V, 200; 201, n. 8; 242, n. 8; 246, n. 10.

[38] See table concluding the present footnote of JM. The Maryland General Assembly had long hesitated to ratify the proposed impost amendment to the Articles of Confederation (*Papers of Madison*, IV, 220; 221, n. 11; 389, n. 16). During most of January and February 1783 Daniel Carroll was Maryland's only delegate in Congress. As chairman of the committee of the whole, he appears to have shared infrequently in the debates on financial issues. Although he had favored providing Congress with a general revenue, he had opposed "abatements" to states which had been main theaters of the war (*JCC*, XXIV, 114–16, 126–27). Maryland had been more inflexible than any other state in opposing the claim of Virginia to territory west and northwest of the Ohio River (*Papers of Madison*, II, 54, n. 3; 74–77; 100–101; 300; 301, n. 4; III, 283, n. 6; 304; 305, n. 2; IV, 131, n. 2; 179, nn. 7, 8; 200–201; 221, n. 11; 340; V, 50; 200; 201, n. 8; 246, n. 10; 378, n. 5).

[39] JM Notes, 29 Jan., and nn. 33, 34; 21 Feb.; JM to Randolph, 25 Feb. 1783, and n. 16; and the table at the close of JM's footnote.

[40] *Papers of Madison*, V, 278; 323, n. 8; 363; 366, nn. 19, 23; Harrison to Delegates, 7 Feb., and nn. 3, 4; JM Notes, 19 Feb. 1783, n. 6. Especially in 1779, 1780, and 1781, the war had been very costly to Virginia, North Carolina, South Carolina, and Georgia, in money disbursed and in the value of destroyed property and lost slaves. Consequently, these states would benefit if the war expenses of all the states were merged into a "common mass" and equitably apportioned among them. In view of the charter claims of Virginia to the Old Northwest and her outlay of "blood and treasure" during the Revolution in seeking to drive British troops out of that area, she reasonably could expect her "sacrifice" for ceding the territory to the United States to appear conspicuously on the credit side of her ledger when a financial accounting with the Confederation should be made. Although these were weighty considerations, JM soon would be less positive that he had correctly assessed the interest of Virginia in regard to "abatements." See Memo. on Revenue Plan, 6 Mar. 1783, ed. n.

[41] See n. 40; also the table at the close of JM's footnote; JM Notes, 29 Jan., and n. 33; JM to Randolph, 25 Feb. 1783, and n. 16. For North Carolina's claim to the area which would become the state of Tennessee, see *Papers of Madison*, II, 73; 76; 77; III, 226, n. 13; IV, 9; 201; 203, n. 16; V, 115–16; 118, n. 13.

[42] See n. 40; also the table at the close of JM's footnote; JM Notes, 27 Jan., n. 13; 29 Jan., and n. 33; JM to Randolph, 25 Feb. 1783, and n. 16. The western lands claimed by South Carolina were "inconsiderable" in area as compared with those of Virginia, North Carolina, and Georgia (*Papers of Madison*, II, 73; III, 226, n. 13; IV, 9; 201–2; 203, n. 16). As "enemies of *every* kind," JM could have cited Indians, European powers, and even the other American states, if the Confederation should dissolve.

[43] JM to Randolph, 25 Feb. 1783, and n. 16. Georgia's interest in "abatements" reflected the presence of enemy troops on her soil from December 1778 to July 1782 (*Papers of Madison*, I, 271, n. 2; IV, 440, n. 5). According to the charter of June 1732 granted to twenty trustees, the western limits of the colony of Georgia were "the south seas" (*ibid.*, IV, 203, n. 16). Even by confining those limits to the Mississippi River, Georgia's "article of territory" was of immense extent and, except for a narrow strip, not overlapped by the claim of any other state. Burdened with a large war debt in proportion to her small population, and menaced by Indians, and perhaps by the Spanish in Florida and Louisiana, Georgia naturally would favor a strong confederation (n. 37) and the merger of her liabilities "in a common mass" (n. 40). See also *Papers of Madison*, II, 73; 77; 197, n. 4; III, 226, n. 13; IV, 9; 15, nn. 13, 14; 17, n. 30; 201; V, 115; 118, n. 13; JM Notes, 14 Jan. 1783, n. 9.

[44] For "the rule" adopted by Congress on 17 February 1783, see JM Notes, 17 Feb. 1783, and n. 1; *JCC*, XXIV, 135–37. This "rule" required each state to count its inhabitants, "distinguishing white from black," but did provide for differentiating freemen and slaves when apportioning a financial requisition among the states. A two-for-one ratio apparently had not been suggested during the debates about what the "rule" should be. John Rutledge expressed regret that the Articles of Confederation barred an allocation of financial quotas solely on the basis of a census, with "certain qualifications as to Slaves." JM and probably most delegates from southern states were of the same mind. Oliver Wolcott favored amending the Articles of Confederation to authorize a census base of apportionment, counting Negroes only between sixteen and sixty years of age. Robert Morris recommended the levying of a poll tax payable by all freemen and all male slaves in that same age bracket. JM also favored a poll tax, "rating blacks somewhat lower than whites" (JM Notes, 14 Jan.; 28 Jan., and nn. 35, 42; 11 Feb., and n. 4; Randolph to JM, 7 Feb. 1783, n. 3). See also Memo. on Revenue Plan, 6 Mar. 1783, ed. n.

[45] JM wrote this sentence at the bottom of a page of his manuscript notes.

[46] With a covering letter of 10 March, Robert Morris, superintendent of finance, submitted to Congress an analysis of the Confederation debt as of 1 January 1783 (Randolph to JM, 15 Jan. 1783, n. 13; NA: PCC, No. 137, II, 199, 205). Although JM clearly took most of his entries from an advance copy of that list or from the ledger entries upon which it was based, he made one mistake in transcribing and probably found his figures for New Hampshire and Connecticut in a source or sources unknown to the present editors. His own column of figures adds to $11,219,-367.80.7 rather than $11,437,410.80.7. Almost all of the discrepancy results from his omission of Georgia, from attributing the sum for that state to South Carolina, and from overlooking the South Carolina total of $218,042.48.3. Adding this amount to $11,219,367.80.7 produces $11,437,410.29, or only about 50 cents less than his own total. Robert Morris' entry for New Hampshire was $300,092.30, for Connecticut, $1,269,677.43, and his total was $11,400,485.64. ⅛.

[47] JM Notes, 27 Jan., n. 13; 30 Jan., n. 6; 20 Feb. 1783, and nn. 6, 7.

Notes on Debates

MS (LC: Madison Papers). For a description of the manuscript of Notes on Debates, see *Papers of Madison*, V, 231–34.

Thursday Feby. 27.

On the report of the Come. on Mr. Morris's letter the injunction of secrecy was taken off without dissent or observation.[1]

The attention of Congress was recalled to the subject of half pay by Messrs. Dyer & Wolcot, in order to introduce a reconsideration of the mode of referring it separately to the States to provide for their own lines.[2]

Mr. Mercer favored the reconsideration,[3] representing the commutation proposed, as tending in common with the funding of other debts, to establish & perpetuate a monied interest in the U. S.[,] that this monied interest would gain the ascendance of the landed interest, would resort to places of luxury & splendor, and by their example & influence, become dangerous to our republican constitutions. He said however that the variances of opinion & indecision of Congress were alarming & required that something should be done; that it wd be better to newmodel the Confederation, or attempt any thing rather than do nothing.[4]

Mr. Madison reminded Congs. that the commutation proposed was introduced as a compromise with those to whom the idea of pensions was obnoxious & observed that those whose scruples had been relieved by it had rendered it no less obnoxious than pensions by stigmatizing it with the name of a perpetuity.[5] He said the public situation was truly deplorable. If the payment of the capital of the public debts was suggested, it was said & truly said to be impossible; if funding them & paying the interest was proposed, it was exclaimed agst. as establishing a dangerous monied interest, as corrupting the public manners, as administering poison to our republican constitutions. He said he wished the revenue to be established to be such as would extinguish the capital as well as pay the interest within the shortest possible period; and was as much opposed to perpetuating the public burdens as any one. But that the discharge of them in some form or other was essential, and that the consequences predicted therefrom could not be more heterogeneous to our republican character & constitutions, than a violation of the maxims of good faith and common honesty.[6] It was agreed that the report for commuting ½ pay, should lie on the table till tomorrow, in order to give an opportunity to the Delegates of Connecticut to make any proposition relative thereto which they should judge proper.[7]

The report of the Comme. consisting of Mr. Ghorum Mr. Hamilton Mr. Madison Mr. Rutlidge & Mr. Fitzimmons was taken up. It proposed that in addition to the impost of 5 PerCt. ad valorem, the States be requested to enable Congs. to collect a duty of $\frac{1}{8}$ of a dollar perbushel on salt imported, of $\frac{6}{90}$ per Gallon on all wines do. and of $\frac{3}{90}$ per Gallon on all rum & brandy do.[8]

On the first article it was observed on the part of the East: States, that this would press peculiarly hard on them on acct. of the salt consumed in the fisheries, and that it would besides be injurious to the national interest by adding to the cost of fish, and a draw back was suggested.[9]

On the other side it was observed that the warmer climate & more dispersed settlements of the Southern States, required a greater consumption of salt for their provisions, that salt might & would be conveyed to the fisheries without previous importation,[10] that the effect of the duty was too inconsiderable to be felt in the cost of fish & that as the rum used in the N. E. States being in a great degree manufactured at home,[11] they would have a greater advantage in this respect, than the other States could have in the article of Salt, that a drawback could not be executed in our complicated governmt. with ease or certainty

Mr. Mercer on this occasion declared that altho' he thought those who opposed a general revenue right in their principles, yet as they appeared to have formed no plan adequate to the public exigences, and he was convinced of the necessity of doing something, he should depart from his first resolutions and strike in with those who were pursuing the plan of a general revenue.[12]

Mr. Holten said that he had come lately into Congress with a pre-determination against any measures for discharging the public engagements other than those pointed out in the confederation, & that he had hitherto acted accordingly. But that he saw now so clearly the necessity of making provision for that object, and the inadequacy of the confederation thereto, that he should concur in recommending to the States a plan of a general revenue.[13]

A question being proposed on the duty on salt there were 9 ays. N. H. alone being no. R. I. not prest.

It was urged by some that the duty on wine should be augmented, but it appeared on discussion & some calculations, that the temptation to smuggling wd. be rendered too strong & the revenue be thereby diminished. Mr. Bland proposed that instead of a duty on the gallon an ad-valorem duty should be laid on wine, and this idea after some loose discussions, was agreed to; few of the members interesting themselves therein, and some of them havg. previously retired from Congress.[14]

[1] According to the journal, the "injunction" had been removed on 26 February (JCC, XXIV, 151; JM Notes, 26 Feb., and n. 14). See also Pa. Packet, 4 Mar.; Pa. Gazette, 5 Mar.; JM to Randolph, 8 Apr. 1783, n. 3.

[2] Eliphalet Dyer and Oliver Wolcott of Connecticut evidently sought to have Congress resume the debate of 25 and 26 February on the Osgood committee's proposals concerning "half pay" so as to enable them to move an amendment similar to the rejected Gilman-Condict motion of 25 February (JM Notes, 25 Feb., and nn. 1, 2, 11; 28 Feb. 1783; JCC, XXIV, 154).

[3] John Francis Mercer's stand on the issue was consistent with that taken by him three days earlier (JM Notes, 25 Feb. 1783, n. 11).

[4] Here and later in his notes for this day, JM suggested that Mercer, by listening to the divergent viewpoints of his fellow delegates, was becoming less confident of remedying the financial ills of Congress without encroaching upon the sovereignty of each state. This new posture was very different from his threat to withdraw from Congress "& do every thing in his power to destroy" the Confederation (JM Notes, 21 Feb.). See also JM Notes, 8 Feb., and n. 3; 12 Feb., and n. 12; 18 Feb.; 19 Feb.; 20 Feb.; JM to Randolph, 18 Feb., and nn. 2, 3; 25 Feb. 1783.

[5] JM Notes, 13 Jan., and nn. 11, 18, 20, 21; 24 Jan.; 25 Jan., and nn. 8, 12; 4 Feb. 1783, and nn. 7, 10, 11, 13–15.

[6] JM Notes, 28 Jan.; 12 Feb., and n. 1; 21 Feb., and nn. 16, 28; JM to Randolph, 28 Jan.; 25 Feb. 1783. JM used "heterogeneous" in the sense of "foreign" or "repugnant" (*Oxford English Dictionary* [1933 ed.], V, 255).

[7] JM Notes, 28 Feb. 1783.

[8] JM Notes, 21 Feb. 1783, n. 28. Although unnoted in the official journal, the "Comme on revenues," as JM designated it, submitted to Congress on 27 February and on 3 March, respectively, small portions of its detailed report (JM Notes, 3 Mar. 1783). The entire report, written almost wholly by JM, was laid before Congress for the first time on 6 March (Report on Restoring Public Credit, 6 Mar. 1783; NA: PCC, No. 186, fol. 84; *JCC*, XXIV, 170–74). Lacking evidence to the contrary, the present editors assume that the drafting of the full report was not completed before that date. In that report JM wrote "$\frac{1}{15}$ of a dollar per Gallon" instead of "$\frac{9}{90}$ per Gallon" and "$\frac{1}{30}$ of a dollar per Gallon" instead of $\frac{9}{90}$ per Gallon." For a discussion of the relative merits of ad valorem and specific duties, see JM Notes, 18 Feb. 1783, and nn. 11, 12.

[9] JM Notes, 29 Jan., and nn. 17, 18, 23; 20 Feb., n. 17; JM to Randolph, 4 Feb. 1783. A drawback is a remittance by the customs office of all or a part of the duty paid on foreign wares if the importer later exports them.

[10] That is, salt from the Bahama Islands or some other customary source of supply would be obtained directly by, or delivered at sea to, a fishing vessel without being brought to a port of the United States.

[11] *Papers of Madison*, II, 17; 18, n. 2.

[12] JM Notes, 12 Feb., and n. 12; 18 Feb.; 19 Feb.; 21 Feb.; JM to Randolph, 18 Feb., and nn. 2, 3; 25 Feb. 1783.

[13] JM Notes, 21 Feb. 1783, and n. 24.

[14] JM Notes, 18 Feb., and nn. 11, 12. For a reversal of the vote on Bland's motion, see JM Notes, 28 Feb. 1783.

Notes on Debates

MS (LC: Madison Papers). For a description of the manuscript of Notes on Debates, see *Papers of Madison*, V, 231–34.

Friday February 28.

A motion was made by Mr. Wolcot and Mr. Dyer to refer the half pay to the States, little differing from the late motion of Mr. Gilman, except that it specified 5 years whole pay as the proper ground of composition with the Officers of the respective lines. On this proposition the arguments used for & agst. Mr. Gilman's motion were recapitulated. It was negatived, Cont. alone answering in the affirmative and no division being called for.[1]

On the question to agree to the report for a commutation of 5 years whole pay, there being 7 ays only it was considered whether this was an appropriation or a new ascertainment of a sum of money necessary for the public service. Some were of opinion at first that it did not fall under that description viz of an appropriation. finally, the contrary opinion was deemed almost unanimously the safest, as well as the most accurate.[2] Another question was whether 7 or 9 votes were to decide doubts whether 7 or 9 were requisite on any question. Some were of opinion that the Secretary[3] ought to make an entry according to his own judgment and that that entry sd. stand unless altered by a positive instruction from Congs. To this it was objected that it wd. make the Secy. the Sovereign in many cases, since a reversal of his entry wd. be impossible, whatever that entry might be; that particularly he might enter 7 votes to be affirmative on a question where 9[4] were necessary, and if supported in it by a few States it wd. [be] irrevocable. It was said by others that the safest rule wd. be to require 9 votes to decide in all cases of doubt whether 9 or 7 were necessary. To this it was objected that one or two States and in any situation 6. States might by raising doubts, stop seven from acting in any case which they disapproved. Fortunately on the case in question there were 9 States of opinion that nine were requisite, so the difficulty was got over for the present.[5]

On a reconsideration of the question whether the duty on wine should be on the quantity or on the value, the mode reported by the Come was reinstated, and the whole report recommited to be included with the 5 PerCt. advalorem in an act of recommendation to the States.[6]

[1] JM Notes, 25 Feb., and nn. 1, 11; 27 Feb. 1783, and n. 2.

[2] New Hampshire, Rhode Island, and New Jersey voted against the recommendation of the Osgood committee. Delaware and Georgia were unrepresented in Congress. Dyer and Wolcott were of opposing views on the issues, thus rendering Connecticut's vote ineffective. Of the Virginia delegates, Mercer was absent, Lee voted "no," and Jones, JM, and Bland, "ay" (JCC, XXIV, 154–55). Article IX of the Articles of Confederation required the affirmative vote of nine or more states for Congress to "appropriate money" (JCC, XIX, 220). By "new ascertainment" JM meant a reassurance of an equivalent of the half pay for life promised to the officers by the resolution of Congress on 21 October 1780 (JM Notes, 25 Feb. 1783, n. 1). Bland introduced the motion, seconded by JM, which led to the decision that to adopt the committee's "proposition" would require the affirmative vote of at least nine states. Of the thirty-two tallied votes, only Dyer's and Mercer's were "no" (JCC, XXIV, 155–56).

[3] Charles Thomson.

[4] JM wrote "nine" above the figure.

[5] See n. 2. The issue seems not to have arisen again in Congress until 5 May 1783 (JM Notes, 5 May 1783, MS in LC: Madison Papers).

[6] JM Notes, 27 Feb., and n. 8; 3 Mar.; Report on Restoring Public Credit, 6 Mar. 1783.

From Edmund Randolph

RC (LC: Madison Papers). Unsigned but in Randolph's hand. Cover addressed by him to "The honble James Madison jr. esq of congress Philadelphia." Docketed by JM, "March 1st. 1783."

RICHMOND. March 1. 1783.

MY DEAR FRIEND

Being here on business, I can not inspect your figures of feby. 18. The drift of them is, however, seen, and I have already met the sentiments half way, by an adherence to my opinion of the necessity of reviving the impost.[1]

A dangerous combination has been formed for counterfeiting tobacco notes and Morris's notes.[2] It extends, like the mountains of America, from south to North. We may hope, that this mint, which has been already been opened with success, will soon be suppressed by the activity of a zealous whig, of genuine honesty. The executive have patronized the measures, which he had adopted for a complete detection.

What renders this scheme of villainy, more perilous, is that it is probable, some of the inspectors have been associated in it; and they, by furnishing marks, weights numbers and names, can always with truth inform the holders of these counterfeits, that such tobacco is to be found in the Warehouses; & yet refuse to deliver the tobacco, when the exporter demands it on these bad notes.[3]

I am told, that the executive have taken a definitive step with respect to the recruiting money. All sums, which have been collected beyond the mountains, are to be retained for the purpose of inlisting; which General Muhlenberg expects may be carried on rapidly. What has been collected below that line, is to be paid into the treasury and from thence distributed into the hands of the different recruiting officers.[4]

My letter of last week miscarried in its journey from my house to the post office, and will therefore go by this post.[5]

[1] JM to Randolph, 18 Feb. 1783, and n. 1. By "figures" Randolph probably meant the encoded portion of that letter which he was unable to decipher because he had not brought the key to Richmond. He had gone there to meet his father's creditors. See Randolph to JM, 1 Feb. 1783, n. 5. For his belief that Congress should revive the impost amendment, see his letters of 1, 7, and 22 Feb. 1783 to JM.

[2] An owner of tobacco, upon depositing it in a public warehouse, received from the inspector a certificate, note, or receipt, recording the weight of, the distinguishing marks on, and the type of tobacco in, each hogshead. This certificate was negotiable and could be used in payment of taxes. If convicted of issuing fraudulent certificates, an inspector was fined, removed from office, and disbarred from hold-

ing any government position in the future. Possibly as a result of the "dangerous combination" to which Randolph referred, the Virginia General Assembly on 28 June 1783 enacted a comprehensive statute which replaced those penalties with "death as in case of felony, without benefit of clergy" and precisely defined the legal form of a printed tobacco note. This law also repeated the provision of earlier legislation making counterfeiting of tobacco notes a capital crime (*JHDV*, May 1783, p. 98; Hening, *Statutes*, IX, 157, 159-60, 502-5, 519; X, 76, 275, 481-82, 508; XI, 94-98, 205-46, and esp. 222, 241-42).

For the promissory notes of Robert Morris, see *Papers of Madison*, IV, 104, n. 1; 361, n. 42; V, 85; 92; 271; 430; 431, n. 4. No Virginia statute provided for the punishment of counterfeiters of those notes. See Randolph to JM, 15 Mar. 1783.

[3] The phrase "south to North" signified that the "dangerous combination" principally included one or more of the inspectors of tobacco in public warehouses in Henrico County and, to the northward, about a dozen residents of Caroline County (*Cal. of Va. State Papers*, III, 466). The inspector most involved was probably Robert Price (d. 1826), who resigned his office at Byrd's warehouses on or about 16 April 1783 (*ibid.*, III, 466; *JCSV*, III, 22, 245; Henrico County Court Records, Will Book 7, p. 7, microfilm in Va. State Library). He seems to have been the inspector whom Randolph called "the cornerstone of the villainy" (Randolph to JM, 29 Mar. 1783). The "zealous whig" was Colonel Samuel Temple (d. 1813), a planter, justice of the peace, and militia officer of Caroline County. From 1792 to 1795 he served in the Virginia General Assembly as senator from the district which included that county (T[homas] E. Campbell, *Colonial Caroline: A History of Caroline County, Virginia* [Richmond, 1954], pp. 259, 266, 274, 348; Swem and Williams, *Register*, pp. 38, 41, 43, 45; Augusta B. Fothergill and John M. Naugle, comps., *Virginia Tax Payers, 1782-87*, p. 125; Caroline County Court Records, Will Book 19, pp. 35-36, microfilm in Va. State Library). For Governor Harrison's support of Temple's measures and for more comment by Randolph on the "scheme," see Randolph to JM, 15 Mar.; 29 Mar. 1783, and n. 4.

[4] For General Muhlenberg, see Harrison to Delegates, 7 Feb., and n. 3. For "the recruiting money," see *Papers of Madison*, V, 93, n. 9; 169; 313; Randolph to JM, 22 Feb. 1783, and n. 7. Recruits were needed west of the Blue Ridge Mountains because of the threat of raids by Indians in Montgomery and Washington counties (McIlwaine, *Official Letters*, III, 456, 457-58; *JCSV*, III, 223, 226, 227). On 1 April 1783 the Council of State advised Governor Harrison to direct the recruiting officers "beyond the blue ridge" to stop "further enlistments of Soldiers for the Continental Service" and "to call into the Treasury the recruiting money collected" there (*ibid.*, III, 238). See also Delegates to Harrison, 8 Apr. 1783, ed. n.

[5] Randolph to JM, 22 Feb., hdn.; JM to Randolph, 18 Mar. 1783, n. 1.

Notes on Debates

MS (LC: Madison Papers). For a description of the manuscript of Notes on Debates, see *Papers of Madison*, V, 231-34.

Monday March 3d.

The Comme. on revenues, reported in addition to the former articles recommended by them,[1] a duty of $\frac{2}{3}$ of a dollar per 112 lbs. on all brown sugars, 1 dollar on all powdered, lumped & clayed sugars; other than loaf sugars, 1⅓ dollar pr. 112 lbs on all loaf sugars, $\frac{1}{30}$ of a dollar per lb on all Bohea Teas, and $\frac{1}{15}$ of a dollar on all finer India Teas.[2] This report without debate or opposition was recommitted to be incorporated with the general plan.[3]

[1] JM Notes, 27 Feb. 1783, and n. 8.

[2] One hundred and twelve pounds, avoirdupois, are a "long hundredweight." One usual step in clarifying or refining sugar was to filter the juice of the cane through clay. "Bohea Teas" are the black, less expensive, varieties.

[3] "This report" and its recommittal are not noted in the official journal. See Report on Restoring Public Credit, 6 Mar. 1783.

Notes on Debates

MS (LC: Madison Papers). For a description of the manuscript of Notes on Debates, see *Papers of Madison*, V, 231–34.

Teusday March 4: & Wednesday March 5.

The motion of Mr. Hamilton on the Journal relative to abatement of the quotas of distressed States was rejected, partly because the principle was disapproved by some, and partly because, it was thought improper to be separated from other objects to be recommended to the States.[1] The latter motive produced the motion for postponing which was lost.[2]

The Committee to whom had been referred the letters of resignation of Mr. Morris reported as their opinion that it was not necessary for Congs. immediately to take any steps thereon. They considered the resignation as conditional, and that if it sd. eventually take place at the time designated, there was no necessity for immediate provision to be made.[3]

Mr. Bland moved that &c (See Journal of Mar: 5)[4]

This motion produced on these two days lengthy & warm debates.[5] Mr. Lee & Mr. Bland on one side disparaging the administration of Mr. Morris', and throwing oblique censure on his character.[6] They considered his letters as an insult to Congs. & Mr. Lee de[c]lared that the man who had published to all the world such a picture of our national character & finances was unfit to be a minister of the latter.[7] On the other side Mr. Wilson & Mr. Hamilton went into a copious defence & Panegyric of Mr. Morris, the ruin in which his resignation if it sd. take effect wd. involve public credit and all the operations dependent on it; and the decency altho' firmness of his letters. The former observed that the declaration of Mr. Morris that he wd. not be the minister of Injustice cd. not be meant to reflect on Congs. because they had declared the funds desired by Mr. Morris to be necessary;[8] and that the friends of the latter could not wish for a more honorable occasion for his retreat from public life, if they did not prefer the public interest to considerations of friendship.[9] Other members were divided as to the propriety of the letters in question. In general however they were thought reprehensible, as in general also a conviction prevailed of the personal merit & public importance of Mr. Morris. All impartial members foresaw the most alarming consequences from his resignation.[10] The prevailing objection to Mr Bland's motion was that its avowed object & tendency was to re-establish a *board* in place of a single minister of finance.[11] Those who apprehended that ultimately this might be unavoidable, thought it so objectionable that nothing but the last necessity would justify it. The motion of Mr. Bland was lost: and a Comme appointed generally on the letters of Mr. Morris.[12]

[1] Alexander Hamilton offered his motion on 4 March (*JCC*, XXIV, 162). For earlier attempts by him and other delegates to have Congress provide for an "abatement," see JM Notes, 8 Feb., and n. 3; 11 Feb., and n. 9; 17 Feb.; 26 Feb., and nn. 8–13, 22, 25, 28, 37, 43; JM to Randolph, 25 Feb. 1783. Hamilton's repeated effort to that end certainly reflected in large degree the occupation by the British of New York City and its environs ever since mid-summer 1776—by far the longest period of their control anywhere in the United States during the Revolution. Of the ten states effectively represented in Congress, only New York voted in favor of Hamilton's motion (*JCC*, XXIV, 163).

In a letter of 5 March explaining to Governor George Clinton their lack of success, Hamilton and William Floyd, the only other delegate in Congress from New York, wrote: "Different motives operated in the dismission. Many were opposed to the principle and others wished to postpone 'till this matter with many others could be taken up on a general plan" (Syrett and Cooke, *Papers of Hamilton*, III, 281). Representing a state which naturally would favor an "abatement," JM was among the "others" who agreed with the "principle" of the motion but voted against it as premature (Harrison to Delegates, 7 Feb.; JM Notes, 26 Feb. 1783).

[2] Prior to the vote mentioned in n. 1, Abraham Clark of New Jersey, seconded by Phillips White of New Hampshire, moved to postpone action on Hamilton's proposal. Clark's motion was unanimously supported by the delegates from six states, including Virginia—thus failing of adoption by a margin of one state (*JCC*, XXIV, 162–63).

[3] JM Notes, 24 Jan., and nn. 20, 23; 26 Feb., and n. 14; 27 Feb. 1783. Although unnoted in the official journal, the Rutledge committee submitted its report on 4 March 1783 (NA: PCC, No. 19, IV, 385; No. 186, fol. 85). The report was debated on that day and the next.

[4] Theodorick Bland, seconded by Arthur Lee, moved that the report of the Rutledge committee "be postponed, in order to take into consideration" their proposal to appoint a committee "to devise the most proper means of arranging the department of finance." The "arranging" which Bland and Lee had in mind was

the replacement of the office of superintendent of finance by a Treasury Board. See JM's sentence near the close of his present notes, and n. 11.

John Rutledge, seconded by Samuel Holten, countered by moving that the report of his committee and the Bland-Lee proposal "be committed." The two Virginians voted for the Rutledge-Holten recommendation but it failed to carry. Congress thereupon rejected the Bland-Lee motion by a vote of 5 to 1. Rutledge voted "no," but his South Carolina colleagues, Ralph Izard and John Lewis Gervais, turned that state's vote in favor of the motion (*JCC*, XXIV, 165–66). See n. 12.

⁵ JM's statement is misleading, for the debate on the Bland-Lee motion, introduced on 5 March, was confined to that day (NA: PCC, No. 36, II, 47–48). The report of the Rutledge committee, submitted on 4 March, was debated without doubt on both that day and the next (NA: PCC, No. 186, fol. 85).

⁶ For earlier attacks upon Robert Morris by Lee and occasionally by Bland, see *Papers of Madison*, IV, 247; 250, nn. 13, 17; 264; 313; 341, n. 4; 343; 419; 447; 449, n. 7; V, 431, n. 4; Harrison to JM, 4 Jan., and n. 3; JM to Randolph, 22 Jan.; Randolph to JM, 7 Feb. 1783. See also Lee's letter of 5 March 1783 to Samuel Adams in Burnett, *Letters*, VII, 67–68.

⁷ Arthur Lee referred to the Morris letter of 24 January 1783 (JM Notes, 24 Jan. 1783, and n. 20). This letter and Morris' letter of 26 February appeared in the *Pennsylvania Packet* of 4 March and in the *Pennsylvania Gazette* of the next day.

⁸ In his letter of 24 January to Congress, Morris had stated, "I should be unworthy of the Confidence reposed in me by my fellow Citizens, If I did not explicitly declare that I will never be the Minister of Injustice" (NA: PCC, No. 137, II, 115–16; JM Notes, 24 Jan., and n. 20; 28 Jan., n. 40). For the resolution of Congress referred to by James Wilson, see JM Notes, 29 Jan. 1783, and n. 13.

⁹ Morris' choice of a time to "retreat" could be defended as "honorable," both for the reason stated by him in n. 8 and because, as he remarked in his letter of 24 January, the "public Danger" from the "common Enemy," which alone had induced him to accept the office of superintendent of finance, had greatly "lessened."

¹⁰ Burnett, *Letters*, VII, 56, 65, n. 4; JM to Randolph, 4 Mar.; 11 Mar. 1783.

¹¹ The word *"board"* was underlined by JM. Between 1775 and 1779 Congress administered its financial operations through a succession of boards, committees, and "offices." An ordinance of 30 July 1779 established a "Board of Treasury" with a structure which remained essentially unchanged until its dissolution on 20 September 1781—nearly three months after Robert Morris began his tenure as superintendent of finance (*JCC*, XIV, 903–7; *Papers of Madison*, III, 137, n. 4; Jennings B. Sanders, *Evolution of Executive Departments of the Continental Congress, 1774–1789* [Chapel Hill, N.C., 1935], pp. 50–74, 132). Morris continued to serve until November 1784. Although Congress on 29 May of that year provided for the creation by 10 November of a Board of Commissioners of the Treasury, the first election of the three commissioners was delayed until 25 January 1785 (Burnett, *Letters*, VII, 486, 523, 538, and n. 2, 541, 544, 606, and n. 3; Harrison to JM, 4 Jan. 1783, n. 5; Jennings B. Sanders, *Evolution of Executive Departments*, pp. 145–47).

¹² The committee of five, with Rutledge as chairman, apparently submitted no report before being discharged on 28 April 1783 (NA: PCC, No. 186, fols. 85, 86; *JCC*, XXIV, 168, and n. 1).

Virginia Delegates to Benjamin Harrison

RC (Jasper E. Crane, Wilmington, Del., 1957). In the hand of John F. Mercer, except for the other four signatures. Cover franked and addressed by him to "His Excellency Benjamin Harrison Esqr. Governor of Virginia." Docketed, "Lr. from the Delegates in Congress—March 4th. 1783."

PHILA. March 4th. 1783

SIR

We have receiv'd your Excellency's Letter of the 26th. Ult, enclosing a copy of the King of Great Britain's speech, wch tho' much mutilated, is in substance, the same with the genuine one transmitted you by Express.

That, & the two Letters of Lord Townshend are the only pecies of intelligence, that bear the marks of authenticity respecting the final adjustment of Peace in Europe.[1]

To this moment Congress are without official information of the formal signing of any Treaty by the belligerent Powers either partially or generally. the Minister of France, is we apprehend, without intelligence on the important head,[2] & we have no reason to suppose that they are in a state of less uncertainty at N York.[3]

Fluctuating reports respecting this subject, as various in their nature, as the interested sources from whence 'tis probable they spring, prevail here. for them we refer to the papers enclosed,[4] &

with much respect, are Yr. Excellency's most obedient & humble servants

> A. LEE
> THEOK: BLAND JR.
> JOS: JONES.
> JOHN F. MERCER
> J MADISON JR.

We fear the certificate respecting Nathan's account has arriv'd too late, to influence the determination of the arbitrators.[5]

[1] JM to Randolph, 4 Feb., and n. 12; 13 Feb., and n. 3; JM Notes, 13 Feb., n. 10; Delegates to Harrison, 18 Feb.; Harrison to Delegates, 21 Feb. 1783, and n. 4. Instead of "26th," Mercer should have written "24th" and "pieces," not "pecies."

[2] The Chevalier de La Luzerne as well as Congress first received official word on 12 March that a preliminary peace treaty between Great Britain and the United States had been agreed upon (JM Notes, 12–15 Mar. 1783; William E. O'Donnell, *Chevalier de La Luzerne*, p. 235).

³ Referring to the "contradictory reports" about the outlook for peace, Washington in a letter of 4 March 1783 to Governor Harrison of Virginia wrote: "The Enemy in New York are as impatient, and as much in the dark as we are on this occasion; not having received a Packet for more than two Months" (Fitzpatrick, *Writings of Washington*, XXVI, 183).

⁴ Probably the *Pennsylvania Packet* of 1 and 4 March and the *Pennsylvania Journal* of 1 March. Items in these papers about the peace negotiations vary from a terse report of the signing of a treaty to those alleging that discussions had "broke off" because of the refusal of either the French or Dutch commissioners to agree to terms acceptable to Great Britain. On 3 March 1783, according to the *Packet* of the next day, an unsubstantiated rumor of Boston origin was "confidently circulated" in Philadelphia that a peace treaty had been concluded at Paris.

⁵ Harrison to Delegates, 15 Feb.; 21 Feb. 1783.

To Edmund Randolph

RC (LC: Madison Papers). Unsigned but in JM's hand. Cover franked by "J. Madison Jr." and addressed by him to "Edmund Randolph Esqr. Richmond." Docketed by Randolph, "James Madison March 4, 1783." The italicized words are those written by JM in the Randolph code, for which see *Papers of Madison*, V, 307; 309, n.1.

PHILADA. March 4. 1783

MY DEAR SIR

The past week has not added a syllable of evidence to our preceding calculations of peace. The inferences from the suspence are as various as the fancies & interests of those who make them.¹ Your letter by last post which came to hand the day after the usual time adopts I conceive the most rational solution, namely, the difficulties & delays incident to so complicated a negociation.²

Provision for the public debts continues to be the wearisome topic of congressional discussion.³ *Mercer declared* that although *he deems* the *opponents of a general revenue right in* principle, *yet as they had no plan and* it was *essential that some thing should be done he should strike in with* the *other side*⁴

A letter from Genl. *Knox* is in Town which I under stand places the *temper and affairs of army in a* less *alarming view* than some preceding *accounts*⁵

The resignation of the Superintendt. of finance with his motives are contained in paper inclosed. It is as you may well suppose a subject of general and anxious conversation. The effect on public credit will be fully anticipated by your knowledge of our affairs.[6] Yesterday's Mail brought me no letter from you. Adieu

Mr. Jefferson is here awaiting further instructions of Congs. which w[ill?] be adapted to the first authorita[tive] advices from Europe.[7]

[1] Delegates to Harrison, 4 Mar. 1783, and n. 4.

[2] Randolph to JM, 15 Feb., and n. 3. See also JM to Jefferson, 18 Feb., and n. 2; JM to Randolph, 18 Feb. 1783. Mail from Richmond usually arrived in Philadelphia on Monday. JM probably received Randolph's letter of the fifteenth on Tuesday, 25 February 1783.

[3] JM Notes, 26 Feb.; 27 Feb.; 28 Feb.; 3 Mar. 1783.

[4] JM to Randolph, 25 Feb., and n. 3; JM Notes, 27 Feb. 1783, and nn. 3, 4. In encoding *"side,"* JM inadvertently used the cipher for "sl" rather than for "si."

[5] The letter of General Henry Knox to which JM referred may have been addressed either to Gouverneur Morris or General Alexander McDougall, both of whom were in Philadelphia. Writing on 21 February from West Point, N.Y., to each of them about the *"temper and affairs"* of Washington's army, Knox was somewhat more optimistic in his comments to Morris than in those to McDougall. On 3 March in a letter to his friend Secretary at War Benjamin Lincoln, Knox strongly urged that "every thing respecting the Army be decided upon before peace takes place," for if the troops were disbanded without a "settlement" of their pay, they would become the country's "tygers and wolves" (Mass. Historical Society: Papers of Henry Knox).

For examples of "preceding *accounts,"* see *Papers of Madison,* V, 159; 162, n. 16; 474, n. 8; JM Notes, 13 Jan., and n. 5; 19 Feb., and n. 12; 20 Feb, and nn. 18–20; 25 Feb., and n. 1; JM to Randolph, 13 Feb., and n. 6; 25 Feb. 1783. See also Syrett and Cooke, *Papers of Hamilton,* III, 254–55, 277–79.

[6] JM Notes, 24 Jan., and nn. 20, 23; 26 Feb., and n. 14, 27 Feb.; 4–5 March 1783, and nn. 3, 4, 6–9, 11, 12.

[7] JM to Jefferson, 15 Feb. 1783, and n. 5.

Memorandum on a Revenue Plan

MS (LC: Jefferson Papers). Three pages of notes, undated and unsigned but in JM's hand. Probably given to Thomas Jefferson in Philadelphia about 6 March 1783. Many years later Jefferson's secretary, Nicholas P. Trist, attached to the memorandum a page bearing the comment, "This is, I believe, in the handwriting of Mr. Madison, *N.P.T.*"

EDITORIAL NOTE

Ca. 6 March 1783. The contents of this memorandum, except as indicated below, are repetitive of JM's long footnote in his notes on debates for 26 February 1783 (*q.v.,* and nn. 15–44). For this reason, only the variations of information or opinion between the two documents are here indicated. The memorandum was given to Jefferson, who had been in Baltimore during much of the debate, on or about 6 March 1783, so that he might understand some of the conflicts of interests which necessarily shaped the recommendations of the committee.

JM entitled the memorandum:

"Plan proposed consists of 1st. permanent revenue. 2. abatements in favor of the States distressed by the war—3. common mass of all reasonable expences incurred by the States without sanction of Congress—4. territorial cessions.

Manner in which the interests of the several States will be affected by these objects."

In this memorandum, except for one instance, JM used the expression "permanent revenue" as a replacement of the term "general revenue" employed in his note. He probably viewed these designations as synonymous, even though the one stresses the duration and the other the scope of the income recommended for the use of Congress.

In his footnote JM stated that "it is presumed in most instances, she [Rhode Island] would be opposed to making a common mass of expences." In the memorandum, on the other hand, JM recorded that Rhode Island would not be "agst. a common mass." This contrast in opinion and the other differences noted in the next two paragraphs suggest that debates or conferences subsequent to 26 February had convinced JM of the need to modify what he had written in his footnote about these particular matters as viewed by Rhode Island, Connecticut, and Pennsylvania.

In the footnote JM wrote that Connecticut's "interest is opposed to abatements, and to a common mass of expences." In the memorandum he noted that Connecticut was "strenous agst. abatements—in favor of common, having often employed militia without sanction of Congss."

Instead of Pennsylvania being "interested against abatements; and against a common mass," as stated in his footnote, JM's memorandum points out that Pennsylvania is "not interested in abatemts. nor common mass, but has espoused both."

JM remarked in his footnote that Virginia was "interested in abatements, and essentially so in a common mass, not only her excentric expenditures being enormous; but many of her necessary ones havg. rcd. no previous or subsequent sanction." The corresponding statement in the memorandum reads: "It is uncertain how the credits of her Citizens may stand in a liquidation of their claims vs U. S—interested somewhat perhaps in abatements—particularly so in a common mass—not only her excentric expenditures being enormous but many of them which have been similar to those allowed to other States, having recd. no sanction of Congs."

Referring in his memorandum to the citizens of North Carolina, JM remarked that "their claims for supplies must be great." In his footnote he had implied rather than explicitly stated this belief.

In the footnote, immediately preceding "a state of the loan office debt," which JM omitted in the present memorandum, he wrote: "it may be proper to include in it ['this plan'] a recommendation to the States to rescind the rule of apportioning pecuniary burdens according to the value of land, & to substitute that of numbers, reckoning two slaves as equal to one free man." The parallel passage at the close of the memorandum reads: "a recommendation is to be included for substituting numbers in place of the value of land as the rule of apportionment. In this all the States are interested if proper deductions be made from the number of Slaves."

The shift from "may be" to "is to be," together with the other factual differences noted above, indicates that JM wrote his memorandum for Jefferson shortly before the report on restoring public credit was delivered to Congress on 6 March. By then JM obviously could inform his friend what the recommendation 'is to be." That report, drafted by JM on behalf of a committee, included a proposal to allocate the financial quotas among the states "in proportion to the number of inhabitants of every age, sex and condition," excepting Indians not taxed and slaves "between the ages of _____ ." See Report on Restoring Public Credit, 6 Mar. 1783.

Report on Restoring Public Credit

MS (NA: PCC, No. 26, fols. 411½, 438–40). In JM's hand, except where otherwise noted. Docketed by Benjamin Bankson, Jr., a clerk in the office of the secretary of Congress: "Report of Mr. Gorham   Mr. Hamilton   Mr. Madison   Mr. FitzSimmons   Mr. Rutledge   Appointed to consider the means of restoring & supporting public Credit & of obtaining from the States substantial funds for funding the whole debt of the United States. Delivered March 6, 1783. Acted on April 18th 1783."

[6 March 1783]

Resolved[1] that it be recommended to the several States as indispensably necessary to the restoration of public credit and the punctual & honorable discharge of the public debts, to vest in the U. S. in Congress assd. a power to levy for the use of the U. S., a duty of 5 PerCt. ad valorem, at the time & place of importation, upon all goods wares and merchandizes of foreign growth and manufactures, which may be imported into any of the said States, from any foreign port, island or plantation, except arms, ammunition, cloathing & other articles imported on account of the United States or any of them, except wool cards, cotton cards & wire for making them, and also except salt during the war:

Also a like duty of 5 PerCt. ad valorem on all prizes & prize goods condemned in the Court of Admiralty of any of these States as lawful prize:[2]

Also to levy a duty of $\frac{1}{8}$ of a dollar per Bushel on all Salt imported as aforesaid after the war. $\frac{1}{15}$ of a dollar per Gallon on all wines $\frac{1}{30}$ of a dollar per Gallon on all rum & brandy $\frac{2}{3}$ of a dollar per 112 lbs. on all brown sugars, 1 dollar per 112 lbs. on all powdered, lump & clayed sugars other than loaf sugars, $1\frac{1}{3}$ dollar[3] on all loaf sugars $\frac{1}{30}$ of a dollar Per lb. on all Bohea Tea and $\frac{1}{15}$ of a dollar per lb on all finer India Teas, imported as aforesaid,[4] after   , in addition to the five per cent above mentioned[5]

Provided that none of the said duties shall be applied to any other purpose than the discharge of the interest or principals of the debts which shall have been contracted on the faith of the U. S. for supporting the present war, nor be continued for a longer term than 25 years; and provided that the collectors of the said duties shall be appointed by the States within which their offices are to be respectively exercised; but when so appointed shall be amenable to, and removeable by the U. S. in Congs. assd. alone and in case any State shall not make such appt. within   after notice given for that purpose, the appointmt may then be made by the U. S. in Congs. assd.[6]

That it be further recommended to the several States to establish for a like term not exceeding 25 years, and to appropriate to the discharge of the Interest & principal of the debts which shall have been contracted on the faith of the U.S. for supporting the present war, substantial & effectual revenues of such nature as they may respectively judge most convenient[7] to the amount of   and in the proportions following, viz.[8]

That an annual account of the proceeds and application of the aforementioned revenues shall be made out & transmitted to the several states distinguishing the proceeds of each of the specified articles, & the amount of the whole revenue received from each State.[9]

the said revenues to be collected by persons appointed as aforesaid; but to be carried to the separate credit of the States within wch. they shall be collected, and be liquidated & adjusted among the States according to the quotas which may from time to time be allotted to them:[10]

That[11] none of the preceding resolutions shall take effect untill all of them shall be acceded to by every State, after Which unanimous accession, however, they shall be considered as forming a mutual compact among all the States, and shall be irrevocable, by any one or more of them without the concurrence of the whole, or of a majority of the U. S. in Congs. assembd.;[12] provided that after the unanimous accession to all the said preceding resolutions, the proposed alteration in the 8th. of the Articles of Confederation shall not hereafter be revoked or varied otherwise than as is pointed out in the 13th. of the Said articles.[13]

That as a further mean[s] as well of hastening the extinguishment of the debts, as of establishing the harmony of the U. States it be recommended to the States which have passed no acts towards complying

with the Resolutions of Congs. of the 6 of Sepr. & 10 of Ocr. 1780, relative to territorial cessions, to make the liberal cessions therein recommended, and to the States wch. may have passed acts complying with the
said resolutions in part only, to revise and complete such compliances.[14]

That in order to remove all objections agst. a retrospective application
of the constitutional rule of proportioning to the Several States the
charges & expences which shall have been supplied for the common defence or general welfare, it be recommended to them to enable Congress
to make such equitable exceptions and abatements as the particular circumstances of the States from time to time during the war may be found
to require.[15]

That conformably to the liberal principles on which these recommendations are founded, and with a view to a more amicable & complete
adjustment of all accounts between the U. S. & individual States, all
reasonable expences which shall have been incurred by the States, without the sanction of Congress, in their defence agst. or attacks upon
British or Savage Enemies, either by sea or by land, and which shall be
supported by satisfactory proofs, shall be considered as part of the
common charges incident to the present war, and be allowed as such;[16]

That as a more convenient and certain rule of ascertaining the proportions to be supplied by the States respectively to the common Treasury,
the following alteration in the articles of confederation & perpetual
Union between these States, be & the same is hereby agreed to in Congress, & the several States are advised to authorize their respective Delegates to subscribe & ratify the same as part of the said instrument of
Union, in the words following to wit:

"So much of the 8th. of the Articles of Confederation and perpetual
Union between the 13 States of America, as is contained in the words
following to wit., 'all charges of war &c. [to the end of the paragraph']¹⁷
is hereby revoked and made void; and in place thereof it is declared &
concluded, the same having been agreed to in a Congress of the U.
States; 'that all charges of war & all other expences that[18] shall be incurred for the common defence or general welfare, and allowed by the
United States in Congress assembled shall be Defrayed out of a common
treasury, which shall be supplied by the several states in proportion to
the number of inhabitants of every age, sex and condition, except Indians not paying taxes in each State; which number shall be triennially
taken & transmitted to the U. S. Congs. assd. in such mode as they shall
direct and appoint; provided always, that in such numeration no persons
shall be included who are[19] bound to servitude for life according to the

laws of the State to which they belong, other than such as may be between the ages of   [' "][20]

[1] For the appointment and personnel of the committee which submitted this report, see JM Notes, 21 Feb. 1783, and n. 29. Although largely drafted by JM, the report includes specific recommendations which he had opposed, a few which he had been the first to suggest, and others which he also had supported. For this reason the report illustrates not so much JM's originality of ideas as his talent for bringing together and clearly expressing in a fairly short document a group of recommendations designed to counterbalance opposing sectional, economic interests and to appeal to all members of Congress except uncompromising nationalists and state-sovereignty advocates. Even so, in at least one important matter of paragraph arrangement, JM as draftsman was obliged to defer to the judgment of a majority of the committee. See JM Notes, 7 Mar. 1783, and n. 2.

[2] Except for the addition of the words, "necessary to the restoration of public credit and the punctual & honorable discharge of the public debts," and the omission of the phrase, "after the first day of May, 1781," the report to this point reproduces almost exactly the first two paragraphs of the 5 per cent impost amendment adopted by Congress on 3 February 1781 (JCC, XIX, 112–13). See also JM Notes, 24 Jan., and n. 20; 28 Jan., and nn. 29–31; 29 Jan., and nn. 18, 20, 25, 38; 12 Feb., and nn. 1, 3; 13 Feb., and n. 1; 18 Feb.; 19 Feb. 1783, and n. 3.

[3] Immediately after this word, "per 112 lbs." was added in the committee's report as printed in the journal of Congress for 6 March and as copied by JM in his notes for the next day. See JCC, XXIV, 171.

[4] JM Notes, 27 Feb., and nn. 8–10, 14; 28 Feb.; 3 Mar. 1783, and nn. 2, 3.

[5] The words following "aforesaid" are in Charles Thomson's hand. For the debate in Congress on the first three paragraphs of the report, see JM Notes, 18 Feb., and nn. 11, 12; 27 Feb., and n. 8; 11 Mar. 1783.

[6] JM Notes, 29 Jan., and n. 25; 12 Feb., and nn. 5–9, 13–15; 19 Feb., and nn. 3, 8, 22, 23; 20 Feb. 1783, and n. 9. By 18 March, "one month" had been entered in the blank space after "within" (JCC, XXIV, 189). As an addition to the closing sentence of this paragraph in the manuscript of the report, but as an immediately succeeding paragraph in the report as printed in the journal of Congress, the following words in Thomson's hand were canceled, "and provided further that an account of the proceeds and application of the said revenues be returned to the different states annually" (JCC, XXIV, 171). This passage, which is omitted in the version of the report copied by JM in his notes for 7 March, was deleted, obviously because its subject is treated in a later paragraph of the report. See n. 9.

[7] The proposal in this paragraph reflects the belief that, even though the states should empower Congress to levy the 5 per cent impost and the tariffs recommended earlier in the report, the resulting revenue would be insufficient to cover the interest and principal of the war debt and the other expenses of Congress. See JM to Randolph, 22 Jan.; 4 Feb.; JM Notes, 27 Jan.; 28 Jan., and n. 11; 29 Jan., and n. 36; 19 Feb., and n. 7; 20 Feb., and n. 14; 21 Feb., and nn. 16, 27; 27 Feb. 1783.

[8] The table, which JM also omitted from the copy of the report in his notes for 7 March, is in the hand of Thomas FitzSimons, a member of the committee (NA: PCC, No. 26, fol. 413). The committee proposed that Congress be furnished annually by the states with a total of $2,000,000, proportioned among them in sums varying between $320,000 from Massachusetts and $24,000 from Georgia (JCC, XXIV, 171–72, n. 4). See JM Notes, 25 Feb.; 21 Mar.; 4 Apr. 1783.

[9] This paragraph, which is in Charles Thomson's hand, appears both in JM's notes for 7 March and in the printed, official copy of the report immediately after, rather than immediately before, the paragraph beginning, "the said revenues to be col-

lected . . ." (NA: PCC, No. 26, fol. 412; *JCC*, XXV, 983–84). Obviously, this reversal of position provides a more logical sequence of subjects than in the present version and the one in *JCC*, XXIV, 172.

The Massachusetts General Court qualified its ratification of the proposed 5 per cent impost amendment by stipulating that Congress must notify each state annually how much money had been collected and how it had been spent (NA: PCC, No. 74, fol. 193; Randolph to JM, 3 Jan., n. 8; JM Notes, 28 Jan., n. 29). John F. Mercer and other delegates had also insisted that the states should be supplied with "full information" (JM Notes, 21 Feb. 1783 and citations in n. 22). See also *Papers of Madison*, V, 407, n. 1.

10 The mode of appointing the collectors and of equitably apportioning to the credit of all the states the revenue from impost duties, which would mainly be paid in the ports of a few of the states, had been frequent subjects of debate. See, for example, JM Notes, 27 Jan.; 28 Jan., and nn. 3, 12, 29; 29 Jan., and nn. 28, 29, 33, 34; 21 Feb., and n. 16; 26 Feb. 1783, and nn. 19, 23.

11 In the space immediately below the last line of the preceding paragraph, JM wrote, "⊙ see 4 page)." On the fourth, or last, page of the manuscript he placed "⊙" before the beginning of the present paragraph. For this reason the editors have transferred the paragraph to the place in the report indicated by JM. In a footnote to his notes of 7 March (*q.v.*, and n. 2), JM pointed out the importance of this change.

12 Judging from JM's notes, Theodorick Bland had been the first delegate to suggest that a grant by the states to Congress should be "irrevocable" as long as Congress or "nine of the States" upheld it (JM Notes, 29 Jan., and n. 36). See also JM Notes, 21 Feb. 1783, and n. 8.

13 The passage beginning after the semicolon and continuing to the close of the paragraph was canceled by JM and is also shown as deleted in *JCC*, XXIV, 172. Both the printed official version of the report and JM's copy of the report in his notes for 7 March omit the expunged words. For the eighth article of the Articles of Confederation, see JM Notes, 9–10 Jan., nn. 3, 8; 14 Jan., nn. 4, 6; 28 Jan. 1783, n. 19. The thirteenth article stipulated that "the Articles of this confederation shall be inviolably observed by every state, and the union shall be perpetual; nor shall any alteration at any time hereafter be made in any of them; unless such alteration be agreed to in a congress of the united states, and be afterwards confirmed by the legislatures of every state" (*JCC*, XIX, 221).

14 For the resolutions of 6 September and 10 October 1780, see *JCC*, XVII, 806–7; XVIII, 915–16. Although Connecticut, New York, Virginia, Massachusetts, North Carolina, South Carolina, and Georgia claimed territory west of the Appalachian Mountains, only the first three of these states had offered to cede some or all of their claims to the United States. Virginia's tender of most of her lands west and northwest of the Ohio River was hedged by many provisos and had been a subject of frequent debate in Congress for over two years. The proposal of Connecticut to yield jurisdiction but not title to her "western reserve" in the Ohio country still awaited the decision of Congress. New York, seeking the support of delegates from other states to her claim to Vermont, had made an unqualified and hence an acceptable offer of her doubtfully legal western claims to Congress. See *Papers of Madison*, III, 210, n. 4; 283, n. 6; 286, n. 5; 301, n. 1; 304, n. 1; IV, 32–34; 34, n. 8; 200–202; 203, n. 16; V, 32, n. 23; 52, n. 14; 115–16; 117, n. 9; 118, n. 14; 119, n. 20; 228, n. 13; 241; 245, nn. 3, 5; 246, nn. 6, 7, 10; 366, n. 12; JM Notes, 30 Jan., n. 2; 26 Feb. 1783, and nn. 20, 24, 29, 37, 38, 40, 42, 43.

Besides the two reasons stated at the outset of this paragraph of the report, satisfactory offers of cession by the five remaining claimant states would be the more timely because of the hope, if not the expectation, that the United States in the treaty of peace would be vested by Great Britain with her title to the territory between the Appalachian watershed and the Mississippi River (*Papers of Madison*, II, 127–35; IV, 4–7; 168–69; V, 23, n. 14; 33; 187; 189, nn. 14, 17; 418, n. 19; 443, n. 2; 444, n. 7; Comment by Jefferson, 25 Jan., and n. 1; JM Notes, 29 Jan.; 30 Jan., n. 2; Randolph to JM, 7 Feb. 1783.

15 *Papers of Madison*, V, 457–58; JM Notes, 26 Feb., and nn. 22, 25, 28, 37, 40, 43; 4–5 Mar., and nn. 1, 2; JM to Randolph, 25 Feb., and citations in n. 7; Memo. on Revenue Plan, 6 Mar. 1783, ed. n.

16 JM interlineated "reasonable" before "expences" as a substitute for a passage immediately following "be allowed as such," which he canceled so heavily as to leave discernible only an occasional word or letter. These vestiges permit no doubt that the deleted passage was the same or nearly the same as the following passage quoted in his footnote to his notes of 7 March (*q.v.* and n. 3): "provided that this allowance shall not be extended to any expences which shall be declared by nine votes in Congress to be manifestly unreasonable."

During emergencies caused by British or Indian invasions, states often had been obliged to spend money and allocate military supplies on behalf of the "common cause" without prior authorization by Congress. Massachusetts, for example, should be enabled by this provision of the report to recover from the Confederation the full cost of the Penobscot expedition; Connecticut to secure compensation for often calling out her "militia without sanction of Congss."; Virginia to gain reimbursement of her "excentric expenditures" in the Northwest; and the citizens of North Carolina to have their "great" claims satisfied (JM Notes, 26 Feb., and n. 22; Memo. on Revenue Plan, 6 Mar. 1783, ed. n.). Although South Carolina and Georgia would have fewer claims of this nature, since occupation by the British army had caused the government in each state to collapse, their ravaged condition would entitle them to correspondingly larger "abatements" in the amount of the financial requisitions which they owed to Congress. See *Papers of Madison*, V, 119, n. 20; JM Notes, 27 Jan., and nn. 13, 27; 17 Feb., and n. 4; 26 Feb. and citations in n. 17; 7 Mar., and n. 4; Memo. on Revenue Plan, 6 Mar. 1783, ed. n.

17 See n. 13. The brackets and the phrase they enclose are in the manuscript of the report.

18 The passage beginning with "that" and continuing through the words "several states" is in the hand of Charles Thomson. For this reason the passage is bracketed in the Hunt edition of the journal of Congress (*JCC*, XXIV, 173, and n. 1).

19 Immediately following "are," JM at first wrote and canceled "deemed slaves."

20 This blank remained unfilled in the other two versions of the report mentioned in n. 13, above. For the issues of how frequently the enumeration should be made and how heavily the slaves should be weighted in apportioning tax quotas among the states, see Randolph to JM, 7 Feb., n. 3; JM to Randolph, 18 Feb.; JM Notes, 14 Jan.; 28 Jan., nn. 35, 42; 7 Feb.; 11 Feb., and nn. 2, 4; 17 Feb., and nn. 1, 3; 26 Feb., and n. 44; 28 Mar.; 1 Apr.; Memo. on Revenue Plan, 6 Mar., ed. n.; Amendment to Report on Public Credit, 28 Mar. 1783, and ed. n. Congress immediately had this report printed as a broadside for distribution to the delegates (*JCC*, XXIV, 174, n. 1; JM Notes, 6 Mar.; 7 Mar. 1783).

Notes on Debates

MS (LC: Madison Papers). For a description of the manuscript of Notes on Debates, see *Papers of Madison*, V, 231–34.

Thursday March 6.

The come. on Revenue made a report which was ordered to be printed for each member, and to be taken up on monday next.[1]

[1] *JCC*, XXIV, 170–74, 174, n. 1; Report on Restoring Public Credit, 6 Mar.; JM Notes, 7 Mar. 1783.

Notes on Debates

MS (LC: Madison Papers). For a description of the manuscript of Notes and Debates, see *Papers of Madison*, V, 231–34.

EDITORIAL NOTE

Except for its first sentence and the footnote, JM's entry for this day is limited to a reproduction of the Report on Restoring Public Credit, 6 March 1783 (*q.v.*), drawn from the printed version of that report distributed the next day to each delegate in Congress. Three copies of this broadside are in NA: PCC, No. 26, fols. 411–13. For the purpose of recording the outcome of the prolonged debates on the report, Charles Thomson or members of his clerical staff marginated each of these copies differently and marked within their text.

To have a convenient means of referring to the particular subject at issue during these debates, JM numbered the paragraphs sequentially from "(1)" to "(12)" in the report copied in his notes for 7 March. See text of notes and nn. 2 and 3, below; also, for example, JM Notes, 21 Mar.; 27 Mar. 1783, and nn. 1, 2. This numbering, the variation mentioned in footnotes 3, 6, 9, 13, and 18 of the Report on Restoring Public Credit, 6 March 1783, and many unimportant differences of abbreviations, capitalization, and punctuation make each of the four versions contrast in minor respects with the other three, even though they almost never differ in their factual contents.

Friday March 7.

Printed copies of the rept. abovementioned were delivered to each member as follows, viz.[1]

. . . . *

* In the draught as laid before the Come. by ___ the (7) paragraph was placed last of all, so as to render the plan indivisible.[2] In the (10) paragraph the word "reason-

able" before the word "expences," was not inserted; but to the paragraph were added "provided that this allowance shall not be extended to any expences which shall be declared by nine votes in Congress to be manifestly unreasonable."[3] In other respects the original draught was unaltered; except that a former resolution of Congress in the words of the (6) paragraph was incorporated by the Secy. before it went to the press.

[1] For the "rept. abovementioned," see Report on Restoring Public Credit, 6 Mar.; JM Notes, 6 Mar. 1783. In his notes for the present day, immediately following the close of his copy of the report, JM placed an asterisk and drew a line in ink across the page of the manuscript to signify that the remainder of his notes for 7 March was in the nature of a footnote to the report as a whole.

[2] The blank should be filled with Madison's name. As already mentioned, his "draught" of the plan for restoring public credit closes with a paragraph beginning: "That none of the preceding resolutions shall take effect untill all of them shall be acceded to by every State, after which unanimous accession, however, they shall be considered as forming a mutual compact among all the States, and shall be irrevocable." Although JM thereby intended "to render the plan indivisible," he either was persuaded or obliged by the other members of "the Come.," upon laying "the draught" before them, to shift this recommendation so as to make it apply only to the first six paragraphs of the report (Report on Restoring Public Credit, 6 Mar., and hdn., and nn. 1, 2, 11, 13; JM to Jefferson, 22 Apr. 1783, and n. 9).

By following the arrangement of JM's manuscript as closely as possible, the reproduction of his report in the present volume makes this "mutual compact" paragraph appear to be the eighth rather than the seventh. JM evidently considered the sixth and what appears to be, from the beginning indentation, the seventh paragraph as only one paragraph. He naturally so assumed for, as he stated in the final sentence of his footnote, the sixth paragraph was lengthened, before Congress sent it "to the press," by an insert in Charles Thomson's hand.

[3] If, as mentioned in n. 2, the sixth and seventh paragraphs of JM's manuscript of the report are counted as one paragraph, what seems to be its eleventh paragraph will become the tenth and correspond in number with the tenth paragraph of the printed report from which JM copied in these notes for 7 March (Report on Restoring Public Credit, 6 Mar. 1783, and n. 16; JCC, XXV, 921–22).

From Edmund Randolph

RC (LC: Madison Papers). Unsigned but in Randolph's hand. Cover missing.

PETTUS's[1] March 7. 1783.

MY DEAR FRIEND

In my letter of last week, I mentioned, I believe, the great probability of Mr. Henry's return to active legislation and my communication to him of the awful crisis, in which America seems to stand, but which his aid might tend to dissipate.[2] As yet I have not received an answer: but I suggested to his recollection the uncontested field now lying before him.[3]

I met some of my father's creditors on monday last. But the most capital were absent. I am afraid, that they are resolved to act with the utmost hostility against me, in order to squander by their rigorous exactions the little fortune, given me by my uncle on my father's death. I shall make one further attempt to a composition of debts: and if I should succeed, my idea of resigning will be adopted.[4] Without it, my pecuniary embarrassments will be so great for the present year, that I fear I must gather my paltry pittances [?] from every last source, to extricate myself from them.[5] Nothing ever pressed more strongly on my mind, than the necessity of the advocation of a liberal policy with respect to continental revenue. And if my difficulties should forbid the assumption of the legislative character, I will not be wanting in remonstrances to my friends out of doors. I have written to the speaker of the delegates on the subject, and the speaker of the senate seems well-satisfied of the propriety of our sentiments.[6]

Mr. J——n has truly stated the modes, in which the Constitution was formed. But he ought to have added, that the people expected at the time of the election of the convention, that they were to be vested with power, of every sort, necessary for political happiness altho' perhaps independence was not a reigning opinion; that they confirmed it by executing it: and that the incroachments, made on it by the assembly, have proceeded either from inadvertency, or emergencies. For it is notorious that they constantly profess a sacred regard to the constitution.[7]

Inclosed is a part of my notes on the question before the court of appeals. Inaccurate as they are (for they were the first rude sketch & the second is lost) you must content yourself with them. The remainder which is equally interesting [?] shall be sent to you by the next post, if I can transcribe in time.[8]

Your favor of the 25 Ulto. has been duly received.[9]

[1] *Papers of Madison*, IV, 148, n. 2.

[2] Randolph's letters of 22 February and 1 March do not mention Patrick Henry. Randolph, who was a correspondent of Henry, regretted that his influential friend had not been present in the October 1782 session of the Virginia General Assembly (*Papers of Madison*, V, 78; 79, n. 16; 217; 262; 282; 339; 340, n. 11; 453). Although Henry attended the May 1783 session, he did not effectively fulfill Randolph's hopes (Randolph to JM, 21 June 1783, MS, Pennsylvania Historical and Museum Commission).

[3] That is, with John Francis Mercer in Congress, there was no one to dispute the domination of the General Assembly by the Lees.

[4] That is, as attorney general of Virginia. See *Papers of Madison*, IV, 160; 162, n. 8; V, 60; 62, n. 20; 308–9; Randolph to JM, 1 Feb., and n. 5; 29 Mar. 1783, and

nn. 1, 3. Possibly among the "most capital" of John Randolph's creditors, and certainly absent, was Arthur Lee (Moncure D. Conway, *Edmund Randolph*, p. 49).

[5] JM to Randolph, 11 Feb., and n. 3; 18 Mar. 1783. A split in the manuscript at the fold obscures several of Randolph's words. The expression "paltry pittances" is suggested by the few remaining vestiges of what he wrote.

[6] Archibald Cary, speaker of the Senate, and John Tyler, Sr., speaker of the House of Delegates of the Virginia General Assembly. See *Papers of Madison*, III, 162, n. 3; IV, 30, n. 2.

[7] Randolph implied that the subject of his paragraph had been suggested to him by a document lately received. Though this perhaps was Jefferson's letter of 15 February (Boyd, *Papers of Jefferson*, VI, 246–49), it almost certainly was the copy by JM of his notes on Jefferson's memorandum for Barbé-Marbois, which had reached Randolph in two installments not long before (JM to Randolph, 7 Jan., n. 10; 18 Feb., and n. 5; 25 Feb. 1783). Judging from JM's surviving notes, a copy of them would hardly have stimulated the comments made by Randolph in the present paragraph; nor would the brevity of the notes have obliged JM to devote two occasions to the preparation of a copy of them. For these reasons JM's existent notes probably are only the portion of a larger whole from which the first installment of the copy sent to Randolph was made. Reinforcing this inference is JM's own statement in the autumn of 1782 that Jefferson's memorandum was "voluminous" (*Papers of Madison*, V, 7–11; 331).

In Jefferson's *Notes on the State of Virginia*, of which his memorandum for Marbois was a forerunner, the beginning pages of the chapter entitled "Constitution" treat of some of the charters of Virginia in a manner obviously reflected in the existing notes taken by JM on the memorandum. Following the references to charters, the remainder of the chapter describes the making of the Virginia Constitution of 1776 and above all criticizes some of its provisions and emphasizes the disregard of them by the public officials of the commonwealth during the war (William Peden, ed., *Notes on the State of Virginia by Thomas Jefferson* [Chapel Hill, N.C., 1955], pp. 110–29).

In his memorandum for Marbois, Jefferson almost surely summarized "the modes in which the Constitution was formed" and its shortcomings both in theory and in practice. Granting that the chapter entitled "Constitution" follows in general the arrangement of the portion of the memorandum on the same subject and that notes by JM on the memorandum were originally considerably longer than now exist, he logically would have devoted his second installment to Randolph to the subjects just mentioned.

That JM did so seems the more probable in view of the similarity between several of Randolph's remarks in the present paragraph and those by Jefferson in his *Notes on the State of Virginia*. Jefferson commented that in the spring of 1776, "Independence, and the establishment of a new form of government, were not even yet the objects of the people at large." At that time, since neither of these objectives had "been opened to the mass of the people," the voters were "not thinking of independance and a permanent republic" when they elected delegates to the convention scheduled to meet in May. Hence the voters could not have vested the delegates with the power to make a constitution, could not have regarded the convention as of higher status than a legislature, and, consequently, must have viewed the constitution as equivalent only to a statute. During the Revolution, the Virginia General Assembly had frequently transgressed this statute and legally could have rescinded it altogether (*Notes* [Peden ed.], pp. 121–24). This disregard of the Constitution had been, Jefferson conceded, "with no ill intention. The views of the present members [of the omnipotent legislature] are perfectly upright. When they are led out of their regular province, it is by art in others, and inadvertence in themselves" (*ibid.*, p. 120). Randolph's remarks clearly express agreement with several of these observations and challenge the accuracy of others. See n. 8, below; also Boyd, *Papers of Jefferson*, VI, 278–80; JM to Randolph, 8 Apr. 1783, n. 10.

⁸ The tear in the manuscript, mentioned in n. 5, renders the phrase "equally interesting" only a probably correct decipherment of what Randolph wrote. The "notes" were for his brief as attorney general in the "Case of the Prisoners" (*Caton* v. *Commonwealth*), which JM had requested (*Papers of Madison*, V, 183–84; 184, n. 3; 217; 218, n. 9; 261; 263; 265, n. 7; 290; 382; 384, n. 4; 474; Randolph to JM, 15 Jan., and n. 6; 7 Feb. 1783, and n. 10). These "notes" in Randolph's hand extend for twelve pages not counting one page bearing only JM's docket, "Notes of Mr. Randolph on the case of Traytors pardoned by Resolve of House of Delegates" (LC: Madison Papers, Vol. 91). In view of this docket, which normally would follow the close of a document, the notes may be both the portion enclosed with the present letter and the "remainder" forwarded at an undetermined time later, even though Randolph's argument appears to be incomplete. In JM's letter of 18 March to Randolph (*q.v.*), receipt was acknowledged of the present letter and its enclosure, but neither man in his correspondence with the other during at least the next three months mentioned the "remainder."

The notes of Randolph have a particular interest when taken together with his criticisms of Jefferson's comments in the memorandum for Marbois. A main premise of Randolph's argument in the "Case of the Prisoners" was that the Form of Government framed by the Virginia Convention of 1776 was a fundamental law or constitution, created to provide "public happiness" and "a touchstone" with which every statute of the General Assembly must conform. This constitution was formed by the representatives of the people, "the fountain of power," and from "the mouth of every civilian do we hear a recurrence to first principles preached." As for the nature of a constitution, continued Randolph, it is "A compact, in which the people themselves are the sole parties and which they alone can abrogate. . . . That we have a constitution in my sense of the word, will not, I presume, be controverted." As pointed out in n. 7, Jefferson had controverted this view.

⁹ *Q.v.*

Notes on Debates

MS (LC: Madison Papers). For a description of the manuscript of Notes on Debates, see *Papers of Madison*, V, 231–34.

Monday. March 10.

See the Journal. much debate passed relative to the proposed commutation of half pay; some wishing it to take place on condition only that a majority of the whole army should concur[;] others preferring the plan expressed on the journal,¹ and not agreed to.²

¹ *JCC*, XXIV, 178–79. The debate focused upon the report of a committee, which Congress had appointed on 7 March (NA: PCC, No. 186, fol. 87). Drafted by Daniel Carroll, the report recommended that the half pay for life guaranteed on 21 October 1780 by Congress should be commuted at its option into either full pay for five years or an equivalent sum in 6 per cent bonds, provided that this offer of commutation should be acceptable to the officers of the continental line of each

state deciding collectively. The already retired officers of those lines, the officers of corps not belonging to those lines, and the officers not included in any of the above categories—each deciding as a group—should have the same choice. During the debate Theodorick Bland sought unsuccessfully to amend in the following respect the proposed mode of exercising the option: "in case the officers of the army or a majority of them will agree to accept the same, to be certified to Congress by a committee from the whole army, authorized for that purpose[,] to consist of a member from each line." This quotation is canceled as printed in *JCC*, XXIV, 178, n. 2.

For the background of the general issue, see JM Notes, 6 Jan., and n. 2; 9–10 Jan.; 13 Jan., and nn. 11, 18, 20, 21; 17 Jan., and n. 6; 24 Jan., and n. 25; 25 Jan., and nn. 8–12; 4 Feb., and nn. 7, 10, 11, 13–15; 25 Feb., and nn. 1–4, 11; 27 Feb., and n. 2; 28 Feb. 1783; *JCC*, XXIV, 93–95, 95, n. 1, 145–48, 149–51, 154–56, 161, and n. 2, 169–70, 170, n. 1, 176.

[2] Eight, rather than the requisite minimum of nine, states voted in favor of the report. Except for John Francis Mercer, the five delegates from Virginia voted "ay" (*JCC*, XXIV, 179).

Notes on Debates

MS (LC: Madison Papers). For a description of the manuscript of Notes on Debates, see *Papers of Madison*, V, 231–34.

Teusday. March 11.

The report entered on Friday the 7 of March was taken into consideration.[1] It had been sent by order of Congs. to the Supt. of Finance for his remarks which were also on the table.[2] These remarks were in substance; that it wd. be better to turn the 5 perCt. ad valorem into a Tariff founded on an enumeration of the several classes of imports; to which ought to [be] added a few articles of exports;[3] that instead of an apportionment of the residue on the States, other general revenues,[4] from a land tax, reduced to $\frac{1}{4}$ of a dollar per Hundred acres, with a house tax regulated by the number of windows,[5] and an excise on all spirituous liquors to be collected at the place of distillery ought to be substituted and as well as the duties on trade made coexistent with the public debts;[6] the whole to be collected by persons appd. by Congs. alone, and that an alternative ought to [be] held out to the States, either to establish these permanent revenues for the interest, or to comply with a constitutional demand of the principal within a very short period.[7]

In order to ascertain the sense of Congs. on these ideas it was proposed that the following short questions sd. be taken:

1. Shall any taxes to operate generally throughout the States be recommended by Congs., other than duties on foreign commerce?

2. Shall the 5 perCt. advalorem be exchanged for a tariff?

3. Shall the alternative be adopted as proposed by the Superintendt. of Finance?

On the 1st question the States were N. H. no Mas: no. Cont. no. N. J. no. Maryd. no Virga. no 6 noes & 5 ays.

On the 2d. question there were 7 ays.

The 3d. question was not put, its impropriety being generally proclaimed.[8]

In consequence of the 2d. vote in favor of a tariff the 3 first paragraphs of the Rept. were recommitted together with the Letter from the Superintendt. of Finance.[9]

On the 4 par: on motion of Mr. Dyer, after the word "war" in "line 5" were inserted "agreeably to the resolution of the 16. of decemr. last."[10]

A motion was made by Mr. Hamilton and Mr. Wilson to strike out the limitation of 25 years and to make the revenue coexistent with the debts.[11] This question was lost, the States being N. H. no Mas: no. Cont. divd. N.Y. ay. N.J. ay. Pa. ay Del: ay. Maryd. ay. Va. no. N. C. ay. S. C. no.

A motion was made by Mr. Hamilton & Mr. Wilson to strike out the clauses relative to the appointment of Collectors, and to provide that the Collectors shd be inhabitants of the States within which they sd. collect; should be nominated by Congs. and appointed by the States, and in case such nomination should not be accepted or rejected within   days it should stand good. On this question there were 5 ays & 6 noes.[12]

---

[1] In the Gaillard Hunt edition of the journals, the manuscript Report on Restoring Public Credit is "entered" on 6 March 1783, the date it was "Delivered" to Charles Thomson and "ordered to be printed" (*JCC*, XXIV, 170–74; Report on Restoring Public Credit, 6 Mar., hdn.; JM Notes, 6 Mar. 1783). The journal for "Friday the 7 of March" omits mention of "Printed copies of the rept." being distributed to the delegates (JM Notes, 7 Mar. 1783).

[2] Robert Morris' "remarks," in the form of a letter of 8 March to the president of Congress, is in Wharton, *Revol. Dipl. Corr.*, VI, 277–81.

[3] If this substitution was agreed to by the states, it would end the long effort to have them authorize Congress to levy a 5 per cent tariff on imports of unspecified varieties. By assenting to Morris' suggestion, the states would make Congress the beneficiary of revenue derived from tariffs of differing ad valorem amounts collected on "classes" of imports precisely defined. Morris also recommended that the request for a levy on prizes be omitted, on the ground that Congress already possessed the power to levy under the provisions of Article IX of the Articles of Confederation. The list of advisable import duties which he enclosed in his letter has not been certainly identified but probably is the basis for the one entered among the proceedings of Congress on 18 March 1783. "I conceive also," wrote Morris, "that a tax might be laid on exports which, without being burdensome, would still be productive" (Wharton, *Revol. Dipl. Corr.*, VI, 280; *JCC*, XXIV, 188; JM Notes, 18 Mar. 1783).

⁴ That is, "the residue" of the annual income needed by Congress. Morris obviously was seeking a speedier and more certain means of deriving money from the states than the unsatisfactory device of requisitions.

⁵ In his letter (n. 2) Morris explained this recommendation by writing: "I am told that the principal objection to a land tax is the inequality. To obviate this objection (although I cannot accede to the force of it), perhaps a reduction of the sum from one dollar to a quarter of a dollar per hundred acres might be expedient; and to supply the deficiency, a tax on houses might be adopted, according to the inclosed rate." The enclosure has not been found. On 20 March 1783 the report of the committee for restoring the public credit "being under debate," a levy on houses was proposed, but there is no entry in the journal respecting "windows." The tax suggested was a half-dollar on each "dwelling-house," plus 2½ per cent of whatever amount its fair rental value exceeded twenty dollars (JCC, XXIV, 200; JM Notes, 28 Jan. 1783, n. 4). For Hamilton's recommendation of a window tax, see JM Notes, 28 Jan. 1783, and n. 43.

⁶ JM may have drawn his reference to an excise on liquor from the missing list of rates enclosed by Morris in his letter of 8 March. Among his recommendations on 29 July 1782 to Congress had been "an excise of one eighth of dollar per gallon, on all distilled spirituous liquors" (JM Notes, 28 Jan. 1783, n. 35). See also Report on Restoring Public Credit, 6 Mar. 1783.

⁷ JM here summarized a portion of the last paragraph of Morris' letter of 8 March. Let Congress issue interest-bearing bonds to each state for its whole outgo "for the public services" during the entire war. Using these bonds or the interest therefrom, each state could then pay whatever it owed on its "own private account." "And on the first requisitions made by Congress for current expenditures," Morris continued, each state "might make payment, either in part, or, perhaps, in the whole, by a discharge of so much of the debt. Thus a degree of simplicity would be introduced into our affairs, and we might avoid the horrors of intestine convulsions." These, he feared, would almost certainly occur if the "accounts among the states" remained unsettled.

Besides introducing "a degree of simplicity" into a most intricate financial situation, Morris certainly was not oblivious of the extent to which his plan, if adopted, would bind the state governments and their creditors to Congress through the possession of United States certificates of debt. If for no better reason, economic considerations would impel the bondholders, whether public or private, to oppose a dissolution of the Union and to favor providing Congress with sufficient revenues to pay its debts. See JM Notes, 27 Jan., and n. 23; 28 Jan. 1783, and nn. 9, 12.

⁸ Except for the contents of JM's next paragraph, none of the proceedings of Congress on 11 March, summarized in his notes for that day, is entered in the official journal.

⁹ For the personnel of the committee and its appointment by Congress, see JM Notes, 21 Feb., and n. 28; Report on Restoring Public Credit, 6 Mar. 1783, hdn. The first three paragraphs of that report (q.v.) were recommitted, together with "so much" of Morris' letter of the eighth "as relates to exchanging the impost of five per cent. ad valorem for a tariff." Also referred to the committee was Morris' letter of 10 March, estimating the "Principal of the Public Debt to the first Day of January, 1783," not including the unknown totals of the "unliquidated Debt," and of "the old continental Bills and Arrearages of Half Pay" (JCC, XXIV, 180–82, 181, nn. 1, 2). See also Randolph to JM, 15 Jan., n. 13; JM Notes, 18 Mar. 1783.

¹⁰ The "motion of Mr. Dyer" refers to the opening lines of the fourth paragraph of the Report on Restoring Public Credit, 6 March 1783 (q.v.), reading: "Provided that none of the said duties shall be applied to any other purpose than the discharge of the interest or principals of the debts which shall have been contracted on the

faith of the U. S. for supporting the present war." For a summary of the resolution adopted by Congress on 16 December 1782, see *Papers of Madison*, V, 407, n. 1.

11 Immediately following the quotation in n. 10 appears the clause, "nor be continued for a longer term than 25 years" (Report on Restoring Public Credit, 6 Mar. 1783, and n. 6).

12 See *ibid.* for the words eventually entered in the blank space and for the passage in the fourth paragraph which the Hamilton-Wilson motion sought to amend. See also JM Notes, 12 Feb. 1783, and n. 15.

Virginia Delegates to Benjamin Harrison

RC (Virginia State Library). In the hand of John Francis Mercer, except for the signatures of the four other delegates. Docketed, "Lr. from the Delegates in Congress—March 11th 1783." Cover franked by Mercer and addressed by him to "His Excelly. Benjamin Harrison Esqr. Governor of Virginia." The second paragraph of the letter explains why Harrison wrote on the cover, "The Treasurer B H."

IN CONGRESS. March 11th. 1783

SIR

Yr. Excellency's Letter of 24th. Feby. is receiv'd & we are sorry that we are not yet enabled by official communications to relieve you from your anxiety on the subject of Peace, whenever they shall arrive, you may be assured that they shall be transmitted to you by express agreably to yr. wish.[1]

We have to remark to your Excellency, that no remittances have been made for sometime [to] the Delegates.[2] it would be superfluous for us to add to yr. Excellency the consequences which arise from the little punctua[lity] we have experienced, in the payment of the appointd [sum?] allowed,[3] besides being exposed to the extortion which is practised here invariably whenever necessity obliges us [to] borrow money, it is not always that money may be had on any terms.[4]

With much respect We have the honor to be Yr. Excellcy's. mo: obedt. & very hble Servants

JOHN F. MERCER
THEOK. BLAND JR.
A. LEE
JOS. JONES.
J. MADISON JR.

1 Harrison to Delegates, 24 Feb. 1783, and n. 3.
2 Delegates to Harrison, 21 Jan., and n. 3; Ambler to JM, 1 Feb. 1783, and nn. 2,

4, 7. Mercer, who had been in Congress for less than five weeks, was probably expressing the acute need of his four colleagues rather than his own. JM had received no money since November 1782 from the treasurer of Virginia (*Papers of Madison*, V, 266, and n. 1). See also Harrison to Delegates, 20 Mar., and n. 3; Ambler to JM, 22 Mar. 1783.

3 By the terms of a statute enacted by the Virginia General Assembly on 1 July 1782, the delegates were to be paid "eight dollars per day . . . quarterly out of such public money as shall hereafter be set apart and appropriated for that use" (Hening, *Statutes*, XI, 31–32).

4 Insofar at least as JM was concerned, he had not "invariably" been subject to "extortion." For his generous treatment by the moneylender, Haym Salomon, see *Papers of Madison*, IV, 108, n. 2; 401, n. 4; V, 170; 205; 206, n. 4.

To Edmund Randolph

RC (LC: Madison Papers). Unsigned but in JM's hand. Cover missing, but the letter was docketed "James Madison March 11, 1783" by Randolph. The words written by JM in the Randolph code are italicized in the present copy. For that code, see JM to Randolph, 7 Jan., and hdn.; 4 Feb. 1783, and n. 10.

PHILADA. March 11th. 1783

MY DEAR SIR

Your favor of the 1st. inst: came to hand yesterday but unaccompanied by that of the preceding week referred to in it.[1]

Another week has passed without affording the least relief from our suspence as to the progress of peace. At New York they are so much in the dark that their curiosity has recourse to the gleanings of the Philada. gazettes.[2] The length of the negociation may be explained, but the delay of all parties to notify its progress is really astonishing. Our last official information is nearly 5 months old & that derived from the royal speech upwards of three months.[3]

The peremptory style & publication of Mr. M's letters have *given offense to many without* & *to some within Congress. His enemys of both* descriptions are *industrious in displayin*[g] *their im*propriety. I wish *they had les*[s] *handle for the purpose.*[4]

The plan before Congress for the arrangemt. of our affairs is to ask from the States a power to levy for a term not exceeding 25. years the 5 perCt. impost, with an additional impost on salt, wine, spirituous liquors, sugars & teas. to recommend to them to establish & appropriate perman[en]t revenues for a like term for the deficiency; the proceeds to be carried to their credit; the whole to be collected by persons amenable to Congs. but appd. by the States; to complete the territorial cessions; to enable Congs. to make abatements in favor of suffering States; Congs. on their part declaring that all reasonable military expences separately incurred by the States without their sanction either by sea or land shall be part of the common mass; and proposing to the States a substitution of numbers in place of a valuation of land;   Slaves to be equal to 1 free man.[5] The fate of this plan in Congs. is uncertain, & still more so among the States. It makes a decent provision for the public debts & seems to comprehend the most dangerous sources of future contests among ourselves. If the substance of it is rejected, and nothing better introduced in its place, I shall consider it as a melancholy proof that narrow & local views prevail over that liberal policy & those mutual concessions which our future tranquility and present reputation call for.

Mr. J.son is still here, agitated as you may suppose with the suspense in which he is kept. He is as anxious as myself for your going into the Legislature. Let me know your final determination on this point.[6]

[1] Randolph to JM, 22 Feb., hdn.; 1 Mar.; JM to Randolph, 18 Mar. 1783.

[2] Delegates to Harrison, 4 Mar., and nn. 2–4; JM to Randolph, 4 Mar.; 12 Mar. 1783. On 15 March 1783 a Loyalist in New York City observed that no European news had been received since 19 January, "except flying and uncertain by way of the West Indies and by some prizes brought into this place" (Thomas Jefferson Wertenbaker, *Father Knickerbocker Rebels: New York City during the Revolution* [New York, 1948], p. 256).

[3] For the speech of King George III to Parliament on 5 December 1782, see JM Notes, 13 Feb., and n. 10. The last official word from the American peace commissioners was dated 14 October and received by Congress on 23 December 1782 (*Papers of Madison*, V, 436; 437, n. 3). For Benjamin Franklin's explanation of the infrequency with which they had written, see Wharton, *Revol. Dipl. Corr.*, VI, 110–11. In anticipating lengthy negotiations, JM assumed that the business of harmonizing the conflicting objectives and pretensions of the powers aligned against Great Britain would be arduous (*Papers of Madison*, V, 33–34, 35, n. 4, 199, 416, 418, n. 19; 436–37; 441–42; 444, n. 11; 466–68; 469, n. 2).

[4] For discussion of Robert Morris' letters, see JM Notes, 26 Feb., and n. 14; 27 Feb.; 4–5 Mar., and nn. 3–9, 12; JM to Randolph, 4 Mar. 1783. JM inadvertently used 536 meaning "X," rather than 526, the correct cipher for "His."

[5] To this point in the paragraph, JM was summarizing the Report on Restoring Public Credit, 6 March 1783 (*q.v.*). The eleventh of March being the weekly post day, JM almost certainly wrote this letter before Congress convened. For this reason he could not have known that on that day the first three paragraphs of "the Report" would be recommitted to have, among other revisions, pepper, molasses, cocoa, and coffee added to the list of dutiable imports. Robert Morris' letter of 8 March, laid before Congress on 10 March, recommended these additions. See JM Notes, 11 Mar., and n. 9; 18 Mar. 1783.

[6] JM to Jefferson, 15 Feb. 1783, and n. 5. On 12 April, eleven days after Congress resolved that Jefferson's "voyage" had been rendered "unnecessary" by the signing of the preliminary treaty of peace, he left for Virginia (*JCC*, XXIV, 226; JM to Randolph, 18 Mar. 1783). For JM's and Jefferson's letters urging Randolph to seek

a seat in the Virginia General Assembly, and for Randolph's decision, see JM to Jefferson, 11 Feb., and n. 14; to Randolph, 11 Feb., and n. 3; Jefferson to JM, 14 Feb. (1st letter), and n. 4; Randolph to JM, 22 Mar. 1783; also Jefferson to Randolph, 15 Feb. 1783 in Boyd, *Papers of Jefferson*, VI, 246–49.

Notes on Debates

MS (LC: Madison Papers). For a description of the manuscript of Notes on Debates, see *Papers of Madison*, V, 231–34. Words italicized in the present copy are those underlined by JM.

Wednesday 12. Th: 13. F. 14. S. 15. of March.

These days were employed in reading the despatches brought on Wednesday morning by Capt. Barney commanding the Washington Packet. They were dated from Decr. 4. to 24. from the Ministers Plenipo: for peace, with journals of preceding transactions, and were accompanied by the Preliminary articles signed on the 30th: of Novr. between the said Ministers & Mr. Oswald the British Minister.[1]

The terms granted to America appeared to Congs. on the whole extremely liberal. It was observed by several however that the stipulation obliging Congs. to recommend to the States a restitution of confiscated property, altho it could scarcely be understood that the States would comply, had the appearance of sacrificing the dignity of Congs. to the pride of the British King.[2]

The separate & secret manner in which our Ministers had proceded with respect to France & the confidential manner with respect to the British Ministers affected different members of Congs. very differently.[3] Many of the most judicious members thought they had all been in some measure ensnared by the dexterity of the British Minister,[4] and particularly disapproved of the conduct of Mr. Jay in submitting to the Enemy his jealousy of the French without even the knowledge of Dr. Franklin, and of the unguarded manner in which he Mr. A. & Dr. F. had given in writing sentiments unfriendly to our Ally, and serving as weapons for the insidious policy of the Enemy.[5]

The separate article was most offensive, being considered as obtained by G: B. not for the sake of the territory ceded to her, but as a means of disuniting the U. S. & France, as inconsistent with the spirit of the Alliance, and a dishonorable departure from the candor rectitude & plain dealing professed by Congs.[6] The dilemma in wch Congs. were placed was sorely felt. If they sd communicate to the F. Minister[7] every thing[,] they exposed their own Ministers, destroyed all confidence in them on the part of France, & might engage them in dangerous factions agst. Congs. which was the more to be apprehended, as the terms obtained by their management were popular in their nature. If Congs. sd. conceal everything, & the F. Court sd. either from the Enemy or otherwise come to the knowledge of it all confidence wd. be at an end between the allies; the enemy might be encouraged by it to make fresh experiments, & the public safety as well as the national honor be endangered. Upon the whole it was thought & observed by many that our Ministers particularly Mr. Jay, instead of making allowances for & affording facilities to France in her delicate situation between Spain & the U. S. had joined with the enemy in taking advantage of it to increase her perplexity; & that they had made the safety of their Country depend on the sincerity of Ld. Shelburne, who [which] was suspected by all the world besides, and even by most of themselves. see Mr. L——'s letter Dcr. 24.[8]

The displeasure of the French Court at the neglect of our Ministers to maintain a confidential intercourse & particularly to communicate the preliminary articles before they were signed, was not only signified to the Secry. of F. A. but to sundry members by the Chevr. de la Luzerne. To the former he shewed a letter from Ct. de Vergennes directing him to remonstrate to Congs. agst. the conduct of the Amr. Ministers; which a subsequent letter countermanded alledging that Docr. F. had given some explanations that had been admitted; & told Mr. Livingston that the American Ministers had deceived him (de Vergennes) by telling him a few days before the preliminary articles were signed, that the agreement on them was at a distance; that when he carried the articles signed into Council, the King expressed great indignation, & asked if the Americans served him thus before peace was made, & whilst they were begging for aids, what was to be expected after peace &c. To several Members he mentioned that the King had been surprized & displeased & that he said he did not think he had such allies to deal with.[9]

No. XI[10]

March 15. 1783. continued

To one of them who asked whether the Ct. of Fr. meant to complain of them to Congs. Mr. Marbois[11] answered that Great powers never *complained* but that they *felt* & *remembered*. It did not appear from any circumstances that the separate article was known to the Court of Fr. or to the Chevr. de la Luzerne¹²

The publication of the preliminary articles excepting the separate article in the Newspapers was not a deliberate act of Congs. A hasty question for enjoining secresy on certain parts of the despaches which included these articles, was lost; and copies havg. been taken by members & some of them handed to the Delegates of the Pena. one of them reached the printer. When the publication appeared Congs. in general regretted it, not only as tending too much to lull the States, but as leading France into suspicions that congress favored the premature signature of the articles and were at least willing to remove in the minds of people the blame of delaying peace from G. B. to France.¹³

¹ Delegates to Harrison, 18 Feb. 1783, and n. 3. The official journal omits mention both of the reading of dispatches on 13 and 15 March and of the convening of Congress on 12 and 14 March (*JCC*, XXIV, 182–84). Charles Thomson's record book lists no dispatches submitted on 13 March. Although he did not differentiate those and other papers laid before Congress on 14 March from those read the next day, he noted the presentation on 12 March of the following items: Benjamin Franklin's journal from 9 May to 1 July 1782; his dispatches of 4, 5, 14, and 24 December 1782; John Jay's dispatch of 12 December, enclosing a copy of Franklin's letter of 26 November to Richard Oswald; a dispatch of 14 December from John Adams, Franklin, Jay, and Henry Laurens, enclosing a copy of the preliminary articles proposed by them; a copy of the preliminary articles proposed by the British commissioners; a copy of an article proposed by the American commissioners; and a copy of the preliminary articles signed on 30 November 1782 (NA: PCC, No. 185, III, 56; Burnett, *Letters*, VII, 71). See also Wharton, *Revol. Dipl. Corr.*, V, 550–86, 842–43, 849–50, 851–53; VI, 74–80, 96–100, 106–7, 110–14, 130, 131–33, 163. For Richard Oswald, see *Papers of Madison*, V, 154, n. 2; JM to James Madison, Sr., 1 Jan., and n. 3; Harrison to Delegates, 4 Jan., n. 3; Rev. James Madison to JM, 16 Jan. 1783, n. 5.

On 14 and 15 March 1783 Congress received the following dispatches and other papers relating to the peace negotiations: Jay's dispatch of 17 November and 14 December, the former enclosing his journal kept at Paris from 23 June to 17 November; Adams' dispatches of 6, 11, 18, and 21 November, and of 4 and 14 December, including extracts from his journal kept at Paris between 2 November and 9 December; Laurens' dispatches of 15 and 24 December; and Jefferson's dispatch of 13 March 1783 (NA: PCC, No. 185, III, 56–57; Wharton, *Revol. Dipl. Corr.*, V, 845–46, 849, 854–58, 869, 872–80; VI, 6–49, 52–54, 56–61, 62–64, 65, 66, 70, 72–74, 82–84, 85–88, 90–93, 103–6, 109, 122–25, 133–37, 138–40, 159–60, 164–65, 298).

² The preliminary articles were not spread on the journal until 15 April 1783, the day on which Congress ratified them (*JCC*, XXIV, 242–51). Article V concerns the "restitution of confiscated property." For relevant statutes of state legislatures, instructions of Congress to its peace commissioners, and efforts by British officials to secure the return of that property to the persons from whom it had been confiscated or sequestered, see *Papers of Madison*, I, 169, n. 13; 239, n. 2; II, 244, n. 2; 245, n. 3; III, 69, n. 2; 121, n. 1; 188, and n. 1; 189, n. 16; IV, 12–13; 16, nn. 27–28; 89; 90, n. 5; 357; 361, nn. 39, 40; 369; 370, n. 3; V, 35; 36, n. 8; 39; 48, n. 7; 74; 80; 81, n. 5; 112, n. 11; 409–10; 410, n. 3; 470, n. 11; JM to Randolph, 7 Jan.; JM Notes, 16 Jan. 1783, and n. 1; Burnett, *Letters*, VII, 79; Wharton, *Revol. Dipl. Corr.*, VI, 9, 77–80, 82, 84, 87, 106.

3 Immediately following this sentence, JM canceled another sentence too heavily to permit all its words to be recovered with assurance. Granting that "The representation of Mr. Jay against M. Ver[gennes] was generally thought however that the separate article was unwarrantable" is at least a nearly accurate rendition, JM probably deleted the sentence both because it is ungrammatical and because it treats a subject to which he decided to devote a complete paragraph.

For samples of the contrasting viewpoints of members of Congress on the preliminary articles, see the letters of Boudinot, Hamilton, and Lee in Burnett, *Letters,* VII, 77–78, 81–87; also JM to Randolph, 18 March 1783. For a thorough and scholarly account of the course of the peace negotiations, especially as influenced by John Jay, see Richard B. Morris, *The Peacemakers,* pp. 282–385.

4 William Petty, Earl of Shelburne. His "dexterity" was believed to consist of having his agents implant in the receptive minds of Jay and Adams a belief that Vergennes was secretly negotiating with the British on behalf of Spain, and to the detriment of the United States. Consequently, in accord with Shelburne's design, Jay and Adams, unknown or not fully known to Vergennes and unknown at the outset even to Franklin, engaged in separate parleys with the British. Shelburne assented the more willingly to extend generous terms of peace to the United States, for he wished to draw her into the British orbit of influence and out of that of France. Not being in Paris until the day before the signing of the "preliminary Articles" on 30 November 1782, Laurens had not shared in these maneuvers but was pleased by their result (*Papers of Madison,* V, 418, n. 17; citations in n. 5, below; n. 8; Randolph to JM, 3 Jan., and n. 14; and JM to Randolph, 12 Mar. 1783).

5 Wharton, *Revol. Dipl. Corr.,* VI, 7, 14–15, 17–21, 27–32, 45–49, 52–54, 57–61, 63, 64, 66, 70, 72, 74, 91, 93, 94–95; JM Notes, 1 Jan., n. 2; 3 Jan. 1783, and n. 2. "Mr. A." is John Adams.

6 The "separate article," appended to the preliminary articles of peace and separately signed by Richard Oswald, British commissioner, and the four American commissioners, reads: "It is hereby understood and agreed, that in case Great Britain, at the conclusion of the present war, shall recover, or be put in possession of West Florida, the line of north boundary between the said province and the United States shall be a line drawn from the mouth of the river Yassous, where it unites with the Mississippi, due east to the river Apalachicola." In Article II of the preliminary articles the southern boundary of the United States from the Mississippi River to the "river Apalachicola" was defined as the "northernmost part of the thirty first degree of north latitude" (*JCC,* XXIV, 246, 250–51). Thus, if Spain in her negotiations of peace with Great Britain succeeded in retaining West Florida, its northern boundary would be about ninety miles farther south than if Great Britain regained that area.

The preamble of the preliminary articles states that although they would comprise the contents of the definitive treaty "to be concluded between the Crown of Great Britain and the said United States," the definitive treaty would not be "concluded until terms of a peace shall be agreed upon between Great Britain and France" (*JCC,* XXIV, 245). For this reason the American peace commissioners had not broken the letter of the Treaty of Alliance between the United States and France, but by not consulting Vergennes during the negotiation of the preliminary articles, they appeared to have violated "the spirit of the Alliance." See JM to Randolph, 7 Jan. 1783, n. 8.

More to the point, the American peace commissioners had violated their instructions of 15 June 1781, wherein Congress had reflected its "candor rectitude & plain dealing" by admonishing them "to make the most candid and confidential communications upon all subjects to the ministers of our generous ally, the King of France; to undertake nothing in the negotiations for peace or truce without their knowledge and concurrence; and ultimately to govern yourselves by their advice and opinion" (*JCC*, XX, 651; *Papers of Madison*, III, 153–54; 154, nn. 3, 5). As the United States in the summer of 1781 had greatly needed French military aid, so in the spring of 1783 Congress earnestly hoped that its desperate financial plight would be eased by the "generous ally." For this reason, many members of Congress judged the offense given to King Louis XVI and Vergennes by the American peace commissioners to be unwise, if not reprehensible.

7 The Chevalier de La Luzerne, minister of King Louis XVI to the United States.

8 In his old age JM without canceling "who," interlineated "which" above "who." For this reason the present editors have inserted a bracketed "which" after the word it was intended to replace. In his dispatch of 24 December 1782 Henry Laurens informed Livingston that the British still viewed the United States as their "*colonies*," a "*reconciliation*" with them as possible, and a general peace as "far distant." "Every engine has been," continued Laurens, "every degree of craft under the mask of returning affection will be, practiced for creating jealousies between the States and their good and great ally" (Wharton, *Revol. Dipl. Corr.*, VI, 165). See also Delegates to Harrison, 18 Mar., and nn. 2, 3; JM Notes, 24 Mar. 1783.

9 Following his instructions from Vergennes, La Luzerne orally informed Robert R. Livingston, secretary for foreign affairs, and several members of Congress of his sovereign's and Vergennes' displeasure, and emphasized in a letter to Washington and in anonymous communications to Philadelphia newspapers that the signing of the preliminary articles did not signify the end of the war. To give added stress to this fact, La Luzerne in a letter on 15 March to Robert Morris, superintendent of finance, pointed out that King Louis XVI would lend the United States six million livres during 1783, rather than the twenty million requested, "to enable them to carry on the war" and with the earnest expectation that Congress would speedily establish a "*solid general revenue*" so as to fulfill to the letter the terms of its financial "*engagements*" in Europe (*JCC*, XXIV, 288–90; William E. O'Donnell, *Chevalier de La Luzerne*, pp. 232–36; George Dangerfield, *Chancellor Robert R. Livingston of New York, 1746–1813* [New York, 1960], pp. 170–75). See also JM Notes, 9–10 Jan., n. 14; 13 Jan., and n. 3; 26 Mar.; JM to Randolph, 22 Jan. 1783, and n. 8.

Although knowledge of this new loan, of the fact that Vergennes had not appeared "displeased" when shown the preliminary articles after they were signed, and of his apparent instruction to La Luzerne not to lodge a formal "complaint" against the conduct of the American peace commissioners must have slightly eased the "dilemma" which members of Congress "sorely felt," they naturally expected that Vergennes would reciprocate to the injury of the United States in the negotiations of the definitive treaty of peace and in the extension of more financial aid. In truth, after Franklin on 17 December had replied ingeniously to Vergennes' muted protest of two days before, the cordial relations between the two men appeared to be unimpaired. After mentioning the "very irregular conduct of their commissioners in regard to us," Vergennes added in his dispatch of 19 December 1782 to La Luzerne: "You may speak of it not in the tone of complaint. I accuse no person; I blame no one, not even Dr. Franklin. He has yielded too easily to the bias of his colleagues, who do not pretend to recognize the rules of courtesy in regard to us. All their attentions have been taken up by the English whom they have met in Paris. If we may judge of the future from what has passed here under our eyes, we shall be but poorly paid for all we have done for the United States and for securing to them a national existence" (Wharton, *Revol. Dipl. Corr.*, VI, 150–52, 152 n.). See also *ibid.*, VI, 113, 133, 140, 143–44.

10 For an explanation of this numeral, see *Papers of Madison*, V, 231, ed. n.

11 François, Marquis de Barbé-Marbois, secretary of the French legation and consul of France in Philadelphia.

12 In his dispatches during December 1782 to La Luzerne, Vergennes apparently did not mention "the separate article," even though an entry in John Adams'

journal permits little doubt that Vergennes knew of the existence but not the contents of the article on or shortly after 5 December (Wharton, *Revol. Dipl. Corr.*, VI, 109). On 19 March, General Sir Guy Carleton and Admiral Robert Digby, having received a copy of the preliminary articles including the separate article, forwarded a copy to Washington for transmission to Congress. Washington's dispatch, enclosing the copy, was received by Congress on 24 March 1783 (Fitzpatrick, *Writings of Washington*, XXVI, 237, n. 48; NA: PCC, No. 152, XI, 179, 183; *JCC*, XXIV, 211, n. 1). The separate article apparently was not published in any newspaper of Philadelphia or New York City during March or April 1783. See JM Notes, 24 Mar. 1783; Richard B. Morris, *The Peacemakers*, pp. 440–42.

13 See n. 2, above. A summary of the preliminary articles, derived from "a kind correspondent," appeared in the *Pennsylvania Packet* of 13 March. That newspaper on 18 March, and the *Pennsylvania Gazette* and *Pennsylvania Journal* the next day, printed the full text, with the exception of the secret article.

Virginia Delegates to Benjamin Harrison

RC (Virginia State Library). In the hand of John Francis Mercer, who signed his own name. Arthur Lee signed for the other delegates. Cover missing, but the delegates were undoubtedly addressing Harrison, even though his name is not shown either at the beginning or the close of the letter. Docketed, "Lr. from the Delegates in Congress—March 12th. 1783." The words italicized in the present copy are those underlined by Mercer.

PHILA. March 12th. 1783.

SIR

We have judged it most advisable to communicate to your Excelly. by Express[1] the purport of the dispat|c|hes from our Ministers at Paris, which have this day arrived by Capt. Barney, who left l'Orient the 17th of Jany. protected by a passport under the signature of his Brittanick Majesty, after having been long detained for the purpose of forwarding advices relative to the negociations for Peace.[2]

These will be found important, altho' not decisive, & we consequently think it our duty, to furnish yr Excelly. with the information requisite to form your own judgement respecting the prospect we have of *a speedy* Peace, not doubting that you will so far diffuse communications (as may appear necessary) on a subject that must influence the measures of the Public & of individuals.[3]

The preliminary Articles of Peace were signed by Mr. Ozwald, Minister Plenipotentiary of Great Britain, & Messrs. Adams, Franklin, Jay & Adams, our Ministers—provisionally, that is to say, to be effective when the definitive treaty may be concluded between France & Great Britain. they are forwarded to us & contain 8 Articles, substantially of the following import[4]

an ample recognition of the independence of the United States & relinquishment on the part of his Brittanick Majesty, for himself[,] heirs & successors, of all claim to right of sovereignty, property or jurisdiction within the limits of the territory of the States, which are fully settled & described in the second Article.[5]

They are affixed much on the principle of the treaty of Paris,[6] but to give you a more accurate idea without a minute detail, the line established, is from the mouth of the River St. Croix to the source, thence north along those mountains which divide the waters that fall[7] on each side into the St. Lawrence & Atlantic Ocean, thence to the head of Connecticut River, thence down the middle of that River to the 45th. degree of Latitude, thence west to the River Iroquois or Cataroquy,[8] thence along the middle of the said River to the Lake Ontario, thence thro' the middle of that Lake & the Lakes Erie, Huron, Superior & the lake of the woods, pursuing the middle of their water communications, thence due west to the Mississippi,[9] thence along the middle of that River to the 31. degree of North latitude, and thence from that intersection nearly an East course to the source of St. Mary's River, thence down the middle of that River to the Atlantic Ocean, together with all Islands in sd. Ocean within 20 Leagues of the Continent.[10]

The great Fisheries to remain free to both nations, with liberty, to cure on the shores subject to either power, & we are also admitted to fish & cure on the shores of Labrador untill they may become settled.[11] Debts due on both sides are to be recovered—no farther confiscations to take place & Congress are earnestly to recommend to the different States to revise those Laws, w[hi]ch forfeit the property of British subjects who have never born Arms against the United States, and all those refugees who have born Arms are to be permitted to make personal application to the different Legislatures to be reinvested, in their Estates on repaying any Sums w[hi]ch may have been bona fide paid by the present possessors.[12]

The subjects of either Power are reciprocally to enjoy in every commercial intercourse all advantages that the subjects of each respective Power enjoy within their own dominions, saving the exclusive rights of the chartered Companies of Brittain, from an interference with which all other British subjects are precluded.[13]

All posts within the territorial limits of the United States at present held by the British troops, are to be evacuated, without carrying any property which may have been seized from the Americans. All Posts taken since the signing of these Preliminaries to be immediately relinquished. These together with a general amnesty on both sides for all offences, & a ceasing of all criminal prosecutions arising on such offences, constitute the ground work of the agreement w[hi]ch has been thus reciprocally signed.[14]

On the 24th. Doctr. Franklin writes that difficulties had intervened between that date & the 15th. of Decr. when his last was dated accompanying the above, in the prosecution of the Negociations between France & Great Britain.[15]

It appears from the Journals of these negociations & the Letters of our Ministers previous to that date that the chief difficulty arose from Gibraltar. France had offered to give G. B. the Island of Guadaloupe for that post & to receive in return from Spain the half of St. Domingo, which belongs now to Spain but Britain obstinately contended for Porto Rico.[16] However to give your Excellency a just idea of the present information of Congress on this subject We transcribe to you quotations from a Letter from the C[o]mte de Vergennes to Doctor Franklin, dated the 24th. transmitted by him to Us. *"Our Negociations* (i.e. between France & G. B.) *are at the same point with yours; but yet far from an end*["], then again *"Our facility has occasioned difficulty*["] and again, *"I do not despair; I rather hope, yet every thing is uncertain*["][17] On the whole I believe the preliminaries between France & Britain are agreed on tho' not signed (an account of them such as we have will be communicated in our next) & that Spain & Holland have made but little progress in their business.[18]

Thus far go the dispatches w[hi]ch we have already perused. matters of importance may yet be behind, & communications of very consequential import are expected from the Minister of France.[19] if from these sources any intelligence may spring, yet unknown, Yr. Excellency may expect it in our next,[20] which will follow this by an Opportunity that will give it a speedy & safe conveyance.

A Copy of the Commission of his Swedish Majesty, to his Minister in France, empowering him to conclude a treaty with the United States, is now transmitted us. the terms in w[hi]ch it is conceived are not only ample but honorary & flattering &c   we are happy to assure Yr. Excellency that some progress has been made in a treaty with that Power.[21]

We are assured that a deputation from the refugees at N York are sent to the legislature of that State requesting to know what terms they are to expect & every thing there portends a very speedy evacuation.[22]

With high respect We have the honor to be Yr. Excellency's most ob: & very humble Servants.

Jos. Jones
James Maddison
Theodorick Bland
Arthur Lee
John F. Mercer

P. S. I find that the Article respecting Commerce altho' adjusted as above, yet was excluded by Mr. O. when about to sign, as several Acts of Parliament stand in the way.[23] The Express who brings you this will apply to yr. Excellency for 24 £ which was the price stipulated. one third however will be repaid us by the Maryland Delegates.[24]

[1] See postscript.

[2] Delegates to Harrison, 18 Feb. 1783, n. 3. The "Washington" had reached Lorient about 1 November 1782 (Wharton, *Revol. Dipl. Corr.*, V, 854).

[3] Harrison to Delegates, 20 Mar. 1783, n. 2.

[4] JM Notes, 12–15 Mar. 1783, and nn. 1, 6. Mercer's "8" should have been 9, and his second "Adams," Laurens.

[5] *JCC*, XXIV, 245–47.

[6] That is, the Treaty of Paris of 1763, concluding the Seven Years' War between Great Britain on the one side and France and Spain on the other, insofar as territories in North America had been at issue in the conflict. See *Papers of Madison*, V, 51, n. 5; 153; 158–59; 161, nn. 6, 9.

[7] Article II reads: "From the north-west angle of Nova Scotia, viz. that angle which is formed by a line drawn due north from the source of St. Croix river to the highlands, along the said highlands, which divide those rivers that empty" etc. (*JCC*, XXIV, 246). This passage, owing to a lack of accurate maps or even of maps which agreed as to the meaning of "St. Croix river," resulted in a boundary dispute between the United States and Canada which the Webster-Ashburton Treaty of 1842 finally adjusted (Richard B. Morris, *The Peacemakers*, pp. 363–67). For a detailed, factual analysis of the geographical ambiguities of the boundaries delineated in Article II and of their solution in a series of treaties between 1794 and 1910, concluded by the United States with Spain or Great Britain, see Charles O. Paullin, *Atlas of the Historical Geography of the United States*, ed. John K. Wright (Washington and New York, 1932) pp. 52–62 and plates 89, 90, 91A, B, and C, 92A and B, 93A, B, D, and E.

[8] The adjective "northwesternmost" immediately before "head" in the "text" of Article II would be difficult to define because, unknown to the peace commissioners, the Connecticut River originated from the confluence of a number of large streams, several of which were joined by lesser watercourses flowing from the northwest. See plate 93A in Charles O. Paullin, *Atlas*. The "Iroquois or Cataroquy" was the St. Lawrence River.

[9] From "Superior" through "Mississippi," the text of Article II reads: "Superiour northward of the isles Royal and Philipeaux to the Long lake; thence through the middle of said Long lake, and the water communication between it and the lake of

the Woods, to the said lake of the Woods; thence through the said lake to the most north-western point thereof, and from thence in a due west course to the river Mississippi" (*JCC*, XXIV, 246). This boundary could not be made effective, partly because of the difficulty in identifying "the Long lake" but mainly because the "highest source" of the Mississippi is south and somewhat east of the most north-western point of the Lake of the Woods. See Charles O. Paullin, *Atlas*, pp. 57–58, 60–61, and plates 91B, 93B.

10 This is a much simplified summary of the latter half of the text of Article II, and, as would be expected, omits mention of the "separate article" concerning the southern boundary of the United States (*JCC*, XXIV, 246–47; JM Notes, 12–15 Mar. 1783, and nn. 6, 12, 13).

11 Article III of the preliminary articles acknowledges "the right" of "the people of the United States" to fish "on the Grand bank, and on all the other banks of Newfoundland, also in the gulf of St. Lawrence, and at all other places in the sea, where the inhabitants of both countries used at any time heretofore to fish." In the same article Great Britain conceded to the people of the United States the "liberty" to fish on all coasts, including that of Newfoundland, and in all "bays and creeks" of "his Britannick Majesty's dominions in America," but they could "dry and cure fish" only on "the unsettled" shores of "Nova Scotia, Magdelen islands and Labrador" (*JCC*, XXIV, 247–48). Mercer was incorrect in writing "subject to either power," for the extension of a "liberty" in Article III was unilateral by Great Britain only, and related solely to coastal lands and waters within her jurisdiction.

12 In this long sentence Mercer summarized the fourth and fifth articles and the first clause of the sixth article of the preliminary peace treaty. Governor Harrison probably would also have been interested in the stipulation of Article V providing that former combatants should have "free liberty" to go anywhere in the United States and remain there "unmolested" for a year while they endeavored to recover their confiscated "estates, rights and properties" (*JCC*, XXIV, 248–49). See also JM to Randolph, 12 Mar. 1783, n. 4.

13 Not conforming with any part of the provisional treaty of peace, this paragraph summarizes the fourth article of an agreement, concluded by the American and British commissioners at Paris on 8 October 1782, concerning the possible terms of such a treaty. The document was to be submitted to King George III for "his majesty's consideration" (Wharton, *Revol. Dipl. Corr.*, V, 805–7).

In his covering letter of 5 December 1782 to Robert R. Livingston, enclosing a copy of the tentative agreement of 8 October as well as copies of other documents, Franklin explained the British refusal to mention commerce in the provisional treaty: "The reason given us for dropping the article relating to commerce was that some statutes were in the way which must be repealed before a treaty of that kind could be well formed, and that this was a matter to be considered in Parliament" (*ibid.*, VI, 113). Before concluding the present dispatch, Mercer was told by his colleagues, or he otherwise ascertained, that the article on commerce was not included in the provisional treaty. See his postscript. An example of a chartered company with "exclusive rights" was the British East India Company.

14 Although the word "amnesty" does not occur in the preliminary articles, it reflects the intent of the signatories respecting the part any person "may have taken in the present war." Except that Mercer's mention of "offences" and "prosecutions" refers to Article VI, his paragraph summarizes Articles VII and IX. Article VII explicitly included, among the items of American "property" which the British must not destroy or carry away, "negroes," "archives, records, deeds and papers belonging to any of said states, or their citizens," and the "American artillery that may be" in the "fortifications" to be evacuated. The same article also stipulated that "all prisoners on both sides shall be set at liberty" (*JCC*, XXIV, 249–50).

In view of Virginia's special concern about her western territory, it is surprising that the delegates did not quote Article VIII, reading: "The navigation of the river Mississippi, from its source to the ocean, shall forever remain free and open to the subjects of Great Britain, and the citizens of the United States" (*JCC*, XXIV, 250).

15 The reference is to Franklin's dispatch of 24–25 December to Livingston, enclosing a copy of Vergennes' note of 25 (not 24) December to Franklin (Wharton, *Revol. Dipl. Corr.*, VI, 163, 168). For quotations from that note, see the next paragraph of the present letter and n. 17, below.

16 Mercer derived this information principally from the 14 December portion of Franklin's dispatch of 5 and 14 December 1782 to Livingston (Wharton, *Revol. Dipl. Corr.*, VI, 113). For the stubborn problem caused by Great Britain's refusal to relinquish Gibraltar despite the determination of Spain to regain it and the obligation of France to endorse her ally's demand, see Richard B. Morris, *The Peacemakers*, pp. 386–410.

17 Except for the last of the three alleged quotations, Mercer distorted what Vergennes had written to Franklin on 25, not 24, December 1782, viz., "I should have been happy could I have informed him [La Luzerne] that our negotiation is advanced as far as yours, but it is far distant as yet. I cannot even foretell what will be the issue of it, for even difficulties proceed from the facility with which we have listened to their proposals. . . . I do not despair, I rather hope; but everything is as yet uncertain" (Wharton, *Revol. Dipl. Corr.*, VI, 168). The tenor of this passage contrasts with that of the portion of an earlier dispatch from Vergennes quoted in n. 18. See also JM to Randolph, 12 Mar. 1783, and n. 10.

18 Delegates to Harrison, 18 Mar. 1783, of which only an abstract has been found by the present editors. The contents of the dispatches and other papers submitted to Congress on 12 March do not justify Mercer's sanguine view about the state of the negotiations between France and Great Britain by 25 December 1782. Mercer, however, may have seen the extracts from John Adams' journal, even though they were not laid before Congress until 14 or 15 March (JM Notes, 12–15 Mar. 1783, n. 1).

In his entry for 5 December 1782 Adams recorded that he was told by La Vauguyon (JM Notes, 29 Jan. 1783, n. 3) that "France and England are agreed, and that there is but one point between England and Spain. England and Holland are not yet so near" (Wharton, *Revol. Dipl. Corr.*, VI, 109). This information is supported by the following passage in Vergennes' dispatch of 19 December 1782 to La Luzerne—the purport of which the latter may have revealed on 12 March 1783 to one or more of his friends in Congress or to Livingston: "There is no essential difficulty at present between France and England, but the King [Louis XVI] has been resolved that all his allies should be satisfied." Vergennes then added that the "fundamental points" with regard to "the interests of Spain" had already been "established and little remains but to settle the forms" (*ibid.*, VI, 152). The negotiations with Holland, being protracted, were not finished by 20 January 1783, when peace commissioners representing Great Britain, France, and Spain signed a "Declaration" stipulating a "cessation of hostilities" as soon as the preliminary peace terms among them had been ratified, and Franklin and Adams signed a separate "Declaration" to the same effect (*ibid.*, VI, 152, 215, 219, 223–25, 226; Jefferson to JM, 7–8 Feb. 1783, n. 13; Richard B. Morris, *The Peacemakers*, pp. 428–29).

19 JM Notes, 12–15 Mar. 1783, nn. 9, 12.

20 Delegates to Harrison, 18 Mar. 1783.

21 The information in this paragraph is based upon the dispatches to Livingston from Adams on 14 December and from Franklin on 24 December 1782. Franklin enclosed a copy of the commission from King Gustavus III (1746–1792) of Sweden to the eminent poet, Gustav Filip, Count Creutz (1731–1785), then ambassador at the court of France and later chancellor of Sweden, to conclude with the United States a treaty of amity and commerce. The commission stated that the independence of

the thirteen United States had been "duly and solidly acknowledged and established." By the date of the present letter, the first draft of the treaty had already
been agreed upon by Creutz and Franklin (Wharton, *Revol. Dipl. Corr.*, VI, 133–
34, 163–64, 276). See also *Papers of Madison*, V, 167–68; 168, nn. 2, 3; 186; 188, n. 7;
Burnett, *Letters*, VII, 263, and n. 2.

22 William Shattuck, who had recently arrived in Philadelphia as an emissary
from Governor George Clinton to reinforce with oral testimony Clinton's dispatch
with many enclosures concerning the continuing outrages to which patriotic New
Yorkers were being subjected in the New Hampshire Grants (Vermont), may have
been the source of the delegates' information about the "deputation from the refugees." Arthur Lee was a member of the committee to which Clinton's letter had
been referred on 4 March 1783 (*JCC*, XXIV, 164, n. 1; Burnett, *Letters*, VII, 66–67;
Syrett and Cooke, *Papers of Hamilton*, III, 282–83, n. 4; *Papers of Madison*, V, 353,
n. 15). Although no reference is made to this "deputation," the *Pennsylvania Packet*
of 11 March and the *Pennsylvania Journal* of 8 and 12 March 1783 emphasized the
odium and detestation with which the Loyalists of New York City regarded King
George III for deserting them and being "the author of their ruin." For Governor
Clinton's implacably hostile attitude toward Loyalists, see E[rnest] Wilder Spaulding, *New York in the Critical Period, 1783–1789* (New York, 1932), pp. 122–28; also
Thomas J. Wertenbaker, *Father Knickerbocker Rebels*, pp. 256–59. The last contingent of British troops did not leave New York City until 25 November 1783
(*ibid.*, pp. 263–67).

23 See n. 13; Mr. "O" was Richard Oswald.

24 The "Express" was William Blake. He was probably the former continental in-
fantryman, William Blake (1730–1798) of Chesterfield County (*Lineage Book of the
National Society of the Daughters of the American Revolution*, CXXXI [1933], 237;
Gwathmey, *Historical Register of Virginians*, p. 68). Blake traveled to Richmond
by way of Baltimore, where he left the Maryland delegates' dispatches that were
forwarded to Annapolis on 15 March. He arrived in Richmond during the evening
of 19 March. The following day the Council of State directed that he be issued a
warrant for $49.00 on the contingent fund (Harrison to Delegates, 20 Mar. 1783;
Burnett, *Letters*, VII, 74, and n. 4, 88; *JCSV*, III, 232).

To Edmund Randolph

RC (LC: Madison Papers). Cover addressed by JM, "Edmund
Randolph Esqr. Richmond. By Express." Docketed by Ran-
dolph, "J. Madison March 12. 1783." For the "Express," see
Delegates to Harrison, 12 Mar. 1783, n. 24.

PHILADA. March 12. 1783

MY DEAR SIR,

Capt. Barney commanding the American packet boat which has been
long expected with official intelligences from our Ministers in Europe
arrived here this morning. He brings a supply of money the sum of
which I cannot as yet specify & comes under a passport from the King
of G. B. The despatches from our Ministers are dated the 5. 14 & 24 of

Decr. Those of the 14th inclose a copy of the preliminary articles provisionally signed between the American & British Plenipotentiaries.[1] The tenor of them is that the U.S. shall be acknowledged & treated with as free, sovereign & independt., that our boundaries shall begin at the mouth of St. Croix, run thence to the ridge dividing the waters of the Atlantic from those of St. Laurence, thence to the head of Cont. river, thence down to 45.° N. L. thence to Cadaraqui, thence thro' the middle of Lakes Ontario, Erie, Huron & Superior to Long Lake, to the lake of the woods & thence due W to the Missi[ssip]pi, thence down the middle of the river to L: 31. thence to Apalichicola, to flint river, to St. Mary's & down the same to the Atlantic,[2] that the fisheries shall be exercised nearly as formerly;[3] that Congress shall earnestly recommend to the States a restitution of Confiscated property a permission to the refugees to come & remain for 1 year within the States to solicit restitution, and that in the most obnoxious cases restitution may be demanded of purchasers on reimbursing them the price of the property,[4] that debts contracted prior to 1775 shall be mutually paid according to sterling value;[5] that all prisoners shall be mutually set at liberty; troops withdrawn & all records & papers restored; that the navigation of the Mississippi from the source to the mouth shall be mutually free for the subjects of G. B. & the Citizens of America,[6] a proposition comprehending the W. I. was offered on the subject of Commerce, but not admitted on the part of G. B.[7]

In the course of the negociation G. B. contended for not only the limits marked out in the Quebec Act, but all ungranted soil, for a contraction of the fisheries, and for absolute stipulations in favr. of the loyalists.[8]

The despatches of the 14th. Speak also of the principal preliminaries between F. & G. B. being settled; but of little progress being made in those between Hold. & Spn. & the latter; & of none between Spn. & U.S.[9]

A letter of the 24. Decr. from Dr. Franklin varies the scene somewhat. It says that uncertainties were arising from the unsettled state of minds in England & incloses a letter from Ct. de Vergennes observing that difficulties had arisen from the very facilities yielded on the part of France; & concluding with these words as well as I can recollect, "Je ne desespere pas. J'espire plutôt; mais tout est incertain."[10]

Franklin's correspondence on this occasion denotes a vigor of intellect, which is astonishing at his age. a letter to the British Minister on the case of the Tories in particular is remarkable for strength of reasoning, of sentiment & of expression.[11] He concludes his letter to Congs. with observing that he is now entering on his 78th. year, 50 of wh[ich] have been spent in the public Service; and that having lived to see like Simeon of old the salvation of his Country, his prayer is that he may be permitted to retire from public life.[12] Mr. Adams has also transmitted a resignation.[13]

The arrival of this intelligence will probably procure from Congs. some final decision with respect to Mr. Jefferson.[14]

Having given you all the facts which hurry wd. admit I leave you to your own conclusion as to the object of them.

Farewell.

J Ma[DISON JR.]

[1] JM Notes, 12–15 Mar., and n. 1; Delegates to Harrison, 12 Mar. 1783, and n. 2. The "Washington" brought 600,000 livres, the first installment of the loan of 6,000,000 livres which King Louis XVI agreed to advance during 1783 (Wharton, *Revol. Dipl. Corr.*, VI, 159–60).

[2] JM Notes, 12–15 Mar., and n. 6; Delegates to Harrison, 12 Mar. 1783, and nn. 6–10.

[3] Delegates to Harrison, 12 Mar. 1783, and n. 11.

[4] *Ibid.*, and n. 12; JM Notes, 12–15 Mar., and n. 2. JM used the phrase "most obnoxious cases" to characterize those Loyalists who had borne arms against the United States. In Article V of the preliminary peace treaty, that category of Loyalists is referred to only as "persons of any other description" (Wharton, *Revol. Dipl. Corr.*, VI, 98–99).

[5] By introducing the phrase "prior to 1775," JM altered the intent of Article IV of the treaty. That article defined the debts as those "heretofore contracted" and "*bona fide*" (*ibid.*, VI, 98). Debts of this description had been incurred as late as 3 July 1776. For John Jay's exhaustive report of 13 October 1786 on the subject of debts owed British creditors, see *JCC*, XXXI, 781–874.

[6] Delegates to Harrison, 12 Mar. 1783, and n. 14.

[7] *Ibid.*, and n. 13.

[8] *Ibid.*, and nn. 2, 6; Wharton, *Revol. Dipl. Corr.*, V, 550, 553, 579, VI, 112–13, 131–32; Richard B. Morris, *The Peacemakers*, pp. 287, 317–18, 344–82. For the Quebec Act of 22 June 1774, see also *Papers of Madison*, IV, 8; 9–10; 14, n. 10; 15, n. 18.

[9] For the dispatches of 14 December 1782, see Wharton *Revol. Dipl. Corr.*, VI, 131–37; JM Notes, 12–15 Mar. 1783, and n. 1.

[10] For Franklin's dispatch of 24–25 December 1782, enclosing a copy of Vergennes' letter to him dated the twenty-fifth, see Wharton, *Revol. Dipl. Corr.*, VI, 163, 168. The delegates in their letter of 12 March 1783 (*q.v.*, and nn. 17, 18) translated the two sentences written in French. According to the copy enclosed by Franklin, Vergennes had written, "Je ne desespere pas, j'espere plutot, mais tout est encore incertain" (NA: PCC, No. 82, II, 335).

[11] In his dispatch of 12 December to Robert R. Livingston, John Jay commented: "Dr. Franklin's firmness and exertions on the subject of the Tories did us much service. I enclose herewith a copy of a letter he wrote [on 26 November] about that matter to Mr. Oswald. It had much weight, and is written with a degree of acuteness and spirit seldom to be met with in persons of his age" (Wharton, *Revol. Dipl. Corr.*, VI, 77–80, 130).

¹² JM refers to Franklin's dispatch of 5 and 14 December 1782 to Livingston (*ibid.*, VI, 110–14). Franklin paraphrased Luke 2:29–32, which in the King James version of the Bible reads: "Lord, now lettest thou thy servant depart in peace, according to thy word: For mine eyes have seen thy salvation, Which thou hast prepared before the face of all people."

¹³ In a dispatch to Livingston on 4 December, John Adams wrote: "As the objects for which I ever consented to leave my family and country are thus far accomplished, I now beg leave to resign all my employments in Europe." If Congress, contrary to his opinion, decided to continue the embassy at The Hague, even though the Treaty of Amity and Commerce with the Netherlands had been concluded, he recommended that his successor as minister plenipotentiary should be Francis Dana. In his dispatch of 14 December 1782 Adams repeated his request to resign and asked Livingston that Congress' acceptance "be transmitted to me several ways by the first ships" (Wharton, *Revol. Dipl. Corr.*, VI, 106, 133–34).

¹⁴ JM Notes, 1 Apr. 1783.

Robert R. Livingston to Virginia Delegates

RC (Virginia State Library). In the hand of a clerk, except for Livingston's signature. Addressed to "The Honorable The Delegates for the Commonwealth of Virginia." Docketed, "Ro. Livingston enclosing Aubrey Memorial." The file copy of the letter is in NA: PCC, No. 119, III, 241.

OFFICE FOR FOREIGN AFFAIRS
15th: March 1783

GENTLEMEN

I have the honor to enclose a translation of a Memorial from Lewis Auby transmitted to me by Dr. Franklin with a letter from the Count De Vergennes accompanying it;¹ which I pray you to submit to your Common Wealth in such way as will most probably procure him the releif he requires, if the State of their accounts with Mr. Pennet will afford them the means

I have the honor to be Gentlemen with great Respect your most obed humble servt

ROBT R LIVINGSTON

¹ Louis Auly, a merchant of Nantes, addressed his undated memorial to Vergennes, who forwarded it with a covering note to Benjamin Franklin on 20 November 1782. When Franklin sent them to Livingston is unclear, but translations of the two documents, in which the memorialist's surname is consistently spelled "Anty," are filed close to Franklin's dispatch of 24 December to the secretary for foreign affairs (NA: PCC, No. 100, II, 304–11). Although Franklin did not mention the Auly memorial in that dispatch, he had commented to Robert Morris ten days

earlier: "Penet, who was employed" by Virginia "as an agent to borrow money here, is broke and absconded. His creditors are all worrying me with their complaints, who have nothing to do with his affairs. I have long since mentioned the inconvenience of the attempts of separate States to borrow money in Europe. They have hurt our credit and produced nothing" (Wharton, *Revol. Dipl. Corr.*, VI, 136). For J. Pierre Penet (d. 1789), whom Virginia had commissioned in 1777 and thereafter to purchase and forward military supplies and to negotiate loans, see Boyd, *Papers of Jefferson*, III, 36, 70, 91; *Papers of Madison*, I, 294, n. 2; IV, 108, n. 2; 175, n. 4; V, 186, n. 3; 195, n. 1; 345, n. 10; Franklin B[enjamin] Hough, *Notices of Peter Penet, and of His Operations among the Oneida Indians, Including a Plan Prepared by Him for the Government of That Tribe . . .* (Lowville, N.Y., 1866).

According to Auly's three-page "Representation" describing his "deplorable situation," he had been reduced to penury by Penet's bankruptcy. Acting as an agent of Penet in fulfilling contracts with Virginia, Auly had used his own funds and credit for buying military matériel, paying export duties and sundry port fees, endorsing some of Penet's bills of exchange, and borrowing money. Since Penet, upon becoming bankrupt, owed Auly over 92,300 livres, the latter pointed out that he had "no hope of recovery but from the Justice of the State of Virginia." The delegates enclosed the translated copy of the memorial in their dispatch of 18 March 1783 to Governor Harrison (*q.v.*). See also Harrison to Delegates, 29 Mar. 1783, and nn. 5, 7, 10, 11, 14.

Before the end of that year Auly arrived in the United States, his name altered to Lewis Abraham Pauly. On 16 December 1783 he "presented" Governor Harrison with a new memorial (Executive Letter Book, 1783–1786, MS in Va. State Library, pp. 245–46), and on 5 April 1785, a little more than three weeks after Pauly had married in Richmond, the state appears to have partially reimbursed him for his financial losses (*Va. Gazette*, 12 Mar. 1785; *JCSV*, III, 431–32). On 28 February 1791 he was recommended "for appointment in the military service" of the United States, but President Washington apparently viewed the suggestion unfavorably (Gaillard Hunt, comp., *Calendar of Applications and Recommendations for Office during the Presidency of George Washington* [Washington, 1901], p. 98).

From Edmund Pendleton

Tr (LC: Force Transcripts). Addressed to "The Honble James Madison, Esq Philadelphia." In the left margin at the top of the transcription, the clerk wrote "MSS McGuire's." See *Papers of Madison*, I, xxii, xxiii.

VIRGA. March 15th. 1783

DEAR SIR

Yr. favr. of the 25th.[1] contains a great many Serious truths very well worth Attention by every friend to America and Particularly those who are concerned in the Public Councils; may the importance of the crisis produce in our approaching Elections men of Abilities to discover, and fortitude to Apply radical Remedies to impending evils,[2] and forsake the horid Quackism of temporary expedients, calculated rather to smother by a kind of Stupor, the disease for the present moment, that it may break out with irresistable violence, than to remove the cause. As you do not mention the Plan agreed on by Congress for making the valuation of lands, which I take to be the great difficulty which formed an objection to that mode of fixing the Quota of each State, I cannot judge of it.[3] That under the Statical influence[4] against the fedral Interest, there will be great partiality in taking it must be supposed, and the only remedie appears to me to be for Congress to refer the Valuation, when returned, to a Committee of one sensible & liberal member from each State; who upon a little enquiry may easily discover the scale wch directs the Value of each, and either raise or lower them, as upon a comparitive view of the whole shall appear just.[5] This method taken by our last Assembly has, I am persuaded, reduced the value of our Lands to equality, much nearer than any of the Various methods theretofore tried.[6] The contentn for an abatement on Account of the unequal pressure of the War, applys strongly in favr of South Carolina & Georgia—perhaps I might Add Virga who suffer'd in 1781 to the full amount of her Quota, I think in Negroes alone, tho' I confess as an Individual I should not think it worth while to claim the exoneration.[7] Those other States from an Infinity of circumstances, were peculiarly distinguishable from all others, and as to the Northern States, who had the most of the War, it appears to me (perhaps wrongly) that the inconveniencys of the War have been over ballanced by the circulation of the money expended amongst them, & other advantages.[8] The Subject of Finance, & how to provide for paying the Public debt and preserving National Credit, is a necessary, Arduous & Important Task, the difficulties of which, will I fear be rather increased than diminished by the Published resignation of the Financier. I have little acquaintance with that Gentln., & less knowledge of his Conduct in office, but from his supposed abilities in that way I can't but fear that his resignation will give an impression of something wrong in our Public Conduct or funds.[9] Should we have Peace, I think our Debts would be immediately liquidated & funded, and funds provided in some mode or other for paying the Annual Interest (wch I think should then be reduced to 5 p ct) & certain Portions of the principal, so as to sink the whole in a reasonable time.[10] I still hope for a confirmation of that desirable Intelligence, notwithstanding the late Marcantile Publication from Baltimore.[11] I feel the necessity & utility, & will not fail to add my mite to the weight of yr exhortation to Mr Randolph to throw off that incumbrance wch deprives us of his great abilities in the Legislature, thrown upon him by a great mistake in forming our Constitution, perhaps we may receive Aid in it by the death of his Aunt, wch has given him a considerable Accession of fortune.[12]

I am now going on a Visit wch will prevent my writing for two succeeding Posts.[13] If not inconvenient I will thank you and Mr Jones to continue your Letters that I may have the pleasure of seeing them on my return.[14] I hope you are at length repd the 12 dollars you advanced[15] for

Dr Sr Yr very affe friend

EDMD PENDLETON

[1] Not found. See Pendleton to JM, 17 and 24 Feb. 1783, ed. n. JM probably included in his letter to Pendleton on 25 February much of what he wrote to Edmund Randolph on that day (q.v.).

[2] Randolph to JM, 15 Jan., and nn. 7, 8; 7 Feb. 1783, and nn. 11, 12.

[3] For the plan of evaluation adopted by Congress, see JM Notes, 17 Feb., and n. 1. See also JM to Randolph, 25 Feb. 1783 and citations in n. 6.

[4] That is, states' rights or state sovereignty.

[5] Pendleton's suggestion conforms closely with the plan mentioned in n. 3, above. For JM's unfavorable view of that solution, see JM Notes, 9–10 Jan.; 14 Jan., and nn. 4, 5; 28 Jan; 31 Jan., and nn. 11, 17; 7 Feb., and n. 11; 17 Feb., and n. 3; JM to Jefferson, 11 Feb.; to Randolph, 18 Feb. 1783, and n. 3.

[6] *Papers of Madison*, V, 311, n. 10; 350, nn. 18, 20; 454, n. 2.

[7] *Ibid.*, IV, 72, n. 3; JM Notes, 27 Jan., n. 27; 28 Jan., n. 19; 31 Jan.; 8 Feb., and n. 3; 10 Feb., n. 14; 11 Feb., n. 2; 17 Feb., nn. 1, 4; 19 Feb., nn. 6, 18; 21 Feb.; 26 Feb., and nn. 22, 24, 28, 31, 37, 38, 40; Randolph to JM, 7 Feb., and n. 3; JM to Randolph, 25 Feb.; Memo. on Revenue Plan, 6 Mar. 1783, ed. n.

[8] Massachusetts, Rhode Island, New York, New Jersey, and Pennsylvania were the theater of "most of the War" until 1780. Among their "advantages" Pendleton probably had in mind the money paid for military supplies and to the British, French, and American troops, and the profits derived from ocean commerce and privateering. See *Papers of Madison*, III, 22–24; 25, n. 27; 142, n. 8; 179; 200; 201, n. 13; 262; 263, n. 9; 339, nn. 2, 3; IV, 250, n. 18; 260; 261, n. 6; 346; 351, nn. 7, 9; 368; 372–75; 414; V, 17; 92; 321–22; 323, n. 8; 375, n. 15; Harrison to Delegates, 7 Feb. 1783.

[9] JM Notes, 24 Jan., and n. 20; 28 Jan., and n. 40; 26 Feb., and n. 14; 4–5 Mar., and nn. 6–9, 11; JM to Randolph, 4 Mar.; 11 Mar. 1783.

[10] Randolph to JM, 15 Jan., and n. 13; JM to Randolph, 28 Jan.; 4 Feb.; 25 Feb.; 11 Mar.; JM Notes, 24 Jan.; 25 Jan., nn. 7, 13; 27 Jan., and nn. 13, 16, 24; 28 Jan.; 29 Jan., and nn. 14, 15; 30 Jan., n. 6; 12 Feb., and n. 9; 17 Feb.; 19 Feb., and n. 7; 20 Feb., and nn. 6, 7, 9; 21 Feb., and n. 27; 11 Mar. 1783, and nn. 3–7, 9.

[11] JM to Randolph, 4 Feb., and n. 12; Jefferson to JM, 7–8 Feb.; Harrison to Delegates, 15 Feb., and n. 2; 21 Feb. 1783, and n. 4.

[12] Harrison to Delegates, 31 Jan., and n. 1; Randolph to JM, 1 Feb., and n. 5; 7 Mar.; JM to Jefferson, 11 Feb., and n. 14; to Randolph, 11 Feb., and n. 3; 25 Feb.; 11 Mar.; 18 Mar.; Jefferson to JM, 14 Feb. 1783 (1st letter), and n. 4. As long as Randolph was attorney general of Virginia, he was barred from serving in the General Assembly by Article III of the "Constitution," reading: "The legislative, executive, and judiciary departments, shall be separate and distinct, so that neither exercise the powers properly belonging to the other; nor shall any person exercise the powers of more than one of them at the same time, except that the justices of the county courts shall be eligible to either House of Assembly" (Hening, *Statutes*, IX, 114).

As presiding officer of the Convention of May 1776, Pendleton had appointed the committee which drafted the Declaration of Rights and Form of Government, but he seems to have contributed little to their contents (David John Mays, *Edmund Pendleton 1721–1803* [2 vols.; Cambridge, Mass., 1952], II, 120–23).

13 Although Pendleton's destination is unknown, he returned to his home on 30 March 1783 (Pendleton to JM, 31 Mar. 1783).

14 *Papers of Madison*, V, 192, and nn. 1, 2.

15 Perhaps the money was to repay JM for purchasing "4 yds good gold lace" for Pendleton. See *Papers of Madison*, V, 272, n. 7; 318; 320, n. 2.

From Edmund Randolph

RC (LC: Madison Papers). Unsigned but in Randolph's hand. Cover addressed by him to "The honble James Madison Jr. esq of congress   Philadelphia." Docketed by JM, "March 15. 1783."

PETTUS'S[1] March 15 1783

MY DEAR SIR

I have not been able as yet to procure your expected favor from the post;[2] nor shall I, until the return of the messenger, who carries this letter to the mail.

We make considerable progress in the detection of the forgeries of the tobacco notes, & Mr. Morris's notes. Of the offenders in the former case, it is hoped, that some considerable examples will be made: and unfortunately for the continent, Morris's notes are not protected by any law, rendering the counterfeiting of them felonious. We must therefore content ourselves with taking a lesser punishment in this case: but the criminal, tho convicted, will still continue to live.[3]

There is a report, that Mr. Morris has actually resigned his superintendancy: and the speculations are various on the subject. Some impute the step to weariness and fatigue; others to an excess of private business; while others, whose disposition is not cordial towards him, ascribe it to a more disagreeable motive. For my part, I conjecture, that he must have been led to this measure by disgust, & want of due support. But even my respect for him will not suffer me to acquit him for resigning at this hour, when fresh vigor may be added to the arms of the enemy, by an assurance, that he abandoned the office thro' despair of our finances; and the affections of France herself, or rather her inclination to succour us with seasonable loans, may be diminished, from the apprehension of her aid, being misapplied, if thrown into other hands than his.[4]

The spirit of opposing laws, as being contrary to the constitution, has reached the executive. They have lately refused to examine into complaints, of a heavy and heinous kind, against a magistrate; alledging, that this would be to assume judiciary power, and that the act of assembly delegating it to the executive, is therefore void. The governor conceives himself obliged to report this bold, and, as I think, mistaken step, to the assembly; by which means you will probably hear more of it. He urged the council to execute the law.[5]

[1] *Papers of Madison*, IV, 148, n. 2.

[2] By 15 March Randolph expected that a letter from JM, probably written about ten days earlier, would be in the post office at Richmond. See JM to Randolph, 4 Mar. 1783.

[3] Randolph to JM, 1 Mar., and nn. 2, 3; 29 Mar. 1783, and n. 4.

[4] Pendleton to JM, 15 Mar. 1783, and citations in n. 9. For Vergennes' respect for Robert Morris as superintendent of finance, see *Papers of Madison*, IV, 316, n. 10. Randolph evidently surmised that the "disgust" of Morris reflected Congress' refusal, owing to the opposition of Arthur Lee and other anti-French and pro–state-sovereignty delegates, to adopt his recommendations for funding the debt and providing a "general revenue." Being unable to pay even the interest due on earlier loans from King Louis XVI, Congress could hardly expect him to extend further monetary aid. For Vergennes' "fear" of Lee, see *Papers of Madison*, V, 427, n. 7.

[5] For the provision of Article III of the Form of Government to which Randolph referred, see Pendleton to JM, 15 Mar. 1783, n. 12. It was probably on 2 December 1778 that the speaker of the Virginia House of Delegates signed into law a bill empowering the governor with the advice of the Council of State to remove any justice of peace from office if they decided that a charge against him of "misconduct, neglect of duty, or mal-practices" had been "proved" (*JHDV*, Oct. 1778, pp. 14, 20, 31–32, 36, 94; Hening, *Statutes*, IX, 478).

On 20 February 1783 Governor Benjamin Harrison laid before Samuel Hardy, Beverley Randolph, and John Marshall, councilors, a memorial from Bartholemew Dandridge, a brother of Mrs. George Washington, accusing John Price Posey, a justice of the peace who in 1780–1781 had been a delegate in the General Assembly from New Kent County, of "diverse gross misdemeanors." These probably comprised alleged thefts by Posey from the estate of the late John Parke Custis, a son of Martha Dandridge Custis Washington by her first husband. Posey may also have condoned "the most shameful Neglect of every species of discipline" by the militia officers of the county. Contrary to the governor's opinion, the councilors held that, because the statute, cited above, violated "the fundamental principles of our constitution" by investing the Executive with judicial power, no consideration should be given to Dandridge's complaint "unless the facts are found in a Court of Justice" (*JCSV*, III, 186–87, 197, 221–22; Swem and Williams, *Register*, p. 11; McIlwaine, *Official Letters*, III, 395, 423; Fitzpatrick, *Writings of Washington*, XXIII, 352–53; XXIV, 139–44, 386–87, 485–87; *Papers of Madison*, IV, 429, n. 3; V, 265, nn. 9, 18).

Having received from the governor and the Council separate statements defending their opposing constitutional views, the Virginia General Assembly at its session of May 1783 took no action except to refer them to the committee of the whole house on the state of the commonwealth. Evidently, however, the position of the councilors prevailed, for on 10 December of that year the General Court found Posey guilty of a misdemeanor and fined him £200. Consequently, on 25 October 1784, the Council of State advised the governor to vacate Posey's commission as justice of peace (*JCSV*, III, 386, 548). See also *ibid.*, III, 497–98; Fitzpatrick, *Writings of Washington*, XXV, 443–46.

In March 1786 Posey was convicted of defrauding Dandridge, the administrator of John Parke Custis' estate. In July of the next year Posey was imprisoned in New Kent County for assaulting the sheriff. Soon escaping from his cell, Posey and some accomplices on the night of 15 July 1787 totally destroyed by fire the county's jail and clerk's office with all its records. Found guilty of arson, he was hanged in Richmond on 25 January 1788 (*Cal. of Va. State Papers*, IV, 95, 225, 329–30, 367, 376, 459; Hening, *Statutes*, XII, 692; *William and Mary Quarterly*, 1st ser., IV [1895–96], 115–16; C[hurchill] G[ibson] Chamberlayne, ed., *The Vestry Book and Register of St. Peter's Parish, New Kent and James City Counties, Virginia, 1684–1786* [Richmond, 1937], p. 591; *Va. Gazette, and Weekly Advertiser*, 19 July, 23 Aug., 18 Oct., 15 Nov., 20 Dec. 1787, 31 Jan. 1788).

Notes on Debates

MS (LC: Madison Papers). For a description of the manuscript of Notes on Debates, see *Papers of Madison*, V, 231–34.

Monday March 17.

A letter was rcd. from Genl Washington inclosing two anonymous & inflammatory exhortations to the army to assemble for the purpose of seeking by other means, that justice which their country shewed no disposition to afford them. The steps taken by the Genl. to avert the gathering storm & his professions of inflexible adherence to his duty to Congress & to his country, excited the most affectionate sentiments towards him.[1] By private letters from the army & other circumstances there appeared good ground for suspecting that the Civil Creditors were intriguing in order to inflame the army into such desperation as wd. produce a general provision for the public debts.[2] These papers were committed to Mr. Gilman Mr. Dyer, Mr. Clark, Mr. Rutlidge & Mr. Mercer. The appt. of These gentlemen was brought about by a few members who wished to saddle with this embarrassment the men who had opposed the measures necessary for satisfying the army viz, the half pay & permanent funds, agst. one or other of which the individuals in question had voted.[3]

This alarming intelligence from the army added to the critical situation to wch our affairs in Europe were reduced by the variance of our ministers with our ally,[4] and to the difficulty of establishing the means of fulfilling the Engagemts. & securing the harmony of the U. S. & to the confusions apprehended from the approaching resignation of the Superintt. of Finance,[5] gave peculiar awe & solemnity to the present moment, & oppressed the minds of Congs. with an anxiety & distress which had been scarcely felt in any period of the revolution.

[1] The official journal of Congress for 17 March omitted mention of the dispatch of 12 March from Washington enclosing an anonymous call for a meeting of general and field officers, the two anonymous "exhortations" to the army, and a copy of his general orders of 11 March 1783. These orders expressed his "disapprobation" of the circular proposing a meeting of the officers on that day "to obtain that redress of Grievances, which they seem to have solicited in vain." In his orders Washington countered this proposal by requesting that the general and field officers, a representative of the staff, and of each company assemble on 15 March "to hear the report of the Committee of the Army to Congress" and to "devise what further measures ought to be adopted as most rational and best calculated to attain" a fulfillment by Congress of its pledges to the officers and troops. In his dispatch, after expressing hope that Congress would approve of the measures he had "taken to dissipate a Storm, which had gathered so suddenly and unexpectedly," Washington reaffirmed his continuing great "zeal in their Service" and for "the wellfare of my Country under the most lively Expectation, that Congress have the best Intentions of doing ample Justice to the Army, as soon as Circumstances will possibly admit" (NA: PCC, No. 152, XI, 105–10, 117; Fitzpatrick, *Writings of Washington*, XXVI, 208–9, 211–12; JM to Randolph, 18 Mar. 1783).

Major John Armstrong, Jr. (JM Notes, 20 Feb. 1783, n. 19), later identified as the writer of the two "exhortations," devoted the first of them to reminding his readers of their manifold hardships during the "seven long Years" wherein they had won independence and peace for their country; to emphasizing that a continuance of their trust in the ultimate justice of a Congress, which "tramples upon your rights, derides your Cries—& insults your distresses" would be "Cowardice"; and to urging immediate resort to a "last Remonstrance" couched in the terms of an ultimatum rather than in the "Milk & Water Stile" of their former petitions. Although by warning against "more moderation and longer forbearance," Armstrong clearly was calling upon his brother officers to reject the counsel of Washington, he closed his "inflammatory" appeal by advising that, if redress was not speedily provided by Congress, "you" should invite "your Illustrious Leader" to guide you "to some unsettled Country, Smile in your turn, and 'mock when their fear cometh' on."

In his second anonymous "exhortation," Armstrong pretended that Washington, even though his general orders had postponed the meeting for four days, substantially endorsed his own proposal. Let that gathering, continued Armstrong, act with the "Energy" he had urged and also with the assurance that, if his advice should prove to be wrong, "I thus publicly pledge my Honor as a soldier, and veracity as a Man, that I will then assume a visible existence, and give my name to the Army, with as little reserve, as I now give my Opinions" (NA: PCC, No. 152, XI, 111–16, 118–23).

[2] On 12 March, in letters of a similar tenor written to Alexander Hamilton and Joseph Jones, Washington remarked that at his headquarters, "it is generally believ'd the Scheme was not only planned, but also digested and matured in Philadelphia," by civilian creditors and "some Members of Congress." They planned to act in concert with the army, which should not disband until it had been paid, and thus "compel the Public, particularly the delinquent States, to do justice." Washington warned Hamilton and Jones of "the ineffable horrors which may be occasioned" if Congress should not soon redress the legitimate grievances of the officers and troops (Fitzpatrick, *Writings of Washington*, XXVI, 213–18). In his reply of 17 March, Hamilton identified himself as one of those "members of Congress" to whom Washington had referred, but not as an advocate of "any combination of *Force*," for "it would only be productive of the horrors of a civil war, might end in the ruin of the Country & would certainly end in the ruin of the army" (Syrett and Cooke, *Papers of Hamilton*, III, 292–93). See also JM Notes, 19 Feb., and nn. 11, 12, 19; 20 Feb., and nn. 18–20; 4–5 Mar. 1783, and n. 5.

³ JM Notes, 13 Jan., and n. 18; 25 Jan.; 28 Jan.; 29 Jan.; 30 Jan.; 4 Feb., and nn. 10, 13; 11 Feb., and n. 3; 12 Feb., and n. 12; 17 Feb., and n. 1; 18 Feb.; 19 Feb.; 20 Feb.; 21 Feb.; 25 Feb., and nn. 1, 2; 27 Feb., and n. 2; 28 Feb.; 10 Mar., and n. 2; 11 Mar.; JM to Randolph, 18 Feb., and n. 3; 25 Feb.; 4 Mar. 1783.
⁴ JM Notes, 12–15 Mar. 1783, and nn. 1–4, 6–8.
⁵ JM Notes, 26 Feb., and n. 14; 27 Feb.; 4–5 Mar., and nn. 3–9, 12; JM to Randolph, 4 Mar.; 11 Mar.; Pendleton to JM, 15 Mar.; Randolph to JM, 15 Mar. 1783, and n. 4.

Notes on Debates

MS (LC: Madison Papers). For a description of the manuscript of Notes on Debates, see *Papers of Madison*, V, 231–34.

Teusday March 18.

On the report of the Committee to whom the 3 paragraphs of the report on revenues¹ (see March 6).² had been recommitted, the said paragraphs were expunged so as to admit the following amendment which took place without³ opposition, viz

"Resolved that it be recommended &c &c (see 1st. ¶)⁴

	Dolr.
Upon all rum of Jamaica proof per Gallon	4/90
Upon all other spirituous liquors	3/90
Upon Madeira wine	12/90
Upon the wines of Lisbon, Oporto, those called Sherry & upon all French wines	6/90
Upon the wines called Malaga or Teneriff⁵	5/90
Upon all other wines	4/90
Upon common Bohea Tea perlb.⁶	6/90
Upon all other Teas	24/90
Upon pepper perlb.	3/90
Upon Brown Sugar perlb	½/90
Upon loaf Sugar	2/90
Upon all other Sugars	1/90
Upon Molasses per Gallon	1/90
Upon Cocoa & Coffee perlb	1/90
Upon salt after the war per Bushel	1/8⁷

And upon all goods except arms, ammunition & cloathing or other articles* imported for the use of the U. S. a duty of 5 perCt. ad valorem:

* The other exception as to Cards & wire for making them &c. was struck out unanimously on the motion of Mr. Clarke; being considered as no longer necessary & contrary to the general policy of encouraging necessary manufactures among ourselves.

provided that there be allowed a bounty of $\frac{1}{8}$ of a dollar for every Quintal of dried fish exported from these U. S. and a like sum for every Barrel of pickled fish, beef or pork, to be paid or allowed to the exporter thereof at the port from which they shall be so exported.[8]

The arguments urged by Mr. Wilson in behalf of his motion [see Journal] for a land tax of $\frac{1}{4}$ of a dollar per 100 Acres,[9] other than those heretofore generally urged were that it was more moderate than had been paid before the revolution & it cd. not be supposed the people wd grudge to pay as the price of their liberty what they formerly paid to their oppressors; that if it was unequal, this inequality wd. be corrected by the States in other taxes, that as the tax on trade would fall cheifly on the inhabitants of the lower Country who consumed the imports, the tax on land wd. affect those who were remote from the Sea & consumed little;[10]

On the opposite side it was alledged that such a tax was repugnant to the popular ideas of equality & particularly wd. never be acceded to by the S. States, at least unless they were to be respectively credited for the amount; and if such credit were to be given, it wd. be best to let the States chuse such taxes as would best suit them.[11]

A letter came in & was read from the Secry. of For Affrs. stating the perplexing alternative to which Congs. were reduced by the secret article relating to West Florida either of dishonoring themselves by becoming a party to the concealment or of wounding the feelings & destroying the influence of our Ministers by disclosing the article to the French Court:[12] and proposing as advisable on the whole

1. that he be authorized to communicate the article in question to The French Minister[13] in such manner as wd. best tend to remove unfavorable impressions which might be made on the Ct. of F. as to the sincerity of Congress or their Ministers.

2. That the sd. Ministers be informed of this communication, and instructed to agree that the limit for W. F. proposed in the separate article be allowed to whatever power the said Colony may be confirmed by a Treaty of peace.

3. That it be declared to be the sense of Congress that the preliminary articles between U. S & G. B. are not to take effect untill peace shall be actually signed between the Kings of F. & G. B.*[14]

---

* This was meant to guard agst. a construction that they were to take effect when peace sd. be agreed on by those powers, & the latter be *ready* to sign, altho the former sd. be restrained untill the other parties sd. be ready for signing

Ordered that tomorrow be assigned for the consideration of the said letter.[15]

[1] In the original report of the committee, the second paragraph recommended a duty on prizes and prize goods (Report on Restoring Public Credit, 6 Mar., and n. 2). In keeping with the recommendation of Robert Morris, that paragraph had been deleted by the committee (JM Notes, 11 Mar. 1783, and n. 2). Hence, the "3 paragraphs" mentioned by JM in the present item represent a complete revision of the original first and third paragraphs and the addition of a provision for a bounty on certain exports.

[2] Above this citation in parentheses JM interlineated "Mar: 6 & 7"—no doubt because his notes for 7 March (q.v.) recorded changes made on that day by Congress in the text of the original report.

[3] Between "expunged" and "without," JM at first wrote, "& the following amendment agreed to be substituted."

[4] That is the first paragraph of the original report as amended between 7 and 18 March. See JCC, XXIV, 118.

[5] These were wines respectively of Spain and of Tenerife in the Canary Islands.

[6] JM Notes, 3 Mar. 1783, n. 2.

[7] JM Notes, 28 Jan., and n. 35; 27 Feb., and nn. 8–10; 3 Mar., n. 2; 11 Mar., and nn. 1–3; Report on Restoring Public Credit, 6 Mar. 1783, and nn. 1–3, 5.

[8] Ibid.; JM Notes, 11 Mar. 1783, and n. 3. A quintal is a hundredweight. By adopting the motion of Abraham Clark, mentioned by JM in his footnote, "wool cards, cotton cards, and wire for making them" would no longer be specifically put on the free list, even though they were not included among the imports recommended to be taxed at the ports of entry. Clark's motion was not entered in the official journal, but the words just quoted are canceled in the manuscript of the revised "3 paragraphs" (n. 1, above), drafted by FitzSimons and submitted to Congress on 18 March (NA: PCC, No. 26, fols. 423 24).

[9] JCC, XXIV, 191. James Wilson's motion, seconded by Alexander Hamilton, would have provided that the tax be levied "on all located and surveyed land within each of the states." At least as early as 27 January, these two men seem to have had in mind a tax on land "to be collected by Congress" (JM Notes, 27 Jan.; 28 Jan., and nn. 3–5, 42; 29 Jan., and n. 19; 7 Feb. 1783, and nn. 5, 8). The brackets are JM's.

[10] That is, "consumed little" of the articles of foreign origin upon which duties would be levied. The assumption, of course, was that the importer would add the amount of the duty to the price which the ultimate consumer would have to pay. See JM Notes, 29 Jan. 1783, and n. 10.

[11] A land tax, unless graduated in rate to reflect the quality of the land, obviously would be unfair, especially to poor people whose holdings were often infertile as well as small. See JM Notes, 14 Jan., and n. 9; 27 Jan., and n. 24; 28 Jan., and nn. 4, 5, 11, 35, 42; 29 Jan., and n. 19; 20 Feb., and n. 14; 11 Mar., and nn. 5, 8; Report on Restoring Public Credit, 6 Mar. 1783, and nn. 7, 8. Wilson's motion failed to carry by a vote of 6 to 4. Every delegate from the states south of Delaware voted "no" (JCC, XXIV, 192).

[12] For Livingston's letter of 18 March to Congress, see Wharton, Revol. Dipl. Corr., VI, 313–16. See also JM Notes, 12–15 Mar., and nn. 6, 12, 13; Delegates to Harrison, 12 Mar. 1783, and n. 10.

[13] The Chevalier de La Luzerne.

[14] The three recommendations are virtually quoted by JM from Livingston's letter to Congress. Following the words "agreed on by" in the footnote, the meaning would be clearer if JM had written: "France and Great Britain; & the latter be ready to sign, although the former might decline to sign until Spain and the Netherlands also indicated readiness to sign their respective peace treaties with Great Britain."

[15] JM Notes, 19 Mar. 1783.

Virginia Delegates to Benjamin Harrison

Printed summary (*Calendar of Virginia State Papers*, III, 458). The original letter has not been found, but the enclosure and a portion of the cover are in the Virginia State Library. On this fragment of the cover is "His Excellency Ben" in the hand of John Francis Mercer and also his signature below the franking word "Free." As a rule the member of the Virginia delegation who drafted its weekly letter to Harrison also addressed the cover. Therefore in this instance Mercer probably was the author, except for the signatures of some or all of his colleagues from Virginia.

The cover docket, "Our Dellegates in Congress March 18. 83 inclosg Auby's Memorial," refers to the memorial of Louis Auly, alias Lewis Abraham Pauly (Livingston to Delegates, 15 Mar. 1783, and n. 1). Clearly having that memorial in mind, Harrison jotted on the cover: "Barclay Peter Penett & co. Livrs 77,502 Interest from Apr. 1782." The abbreviation "Livrs," for Livres, is written immediately above "77,502."

[PHILADELPHIA, 18 March 1783]

The import of the last Dispatches received by Capt: Burney had been communicated. A Letter from Mr. Laurens received at the same time had not been read in Congress. Its date was posterior to those of his colleagues,[1] and conveyed strong suspicions of the designs of the Court of London—that their plan was to disunite the belligerent Powers & he thinks the spirit of the English high "for the prosecution of the war against France."[2]

This minister's reflections were wise and deserved "the most serious attention." He recommends we "should ardently adhere in all points to every engagement with the Court of France," whose views he did not suspect, and cautions us against "trusting to our new but half-made Friends."[3] The news-paper reports of the Parliamentary debates discovered indecision, even in the Cabinet of the British King, consequently he inferred Ld: Shelburne had not disclosed his ultimate views even to them.[4]

. . . .

Refer to sundry claims against the State for goods furnished by French Houses &c. and recommends Mr. Barclay the consul in France, be appointed to settle them.[5] P. S.—By a letter from Genl: Washington, rec'd the day before, they "find the army in a situation highly alarming & truly critical." They "trust much to the prudence & discretion of the General to prevent desperate measures."[6]

[1] Perhaps this summary should have read "posterior to most of those," for Franklin's dispatch of 24 December 1782 bore the same date as that of Laurens' (JM Notes, 12–15 Mar. 1783, and n. 1). "Capt: Burney" was Captain Joshua Barney.

[2] *Ibid.*, and n. 8. For Laurens' dispatch, see Wharton, *Revol. Dipl. Corr.*, VI, 164–65.

[3] Laurens wrote: "I see no cause for entertaining more particular jealousy than ought to be kept upon guard against every negociating court in the world, nor half so much as should at this moment be upon the watch against every motion arising from our new half friends"—that is, the English.

[4] The information conveyed in this sentence was derived by the delegates from the *Pennsylvania Journal* of 15 March and the *Pennsylvania Packet* of 15 and 18 March rather than from Laurens' dispatch. The excerpts in these newspapers from the debates in the House of Commons on 9, 11, and 14 December and in the House of Lords on 13 December make clear that Shelburne, supported by his cabinet colleague the Duke of Richmond, contended that the recognition of American independence would become irrevocable only after the conclusion of peace between Great Britain and France. Simultaneously in the House of Commons the younger William Pitt, chancellor of the exchequer, supported by his cabinet colleague Thomas Townshend, as well as by Edmund Burke and Charles James Fox, held that the acknowledgment of American independence had been "free and unbounded," no matter whether the war against their country's remaining foes should end. Pressed by his opponents in the debate to reveal the position of George III on this issue, Shelburne refused on the grounds that he was "bound, by his office, to keep the secrets of the king." See Richard B. Morris, *The Peacemakers*, pp. 411–14.

[5] Livingston to Delegates, 15 Mar., and n. 1; Harrison to Delegates, 29 Mar. 1783.

[6] JM Notes, 17 Mar. 1783, and nn. 1, 2.

To Edmund Randolph

RC (LC: Madison Papers). Unsigned but in JM's hand. Docketed by Randolph, "J Madison." Below this appears "March 18, 1783," probably in the hand of Randolph's clerk. In his old age JM added after his name on the docket, "X in part," without further specifying what part of the letter he designated for later publication. In the earliest comprehensive edition of his writings, the first and last paragraphs of the letter are omitted (Madison, *Papers* [Gilpin ed.], I, 517–19). Italicized words are those which JM enciphered in the Randolph code. See *Papers of Madison*, V, 307; 309, n. 1; 339, n. 5.

PHILADA. March 18. 1783

My dear Sir

I recd. yesterday your favor of the 7. inst: together with that of the 22. Ulto. which ought to have been brought by the preceding mail.[1] I regret much the uncertainty which attends your going into the Legislature. Is it possible that the difference between the amt. of your salary from the State and of the profits from which your office excludes you can form an essential article in your pecuniary plans? I am far from being singular in supposing that the business on the opposite side would be a much more productive fund.[2]

My letter by Express communicated to you the outlines of the intelligence brought by Capt: Barney from our Ministers in Europe.[3] The tediousness of the Cypher does not permit me now to enter into detail.[4] I can only add that notwithstanding the flattering aspect of the preliminary articles there are various circumstances which check our confidence in them, as there are some which will *detract from our joy* if they should be *finally established*[5] To explain this it must suffice that The latest letters from our Ministers express the greatest *jealousy of G B*[6] and secondly that the situation of *France between* the *interfering claims of Spain & U S* to which may perhaps be added some particular *views of her own* having carried *her into a discountenance of* claims,[7] the *suspicions of our ministers* on *that side* gave an opportunity to *British address to decoy them into a* degree *of confidence* which seems to leave their *own reputations* as well as the *safety of their country at the mercy of Shelburne*[8] In this *business Jay has taken the lead* & proceeded to *a length of which you* can *form little idea. Adams has followed with* cordiality. *Franklin has been dragged into it.*[9] *Laurens* in his *separate letter* professes a *violent suspicion of G B* and *good will & confidence toward France*[10] The *dilemma to which Congress are* reduced is *infinitely perplexing* If *they abet the procedings of their ministers all* confidence *with France is at an end* which in the event of *a renewal of the war must be dread*full as in *that of peace it may* be *dishonourable. If they avow the conduct of their ministers* by *their* usual *frankness of communication* the most serious *inconveniences* also *present* themselves. The torment of this *dilemma can not be justly conveyed* with*out a* fuller *recital of facts than is permitted.* I wish you not to hazard even an interlined decypherment of those which I have deposited in your confidence.[11]

Despatches were yesterday recd. from Genl Washington which have *revived & increased our apprehenseons on that side.* There seems to be reason to *suspect that* the *intriegues of* the *civil creditors fan* the *discontents of* the *army. The conduct of Washington* does equal honor to *his prudence and to his virtue*[12]

The state *of our foreign affairs and of the army* combined with the difficulty and uncertainty of providing for justice & for our finances & with the *approaching exit of Morris give a peculiar solemnity to* the *present moment* God send us a Speedy & *honourable deliverance from every danger.*[13] pray hasten the new Cypher which you have promised.[14]

I have not yet perused your notes but thank you for them.[15] Mr. J.n is still left in dubio as to his destination. Before the next post the final decision of Congs. will probably take place.[16] The paper inclosed to Mr. Ambler will give you the first part of the parliamentary debates, as the one herewith inclosed will the preliminary articles. The eagerness of the opposition for them portends violent altercations. The liberality of the articles to the U.S. will probably be the ground of Attack from the old Ministry; the omission of Commerce that of Fox's division.[17]

Farewell.

[1] Randolph to JM, 22 Feb., and hdn.; 7 Mar. 1783.

[2] JM to Randolph, 11 Feb., and n. 3; Randolph to JM, 29 Mar. 1783.

[3] JM Notes, 12–15 Mar., and n. 15; JM to Randolph, 12 Mar. 1783.

[4] JM to Randolph, 4 Feb. 1783, and n. 10.

[5] JM Notes, 12–15 Mar., and nn. 2, 6, 12; Delegates to Harrison, 12 Mar., and n. 12; JM to Randolph, 12 Mar. 1783, and nn. 4 and 5.

[6] JM erroneously encoded "sy" in "jealousy" as 246 symbolizing "sl." Both here and later in the paragraph, JM underlined the ciphers for "G B."

[7] JM underlined the ciphers for "U S." The antecedent of "her" is "France." The misspelling of "discountenance" reflects JM's coding of the word. Having failed in concert with Spain to drive the British from Gibraltar, France was the more obligated to support the claims of Spain to control the navigation of the Mississippi River and to possess the territory between the Appalachian Mountains and the Mississippi south of the Ohio River. John Jay and John Adams also suspected that Vergennes was the more willing to back Spain in these regards in order to assure that the United States would remain weak after the war and hence continue to be dependent upon France. See *Papers of Madison*, V, 416; 418, n. 19; 441–42; 443, n. 2; 444, n. 7; 467; 470, n. 16; JM Notes, 12–15 Mar., and n. 4; 19 Mar., and n. 24; Delegates to Harrison, 12 Mar. 1783, and n. 16.

[8] JM Notes, 18 Mar., and n. 14; 19 Mar.; Delegates to Harrison, 18 Mar. 1783, and nn. 3, 4. In encoding "suspicions" and "side," both in this sentence and later in the letter, JM used the cipher for "sw" rather than for "su" in the first of these words, and the cipher for "sl" rather than for "si" in the second.

[9] *Papers of Madison*, V, 172, n. 8; 418, n. 19; 438, nn. 5, 7, 9; 443, n. 2; JM Notes, 3 Jan., and n. 2; JM to Jefferson, 11 Feb., and n. 10; Jefferson to JM, 14 Feb. 1783 (2d letter), and n. 7.

[10] Delegates to Harrison, 18 Mar. 1783, and nn. 2, 3. JM probably used the word "professes" because in the autumn of 1782 he had deemed Laurens to be too friendly

toward the British (*Papers of Madison,* V, 140–41; 143–45; 159–60; 329–30). The ampersand between "good will" and "confidence" was interpolated by Randolph.

[11] Disregarding JM's wish, which might better have been expressed before he began enciphering, Randolph interlineated a decoding. In cautioning Randolph, who was no longer a delegate from Virginia, JM almost surely recalled his own criticism of David Howell for divulging information which Congress had designated confidential. See *Papers of Madison,* V, 372–73; 397; 398, n. 10; 419–20; 420, nn. 4, 6; 421, n. 10; JM Notes, 3 Jan., and n. 3; 9–10 Jan., and n. 21; 19 Mar., and n. 19; JM to Randolph, 14 Jan. 1783, n. 5.

[12] JM Notes, 17 Mar. 1783, and nn. 1, 2. The misspellings of "apprehensions" and "intrigues" resulted from faulty encoding by JM. In encoding the first syllable of "Washington," he wrote 491 symbolizing "way" rather than 490 for "wash."

[13] JM Notes, 24 Jan., and n. 20; 28 Jan., and n. 40; 26 Feb., and n. 14; 27 Feb.; 4–5 Mar., and nn. 3, 4, 7–9, 11, 12; JM to Randolph, 4 Mar.; 11 Mar., and n. 4; Randolph to JM, 15 Mar. 1783, and n. 4. JM encoded "approaching" as "approaccing" and underlined the ciphers for "honourable."

[14] Although Randolph did not comply, neither he nor JM found occasion to employ the cipher in their letters to each other during the remainder of the time-span of the present volume.

[15] Randolph to JM, 7 Mar. 1783, and n. 8.

[16] JM to Randolph, 11 Mar. 1783, n. 6.

[17] Jacquelin Ambler, the treasurer of Virginia. See JM Notes, 12–15 Mar., and n. 13; Delegates to Harrison, 18 Mar., and n. 4. The "old Ministry" was that of the Marquis of Rockingham, who died on 1 July, 1782. Charles James Fox, a Rockingham Whig, had declined to serve in the cabinet of the Earl of Shelburne (*Papers of Madison,* V, 211, n. 17). For the refusal of Shelburne to include an article on commerce in the preliminary treaty of peace, see Delegates to Harrison, 12 Mar. 1783, and n. 13.

Notes on Debates

MS (LC: Madison Papers). For a description of the manuscript of Notes on Debates, see *Papers of Madison,* V, 231–34.

Wednesday March 19. 17[83]

A letter was read from the Superintendt. of Finance inclosing letters from Docr. Franklin accompd. with extracts from the Ct. de Vergennes relative to money-affairs, the Supt. thereupon declaring roundly that our credit was at an end & that no further pecuniary aids were to be expected from Europe.[1] Mr. Rutlidge denied these assertions & expressed some indignation at them.[2] Mr. Bland said that as the Supt. was of this opinion it would be absurd for him to be Minister of Finance and moved that the come. on his motion for arranging the department might be instructed to report without loss of time. This motion was negatived as censuring the Come. but it was understood to be the sense of Congs. that they sd. report.[3]

The order of the day viz the letter from the Secretary of Fr. Afrs. was taken up.[4]

Mr. Wolcot conceived it unnecessary to waste time on the subject as he presumed Congs. would never so far censure the Ministers who had obtained such terms for this Country; as to disavow their conduct.[5]

Mr. Clarke was decided agst. communicating the separate article,[6] which wd. be sacrificing meritorious Ministers, & wd. rather injure than relieve our national honour. He admitted that the separate article put an advantage into the hands of the Enemy,[7] but did not on the whole deem it of any very great consequence. He thought Congress ought to go no farther than to inform the Ministers that they were sorry for the necessity which had led them into the part they had taken, & to leave them to get rid of the embarrassmt. as to the separate article in such way as they sd. judge best. This expedient would save Congress & spare our Ministers who might have been governed by reasons not known to Congress.[8]

Mr. Mercer said that not meaning to give offence anywhere he should speak his sentiments freely. He gave it as his clear & decided opinion that the Ministers had insulted Congress by sending them assertions without proof as reasons for violating their instructions, & throwing themselves into the confidence of G. B.[9] He observed that France in order to make herself equal to the Enemy had been obliged to call for aid & had drawn Spain agst. her interest into the war: that it was not improbable that She had entered into some specific engagements for that purpose; that hence might be deduced the perplexity of her situation, of which advantage had been taken by G. B.—an advantage in which our Ministers had concurred for sowing jealousies between F. & U. S. & of which further advantage wd. be taken to alienate the minds of the people of this Country from their ally by presenting him as the obstacle to peace.[10] The British Court he said havg gained this point may easily frustrate the negociation & renew the war agst. divided enemies. He approved of the conduct of the Count de Vergennes in promoting a treaty under the 1st. Commisson. to Oswald as preferring the substance to the shadow & proceeding from a desire of peace.[11] The conduct of our Ministers throughout, particularly in giving in writing every thing called for by British Ministers expressive of distrust of France[12] was a mixture of follies which had no example, was a tragedy to America & a comedy to all the world beside. He felt inexpressible indignation at their meanly stooping as it were to lick the dust from the feet of a nation whose hands were still dyed with the blood of their fellow-citizens. He reprobated the chicane & low cunning wch. marked the journals transmitted to congress,[13] and contrasted them with the honesty & good faith which became all nations & particularly an infant republic. They proved that America had at once all the follies of youth and all the vices of old age: thinks it wd. [be] necessary to recall our Ministers: fears that France may be already acquainted with all the transactions of our Ministers, even with the separate article, & may be only awaiting the reception given to it by Congs. to see how far her hopes of cutting off the right arm of G. B. by supporting our revolution may have been well founded: and in case of our basely disappointing her, may league with our Enemy for our destruction and for a division of the spoils. He was aware of the risks to which such a league wd. expose France of finally losing her share, but supposed that the British Islands might be made hostages for her security.[14] He said America was too prone to depreciate political merit, & to suspect where there was no danger: that the honor of the King of F. was dear to him, that he never wd. betray or injure us unless he sd. be provoked & justified by treachery on our part. For the present he acquiesced in the proposition of the Secy. of Fr. As. But when the question sd. come to be put, he sd. be for a much more decisive resolution.

Mr. Rutlidge said he hoped the character of our ministers wd. not be affected, much less their recall produced by declamations agst. them: and that facts would be ascertained & stated before any decision sd. be passed: that the Ct. de Vergennes had expressly declared to our Ministers his desire that they might treat apart; alluded to & animadverted upon the instruction which sumbmitted them to French Councils;[15] was of opinion that the separate article did not concern France & therefore there was no necessity for communicating it to her; & that as to Spain she deserved nothing at our hands.[16] she had treated us in a manner that forfeited all claim to our good offices or our confidence. she had not as had been supposed entered into the present war as an ally to our ally and for our support; but as she herself had declared, as a principal & on her own account.[17] He sd. he was for adhering religiously to the Spirit & letter of the treaty with France, that our Ministers had done so; & if recalled or censured for the part they had acted, he was sure no man of spirit would take their place. He concluded with moving that the letter from the Secy. for F. A. might be referred to a special comme. who might enquire into all the facts relative to the subject of it. Mr. Holten 2ded. the motion.

Mr. Williamson was opposed to harsh treatment of Ministers who had shewn great ability. He said they had not infringed the Treaty,[18] and as they had recd. the concurrence of the Ct. de Vergennes for treating apart, they had not in that respect violated their instruction. He proposed that Congress sd. express to the Ministers their concern at the separate article & leave them to get over the embarrassment as they shd. find best.

Mr. Mercer in answer to Mr. Rutlidge said that his language with respect to the Ministers was justified by their refusal to obey instructions, censured wth. great warmth the servile confidence of Mr. Jay in particular in the British Ministers. He said the separate article was a reproach to our character, and that if Congress wd. not themselves disclose it he himself would disclose it to his Constituents who would disdain to be United with those who patronize such dishonorable proceedings. He was called to order by the Presidt. who said that the article in question was under an injunction of secrecy & he cd. not permit the orders of the House to be trampled upon.[19]

Mr. Lee took notice that obligations in national affairs as well as others ought to be reciprocal & he did not know that France had ever bound herself to like engagements as to concert of negociation with those into which America had at different times been drawn:[20] He thought it highly improper to censure Ministers who had negociated well, said that it was agreeable to practice & necessary to the end proposed, for Ministers in particular emergencies to swerve from strict instructions.[21] France he said wanted to sacrifice our interests to her own or to those of Spain, that the French answer to the British Memorial contained a passage which deserved attention on this subject. She answered the reproaches of perfidy contained in that Memorial by observing that obligations being reciprocal, a breach on one side absolved the other.[22] The Ct. de Vergennes he was sure was too much a master of negociation not to approve the management of our Ministers instead of condemning it.[23] No man lamented more than he did any diminution of the confidence between this country & France, but if the misfortune should ensue it could not be denied that it originated with France, who has endeavoured to sacrifice our territorial rights, those very rights which by the Treaty she had guarantied to us.[24] He wished the preliminary articles had not been signed without the knowledge of France but was persuaded that in whatever light she might view it, she was too sensible of the necessity of our Independence to her safety ever to abandon it. But let no censure fall on our Ministers who had upon the whole done what was best. He introduced the instruction of June 15. 1781 proclaimed it to be the greatest opprobrium and stain to this

Country which it had ever exposed itself to, & that it was in his judgment the true cause of that distrust & coldness which prevailed between our Ministers & the French Court, inasmuch as it could not be viewed by the former without irritation & disgust.[25] He was not surprized that those who considered France as the Patron rather than the ally of this Country should be disposed to be obsequious to her, but he was not of that number.

Mr. Hamilton urged the propriety of proceeding with coolness and circumspection. He thought it proper in order to form a right judgment of the conduct of our Ministers, that the views of the French & British Courts should be examined. He admitted it as not improbable that it had been the policy of France to procrastinate the definitive acknowledgmt. of our Independence on the part of G. B. in order to keep us more knit to herself & untill her own interests could be negociated. The arguments however urged by our Ministers on this subject, although strong, were not conclusive; as it was not certain, that this policy & not a desire of excluding obstacles to peace, had produced the opposition of the French Court to our demands.[26] Caution & vigilance he thought were justified by the appearance & these alone. But compare this policy with that of G. B. survey the past cruelty & present duplicity of her councils, behold her watching every occasion & trying every project for dissolving the honorable ties which bind the U. S. to their ally,[27] & then say on which side our resentments & jealousies ought to lie. With respect to the instruction submitting our Ministers to the advice of France, he had disapproved it uniformly since it had come to his knowledge, but he had always judged it improper to repeal it.[28] He disapproved also highly of the conduct of our Ministers in not shewing the preliminary articles to our Ally before they signed them, and still more so of their agreeing to the separate article. This conduct gave an advantage to the Enemy which they would not fail to improve for the purpose of inspiring France with indignation & distrust of the U. S. He did not apprehend (with Mr. Mercer) any danger of a coalition between F. & G. B. against America, but foresaw the destruction of mutual Confidence between F. & U. S. which wd. be likely to ensue, & the danger which would result from it in case the war should be continued. He observed that Spain was an unwise nation, her policy narrow & jealous, her King old her Court divided & the heir apparent notoriously attached to G. B.[29] From these circumstances he inferred an apprehension that when Spain sd. come to know the part taken by America with respect to her, a separate treaty of peace might be resorted to. He thought a middle course best with respect to our Ministers; that they ought to be commended in general, but that the communication of the separate article ought to take place. He observed that our Ministers were divided as to the policy of the Ct. of France, but that they all were agreed in the necessity of being on the watch against G. B. He apprehended that if the ministers were to be recalled or reprehended, that they would be disgusted & head & foment parties in this Country. He observed particularly with respect to Mr. Jay that altho' he was a man of profound sagacity & pure integrity, yet he was of a suspicious temper, & that this trait might explain the extraordinary jealousies which he professed.[30] He finally proposed that the Ministers sd. be commended & the separate articles communicated. This motion was 2ded. by Mr. Osgood, as compared however with the proposition of the Secy. for F. A. and so far only as to be referred to a Committee.[31]

Mr. Peters favored a moderate course as most advisable. He thought it necessary that the separate art: sd. be communicated, but that it wd. be less painful to the feelings of the Ministers if the doing it was left to themselves; and was also in favor of giving the territory annexed by the separate art: to W. Florida[32] to such power as might be invested with that Colony in the Treaty of peace.

Mr. Bland said he was glad that every one seemed at length to be struck with the impropriety of the instruction submitting our Ministers to the advice of the French Court. He represented it as the cause of all our difficulties & moved that it might be referred to the come. with the several propositions which had been made. Mr. Lee 2ded. the motion.

Mr. Wilson objected to Mr. Blands motion as not being in order.[33] When moved in order perhaps he might not oppose the substance of it. He said he had never seen nor heard of the instruction it referred to untill this morning; and that it had really astonished him; that this Country ought to maintain an upright posture between all nations. But however objectionable this step might have been in Congs. the magninimity of our Ally in declining to obtrude his advice on our Ministers ought to have been a fresh motive, to their confidence and respect. Altho they deserve commendation in general for their services; in this respect they do not. He was [of the] opinion that the spirit of the treaty with France forbade the signing of the preliminary articles without her previous consent; and that the separate article ought to be disclosed;[34] but as the merits of our Ministers entitled them to the mildest & most delicate mode in which it cd. be done, he wished the communication to be left to themselves as they wd. be the best judges of the explanation which ought to be made for the concealment; & their feelings wd. be less wounded than if it were made without their intervention. He observed that the separate article was not important in itself & became so only by the mysterious silence in which it was wrapt up. A candid and open declaration from our Ministers of the circumstances under which they acted & the necessity produced by them of pursuing the course marked out by the interest of their Country, wd. have been satisfactory to our ally, wd. have saved their own honor, and would have not endangered the objects for which they were negociating.

Mr. Higginson contended that the facts stated by our Ministers justified the part they had taken.

Mr. Madison expressed his surprize at the attempts made to fix the blame of all our embarrassments on the instruction of June 15, 1781, when it appeared that no use had been made of the power given by it to the Ct. of France,[35] that our Ministers had construed it in such a way as to leave them at full liberty; and that no one in Congs. pretended to blame them on that acct. For himself he was persuaded that their construction was just; the advice of France having been made a guide to them only in cases where the question respected the concessions of the U. S. to G. B. necessary & proper for obtaining peace & an acknowledgt. of Indepe.; not where it respected concessions to other powers & for other purposes. He reminded Congress of the change which had taken place in our affairs since that instruction was passed, and remarked the probability that many who were now perhaps loudest in disclaiming, would under the circumstances of that period have been the foremost to adopt it.*[36] He admitted that the change of circumstances had rendered it inapplicable, but thought an express repeal of it might at this crisis at least have a bad effect. The instructions he observed for disregarding which our Ministers had been blamed, and which if obeyed would have prevented the dilemma now felt, were those which required them to act in concert & in confidence with our ally: & these instructions he said had been repeatedly confirmed in every stage of the revolution by unanimous votes of Congress;[37] Several of the gentlemen present† who now justified our Ministers having concurred in them, and one˟ of them, hav-

---

* The Committee who reported the instruction were Mr Carroll, Mr. Jones, Mr Witherspoon, Mr. Sullivan & Mr. Mathews. Mr. Witherspoon was particularly prominent throughout.

† Mr. Bland, Lee, & Rutlidge

˟ Mr. Rutlidge; he formed in the Come the first draught of the declaration made in Sept. last & the instruction abt. the same time. This was considerably altered but not in that respect.

ing penned two of the Acts, in one of which Congs. went farther than they had done in any preceding act; by declaring that they would not make peace untill the interests of our allies & friends as well as of the U. S. sd. be provided for.[38]

As to the propriety of communicating to our Ally the separate article, he thought it resulted clearly from considerations both of national honor & national security. He said that Congress having repeatedly assured their ally that they would take no step in a negociation but in concert & in confidence with him, and havg. even published to the world solemn declarations to the same effect,[39] would if they abetted this concealment of their Ministers be considered by all nations as devoid of all constancy & good faith; unless a breach of these assurances & declarations cd. be justified by an absolute necessity or some perfidy on the part of France; that it was manifest no such necessity could be pleaded, & as to perfidy on the part of France, nothing but suspicious & equivocal circumstances had been quoted in evidence of it; & even in these it appeared that our Ministers were divided;[40] that the embarrassmt. in which France was placed by the interfering claims of Spain & the U. S. must have been foreseen by our Ministers, and that the impartial public would expect that instead of co-operating with G. B. in taking advantage of this embarrassment, they ought to have made every allowance & given every facility to it consistent with a regard to the rights of their Constituents; that admiting every fact alledged by our Ministers to be true, it could by no means be inferred that the opposition made by France to our claims, was the effect of any hostile or ambitious designs agst. them, or of any other design than that of reconciling them with those of Spain; that the hostile aspect wch. the separate art: as well as the concealment of it bore to Spain, would be regarded by the impartial world as a dishonorable alliance with our enemies against the interests of our friends; that notwithstanding the disappointments & even indignities which the U S. had recd from Spain it could neither be denied nor concealed that the former had derived many substantial advantages, from her taking part in the war & had even obtained some pecuniary aids; that the U. S. had made professions corresponding with these obligations: that they had testified the important light in which they considered the support resulting to their cause from the arms of Spain by the importunity with which they had courted her alliance; by the concessions with which they had offered to purchase it, and by the anxiety which they expressed at every appearance of her separate negociations for a peace with the common Enemy.[41]

That our national safety would be endangered by Congress making themselves a party to the concealment of the separate article, he thought could be questioned by no one. No definitive treaty of peace he observed had as yet taken place, the important articles between some of the belligerent parties had not even been adjusted, our insidious enemy was evidently labouring to sow dissentions among them, the incaution of our Ministers had but too much facilitated them between the U. S. and France; a renewal of the war therefore in some form or other was still to be apprehended[42] & what would be our situation if France & Spain had no confidence in us: and what confidence could they have if we did not disclaim the policy which had been followed by our Ministers.

He took notice of the intimation given by the British Minister to Mr. Adams of an intended expedition from N. York agst. W. Florida, as a proof of the illicit confidence into which our Ministers had been drawn, & urged the indispensable duty of Congs. to communicate it to those concerned in it.[43] He hoped that if a Come. sd. be appd. for wch. however he saw no necessity that this wd. be included in their report & that their report wd. be made with as little delay as possible.

In the event the Lettr from Secy of F. A. with all the despatches & the several propositions which had been made, were committed to Mr. Wilson, Mr. Ghorum, Mr. Rutlidge, Mr. Clarke & Mr. Hamilton.[44]

[1] In his letter of 17 March 1783 to Congress, enclosing copies of Benjamin Franklin's dispatches to him of 14 and 23 December, and a translation of Vergennes' note of 15 December 1782 to Franklin, Robert Morris presented a most dismal account of the financial condition of Congress to warrant his conclusions that *"there is no hope of any further pecuniary aid from Europe"* and *"our public credit is gone."* After expressing "a contempt" for critics who blamed him for this situation and after reminding Congress that the sorry state of affairs would have been avoided if his recommendations had been adopted, Morris added, "I pray to be dismissed" as superintendent of finance (Wharton, *Revol. Dipl. Corr.,* VI, 134–36, 140–41, 159–60, 308–11). On 19 March Morris submitted to Congress La Luzerne's letter of equally discouraging tenor, written to him four days before (NA: PCC, No. 185, III, 58; No. 186, fol. 89).

[2] John Rutledge, who evidently was much more hopeful than Morris that the states would come to the financial rescue of Congress, may also have quoted Franklin's letter of 23 December 1782 to the effect that Vergennes had already supplied 600,000 of the French loan of 6,000,000 livres for 1783 and promised to pay the remainder "quarterly" during that year (Wharton, *Revol. Dipl. Corr.,* VI, 160). Morris, however, could retort that even that amount, which was 14,000,000 livres less than the total sought, had been loaned in the expectation that the war would continue and that Congress would assure itself of a sufficient "general revenue" to restore public credit (JM Notes, 12–15 Mar. 1783, n. 7).

[3] After rejecting on 5 March Theodorick Bland's motion to have a committee "devise the most proper means of arranging the department of finance," Congress on that day appointed a committee, John Rutledge, chairman, "to devise the most

proper steps to be taken in consequence of" the impending resignation of Morris (*JCC*, XXIV, 165–66, 168, and n. 1; JM Notes, 4–5 Mar. 1783, and nn. 4, 12). Bland evidently considered that this directive included the purport of his own unsuccessful motion. The journal for 19 March records neither the reference to that committee of Morris' letter of 17 March 1783, nor Bland's motion to have the committee report "without loss of time."

⁴ JM Notes, 18 Mar. 1783, and nn. 12, 13.

⁵ Oliver Wolcott's meaning will become clearer if "favorable" or a word of similar connotation is interpolated between "such" and "terms."

⁶ JM Notes, 12–15 Mar., and nn. 6, 12, 13; 18 Mar.; JM to Randolph, 18 Mar. 1783, and n. 5.

⁷ That is, France would be alienated from the United States if, as seemed likely, Great Britain should reveal to Vergennes the secret article in her preliminary treaty of peace with the United States.

⁸ Abraham Clark's proposal ran counter to that of Robert R. Livingston, secretary for foreign affairs, who wished to be authorized by Congress to inform La Luzerne of the secret article (JM Notes, 18 Mar. 1783).

⁹ John Francis Mercer probably was referring above all to John Jay's long dispatch of 17 November 1782 and John Adams' brief one of the next day, both addressed to Livingston (Wharton, *Revol. Dipl. Corr.*, VI, 11–49, 51–52). Granting that JM's record is accurate, Mercer's indictment of Jay for making "assertions without proof" was much too severe. Jay, however, had reminded Benjamin Vaughan, an agent of the Earl of Shelburne, that Great Britain's own interest should impel her "to make friends of those whom she could not subdue" and "to cut the cords which tied us to France" (*ibid.*, VI, 29–30). For Vaughan, see Comment by Jefferson, 25 Jan. 1783, and n. 1.

In their joint dispatch of 14 December to Livingston, the four American peace commissioners admitted that, by not always taking Vergennes into their confidence, they had "deviated from the spirit of our instructions" of 15 June 1781, but they justified their deviation by mentioning his resistance to what they were expected by Congress to achieve in regard to "the boundaries, the refugees, and fisheries" (Wharton, *Revol. Dipl. Corr.*, VI, 133; JM Notes, 12–15 Mar. 1783, n. 6). In his dispatch of 18 November, Adams commented to Livingston that, if Congress really had wanted the American commissioners "to consult and communicate with French ministers upon all occasions and follow their advice," it would have been "better to constitute the Count de Vergennes our sole minister, and give him full powers to make peace, and treat with all Europe." As a guide to his own conduct, Adams assumed that Congress meant the instructions to accord with the demands of "reason, necessity, and the nature of things" (Wharton, *Revol. Dipl. Corr.*, VI, 52–54). See also *ibid.*, V, 854–55.

¹⁰ King Charles III of Spain concluded with France at Aranjuez on 12 April 1779 a secret "convention" wherein, among other guarantees, France pledged, if Spain entered the conflict, to continue the war until Great Britain agreed to retrocede Gibraltar to Spain. Although Charles III declared war on Great Britain in June 1779, he encouraged agents of the ministry of Lord North, for about three years thereafter, to believe that, if Great Britain would abandon Gibraltar, Spain would withdraw from the war (*Papers of Madison*, II, 223; 225, n. 2; 226; III, 130; 131, n. 3).

Among other "specific arrangements" stipulated in the convention of Aranjuez, France promised to help Spain recover Pensacola and Mobile from Great Britain and to admit Spaniards, but presumably no other foreigners, to the Newfoundland fisheries. On her part, Spain agreed neither to resist having the United States win her independence nor, except after consulting France, to make a pact with the United States or any other country about that independence (Richard B. Morris, *The Peacemakers*, pp. 14–16). For the convention of Aranjuez, see Henry Doniol, *Histoire de la participation de la France à l'éstablissement des États-Unis d'Amérique* (5 vols.; Paris, 1886–92), III, 806–9.

11 John Jay declined to negotiate with Richard Oswald under his commission of 7 August 1782, in which King George III designated him to be "our commissioner" to treat with the commissioner or commissioners of the thirteen "colonies or plantations." Vergennes believed that this wording was satisfactory because "an acknowledgment of our independence, instead of preceding, must in the natural course of things be the effect of the treaty, and that it would not be reasonable to expect the effect before the cause" (Wharton, *Revol. Dipl. Corr.*, V, 613–14, 614 n.; VI, 14–15, 17–18; *Papers of Madison*, V, 172, n. 13; 418, n. 17).

12 Although Shelburne no doubt had been aware of and fostered Jay's and Adams' "distrust of France," he probably did not realize that at least two of the dispatches he received from Oswald had been largely drafted by Jay (Wharton, *Revol. Dipl. Corr.*, VI, 16–17, 19, 46).

13 For the journals referred to by Mercer, see JM Notes, 12–15 Mar. 1783, n. 1.

14 Although by joining with Great Britain in a renewed war, France would incur "risks" because her navy was feeble compared with that of her new ally, she might assure herself of "a division of the spoils" resulting from "our destruction," by occupying the rich "sugar islands" of Great Britain in the Caribbean Sea.

15 For the instructions of 15 June 1781, see *Papers of Madison*, III, 152, n. 10; 154, nn. 3, 5; V, 33–35; 35, n. 4; 36, n. 9; 466–67.

16 The "separate article" concerning the southern boundary of the United States did not affect France directly, but she had promised in the convention of Aranjuez to help Spain recover the coast of West Florida from the British (n. 10). See also *Papers of Madison*, I, 218, n. 6; II, 135, n. 11.

17 *Papers of Madison*, II, 108, n. 9; 196, n. 4; 239, n. 5; 273; III, 101–4; 104, n. 3; 142, n. 8; 170, n. 3; 196–97; 263, n. 6; 278–79; 280, nn. 11, 12; IV, 5–6; 168–69; 169, nn. 3, 5; 215; 216, n. 6; 230, n. 19; 342, n. 1; V, 14; 21, n. 4; 23–24; 35, n. 4; 416; 418, n. 19; 441–42; 444, nn. 7, 11.

18 That is, Article VIII of the Treaty of Alliance between the United States and France, pledging joint action in concluding "either truce or peace with Great Britain" (*JCC*, XI, 451).

19 The journal of Congress does not mention "the orders," presumably of 12 March, enjoining secrecy respecting the separate article. About three months earlier the case of David Howell had demonstrated the inability of Congress to prevent a delegate from revealing secret information to the general assembly of his sovereign state (*Papers of Madison*, V, 419–20; 420, nn. 4, 6; 421, n. 10; JM Notes, 9 10 Jan. 1783, and nn. 21, 22).

20 If JM's sentence to this point is hastily read, he will appear to have Arthur Lee take a position contrary to a stipulation in the Treaty of Alliance between the United States and France (n. 18). Lee most probably meant that Congress should have rescinded the instructions of 15 June 1781 limiting the American peace commission to actions approved by the court of France as soon as it became clear that King Louis XVI would not reciprocally circumscribe the freedom of Vergennes in the negotiations. Lee had tried without success to induce Congress to amend or cancel those instructions (*Papers of Madison*, IV, 435; 436–37; 438, nn. 2, 7; V, 15, nn. 3, 4; 33–35; 35, n. 4; 36, n. 9; 466–68; 469, n. 2).

21 In a recent letter to James Warren, Lee had extolled the conduct of John Adams and John Jay during the negotiations but charged "old Franklin" with "treachery" (Burnett, *Letters*, VIII, 78). See also JM to Randolph, 1 Apr. 1783, n. 5.

22 Lee probably referred to "A Manifesto, published at Paris [1779], displaying the Motives and Conduct of his Most Christian Majesty toward England," and "The Justifying Memorial of the King of Great Britain, in Answer to the Exposition, Etc. of the Court of France." These were published in *The Annual Register*,

or a View of the History, Politics, and Literature, for the Year 1779 (London, Printed for J. Dodsley, 1780), pp. 390–412, and esp. p. 391. The author of the French "Manifesto" charged that although his country had scrupulously observed every commercial stipulation in the Treaty of Utrecht, the "Court of London, and England" had violated it "daily." On 29 July 1778 King George III, to vindicate "the honour of his Crown" had ordered "general reprisals" against France for seizing British ships and goods "contrary to the faith of treaties" (*The Remembrancer, or Impartial Repository of Public Events, for the Year, 1778* [London: John Almon, 1778], pp. 118–20, 255). See also JCC, XVIII, 818–19; Burnett, *Letters,* III, 240, 252; *Papers of Madison,* II, 80, n. 1.

23 JM Notes, 12–15 Mar. 1783, and n. 7.

24 JM to Randolph, 18 Mar. 1783, and n. 7. As a Virginian, Lee must have been aroused by Jay's well-founded suspicion, expressed in the minister's dispatch of 17 November 1782, that France supported the Spanish aspiration to confine the United States by boundaries east of the Mississippi River (Wharton, *Revol. Dipl. Corr.,* VI, 25–27, 31, 46–47; Richard B. Morris, *The Peacemakers,* pp. 320–40). Articles V, VI, and XI of the Treaty of Alliance between France and the United States committed France to recognize American possession of conquered British territory "remaining in the northern parts of America, or the islands of Bermudas" (*JCC,* XI, 450, 451–52). At the time of the signing of the preliminary peace, Virginia troops effectively held the district of Kentucky and small areas north of the Ohio River, but most of the vast region between the Appalachian Mountains and the Mississippi River was not under American control; nor had France bound herself to recognize as valid the territorial claims to that area, based upon American interpretations of British royal charters.

25 JM Notes, 12–15 Mar. 1783, and n. 6; also n. 9, above.

26 Wharton, *Revol. Dipl. Corr.,* VI, 27, 30, 45–46, 48, 49–51, 95 n., 107–8, 140, 150 n., 150–52, 166–68.

27 Hamilton could have cited examples ranging from the Earl of Carlisle's mission in 1778 to the efforts of the British ministry in 1782 to have Washington or Congress negotiate with General Carleton and Admiral Digby for peace (*Papers of Madison,* III, 273, n. 2; V, 3; 5, n. 2; 39, n. 1; 46; 47, n. 4; 76; 247, n. 20; 258, n. 2; Wharton, *Revol. Dipl. Corr.,* VI, 35–36).

28 JM also had opposed its "repeal" (*Papers of Madison,* V, 33–35; 36, n. 9; 408).

29 Charles III, sixty-seven years of age, had designated his son Charles (1748–1819), Prince of the Asturias, as heir-apparent (Wharton, *Revol. Dipl. Corr.,* IV, 842).

30 JM Notes, 1 Jan. 1783, n. 2; Wharton, *Revol. Dipl. Corr.,* V, 849; Richard B. Morris, *The Peacemakers,* pp. 235–36, 245–46, 297–303, 310.

31 In his motion Hamilton proposed that Livingston inform La Luzerne of the separate article and explain to the American peace commissioners the reasons justifying the disclosure (*JCC,* XXIV, 194). For the effect of Samuel Osgood's qualifying second of the motion, see JM's final paragraph.

32 JM Notes, 12–15 Mar. 1783, n. 6.

33 The Bland-Lee motion was a violation of the fifteenth rule of the rules of procedure adopted on 4 May 1781. That rule barred the admittance of a new proposition "under colour of" an amendment to the original motion until the latter should be "postponed or disagreed to" (*JCC,* XX, 479).

34 JM Notes, 12–15 Mar. 1783, nn. 6, 7, 12.

35 Obeying the directions of Congress, Franklin had presented "the instructions relative to the negotiations for peace" to Vergennes in September 1781 (Wharton, *Revol. Dipl. Corr.,* IV, 511, 709).

36 Of these five members of the committee, which had been appointed on 28 May 1781, John Sullivan of New Hampshire, John Mathews of South Carolina, and John Witherspoon of New Jersey were no longer in Congress. Among these instructions,

the paragraph which was central in the present debate had been drafted by Wither-spoon and supported by JM as well as by many other delegates (*JCC*, XX, 562, 606, 627, 650). See also *Papers of Madison*, V, 466–67, and citations in 469, n. 8; Burnett, *Letters*, VII, 111–17.

37 Congress "confirmed" the instructions of 15 June 1781 on 31 May and 4 Octo-ber 1782, but only in the latter instance had the vote been clearly "unanimous" (*JCC*, XXII, 311–13; XXIII, 638; *Papers of Madison*, IV, 302–4; V, 181; 182, n. 5). JM might have been more accurate if he had said that those instructions had repeat-edly withstood the assaults of Arthur Lee and like-minded critics. See n. 20.

38 On 4 October 1782 Bland, Lee, and Rutledge were among the delegates who "*Resolved, unanimously,* That Congress . . . will inviolably adhere to the treaty of alliance with his Most Christian Majesty, and conclude neither a seperate peace or truce with Great Britain" (*JCC*, XXIII, 636, 638). This resolution was an outgrowth of a report by a committee, appointed on 24 September with James Duane, chairman, and JM and Rutledge among its other members. The report, adopted by Congress on 3 October, included: "That his Most Christian Majesty's declaration to the Brit-ish minister at Paris, that he will neither treat nor terminate any negotiation unless the interests of his allies and friends shall be considered and determined, is entirely correspondent to the part which these United States are resolved to take in any negotiation for peace" (*JCC*, XXIII, 603, 633). Based upon this report were the resolutions in the hand of Duane and JM, rather than Rutledge, adopted the next day (*JCC*, XXIII, 639, n. 1; *Papers of Madison*, V, 180–81). They include the reso-lution quoted at the beginning of this note.

39 By adopting the report of 3 October 1782, Congress declared: "That they will hearken to no propositions for peace which shall not be discussed in confidence and in concert with his Most Christian Majesty, agreeably to the declaration made to his minister plenipotentiary on the 31 day of May last" (*JCC*, XXIII, 633). See also *Papers of Madison*, IV, 302–4.

40 That is, Franklin seldom shared the distrust manifested by Jay and his "very able and agreeable coadjutor," Adams, in the attitude and actions of Vergennes with regard to the best interests of the United States during the peace negotiations. Henry Laurens, of course, arrived in Paris too late to share importantly in this dif-ference of outlook (Wharton, *Revol. Dipl. Corr.*, VI, 14–17, 20, 23–30, 47–48, 133). See also *Papers of Madison*, V, 418, n. 17; 438, nn. 7, 9; 443, n. 2; JM Notes, 12–15 Mar., n. 4; JM to Randolph, 18 Mar. 1783, and n. 7.

41 *Papers of Madison*, II, 273; III, 101–4; 104, n. 3; 105, n. 5; 170, n. 3; 263, n. 6; 280, n. 11; IV, 5–6; 14, n. 7; 168–69; 170, n. 5; 190; 215; 216, n. 6; 224, n. 3; V, 21, n. 4; 23–24; 35, n. 4; 418, n. 19; 474, n. 9; 444, n. 11; Wharton, *Revol. Dipl. Corr.*, I, 442; II, 213, 304, 323, 390; III, 290, 335–37, 476, 603, 721–22; IV, 59, 66, 228, 346, 386.

42 JM Notes, 12–15 Mar., nn. 7, 8; Delegates to Harrison, 12 Mar., and nn. 15–18; JM to Randolph, 18 Mar. 1783.

43 From a conference with Richard Oswald on 2 November 1782, Adams con-cluded that, upon evacuating New York City, the British troops would be taken to the Gulf of Mexico to recover West Florida from Spain (Wharton, *Revol. Dipl. Corr.*, V, 845–46, 857). Unknown to Congress, and apparently to the other Ameri-can commissioners, Jay had proposed that expedition to Oswald (Richard Morris, *The Peacemakers*, p. 344).

44 JM interlineated "In the event" above a canceled "On the question." Unmen-tioned in the official journal of 19 March, the names of the committee members were listed by Charles Thomson in his committee book with the notation of a re-ferral to them of "Report of the secy for foreign Affairs on the communications from the Ministers for negotiatg a peace. 3 Motions thereon. the preliminary Articles. the ministers letters & communications respecting the negotiations" (NA: PCC, No. 186, fol. 89). See JM Notes, 22 Mar. 1783.

Notes on Debates

MS (LC: Madison Papers). For a description of the manuscript of Notes on Debates, see *Papers of Madison*, V, 231–34. JM underscored the three words which are italicized below.

Thursday March 20.

An instruction from the Legislature of Virga. to their Delegates agst. admitting into Treaty of peace any stipulation for restoring confiscated property was laid before Congress.[1]

Also resolutions of the Executive Council of Penna. requesting the Delegates of that State to endeavor to obtain at least a reasonable term for making the payment of British debts stipulated in the preliminary articles lately recd.[2]

These papers were committed to Mr. Osgood, Mr. Mercer & Mr. Fitzimmons.[3]

Mr. Dyer whose vote on the   day of   frustrated the commutation of the half pay made a proposition substantially the same wch was committed. This seemed to be extorted from him by the critical state of our affairs, himself personally & his State being opposed to it.[4]

The Motion of Mr. Hamilton on the journals was meant as a testimony on his part of the insufficiency of the report of the Come. as to the establishmt. of revenues, and as a final trial of the sense of Congs. with respect to the practicability & necessity of a *general* revenue equal to the public wants. The debates on it were cheifly a repetition of those used on former questions relative to that subject.[5]

Mr. Fitzimmons on this occasion declared that on mature reflection he was convinced that a *complete* general revenue was unattainable from the States, was impractical in the hands of Congress, and that the modified provision reported by the Come. if established by the States wd. restore public credit among ourselves. He apprehended however that no *limited* funds wd. procure loans abroad, which wd. require funds commensurate to their duration.[6]

Mr. Higginson described all attempts of Congs. to provide for the public debts out of the mode prescribed by the Confederation, as nugatory:[7] sd that the States wd. disregard them[,] that the impost of 5 peCt. had passed in Massts. by 2 voices only in the lower, & one in the upper house; & that the Govr. had never formally assented to the law; that it was probable this law wd. be repealed; & almost certain that the extensive plans of Congress would be reprobated.[8]

¹ *Papers of Madison*, V, 409–10; 410, nn.; Harrison to Delegates, 4 Jan. 1783, and n. 5.

² *JCC*, XXIV, 204, n. 1; Delegates to Harrison, 12 Mar., and n. 12; JM to Randolph, 12 Mar. 1783, and n. 5.

³ This committee, which reported on 1 April, was supplanted on 20 May by a new committee comprising Mercer, FitzSimons, and Bland. Mercer, as chairman, replaced Osgood, who had left Congress about 30 April. The new committee's report of 29 May was recommitted on that day (NA: PCC, No. 186, fols. 89, 103; JM Notes, 20 and 29 May 1783 [LC: Madison Papers]; *JCC*, XXIV, 348; Burnett, *Letters*, VII, lxviii).

⁴ JM refers to 10 March 1783, when Congress failed to adopt by a margin of one vote a committee's report, drafted by Daniel Carroll, on the commutation of half pay for retired officers of the continental line. If in that tally Eliphalet Dyer had voted "ay" rather than "no," Connecticut would have been in the affirmative column—thus enabling the committee's recommendation to carry (*JCC*, XXIV, 178–79; JM Notes, 10 Mar. 1783, and nn. 1, 2). Following that vote, the report was returned to the committee, including Dyer, which had submitted it. Ten days later the committee reintroduced almost the same proposal, but Dyer was the author of the long justificatory statement prefacing the recommendations. After Bland had seconded the committee's motion to adopt, the report and the army memorial, which had occasioned the long deliberations on the half-pay issue, were referred to a new committee comprising Alexander Hamilton, chairman, Dyer, and Gunning Bedford, Jr., of Delaware (*JCC*, XXIV, 202–3, 203, n. 1).

Recalling this episode, JM told Nicholas P. Trist on 15 July 1827: "On the question for paying the army, we had eight States; it required nine. It turned on the vote of Connecticut. These representatives were Dyer, a man of gentlemanly manners, who had seen the world (he had been to England) but not of very sound principle. Wolcott, an honest man. Wolcott determined he would brave the storm that awaited him at home. Dyer hung back. He was of course very much pressed. At length, he consented, on condition that it should be referred to a committee, and that he should be allowed to write a preamble. In this he was indulged" (Henry S. Randall, *The Life of Thomas Jefferson* [3 vols.; New York, 1858], II, 325–26 n.). See also JM Notes, 4 Feb. 1783, n. 10. The rest of Madison's reminiscence about Dyer and his preamble relates to the session of Congress on 22 March. See JM Notes, 22 Mar. 1783, and n. 3.

⁵ For the original and amended "report of the Come.," see Report on Restoring Public Credit, 6 Mar., and nn. 1–3, 6–10; JM Notes, 7 Mar., and nn. 2, 3; 11 Mar., and nn. 3–6, 9–12; 18 Mar. 1783, and nn. 1, 3, 4, 8, 9, 11. This report "being under debate," Hamilton introduced a motion, seconded by James Wilson, to postpone its further consideration "in order to take up" a plan designed to provide an amount of "revenue equal to the public wants." The Hamilton-Wilson proposal, unlike the amended report, would have (1) the customs collectors nominated by Congress; (2) a land tax and a house tax "to be credited to each State in which they shall arise"; (3) the impost revenues "to pass to the general benefit of the United States, without credit for the proceeds to any particular states"; (4) these sources of public funds to continue, not for twenty-five years only, but until the "principal of the debt due by the United States at the termination of the present war shall be finally discharged"; and (5) Congress inform each state annually of the amount of the public debt and of the proceeds and disposition of income, so that "all doubts and apprehensions, respecting the perpetuity of the public debt, may be effectually removed" (*JCC*, XXIV, 195–200).

⁶ That is, if the sources of public funds were limited in duration to twenty-five years.

[7] The "mode" was requisitions upon the states by quotas, as stipulated by Article VIII of the Articles of Confederation (*JCC*, XIX, 217).

[8] JM Notes, 28 Jan. 1783, n. 29. The journal of the House of Representatives of the General Court of Massachusetts for the January session of 1782 notes the passage by that house and the Senate of the bill ratifying the impost amendment to the Articles of Confederation, and also the long delay before Governor John Hancock signed the bill, but does not record the vote (*Journal of the House of Representatives of the General Court of Massachusetts, March 1780–January 1800*, fols. 644, 657, 756–57).

The Hamilton-Wilson motion was defeated by a vote of 7 states to 4. Bland was the only Virginia delegate who voted for "postponing" a further consideration of the amended report (*JCC*, XXIV, 201–2).

Benjamin Harrison to Virginia Delegates

FC (Virginia State Library). In the hand of Thomas Meriwether. Addressed to "The Virginia Delegates in Congress."

In Council March 20th. 1783

Gentlemen

Your acceptable favor of the 12th. Instant[1] reached me last Evening, the acknowledgement of our Independence gives me great Pleasure, for tho' the Peace is not finally concluded, yet we may safely look on that Part of it, as certain and not to be retracted. I shall make such Parts of your Letter public as may be necessary for the Information of the Public who the Speculators of your Town intended to have imposed on, by dispatching an Express to Nelson of this Place informing him that Doctor Franklin had declared to Congress that all Negotiations were at an End and that there would be another Campaign at least.[2]

I understand the Treasurer made you a remittance last Week. I shall nevertheless send him your Letter and call on him to make it more ample.[3]

Will you be so obliging as to send us Hutchings's new Map of America which we want exceedingly.[4] I am with great respect

Yrs: &c.

B. H.

[1] *Q.v.*, and n. 24.

[2] Harrison to Delegates, 31 Jan.; JM to Randolph, 13 Feb., and n. 3; Delegates to Harrison, 12 Mar. 1783. The *Virginia Gazette* of 22 March 1783 printed a summary of the terms of the provisional peace treaty between Great Britain and the United States. The issue of 29 March carried the entire text, except the secret article. The

same paper on 15 March had mentioned the alleged letter of Franklin, said to have been received on 26 December 1782 by "an American gentleman in public character at l'Orient," stating "that all hopes of peace were at an end."

Nelson was probably Alexander Nelson (1749–1834), a native of Ireland who came as a boy to Philadelphia, where he was patronized by Robert Morris. Moving to Virginia during the Revolution, Nelson became a partner in the Richmond merchant-shipping firm of Nelson, Heron, and Company (*Va. Gazette*, 12 Apr., 19 Apr., 28 June 1783). Jefferson was told in 1785 that Nelson was an unusually able businessman of "unsullied Reputation" (Boyd, *Papers of Jefferson*, VIII, 646). Nelson later resided about six miles from Staunton in Augusta County (Jos. A. Waddell, *Annals of Augusta County, Virginia* . . . [Richmond, 1886], p. 225; Olive Nelson Gibson, *Descendants of John Nelson, Sr.—Mary Toby, Stafford County, Virginia, 1740–1959* . . . [Redlands, Calif., 1961], p. 14).

[3] Delegates to Harrison, 12 Mar. 1783, and n. 3. Jacquelin Ambler's letter of "last Week" has not been found, but it was addressed to JM and enclosed bills on Philadelphia for £500 Virginia currency for apportionment among the Virginia delegates as they should see fit. See Ambler to JM, 22 Mar.; also George Webb to Theodorick Bland, 14 Mar. (MS in Charles Campbell Collection of Bland Papers in Va. Historical Society) and James Mercer to John Francis Mercer, Apr. 1783, in *Va. Mag. Hist. and Biog.*, LIX (1951), 94.

[4] This request seems neither to have been fulfilled by the delegates nor mentioned again by Governor Harrison. For the possibility that his letter was lost in transmission, see their letter of 1 April 1783 to Harrison. In 1780 Thomas Hutchins (1730–1789), a native of New Jersey, had resigned his commission as a captain in the British army because "he would not bear arms against his countrymen." On 11 July 1781, about two months after Congress appointed him "geographer to the southern army," his title and that of "the geographer to the main army" were altered by Congress to "Geographer to the United States of America" (*JCC*, XX, 436, 738).

Governor Harrison was referring to "A New Map of the Western Parts of Virginia, Pennsylvania, Maryland and North Carolina; Comprehending the Rivers Ohio, and all Rivers, which Fall into It; Part of the River Missis[s]ippi, the Whole of the Illinois River, Lake Erie; Part of the Lakes Huron, Michigan &c. And All the Country Bordering on These Lakes and Rivers." Hutchins had folded this map in his *A Topographical Description of Virginia, Pennsylvania, Maryland, and North Carolina, Comprehending the Rivers Ohio, Kenhawa, S[c]ioto, Cherokee, Wabash, Illinois, Missis[s]ippi, &c.* (London, 1778), based on his surveys made during and just after the French and Indian War. In 1781 JM had procured a copy of this work for Jefferson (*Papers of Madison*, III, 98, n. 1). In the French edition of Hutchins' little volume, published in Paris in 1781, his maps were much reduced in size.

In 1783 and 1784 Hutchins was a member of the commission appointed by Pennsylvania to determine the western portion of the boundary between that state and Virginia (Anna M. Quattrocchi, "Thomas Hutchins in Western Pennsylvania," *Pa. History*, XVI [1949], 37–38).

Notes on Debates

MS (LC: Madison Papers). For a description of the manuscript of Notes on Debates, see *Papers of Madison*, V, 231–34.

Friday March 21.

The Report of Revenue was taken into consideration; and the 5 & 6 paragraphs after discussion being judged not sufficiently explicit were recommitted to be made more so.[1]

A motion was made by Mr. Clarke 2ded. by Mr. Bland to complete so much of the report as related to an impost on Trade & send it to the States immediately apart from the residue.[2]

In support of this motion, it was urged that the Impost was distinct in its nature was more likely to be adopted, & ought not therefore to be delayed or hazarded by a connection with the other parts of the Report. On the other side it was contended that it was the duty of Congs. to provide a system adequate to the public exigences; & that such a system wd. be more likely to be adopted by the States than any partial or detached provision, as it would comprize objects agreeable as well as disagreeable to each of the States, and as all of them wd feel a greater readiness to make mutual concessions & to disregard local considerations in proportion to the magnitude of the object held out to them.[3]

The motion was disagreed to: N. J. being in favor of it & several other States divided.[4]

[1] JM Notes, 20 Mar. 1783, and citations in n. 5. The fifth paragraph of the report recommended that for twenty-five years each state should establish "substantial & effectual revenues," sufficient to provide its equitable share of an annual unspecified total, which would be applied to the interest and principal of the public debt. These revenues, according to the sixth paragraph, were to be credited to each state "within wch. they shall be collected, and be liquidated & adjusted among the States" proportionately "to the quotas which may from time to time be allotted to them" (Report on Restoring Public Credit, 6 Mar. 1783, and nn. 7–10; *JCC*, XXIV, 171–72). See also Amendment to Report on Public Credit, 27 Mar. 1783.

[2] This motion referred to the fourth paragraph of the report, as submitted on 6 March, and to the first three paragraphs, as amended and passed "without opposition" on 18 March 1783 (Report on Restoring Public Credit, 6 Mar. and nn. 1–6; 18 Mar. 1783, and n. 1; *JCC*, XXIV, 170–71).

[3] JM Notes, 28 Jan., and nn. 19, 35; 29 Jan.; 20 Feb., n. 14; 21 Feb.; 26 Feb.; Report on Restoring Credit, 6 Mar. 1783, n. 10.

[4] New Jersey and Delaware supported the motion; Massachusetts, Connecticut, New York, Pennsylvania, Maryland, and South Carolina opposed the motion; the ballots of New Hampshire, Virginia, and North Carolina were ineffective because their delegates divided equally in voting; Rhode Island was represented by only one delegate; and Georgia was still unrepresented. Among the Virginia delegates Madison and Mercer voted "no"; Bland and Lee, "ay"; Jones was absent (*JCC*, XXIV, 205–6).

Notes on Debates

MS (LC: Madison Papers). For a description of the manuscript of Notes on Debates, see *Papers of Madison*, V, 231–34.

Saturday 22. March.

A letter was recd. from Genl Washington inclosing his address to the convention of Officers with the result of their consultations.[1] This dissipation of the cloud which seemed to have been gathering afforded great pleasure on the whole to Congress; but it was observable that the part which the Genl. had found it necessary & thought it his duty to take, would give birth to events much more serious if they sd. not be obviated by the establishment of such funds as the Genl. as well as the army had declared to be necessary.[2]

The report of the come. on Mr. Dyer's motion in favor of a commutation for the half pay was agreed to. The preamble was objected to, but admitted at the entreaty of Mr. Dyer who supposed the considerations recited in it wd. tend to reconcile the State of Cont. to the measure.[3]

An order passed for granting 35 licences for vessels belonging to Nantucket to secure the whaling vessels agst. the penalty for double papers. This order was in consequence of a deputation to Congs. representing the exposed situation of that island, the importance of the Whale fishery to the U. S. the danger of its being usurped by other nations & the concurrenc of the Enemy in neutralizing such a number of Vessels as wd. carry on the fisheries in an extent necessary for the support of the inhabitants.[4]

The Come. to whom was referred the letter from the Secy. of F. A. with the foreign despatches &c reported[5]

1. That our Ministers be thanked for their zeal & services in negociating the preliminary articles:

2. that they be instructed to make a communication of the separate article[6] to the Court of France in such way as would best get over the concealment.

3. that the Secy. of F. A. inform them that it is the wish of Congress that the preliminary articles had been communicated to the Court of France before they had been executed.

Mr. Dyer said he was opposed to the whole report; that he fully approved of every step taken by our Ministers as well towards G. B. as towards France, that the separate article did not concern the interests of France[7] & therefore could not involve the good faith of the U. S

Mr. Lee agreed fully with Mr. Dyer, said that a special report of facts ought to have been made as necessary for enabling Congs. to form a just opinion of the Conduct of the Ministers, and moved that the report might be recommitted. Mr. Wolcot 2ded. the motion which was evidently made for the sole purpose of delay. It was opposed by Mr. Clarke, Mr. Wilson & Mr. Ghorum the 1[s]t & last of whom had however no objection to postponing; by Mr. Mercer who repeated his abhorrence of the confidence shewn by our Ministers to those of G. B.[8] said that ct.[9] was about to realize the case of those kicked down the ladder by wch. they had been elevated, & of the viper which was ready to destroy the family of the man in whose bosom it had been restored to life,[10] observed that it was unwise to prefer G. B. to Spain as our Neighbours in W. Florida.

Mr. Higgenson supported the sentiments of Mr. Lee. sd. that the Ct. de V. had released our Ministers & that he agreed with those who thought the instruction of June 15. cd. relate only to questions directly between G. B. & U. S.[11]

Mr. Holten thought there was no sufficient evidence for praise or blame; and that both ought to be suspended untill the true reasons sd. be stated by the Ministers. He supposed that the separate article had been made an ultimatum of the preliminaries by G. B. & that there might also be secret arts: between G. B. & F.[12] If the latter were displeased he conceived that she wd. officially notify it.[13] Mr. Rutlidge was agst. recommitting but for postponing. The motion for recomg. was disagreed to, but several states being for postponing, the vote was no index as to the main question.[14] (continued see No. XII)[15]

No. XII

Saturday March 22. 1783. continued

It had been talked of among sundry members as very singular that the British Minister should have confided to Mr. Adams an intended expedition from N. Y. agst. W. Florida; as very reprehensible in the latter to become the depository of secrets hostile to the Friends of his Country, and that every motive of honor & prudence made it the duty of Congs. to impart the matter to the Spaniards.[16] To this effect a motion was made by Mr. Mercer 2ded. by Mr. Madison. But it being near the usual hour of adjournment, the house being agitated by the debates on the separate article: and a large proportion of members predetermined agst. every measure wch. seemed in any manner to blame the Ministers; & the

Eastern delegates in general extremely jealous of the honor of Mr. Adams, an adjournment was pressed & carried without any vote on the motion.

[1] For Washington's letter of 18 March, enclosing his address "To the Officers of the Army" and their resolutions, both dated 15 March, see Fitzpatrick, *Writings of Washington*, XXVI, 222–27, 228, 229–32; *JCC*, XXIV, 306–11. See also JM Notes, 17 Mar., and nn. 1, 2; JM to Randolph, 18 Mar. 1783.

[2] In his address to the officers, Washington pledged his "Services to the utmost of" his "abilities" to secure "compleat justice" for them from Congress. He appealed to them to share his "full confidence in the purity of the intentions of Congress" and in its determination to have their accounts "fairly liquidated" before their "dissolution as an Army." In his letter, after "earnestly entreating" Congress to reach a "most speedy decision" about "the subjects of the late address from the Army," Washington expressed his "decided opinion" that "the establishment of funds, and security of the payment of all the just demands of the Army will be the most certain means of preserving the National faith and future tranquillity of this extensive continent." For the memorial from the army and the debates in Congress resulting therefrom, see JM Notes, 10 Mar., and citations in nn. 1 and 2; 17 Mar., and n. 1; 20 Mar., and n. 4; JM to Randolph, 4 Mar. 1783, and n. 5.

On 22 March Washington's "address" of 15 March, and his letter of 18 March were referred by Congress to a committee, with Samuel Osgood as chairman (*JCC*, XXIV, 210, n. 1). The report of this committee on 1 April 1783 is unnoted both in the official journal and in JM's notes for that day. See NA: PCC, No. 186, fol. 90.

[3] JM Notes, 20 Mar. 1783, and n. 4. JM's reminiscence, partly quoted in that footnote, closed with these words: "The resolution being adopted—the preamble came under consideration. Whereupon a good many criticisms were made upon the preamble (not in earnest; but some of the members felt provoked at the uneasiness which D. had caused them to experience), and he was kept for an hour as pale as a sheet under the apprehension that his preamble would be rejected." Evidently Eliphalet Dyer wrote the preamble, even though it and the resolutions introduced by it are in the hand of Alexander Hamilton, chairman of the committee to which an earlier report on the army memorial had been referred on 20 March. During the debate on 22 March, Congress slightly amended the committee's report and rejected substitute resolutions offered by Oliver Wolcott and seconded by Jonathan Arnold. Congress adopted the report by a vote of 9 to 2 (New Hampshire and New Jersey) (*JCC*, XXIV, 207–10).

[4] On 11 March Congress referred to a committee, with Nathaniel Gorham as chairman, a memorial signed by Samuel Starbuck and William Rotch on behalf of the inhabitants of the island of Nantucket (*JCC*, XXIV, 182, n. 1). After portraying their "poverty and distress" during the Revolution because of lack of military aid from Congress or Massachusetts, frequent invasion by the British, and the capture of many whaling ships by the enemy—thus ruining almost the sole industry of Nantucket—the memorial admitted that the islanders' desperate plight late in the war led them to accept British passports for a few of their vessels. Thereupon several of them had been captured by American privateers and condemned by American admiralty courts. "The coersive law of necessity," the memorial continued, "may compel" Nantucket families "to relinquish the tender ties of natural affection" for their native land and to succumb to British enticements in the form of protection by a strong navy and a bounty on whale products. After emphasizing the value of these to the United States, the memorial closed by praying Congress

speedily, through the issuance of passports, to enable the islanders to "Employ a few Vessels in Whale Fishery, unmolested from American Cruisers" (NA: PCC, No. 41, VII, 91–94).

On 18 March the committee recommended that any Nantucket whaler, provided the boat have aboard only "whaling utensils," "the produce of fish taken," and the necessary supplies for the captain and crew, be permitted to operate under one passport issued by the British and a certificate issued by the selectmen of the town of Nantucket. This report thus recommended that Congress exempt Nantucket whalers from the penalty stipulated by the ordinance of 4 December 1781, making any ship with "double papers" subject to "condemnation, unless good cause be shown to the contrary" (JCC, XXI, 1156; Papers of Madison, III, 240; 339, n. 2).

After the report was read for a second and third time on 19 and 20 March, respectively, it was returned to the committee with the instruction to suggest the form of a passport. This document, approved by Congress on 22 March, embodied the provisos mentioned above, had to be renewed every year, and would be issued only to a whaling captain who had a paper from the selectmen attesting to his name and the names of his crew and that his vessel was "bona fide, the property of the inhabitants" of Nantucket (NA: PCC, No. 49, 261–64; JCC, XXIV, 187, 195, 206–7).

In his autobiography, Rotch mentioned the "great civility" shown to him by JM and other members of Congress, with the exception of "the Massachusetts members." Congress, Rotch continued, "actually granted to us thirty-five permits for the whale fishery" ("An Autobiographical Memoir of William Rotch Written in the Eightieth Year of His Age," New England Historical and Genealogical Register, XXXII [1878], 153).

⁵ For the letter of Robert R. Livingston and its referral to a committee, see JM Notes, 18 Mar. and nn. 12, 14; 19 Mar., and n. 44. The committee's report, which was submitted to Congress on 21 March 1783, is not mentioned in the official journal of that day or the next, and the manuscript of the report has not been found (NA: PCC, No. 186, fol. 89).

⁶ JM Notes, 12–15 Mar. 1783, n. 6.

⁷ JM to Randolph, 18 Mar., and n. 7; JM Notes, 19 Mar. 1783, and n. 16.

⁸ JM Notes, 19 Mar. 1783, nn. 9–12.

⁹ The court of St. James.

¹⁰ By his remarks Mercer indicated his distaste for placing confidence in the British court, which was about to attain its objective of causing the United States to turn on the ally that had made possible its independence. He may have derived the "kicked-down-the-ladder" metaphor from Shakespeare, Richard II, Act 5, scene 1, line 55. The viper-in-the-bosom metaphor dates at least as early as Aesop (ca. 620–560 B.C.), whose fables in Greek were versified in Latin by Phaedrus (early 1st century A.D.) in his Fabulae Aesopiae. The viper story is No. XIX of Book IV. See G[eorge] H[erbert] Nall, ed., The Fables of Phaedrus (London, 1946), p. 45.

¹¹ JM Notes, 12–15 Mar., n. 6; 19 Mar. 1783, n. 9; Burnett, Letters, VII, 122.

¹² JM Notes, 12–15 Mar. 1783, n. 6.

¹³ Ibid., n. 7; JM Notes, 19 Mar. 1783, and n. 12.

¹⁴ See n. 5. The defeat of the Lee-Wolcott motion left unanswered, of course, the main question of whether and by whom the separate article should be revealed to Vergennes and the extent to which, if at all, the American peace commissioners should be censured for their conduct during the negotiations.

¹⁵ JM's parenthetical expression is at the close of the final page of segment No. XI of his notes. For a probable explanation of the Roman numeral, see Papers of Madison, V, 231.

¹⁶ JM Notes, 19 Mar., and n. 43; Delegates to Harrison, 24 Mar. 1783, and n. 4.

From Jacquelin Ambler

RC (LC: Madison Papers). Addressed to "The Honobl. James Madison of Congress Philadelphia." Docketed by JM, "Mar: 22 1783. J. A. bala. due at end of 1782 £865-8-3 Virga. currency."

RICHMOND VIRGA. 22. Mar 83

DEAR SIR

The Auditors have at length adjusted your Accot. on their Books to the 31st December last; the Bal[ance] then due you from the Commonwealth appears to be £865.. 8.. 3.[1] By last Mail I transmitted you Bills on Phila. to the amount of £500. Virga. Curry. with a request that you would inform me by the succeeding Post how it might be divided among the Gentlemen Delegates, that such might be duly charged in the Auditor's Books.[2] Mr. Ross was so obliging as to assist me in this remittance otherwise it would have been out of my power to have made one for that Sum.[3] Some difficulties have arisen with respect to the settlement of the Sherifs Accounts with the Auditors which will probably keep the Treasury low until the Meeting of the Assembly.[4]

I congratulate you on the agreeable prospect which the late Accounts from Europe give us of a general Peace.[5] God grant it may be long & happy.

Yr. affect Servt

J. AMBLER

[1] Delegates to Harrison, 21 Jan., and n. 3; Ambler to JM, 8 Feb. 1783, and nn. 2, 3. This balance, also shown at the close of the credit column of the treasurer's record of JM's account, was the amount which Virginia still owed JM at the close of 1782 for his services as a delegate in Congress during the preceding three years and as reimbursement for a few miscellaneous expenses incurred by him in Philadelphia on the state's behalf. From time to time during those years the treasurer of Virginia had forwarded to him a total of £1613 5s. 9d. (Commonwealth of Virginia in Accompt with James Madison, junr., MS in Va. State Library).

[2] Harrison to Delegates, 20 Mar. 1783, and n. 3. One of the two "Bills" was drawn on Samuel Inglis and Company and the other on William Turnbull and Company, both of Philadelphia (Commonwealth of Virginia in Accompt with James Madison, junr., MS in Va. State Library). See also *Papers of Madison*, II, 172, n. 2; V, 148; 150, n. 16; Receipt of Delegates, 27 Mar. 1783; *Pa. Archives*, 3d ser., XVI, 321–22.

[3] David Ross (*Papers of Madison*, III, 60, n. 8).

[4] *Ibid.*, V, 182, n. 1; *Cal. of Va. State Papers*, III, 459; Ambler to JM, 1 Feb., and nn. 6, 7; 8 Feb. 1783.

[5] Delegates to Harrison, 12 Mar. 1783, n. 3.

From Edmund Randolph

RC (LC: Madison Papers). Unsigned but in Randolph's hand. Cover addressed by Randolph to "The honble James Madison jr. esq of congress Philadelphia." Docketed by JM, "March 22. 1783."

RICHMOND March 22. 1783

MY DEAR SIR

Your favors by the post and the express[1] reached me at the same time with a letter from Dr Lee, dated on the 11th. of decr. (I presume it should have been march). 1783.[2] Having read his first, I was astonished at this passage. "We are still as we were, and always shall be, while Dr. Franklin presides in Europe, utterly in the dark as to the progress of the negotiations at Paris. I am too well acquainted with the European cabinets, not to fear that a continuation of the war, so grievous to us, will be the consequence of these protracted negotiations. I wish I may be deceived." The contrast, which your eulogium on Franklin presented, was truly grateful to my mind, being a complete antidote to the insinuation of Mr. Lee.[3]

The humiliation of G. B. seems now proportionate to her former arrogance. So lukewarm in the patronage of the Tories, as to desert them rather than risque a new campaign,[4] so profuse in her surrender of territory, so satisfactory in her recognition of independence,[5] she must begin to doubt her own identity. But may not the treaty be so worded, as to give congress a substitution in the place of the King of G. B. with respect to ungranted soil? If so, will not the argument against particular states be stronger, than it ever could have been under the confederation only? For [I] imagine, that the power of congress to accept territory by treaty will not be denied. This will throw a plausibility against us, which never before existed in the contest with congress.[6]

I cannot procure a regular accession of my father's creditors to my proposals: and without that it is not possible for me to go into the legislature. I am now on my way to Wmsburg., to endeavour at the proper accommodation.[7] But having omitted to declare myself hitherto from an uncertainty of my being able to accept a seat in the house, and the election being at hand, no farther remote than the first monday in next month, and the candidates having been active, and indefatigable, I might possibly expose myself to a mortification, were I to step forward at this late hour.[8] But be the final issue what it will, I shall promote the impost.[9]

Lucius has expressed the destructiveness of Mr. Morris's resignation in colours not very tender, nor yet very extravagant on the score of cruelty. At such a season to quit his office, even if it were steeped to the lips in poverty and difficulty! Personal embarrassments from personal engagements he might have avoided. He ought to have avoided an obedience to that impulse of petulance, which caused him to proclaim the bankruptcy of America.[10]

We have no internal news.

Betsy and myself are very solicitous to hear of Mrs. House's and Mrs. Triste's welfare. She will not inquire into this, by her own pen altho' she has set one hundred days for writing to the latter. I can urge nothing in her behalf: but to assure Mrs. T. that her shameful neglect does not proceed from a want of a sincere regard for her.[11]

[1] JM to Randolph, 11 Mar.; 12 Mar. 1783.

[2] Although Arthur Lee's letter to Randolph has not been found, its contents probably resembled those of Lee's letter written on 12 March to James Warren (Burnett, *Letters*, VII, 77–78). See also JM to Randolph, 1 Apr. 1783, and n. 5.

[3] *Papers of Madison*, II, 108, n. 10; 147, n. 1; 167, n. 4; 218, n. 2; 258; IV, 250, nn. 13, 17; V, 33, hdn.; 187; 427, n. 7; Jefferson to JM, 31 Jan., n. 9; JM Notes, 12–15 Mar., n. 7; 19 Mar., and nn. 20, 21; Delegates to Harrison, 12 Mar., and nn. 16–18; 18 Mar., and n. 2; JM to Randolph, 12 Mar., and n. 10; 1 Apr. 1783.

[4] JM Notes, 12–15 Mar., and n. 2; Delegates to Harrison, 12 Mar., and n. 12; JM to Randolph, 12 Mar. 1783, and nn. 4, 11. See also *Papers of Madison*, V, 233, and citations in 224, n. 5.

[5] Delegates to Harrison, 12 Mar. 1783, and nn. 7–10.

[6] *Papers of Madison*, V, 56–57; 69; 83; 84, n. 6; 115–16; 119, n. 20; 292, n. 19; JM Notes, 19 Mar., and n. 24; JM to Randolph, 1 Apr. 1783.

[7] Randolph to JM, 1 Feb., and n. 5; 7 Mar., and n. 4; 29 Mar. 1783.

[8] Randolph to JM, 15 Jan., and n. 7; 7 Feb.; 1 Mar.; JM to Jefferson, 11 Feb., and n. 14; JM to Randolph, 11 Feb., and n. 3; 25 Feb.; 11 Mar.; 18 Mar. 1783.

[9] Randolph to JM, 3 Jan., and nn. 2, 10; 1 Feb.; 7 Mar.; Harrison to JM, 1 Jan., and nn. 1, 4; JM to Randolph, 22 Jan., and n. 7; 18 Feb. 1783, and n. 1.

[10] Randolph's comments upon Robert Morris' letter of resignation as superintendent of finance suggest those made in Congress by Arthur Lee (JM Notes, 4–5 Mar., and nn. 6, 7). See also JM to Randolph, 4 Mar.; 11 Mar.; Randolph to JM, 15 Mar. 1783, and n. 4. For attacks on Morris in two essays signed by "Lucius," see the issues of the *Freeman's Journal: or, the North-American Intelligencer*, published in Philadelphia by Francis Bailey, for 5 and 12 March 1783.

[11] *Papers of Madison*, V, 205–6; 226; Jefferson to JM, 31 Jan. 1783, n. 29.

Notes on Debates

MS (LC: Madison Papers). For a description of the manuscript of Notes on Debates, see *Papers of Madison*, V, 231–34.

Monday March 24th.

On the day preceding this, intelligence arrived which was this day laid before Congs. that the preliminaries for a general peace had been signed on the 20th. of Jany. This intelligence was brought by a French cutter from Cadiz despatched by Ct. d'Estaing to notify the event to all vessels at sea, and engaged by the zeal of the Marquis de la Fayette to convey it to Congress.[1] This confirmation of peace produced the greater joy, as the preceding delay, the cautions of Mr. Lauren's Letter of the 24 of Decr. and the general suspicions of Ld. Shelburne's sincerity had rendered an immediate & general peace extremely problematical in the minds of many.[2]

A letter was recd. from Genl. Carlton thro' Genl. Washington inclosing a copy of the preliminary articles between G. B. & the U. S. with the separate article annexed.[3]

Mr. Carroll after taking notice of the embarrassment under which Congs. were placed by the injunction of secrecy as to the separate article after it had probably been disclosed in Europe & it now appeared was known at N. York,[4] called the attention of Congs. again to that subject.

Mr. Wolcot still contended that it would be premature to take any step relative to it, untill further communications should be recd. from our Ministers.[5]

Mr. Gilman being of the same opinion, moved that the business be postponed. Mr. Lee 2ded it.[6]

Mr. Wilson conceived it indispensably necessary that something should be done;[7] that Congs. deceived themselves if they supposed that the separate art: was any secret at N. York after it had been announced to them from Sr. Guy Carlton. He professed a high respect for the character of the Ministers which had received fresh honor from the remarkable steadiness and great abilities displayed in the negociations, but that their conduct with respect to the separate article could not be justified. He did not consider it as any violation of the instruction of June 15th. 1781.[8] The Ct. de Vergennes having happily released them from the obligation of it;[9] But he considered it with the signing of the preliminaries secretly as a violation of the spirit of the Treaty of Alliance as well as of the unanimous professions to the Court of France, unanimous instructions to our Ministers, & unanimous declarations to the world, that nothing should be discussed towards peace but in confidence and in concert with our ally.[10] He made great allowance for the ministers, saw how they were affected, and the reasons of it, but could not subscribe to the opinion that Congs. ought to pass over the separate article in the manner that had been urged: Congs. ought he said to disapprove of it in the softest terms that could be devised & at all events not to take part in its concealment.

Mr. Bland treated the separate article with levity and ridicule; as in no respect concerning France, but Spain with whom we had nothing to do.[11]

Mr. Carroll thought that unless some thing expressive of our disapprobation of the article & of its concealment was done, that it would be an indelible stain on our character.

Mr. Clarke contended that it was still improper to take any step, either for communicating officially, or for taking off the injunction of secresy. that the article concerned Spain, and not France, but that if it sd. be communicated to the latter she would hold herself bound to communicate it to the former that hence an embarrassment might ensue; that it was probably this consideration which led the Ministers to the concealment, and he thought they had acted right. He described the awkwardness attending a communication of it under present circumstances; remarking finally that nothing had been done contrary to the Treaty, and that we were in possession of sufficient[x] materials to justify the suspicions wch. had been manifested.[12]

Mr. Rutlidge was strenuous for postponing the subject, said that Congs. had no occasion to meddle with it, that the Ministers had done right, that they had maintained the honor of the U. S. after Congress had given it up; that the manoeuvre practiced by them was common in all courts & was justifiable agst. Spain who alone was affected by it; that instructions ought to be disregarded whenever the public good required it; and that he himself would never be bound by them when he thought them improper.[13]

Mr. Mercer combated the dangerous tendency of the Doctrine maintained by Mr. Rutlidge with regard to instructions; and observed that the Delegates of Virga. havg been unanimously instructed not to conclude or discuss any Treaty of peace but in confidence & in concert with

[x] alluding probably to the intercepted letter from Mr. de Marbois.

his M. C. M. he conceived himself as much bound as he was of himself inclined to disapprove every other mode of proceeding, and that he should call for the yeas & nays on the question for his justification to his constituents.[14]

Mr. Bland tartly said that he of course, was instructed as well as his colleague & sd. himself require the yeas & nays to justify an opposite conduct; that the instructions from his constituents went no farther than to prohibit any *Treaty* without the concurrence of our ally*; which prohibition had not been violated in the case before Congress.[15]

Mr. Lee was for postponing & burying in oblivion the whole transaction; he sd that delicacy to France required this: since if any thing should be done implying censure on our Ministers, it must & ought to be done in such a way, as to fall ultimately on France whose unfaithful conduct had produced & justified that of our Ministers. In all national intercourse he said a reciprocity was to be understood; and as France had not communicated her views & proceedings to the American Plenipotentiaries, the latter were not bound to communicate theirs. All instructions he conceived to be conditional in favor of the public good;[16] and he cited the case mentioned by Sr. Wm. Temple in which the Dutch ministers concluded of themselves an act wch. required the previous sanction of all the members of the Republic[17]

Mr. Hamilton said that whilst he despised the man who wd. enslave himself to the policy even of our Friends, he could not but lament the overweening readiness which appeared in many, to suspect every thing on that side & to throw themselves into the bosom of our enemies. He urged the necessity of vindicating our public honor by renouncing that concealment to which it was the wish of so many to make us parties.[18]

Mr. Wilson in answer to Mr. Lee observed that the case mentioned by Sr. Wm. T. was utterly inapplicable to the case in question;[19] adding that the conduct of France had not on the principle of reciprocity justified our Ministers in signing the provisional preliminaries without her knowledge, no such step having been taken on her part. But whilst he found it to be his duty thus to note the faults of these gentlemen, he with much greater pleasure gave them praise for their firmness in refusing to treat with the British Negociator until he had produced a proper commission, in contending for the fisheries, and in adhering to our Western claims.[20]

Congress adjourned without any question[21]

* this construction of the instructions was palpably wrong

AMERICA

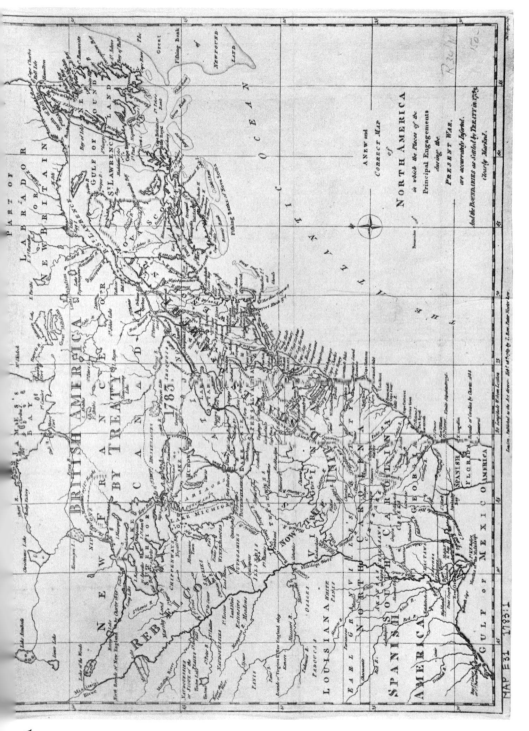

The remaining clafs of creditors is compofed partly of fuch of our fellow citizens as originally lent to the public the ufe of their funds, or have fince manifefted moft confidence in their country, by receiving transfers from the lenders; and partly of thofe whofe property has been either advanced or affumed for the public fervice. To difcriminate the merits of thefe feveral defcriptions of creditors would be a tafk equally unneceffary and invidious. If the voice of humanity plead more loudly in favor of fome than of others, the voice of policy, no lefs than of juftice, pleads in favor of all. A wife nation will never permit thofe who relieve the wants of their country, or who rely moft on its faith, its firmnefs, and its refources, when either of them is diftrufted, to fuffer by the event.

Let it be remembered finally, that it has ever been the pride and boaft of America, that the rights for which fhe contended, were the rights of human nature. By the bleffing of the author of thefe rights, on the means exerted for their defence, they have prevailed againft all oppofition, and form the bafis of thirteen independent ftates. No inftance has heretofore occurred nor can any inftance be expected hereafter to occur, in which the unadulterated forms of republican government can pretend to fo fair an opportunity of juftifying themfelves by their fruits. In this view the citizens of the United States are refponfible for the greateft truft ever confided to a political fociety. If juftice, good faith, honor, gratitude, and all the other qualities which enoble the character of a nation, and fulfil the ends of government, be the fruits of our eftablifhments, the caufe of liberty will acquire a dignity and luftre which it has never yet enjoyed: and an example will be fet which cannot but have the moft favorable influence on the rights of mankind. If on the other fide, our governments fhould be unfortunately blotted with the reverfe of thefe cardinal and effential virtues, the great caufe which we have engaged to vindicate, will be difhonored and betrayed; the laft and faireft experiment in favor of the rights of human nature will be turned againft them, and their patrons and friends expofed to be infulted and filenced by the votaries of tyranny and ufurpation.

By order of the United States in Congrefs affembled:

EXCERPT FROM MADISON'S
"ADDRESS TO THE STATES"

1 Jefferson to JM, 7–8 Feb., n. 13; Delegates to Harrison, 12 Mar. 1783, n. 18. For Vice Admiral Comte d'Estaing, see *Papers of Madison*, II, 316, n. 6; III, 6, n. 2. On 1 February 1783 a courier from Paris delivered to Lafayette in Cadiz a dispatch announcing the signing of "the preliminaries for a general peace." Eager to return to Washington's headquarters, Lafayette was serving temporarily as quartermaster general of a Franco-Spanish army assembled to form part of an amphibious expedition, commanded by d'Estaing, against the British in the West Indies and New York City. The corvette "Triomphe," sent by d'Estaing on 14 February to inform French men-of-war of the end of hostilities, carried letters from Lafayette to the president of Congress, Washington, Livingston, and other prominent Americans (Louis Gottschalk, *Lafayette and the Close of the American Revolution* [Chicago, 1942], pp. 387–88, 394–95, 399–406; Wharton, *Revol. Dipl. Corr.*, VI, 237–40; *JCC*, XXIV, 211, n. 1). On 24 March 1783 Congress directed Robert Morris, as agent of marine, "immediately to recall all armed vessels cruising under commissions from the United States of America" (*JCC*, XXIV, 211). Morris' notification was issued the next day.

2 JM Notes, 12–15 Mar., and nn. 4, 7, 8; 18 Mar., and nn. 1–3; 19 Mar., and nn. 7, 10, 42; 22 Mar.; Delegates to Harrison, 12 Mar., nn. 16–18; 18 Mar., and nn. 2, 4; JM to Randolph, 18 Mar. 1783, and nn. 7, 10, 17.

3 JM Notes, 12–15 Mar., n. 12. For the "separate article," see *ibid.*, n. 6; 18 Mar., and n. 14; 19 Mar.; JM to Randolph, 18 Mar. 1783, and n. 5.

4 JM Notes, 12–15 Mar. 1783, n. 12.

5 JM Notes, 19 Mar., and n. 5; 22 Mar. 1783, and n. 14.

6 For Arthur Lee's view of the issue of the "separate article," see JM Notes, 19 Mar., and nn. 20–22, 24; 22 Mar. 1783, and n. 14.

7 For James Wilson's earlier remarks on the general subject, see JM Notes, 19 Mar., and n. 33; 20 Mar. 1783.

8 JM Notes, 12–15 Mar., and n. 6; 19 Mar., and nn. 9, 35; 20 Mar. 1783.

9 JM Notes, 12–15 Mar., and n. 7; 19 Mar. 1783, and nn. 12, 15.

10 JM Notes, 12–15 Mar. 1783, and nn. 6, 37–39.

11 For Theodorick Bland's previous comments on the issue, see JM Notes, 19 Mar. 1783. For Spain, see *ibid.*, and n. 16 and citations in n. 17. For the contrasting view of Bland's colleague, JM, see *ibid.*, and nn. 36–39.

12 The ink and handwriting of the two footnotes strongly suggest that JM wrote them and his text at about the same time. Abraham Clark may have been alluding to Jay's dispatch of 17 November 1783 rather than to Barbé-Marbois' letter (Wharton, *Revol. Dipl. Corr.*, VI, 21–32, 46–47). For Clark's earlier remarks on the subject, see JM Notes, 19 Mar., and nn. 7, 8, 33; also *ibid.*, n. 9. For Barbé-Marbois' letter, see *Papers of Madison*, V, 441; 443, n. 2; 444, n. 5; 466; 468; JM Notes, 1 Jan., and n. 2; 3 Jan. 1783, and n. 2.

13 John Rutledge was re-emphasizing the position he had taken on 19 and 22 March (JM Notes, 19 Mar., n. 16, and citations in n. 17; 22 Mar.). See also *Papers of Madison*, V, 33–35; 35, n. 4; 53–54; 172, n. 8; 418, n. 19; 438, nn. 5, 7; 469, n. 2; Rev. James Madison to JM, 16 Jan., n. 6; Comment by Jefferson, 25 Jan., and n. 1; JM to Jefferson, 11 Feb., n. 11; to Randolph, 18 Mar., and n. 7; JM Notes, 19 Mar. 1783, and n. 9.

14 For the "instructions," see *Papers of Madison*, IV, 271–72; 272, n. 3; V, 408, and n. 2; Harrison to Delegates, 4 Jan., n. 5. For John Francis Mercer's previous comments on the conduct of the American peace commissioners, see JM Notes, 19 Mar., and nn. 9–12; 22 Mar., and n. 10. For JM's view of the binding force of instructions from state legislatures to delegates in Congress, see JM Notes, 28 Jan. 1783, and n. 32.

15 JM's comment in his footnote reflects the instruction of the Virginia General

Assembly to the delegates "not to consent to open a communication with any agent or minister from his Britannic Majesty, upon the subject of a peace, separate from our great Ally the King of France" (*Papers of Madison*, V, 408). See also JM Notes, 19 Mar. 1783, and nn. 33, 38.

[16] For Arthur Lee's comments upon the matter at issue, see JM Notes, 19 Mar., and nn. 9, 20–22, 24; 22 Mar. 1783, and n. 14. See also citations in n. 13, above.

[17] In his "Observations upon the United Provinces of the Netherlands," Sir William Temple related that King Charles II of England instructed him in January 1668 to propose to the States-General a "League of Mutual Defence" for protection against the armies of Louis XIV of France, which already had overrun the Spanish provinces of Flanders. So obvious to the members of the States-General were the value of such a "League" and the need of forming it speedily that they unanimously decided to violate the terms of the Dutch articles of union by signing the agreement without first gaining the approval of the separate provinces and the cities therein. Thus they "ventured their heads," but their action was so patently to the advantage of the Netherlands that they later "were applauded by all the Members of every Province" (*The Works of Sir William Temple, Bart . . . to which is prefixed, the Life and Character of Sir William Temple, written by a Particular Friend* [2 vols.; London, 1740], p. 36). JM knew at least of the existence of this work (Report on Books, 23 Jan. 1783, item 167).

Sir William Temple (1628–1699) was the ambassador from the Court of St. James to the United Provinces of the Netherlands from 1668 to 1672 and 1674 to 1679. In 1681, following two years of service as a privy councilor and member of Parliament, he retired to his estate in Ireland. There, with the assistance of Jonathan Swift, he prepared his memoirs and other literary works.

[18] That is, the "concealment" of the secret article of the preliminary treaty. Alexander Hamilton was repeating the recommendation he had made five days earlier (JM Notes, 19 Mar. 1783, and n. 31).

[19] In contrast with the episode mentioned in n. 17, the American peace commissioners were not members of Congress and had violated its instructions rather than the Articles of Confederation.

[20] *Papers of Madison*, V, 23, n. 14; 33; 187; 189, nn. 14, 17; 418, nn. 17, 19; 437, n. 4; 438, n. 5; Delegates to Harrison, 12 Mar., and nn. 7–9, 11, 14; JM Notes, 19 Mar. 1783, and nn. 9–11, 24.

[21] That is, Congress adjourned without voting on any motion. For a further record of discussions in Congress on 24 March, see JM Notes, 31 Mar. 1783.

Virginia Delegates to Benjamin Harrison

RC (Virginia State Library). In the hand of John Francis Mercer, except for the signatures of the other delegates. Cover addressed by Mercer to "His Excellency Benjamin Harrison Esqr. Governor of Virginia." Mercer signed his name on the lower left, and wrote "(On public Service)" on the upper right portion of the cover. The letter was carried to Richmond by a special courier. The cover is docketed, "Lr. from Delegates in Congress March 24th. 83."

PHILADELPHIA March 24th. 1783.

SIR

We have the pleasure of congratulating your Excellency on the result of the Negociations in Europe, which have at length happily terminated in a general Pacification.

The Triumph a french Sloop of War, commanded by the Chevalier du Quêne, arriv'd here the last Evening, dispatchd from Cadiz the 14th. of Feby by the Marquiss of Fayette & the C[o]mte D'Estaign, on a supposition, which the event has justified, that she might reach America, before any Packett which shoud sail either from Brest or L'Orient:[1]

The orders of the C[o]mte d'Estaign to the Ch: du Quêne contain a proclamation of the cessation of Hostilities, & the communications from the Marquiss of Fayette, convey the heads of the Preliminary Articles of the General Peace, which were signed the 20th. January at Paris.[2] These leave the decisive terms respecting the United States as affixed by the partial Agreement between America & G. Britain[3] (our southern boundary being restricted to the 32 degree). The other belligerent Powers are in general reinstated in those Possessions which they held previous to the War, with Exception that G. Britain cedes to France, Tobago, St. Vincents & Senegal, who on her part recedes from her right to fish on great Part of the Coast, which she held by the treaty of 63. She cedes to Spain, The Floridas & Minorca, & retains Negapatam in the East Indies,[4] If any thing can add to this happy event, it is that the late confusion in the Army, thro' the prudence of the Commander in chief, has terminated in a manner wch reflects additional honor on that band of Patriots.[5]

With the highest Respect We have the honor to be Yr Excellencys Most Ob' & very hble Servants

> JOS: JONES
> THEOK. BLAND JR.
> J. MADISON JR.
> A. LEE
> JOHN F. MERCER

Congress have just now directed the Agent of Marine to recall all armed naval Commissions & the Minister of Foreign Affairs to make the necessary communications to Sr. Guy Carleton & Admiral Digby, which will produce an immediate cessation of hostilities[6] We shall draw on you for 24 £ the price agreed on for the Express:[7]

> JOHN F. MERCER

¹ JM Notes, 24 Mar. 1783, and n. 1. For Lieutenant (later Rear Admiral) Pierre Claude, Chevalier (later Marquis) du Quesne (1751–1834), see Baron Ludovic de Contenson, *La Société des Cincinnati de France et la Guerre d'Amérique*, p. 249.

² La Luzerne immediately released for publication an English translation of the "Orders, in form of a Passport" issued by d'Estaing to "monsieur the chevalier Duquesne, lieutenant commanding his majesty's cutter, Triumph" (*Pa. Packet*, 25 Mar. 1783). The same issue of the *Packet* printed the "heads of the preliminaries of peace, signed the 20th of January" 1783. These, too, had been dispatched to La Luzerne by d'Estaing. For the "proclamation," see JM to Maury, 24 Mar. 1783, and n. 2.

³ That is, by the preliminary articles of peace between Great Britain and the United States, 30 November 1782. See JM Notes, 12–15 Mar., and nn. 2, 6; Delegates to Harrison, 12 Mar. 1783, and nn. 6–14.

⁴ Although Mercer intended only to report "in general" about the territorial provisions of the preliminary peace treaty of Great Britain with France and of Great Britain with Spain, several of his facts were inaccurate. In the West Indies, St. Lucia and Tobago were returned and ceded, respectively, by Great Britain to France, while France restored all the islands, including St. Vincent, which she had conquered from Great Britain. France regained possession of the islands of St. Pierre and Miquelon but relinquished her right under the Treaty of Utrecht (1713) to fish on the coast of Newfoundland between Cape Bonavista and Cape St. John.

Although Spain returned the Bahama Islands to Great Britain, the latter ceded the Mediterranean island of Minorca and East Florida to Spain and agreed that Spain "shall keep West Florida." The northern boundary of West Florida was not defined in the treaty but presumably, as Mercer surmised, would be the thirty-second parallel of north latitude, thus confirming Article II of the preliminary treaty between Great Britain and the United States (JM Notes, 12–15 Mar. 1783, n. 6). His statement concerning Senegal was correct, except that France guaranteed Great Britain there "the possession of Fort James, and of the river Gambia." Great Britain restored to France her posts in India (Frances Gardiner Davenport and Charles Oscar Paullin, eds., *European Treaties Bearing on the History of the United States and Its Dependencies* [4 vols.; Washington, 1917–37], IV, 147–48, 150; *Hansard's Parliamentary Debates*, XXIII, cols. 346–54). In the preliminary treaty of peace of 2 September 1783 between Great Britain and the Netherlands, Trincomalee in Ceylon was returned to the Dutch, but unless they "shall hereafter have an equivalent to offer" the British, Negapatam in India would remain under the British flag (*Hansard's Parliamentary Debates*, XXIII, cols. 1158–60).

⁵ JM Notes, 22 Mar. 1783, and nn. 1, 2.

⁶ JM Notes, 24 Mar., n. 1. For Morris' notification of "recall," dated 25 March, see *Va. Gazette*, 12 Apr. 1783.

⁷ See hdn. The unidentified "Express" delivered this letter to Harrison on 30 or 31 March 1783 (*JCSV*, III, 237).

To James Maury

RC (LC: Madison Papers). Although the cover is missing and the name of the addressee does not appear in the letter, its contents strongly suggest that JM was writing to James Maury of Fredericksburg, Va. Stan. V. Henkels Catalogue No. 694 (1892), p. 122, prints a portion of the letter and adds at the close, "*To J. Maury.*" For Maury, see *Papers of Madison*, I, 114, n. 8.

PHILA. March 24—1783

DEAR SIR

By a cutter despatched by the Ct. d'Estaing & the Marquis de la fayette from Cadiz on Feby 14 & which arrived here last evening we have it confirmed that the preliminary articles for a general peace were signed in Jany.[1] The day of the signature as well as of the cessation of hostilities are omitted in the abstract rcd. by the Secretary of F. A.[2] The changes produced in the possessions of the belligerent parties as nearly as I can recollect them are that as to the Fisheries France cedes to G. B. the Coast from Cape Bonavista &c in N. foundland, & with some small exceptions makes restitution in W. Indies. In the W. Indies she receives back St. Lucia. In the E. Indies her losses are also restored. Spain retains Minorca & W. Florida which is to extend to 32°. N. L. from Mississippi to head of St. Mary's. G. B. cedes to her E. Florida & receives back the Bahamas. The Dutch possessions in general are restored. There are a few conditions annexed which I do no[t] call to mind.[3] Nothing is said as to the Navigation of the Mississippi. I beg the favr. of you to [send?] this as soon as you shall have perused it to my father.[4] & am Dr Sir

Yr friend & Servt.

J. MADISON JR.

P.S. The Preliminiaries appr. to have [been] signed on the 20th. of Jany.

[1] JM Notes, 24 Mar., and n. 1; Delegates to Harrison, 24 Mar. 1783, and nn. 1, 2.
[2] Lafayette's letter of 5 February from Cadiz to Robert R. Livingston, secretary for foreign affairs, summarizes many of "the preliminary articles" but fails to mention 20 January 1783 as the day when they were signed (NA: PCC, No. 156, fols. 316–21). From the postscript (q.v.), it is obvious that before sealing the present letter JM had been told only of the probable date. This uncertainty contrasts with the unqualified assertion of the date in his letter to Randolph and in the letter of the delegates to Harrison on 24 March (qq.v.). For this reason, JM almost certainly wrote to Maury early that morning before Congress convened and before the other two letters were penned.
Although Alleyne Fitzherbert, the English commissioner who signed the preliminary treaty of a general peace, released on 20 January a "Declaration" suspending hostilities, to which Adams and Franklin on behalf of the United States appended their formal assent on the same day, the "Proclamation" of King George III of England "declaring the cessation of arms" was not issued until 14 February 1783 (Wharton, Revol. Dipl. Corr., VI, 223–24, 251–52). See also Delegates to Harrison, 25 Mar., and n. 4. For Fitzherbert, see Jefferson to JM, 7–8 Feb. 1783, n. 12.
[3] Delegates to Harrison, 24 Mar. 1783, and nn. 3, 4.
[4] James Madison, Sr., at Montpelier, about thirty-five miles west of Fredericksburg.

To Edmund Randolph

RC (LC: Madison Papers). Cover addressed, "Edmd Randolph Esqr. per Express. Richmond." Docketed by Randolph, "Jas. Madison jr. Congress. private March. 24. 1783."

PHILADA. March 24, 1783.

DEAR SIR

The express by whom I send this conveys to the Governor the welcome event of a general peace.[1] The preliminary articles were signed on the 20th. of Jany. The day to which hostilities are limited is omitted in the abstract of the preliminaries transmitted to Congs.[2] This intelligence altho' not from our Ministers is authenticated beyond all possibility of doubt.[3] For the outlines of the Articles I refer to the letter to the Govr. & for the articles themselves as recd. by Congs. to my letter by tomorrows post.[4]

I am &c.

J. MADISON JR.

[1] Delegates to Harrison, 24 Mar. 1783, and hdn., and n. 7.
[2] JM to Maury, 24 Mar., and n. 2; Delegates to Harrison, 25 Mar. 1783, n. 4.
[3] Delegates to Harrison, 24 Mar. 1783, and n. 2.
[4] JM to Randolph, 25 Mar. 1783.

Virginia Delegates to Benjamin Harrison

RC (Virginia State Library). In the hand of John Francis Mercer, except for the two other signatures. Cover missing. Docketed, "March 25th. 1783 Letter from Repsts in Congress."

IN CONGRESS. March 25th. 1783.

SIR

Having dispatched an Express yesterday,[1] by whom we communicated to your Excellency, the substance of the important & happy advices, receiv'd by the Ch: du Quesne.[2] We now enclose yr. Excellency the days papers,[3] in which you will no doubt find many interesting particulars, & have to add, that the Ch: du Quesne, informs us that he has a table, ascertaining the different periods, established for the cessation of Hostilities in different Quarters. viz. in Europe & thence to the Azores within 10 Days after the signing the Preliminaries on the 20th. of January, within two months in America & within four months in the East Indies.[4]

We have the honor to be with much respect Yr Excellency's most obedient & very hble Servts,

JOHN F MERCER
THEOK: BLAND JR.
J MADISON JR.

[1] Delegates to Harrison, 24 Mar. 1783, and hdn., and n. 7.

[2] *Ibid.*, and nn. 1, 2.

[3] Probably the *Pennsylvania Packet* and the *Pennsylvania Journal.*

[4] Either du Quesne was in error or Mercer misunderstood him. By the terms of the two preliminary general peace treaties, one of them between Great Britain and France and the other between Great Britain and Spain, the time periods after the ratification, rather than after 20 January, beyond which captures at sea would become unlawful were (1) twelve days in the English Channel and North Sea, (2) one month in the ocean from the North Sea and English Channel to the Canary Islands "inclusively," and in the Mediterranean, (3) two months in the ocean from the Canaries to the equator, and (4) five months in all other parts of the world "without any exception" (Frances G. Davenport and Charles O. Paullin, eds., *European Treaties*, IV, 148–49, 151; *Hansard's Parliamentary Debates*, XIII, cols. 350, 353–54).

To Edmund Randolph

RC (LC: Madison Papers). Unsigned but in JM's hand. Cover franked and addressed by him to "Edmund Randolph [Esq]r. Richmond." Docketed by Randolph, "Honble Jas. Madison, March 25 1783." Probably after recovering the letter and noting that Randolph's "3" in the year could easily be mistaken for a "5," JM added "1783" to the docket.

PHILADA. March 25, 1783.

SIR

Your[1] favor of the 15th. inst:[2] was duly recd. yesterday. Mine by yesterday's Express[3] will have notified the consummation of our wishes by a settlement of the preliminaries of a general peace on the 20th. of Jany. The inclosed Gazette[4] will add all the circumstances under which the happy event is brought to us.—happy it may be indeed called whether we consider the immediate blessing[s w]hich it confers, or the cruel distresses and embarrassments from w[hich it] saves us.[5] The pecuniary aid of France for the year 1783. had been unalterably limited to 6 Million of livres. The greatest part of this sum had been anticipated and how our army could have been kept together for three months is utterly beyond my solution.[6] As it is, God only knows how the plans in agitation for satisfying their just expectations will terminate; or what will be the issue in case they should be abortive. The effects of the anonymous addresses mentioned in my last[7] on the irritable state of their minds, have been effectually obviat[ed by the] seasonable & judicious steps taken by the Commander in Ch[ief]. The manner however in which he found it necessary, and indeed felt it to be his duty, to espouse their interests enforces in the highest degree the establishment of adequate and certain revenues.[8] The provision reported by a Committee on this subject and of which I sketched you the import, is still before Congress. The past deliberations upon it do not with certainty prognosticate its fate. I fear it calls for more liberality & greater mutual confidence than will be found in the American Councils.[9]

[1] Many years later JM or someone at his bidding placed brackets at the beginning and close of the text of this letter, thus designating it for inclusion in the first comprehensive edition of his writings. See Madison, *Papers* (Gilpin ed.), I, 519–20.

[2] *Q.v.*

[3] *Q.v.*

[4] Probably the *Pennsylvania Packet* of 25 March 1783.

[5] No doubt the partial release of Congress from the dilemma caused by the "secret" or "separate" article in the preliminary peace treaty of 30 November 1782 between Great Britain and the United States was among the blessings conferred by the news of the preliminary general articles of peace. See JM Notes, 24 Mar. and citations in nn. 2–16; 15 Apr., n. 2; Delegates to Harrison, 24 Mar. 1783, and n. 4.

[6] JM Notes, 12–15 Mar., nn. 6, 9; 19 Mar., and nn. 1, 2; JM to Randolph, 12 Mar. 1783, n. 1; William E. O'Donnell, *Chevalier de La Luzerne*, pp. 244–45; Clarence L. Ver Steeg, *Robert Morris*, pp. 183, 252, nn. 51–53. JM reflects the quandary which Robert Morris, superintendent of finance, forcibly presented to Congress in his letter of 17 March 1783. Morris stated that even if loans totaling about six million livres were derived from France for use in 1783, nearly one half of that sum had already been pledged to cover debts due in 1782. For this reason and because most of the states were greatly delinquent in paying their financial quotas, he did not see how the promise made to the discontented army could be fulfilled (Wharton, *Revol. Dipl. Corr.*, VI, 308–11).

[7] JM refers to his letter of 18 rather than 24 March.

[8] JM Notes, 22 Mar. 1783, and nn. 1, 2.

[9] JM to Randolph, 11 Mar. 1783, and n. 5. See also JM Notes, 17 Mar. and citations in n. 3; 18 Mar.; 21 Mar.; 22 Mar. 1783, and n. 2; Burnett, *Letters*, VII, 106–9.

Notes on Debates

MS (LC: Madison Papers). For a description of the manuscript of Notes on Debates, see *Papers of Madison*, V, 231–34. Immediately above his entry for this day, JM wrote "Teusday No Congress."

Wednesday March 26.

Communication was made thro' the Secy of F. A. by the Minister of France, as to the late negociation, from letters recd. by him from Ct. de Vergennes dated in Decr. last, & brought by the Washington packet.[1] This communication shewed though delicately that France was displeased with our Ministers for signing the prely. arts. separately; that she had laboured by recommending mutual concessions to compromise disputes between Spain & the U. S., and that she was apprehensive that G. B. would hereafter, as they already had, endeavor to sow discords between them. It signified that the "intimacy between our Ministers & those of G. B." furnished a handle for this purpose.[2]

Besides the public communication to Congress other parts of Letters from the Ct. de Vergennes were privately communicated to the Presidt. of Congs. & to sundry members, expressing more particularly the dissatisfaction of the Ct. of F. at the conduct of our Ministers; and urging the necessity of establishing permanent revenues for paying our debts & supporting a national character.[3] The substance of these private communications as taken on the 23. instant by the President is as follows:

Finance.[4] "That the Ct. de Vergennes was alarmed at the extravagant demands of Docr. Franklin in behalf of the U. S.; that he was surprized at the same time that the inhabitants paid so little attention to doing something for themselves: If they could not be brought to give adequate funds for their defence during a dangerous war, it was not likely that so desireable an end could be accomplished when their fears were allayed by a general peace[;] that this reasoning affected the credit of the U. S. and no one could be found who would risque their money under such circumstances; that the King would be glad to know what funds were provided for the security and payment of the 10 Million borrowed by him in Holland;[5] that the Count de Vergennes hardly dared to report in favor of the U. S. to the King & Council, as money was so scarce that it would be with the greatest difficulty that even a small part of the requisition could be complied with. The causes of this scarcity were, a five year's war which had increased the expences of Government to an enormous amount, the exportation of

393

large sums of specie to America for the support & pay of both French & English armies, the loans to America, the stoppage of Bullion in S. America which prevented its flowing in the usual channels.*"[6] A letter of later date added

"That he had received the Chevrs. letter of Ocr. and rejoiced to find that Congress had provided funds for their debts, which gave him great encouragemt. and had prevailed on the Comptroller General to join him in a report to his Majesty & Council for 6 Million of livres for the U. S. to support the war,[7] but assures the Chevalier de la Luzerne, that he must never again consent to a further application."

Negociations[8]   "He complains of being treated with great indelicacy by the American Commissrs. they having signed the Treaty without any confidential communication, that had France treated America with the same indelicacy she might have signed her Treaty first as every thing between France & England was settled, but the King chose to keep faith with his allies, and therefore always refused to do any thing definitively, till all his allies were ready; that this conduct had delayed the definitive Treaty,[9] England having considered herself as greatly strengthened by America; that Docr. Franklin waited on Ct. de Vergennes & acknowledged the indelicacy of their behavior & had prevailed on him to bury it in oblivion: that the English were endeavoring all in their power to sow seeds of discords between our Commissrs. & the Court of Spain, representing our claims to the Westward as extravagant and inadmissible, that it became Congress to be attentive to this business, & to prevent the ill effects that it might be attended with, that the King had informed the Court of Spain, that tho' he heartily wished that the U. S. might enjoy a cordial coalition with his Cat: Majesty, yet he should leave the whole affair entirely to the two States and not interfere otherwise than as by his counsel & advice when asked, that altho' the U S. had not been so well treated by Spain as might have been expected, yet that his Majesty wished that America might reap the advantage of a beneficial Treaty with Spain.[10] That as the peace was not yet certain, it became all the powers at war, to be ready for a vigorous campaign, and hoped Congs. would exert themselves to aid the common cause by some offensive operations against the Enemy, but if the British should evacuate the U. S. the King earnestly hoped Congs. would take the most decided measures to prevent any intercourse with the British, and particularly in the way of merchandise or supplying them with provisions, wch. would

---

* another cause mentioned was the large balance of specie in favor of the Nn. powers during the war.

prove of the most dangerous tendency to the campaign in the W. Indies, that the British now had hopes of opening an extensive trade with America, tho' the war should continue, which if they should be disappointed in, might hasten the definitive Treaty, as it would raise a clamor among the people of England.[11]

The Chevr. added that as he had misinformed his Court with regard to Congs. having funded their debts, on which presumption, the 6 Milon. had been granted, he hoped Congs. would enable him in his next despatches to give some satisfactory account to his Court on this head."[12]

[1] Enclosed in a covering note from Robert R. Livingston to the president of Congress were "Minutes of a verbal communication" by La Luzerne on 22 March 1783. The contents of these "Minutes," although they mention explicitly only Vergennes' dispatches of 19 November, 19 December, and 20 December, permit little doubt that La Luzerne also revealed the substance of Vergennes' dispatches of 21 and 24 December 1782 (NA: PCC, No. 113, fols. 272–78; No. 119, fols. 250–51; No. 185, III, 59; Wharton, *Revol. Dipl. Corr.*, VI, 150–52, 152 n., 330–32).

[2] According to the "Minutes," British "emissaries" were busily endeavoring "to inspire Spain with apprehension" concerning the United States as a neighbor of Louisiana and the Floridas. See also JM Notes, 12–15 Mar., and nn. 4, 6–8; 19 Mar., and nn. 9, 10, 16; 22 Mar., and n. 14; JM to Randolph, 18 Mar. 1783, and n. 7.

[3] In his dispatch of 19 December Vergennes had instructed La Luzerne to inform "the most influential members of Congress" of the "very irregular conduct" of their peace commissioners. The "Minutes" state that Vergennes' dispatches of 19 November and 19 December 1782 dealt wholly with financial matters of which Congress already had been informed by Robert Morris, superintendent of finance, in his letters of 17 and 19 March 1783, and their enclosures (NA: PCC, No. 137, II, 232–33; JM Notes, 19 Mar. 1783, and nn. 1–3; Wharton, *Revol. Dipl. Corr.*, VI, 150–52, 159–60).

[4] Under this caption much of the first half of the first paragraph and all of the second closely resemble the contents of La Luzerne's coldly formal letter of 15 March 1783 to Morris (NA: PCC, No. 137, II, 232–33). That letter appears to paraphrase Vergennes' dispatches of 19 and 21 December 1782 to La Luzerne, reminding him that, contrary to his assurances in an earlier dispatch, Congress had neither paid the interest due on loans from the royal treasury and Dutch bankers nor provided sources of domestic revenue adequate to restore American credit in Europe. Vergennes' missing dispatch of 19 November 1782 to La Luzerne probably was the source of the explanation of France's scarcity of money, as recorded in the latter half of the first paragraph under the caption "Finance." See n. 6.

[5] *Papers of Madison*, V, 156, n. 7; 158, n. 7; 362; 424, n. 9; 450, n. 5; 451, n. 14; JM Notes, 19 Mar. 1783, n. 2.

[6] On 17 November 1782, in Paris, Lafayette informed John Adams that the French controller general of finance had expressed the view that the royal treasury was unable to loan the United States additional funds. The minister pointed out that the "American war" had already cost France 250,000,000 livres and that there must be a "great deal of money in America," for specie had been sent in large quantities by both the French and the British to pay and subsist their troops. Lafayette reminded the minister that most of the British gold had benefited "the Tories within the lines"

of the enemy (Wharton, *Revol. Dipl. Corr.*, VI, 9). See also *ibid.*, V, 873–74; Pendleton to JM, 15 Mar. 1783, n. 8.

As soon as Spain entered the war in 1779, the British navy virtually stopped the flow of bullion from Mexican and South American ports to Spain. She had customarily exported specie to settle her adverse trade balances with France and other European powers (Richard Herr, *The Eighteenth-Century Revolution in Spain* [Princeton, 1958], pp. 145–46). During the war, France was largely dependent upon Scandinavian countries for the timber and naval stores required for enlarging her navy.

[7] JM Notes, 24 Jan., n. 18; 12–15 Mar., n. 7; JM to Randolph, 12 Mar., n. 1. Jean François Joly de Fleury (1718–1804) was French controller general of finance from May 1781 to March 1783.

[8] JM's two paragraphs on this subject summarize information contained in the "minutes" and the letters of Franklin to Vergennes, 29 November and 17 December; Vergennes to Franklin, 15 and 25 December; Vergennes to La Luzerne, 19 and 24 December 1782; and La Luzerne to Livingston, 15 March 1783 (Wharton, *Revol. Dipl. Corr.*, VI, 90, 140, 143, 150–52, 168).

[9] JM Notes, 12–15 Mar., and n. 4; 19 Mar., and nn. 38, 39; 24 Mar., and n. 15; Delegates to Harrison, 12 Mar., and n. 18; Livingston to Congress, 18 March 1783 (NA: PCC, No. 119, fols. 251–59; Wharton, *Revol. Dipl. Corr.*, VI, 166–67).

[10] JM Notes, 12–15 Mar., and nn. 4, 7, 8; 19 Mar., and citations in n. 17; 22 Mar.; 24 Mar.; JM to Randolph, 18 Mar. 1783, and n. 7.

[11] JM Notes, 12–15 Mar., and n. 7; 19 Mar.; Delegates to Harrison, 12 Mar., and n. 17; 18 Mar., and n. 2; JM to Randolph, 12 Mar., and n. 10; 18 Mar. 1783.

[12] La Luzerne to Robert Morris, 15 Mar.; and Morris to Congress, 17 Mar. 1783 (NA: PCC, No. 137, II, 232–33; Wharton, *Revol. Dipl. Corr.*, VI, 301–3, 308–11). See also *ibid.*, VI, 338–40.

Annotations on Copy of Report on Restoring Public Credit

MS (LC: Jefferson Papers, IX, fol. 1458).

EDITORIAL NOTE

Although it would be reasonable to expect that JM, on the eve of Jefferson's departure on 12 April from Philadelphia for Virginia, annotated for his friend's information a printed copy of the original report on restoring public credit so as to indicate the major changes made by Congress in the report before that date, it appears that he either wrote these annotations prior to 27 March 1783 or, if later, failed to point out an important amendment adopted on that day. The paragraph numbers mentioned below conform with the sequence of paragraphs of the report as printed in *JCC*, XXIV, 170–74, which varies slightly from the text as printed in the Report on Restoring Public Credit of 6 March. See also Memo. on a Revenue Plan, 6 Mar., and hdn.; JM Notes, 7 Mar., and ed. n., nn. 2, 3; JM to Jefferson, 22 Apr., and n. 9; to Randolph, 22 Apr. 1783; Boyd, *Papers of Jefferson*, VI, 263–64, n.

[*ca.* 26 March 1783]

JM wrote:

(a) in the left margin opposite the beginning of the fourth paragraph, "Tuesday Mar: 11. on motion of Mr Dyer, amendt. agreeably to the Resolution of 16 day of decmr."[1]

(b) within the blank space in the fourth paragraph near its close, "one month"[2]

(c) within the blank space in the fifth paragraph near its close, "2. mi drs. annuly."[3]

(d) after the final words of the sixth paragraph, "according to such rule as is or may be prescribed by the Arts. of Confederation"[4]

[1] JM Notes, 11 Mar. 1783, and n. 10.

[2] Congress probably agreed to this insertion on 18 March (Report on Restoring Public Credit, 6 Mar. 1783, n. 6).

[3] It was not until 7 April that Congress accepted an amendment, offered three days earlier, to requisition the states annually for $1,500,000 rather than $2,000,000 (JM Notes, 4 Apr.; 7 Apr. 1783; *JCC*, XXIV, 231).

[4] The sixth paragraph, "being judged not sufficiently explicit," was recommitted on 21 March (JM Notes, 21 Mar. 1783). By 27 March the clause no longer stood "after the final words" but in slightly altered form had been inserted within an enlarged sixth paragraph of the original report (Amendment to Report on Public Credit, 27 Mar., and nn. 2, 6; JM Notes, 27 Mar., and n. 3; *JCC*, XXIV, 189, 214, 258). For this reason, and because JM made no note of the other extensive revisions of the sixth paragraph adopted by Congress on 27 March, he probably annotated the copy for Jefferson before that date.

Amendment to Report on Restoring Public Credit

MS (NA: PCC, No. 26, verso of fol. 412). Written by JM on a printed copy of the report as laid before "each member" of Congress on 7 March. See Report on Restoring Public Credit, 6 Mar. hdn.; JM Notes, 6 Mar.; 7 Mar. 1783.

[27 March 1783]

That[1] it be further recommended to the several states, to establish for a Term limited to 25 Years, and to appropriate to the discharge of the Interest & principal of the debts which shall have been contracted on the faith of the US. for supporting the present war, substantial & effective Revenues of such nature as they may judge most convenient[2] for supplying their respective proportions of 2 Millions of Dollrs annually, which proportions shall be fixed & equalized from time to time according to the rule which is or may be prescribed by the Articles of Confederation,[3] and in case the revenues established by any State, shall at any Time yield a Sum exceeding its actual proportion, the excess shall be refunded to it, and in case the Revenues of any State shall be found to be deficient, the immediate deficiency shall be made up by such State with as little delay as possible,[4] & a future deficiency guarded agst by an Enlargement of the Revenues established,[5] provided that until the Rule of the confederation can be carried into practice, the proportions of the sd. 2000000 of Dollrs. shall be as follows—viz.[6]

[1] For the background of the report to which the present amendment pertains, see JM Notes, 21 Feb., and n. 29; 27 Feb., and n. 8; 3 Mar. and n. 3; 7 Mar., ed. n., and nn. 2, 3; 11 Mar., and nn. 9, 10; 18 Mar., and nn. 1, 8; 20 Mar., and n. 25; Report on Restoring Public Credit, 6 Mar. 1783, and nn. 3, 5, 8, 9, 11, 16, 18, 20. On 21 March, after discussing the "5 & 6 paragraphs" of the report, Congress recommitted them to be made more explicit (JM Notes, 21 Mar. 1783, and n. 1). The present amendment, which, together with all other business before Congress on 27 March, is omitted in the journal, was offered in compliance with that instruction.

[2] The portion of this amendment following the word "convenient" merges, with an exception mentioned in n. 4, and greatly alters the fifth and sixth paragraphs of the printed report laid before Congress on 7 March 1783 (JCC, XXIV, 171–72). All taxes, other than duties specified in the first four paragraphs of that report, obviously were to be selected by the states rather than by Congress.

[3] Randolph to JM, 3 Jan., and n. 4; JM Notes, 9–10 Jan., nn. 3, 8; 14 Jan., nn. 4, 6; 31 Jan.; 11 Feb., and nn. 2, 4; 17 Feb., and n. 3; JM to Jefferson, 11 Feb.; to Randolph, 18 Feb. 1783. Besides stipulating for the first time a definite amount of money to be requisitioned annually from the states, the committee suggested that the eighth article of the Articles of Confederation, with which Congress had never been able to conform in apportioning quotas, should be amended. For the amendment recommended, see Amendment to Report on Public Credit, 28 Mar. 1783.

[4] JM Notes, 28 Jan. 1783, and n. 19. From "and in case" through "as possible," the amendment changes the recommendation of the sixth paragraph of the committee's printed report, laid before Congress on 7 March, but, unlike that paragraph, omits mention of how the collectors of "the revenues" were to be appointed. The apparent lack of future debate upon this controversial issue and also the fourth paragraph of the report, as finally adopted on 18 April, lead to the inference that the present amendment implicitly shortened the sixth paragraph to read: "The said last mentioned revenues to be collected by persons appointed as aforesaid, but to be carried to the separate credit of the states within which they shall be collected" (JCC, XXIV, 172, 259). The "appointed as aforesaid" refers to the mode specified in the fourth paragraph of the printed report or in the second paragraph as adopted on 18 April 1783 (JCC, XXIV, 171, 258).

[5] That is, every state which had been "deficient" should thereafter raise sufficient additional revenue to meet its allotted quota in full.

[6] For the debate upon, and the adoption of, this amendment, see JM Notes, 27 March 1783. The state-by-state quotas, ranging upward from $24,000 for Georgia to $320,000 for Massachusetts, appear in the hand of Thomas FitzSimons, a member of the committee, along the right margin of a printed copy of the report submitted to Congress on 7 March 1783 (NA: PCC, No. 26, fol. 413). For alterations in this list of quotas, see JM Notes, 4 Apr. 1783.

Notes on Debates

MS (LC: Madison Papers). For a description of the manuscript of Notes on Debates, see *Papers of Madison*, V, 231–34. The six words italicized in the present copy are those underlined by JM.

Thursday Mar. 27.

this day not noted in the Journal as in some other instances[1]

Revenues taken up as reported Mar. 7.[2]

The 5. paragraph in the report on Revenue havg. been judged not sufficiently explicit, and recommitted to be made more so, the following paragraph was recd. in its place viz "That it be further recommended to the several States, to establish for a term limited to 25. Years, and to appropriate" &c [to the word 2 Million of dollars annually]. "which proportions shall be fixed and equalized from time to time according to such rule as is or may be prescribed by the articles of Confederation: and in case the revenues so established and appropriated by any State shall at any time yield a sum exceeding its proportion, the excess shall be refunded to it, and in case the same shall be found to be defective the immediate deficiency shall be made good as soon as possible, and a future deficiency guarded against by an enlargement of the Revenues established provided that untill the rule of the confederation can be applied, the proportions of the 2,000,000 of dollars aforesaid, shall be as follows: viz . . . This amendment was accepted,[3] a motion of Mr. Clark to restrain this apportionmt. in the first instance to the term of 2 years, being first negatived. He contended that a valuation of land would prob[ab]ly never take place, and that it was uncertain whether the rule of numbers wd. be substituted and therefore that the first apportionment might be continued throughout the 25 years, altho it must be founded on the present relative wealth of the States which would vary every year, in favor of those which are the least populous.[4]

This reasoning was not denied, but it was thought that such a limitation might leave an interval in which no apportionment wd. exist, when a confusion would proceed, & that an apprehension of it would destroy public Credit.

A motion was made by Mr. Bland 2ded. by Mr. Lee to go back to the first part of the report & instead of the words "*levy*" an impost of 5 PerCt. to substitute the word "collect" an impost &c.[5] It was urged in favor of this motion that the first word imported a Legislative idea, &

the latter an executive only, and consequently the latter might be less obnoxious to the States.[6] On the other side it was said that the States would be governed more by things than by terms; that if the meaning of both was the same, an alteration was unnecessary; that if not, as seemed to be the case, an alteration would be improper. It was particularly apprehended that if the term "collect" were to be used, the States might themselves fix the *mode* of collection; whereas it was indispensable that Congs. sd. have that power as well that it might be varied from time to time as circumstances or experience sd. dictate, as that a uniformity might be observed throughout the States.[7] On the motion of Mr. Clarke the negative was voted by a large Majority there being 4 ays only.

On (8) parag:[8] there was no argt. nor opposition

The (9) paragraph being considered by several as inaccurate in point of phraseology; a motion was made by Mr. Madison to postpone it to take into consideration the following towit "That in order to remove all objections against a retrospective application of the constitutional rule to the final apportionment on the several States, of the monies & supplies actually contributed in pursuance of requisitions of Congress, it be recommended to the States to enable the U. S. in Congs. assembd. to make such equitable abatements & alterations as the particular circumstances of the States from time to time during the war may require, and as will divide the burden of such actual contributions among them in proportion to their respective abilities at the period at which they were made."[9] On a question for striking out, the original paragraph was agreed to without opposition: On the question to insert the amendment of Mr. M, the votes of the States were 5 ays, 6 noes, viz N.H. no, Cont. no, N.J. no, Delr. no, Maryd. no, S.C. no. The rest ay.

On (10) paragraph relative to expences incurred by the States without the sanction of Congs. Mr. Clarke exclaimed agst. the unreasonbleness of burdening the Union with all the extravagant expenditures of particular States: and moved that it might be struck out of the Report. Mr. Helmsly 2ded. the motion.[10] Mr. Madison said that the effects of rejecting this paragraph wd. be so extensive that a full consideration of it ought at least to preceede such a step, that the expences referred to in the paragraph were in part such as would have been previously sanctioned by Congs. if application cd. have been made; since similar ones had been so with respect to States within the vicinity of Congs. and therefore complaints of injustice would follow a refusal, that another part of the expences had been incurred in support of claims to the territory of which cessions were asked by Congs. and therefore these cd. not be expected, if the expences incident to them should be rejected; that it was probable if no previous assurance were given on this point, it would be made a condition by the States ceding, as the Cessions of territory would be made a condition by the States most anxious to obtain them; that by these mean[s] the whole plan would be either defeated,[11] or the part thereof in question be ultimately forced on Congs. whilst they might with a good grace yield it in the first instance; not to mention that these unliquidated & unallowed claims would produce hereafter such contests & heats among the States as wd. probably destroy the plan even if it sd. be acceded to by the States without this paragraph.[12]

Mr. Dyer was in favor of the paragraph.[13] Mr. Rutledge opposed it as letting in a flood of claims which were founded on extravagant projects of the States.[14]

Mr. Higgenson & Mr Ghorum were earnest in favor of it, remarking that the distance of Massachusetts from Congs. had denied a previous sanction to the Militia operations agst. General Burgoyne &c. The Penobscot expedition also had great weight with them.[15]

Mr. Williamson was in favor of it.[16]

Mr. Wilson said he had always considered this Country with respect to the war, as forming one community; and that the States which by their remoteness from Congs. had been obliged to incur expences for their defence without previous sanction, ought to be placed on the same footing with those which had obtained this security; but he could not agree to put them on a better which wd. be the case if their expences sd. be sanctioned in the lump: he proposed therefore that these expences sd. be limited to such as had been incurred in a *necessary defence;* and of which the object in each case sd. be approved by Congress:[17]

Mr. Madison agreed that the expressions in the paragh: were very loose,[18] & that it wd. be proper to make them as definite as the case wd. admit; he supposed however that all operations agst. the enemy within the limits assigned to the U. S. might be considered as defensive, & in that view the expedition agst. Penobscot might be so called. He observed that the term *necessary* left a discretion in the Judge as well as the term *reasonable:* and that it wd. be best perhaps for Congress to determine & declare that they wd. constitute a tribunal of impartial persons to decide on oath as to the propriety of claims of States not authorized heretofore by Congs. He sd. this wd. be a better security to the States & wd. be more satisfactory than the decisions of Congs., the members of wch. did not act on oath, & brought with them the spirit of advocates for their respective states rather than of impartial judges between them. He moved that the clause with Mr. Wilsons proposition be recommitted; which was agreed to without opposition.[19]

(11& 12 paraghs.)[20] Mr. Bland opposed it: said that the value of land was the best rule, and that at any rate no change sd. be attempted untill its practicability sd. be tried.[21]

Mr. Madison thought the value of land, could never be justly or satisfactorily obtained; that it wd. ever be a source of contentions among the States, and that as a repetition of the valuation would be within the course of the 25. years, it wd. unless exchanged for a more simple rule mar the whole plan[22]

Mr. Ghorum was in favr. of the paraghs. He represented in strong terms the inequality & clamors produced by valuations of land in the State of Mas:ts. & the probability of the evils being increased among the States themselves which were less tied together & more likely to be jealous of each other.[23]

Mr. Williamson was in favr. of paraghs.[24]

Mr. Wilson was strenuous in favor of it. sd. he was in Congs. when the article of Confederation directing a value of land was agreed to, that it was the effect of the impossibility of compromising the different ideas of the Eastern & Southern States as to the value of Slaves compared with the Whites, the alternative in question.[25]

Mr. Clarke was in favor of it. He said that he was also in Congs. when this article was decided, that the Southern States wd. have agreed to numbers, in preference to the value of land if $\frac{1}{2}$ their slaves only sd. be included: but that the Eastern States would not concur in that proportion.[26]

It was agreed on all sides that instead of fixing the proportion by ages as the report proposed it would be best to fix the proportion in absolute numbers. With this view & that the blank might be filled up, the clause was recommitted.[27]

---

[1] Immediately preceding this comment, JM drew an index fist. For examples of the official journal's failure to mention other days when Congress convened, see JM Notes, 13 Feb., and n. 1; 19 Feb., and n. 1; 12–15 Mar. 1783, and n. 1.

[2] JM Notes, 7 Mar., and ed. n.; Amendment to Report on Public Credit, 27 Mar. 1783.

[3] This copy of most of the amendment which JM introduced on behalf of the committee on the restoration of credit differs occasionally from the wording of the manuscript of the amendment. See Amendment to the Report on Public Credit, 27 Mar. 1783. These variations may reflect inaccurate copying by JM, minor amendments adopted on 27 March, or both. JM's notation of the passage of the amendment obviously implies only that its factual contents and statements of purpose remain unchanged. The brackets and the passage enclosed in them are JM's.

[4] Abraham Clark's motion was to amend the proviso which closed JM's proposed amendment, except for the list of state-by-state quotas appended by Thomas Fitz-Simons (Amendment to the Report on Public Credit, 27 Mar. 1783, and n. 6). Clark was by no means the first delegate who expressed doubt whether an acceptable valuation of land, as stipulated by the eighth article of the Articles of Confederation, would ever be made or whether all the states would ever consent to amend that article so as to provide a more practical basis upon which to apportion financial quotas. See JM Notes, 9–10 Jan., and nn. 3, 8; 14 Jan., and nn. 4, 6, 7, 9; 28 Jan., and nn. 19, 42; 31 Jan., and nn. 11, 17; 4 Feb.; 5–6 Feb., and nn. 7, 9; 7 Feb., and nn. 9, 10, 12; 8 Feb., and n. 4; 10 Feb.; 11 Feb., and nn. 2–6, 8–11; 12 Feb., and n. 14; 17 Feb.; JM to Randolph, 14 Jan.; 4 Feb.; 18 Feb., and n. 3; Randolph to JM, 7 Feb.; JM to Jefferson, 11 Feb. 1783. Clark meant that if an allotment of financial quotas as of 1783 should not be frequently revised by Congress, every state which then was relatively poor in wealth and small in population would thereafter, as it grew in both those respects, pay year after year a decreasingly equitable proportion of the total sum requisitioned from the states.

[5] The substitution recommended by the Bland-Lee motion would affect the first and second paragraphs of the committee's report (Report on Restoring Public Credit, 6 Mar.; JM Notes, 18 Mar. 1783, n. 1).

[6] JM Notes, 21 Feb. 1783, and n. 4.

[7] If "the States" should construe "collect" to mean that "the *mode* of collection" was under their control, they thereby would negate the provision of the third paragraph of the committee's report making "the collectors" of the imposts "amenable to" Congress (Report on Restoring Public Credit, 6 Mar.; JM Notes, 18 Mar. 1783, n. 1).

[8] Report on Restoring Public Credit, 6 Mar., n. 14; JM Notes, 18 Mar. 1783, n. 1.

[9] Report on Restoring Public Credit, 6 Mar., and the citations in n. 15; JM Notes, 18 Mar. 1783, n. 1.

[10] Report on Restoring Public Credit, 6 Mar., and n. 16; JM Notes, 18 Mar. 1783, n. 1. In 1783 William Hemsley, a delegate from Maryland, had first attended Congress on 25 February (*JCC*, XXIV, 145; Burnett, *Letters*, VI, xlv; VII, lxvii). His support of Abraham Clark of New Jersey on this issue was to be expected, for Maryland remained immune from invasion by the British during the Revolution. Although New Jersey had been a principal theater of the war from 1776 to 1779, her proximity to the meeting place of Congress usually enabled her, before contracting extraordinary military expenses, to obtain guarantees of eventual reimbursement from the treasury of the Confederation (JM Notes, 26 Feb. 1783, and nn. 31, 38).

[11] JM was emphasizing the close relationship between the tenth paragraph of the report and the eighth, which requested Virginia and five other states to make "liberal cessions" of their lands west of the Appalachian Mountains to the United States. See *Papers of Madison*, II, 72–77; Report on Restoring Public Credit, 6 Mar., and n. 14; JM Notes, 7 Mar. 1783, and n. 2.

[12] Viewing the two paragraphs as embodying an equitable compromise, JM was urging Congress to accept it with "good grace" rather than perforce eventually, as perhaps the only means of preventing the failure of the entire plan for restoring public credit. For the "unliquidated & unallowed claims," see Randolph to JM, 15 Jan., n. 13; JM Notes, 27 Jan., n. 13; 21 Feb.; 26 Feb., and nn. 17, 28, 40, 43; Memo. on Revenue Plan, 6 Mar. 1783, ed. n.

[13] Eliphalet Dyer voiced the interest of Connecticut, which, besides attaching provisos to her still pending offer to cede her trans-Appalachian land to the United States, had incurred indebtedness by frequently calling out her militia without prior authorization of Congress (Memo. on Revenue Plan, 6 Mar. 1783). See also Article VI, paragraph 5, of the Articles of Confederation (*JCC*, XIX, 216).

14 John Rutledge represented a state which claimed little territory west of the Appalachians. In accord with JM's expectation, as recorded in his notes of 26 February 1783 (*q.v.*, and nn. 40, 42), Rutledge evidently believed that for Congress to invite "a flood" of controversial claims would be disadvantageous to South Carolinians who were owed by the United States a disproportionately large total of valid debts.

15 On 23 July 1777 William Sever, president of the council of Massachusetts, wrote to John Hancock, president of Congress, informing him of the large number of militia from the western counties of the state which had been dispatched to aid "the northern army," commanded by General Horatio Gates, resist the British troops led by General John Burgoyne (NA: PCC, No. 65, I, 203–6; *JCC*, VIII, 601–2; JM Notes, 31 Jan., and n. 4). For the Penobscot expedition, see JM Notes, 26 Feb. 1783, n. 22.

16 Hugh Williamson's support reflected North Carolina's heavy expenses occasioned by the presence of British and Loyalist troops within her borders from 1780 to 1782 (NA: PCC, No. 72, fols. 87–89; 101–4; *Papers of Madison*, II, 107, n. 5; 185, n. 8; III, 9, n. 1; IV, 272–73).

17 *Papers of Madison*, V, 56–57; JM Notes, 27 Jan. 1783.

18 In the tenth paragraph, the passage at issue reads: "all reasonable expences which shall have been incurred by the states without the sanction of Congress, in their defence against, or attacks upon British or savage enemies, either by sea or by land, and which shall be supported by satisfactory proofs, shall be considered as part of the common charges incident to the present war, and be allowed as such" (*JCC*, XXIV, 173).

19 *Ibid.* For JM's effort on behalf of the committee to meet James Wilson's objection, see Amendment to Report on Public Credit, 17 April 1783.

20 These paragraphs contained the recommendation that the eighth article of the Articles of Confederation be amended for the purpose of substituting the number of persons, with some exceptions, for the value of land as the basis upon which the amount of the financial quota of each state should be determined by Congress (*JCC*, XXIV, 173–74).

21 Theodorick Bland and Arthur Lee had been among the most vocal delegates in opposing an abandonment of land evaluation as a gauge for apportionment by Congress of its monetary requisition among the states (JM Notes, 27 Jan., and n. 29; 28 Jan., and n. 5; 31 Jan.; 5–6 Feb., and n. 13; 10 Feb.; 11 Feb. 1783).

22 JM here repeated what he often had said before. See n. 4.

23 According to JM's previous notes, Nathaniel Gorham was wavering in his views of the efficacy of land evaluation. See JM Notes, 14 Jan., n. 4; 31 Jan., and n. 10; 11 Feb. 1783, and n. 9.

24 JM Notes, 31 Jan.; 7 Feb. 1783, and n. 6.

25 As a member of Congress James Wilson had shared during the latter half of 1776 in the frequent debates concerning the standard to be used in allocating financial quotas among the states. The first two printed drafts of the Articles of Confederation provided for the relative number of white inhabitants rather than their wealth to be the gauge (*JCC*, III, 327; V, 433, 548, 596, 677–78; VI, 1079–82, 1098–1102, 1105–6). On 14 October 1777, after another year of intermittent discussion of the issue and about a month after Wilson left Congress, the delegates by a sectional vote substituted land values for population as a basis for apportioning financial quotas. The New England delegates voted unanimously against this change, while those from New York and Pennsylvania deadlocked in the tally (*JCC*, VIII, 735, 746; IX, 801–2). On 15 November 1777 Congress adopted the Articles of Confederation, including the controversial eighth article (*JCC*, IX, 907–25, and esp. 913–14).

See also JM Notes, 7 Feb., and n. 7; 11 Feb., and n. 2; JM to Randolph, 11 Mar. 1783.

[26] JCC, VI, 1002, 1079. Abraham Clark did not attend Congress on 14 October 1777 when the ninth (which soon would be the eighth) article of the Articles of Confederation was adopted (JCC, IX, 801–2, 833, 913–14).

[27] After stipulating that the "common treasury" of the United States would be "supplied" by allocating the "expences" among the states "in proportion to the number of inhabitants," counted "triennially," except for Indians not taxed, the twelfth paragraph closed with the proviso, "that in such numeration no persons shall be included who are bound to servitude for life, according to the laws of the state to which they belong, other than such as may be between the ages of   " (NA: PCC, No. 26, fol. 412; JCC, XXIV, 173–74). For JM's effort on behalf of the committee to express what he believed to be "agreed on all sides," see Amendment to Report on Public Credit, 28 March 1783.

Virginia Delegates to Virginia Auditors of Public Accounts

MS (Virginia State Library). In JM's hand, except for the signatures of the other four delegates.

PHILADA. March 27th. 1783.

We have received in consequence of two bills of Exchange remitted by J. Ambler Esq. each of us one hundred pounds Virga. currency;[1] and request the Auditors of the Commonwealth of Virginia to issue warrants to that amount and charge the same to us in part of our Salaries as Delegates to Congress.[2]

> J. MADISON JR.
> JOS: JONES
> THEOK: BLAND JR.
> ARTHUR LEE
> JOHN F. MERCER

N. B. out of the above the Charges of discount on the negotiating the said Bills to be credited to the delegates amount to Six dollars

[1] Ambler to JM, 22 Mar. 1783, and n. 2.
[2] Ambler to JM, 12 Apr. 1783. For "the Auditors," see Ambler to JM, 1 Feb. 1783, n. 1.

Amendment to Report on Restoring Public Credit

MS (NA: PCC, No. 26, fols. 433–34).

EDITORIAL NOTE

For the background of this amendment, see Report on Restoring Public Credit, 6 Mar., and n. 20; JM Notes, 27 Mar. 1783, and n. 27. JM's notes for 28 March (*q.v.*) permit no doubt that the wording of the amendment on the first page of his manuscript (fol. 433, cited above) includes at least one revision resulting from the discussion in Congress following the submission of the amendment. Effort has been made to restore JM's original wording in the present text.

Most probably during the course of the debate, which focused upon the fractional weight to be given to slaves in allocating tax quotas among the states in proportion to their population, JM attempted on the second page (fol. 434) either to rephrase that portion of the amendment or to record the changes in it suggested and rejected during a part of the lengthy discussion. The legible residue of his jottings, which he partially effaced by heavy erasures, reads: "in proportion to the number of white Inhabitants of every age, sex & condition, and of the $\frac{1}{2}$ of the number of all other inhabitants; which numbers shall be triennially taken & transmitted to the U. S. in Congs. Assembd. in such mode as they shall direct & appoint."

On the second page there are other notations bearing upon the debate of 28 March, but they are not in JM's hand. For these, see JM Notes, 28 March 1783, n. 2.

[28 March 1783]

Rept of Come. to whom was transmitted the last paragraph of the Report on the establishmt. of a Revenue &c[1]

All charges of war, and all other expences that have been or shall be incurred for the common defense or general welfare, & allowed by the U. S. in Congs. assembd. except so far as shall be otherwise provided for shall be defrayed out of a common Treasury, which shall be supplied by the several States in proportion to[2] the whole number of free[3] inhabitants & one half of the number of all other inhabitants[4] of every age sex and condition except Indians not paying Taxes in each State; which number shall be triennially taken & transmitted to the U. S. in Congs. assembled, in such mode as they shall direct & appoint.[5]

---

[1] Preceding the amendment, as entered in the journal, appear the eleventh paragraph of the printed report on restoring public credit and the first seven lines of the twelfth paragraph, revised to include the first sentence of Article VIII of the Articles of Confederation, which the committee recommended to be "revoked and

made void" by Congress' adoption of the amendment and its ratification by the states (*JCC*, XIX, 217; XXIV, 198, 214–15).

[2] To this point the amendment varies the wording of Article VIII of the Articles of Confederation only in the following respects: (1) substituting "have been or shall be incurred" for "shall be incurred," and (2) inserting "except so far as shall be otherwise provided for" just before "shall be defrayed." The first of these changes was needed to cover past as well as future debts, while the second reflected the hope that the states would empower Congress to levy duties on many varieties of imported goods, as specified in the first three paragraphs of the committee's printed report (*JCC*, XIX, 217; XXIV, 195–96).

[3] JM at first interlineated "free white" and then canceled "white." This latter change was made during the debate in Congress (*JCC*, XXIV, 215).

[4] For conclusive evidence that the amendment as presented to Congress recommended "one half" rather than the "three fifths" interlineated above a partially erased "one half" in the manuscript, see JM Notes, 28 Mar.; *JCC*, XXIV, 215. See also JM Notes, 26 Feb. 1783, and n. 44.

[5] The passage beginning with "of every age" and continuing to the close of the amendment was taken verbatim from the final paragraph of the Report on Restoring Public Credit, 6 March 1783 (*q.v.*). Inadvertently the word "age" was omitted from the passage as entered in the journal for 28 March (*JCC*, XXIV, 215). See also *JCC*, XXIV, 223, 260.

Notes on Debates

MS (LC: Madison Papers). For a description of the manuscript of Notes on Debates, see *Papers of Madison*, V, 231–34.

Friday March 28.

The Come. last mentd. reported that two blacks be rated as equal to one freeman.[1]

Mr. Wolcot was for rating them as 4 to 3.

Mr. Carrol as 4 to 1.

Mr. Williamson sd. he was principled agst. slavery; & that he thought slaves an incumbrance to Society instead of increasing its ability to pay taxes.

Mr. Higgenson as 4 to 3.

Mr. Rutlidge sd. for the sake of the object he wd. agree to rate Slaves, as 2 to 1, but he sincerely thought 3 to 1. would be a juster proportion

Mr. Holten—as 4 to 3.

Mr. Osgood sd. he cd not go beyond 4 to 3.

On a question for rating them as 3 to 2, the votes were N. H. ay. Mas: no. R.I. divd. Cont. ay. N.J. ay. Pa. ay. Delr. ay. Maryd. no Virga. no N.C. no. S. C. no[2]

The paragraph was then postponed by general consent; some wishing for further time to deliberate on it; but it appearing to be the general opinion that no compromise wd. be agreed to

After some further discussions on the report in which the necessity of some simple & practicable rule of apportionment came fully into view, Mr. Madison said that in order to give a proof of the sincerity of his professions of liberality he wd. propose that Slaves should be rated as 5 to 3. Mr. Rutlidge 2ded. motion. Mr. Wilson sd. he wd. sacrifice his opinion to this compromise.

Mr. Lee was agst. changing the rule, but gave it as his opinion that 2 Slaves were not equal to 1 freeman.

On the question for 5 to 3, it passed in the affirmative N.H. ay. Mas: divd. R. I. no. Cont. no. N.J. ay. Pa. ay Maryd. ay. Va. ay N.C. ay. S.C. ay.

A motion was then made by Mr. Bland 2ded. by Mr. Lee to strike out the clause so amended, and on the question, "shall it stand" it passed in the negative. N.H. ay. Mas. no. R.I. no. Con no N.J. ay. Pa. ay. Del. no. Mar. ay. Virga. ay. N.C. ay. S.C. no. so the clause was struck out.[3]

The arguments used by those who were for rating slaves high were; that the expence of feeding & cloathing them was as far below that incident to freemen, as their industry & ingenuity were below those of freemen: and that the warm climate within wch. the States having slaves lay, compared wth. the rigorous climate & inferior fertility of the others, ought to have great weight in the case & that the exports of the former states were greater than of latter.[4] on the other side it was said that Slaves were not put to labour as young as the children of laboring families, that having no interest in their labor they did as little as possible, & omitted every exertion of thought requisite to facilitate & expedite it: that if the exports of the States having slaves exceeded those of the others, their imports were in proportion, Slaves being employed wholly in agriculture, not in manufactures: & that in fact the balance of trade formerly was much more agst. the So. States than the others.

on the main question, see Journal[5]

[1] Amendment to Report on Public Credit, 28 Mar. 1783, and ed. n., and n. 4.

[2] This proposal may have been made by JM as a compromise between the 2 for 1 recommended by the committee and the 4 for 3 evidently desired by some New England delegates. On fol. 434 of NA: PCC, No. 26, the following was noted, apparently by Benjamin Bankson, Jr., a clerk in the office of the secretary of Congress: "The latter clause of the report of the Comee. being recommitted the Commite reported the enclosed in lieu thereof and motion being made to fill the blank before the words 'the number of all other inhabitants' with the words 'two thirds of.' Question taken 5 ayes 4 Noes 2 divided. N H a[y] Mass. div. R I divd Con ay N J ay Pens ay Delr ay Maryland, Virg. N. Car. & [S] Cr. no So the

question was lost & this part relative to an alteration of the Art: of Confederation was [bis] postponed   March 28. 1783." This tally is identical with that of JM in his notes, except that he recorded Massachusetts as "no" rather than "div"—a distinction which leaves unchanged the outcome of the poll. Georgia was not represented in Congress, and William Floyd was the only delegate present from New York.

3 JM's use of the word "clause" is misleading, for only the words "three-fifths of" were struck out, leaving the "clause," "in proportion to the whole number of free inhabitants and   the number of all other inhabitants" (JCC, XXIV, 214-15, 215, n. 1).

4 JM to Randolph, 25 Feb., and n. 16; JM Notes, 26 Feb. 1783.

5 The "main question" was whether the twelfth and thirteenth paragraphs of the report of 6 March by the committee on restoring public credit should be adopted. Those paragraphs were evidently treated as one, since they were interdependent. Bland and Lee moved that they be struck out. The question as put was "shall the paragraph, as amended, stand as part of the report?" Except that William Floyd, who was now present to cast a lone, ineffective "ay" vote for New York, the ballot was identical with that recorded by JM for the first Bland-Lee motion, six states voting "ay," five "no." "So the question was lost, and the paragraph struck out" (JCC, XXIV, 173-74, 215-16; NA: PCC, No. 26, fol. 411; Report on Restoring Public Credit, 6 Mar. 1783; and n. 20). For a reconsideration by Congress of the issue, see JM Notes, 1 April 1783.

Motion for Reports by Superintendent of Finance

MS (NA: PCC, No. 36, II, 49). In JM's hand. Docketed, "Motion of Mr Madison Seconded by Mr Wilson, March 29th 1783."

[29 March 1783]

That[1] it be the duty of the Superintendt of Finance with as little delay as may be & thereafter on the   day of   [2] in every year to lay before the U. S. in Congss. assmbd. a state of all monies receiv'd into his Departmt. with the times when & the persons from whom they shall have been received; and also a state of all payments made immediately under his warrant with the t[im]es when the persons to whom & the purposes for which such warrants shall have been issued; that he also at periods aforesaid lay before the U. S. in Congr. assembd. copies of the receipts given to him for all such warrants, with the amounts of the estimates or substance of the other documents on which the warrants shall have been issued; and also a report from the Comptroller's office[3] [o]f how far monies issued under warrants of the sd. Superintendt. as aforesaid shall have been finally & satisfactorily accounted for.[4]

1 JM introduced this motion, seconded by James Wilson, after unsuccessful attempts had been made to commit or defer debate upon a motion offered by Arthur Lee and seconded by Samuel Holten of Massachusetts. Lee's motion, in line with his many earlier efforts to embarrass Robert Morris, would have required the superin-

tendent of finance to submit to Congress "immediately" a month-by-month report, covering his entire tenure, of the "monies" he had received "for the public use" and a detailed statement of why and to whom he had disbursed those funds (*JCC*, XXIV, 216–19; JM Notes, 29 Mar. 1783, and n. 7). See also *Papers of Madison*, IV, 343, ed. n.; 419; 435; 449, n. 7; V, 4, ed. n.; 15, n. 3; JM Notes, 12 Feb., n. 7; 4–5 Mar. 1783, and n. 4, and citations in n. 6; *JCC*, XXIV, 165–67.

2 Had his motion carried, JM perhaps then would have tried to gain acceptance of a date sufficiently deferred to give Morris ample time to prepare a report, perhaps 14 May, the anniversary of Morris' acceptance of appointment as superintendent of finance, or 20 September, that of his assumption of the full duties of the office in 1781 (Jennings B. Sanders, *Evolution of Executive Departments,* pp. 130–32).

3 James Milligan (d. 1818) of Philadelphia, whom Congress on 13 October 1781 had elected as "comptroller" of the treasury, "was authorized to 'inspect and superintend the settlement of public accounts, and all subordinate officers concerned therein'" (American Antiquarian Society, comp., *Index of Obituaries in Massachusetts Centinel and Columbian Centinel, 1784 to 1840* [5 vols.; Boston, 1961], IV, 3116; *JCC*, XXI, 1050; Clarence L. Ver Steeg, *Robert Morris*, p. 80). Ever since the summer of 1775, when Congress included Milligan among the men authorized to "sign and number" bills of credit, he had held a succession of increasingly important positions relating to finance. For nearly a year immediately prior to his election as comptroller, he served as auditor general. See *JCC*, II, 207; III, 258; IV, 194; V, 612; VII, 715; IX, 999; X, 113; XII, 1096; XV, 1251.

4 This motion failed to carry, but the Lee-Holten proposal did not come to a vote before Congress adjourned. See JM Notes, 29 Mar. 1783, and n. 7.

Notes on Debates

MS (LC: Madison Papers). For a description of the manuscript of Notes on Debates, see *Papers of Madison*, V, 231–34.

Saturday. March 29.

The objections urged agst. the motion of Mr. Lee on the Journal calling for specific Report of the Supt. of Finance as to monies passing thro' his hands[1] were that the information demanded from the office of Finance had during a great part of the period been laid before Congress & was then actually on the Table,[2] that the term *"application"* of money was too indefinite,[3] no two friends of the motion agreeing in the meaning of it and that if it meant no more than immediate payments under the warrants of the Superintendt to those who were to expend the money, it was unnecessary[,] the Superintendt being already impressed with his duty on that subject; that if it meant the ultimate payment for articles or services for the public, it imposed a task that wd. be impracticable to the Superintdt., and useless to Congress, who could no[t] otherwise examine them than through the department of accounts, & the Committees appd. half yearly for enquiring into the whole proceedings;[4] & that if the motion were free from those objections, it ought to be so varied as to oblige the office of Finance to report the information periodically; since it would otherwise depend on the memory & vigilance of members, and wd. moreover have the aspect of suspicion towards the Officer called upon.—N.B. as the motion was made at first, the word "immediately" was used; which was changed for the words "as soon as may be" at the instance of Mr. Holten.[5]

The object of the motion of Mr. Madison[6] was to define & comprehend every information practicable & necessary for Congs. to know, & to enable them to judge of the fidelity of their Minister: and to make it a permanent part of his duty to afford it. The clause respecting copies of receipts was found on discussion not to accord with the mode of conducting business & to be too voluminous a task; but the question was taken without a convenient opportunity of correcting it. The motion was negatived see the Journal[7]

[1] Reports by Superintendent of Finance, 29 Mar. 1783, n. 1.

[2] Robert Morris, superintendent of finance, had provided Congress a detailed report of receipts and expenditures from July 1781, when he commenced to serve, until the close of that year (*Papers of Madison*, IV, 188, n. 3). Either by his own initiative or by direction of Congress, he also had frequently reported upon particular subjects germane to the wide range of his responsibilities. See, for example, *ibid.*, V, 52, n. 14; 129, n. 13; 162, n. 15; 175, n. 8; 293, n. 2; JM Notes, 13 Jan., n. 5; 27 Jan., n. 13; Randolph to JM, 15 Jan. 1783, and n. 13.

[3] Reports by Superintendent of Finance, 29 Mar. 1783, n. 1.

[4] By "department of accounts," JM meant the office of the comptroller, which was one of the four main divisions of the "Treasury," headed by the superintendent of finance (*ibid.*, n. 3; *JCC*, XXI, 948–51). For "the Committees," see *Papers of Madison*, IV, 335, ed. n.; 343–44; 344, n. 5; *JCC*, XXIV, 37, 222 and n. 1, 396–99.

[5] *JCC*, XXIV, 216; Reports by Superintendent of Finance, 29 Mar. 1783, n. 1.

[6] *Ibid.*, and n. 1.

[7] By a vote of 7 to 4, Congress refused to postpone debate on Lee's proposal "in order to take into consideration" JM's substitute motion. JM was supported only by New York, New Jersey, Pennsylvania, and Maryland. After "farther debate" without reaching a decision, "an adjournment was called for and carried" (*JCC*, XXIV, 218–19; Reports by Superintendent of Finance, 29 Mar. 1783, n. 4).

Benjamin Harrison to Virginia Delegates

FC (Virginia State Library). In the hand of Thomas Meriwether. Addressed to "Virginia Delegates in Congress."

GENTLEMEN,   IN COUNCIL March 29th. 1783.

Your favor of the 18th. of March came safe to hand, by which I find our Prospects of Peace are greatly lessen'd since the perusal of Mr.

Lawrence's Letter   it is however some consolation to me to know that the reports spread abroad by the Enemies of the French Alliance are on this as they have been on all other occasions false and malitious and grounded on ill founded Prejudices, to say no worse of them.[1] It is a Matter of serious concern and chagrin to me that the Affairs of Penet & Co. have taken the turn they have[2] tho' it was to be expected from the Conduct of the Assembly, whose interference with the Executive Department, by taking from them Vessels that were prepared to make remittances according to their most sacred Promises have brought it about, the intentions of some Gentlemen are fully answered in bringing me into Contempt for destroying the Public faith. I wish they had recollected that thro' me they would deeply wound their Country.[3] Mr. Barclay has been appointed Agent for the State ever since the 6th. of September last, and I am happy to find from his Letters by Capt. Barney that he has taken the trust upon him and has entered into the Discharge of it.[4] the first Thing recommended to him was to use every Method in his Power to prevent Penets doing more Mischief to the State by advertizing the People of Europe that his Powers were recalled, which he has done; his next care was to inform us what Contracts he had entered into that were really on Account of the State, to settle such Accounts and give me a full State of them which I expect he will do by the first Opportunity,[5] as soon as they arrive you shall have them in Order to your laying them before any Person or Persons who may have a Claim against us on his Account.[6] The Goods ship'd by Penet & Co. in the Duke of Linster and Franklin amounted to 77502. Livers Tournois and no more as may be made appear by Letters and Invoices.[7] they ship'd another Parcel of Goods in the Schooner Committee which were taken and retaken and carried into Rode Island.[8] their amount I do not exactly know, but suppose from examining the commercial Agents[9] Books when the Accounts of the whole transactions are settled there will be a Ballance of nearly the first Sum due to the Company, be it more or less it is at present attach'd by a mr. Bourdeaux of South Carolina and Coulignac & Co. of Nantes have demanded it alledging that the Money for the Purchase of the Goods was advanced by them.[10] Mr. Auby says the same thing and therefore claims Payment. I leave you to determine whither both of them can be in the right.[11] As far as I am able to jud[g]e these Gentlemen and perhaps some others have been taken in by Penet who was an adventurer and a very bad Man and may Perhaps have in some Measure imposed on them by shewing the Powers he had from this Government, but they never could have advanced the Money to the State or intended to look to it for Payment as will appear by Penets Letters who tells us he could obtain nothing on his Powers till Doctor Franklin should authenticate them which the Doctor Prudently declined,[12] and the State never thought fit to ask the favor of him to do it, but rather rejoiced on his refusal. This is as full a State of the Transactions of Penet and his Demands against us as I can at present give you. when what is due will be paid I know not, or to whom it will be paid, if it should be left to me I shall give it to those who really furnish'd the Goods and to no other Person. The Account was given in to the Assembly by the commercial Agent in his List of Debts, and by them ordered to be paid when the Treasurer should be in Cash and I suppose will be so if the Gentlemen can settle the Matter amongst themselves who is to receive it.[13] I am altogether disappointed in my Expectations of Arms and Ammunition from France Mr. Barclay informs me the Count De Vergen[nes] has revoked his Powers and will not furnish them. is not this refusal to be attributed to our Breach of Faith?[14] if we have an Invasion and our Country is once more overrun by the Enemy for want of them what ought to be the Portion of those who occasioned it? I dare say you will join with me in saying a Rope. With respect I am Gentlemen Yrs: &c.

B. H.

[1] Delegates to Harrison, 18 Mar. 1783, and nn. 2 and 3. Harrison's comment must have been galling to Arthur Lee, if he read this letter after his return to Philadelphia on 24 April. See JM Notes, 13 Feb., and n. 6; Randolph to JM, 15 Mar., and n. 4; JM to Randolph, 1 Apr. 1783, and n. 9.

[2] For the bankruptcy of Penet d'Acosta Frères et Cie of Nantes, see *Papers of Madison*, IV, 108, 1st n. 2; 175, n. 4; V, 185; 186, n. 3; 195, n. 1.

[3] By "most sacred Promises," Harrison probably referred to the resolutions of the Virginia General Assembly in May 1782 (McIlwaine, *Official Letters*, III, 238–39). The Assembly in its session of May 1779, when Harrison was speaker of the House of Delegates, had empowered Governor Jefferson to contract with the Penet company for "the most speedy importation of arms and military stores" from France (*JHDV*, May 1779, p. 66; McIlwaine, *Official Letters*, II, 23–28, and esp. 25–26; Hening, *Statutes*, X, 15). Thereafter until January 1782 the company served as Virginia's foreign agent for the purchase of similar articles (*JCSV*, III, 34). The "Gentlemen" who influenced the Assembly in its May 1782 session to thwart Governor Harrison's plan to use state-owned vessels for transporting war matériel from France are unknown, but probably included Arthur and Richard Henry Lee (*Papers of Madison*, IV, 42, and n. 1; 43, nn. 2, 4; 44, n. 5; 307, n. 11; 356–57; 361, nn. 33, 34, 36; V, 195, n. 1; 355; Harrison to JM, 4 Jan. 1783, and nn. 3, 6; McIlwaine, *Official Letters*, III, 241, 350–51).

[4] For Thomas Barclay, whose appointment by Virginia preceded by over two months his appointment by Congress to settle the accounts of the United States in Europe, see *JCSV*, III, 142; *Papers of Madison*, IV, 113, n. 6; 280, n. 4; 291, n. 20; 325, n. 3; V, 195, n. 1; 290, n. 4. For Captain Joshua Barney, see Delegates to Harrison, 18 Feb. 1783, n. 3.

5 Harrison was summarizing what he had written about the Penet affair to Barclay in letters of 6 September and 11 November, and especially to George Mason, Jr., in Nantes on 30 September 1782 (McIlwaine, *Official Letters*, III, 318–19, 335–36, 374). See also *ibid.*, III, 328–29, 378–80.

6 JM's term as delegate from Virginia had terminated before Harrison on 26 December 1783 acknowledged to Barclay receipt of his letter concerning the Penet company's "Accounts" with Virginia (Executive Letter Book, 1783–1786, p. 254, MS in Va. State Library).

7 For the ship "Franklin," which docked at Philadelphia on 21 June 1781 with a cargo including "Merchandise" for Virginia bought by Penet and Company with money borrowed from Coulignac and Company, see *Papers of Madison*, III, 184–85; 185, nn. 4, 5; 186, nn. 7–10; 191, n. 3; 231, and n. 1. The ship "Duke of Leinster," while carrying some of the same consignment of goods, was captured at sea by the British. The bankruptcy of Penet accounts for the appeal to Virginia by Coulignac and Company in August 1782 for £85 14s. 6d. as reimbursement to that firm for the wares which it had purchased on Penet's account for shipment in the two vessels (*Cal. of Va. State Papers*, III, 260). In a letter on 29 March 1783 to Barclay, Harrison stated that the "books" of the commercial agent of Virginia showed that the state owed Penet a balance of 77,502 livres tournois for the cargoes of those ships and of "Le Comité" (Executive Letter Book, 1783–1786, p. 83, MS in Va. State Library).

8 For the complicated and long-extended issue of the goods aboard "Le Comité," see *Papers of Madison*, I, 295, n. 2; II, 228, and n. 4; 247, n. 2; 313, and nn. 4, 6, 8; III, 47, n. 10; 109, n. 6.

9 David Ross, commercial agent of Virginia from 27 December 1780 to 2 April 1782, and William Hay, from 24 May to 21 October 1782 (*JCSV*, II, 278; III, 97; McIlwaine, *Official Letters*, II, 317; III, 234, n. 56; *Papers of Madison*, V, 218, n. 6).

10 Daniel Bordeaux (d. 1815) was a prominent merchant and slave trader of Charleston (*South Carolina Historical and Genealogical Magazine*, XL [1939], 67; LXV [1964], 211).

11 For Louis Auly, alias Lewis Abraham Pauly, see Livingston to Delegates, 15 Mar., and n. 1; Delegates to Harrison, 18 Mar. 1783, and hdn. In his memorial, Auly claimed that by loaning money to Penet, endorsing his defaulted notes, and paying other charges—all connected with Penet's activities as agent of Virginia—he was owed by Penet a total of about 92,352 livres tournois. Of this sum, "Judgement has been obtained at the Consulate of Nantz against Penet" for 46,535 livres, expended by Auly for the "divers Articles" shipped in the "Franklin" and "Duke of Leinster." The exports had also cost Auly, on Penet's behalf, over 2,624 livres for "duties, expences, & commission." To enable Penet to render other services for Virginia, Auly claimed that he had endorsed Penet's "Bills drawn on Pauly of Paris" for a loan of 36,400 livres (*Papers of Madison*, IV, 175, n. 4).

12 In his letter of 6 December 1782 to Harrison, Barclay enclosed the copy of an "advertisement" intended to be placed in "the Paris Gazette and some other General Papers," as a warning that Barclay alone was authorized to act as Virginia's agent abroad (MS in Va. State Library). Besides the advertisement, Barclay's letter originally enclosed a copy of a letter of 11 November 1782 to "Penet De Costa freres & Co," to which he had "never received any answer"; a copy of a letter to Vergennes respecting the provision of French military matériel for Virginia; and a copy of Vergennes' reply. See also *Papers of Madison*, IV, 42, and n. 1; 227; 230, n. 21; 233, n. 1; 285, nn. 11, 13; 308–9; 313; 316, n. 14; 325, n. 3; V, 278; 279, nn. 3, 4; McIlwaine, *Official Letters*, III, 210–11.

13 *Cal. of Va. State Papers*, III, 328, 340, 344, 403, 447–48; McIlwaine, *Official Letters*, III, 234, 348; *JHDV*, Oct. 1782, pp. 40, 90. Virginia's debt to David Ross for advances of money and goods during his tenure as commercial agent was still unpaid in the autumn of 1787 (Hening, *Statutes*, XII, 428).

[14] McIlwaine, *Official Letters*, III, 378. In his letter of 29 March 1783 to Barclay (n. 12), Harrison expressed regret because the Comte de Vergennes had refused "to furnish the Arms and Ammunition that are so much wanted for the Defence of the State," and asked Barclay to seek a "Loan of one half of" the munitions "formerly required." Harrison also directed Barclay to secure vouchers from the creditors of Penet, insofar as his transactions for Virginia were concerned, and to forward them as soon as possible (Executive Letter Book, 1783–1786, MS in Va. State Library, pp. 83–86). Over two months elapsed before Harrison again mentioned the Penet issue in a letter to the delegates (Harrison to Delegates, 31 May 1783, MS in Va. State Library).

From Edmund Randolph

RC (LC: Madison Papers). Unsigned but in Randolph's hand. Cover addressed by him to "The honble James Madison jr. esq. of congress Philadelphia." Docketed by JM, "March 29th. 1783."

RICHMOND March 29. 1783.

MY DEAR SIR

I have just returned from Wmsburg, the seat of a majority of the keenest pursuers of my father's estate. Nothing, I believe, will content them, but a fair experiment at law: and to guard against this is my object in retaining for the present my office of Attorney general.[1] I do not mean, however, by this, that the adhering to it would be desireable by me at any other [se]ason, than this. For at no other would the salary be equal, [a]s you rightly conceive, to the profits of the other side.[2] But it is easily foreseen, that the next session will limit, if not wholly abolish, executions, and thus cut off the means of supporting my family, except with great difficulty.[3]

Among the confederates in forging tobacco notes, &c., two penitents have appeared. Their evidence will be pointed against the inspector, who has been the cornerstone of the villainy. But it is suggested, and with much shew of truth, that an inspector cannot forge his own name. If it should be so adjudged, his acquittal is certain.[4]

While in Wmsburg, I found a cause depending in the admiralty, the capital point of which is, to decide, whether a capture by a vessel not commissioned, pursuing indeed the course of her voyage, but not repelling a previous attack, is legal. The ordinance is to my apprehension clear enough against my client, the captor: and yet in the eccentricity of human opinion we may catch some advantage, by shewing, that altho' it enumerates certain persons, capable of capturing, it does not in express terms, exclude all others and therefore as the right of capturing without

415

a commission exists, according to Grotius and Lee under the law of nations, it still exists, the ordinance having no negative words.[5]

Mr. Wm. Short will probably lose his election. Dr. Walker, who is one of the candidates, will undoubtedly be chosen, and Colo. Nicholas, who is the other, has the murmur of the people strongly in his favor.[6] The latter gentleman was at the first breaking of the impost to him, vehement against its revival: but he has seen the subject since in a more dispassionate light, and will, I believe, adopt fit measures for our salvation.[7]

In the neighbouring county of New-Kent, I have been informed, that one of the candidates, whose interest seems to increase, makes his court to the freeholders by declaring himself against executions and taxes.[8] The suspension of the former I advocate now, as I always have: and if british debts should be soon recoverable, that suspension ought not to be taken off, until many years after the firm establishment of our government.[9] I do not discover, that the provisional articles fix a future day for their recovery. If recoverable immediately, may they not indanger us, by the possibility of a relapse into the arms of G. B. if not by a restoration of dependence, at least by a destructive connection? Let a merciless british creditor grant indulgence on condition of favoring G. B. in some particular form.[10] What is to be the consequence?

I wish to learn, whether Congress assented to the publication of Mr. Morris's letter of resignation? This letter, united with Rivington's late account of all the monthly payments from the different states, will constitute a delightful regale of Shelburne's duplicity.[11]

---

[1] In retaining the attorney generalship, Randolph evidently planned to shield himself behind a privilege of office long established in English legal precedent. He could not be sued in a Virginia inferior court because he was an officer of the state superior courts. During sessions of the superior courts, a suit entered therein against him would be deferred, for he would then be engaged in the performance of public duty (Edward Jenks, "The Story of *Habeas Corpus*," in Association of American Law Schools, a committee, comp. and ed., *Select Essays in Anglo-American Legal History* [3 vols.; Boston, 1907–9], II, 531–48).

[2] JM to Randolph, 11 Feb., and n. 3; 18 Mar. 1783.

[3] By "executions" Randolph referred to the enforcement of judgments respecting private debts. A statute of 1 July 1782, as amended on 22 December 1782, suspended the payment of debts owed to British creditors (*Papers of Madison*, IV, 361, n. 40; V, 264, n. 2; 310, n. 10). Randolph implied that by continuing as attorney general during the present "[se]ason," he might be freed, by effecting a settlement with his father's creditors, to resume his private practice, but a stay law would no doubt lessen his income by reducing the number of his clients. See Randolph to JM, 1 Feb., and n. 5; 7 Mar.; 22 Mar. 1783.

[4] Randolph to JM, 1 Mar., and nn. 2, 3; 15 Mar. 1783. Thomas Chiles of Caroline County was the "penitent" who, by turning state's evidence in exchange for an

executive pardon, enabled Colonel Samuel Temple to arrest the other "confederates" (*JCSV*, III, 230–31; *Va. Gazette*, 29 Mar. 1783). Being a key witness and fearing that his confession had imperiled his life, Chiles was protected, at least until after the trial, by a guard of militia provided at Governor Harrison's direction (*JCSV*, III, 241, 268; *Cal. of Va. State Papers*, III, 466, 474). By 1785, perhaps still apprehensive for his own safety, Chiles had left Caroline County (Caroline County Court Records, Personal Property Tax Books, 1783–1785, MSS in Va. State Library).

The most notorious of the criminals was John Purcell. After his escape from the jail at Fredericksburg, his recapture, and his conviction for forgery by the General Court, he escaped from the "public Gaol" at Richmond on 27 October 1783. There were grounds for believing that he had fled to North Carolina (*JCSV*, III, 304, 380; *Va. Gazette*, 29 Mar.; 1, 8, and 22 Nov. 1783; Caroline County Court Records, Order Book, 1781–1785, p. 216, microfilm in Va. State Library; Harrison to the governors of North and South Carolina, 10 Dec. 1783, in Executive Letter Book, 1783–1786, pp. 68, 243–44, MS in Va. State Library).

⁵ The "cause" has not been identified. The crux of the matter, legally considered, was the stipulation of the ordinance, largely drafted by Randolph and enacted by Congress on 4 December 1781, confining a legitimate prize to one taken by a vessel which had participated in the fight. Neither the ordinance nor Hugo Grotius in *De jure belli ac pacis* required the captor to be "commissioned" with a letter of marque, but Grotius failed to mention the obligation of the captor to have taken part in the battle occasioning the capture (*JCC*, XXI, 1153–58, esp. p. 1156; *Papers of Madison*, III, 217–21; 235–43, esp. 238; Hugo Grotius, *De jure belli ac pacis*, II, [1925], 626–27, 663–66, 788–90).

"Lee" was Sir George Lee (1700–1758), dean of arches and a lord commissioner of appeals in prize cases, 1753–1758. Randolph probably had consulted Sir George Lee, Sir George Paul, *et al.*, *Report on Procedure in Prize Cases* (London, 1753). "It was a principle of English and foreign Admiralty law that a captor without commission had no legal title to his prize," although exceptions were occasionally made (Richard Pares, *Colonial Blockade and Neutral Rights, 1739–1763* [Oxford, 1938], pp. 3 and n., 101, 105, 146).

⁶ About a week after Randolph wrote the present letter, elections to the Senate and House of Delegates of the General Assembly were held in Virginia. In Albemarle County neither Dr. Thomas Walker, who was seeking re-election as a delegate, nor William Short, who had entered the lists for the first time, was elected. Those chosen were George Nicholas and Edward Carter (Swem and Williams, *Register*, p. 17). For Walker, see *Papers of Madison*, I, 242, n. 3; for Short, *ibid.*, III, 270, n. 2.

George Nicholas (*ca.* 1749–1799), who had moved to Albemarle County after serving as a delegate from Hanover County in 1781, was elected in 1783 and again in 1786–1788 (Swem and Williams, *Register*, pp. 17, 23, 26). A son of Robert Carter Nicholas, he was graduated from the College of William and Mary in 1772, rose to the rank of lieutenant colonel in the continental army between 1776 and 1777, and served as an aide-de-camp to Governor Thomas Nelson in 1781 (McIlwaine, *Official Letters*, I, 98 and n. 124, 105; III, 48, 61; *JCSV*, I, 73, 325, 339; II, 468). Admitted to the bar in the autumn of 1778, Nicholas was appointed acting attorney general of Virginia during Randolph's absence as a delegate to Congress late in 1781 and early in 1782 (*JCSV*, II, 187, 402; III, 4). In the session of May 1781 of the General Assembly, probably influenced by Patrick Henry, Nicholas was among the delegates most critical of Thomas Jefferson's conduct as governor (Boyd, *Papers of Jefferson*, IV, 261–62, 264, 268; VI, 105–9), but subsequently became Jefferson's firm supporter. In 1788 Nicholas was a prominent member of the Virginia convention that ratified the Federal Constitution. After moving to Kentucky in 1790, he served as principal draftsman of the first constitution of that state and its first attorney general.

Between 1785 and 1795 he corresponded frequently with JM (LC: Madison Papers). See Huntley Dupre, "The Political Ideas of George Nicholas," *Register of the Kentucky State Historical Society*, XXXIX [1941], 201–23.

⁷ The vote on 6 and 7 December 1782, by which the Virginia General Assembly repealed its ratification of the proposed impost amendment to the Articles of Confederation, was not tallied in the journal of the House of Delegates (*JHDV*, Oct. 1782, pp. 55, 58). There is no evidence that a serious attempt was made in the session of May 1783 of the General Assembly to revive the impost act.

⁸ New Kent County is immediately east of Henrico County, where Randolph lived. In the April elections the incumbents, Colonel William Dandridge, Jr. (1743–1822), and John Watkins (d. *ca.* 1787), were re-elected as delegates from New Kent County to the Virginia General Assembly (*Lineage Book of the National Society of the Daughters of the American Revolution*, CXL [1934], 100; New Kent County Records, Personal Property Tax Book, 1787, MS in Va. State Library; Swem and Williams, *Register*, pp. 16, 18). Possibly Randolph's reference was to an unsuccessful candidate. If he meant either of the incumbents, Dandridge was considerably the larger holder of realty and personalty, but by the same token he could have been the larger debtor (New Kent County Records, Land Tax Books, 1783–1787; Property Tax Books, 1783–1787, MSS in Va. State Library). On 20 June 1783 a vote was tallied in the House of Delegates on a motion to suspend until the October session further consideration of a bill "for the relief of debtors." Neither Dandridge's nor Watkins' name appears in the tally (*JHDV*, May 1783, p. 70).

⁹ Randolph to JM, 7 Feb.; 15 Feb.; 9 May; 24 May 1783. Randolph's point of view may have reflected in some degree the pressure upon him by his father's creditors (Randolph to JM, 7 Mar. 1783, and citations in n. 4). See also *Papers of Madison*, IV, 357–58; 361, n. 40.

¹⁰ Article IV of the provisional articles of peace between Great Britain and the United States stated only: "It is agreed that creditors on either side shall meet with no lawful impediment to the recovery of the full value, in sterling money, of all *bona fide* debts heretofore contracted" (Wharton, *Revol. Dipl. Corr.*, VI, 98). See JM to Randolph, 8 Apr. 1783, and n. 2.

¹¹ Randolph to JM, 15 Jan., and n. 13; 15 Mar.; 22 Mar. 1783, and n. 10; JM Notes, 26 Feb., and n. 14; 27 Feb. 1783. For James Rivington, publisher of the *Royal Gazette* of New York City, see *Papers of Madison*, I, 133, n. 5. For the Earl of Shelburne's alleged duplicity, see Randolph to JM, 3 Jan.; Delegates to Harrison, 18 Mar., n. 4; JM Notes, 12–15 Mar., and n. 4; 19 Mar. 1783, and nn. 7, 12.

Report on Robert R. Livingston's Funds

MS (NA: PCC, No. 19, III, fol. 595). In JM's hand, except as mentioned in n. 4, below. Docketed by Charles Thomson: "Report of Mr Madison Mr Rutlidge Mr Fitzsimmons On Letter 28 March Secy forn Affairs. delivered March 31. 1783. Recd. Entd. Debated May 16 1783 postponed. March 1. 1785 Referred to Mr [Samuel] Hardy Mr [John] Beatty Mr [Elbridge] Gerry."

[31 March 1783]

The Committee to whom was refd. a letter from the Secy. of F. A. of the 28th. inst; informing Congs. that there remain in his hands about

7300 dollars, savd. from the Salaries of the Foreign Ministers by the course of Exchange during the last year; and requesting some order of Congs. relative to the disposition thereof;[1] Recommend that in consideration of the expences incurred by the sd Secy since his appt. beyond the Salary annexed to it; as appears by his letter of   day of   [2] & of the extra ser[v]ice [dis]charged by him in transacting the business from which the savings abovemd. have resulted,[3] he be allowed to retain   dollars out of the same, & that he be directed to place the residue in the hands of the Superintendent. of Finance.[4]

[1] In his letter of 28 March to President Elias Boudinot, Livingston pointed out that, preparatory to "leaving" the Department of Foreign Affairs on 1 April, he wished to settle all of his financial accounts. Among these was a balance of 38,332 livres, equivalent "at par to about" $7,310 (Wharton, *Revol. Dipl. Corr.*, VI, 350–51). For the referral of the letter to the committee on 28 March 1783, see NA: PCC, No. 186, fol. 90.

[2] In his letter of 2 December 1782, making known to Congress his intention of resigning, Livingston stated that his annual expenses as secretary for foreign affairs exceeded his $4,000 salary by at least $3,000 (*Papers of Madison*, V, 338, n. 4).

[3] In his letter of 28 March 1783, Livingston mentioned that his "extra service" had included acting, at "some trouble and risk," as disbursing "agent" for Henry Laurens, one of the American peace commissioners (Wharton, *Revol. Dipl. Corr.*, VI, 351). In similar fashion Livingston had helped John Adams and Francis Dana, minister-designate to the court of Tsarina Catherine the Great of Russia (*ibid.*, V, 862–63; VI, 375). The regulations of 10 January 1781, by which the duties of the secretary for foreign affairs were defined, did not oblige him to act as a disbursing agent (*JCC*, XIX, 43–44). He could have served in this capacity only by authorization of Robert Morris. On 14 September 1782 Congress adopted JM's motion to inform the "several public ministers" overseas "that the care and management of all monies" obtained in Europe could be "disposed of" only by the superintendent of finance in accord with appropriations made by Congress (*Papers of Madison*, V, 124–25). The salaries of those "public ministers" were derived from the foreign loans.

[4] Robert Morris. On 8 May 1783, upon the recommendation of a committee, Congress resolved that henceforward the secretary for foreign affairs should share in determining the political and economic policies of the United States in its international relations but failed to act upon the committee's proposal to increase his salary to $8,000. The next day Livingston informed Congress that financial considerations obliged him to resign (*Papers of Madison*, V, 337, n. 2; *JCC*, XXIV, 334–35, 336–37). Expectation that there soon would be a final accounting with him may partially explain why action on the present report was postponed after being debated on 16 May 1783.

On the manuscript are notes, not written by JM, which perhaps further reveal the nature of that debate and the reason for the inconclusive outcome. Immediately following "disposition thereof" is a single bracket, inserted heavily in ink. Along the left margin, embracing all of the committee's proposal after the word "Recommend," is a wavy, ink-drawn, single parenthesis, curving below the last line of the report. Below this Abraham Clark wrote, "Whereupon ordered that the money in the hands of the secretary of foreign affairs be paid to the Superintendt of finance." This passage is canceled with crosshatches in ink. Below the passage is a second one, also in Clark's hand and deleted, reading, "Whereupon ordered that the money in the hands of the secretary of foreign affairs, saved from the salaries of foreign ministers by the Course of exchange, be placed in the hands of the Superindt of finance." These two attempted emendations appear to signify, for reasons noted below, that, after the debate on 16 May had demonstrated the unacceptability of the committee's recommendation, the manuscript of the report was handed to Clark.

On the docket page of the manuscript, Clark erroneously noted that Livingston had been appointed on 4, instead of 10, August 1781; that his personal expenses connected with the office dated from 1 October 1781; that during the fourteen months from that date to 2 December 1782, when he expressed his intention of resigning, he claimed to have spent $3,000, or $214 a month, more than his salary; and, therefore, that his out-of-pocket costs from 2 December 1782 to the close of May 1783 would be about $1,200, making a total of $4,500. The fact that Clark extended the estimate until the close of May makes almost certain that he wrote these jottings and his suggested amendments to the committee's report during the debate on 16 May. See *JCC*, XXI, 851–52, 1028; XXIII, 759; Wharton, *Revol. Dipl. Corr.*, VI, 100.

On 4 June 1783 Congress thanked Livingston "for his services during his continuance in office" (*JCC*, XXIV, 382). See also Boyd, *Papers of Jefferson*, VI, 275–76; George Dangerfield, *Chancellor Robert R. Livingston*, pp. 177–80.

Notes on Debates

MS (LC: Madison Papers). For a description of the manuscript of Notes on Debates, see *Papers of Madison*, V, 231–34.

Monday March 31.

A letter was recd. from the Govr, of R. Island with resolutions of the Legislature of that State justifying the conduct of Mr. Howell.[1]

On the arrival of the French Cutter with the acct of the signing of the general preliminaries, it was thought fit by Congress to hasten the effect of them by calling in the American Cruisers.[2] It was also thought by all not amiss to notify simply the Intelligence to the British Commanders at N.Y.[3] In addition to this it was proposed by the Secy. of F. A. and urged by the Delegates of Pa. by Mr. Lee, Mr. Rutlidge & others, that Congress should signify their desire & expectation that hostilities sd. be suspended at sea on the part of the Enemy.[4] The arguments urged were that the effusion of blood might be immediately stopped & the trade of this Country rescued from depredation. It was observed on the other side that such a proposition derogated from the dignity of Congs.; shewed an undue precipitancy; that the intelligence was not authentic enough to justify the British commander in complying with such an overture; and therefore that Congs. would be exposed to the mortification of a refusal. The former considerations prevailed & a *verbal* sanction was given to Mr. Livingston's expressing to the sd. Commanders the expectation of Congs. &c. This day their answers were recd. addressed to Robt. R. Livingston Esqr. &c&c&c. declining to accede to the stopping of hostilities at sea, & urging the necessity of authentic orders from G. B. for that purpose.[5] With their letters Mr. Livingston communicated resolutions proposed from his office, "that inconsequence of these letters the orders to the American Cruisers sd. be revoked; and that the Executives sd. be requested to embargo all vessels.["] Congs. were generally sensible after the rect. of these papers that they had committed themselves in proposing to the British Commanders at N.Y. a stop to naval hostilities; & were exceedingly at a loss to extricate themselves. On one side they were unwilling to publish to the world the affront they had recd. especially as no written order had been given for the correspondence and on the other it was necessary that the continuance of hostilities at sea should be made known to American Citizens. Some were in favor of the revocation of hostilities. others proposed as Col: Bland & Genl. Mifflin, that the Secy of F. A. should be directed verbally to publish the letters from Carlton & Digby. This was negatived. The superinscription was animadverted upon particularly by Mr. Mercer, who said that the letters ought to have been sent back unopened. Finally it was agreed that any member might take copies & send them to the press & that the subject should lie over for further consideration[6]

1 JM Notes, 3 Jan., and n. 3; 9–10 Jan., and n. 21; 4 Feb., n. 14; JM to Randolph, 14 Jan. 1783, and n. 5; JCC, XXIV, 222, n. 2. The resolutions of the Rhode Island General Assembly are printed in William R. Staples, Rhode Island in the Continental Congress, pp. 427–28.

2 From the opening of this paragraph to the sentence beginning "This day their answers," JM summarized proceedings of Congress on 24 March. See JM Notes, 24 Mar., and n. 1; Delegates to Harrison, 25 Mar. 1783, and nn. 2, 4.

3 General Sir Guy Carleton and Admiral Robert Digby (Papers of Madison, I, 291, n. 2; III, 198, n. 6).

4 In separate dispatches of 24 March, carried under flag by Lewis Morris, Jr., one of Robert R. Livingston's secretaries, Livingston expressed to Carleton and Digby hope that they would follow the example of the French and of Congress by "adopting such measures as humanity dictates" to "prevent the further effusion of blood at sea" (Wharton, Revol. Dipl. Corr., VI, 336–37; Burnett, Letters, VII, 102, n. 4; Fitzpatrick, Writings of Washington, XXV, 413, and nn. 15, 16; XXVI, 258 n.). The delegates from Pennsylvania, present in Congress, were Thomas Mifflin, Thomas FitzSimons, Richard Peters, James Wilson, and Joseph Montgomery (JCC, XXIV, 219, 224).

5 The significance of JM's underlining of "verbal" becomes clear later in his notes for this day. Copies in the Papers of the Continental Congress show Carleton's reply of 26 March to have been addressed to "Robert R. Livingston, Esq. &c &c," and Digby's of 27 March to "Robert R. Livingston, Esqr." Both answers reached Livingston on 30 March, the day on which he sent them, with a brief covering note, to Congress (NA: PCC, No. 119, fols. 261–64; Wharton, Revol. Dipl. Corr., VI,

346). The British commanders suggested that upon receiving official notification of peace, which they daily expected, there should be a general release of prisoners as well as a cessation of war at sea. Digby further recommended that until that word reached the British headquarters in New York City, Congress could protect American ships by forbidding them to leave port.

6 For the "superinscription," see n. 5; also Delegates to Harrison, 1 Apr. 1783; Burnett, *Letters*, VII, 121–22, 125, 128, 132. The letters of Carleton and Digby to Livingston are printed in the *Pennsylvania Gazette* of 2 April and the *Pennsylvania Packet* of 3 April 1783.

Congress apparently gave no "further consideration" to the dilemma before it was resolved on 9 April by the receipt of dispatches from Carleton and Digby enclosing copies of the preliminary articles of peace between Great Britain, France, and Spain, signed on 20 January; the British peace commissioners' "Declaration of the Cessation of Hostilities" on that day; and the announcement of King George III on 14 February proclaiming "a Cessation of Arms." See Jefferson to JM, 7–8 Feb., nn. 3, 4, 8; *Pa. Packet* broadside of 9 Apr.; JM Notes, 10 Apr. 1783; Wharton, *Revol. Dipl. Corr.*, VI, 223–24, 251–52.

From Edmund Pendleton

Tr (LC: Force Transcripts). In the left margin at the top of the transcription, Peter Force's clerk wrote "MSS [Mc]Guire's." See *Papers of Madison*, I, xxii, xxiii. A passage, also taken from the original letter, but occasionally varying in spelling, punctuation, and capitalization from the present text, is in Stan. V. Henkel's Catalogue No. 694 (1892), p. 92.

EDMUNDSBURY,[1] March 31st, 1783

MY DEAR SIR:

I yesterday evening return'd from my Visit and found yr favr of the 24th (that of the 11th I believe has been acknowledged) conveying me the long wish'd for & glorious Intelligence; which I cordially wish we may have virtue & social spirit enough to reap the full fruits of:[2] I think the Peace upon the whole a very liberal one;[3] and therefore most likely to be durable—never was so Important a Revolution as Ours, so cheaply, and in so short a time purchased; the value of which, I hope we shall not estimate by the price, but by its Intrinsic worth. The Payment of British debts does not set well on the stomachs of people in general here; you know my sentiments always were that a National War, tho' it might suspend, ought not to destroy the Contracts or engagements of Individuals.[4] The restitution of confiscated property, is touched so gently, as to produce no effect I imagine, tho' for myself I declare, that in this state, I believe it would produce in general, good rather than evil, the lands being in the hands of worse Citizens than they were taken from:[5] how-

422

ever I am my self no ways concerned either with the debts or property, and therefore shall leave it to the Legislature whose province it is to determine how the treaty is to be performed.[6] It is probably on these Accounts that contests are very warm amongst the Land estates[7] for our approaching Elections, which commence this week, & we shall soon see what is like to be the cast of them.[8] We have in Goal several notorious forgers of Inspn & Mr Morris's notes, and are hunting more of the Party discovered by two of the Gang, who have received their pardons in reward for the discovery. One case is a singular one and engages the ingenuity of the Bar; it is of an Inspection of tobo charged wth Forging the notes of his own Inspection,[9] which those Gentn say is no Felony, but a breach of Trust, since by his office he had power to Issue the notes; and argue that the Objection is strongly fortified by a clause in the tobacco Laws, which subjects the Insprs. to a disability to hold any office & to a pecuniary Penalty for issuing notes for tobacco not actually received into the Warehouses, which they urges is all this man's offence —how the[y] will succeed will soon be determined.[10] My journey has so shaken my nerves that I can scarcely write—so begging my Complts to Mr Jones & joining in cordial congratulations wth you both on the memorable 20th of Jany[11] I conclude

    Yr very Affe friend

EDMD PENDLETON

1 Pendleton to JM, 17 and 24 Feb. 1783, and n. 2.

2 Pendleton to JM, 15 Mar. 1783, and n. 13. JM's letters of 11 and 24 March to Pendleton have not been found. See Pendleton to JM, 17 and 24 Feb., n. 3. In order to reach Pendleton by 30 March, JM's letter of 24 March must have been delivered at Edmundsbury, Caroline County, by the special courier who left Philadelphia on the twenty-fourth with letters of that date from the Virginia delegates to Harrison and from JM to James Maury and to Edmund Randolph (qq.v.).

3 Delegates to Harrison, 24 Mar. 1783, and nn. 1–4.

4 Papers of Madison, IV, 361, n. 39; V, 409; JM Notes, 16 Jan., and n. 4; 20 Mar., and n. 2; JM to Randolph, 12 Mar. 1783, and n. 5.

5 Papers of Madison, IV, 361, n. 38; V, 80; 81, n. 5; 110; 111, n. 8; 111–12; 112, n. 11; JM Notes, 12–15 Mar.; Delegates to Harrison, 12 Mar. 1783, and n. 12.

6 Randolph to JM, 29 Mar. 1783, and n. 10.

7 If "Land estates" is not an erroneous transcription by Peter Force's clerk, Pendleton probably meant plantation owners who owed British creditors for debts incurred before the Revolution, and who in some instances had increased their landed "Estates" by purchasing acreage which Virginia had confiscated from absentee British or Loyalist titleholders.

8 Randolph to JM, 29 Mar. 1783, and n. 6. In the April elections the voters of Caroline County, where Pendleton lived, returned Robert Gilchrist to the Virginia House of Delegates but replaced John Page with John Taylor (Swem and Williams, Register, pp. 15, 17). For Gilchrist, see Papers of Madison, IV, 171–72; 173, n. 14. Although John Taylor of Caroline, only thirty years of age, had already served

three terms as a delegate, he was still at the outset of his distinguished career (*ibid.*, III, 37, n. 16; Swem and Williams, *Register*, pp. 8, 11, 13). See Pendleton to JM, 14 Apr. 1783. The earliest extant land-tax records for Caroline County show that each of these men was a substantial owner in his home county. In 1787 Gilchrist paid taxes on 1,510 acres of land, Page on 3,992½, and Taylor on 1,123 (Caroline County Land-Tax Book, 1787, MS in Va. State Library).

9 Instead of "Inspection of tobo" Pendleton probably wrote "Inspector of tobo." See Randolph to JM, 29 Mar., and n. 4. For Robert Morris' notes, see *Papers of Madison*, V, 271; 430; 431, n. 4; Randolph to JM, 1 Mar. 1783, n. 2. For the law of 2 July 1782, to which Pendleton referred, see Minute Book, House of Delegates, May 1782, p. 86, MS in Va. State Library; Hening, *Statutes*, XI, 95–98. On 28 June 1783 the loopholes existing in that measure were closed by the enactment of a long and detailed statute. See Randolph to JM, 1 Mar. 1783, n. 2.

10 *Ibid.*, n. 2. The copyist probably erred in adding an "s" to "urges."

11 Joseph Jones, who took weekly turns with JM in corresponding with Pendleton (*Papers of Madison*, V, 97; 98, n. 12; 158, nn. 6, 8). For the "memorable 20th of Jany," see JM Notes, 31 Mar. 1783, n. 6.

Notes on Debates

MS (LC: Madison Papers). For a description of the manuscript of Notes on Debates, see *Papers of Madison*, V, 231–34.

No. XIII[1]

Tuesday April 1. 1783.

Mr. Ghorum called for the order of the day to wit the Report on Revenue &c.[2] and observed as a cogent reason for hastening that business that the Eastern States at the invitation of the Legislature of Massts. were with N.Y. about to form a convention for regulating matters of common concern, & that if any plan sd. be sent out by Congs. during their session, they would probably cooperate with Congs. in giving effect to it.[3]

Mr. Mercer expressed great disquietude at this information, considered it as a dangerous precedent, & that it behoved the Gentleman to explain fully the objects of the Convention, as it would be necessary for the S. States to be otherwise very circumspect in agreeing to any plans on a supposition that the general confederacy was to continue.[4]

Mr. Osgood said that the sole object was to guard agst. an interference of taxes among States, whose local situation required such precautions: and that if nothing was defi[ni]tively concluded without the previous communication to & sanction of Congs. the confederation could not be said to be in any manner departed from; but that in fact nothing was intended that could be drawn within the purview of the fœderal articles.[5]

Mr. Bland said he had always considered those Conventions as improper & contravening the spirit of the fœderal Governmt. He said they had the appearance of young Congresses.[6]

Mr. Ghorum explains as Mr. Osgood.

Mr. Madison & Mr. Hamilton disapproved of these partial conventions, not as absolute violations of the Confederacy, but as ultimately leading to them & in the mean time exciting pernicious jealousies; the latter observing that he wished instead of them to see a general Convention take place & that he sd. soon in pursuance of instructions from his Constituents, propose to Congs. a plan for that purpose. the object wd. be to strengthen the fœderal Constitution.[7]

Mr. White informed Congs. that N. Hampshire had declined to accede to the plan of the Convention on foot.[8]

Mr. Higginson said that no Gentleman need be alarmed at any rate for it was pretty certain that the Convention would not take place. He wished with Mr. Hamilton to see a General Convention for the purpose of revising and amending the fœderal Government.[9]

These observations having put an end to the subject, Congs. resumed the Report on Revenue &c. Mr. Hamilton who had been absent when the last question was taken for substituting numbers in place of the value of land, moved to reconsider that vote.[10] He was 2ded. by Mr. Osgood. See the Journal. Those who voted differently from their former votes were influenced by the conviction of the necessity of the change & despair on both sides of a more favorable rate of the Slaves. The rate of ⅗ was agreed to without opposition.[11] On a preliminary question The apportionmt. of the sum & revision of the same refd. to Grand Come.[12] The Report as to the Resignation of Foreign Ministers was taken up & on the case of Mr. Jefferson. See Journal.[13] The Eastern delegates were averse to doing any thing as to Mr. Adams, untill further advices sd. be recd.[14] Mr. Laurens was indulged not without some opposition. The acceptance of his resignation was particularly enforced by Mr. Izard.[15]

[1] For a probable explanation of the Roman numeral, see *Papers of Madison*, V, 231.

[2] Amendment to Report on Public Credit, 28 Mar., and ed. n., and nn. 1, 2, 4, 5; JM Notes, 28 Mar., and nn. 2, 3, 5.

Although unnoted in the journal, Nathaniel Gorham's "call" is *ipso facto* evidence that Congress at the close of the inconclusive discussion on 28 March provided that the issue should either be made the standing order of the day or be taken up specifically on 1 April 1783.

[3] On 13 February the Massachusetts General Court resolved to have Governor John Hancock invite the other New England states and New York to elect com-

missioners to join with three from Massachusetts at Hartford on 30 April 1783 to consider "the necessity of adopting within the said States for their respective Uses such General & uniform system of Taxation by import & excise as may be thought advantageous to the Said States" (Hugh Hastings and J. A. Holden, eds., *Public Papers of George Clinton*, VIII, 65).

4 A meeting of commissioners from New York and the New England states in November 1780 had considered means of conferring more power on the Continental Congress. See *Papers of Madison*, II, 318–19; E. Wilder Spaulding, *New York in the Critical Period*, pp. 163–64.

5 No provision was included in the brief resolution, mentioned in n. 3, for submitting whatever should be agreed upon by the convention to Congress, either for its information or sanction.

6 Members of Congress who held that the convention would violate the "spirit" of the Confederation probably had in mind the following portion of Article VI of the Articles of Confederation: "No two or more states shall enter into any treaty, confederation or alliance whatever between them, without the consent of the united states in congress assembled, specifying accurately the purposes for which the same is to be entered into, and how long it shall continue" (*JCC*, XIX, 216).

7 Many years after writing his notes, JM inserted his surname in place of an "M." For examples of these "partial conventions," see Edmund C. Burnett, *The Continental Congress*, pp. 423, 484–87; *Papers of Madison*, II, 318–19; Boyd, *Papers of Jefferson*, IV, 138–41; Syrett and Cooke, *Papers of Hamilton*, II, 400–18.

Hamilton was referring to resolutions, adopted by the legislature of New York on 20–21 July 1782, calling for "a general Convention of the States, specially authorised to revise and amend the Confederation." Forwarded to Congress on 4 August 1782, these resolutions were still tied up in committee (*ibid.*, III, 110–13 and nn. 2, 4). Although clearly impatient with this procrastination, Hamilton did not draft his own "plan" until July 1783, when Congress was at Princeton. During that month, his last in Congress until 1788, Hamilton found so little support for his proposals that he did not submit them before returning to New York (*ibid.*, III, 420–26; Burnett, *Letters*, VII, lxxi; VIII, xci).

8 On 1 March 1783 the New Hampshire House of Representatives resolved that "the method of laying impost duties proposed" by Massachusetts "will be unequal & hurtful to this State; and as this State impowered Congress to lay such Duties, which they still think preferable to the method proposed by the said Resolve, that it is not best to appoint Delegates as therein proposed" (Nathaniel Bouton *et al.*, comp. and eds., *New Hampshire Provincial and State Papers* [34 vols. to date; Concord, 1867——], VIII, 971–72). Rhode Island and New York also appear to have declined. In a letter to Governor Hancock on 28 February 1783, Governor William Greene of Rhode Island wrote that he had referred the invitation to the General Assembly, but it seems to have adjourned without acting upon the proposal (John Russell Bartlett, ed., *Records of the State of Rhode Island and Providence Plantations in New England* [10 vols.; Providence, 1856–65], IX, 634–76, 685). Although Governor Jonathan Trumbull and the Council of Safety of Connecticut on 24 March 1783 accepted Hancock's invitation by appointing three delegates, the meeting at Hartford evidently did not convene (Charles J. Hoadly *et al.*, eds., *Public Records of Connecticut*, V, 101–2).

9 In a letter of 8 February 1787 to Henry Knox, Stephen Higginson remarked that in 1783 he had "pressed upon Mr. Maddison and others the Idea of a special Convention, for the purpose of revising the Confederation, and increasing the powers of the Union," but they "were as much opposed to this Idea, as I was to the measures they were then pursuing, to effect, as they said, the same thing" (*Annual Report of the American Historical Association for the Year 1896* [2 vols.; Washington, 1897], I, 745).

10 JM Notes on Debates, 28 Mar. 1783. On that day a committee's report, amended so as to apportion tax quotas among the states in accord with the whole number of free inhabitants and three-fifths, rather than one-half, of the number of all other inhabitants, except Indians not taxed, was rejected by a vote of 6 to 5. The vote of New York was ineffective because William Floyd, although in favor of the amendment, was the only delegate present from that state. If Hamilton had attended, the amended report would have been adopted by a 7-to-5 margin (JCC, XXIV, 215–16).

11 By "without opposition," JM meant only that there was no oral dissent respecting "the rate of 3/5," but Massachusetts and Rhode Island still refused to agree to the amended report as a whole. Its adoption was assured by Oliver Wolcott and Eliphalet Dyer of Connecticut, Thomas Sim Lee of Maryland, and John Rutledge and Ralph Izard of South Carolina reversing their votes of 28 March (JCC, XXIV, 222–24).

In a printed copy of the report of the committee on restoring public credit, Benjamin Bankson, Jr., a clerk in the office of the secretary of Congress, embraced in a parenthesis so much of the twelfth paragraph as had been amended by the vote, just mentioned, and wrote alongside the parenthesis, "Aprill 1. reconsidered & report amended & adopted" (NA: PCC, No. 26, fol. 412). See also Report on Restoring Public Credit, 6 Mar., and n. 20; JM Notes, 7 Mar. 1783, ed. n.

12 For a "preliminary question" submitted to the grand committee, see JM Notes, 4 Apr. 1783.

13 On 15 March Congress appointed a committee, Samuel Osgood, chairman, to report on the desire to resign expressed by John Adams in his dispatch of 4 December and by Henry Laurens, in his of 15 December 1782. In a letter to Congress on 26 February 1783, Robert R. Livingston queried whether Francis Dana should not be recalled as minister-designate to the court of Catherine the Great, since his dispatches had pointed out that British interference would most probably restrain the tsarina from recognizing the independence of the United States. This issue, too, was referred by Congress to the committee for consideration.

Congress also instructed the committee to recommend a reply to Jefferson's request of 13 March 1783 for a decision "on the expediency of continuing or of countermanding my mission to Europe" as a peace commissioner (NA: PCC, No. 185, III, 57; No. 186, fol. 88; JM Notes, 12–15 Mar., and n. 1; JM to Randolph, 12 Mar. 1783, and n. 13; Boyd, Papers of Jefferson, VI, 257; Wharton, Revol. Dipl. Corr., V, 752–53, 780–83, 812–14; VI, 106, 133–34, 138–40, 264–65). On 1 April 1783 Congress by a vote of 8 to 1 authorized Livingston to thank Jefferson for his "readiness" to be of public service, but to inform him that "the object" of his "appointment" was "so far advanced" as to render it unnecessary for him to pursue his voyage (JCC, XXIV, 226, and n. 2; Boyd, Papers of Jefferson, VI, 259–60; JM to Randolph, 8 Apr. 1783).

14 Although the Osgood committee recommended that John Adams "have leave to return to America," Congress postponed accepting his resignation (JCC, XXIV, 225; Wharton, Revol. Dipl. Corr., VI, 375). Congress adopted the committee's proposal that Francis Dana be free to return to America, provided he complete any "negociation with the Court of St. Petersburg" in which he may be engaged "at the time of receiving this Resolution" (JCC, XXIV, 226, 227, 267). Dana received this resolution on 21 July, left St. Petersburg about a month later, and reached Boston on 18 December 1783 (W[illiam] P[enn] Cresson, Francis Dana: A Puritan Diplomat at the Court of Catherine the Great [New York, 1930], pp. 303, 317–18).

15 Knowing that the South Carolina General Assembly had elected Henry Laurens to be a delegate in Congress, Ralph Izard probably was the more insistent that Congress sanction Laurens' return to America (JCC, XXIV, 226; Burnett, Letters, VII, lxxv, 137). Laurens did not arrive in the United States until 3 August 1784 (ibid., VII, 585).

Virginia Delegates to Benjamin Harrison

RC (Virginia State Library). In hand of Theodorick Bland, Jr., except for the signatures of the other delegates. Cover franked by Bland and addressed by him to "His Excelly. Benjn: Harrison Esqr. Govr. of Virginia." Docketed, "Letter fr. Virga. Dels Apl 1. 83."

PHILADELPHIA April 1st 1783

Sr.

Your Excelly. will have received by our Express the important Intelligence brought by the Triomphe.[1]

That Intelligence (together with Authenticated Copies of Count D'Estaings dispatches relating to Peace which were received by the Minister of France) was sent into New York immediately by An officer in the department of foreign Affairs, and proposals, founded on the presumption of their Authenticity, were made to Sr. Guy Carleton and Admiral Digby by Congress, that a Suspension of Hostilities should immediately take place both by Sea and Land, that a Stop might be put to the further effusion of Human Blood.[2] However Humane the motives might be which dictated these proposals, we find, the Application has not Succeeded. The British Commanders have Informd Congress that no Authority has reached them from their Court—they could not therefore think themselves Justified in taking such a step—thus Untill that shall arrive, every thing remains with the British in Statu quo, altho the Hands of the French Naval Force in America are tied.[3] Your Excelly will no doubt Judge it proper that this Intelligence may be conveyed as speedily as possible to our Sea Ports, to prevent the Risque which Vessels Sailing in this Critical Juncture might run.[4]

We sincerely wish that your Excelly wd. be pleased to urge to the Assembly at their next meeting, the making a provision for Establishing a Credit for the Delegates in this Place or where Congress may sit, so that they may be Enabled to draw their Salaries as they become due, that they may no longer be Subject to that uncertainty which they have hitherto Experienced, which lays them under every disadvantage in their expenditure, Exposes them to be obliged to borrow frequently on the most Humiliating terms to supply their real necessities, and consigns them to the Hands of Extortionate Usury. [5]

428

We received no Public letter by the last Post.[6]
We are with the most perfect respect Yr. Excellys most obedt. svts

THEOK: BLAND JR.
A. LEE
J. MADISON JR
JOS: JONES.

[1] Delegates to Harrison, 24 Mar., and hdn., and n. 7; 25 Mar. 1783, and n. 4.
[2] Delegates to Harrison, 24 Mar., n. 2; JM Notes, 31 Mar. 1783, and nn. 2–4.
[3] JM Notes, 31 Mar. 1783, and nn. 5, 6.
[4] The *Virginia Gazette* of 5 April printed a copy, attested as accurate by La Luzerne, of the orders directing ships of the French navy to cease hostilities at sea. This issue of the *Gazette* also included a report that Congress had provided for a similar order to be communicated by Robert Morris to American armed vessels, and for Carleton and Digby to be notified thereof. A week later the same newspaper added immediately below a copy of Morris's circular letter of 25 March a statement that the British commanders, lacking orders from King George III, had refused to follow Congress' example. Although the editor of the *Virginia Gazette* probably derived this information from Governor Harrison, there is no other evidence that he "conveyed" the delegates' word of British non-compliance "as speedily as possible to our Sea Ports." See also *Cal. of Va. State Papers*, III, 460–61, 464.
[5] Harrison to Delegates, 12 Apr., and n. 2. See also Delegates to Harrison, 11 Mar. 1783, and n. 4.
[6] Harrison's letter of 20 March, which should have reached Philadelphia "by the last Post," possibly never was received by the delegates. See Harrison to Delegates, 20 March 1783, n. 4.

To Edmund Randolph

RC (LC: Madison Papers). Lacks complimentary close and signature but in JM's hand. Cover missing. Docketed by Randolph, "J. Madison April 1. 1783."

PHILADA. April 1. 1783.

MY DEAR FRIEND

Your favor of the 22. Ulto. verifies my fears that some disappointment would defeat your plan of going into the Legislature.[1] I regret it the more as every day teaches me more & more the necessity of such measures as I know you would have patronized; and as we are losing ground so fast in the temper of the States as to require every possible support. Unless some speedy & adequate provision be made beyond that of the Confederation, the most dismal alternative stares me in the face.[2] And yesterday's post brought us information that the bill repealing the impost had passed the lower house of Massts. and one of like import had made equal progress in the Legislature of S. Carolina.[3] These defections are alarming, but if a few enlightened & disinterested members would step forward in each Legislature as advocates for the necessary plans, I see with so much force the considerations that might be urged, that my hopes would still prevail. If advantage should be taken of popular pre-possessions on one side without such counter-efforts, there is, to be sure, room for nothing but despair.

The extract from [Lee]'s letter recited in yours astonishes me more than it could do you, because I must be more sensible of its contrast to truth.[4] High as my opinion of the object of it was, the judgment & acuteness & patriotism displayed in the last despatches from him, have really enhanced it. So far are they in particular from studiously leaving us in the dark, that some of them are of as late date as any, if not later than those from several & perhaps as voluminous as all the rest put together.[5]

The zeal of Congs. to hasten the effect of the general preliminaries, led them (precipitately as I conceive) to authorise the Secy. of F. A. to notify to Sr. G. Carlton & Adml Digby, the intelligence rcd. by the French Cutter on that subject, with their recall of American Cruisers, in order that correspondent measures might be taken at N. Y. The answers from these Commanders were addressed to Robt. R. Livingston Esqr &c &c &c. and imported that they could not suspend hostilities at sea with-out proper authority from their Sovereign; but as Congress placed full reliance on the authenticity of the intelligence they supposed no objec-tion cd. lie on their part agst. releasing all prisoners &c. A letter from Digby to the French Minister is I am told remarkably su[r]ly & indecent even for a British Admiral.[6] We have recd. no official report of the sign-ing of the General Preliminaries, nor any further particulars relative to them. Your surmize as to the dangerous phraseology which may be used in designating our limits, may be realized, if our Ministers are not cautious, or sd. yield to improper considerations. But I trust that no such defaults will happen on that side: & that even if they should, the lan-guage used by Congress in all their own acts on that head will overpower any arguments that may be drawn from acts of their Ministers.[7]

Mrs. Randolph's & your good wishes were recd. by Mrs. House & Mrs Trist with marks of unfiegned affection. The latter will however speak for herself.[8]

Docr. Lee sets off to day or tomorrow for Virga. but talks of return-ing hither before the meeting of the Legislature, which however he means to attend. His immediate object I suppose is to attend the County election.[9]

¹ *Q.v.*

² By "temper of the States," JM meant their growing unwillingness to compromise and their increasing stress upon state sovereignty, along with numerous evidences of sectionalism. The "dismal alternative" would be a dissolution of the Confederation, possibly accompanied by military coups and civic tumult (JM Notes, 13 Jan. 1783, and n. 17).

³ Neither of these states, however, rescinded its ratification of the proposed 5 per cent impost amendment of the Articles of Confederation. See *JCC*, XXII, 213, n. 1, 361.

⁴ Randolph to JM, 22 Mar. 1783, and n. 2.

⁵ JM's reference is to Benjamin Franklin. See JM Notes, 12–15 Mar., n. 1; JM to Randolph, 12 Mar. 1783, and nn. 11, 12. On 12 March, the same day on which Arthur Lee wrote his missing letter to Randolph, Lee commented as follows in a letter to James Warren: "There never I think existed a man more meanly envious and selfish than Dr. Franklin. The reason probably why it is not seen so as to make men dispise him is, that men in general listen much to professions, and look little to actions" (Burnett, *Letters*, VII, 77–78).

⁶ JM Notes, 31 Mar. 1783, and nn. 2–6.

⁷ Randolph to JM, 22 Mar. and citations in n. 6. See also JM Notes, 9 Apr. 1783.

⁸ Randolph to JM, 22 Mar. 1783 and citations in n. 11. Any letter which Mrs. Nicholas Trist may have written to Mrs. Randolph is now missing.

⁹ *Papers of Madison*, V, 455, nn. 6, 10. Lee appears to have left Philadelphia on 1 April. He was again in Congress on 24 April (*JCC*, XXIV, 224, 275–76). He returned to Virginia in May, setting out from Philadelphia on the twelfth and first attending the House of Delegates on the twenty-fourth (*JHDV*, May 1783, p. 19). See also Pendleton to JM, 31 Mar.; 14 Apr. 1783.

Notes on Debates

MS (LC: Madison Papers). For a description of the manuscript of Notes on Debates, see *Papers of Madison*, V, 231–34.

EDITORIAL NOTE

JM prefaced the present notes by writing, "Wednesday apl. 3. Thursday Apl. 4. Friday apr. 5. Saturday apr. 6. See Journals." He thereby confused either the days or the dates, for 3 April in 1783 was a Thursday and the fourth, fifth, and sixth were Friday, Saturday, and Sunday, respectively. Between 3 and 6 April, Congress convened only on 4 April (NA: PCC, No. 185, III, 60; No. 186, fols. 171–72; *JCC*, XXIV, 227–30).

The notes below are confined to the contents of, rather than the debate on the report of the grand committee, and to the appointment of a committee to propose "the proper arrangements to be taken in consequence of peace." Congress named this latter committee on 4 April. The report of the grand committee, which was adopted on 7 April, is in NA: PCC, No. 26, fols. 399–401. See also NA: PCC, No. 186, fol. 172; *JCC*, XXIV, 230–31; JM Notes, 7 April 1783. Although Charles Thomson's committee book, the docket of the manuscript report of the grand committee, and the journal omit mention of the report being submitted to Congress on 4 April, they at

least record nothing which bars the conclusion that the report was first presented on that day (*JCC*, XXIV, 227–29). If this conclusion is correct, all the
present notes refer only to the session of 4 April 1783.

[Friday, 4 April]

The Grand Come. appointed to consider the proportions for the blank
in the Report on Revenue &c.[1] reported the following grounded on the
number of Inhabitants in each State; observing that N.H. R.I. Cont. &
Mard. had produced authentic documents of their numbers;[2] & that in
fixing the numbers of other States, they had been governed by such information as they could obtain. They also reduced the interest of aggregate debt. 2,500,000 Drs.[3]

	No. of Inhabts.[4]	proportions of 1000[5]	proportions of $1\frac{1}{2}$ Miln[6]
N.H.	82,200	35	52,500
Mas:	350,000	148	222,000
R.I.	50,400	21	31,500
Cont.	206,000	87	130,500
N.Y.	200,000	85	127,500
N.J.	130,000	55	82,500
Pena.	320,000	136	204,000
Del:	35,000	15	22,500
Mard.	220,700	94	141,000
Virga.	400,000	169	253,000
N.C.	170,000	72	108,000
S.C.	170,000	72	108,000
Georga.	25,000	11	16,500
	2,359,300	1000	1,500,000

Annual Intst.
of debt[7] after
deducting
1000....[8] Drs.
expected from
Impost on
Trade.

A Come. consisting of Mr. Hamilton, Mr. Madison &[9] was appointd
to report the proper arrangements to be taken in consequence of peace.

The object was to provide a system for foreign affairs, for Indian affairs, for military & naval peace establishments; and also to carry into execution the regulation of weights & measures & other articles of the Confederation not attended to during the war. To the same Come. was referred a resolution of the Executive Council of Pa. requesting the Delegates of that State to urge Congs. to establish a general peace with the Indians.[10]

[1] JM Notes, 1 Apr. 1783, and n. 12. The "blank" to which JM referred was in the fifth paragraph of the Report on Restoring Public Credit, submitted to Congress on 6 Mar. 1783 (*q.v.*, and n. 8).

[2] *Papers of Madison*, IV, 122; 123, n. 3; 356; 360, n. 28; Amendment to Report on Public Credit, 27 Mar., and n. 6; JM Notes, 27 Mar. 1783, and nn. 4, 27; Burnett, *Letters*, VI, 257, 261, n. 3, 278. A census taken in New Hampshire in 1775 showed its population to be 81,539 whites and 661 Negroes (NA: PCC, No. 64, fols. 221–23). A similar tally, made in Rhode Island in 1774, enumerated 54,453 whites and 3,768 Negroes in that colony (Stella H. Sutherland, *Population Distribution in Colonial America*, pp. 20–21). In the same year 191,392 whites and 6,464 Negroes were counted in Connecticut (NA: PCC, No. 59, X, 217; Charles J. Hoadly *et al.*, eds., *Public Records of Connecticut*, XIV, 491). In March 1782 the people in Maryland were reported to comprise 170,688 whites and 83,362 Negroes (NA: PCC, No. 75, fols. 310–11).

[3] This was the approximate sum estimated to be needed annually to pay the interest on the "liquidated" domestic and foreign debts totaling about $42,000,375, "as far as they can now be ascertained" (Address to States, 25 Apr. 1783, and n. 5). Of the $2,500,000, about $1,000,000 was expected to accrue from the recommended tariffs on foreign imports, thus leaving a "reduced" sum of $1,500,000 to be requisitioned from the states. This also was a much "reduced" requisition as compared with the $8,000,000 of 1782 and the $2,000,000 of 1783 (*Papers of Madison*, V, 129, n. 13; 211, n. 10; 289; 291, n. 11; JCC, XXI, 1090; XXIII, 666).

[4] *Papers of Madison*, IV, 123, n. 3. In the manuscript of the report, as in JM's notes, the population of South Carolina was shown originally as 170,000 and the total population of the thirteen states as 2,359,300. In the manuscript of the report, the "5" written over the "7" in "170,000" and the "2,339,300" entered below the former total reflect the outcome of the debate on 7 April (NA: PCC, No. 26, fol. 399; JCC, XXIV, 231; JM Notes, 7 Apr. 1783). JM obviously copied the committee's draft of the report as it was submitted on 4 April rather than as it was revised during the debate three days later. For comments upon the population of Virginia, see *Papers of Madison*, V, 8; 351, nn. 21, 22; Randolph to JM, 7 Feb. 1783, n. 3.

[5] If JM had used 2,359.3 as his divisor, the "proportions of 1,000" would have been incorrect. Almost certainly he did not enter in his notes for 4 April the figures in the proportions column until 7 April, and then he copied those in the report by the committee. This committee, by reducing the population figure of South Carolina by 20,000, had a divisor of 2,339.3 rather than 2,359.3. Using 2,339.3, the figures in the second column of the committee's report are correct with two minor exceptions. The figure for Connecticut should be 88.1 rather than 88.2 and that for New York 85.4 rather than 85.6. Although JM copied accurately in his notes the figures in the third column of the report, it is not clear how the committee arrived at several of them. In some instances it obviously raised to the next highest integer a proportion

in which the decimal fraction exceeded six tenths, and eliminated any fraction below six tenths, but it seems arbitrarily to have dropped Massachusetts' true proportion from 149.6 to 148, Connecticut's from 88.2 to 87, Pennsylvania's from 136.8 to 136, and Virginia's from 171 to 169. The committee furthermore neglected to take into account its reduction of 20,000 in South Carolina's population figure (*JCC*, XXIV, 231).

By 18 April 1783, when Congress adopted the plan for restoring public credit including the state-by-state requisition quotas, the overcharge of South Carolina had been altered by correctly deducting $11,817 from her quota. The quotas of Delaware and Georgia had also been reduced by $57 and $470, respectively. These three figures total $12,344. This sum had been distributed proportionately among the quotas of the other nine states so as to retain the full requisition of $1,500,000 (*JCC*, XXIV, 259).

6 The quota of each state in this column was derived by multiplying 1,500 thousands ($1,500,000) by the appropriate figure in the preceding column for that state. Virginia's proportion, miscopied by JM, was $253,500.

7 In reality, $1,500,000 was not the annual interest on the debt. See n. 3. JM's figures actually total to $1,499,500, but see n. 6 for error of $500 in the figure for Virginia.

8 JM meant $1,000,000. An earlier estimate of the annual income to be derived from collecting a 5 per cent impost had been $600,000, but that figure had assumed a continuance of hostilities (JM Notes, 29 Jan. 1783, n. 20). The foreign trade of the United States obviously should be larger in peacetime.

9 Many years after he penned his notes, JM interlineated "See Journal" above "Madison &." Although Congress on 4 April appointed Alexander Hamilton, chairman, and JM, Samuel Osgood, Oliver Ellsworth, and James Wilson as the other members of the committee, the journal does not record the personnel of the committee until 21 April 1783 (NA: PCC, No. 186, fol. 92; *JCC*, XXIV, 264).

10 On 3 April President John Dickinson in Council expressed to the delegates in Congress from Pennsylvania his earnest desire, as "indispensably necessary" to the welfare of the state, that they use their "utmost exertions" to have Congress adopt speedily "the most effectual measures for making a peace with all the Indian nations" (NA: PCC, No. 69, fol. 435). The committee's first report, submitted on 21 April 1783, cited Dickinson's letter as a particular justification for recommending to Congress a general policy for dealing with all Indian tribes "preparatory to" a "final pacification" (*JCC*, XXIV, 264).

Besides "regulating the trade and managing all affairs with the Indians, not members of any of the states," and "fixing the standard of weights and measures throughout the united states," Article IX of the Articles of Confederation also delegated to Congress the "sole and exclusive right and power of regulating the alloy and value of coin struck by their own authority, or by that of the respective states" (*JCC*, XIX, 219). A proposal by Bridgen and Waller, merchants of London, to provide copper coins for the United States was enclosed by Benjamin Franklin in his dispatch of 24 December 1782 to Robert R. Livingston and apparently referred to the committee on 6 May 1783 (Wharton, *Revol. Dipl. Corr.*, VI, 163; NA: PCC, No. 186, fol. 93). Following a recommendation by Robert Morris, Congress on 21 February 1782 had approved "the establishment of a mint," but the resolution was not made effective either in that year or in 1783 (*JCC*, XXII, 9, 87; Clarence L. Ver Steeg, *Robert Morris*, pp. 88–89, and nn. 24–26). The committee made no report to Congress on that subject or on weights and measures.

For the committee and the military "peace establishment," see Burnett, *Letters*, VII, 131–32, 132, n. 2; Syrett and Cooke, *Papers of Hamilton*, III, 311–13, 321–22; Fitzpatrick, *Writings of Washington*, XXVI, 291, and n. 6, 291–96.

Notes on Debates

MS (LC: Madison Papers). For a description of the manuscript of Notes on Debates, see *Papers of Madison*, V, 231–34.

Monday April 7.

The sense of Congs. having been taken on the truth of the numbers reported by the Grand Committee, the no. allotted to S.C. was reduced to 150,000. on the representation of the Delegates of that States.[1] The Delegates of N.J. contended also for a reduction, but were unsuccessful. Those of Virga also, on the principle that Congs. ought not to depart from the relative numbers given in 1775,[2] without being also required by actual returns which had not been obtained either from that State, or others whose relation wd. be varied: To this reasoning were opposed the verbal & credible information recd. from different persons & particularly Mr. Mercer, which made the no. of Inhabitants in Va. after deducting ⅔ of the Slaves, exceed the number allotted to that State.[3] Congs. were almost unanimous agst. the reduction. A motion was made by Mr. Gervais 2d. by Mr. Madison to reduce the no. of Georgia to 15,000. on the probability that their real no. did not exceed it, & the cruelty of overloading a State which had been so much torn & exhausted by the war. The motion met with little support & was almost unanimously negatived.[4]

A letter was recd. from Genl. Washington expressing the joy of the army at the signing of the general preliminaries notified to him & their satisfaction at the commutation of half pay agreed to by Congs.[5]

[1] JM Notes, 4 Apr. 1783, and nn. 4 6. JM obviously should have written "State." Although the journal for 7 April makes clear that Congress amended the report of the grand committee by reducing the estimated population of South Carolina from 170,000 to 150,000, the session of that day evidently adjourned without proportionately lowering the financial quota of the state from $108,000 to $96,183 (*JCC*, XXIV, 231). By 18 April, when Congress adopted the amended report of the grand committee, this needed adjustment had been made, along with an increase in the quota of every other state except Georgia and Delaware (*JCC*, XXIV, 259; Burnett, *Letters*, VII, 128, and n. 3).

[2] The "principle" could be defended on the ground that three of the four state censuses, which had been available to the grand committee for estimating financial quotas, had been taken in 1774 or 1775 (JM Notes, 4 Apr. 1783, n. 2). According to the colony-by-colony population schedule adopted by Congress on 29 July 1775, Virginia's "Inhabitants, of all ages, including negroes and mulattoes" numbered 496,278 (*JCC*, II, 221–22). This figure was 16.5 per cent of the total population of the thirteen colonies at that time, as compared with the 17.1 per cent as estimated in the grand committee's report. If the delegates of Virginia meant that the figures of

1775 should be revised so as to take into account only three-fifths of the slaves, her advantage from using the 1775 rather than the 1783 estimate in allocating financial quotas obviously would have been much greater than the difference between those two percentages. The exact number of slaves in Virginia in 1775 is unknown. In 1782 Jefferson judged that they comprised over 47 per cent of the population. Many years later a scholar concluded that 42 per cent would be approximately accurate on the eve of the Revolution (*Papers of Madison*, V, 351, nn. 21, 22; Stella H. Sutherland, *Population Distribution in Colonial America*, p. 202). See also *Papers of Madison*, V, 129, n. 13.

[3] Of the "different persons" only John F. Mercer is identifiable.

[4] By 18 April 1783 Georgia's quota had been lowered from $25,000 to $16,030 (*JCC*, XXIV, 231, 259). Between about 2 November 1782 and 30 June 1784 there was no delegate in Congress from Georgia to speak on her behalf (Burnett, *Letters*, VI, xliv–xlv; VII, lxvi; *JCC*, XXIV, 836–37). From the close of 1778 to the close of 1781 the British had occupied most of the coastal area of Georgia. Thereafter until 12 July 1782, when they evacuated Savannah, they were confined to that seaport and its environs. During the entire period the civil government of the patriots was "feeble, uncertain, and peripatetic," and their armed strife with Loyalists was almost unceasing (Charles C[olcock] Jones, Jr., *The History of Georgia* [2 vols.; Boston, 1883], II, 417–41).

[5] *JCC*, XXIV, 232, n. 1. In his letter of 30 March, Washington acknowledged President Elias Boudinot's of 23 March (Burnett, *Letters*, VII, 93–94; Fitzpatrick, *Writings of Washington*, XXIV, 273). See also JM Notes, 22 Mar., and n. 3; 24 Mar. 1783, and n. 1.

Notes on Debates

MS (LC: Madison Papers). For a description of the manuscript of Notes on Debates, see *Papers of Madison*, V, 231–34.

Tuesday April 8th.[1]

Estimate of the debt of the U.S. reported by the Grand Committee:[2]

Foreign debt

To the Farmers General of France............... Livrs.	1,000,000[3]	
To Beaumarchais.............................	3,000,000[4]	
To King of France to end of 1782.................	28,000,000[5]	
To do.................for 1783................	6,000,000[6]	
		Dollars
	Livrs. 38,000,000 = 7,037,037[7]	
Recd. on loan in Holland...................... Florins 1,678,000 =	671,200[8]	
Borrowed in Spain by Mr. Jay....................................	150,000[9]	
Int. on Dutch one year at 4 prCt..................................	26,848[10]	

Total for: debt..7,885,085

Domestic debt.

	Dollars
Loan office	11,463,802
Int. unpaid for 1781	190,000
do............1782	687,823[11]
Credit to sundry persons } on Treasury books }	638,042[12]
army debt *to 31 Dr. 1782*	5,635,618[13]
unliquidated do	8,000,000[14]
deficiencies in 1783	2,000,000[15]

Total dom: debt....28,615,290

Aggregate debt....36,500,375[16]

Interest

On for: debt, 7,885,085, at 4 PerCt	315,403[17]
On dom: do.. 28,615,290, at 6 do	1,716,917
On Com: ½pay, estimd. 5,000,000 at 6 do	300,000
Bounty to be pd estimd. 500,000 at do	30,000[18]

2,362,320 Aggreg: of Int.

A motion was made by Mr. Hamilton who had been absent on the question on the 9th. parag: of the report on Revenue assessing quotas, to reconsider the same. Mr. Floyd who being the only delegate from N.Y. then present on that question, cd. not vote, 2ded. the motion. For the argts. repeated see the former remarks on the 7. apl.[19]

On the question the votes were Mas: no. R.I. no. Cont. no. N.Y. ay. N.J. no. Pa. ay. Maryd. no. Virga. ay. S.C. no.

[1] Congress met on this date, even though the journal omits mention of the session (NA: PCC, No. 185, III, 61).

[2] JM Notes, 4 Apr.; 7 Apr. 1783. With approximate accuracy, JM copied the estimate of debt from a manuscript, apparently in Charles Thomson's hand (NA: PCC, No. 26, fol. 403). A similar analysis, spread on the journal for 29 April 1783, differs considerably, especially in its sections entitled "Domestic Debt" and "Annual Interest of the debt of the United States," from the corresponding sections in the present notes (*JCC*, XXIV, 286).

[3] The "tobacco contract" was concluded in March 1777 by the American commissioners in Paris with "the Farmers General," the organization that "farmed," or collected, the royal taxes. In accord with the terms of the agreement, the farmers-general, which also exercised the monopoly over the purchase and sale of tobacco in France, advanced 1,000,000 livres in part payment on 4,000 or 5,000 hogsheads of Maryland and Virginia tobacco. British captures of French and American ships at sea appear to be the main reason why the tobacco failed to reach the consignees (Wharton, *Revol. Dipl. Corr.*, II, 249–50, 270, 284, 290–91; *JCC*, IX, 983). See also NA: PCC, No. 135, I, 282–87, 137; II, 201; JM Notes, 29 Jan. 1783, n. 17.

[4] *Papers of Madison*, I, 246, n. 5; II, 60, n. 7; IV, 287; 289–90, n. 4.

[5] *Ibid.*, V, 424, n. 9.

[6] *Ibid.*, V, 22, n. 4; JM Notes, 19 Mar., n. 2; 26 Mar. 1783.

[7] JM Notes, 29 Jan. 1783, and n. 15. A specie dollar was equated with 5.4 livres.

[8] *Papers of Madison,* V, 424, n. 9; 450, n. 5; JM Notes, 9–10 Jan. 1783, n. 12. JM wrote "Recd. on" because the Amsterdam bankers originally had promised to lend $10,000,000 (Wharton, *Revol. Dipl. Corr.,* V, 515). One specie dollar was equated with 2.5 florins.

[9] *Papers of Madison,* V, 21, n. 4; 424, n. 9; Wharton, *Revol. Dipl. Corr.,* IV, 59, 70, 101, 228, 346, 386; V, 68.

[10] *Papers of Madison,* V, 451, n. 14. Between "Dutch" and "one," "loan" obviously should be interpolated.

[11] JM should have written "687,828" (NA: PCC, No. 26, fol. 403; No. 137, II, 205; *JCC,* XXIV, 286). For the loan-office certificates and the unpaid interest thereon, see *Papers of Madison,* IV, 388, n. 13; V, 294, n. 1; 380, n. 11; JM Notes, 27 Jan., n. 13; 30 Jan., and nn. 4, 6; 26 Feb. 1783 and n. 46.

[12] This entry is separated into four categories under the general caption "Liquidated Debt" in a report of 3 March 1783 by Joseph Nourse, register of the treasury (NA: PCC, 137, II, 207).

[13] JM Notes, 13 Jan., n. 5; 27 Jan. 1783, n. 13; *JCC,* XXIV, 286.

[14] Although neither Robert Morris nor anyone else knew the exact amount of the unliquidated debt, it was assumed to total about this figure. See Randolph to JM, 15 Jan., n. 13; JM Notes, 27 Jan., n. 13; 26 Feb.; 11 Mar. 1783, n. 9; *JCC,* XXIV, 180–81.

[15] The "deficiencies" had resulted largely from the arrears of the states in complying with the requisitions of Congress. Although, as compared with the amounts sought in previous years, the $2,000,000 for 1783 was small, five states had remitted nothing by 30 April; and the other eight, a total of only $259,682.78 (NA: PCC, No. 137, II, 455; *Papers of Madison,* V, 211, n. 10). At the close of 1782 there had been $7,577,838.27 still unpaid on the requisition of $8,000,000 for that year (NA: PCC, No. 142, II, 159; *Papers of Madison,* V, 162, n. 15; 423, n. 2; JM Notes, 27 Jan., n. 12; 30 Jan. 1783, n. 4; Clarence L. Ver Steeg, *Robert Morris,* p. 136).

[16] Both this total and the one immediately above it are accurate, but in checking JM's addition of the items comprising the latter, his mistake, mentioned in n. 11, above, must be taken into account. In a revised version of this "Estimate of the debt of the U. S." in the journal of Congress, the following entries were added to the analysis of the domestic debt: "Commutation to the army, agreeable to the act of 22 March last, 5,000,000," and "Bounty due to privates, 500,000" (*JCC,* XXIV, 286). See also *JCC,* XXIV, 180–81, 207–10; JM Notes, 27 Jan., and n. 13; 29 Jan., and n. 15; 22 Mar. 1783, and n. 3. Acting as agents of Congress in fulfilling its pledge made in the ordinances of 3 and 21 October 1780, the states had paid the money bounty of "not exceeding fifty dollars" to each recruit at the time of his enlistment for the duration of the war (*Papers of Madison,* IV, 24; 25, n. 3; V, 93, n. 9).

[17] In the revised version, mentioned in n. 16, above, the title of this item is "On the foreign debt, part at 4 and part at 5 per cent.," and the amount, $369,038.6. This correction in the interest reflects, for example, the terms of several contracts made with the court of France and Dutch bankers (NA: PCC, No. 137, I, 11, 18, 163, 166; E. James Ferguson, *Power of the Purse,* pp. 40–42, 235, and n. 35; Clarence L. Ver Steeg, *Robert Morris,* p. 137).

[18] Six per cent of $28,615,290 is $1,716,917.40. The revised version in the journal consolidates with this annual interest the $300,000 and $30,000 items, thus arriving at $2,046,917.40 as the total yearly interest "On the domestic debt, at 6 per cent" (*JCC,* XXIV, 286). See also n. 16, above; JM Notes, 25 Jan. 1783, n. 11; *JCC,* XXIV, 207.

[19] JM Notes, 1 Apr., and n. 10; 4 Apr., and ed. n.; 7 Apr. 1783. If the purpose of Alexander Hamilton and William Floyd was to gain a reduction in New York's quota of $127,500 as recommended by the grand committee, they were unsuccessful, for that quota was increased to $128,243 before Congress adopted the allocation schedule on 18 April 1783 (*JCC,* XXIV, 259).

Virginia Delegates to Benjamin Harrison

Letter not found.

EDITORIAL NOTE

Ca. 8 April 1783. In his letter to the delegates on 19 April, Governor Harrison mentioned that "by the last Post" he had received their "favor" dealing with the claims of Simon Nathan and Oliver Pollock against the state of Virginia. See Harrison to Delegates, 19 April, and nn. 1–7, and especially the closing paragraph of n. 5. Harrison almost certainly referred the now missing letter to the Virginia General Assembly on 5 May 1783 (Executive Letter Book, 1783–1786, pp. 109–12, MS in Va. State Library; *JHDV*, May 1783, p. 83). That letter may have touched upon several of the topics alluded to by JM in his letter to Randolph on 8 April, and probably also reported that Congress four days earlier had resolved "that the several States be required to suspend all enlistments for any regiment or corps in the United States" (Randolph to JM, 1 Mar., n. 4; JM to Randolph, 8 Apr.; *Va. Gazette*, 19 Apr. 1783).

To Edmund Randolph

RC (LC: Madison Papers). Unsigned but in JM's hand. Cover addressed by him to "E. Randolph Esqr." Carried to Richmond by "a private hand" (Delegates to Harrison, 10 Apr.; JM to Randolph, 15 Apr. 1783). Docketed by Randolph, "J. Madison Jr. April 8th. 1783."

PHILADA. Apl. 8. 1783.

MY DEAR SIR

Your favor of the 29th. ult:[1] was duly recd. yesterday. Your apprehensions from the article in favor of British Creditors, correspond with those entertained by all whose remarks I have heard upon it. My hope is that in the definitive treaty the danger may be removed by a suspension of their demands for a reasonable term after peace.[2]

The publication of Mr. M's letters was neither previously assented to nor known by Congress. Whether it was the act of Mr. M. himself is even unknown to them. After the injunction of secresy was taken off, the curiosity of any individual, or the interest of the printer might obtain copies for the press.[3]

The imperfect information brought by the French Cutter is all that we have yet recd. relative to peace. It is reported from N. York that similar intelligence has been brought thither by a vessel from Lisbon. Hostilities however continue to devour our commerce.[4]

The report on revenue of which I gave you the outlines[5] is still in an unfinished State; but in a way I flatter myself of being ultimately & substantially adopted. The admission into the common mass, of all expences of the war not authorised by Congress is the remaining article of difficulty. Even this however under some qualifications is so respectably patronized & so intimately linked with the art[i]cle concerning the back lands that I do not despair altogether of seeing that also finally comprehended.[6] A change of the valuation of the Lands for the number of Inhabitants deducting $\frac{2}{5}$ of the Slaves, has recd. a tacit sanction & unless hereafter expunged will go forth in the general recommendation, as material to future harmony & justice among the members of the Confederacy. The deduction of $\frac{2}{5}$ was a compromise between the wide opinions & demands of the Southern & other States.[7]

A letter was recd. yesterday from Genl Washington in answer to a notification from the Presidt. of the signing the Genl. preliminaries on the 20th Jany. expressing the joy of the army at the glorious event and the satisfaction they have recd. from the act of Congs. commuting the half pay &c.[8]

The Mission of Mr. Jefferson has been entirely superceded by the last advices. He will set out in a few days for Virga. and means to pass through Richmond.[9] To his information I refer for details which my late correspondence may have omitted. As his services are not required, at least for the present, in Europe, it is to be most devoutly wished that they could be engaged at the present crisis at home.[10]

[1] Q.v.

[2] Randolph to JM, 29 Mar. 1783, and nn. 9, 10. On 15 April and 6 August Congress and King George III, respectively, ratified the preliminary treaty of peace, including Article IV favoring British creditors. The provisions of this treaty and of the definitive treaty of peace, signed on 3 September, were identical. The American commissioners, who were instructed by Congress on 30 May 1783 to have Article IV amended so as to bar suits to recover debts until three years after the signing of the definitive treaty, found that this change could only be gained by surrendering more rights or privileges granted to the United States in the treaty than Congress would ever accept (Wharton, *Revol. Dipl. Corr.*, VI, 569, 581, 602, 633, 646, 669; *JCC*, XXIV, 241–51, 369–76, 812; JM Notes, 14 Apr.; 15 Apr. 1783).

[3] On 26 February Congress had complied with the request of that day from Robert Morris that he be permitted to inform his creditors of his intention to resign

on 31 May as superintendent of finance. Congress did not specifically authorize him to announce his intention in the newspapers, although making known the fact to all his creditors would be almost equivalent to its publication. What shocked Randolph was the appearance in the *Pennsylvania Packet* of 4 March and in the *Pennsylvania Gazette* of the next day of a copy of Morris' letter of 24 January 1783 to Congress, stating that his "Ideas of Integrity" would compel him to retire from office unless Congress stopped incurring new debts before providing the means to pay old ones (JM Notes, 24 Jan., and n. 20; 26 Feb., and n. 14; 27 Feb.; 4–5 Mar., and n. 7; JM to Randolph, 4 Mar.; 11 Mar.; Randolph to JM, 29 Mar. 1783). Without revealing his source, the editor of the *Packet* expressed his happiness because, in view of the "much conversation" occasioned by the resignation, he was "able to furnish his customers" with copies of Morris' two letters of resignation. According to his confidant Hamilton, it was Morris himself who caused these letters to be published (Clarence L. Ver Steeg, *Robert Morris*, pp. 170–71, 248, n. 23, 249, n. 25; Syrett and Cooke, *Papers of Hamilton*, III, 319–20).

4 Jefferson to JM, 7–8 Feb., and nn. 3, 4, 8; JM Notes, 31 Mar., and nn. 2, 4–6; Delegates to Harrison, 1 Apr., and n. 4; JM to Randolph, 1 Apr. 1783. JM must have been told orally of the arrival in New York Harbor early in the morning of 7 April of a ship from Lisbon. This news was first published in the *Pennsylvania Gazette* of 9 April. Captain Henry James Reynett, an aide-de-camp of General Sir Guy Carleton, reached Philadelphia on the evening of 8 April, bringing among other "authentic" documents confirming the cessation of hostilities between Great Britain, France, and Spain, a notification from Carleton and Admiral Digby that they had dispatched a vessel "to call in the British cruisers now on our coasts" (Worthington Chauncey Ford, comp., *British Officers Serving in the American Revolution, 1774–1783* [Brooklyn, N. Y., 1897], p. 150; *Pa. Packet*, 10 Apr.; *Pa. Journal*, 12 Apr.). See also JM Notes, 10 April 1783; Fitzpatrick, *Writings of Washington*, XXVI, 308.

5 JM to Randolph, 11 Mar.; 25 Mar. 1783.

6 For Congress to assume the reasonable but unauthorized military expenses of the states and for Congress to urge states which claimed trans-Appalachian lands to cede them to the United States were "intimately linked" proposals of the "report on revenue." Massachusetts, Connecticut, Virginia, and North Carolina each asserted a valid title to western territory and also a right to be reimbursed for war costs. Virginia, for example, might find Congress more willing to admit her expenses "into the common mass" if she mitigated the provisos attached to her offer to cede her lands north and west of the Ohio River. See *Papers of Madison*, IV, 221, n. 11; V, 119, n. 20; 246, n. 7; 292, n. 19; JM Notes, 26 Feb., and nn. 15–44; Memo. on Revenue Plan, 6 Mar., ed. n.; Report on Restoring Public Credit, 6 Mar. 1783, and n. 14.

7 JM Notes, 1 Apr.; 7 Apr. 1783, and n. 2.

8 JM Notes, 7 Apr. 1783, and n. 5.

9 JM Notes, 1 Apr., and n. 13. Jefferson left Philadelphia on 12 April (JM to Randolph, 15 Apr. 1783).

10 Many years later JM or someone at his bidding placed a single bracket at the close of this sentence. Henry D. Gilpin, the editor of the first comprehensive edition of JM's writings, interpreted the bracket as a clearance by JM to publish the entire letter (Madison, *Papers* [Gilpin ed], I, 522–24). Shortly after his return to Monticello, Jefferson centered his attention upon drafting a new constitution for Virginia. He hoped that the General Assembly would find the outcome of his labors a decided improvement upon the Form of Government adopted in 1776 (Randolph to JM, 7 Mar. 1783, nn. 7, 8; Boyd, *Papers of Jefferson*, II, 315; VI, 278–84, 294–308).

Notes on Debates

MS (LC: Madison Papers). For a description of the manuscript of Notes on Debates, see *Papers of Madison*, V, 231–34.

Wednesday April 9.

A memorial was recd. from Genl. Hazen in behalf of the Canadians who had engaged in the cause of the U.S. praying that a tract of vacant land on L. Erie might be allotted to them.[1]

Mr. Wilson thereupon moved that a Come. be appointed to consider and report to Congress the measures proper to be taken with respect to the Western Country. In support of his motion he observed on the importance of that Country, the danger from immediate emigrations of its being lost to the public; & the necessity on the part of Congress of taking care of the fœderal interests in the formation of New States, which could not take place by the authority of any particular States.[2]

Mr. Madison observed that the appointment of such a Come. could not be necessary at this juncture & might be injurious, that Congs. were about to take in the report on Revenue &c. the only step that could now be properly taken, viz to call again on the States claiming the W. Territory to cede the same;[3] that until the result sd. be known every thing wd. be premature & wd. excite in the States irritations & jealousies that might frustrate the Cessions; that it was indispensable to obtain these cessions in order to compromise the disputes, & to derive advantage from the territory to the U. S.;[4] that if the motion meant merely to prevent irregular settlements, a recommendation to that effect ought to be made to the States, that if ascertaining & disposing of garrisons proper to be kept up in that Country was the object it was already in the hands of the Come. on the peace arrangements; but might be expressly referred to them.[5]

Mr. Mercer supported the same ideas.

Mr. Clarke considered the motion as no wise connected with peace arrangements; his object was to define the western limits of the States which Congs. alone cd. do, and which it was necessary they sd. do in order to know what territory properly belonged to the U. S. and what steps ought to be taken relative to it. He disapproved of repeatedly courting the States to make *cessions* wch. Congs. stood in no need of.[6]

Mr. Wilson seemed to consider as the property of the U. S. all territory over which particular States had not exercised jurisdiction particularly N. W. of Ohio, & said that within the Country confirmed to the

U. S. by the Provisional articles, there must be a large Country over which no particular claims extended.[7]

It was answered that the exercise of jurisdiction was not the criterion of the territorial right of the States; that Pa. had maintained always a contrary doctrine; that if it were a criterion Va. had exercised jurisdiction over the Illinois & other places conquered N. W. of the Ohio:[8] that it was uncertain whether limits of the U. S. as fixed by the Prov:1. Arts: did comprehend any territory out of the claims of the individual States: that sd. it be the case a dicision or examination of the point had best be put off till it sd. be seen whether Cessions of the States wd. not render it unnecessary; that it cd. not be immediately necessary for the purpose of preventing settlemts. on such extra lands, since they must lie too remote to be in danger of it.[9]

Congress refused to refer the motion to the Come. on peace arrangents, and by a large majority referred it to a special Come. viz Messrs. Osgood, Wilson, Madison, Carrol & Williamson; to whom was also referred the Meml. of Genl. Hazen.[10]

On the preceding question Cont. was strenuous in favr. of Mr. Wilsons motion.[11]

A motion was made by Mr. Dyer to strike out the drawback on salt fish &c.. Mr. Ghorum protested in the most solemn manner that Massts. wd. never accede to the plan without the drawback. The motion was very little supported.[12]

[1] Moses Hazen, brevet brigadier general, petitioned Congress to grant to the Canadian refugees under his command, and to other Canadians who had fled with their families to the United States, a huge tract of land comprising what would become much of southeast Michigan and northwest Ohio, with a frontage on Lake Erie from the mouth of the Huron River on the north to six miles east of the mouth of the Maumee River. Hazen pointed out that this area, once a part of the "Province of Canada," was now "under the sovereignty of the United States" (NA: PCC, No. 42, III, 451–54).

After long service as an enlisted man and officer in the French and Indian War, Hazen (1733–1803), a native of Haverhill, Mass., settled near St. John on the Richelieu River, Canada. In recognition of this military experience, of the confiscation by the British of his large estate, and of his assistance to the Montgomery-Arnold expedition in the autumn of 1775, Congress on 22 January 1776 unanimously elected him to be the "Colonel commandant" of the "second Canadian Regiment" (JCC, IV, 78, 192, 198–99; VI, 900).

Although Hazen's vigorous recruiting made the personnel of the regiment largely Canadian at the outset of its notable service, his command came to include, in accord with an act of Congress of 3 October 1780, a miscellany of foreign-born "non-commissioned officers and privates" who had belonged to "any of the reduced regiments and corps" (JCC, XVIII, 896). The penchant of Hazen for embroiling himself in controversies and the fact that his regiment was a unit apart from the normal structure of the continental establishment long delayed his promotion. Finally on 29 June, 1781, yielding to Washington's recommendation and following a reorganization which associated the regiment with the New York and New Jersey continental lines, Congress appointed Hazen "a Brigadier in the Army of the United States by Brevet" (*JCC*, XX, 540, 711–12; Fitzpatrick, *Writings of Washington*, XXI, 326–27). After leading a brigade through the Yorktown campaign, he commanded the detachment, including the Canadian regiment, which guarded British prisoners and trained recruits at Lancaster, Pa. (*JCC*, XXIII, *passim;* XXIV, 74, 107–10; NA: PCC, No. 78, XII, 285–97). Hazen and his regiment had rejoined Washington's main army about four months before he presented his memorial to Congress (*JCC*, XXV, 234, 348, 400; XXVI, 282; *Pa. Journal*, 9 Nov. 1783).

[2] According to Article XI of the Articles of Confederation, Canada was welcome to join "this union; but no other colony shall be admitted into the same, unless such admission be agreed to by nine states." Article IX further stipulated that "no state shall be deprived of territory for the benefit of the united states" (*JCC*, XIX, 218, 221). See also *JCC*, XVIII, 915; *Papers of Madison*, V, 246, n. 7.

For the first time since Congress on 29 October 1782 had accepted New York's cession of her western claims, the complex issue of the lands west of the Appalachian Mountains was revived by the motion of James Wilson (*ibid.*, III, 303, n. 4; IV, 34, n. 8; V, 245, nn. 3, 5; 246, n. 10; *JCC*, XXIII, 694). His motion was posited upon the controversial assumption that Congress, having received Great Britain's title "to the Western Country," could govern it, control migration to it, derive desperately needed revenue from selling its land, confirm or refuse to confirm the alleged titles conferred by Great Britain or Indian tribes upon land companies, and prescribe the rules for the formation of new states in the area. All these matters had been debated many times in Congress but were now placed in a new context by Great Britain's transfer to the United States, rather than to the six claimant states, of her rights of jurisdiction and soil in the West. Members of Congress from Massachusetts, Connecticut, Virginia, North Carolina, South Carolina, and Georgia, with boundaries extending beyond the mountains, could plausibly contend that Congress could be no more than trustee, on behalf of those states, of all rights possessed by Great Britain in the West prior to 4 July 1776. Furthermore, the vacating by Great Britain of her title could not annul equally valid titles to the same area. For the long background of the issue, see the indexes of *Papers of Madison*, II, III, IV, and V, especially under Continental Congress, actions; Western lands; Madison, James, Jr., views of western lands; Virginia, western land claims of.

[3] Report on Restoring Public Credit, 6 Mar. 1783, and n. 14.

[4] Among "the disputes," JM may have had in mind the overlapping claims of Virginia, Connecticut, and Massachusetts to land in the territory north and west of the Ohio River. See JM Notes, 27 Mar., and n. 11.

[5] JM Notes, 4 Apr. 1783, and ed. n., and n. 10.

[6] This extreme view, often expressed before by delegates from the "landless" states, was now advanced even more confidently by Abraham Clark of New Jersey because of the cession to the United States by Great Britain of her title to the West. See *Papers of Madison*, II, 72–77; IV, 32–33; 35, nn. 9, 10; 179, nn. 7, 8; V, 82–83; 84, n. 6; 200; 201, n. 8.

[7] If the only true test of ownership to the area north and west of the Ohio River was the exercise of effective jurisdiction there, Massachusetts and Connecticut obviously had no defensible claims whatsoever, and Virginia's valid title would be restricted to a few posts precariously held. Wilson's argument could readily be turned against him, for Congress had not even attempted to govern in that region (*Papers of Madison*, I, 261–62; 263, n. 10; III, 210, n. 4).

[8] Using this "criterion," Virginians could point to the campaigns of George

Rogers Clark, the creation of the county of Illinois by the Virginia General Assembly on 18 December 1778, and to the civil government of that county, centering at Kaskaskia, beginning in May of the next year (*Papers of Madison,* I, 219, n. 9; 274–77; 277, nn. 2, 3; II, 24, and nn. 2, 3; 105, n. 4; III, 342–43; 345, n. 7; 346, nn. 9, 10; IV, 120, n. 5; 439, n. 1). Pennsylvania had maintained a "contrary doctrine" during her boundary dispute with Virginia in the Monongahela River and Youghiogheny River valleys (*Colonial Records of Pa.,* XIII, 79, 541–42, 685–86; *Papers of Madison,* IV, 184–87; 276–77; 277, nn. 5, 8, 9). For a boundary controversy with Maryland decided in Pennsylvania's favor by applying a contrary principle, see Randolph to JM, 15 Feb. 1783, n. 7.

9 If the grant of "Virginia" to the London Company of Virginia in the charter of 1609 was still valid, the state appeared to have a legal title to all of the Northwest Territory, with the possible exception of small areas in what became western Wisconsin, east central Minnesota, and northeastern Ohio (*Papers of Madison,* II, 72–78; III, 14, n. 17; 284–86; 304–5; IV, 32–34; V, 117, n. 7; 292, n. 19; Randolph to JM, 15 Feb. 1783, and nn. 5, 6). The last of these three, which probably would be the first to be entered by white settlers, was within the area embraced in the claims of Massachusetts and Connecticut. Congress accepted their cessions on 19 April 1785 and 14 September 1786, respectively (*Papers of Madison,* II, 73–74; IV, 34, n. 8; V, 118, n. 15; 119, n. 20; *JCC,* XXXI, 654–55; Edmund C. Burnett, *The Continental Congress,* p. 626).

10 The report of this committee, insofar as the memorial was concerned, was rendered on 22 April and adopted the next day. Congress promised that whenever it "can consistently make grants of land, they will reward in this way, as far as may be consistent, the officers, men and others, refugees from Canada" (NA: PCC, No. 186, fol. 93; *JCC,* XXIV, 268–69).

11 JM probably made particular note of the "strenuous" support by Eliphalet Dyer, Oliver Ellsworth, and Oliver Wolcott, in view of the continuing refusal of Congress to accept Connecticut's and Virginia's offers of cession because of the proviso attached to each offer. A regard for the interests of Connecticut would seem to require her delegates to join with those of Virginia in opposing Wilson's motion. See also *Papers of Madison,* V, 243; 247, n. 16; JM Notes, 18 Apr. 1783, and nn. 2–6.

12 JM Notes, 27 Feb., and n. 9; 11 Mar., and n. 3; 18 Mar. 1783, and n. 8.

Notes on Debates

MS (LC: Madison Papers). For a description of the manuscript of Notes on Debates, see *Papers of Madison,* V, 231–34.

Thursday Apl. 10.

Letters rcd. from Genl. Carlton & Admiral Digby inclosing British proclamation of cessation of arms[1] &c also Letters from Docr. Franklin & Mr. Adams, notifying the conclusion of Preliminaries between G. B. & F. & Spain, with a declaration entered into with Mr. Fitzherbert applying the epochs of cessation to the case of G. B. & U. S.[2] These papers were referred to Secy. of F. A. to report a proclamation for Congs. at 6 OClock—at which time Congs. met & recd. report nearly as it stands on the Journal of Friday, Apl. 11. After some consideration of the Report as to the accuracy & propriety of which a diversity of sentiments prevailed, they postponed it till next day.[3] They Secy also reported a Resolution directing Secy. at War and Agent of Marine to discharge all prisoners of war.[4]

[1] JM to Randolph, 8 Apr. 1783, and n. 4.

[2] The dispatches to Livingston, secretary for foreign affairs, were John Adams' of 22 and 23 January and Benjamin Franklin's of 21 January, enclosing a copy of the document signed by Alleyne Fitzherbert, announcing a cessation of the war by Great Britain against France, Spain, and the United States. Appended to this document were three brief paragraphs in which Franklin and Adams "reciprocally declare" that the United States will "cause to cease all hostilities against his Britannic majesty, his subjects and possessions, at the terms or periods agreed" by Great Britain, France, and Spain (NA: PCC, No. 185, III, 61; Wharton, *Revol. Dipl. Corr.*, VI, 223–25, 226–27). For Fitzherbert, see Jefferson to JM, 7–8 Feb., n. 12. For the "terms or periods," see Delegates to Harrison, 25 Mar., and n. 4. See also Delegates to Harrison, 24 Mar., and n. 2; 1 Apr. and n. 4; JM Notes, 24 Mar., and n. 1; 31 Mar.; JM to Maury, 24 Mar., and n. 2; JM to Randolph, 1 Apr. 1783.

[3] *JCC*, XXIV, 238–40. For the debate on "the Report" and the few changes of any significance which were made in its text before it was adopted, see JM Notes, 11 Apr. 1783.

[4] JM inadvertently wrote "They" instead of "The" before "Secy" (Robert R. Livingston). The "Secy at War" was Benjamin Lincoln, and the "Agent of Marine," Robert Morris. For the issue of discharging "all prisoners of war," see JM Notes, 12 Apr.; 14 Apr. 1783.

Virginia Delegates to Benjamin Harrison

RC (Virginia State Library). In the hand of Theodorick Bland. Cover addressed by him to "His Excellency Benjn: Harrison Esqr. Governor of Virginia." Bland also wrote on another fold of the cover, "Delegates—Apr. 10th." At the opposite side of the same fold appears the docket, "Letter from the Delegates in Congress. April 10th 1783."

PHILADELPHIA April 10th 1783

SR.

We take the opportunity by a Gentn. who sets off to North Carolina tomorrow; and whose route lays through Richmond[1] to Communicate to Yr. Excellency copies of Papers sent by Sr. Guy Carleton & Admiral Digby and brought by an Aid of the Former Yesterday to the Office of Foreign Affairs.[2] we believe them to be Perfectly Authentic and as they are a full Confirmation of what we have before informd your Excelly[3] they need no further Comment.

We sincerely congratulate Your Excelly and our fellow Citizens on the Happy Event

We take the liberty to inform Your Excelly that the State of New York has made an offer to Congress of a tract of land included in the boundaries of the Township of Kingston or Esopus on the North River, accompanied by a provisional act of Incorporation, granting certain Privilidges of Jurisdiction in civil matters—except in cases concerning the Property of the Soil &c. the Policy of which is to Induce Congress to fix their residence in that State.[4]

The Delegates of Virginia and Maryland,[5] conceiving that a more Central Situation for Congress, accompanied with other equal or superior advantages might possibly be more agreeable, and that an Offer of a Small tract of Territory by Virginia & Maryland in the Neighbourhood of George Town on Potowmack might meet with the Acceptance of Congress in Preference to that offerd by New York, especially if a more ample and Enlarged Jurisdiction shd be Annexd thereto—have Conceived it their Duty to inform their states respectively of the steps taken by New York—that if they think proper they may Conjointly adopt such p[o]licy as they may deem most Eligible to Induce Congress to fix their Residence in a Place which we Humbly Conceive wd. be not only more Generally agreeable to the States, but wd. be so manifestly advantageous to the states Immediately in the Vicinage of the Seat of General Government.[6]

We shall endeavor to procure before the Assembly sits a copy of the Grant of New York with the Boundaries therein assigned for the Jurisdiction of Congress, which will be transmitted to your Excelly to be laid before them[7]

Since writing the above, Official dispatches from Mr. Adams, Mr. Franklin & Mr. Jay, have arrived announcing the Signature & ratification of the Preliminary Articles by the Belligerent Powers, as mentiond in the Enclosed Proclamation, and an agreement between the Said Powers, to an Arm[i]stice, which we Expect will this day be Proclaimed by order of Congress and transmitted to the Respective States.[8] the same dispatches inform us, that the Definitive treaty is not yet signed, the terms not yet having been adjusted between the Court of Great Britain & the Seven U. Provinces.[9]

The British Prints inform us that in a Division on a debate in their House of Commons, on a Paragraph in their address to their King for approving the Peace a Majority of Sixteen were against the approbation —North & Fox violently opposing the Ministry. the vote for approving

447

was carried in the Lords. how this temper of the Commons may effect the Politics of Europe, or the Ministry of Great Britain time must determine[10]

with the most perfect respect we are Yr. Excelly's most obedt. Serts. (Signed in behalf and at the request of the Delegates)[11]

THEOK. BLAND JR.

[1] The "Gentn." was a "Mr. Sitgreaves," who also carried JM's letter of the same date to Edmund Randolph (JM to Randolph, 10 Apr. 1783, hdn.). John Sitgreaves (1757–1802), English-born and a resident of New Bern, N. C., was a lawyer, a war veteran, and clerk of the state Senate from 1778 to 1779. While a member of the Commons House of the North Carolina General Assembly, 1784 and 1786–1789, he served as its speaker in 1787 and 1788. In 1785 he attended Congress briefly as a delegate. From 1789 until his death he was judge of the federal district court in North Carolina.

[2] JM to Randolph, 8 Apr. 1783, and n. 4.

[3] Delegates to Harrison, 24 Mar., and n. 2; 25 Mar., and n. 4; 1 Apr. 1783, and n. 4.

[4] On 20 March 1783 Governor George Clinton, writing from the seat of New York's government at Kingston, enclosed with his strong letter of endorsement to Elias Boudinot, president of Congress, (1) a copy of the resolutions of the "Trustees of the Freeholders and Commonalty of the Town[ship] of Kingston," 7 March, offering Congress a "Mile Square, or an Equivalent Quantity in any part of the Common Lands"; (2) a map of that township, showing the many areas, even with a frontage along the North (Hudson) River, which were available for Congress to select as "a fixed residence," because they were not privately owned; and (3) a copy of a joint resolution of both houses of the legislature on 12 and 14 March, pledging to incorporate any square mile or equivalent acreage which Congress might choose within that township, and guaranteeing "exempt jurisdiction" in almost all "civil matters" to the officials of Congress (NA: PCC, No. 46, fols. 1–13). Congress received these documents on 4 April and referred them to a committee, Rutledge chairman, three days later (JCC, XXIV, 229, n. 2).

[5] The Maryland delegates present in Congress on 9 April were Thomas Sim Lee and Daniel Carroll (JCC, XXIV, 233).

[6] Apparently this is the earliest suggestion of the site which eventually was chosen for the national capital.

[7] When Joseph Jones left Philadelphia on 6 or 7 May, he probably took the "copy" with him and gave it to Harrison upon arriving in Richmond two weeks later to attend the session of the Virginia legislature. The governor referred the papers to the House of Delegates on 12 June (JM to Randolph, 6 May 1783 in LC: Madison Papers; Cal. of Va. State Papers, III, 493; JHDV, May 1783, p. 50).

[8] If Charles Thomson's record of the dates on which dispatches arrived is complete and accurate, Congress received no dispatch from Jay along with the dispatches from Adams and Franklin, and neither had received nor would receive any communication from Jay for three or more weeks (NA: PCC, No. 185, III, 56–57). Bland probably should have written "Mr. Laurens," whose dispatch of 9 January, along with those from Adams and Franklin, was laid before Congress (NA: PCC, No. 185, III, 61; Wharton, Revol. Dipl. Corr., VI, 200; JM Notes, 10 Apr. 1783, n. 2). The "Proclamation," of which Bland enclosed a copy, was not adopted by Congress until 11 April (JM Notes, 11 Apr. 1783).

[9] In his dispatch of 22 January to Robert R. Livingston, Adams remarked: "The King of Great Britain has made a declaration concerning the terms that he will

allow to the Dutch; but they are not such as will give satisfaction to that unfortunate nation" (Wharton, *Revol. Dipl. Corr.*, VI, 226). An article, dated at Leyden on 16 January and published in the *Pennsylvania Packet* of 12 April 1783, summarizes the contents of King George III's "declaration" and why the States-General of the Netherlands would not accept its rigorous terms. For the preliminary treaty of peace of 2 September 1783 between Great Britain and the Netherlands, see Delegates to Harrison, 24 March 1783, n. 4.

10 Besides London newspapers, "British Prints" may mean reprints in Rivington's *Royal Gazette* of New York City. Extracts from the debates in each house of Parliament on 17 and 18 February appear in the *Pennsylvania Packet* of 15 April 1783. By a vote of 72 to 59 the House of Lords resolved to prepare "an humble address," thanking the king for relieving his subjects of the "bothersome and expensive war." In the House of Commons, after a nightlong discussion, the ministry of the Earl of Shelburne evidently decided to ward off defeat by not bringing to a vote an "address to the throne" of similar tenor.

The session closed with the opposition, comprising an unusual coalition of the adherents of Charles James Fox and Lord North, carrying by a vote of 224 to 208 an amendment to the proposed address, praying the king "to concert with his parliament" in measures to extend British commerce. A second amendment, begging the king to bestow his particular favor upon the American Loyalists, was also sponsored by the opposition and passed by an unrecorded vote (*Hansard's Parliamentary Debates*, XVI, cols. 373–435, esp. cols. 374–75; cols. 436–93, esp. cols. 438–39, 493). For the ministry of the Earl of Shelburne, see *Papers of Madison*, V, 120, n. 33; 210; 211, nn. 17–23. For the resignation of Shelburne on 24 February, see JM to Randolph, 29 Apr. 1783, and n. 3.

11 Joseph Jones, JM, and John Francis Mercer. Arthur Lee had left Philadelphia to return to Virginia (JM to Randolph, 1 Apr. 1783, n. 9).

To Edmund Randolph

RC (LC: Madison Papers). JM wrote on the cover only his own signature and "Edmund Randolph." On the cover in another hand appears also "Favd. by Mr. Sitgreaves" (Delegates to Harrison, 10 Apr. 1783, n. 1). Randolph docketed the cover of the present letter, "J. Madison. April 10, 1783," and wrote "J. Madison" in the left margin of the text.

PHILADA. Apl. 10. 1783

DEAR SIR,

The important contents of the inclosed paper[1] were brough[t] hither yesterday[2] by a British officer sent for that purpose by Sr. G. Carlton. To day Congs. recd. letters from Dr. F. & Mr. Adams[3] inclosing a declaration entered into by them & the British Plenipoy. by which the epochs at which hostilities are to cease between France & G. B. are adopted between the latter & America. a great diversity of opinion pre-

449

vails as to the time at which they were to cease on this Coast.[4] The Merchants & the lawyers are most affected by the question.[5] Yrs affy.

J. MADISON JR

[1] Probably the *Pennsylvania Packet* of 10 April 1783.

[2] If the *Pennsylvania Journal* of 12 April is correct, the "British officer" had reached Philadelphia on the evening of 8 April rather than "yesterday" (JM to Randolph, 8 April 1783, n. 4).

[3] JM Notes, 10 Apr. 1783, and n. 2.

[4] For "the epochs," see Delegates to Harrison, 25 Mar., n. 4; JM Notes, 10 Apr., nn. 2, 3. For the ambiguity about "the time," see JM Notes, 11 Apr. 1783, and n. 3.

[5] For illustrations of why merchants and lawyers were especially "affected," see JM to Randolph, 15 Apr.; JM Notes, 18 Apr. 1783, and n. 1; Burnett, *Letters*, VI, 136, 137, first n. 2, 138–39.

Notes on Debates

MS (LC: Madison Papers). For a description of the manuscript of Notes on Debates, see *Papers of Madison*, V, 231–34.

Friday. Apl. 11.

This day was spent on discussing the Proclamation which passed.[1] Mr. Wilson proposed an abreviation of it which was disagreed to.[2] The difficultys attending it were that 1st. the Agreemt of our Ministers with Fitzherbert that the Epochs with Spain as well as France sd. be applied to U S. to be computed from the ratifications which happened at different times, the former on the 3d. the latter the 9th. of Feby. 2d. the circumstance of the Epochs having passed at wch the Cessation of hostilities was to be enjoined.[3] The impatience of Congs. did not admit of proper attention to these & some other points of the Proclamation; particularly the authoritative stile of enjoining an observance on the U.S. the Govrs. &c. It was agst. these absurdities & improprities that the *solitary no* of Mr. Mercer was pointed. See the Journal.[4]

[1] That is, the proclamation, drafted by Robert R. Livingston, declaring the "cessation of arms, as well by sea as by land, agreed upon between the United States of America and his Britannic Majesty; and enjoining the observance thereof" (NA: PCC, No. 79, III, 153–57; *JCC*, XXIV, 238–40; JM Notes, 10 Apr. 1783).

[2] The draft of James Wilson's substitute proposal, slightly amended by Alexander Hamilton, is in NA: PCC, No. 25, II, 196. See also *JCC*, XXIV, 242, n. 1.

[3] The "difficultys" concerning the date when hostilities, especially at sea, between Great Britain and the United States should cease arose from the following circumstances: (1) Although no specific date was mentioned in the preliminary peace

treaty of 30 November 1782, Articles VI and VII could be interpreted to mean "all hostilities both by sea and land" should end "at the time of the Ratification of the Treaty in America" (Hunter Miller, ed., *Treaties and Other International Acts*, II, 99). See also JM Notes, 14 Apr. 1783, and n. 3. Congress had received an official copy of that treaty on 12 March but delayed ratifying it until 15 April, thus conforming with the pledge given in Articles I and VIII of the Treaty of Alliance between the United States and France (Hunter Miller, ed., *Treaties* II, 36, 38; JM Notes, 12–15 Mar., and nn. 1, 2; 10 Apr., and n. 2; 15 Apr. 1783; *JCC*, XXIV, 242–51).

(2) Although on behalf of the United States, Franklin and Adams on 20 January 1783 had subscribed to Articles XXII and XXIII of the preliminary peace treaty signed on that day between Great Britain and France and the similar articles, X and XI, of the treaty concluded also on that day between Great Britain and Spain, they apparently had not realized that those articles, which stipulated the dates when captures of ships and cargoes by the belligerents in various areas of the Atlantic Ocean would become unlawful, were both indefinite and, because of the time-distance involved, impracticable insofar as Great Britain and the United States were concerned (Wharton, *Revol. Dipl. Corr.*, VI, 223–24). Of prime importance to the United States, because of the span in degrees of latitude of her ocean coastline, was the provision in each of those treaties that, beginning one month after its ratification, captures "from the Channel and North Seas, as far as the Canary Islands, inclusively, whether in the Ocean or in the Mediterranean," would become invalid. As JM noted, the two ratifications had occurred on different dates and the month's extension beyond them had lapsed, at the latest, on 9 March. Exactly one month after that deadline, "authentic" texts of those treaties, translated into English, had finally been laid before Congress and published in the newspapers of Philadelphia (Delegates to Harrison, 25 Mar., n. 4; *Pa. Packet*, supplement, 9 Apr.; JM Notes, 10 Apr., and n. 2; JM to Randolph, 10 Apr. 1783).

(3) King George III's proclamation of 14 February, of which a copy had reached Congress on 9 April from General Sir Guy Carleton, stated that one month after 3 February, which was the date of the exchange of ratifications of the preliminary peace treaty between Great Britain and France, hostilities in the North American waters of the Atlantic Ocean would end with the United States as well as with France (Wharton, *Revol. Dipl. Corr.*, VI, 251–52; JM Notes, 10 Apr. 1783). Obviously, being a terminal date over five weeks in the past on 11 April, the proclamation only compounded rather than resolved the "difficultys." Of more practical help, except to lawyers who needed a precise and official date for the termination of hostilities, and to American merchants and shipowners who had lost property at sea to the enemy after 3 March, was the assurance from Carleton and Admiral Robert Digby that they were recalling "the British cruisers now on our coasts." As early as 24 March Congress had been told that the French were similarly informing their men-of-war in American waters (JM Notes, 31 Mar., and nn. 2, 4–6; JM to Randolph, 8 Apr., and n. 4; Delegates to Harrison, 10 Apr.; *Pa. Packet*, 10 Apr. 1783).

4 Bearing in mind the difference in ratification dates of the Anglo-French and Anglo-Spanish preliminary treaties of peace and the similarly obsolescent date proclaimed by King George III for the ending of the Anglo-American war at sea, "absurdities" accurately characterizes portions of Livingston's draft, and especially the terminal "whereas" clause in his second paragraph, reading, "and whereas it is our will and pleasure, that the cessation of hostilities between the United States of America and his Britannic Majesty, should be conformable to the epochs fixed between their Most Christian and Britannic Majesties."

John Francis Mercer and other zealous republicans undoubtedly objected to the regal tone of the proposed proclamation. In the second of six paragraphs Congress was made to say, "it is our will and pleasure"; in the third, "we hereby strictly charge and command all our . . . subjects"; and in the fourth, "we do further strictly charge and require all the governors and others, the executive powers of these United States respectively, to cause this our proclamation to be made public." Although the delegates restrained their "impatience" long enough to soften the haughty phraseology by deleting "strictly charge and" insofar as it related to state executives, and to make a few other alterations in the draft, they felt impelled to adopt and issue the proclamation with a minimum of delay. See *JCC*, XXIV, 238–41; *Pa. Journal*, 12 Apr.; Randolph to JM, 26 Apr. 1783. JM underlined the two words italicized in the present copy.

Notes on Debates

MS (LC: Madison Papers). For a description of the manuscript of Notes on Debates, see *Papers of Madison*, V, 231–34.

Saturday Apl. 12.

A letter of the 16th. of Decr. O. S. was rcd. from Mr. Dana, in which he intimates that in consequence of news of peace taking place & independance being acknowledged by G. B. he expected soon to take his proper station at the Ct. of St. Petersburg, & to be engaged in forming a Commercial Treaty with her Imperial Majesty.[1]

Mr. Madison observed that as no powers or instructions had been given to Mr. Dana relative to a Treaty of Commerce, he apprehended there must be some mistake on the part of Mr. Dana, that it wd. be proper to enquire into the matter & let him know the intentions of Congs. on this subject.[2] The letter was committed to Mr. Madison Mr. Gorhum & Mr Fitzsimmons.[3]

Mr. Rutlidge observed that as the instructions to Foreign Ministers now stood it was conceived they had no powers for commercial stipulations other than such as might be comprehended in a definitive Treaty of Peace with G. B.[4] He said he did not pretend to commercial knowledge but thought it wd. be well for the U. S. to enter into commercial Treaties with all nations & particularly with G. B. He moved therefore that the Come. sd. be instructed to prepare a general report for that purpose.

Mr. Madison & Mr. Fitzsimmons thought it wd. be proper to be very circumspect in fettering our trade with stipulations to foreigners, that as our stipulations wd. extend to all the possessions of the U. S. necessarily— & those of foreign Nations havg. colonies to part of their possessions only;[5] and as the most favd. nations enjoyd greater privileges in U. S. than elsewheres, The U. S. gave an advantage in Treaties on this subject,[6] & finally that negociations ought to be carried on here, or our Ministers directed to conclude nothing without previously reporting every thing for the sanction of Congs. It was at length agreed that the Come. sd. report the general State of instructions existing on the subject of commercial Treaties[7]

Congress took into consideration the report of Secy. for F. A. for immediately setting at liberty all prisoners of war,[8] & ratifying the provisional articles. Several members were extremely urgent on this point from motives of Œconomy. Others doubted whether Congs. were bound thereto, & if not bound whether it would be proper. The first question depended on the import of the provisional articles, which were very differently interpreted by different members. after much discussion from which a general opinion arose of extreme inaccuracy & ambiguity as to the force of those articles, the business was committed to Mr. Madison, Mr. Peters & Mr. Hamilton who were also to report on the expediency of ratifying the said articles immediately.[9]

[1] The dispatch to Robert R. Livingston, secretary for foreign affairs, from Francis Dana, minister-designate to Russia, is printed in Wharton, *Revol. Dipl. Corr.*, VI, 170–71.

[2] In view of Dana's commission and instructions of 19 December 1780, JM's statement was inexact. As Livingston informed Dana in a dispatch of 1 May 1783: "With respect to a commercial treaty, none can be signed by you. Your powers only extend to 'communicate with her Imperial Majesty's ministers on the subject of a treaty,' &c., but not to sign it" (*JCC*, XVIII, 1166–73, and esp. 1172; Wharton, *Revol. Dipl. Corr.*, VI, 403).

[3] Before Thomas FitzSimons reported for this committee on 22 April 1783, Congress had also referred to his committee Livingston's letter of the day before, enclosing Dana's dispatch of 19 December (O.S.) 1782, "just received" (*ibid.*, VI, 171–72, 300, *JCC*, XXIV, 267, and n. 1, 318–57).

[4] *Papers of Madison*, V, illustration opp. p. 416; also 476, and nn. 2, 3; 477, nn. 4, 5.

[5] Lacking colonies, the United States, in contrast with Great Britain and many of the powers of western Europe, had no navigation acts or their mercantilistic equivalents obliging colonists to restrict most of their trade to or through the mother country. See *Papers of Madison*, V, 476; 477, n. 4; JM Notes, 27 Jan. 1783, n. 10.

[6] The reference was especially to the second, third, fourth, and fifth articles of the Treaty of Amity and Commerce with France and to the second, third, and ninth articles of the similar treaty with the Netherlands (*JCC*, XI, 423–25; XXIV, 69, 71). See also *Papers of Madison*, III, 189, n. 6; IV, 13; 16, n. 29; 392; 393, n. 17; 410–11.

[7] A note by Charles Thomson in one of his record books indicates that no report on this subject was rendered by the committee before it was superseded on 6 May by a new committee (NA: PCC, No. 186, fol. 94). On 28 April the arrival of John Adams' dispatch of 5 February 1783 concerning a commercial treaty with Great Britain led Congress to appoint a committee, Hamilton, chairman, on that particular phase of the general problem (Wharton, *Revol. Dipl. Corr.*, VI, 242–47; NA: PCC, No. 186, fol. 97).

8 JM Notes, 10 Apr., and n. 4. On 11 April Livingston recommended that Congress have Benjamin Lincoln, secretary at war, and Robert Morris, agent of marine, "take order" for the immediate discharge of all prisoners at war, "as well those upon Parole, as others in actual Confinement." On that day Livingston wrote to General Sir Guy Carleton, and on 12 April to Admiral Robert Digby, informing them of his recommendation to Congress (NA: PCC, No. 52, fols. 225–32; No. 79, III, 149, 165–71, 178). See also JM Notes, 15 Apr. 1783, and n. 2; JCC, XXIV, 242–43.

9 For the report of the committee and the differences of opinion concerning "the import of the provisional articles" of peace, see JM Notes, 14 April 1783.

From Jacquelin Ambler

RC (LC: Madison Papers). Addressed to "The Honobl. James Madison of Congress Philadelphia." Docketed by JM, "Apl. 12. 1783."

RICHMOND VIRGINIA 12th April 1783

DEAR SIR

The Auditors, to my great surprize, excuse themselves from issuing Warrants on Account, to the Delegates in Congress, unless their respective Accounts are first transmitted; so that I have only the Certificate sent me in your last as my Voucher for the payment of the £500.[1] the Act requires no more of me than to pay them on their order *at the Treasury* quarterly, as the means may be in my power; but, sensible of the difficulties which would result to them at so great a distance in being left on the same footing with the Officers of Government here, I have taken the liberty to vest the Money in what I conceived to be a better remittance:[2]—if, the Gentlemen Delegates have leizure & inclination to transmit their Accounts quarterly to the Auditors, it will indeed save them an entry or two more on their Books; & the Receipts in the Treasury will be more regular on the Auditors issuing their warrants.[3] if otherwise, I have no doubt but the Assembly on being informed of the circumstances, will admit such a Certificate as you sent me a sufficient Voucher.[4]

I had great expectations of being able to remit another £500. by this days Mail; but the Bill cannot be procured until next Week.[5]

Mr. Digby has not yet made a sufficient fortune I suppose, & wishes a few more Prizes. I hope he will be disappointed.[6]

I am Dr Sir Yr. Affect. Serv.

J. A.

[1] For the members of the Board of Auditors, see Ambler to JM, 1 Feb. See also Ambler to JM, 22 Mar. 1783, and n. 2. Ambler's "surprize" was occasioned by the auditors' insistence that each of the delegates send his own "Certificate" rather than the jointly signed receipt which they had forwarded to Ambler on or about 27 March (Receipt of Delegates, 27 Mar. 1783). The law creating the Board of Auditors, enacted by the Virginia General Assembly in December 1778, directed them "to give warrants on the treasurer for the payment or advance of wages to our delegates in congress, debiting each delegate respectively with the warrant given in his name, and requiring account thereof to be rendered within three months after the expiration of his appointment" (*JHDV*, Oct. 1778, p. 111; Hening, *Statutes*, IX, 537).

[2] Harrison to Delegates, 12 Apr., n. 2. In their letter of 1 Apr. 1783 to Harrison (*q.v.*), the delegates had expressed a wish to be enabled to draw their quarterly salary from a source in Philadelphia rather than from the treasury in Richmond. Ambler seems to have responded to the request by underlining the words "at the Treasury"—italicized in the present copy—to emphasize what the law required him to do. Ambler's "better remittance" to the delegates, from which JM received one-fifth, was in the form "of two bills of exchange one for £300 on Saml Inglis & Co. and the other for £200 on Wm. Turnbul & Co" (MS in Va. State Library). These sums are in Virginia pounds, but on Ambler's ledger for the quarter, March to May 1783, they are entered in Virginia dollars, at a 3⅓ exchange ratio, as $1,000 on Inglis & Co. and $666⅔ on Turnbull & Co. (MS in Va. State Library). See also *Papers of Madison*, II, 172, n. 2; 237, n. 7; 252; V, 148; 150, n. 16; Ambler to JM, 22 Mar. 1783, and n. 2.

[3] JM's quarterly statement of accounts was dated 28 May 1783.

[4] Receipt of Delegates, 27 Mar. 1783.

[5] Ambler to JM, 19 Apr. 1783.

[6] JM to Jefferson, 13 Feb.; to Randolph, 8 Apr., and n. 4; JM Notes, 11 Apr. 1783, and n. 3.

Benjamin Harrison to Virginia Delegates

FC (Virginia State Library). In the hand of Thomas Meriwether. Addressed to "Virginia Delegates in Congress."

COUNCIL CHAMBER April 12th. 1783.

GENTLEMEN

Severe rheumatic Pains prevent my doing more than acknowledge the receipt of yours favor of the 1st. Instant[1] and informing you that I shall lay it before the Assembly if you desire it but I really do not know what they can do more than is already done,[2] the Treasurer is directed to Pay your Salarys quarterly out of any Money that shall come to his Hands, if it is not done the fault must either be in him or your Agents.[3]

I am with respect Gentlemen yrs: &c.

B. H.

[1] *Q.v.* Harrison's affliction probably accounts for the recess in the meetings of the Virginia Council of State from 15 to 19 April and the almost complete suspension of

letter writing by the governor during the same period (Executive Letterbook, 1783–1786, p. 100, and Executive Letterbook of War Office, 1783–1786, p. 42, MSS in Va. State Library; *JCSV*, III, 77).

[2] In their letter of 1 April 1783, the delegates asked Harrison to recommend to the Virginia General Assembly that it establish "a Credit" in Philadelphia to enable them "to draw their Salaries" when due rather than to have to resort to usurers for loans. On 1 July 1782 the Assembly had enacted a law assuring the delegates that their salaries would "be paid them quarterly out of such public money as shall hereafter be set apart and appropriated for that use" (Minutes of the House of Delegates, 6 May 1782–2 July 1782, p. 85, MS in Va. State Library; Hening, *Statutes*, XI, 32).

[3] See Ambler, "the Treasurer," to JM, 12 April 1783, and nn.

Notes on Debates

MS (LC: Madison Papers). For a description of the manuscript of Notes on Debates, see *Papers of Madison*, V, 231–34. The words italicized in the present copy are those which were underlined by JM.

Monday April 14.[1]

The Committee on the report of Secretary of foreign Affrs. reported as follows, Mr. Hamilton dissenting:[2]

1. That it does not appear that Congress are any wise bound to go into the ratification proposed. "The Treaty" of which a ratification is to take place, as mentioned in the 6th. of the provisional articles, is described in the title of those articles to be "a Treaty of peace proposed to be concluded between the Crown of G. B and the said U. S. but which is not to be concluded until terms of peace shall be agreed upon between G. B. & France"; The act to be ratified therefore is not the provl. articles themselves; but an act *distinct, future,* and *even contingent:*[3] again altho' the Declaratory act entered into on the 20th Jany. last, between the American & British Plenipotentiaries relative to a cessation of hostilities, seems to consider the contingency on which the provl. articles were suspended as having taken place, yet that act cannot itself be considered as the *"Treaty of peace meant to be concluded*["]; nor does it stipulate that either the provl. articles or the act itself should be ratified in America; it only engages that the U. S. shall cause hostilities to cease on their part, an engagement which was duly fulfilled by the Proclamation issued on the 11th. instant[4]—lastly it does not appear from the correspondence of the American Ministers, or from any other information either that such ratification was expected from the U. S. or intended on the part of

G. B: still less that any exchange of mutual ratifications has been in contemplation.[5]

2. If Congress are not bound to ratify the articles in question, the Come. are of opinion that it is inexpedient for them to go immediately into such an act; inasmuch as it might be thought to argue that Congress meant to give to those articles the quality & effect of a definitive Treaty of peace with G. B. tho neither their allies nor friends have as yet proceeded farther than to sign preliminary articles;[6] and inasmuch as it may oblige Congs. to fulfil immediately all the stipulations contained in the provl. articles tho' they have no evidence that a correspondent obligation will be assumed by the other party.[7]

3. If the ratification in question be neither obligatory nor expedient, the Come are of opinion, that an immediate discharge of all prisoners of war on the part of the U.S. is premature and unadvisable; especially as such a step may possibly lessen the force of demands for a reimbursement of the sums expended in the subsistance of the prisoners.[8]

Upon these considerations the Come. recommend that a decision of Congs. on the papers referred to them be postponed.

On this subject a variety of sentiments prevailed:

Mr. Dyer, on a principle of frugality was strenuous for a liberation of the Prisoners.

Mr. Williamson thought Congs. not obliged to discharge the prisoners previous to a definitive treaty, but was willing to go into the measure as soon as the public honor would permit. He wished us to move pari passu with the British Commander. He suspected that that place would be held till the interests of the Tories should be provided for.[9]

Mr. Hamilton contended that Congress were bound by the tenor of the Provl. Treaty immediately to Ratify it and to execute the several stipulations inserted in it; particularly that relating to discharge of Prisoners.[10]

Mr. Bland thought Congs. not bound.

Mr. Elseworth was strenuous for the obligation and policy of going into an immediate execution of the Treaty. He supposed that a ready & generous execution on our part wd. accelerate the like on the other part.

Mr. Wilson was not surprized that the obscurity of Treaty sd. produce a varity of ideas.[11] He thought upon the whole that the Treaty was to be regarded as "contingently definitive."

The Report of the Come. being not consonant to the prevailing sense of Congs. it was laid aside.

¹ The journal of Congress omits mention of a session on this date (*JCC*, XXIV, 241, and n. 2).

² JM Notes, 12 Apr. and n. 9. The manuscript of the committee's report has not been found. In view of Alexander Hamilton's dissent, the report must have been drafted either by JM, chairman, or Richard Peters. See JM Notes, 15 Apr. 1783, n. 2.

³ Barring differences in abbreviation, punctuation, and capitalization, JM quoted accurately from "the title" or preamble of the "articles of the proposed treaty" agreed upon by the commissioners of the United States and Great Britain on 30 November 1782 (*JCC*, XXIV, 244–45; JM Notes, 12–15 Mar., and nn. 1, 2, 13; Delegates to Harrison, 12 Mar. 1783, and nn. 6–12, 14). In the concluding article, IX, the document is also designated as "these articles" rather than as a treaty (*JCC*, XXIV, 250). Except in the preamble, the word "treaty" is used in the document only in the phrase in Article VI, reading "at the time of the ratification of the treaty in America" (*JCC*, XXIV, 249). The phrase, together with the preamble and Article IX, justifies JM's position that Congress was not "bound to ratify" the provisional document. An acceptance of it by Congress could not formally end the war but would reconfirm the suspension of hostilities and make known that a definitive treaty of peace embodying those articles would be ratified. See JM Notes, 31 Mar., and nn. 2, 4–6; 12 Apr. 1783.

Besides being justified by the text of the document, JM and a minority of the delegates in Congress probably also opposed ratification because it would imply that all the provisional articles, including those favoring British creditors and owners of confiscated property, should immediately become effective (*Papers of Madison*, V, 81, n. 5; 112, n. 11; JM Notes, 16 Jan., and n. 4; 12–15 Mar., and n. 2; 20 Mar.; Delegates to Harrison, 12 Mar., n. 12; JM to Randolph, 12 Mar., nn. 4, 5; 8 Apr., and n. 2; Randolph to JM, 29 Mar. 1783, and n. 10; Burnett, *Letters*, VII, 136). An opposing consideration was the possibility that the postponement would prevent an immediate release of prisoners of war and reduce the number of slaves, taken by the British, which they eventually would return (*Papers of Madison*, V, 111–12; 112, nn. 1, 11; 113; Delegates to Harrison, 12 Mar., and n. 14; JM Notes, 12 Apr. 1783, and n. 7; Burnett, *Letters*, VII, 139).

⁴ For the "Declaratory act," see JM Notes, 24 Mar., and n. 1; 10 Apr., and n. 2; 11 Apr., and nn. 1, 3, 4; JM to Maury, 24 Mar., n. 2; Delegates to Harrison 10 Apr., and nn. 8, 10; JM to Randolph, 10 Apr. 1783.

⁵ JM Notes, 12–15 Mar., n. 1; 24 Mar., and n. 1; Delegates to Harrison, 18 Mar., nn. 2, 4; JM to Randolph, 10 Apr. 1783.

⁶ JM Notes, 11 Apr. 1783, and n. 3.

⁷ The "correspondent obligation," besides that mentioned in n. 3, would include withdrawal by Great Britain of her troops from wherever they were stationed within the territory ceded by her to the United States (*JCC*, 246–47, 249–50; JM Notes, 26 Feb. 1783, and n. 22).

⁸ *Papers of Madison*, V, 105, n. 8; 191, n. 27; 255; 257, n. 18; Delegates to Harrison, 12 Mar. 1783, n. 14.

⁹ By "that place," Hugh Williamson meant New York City. For its discontented Tories (Loyalists), see *Papers of Madison*, V, 46; 48, n. 7; 51, n. 6; 102, n. 6; 109; 223; Delegates to Harrison, 12 Mar. 1783, and n. 22.

¹⁰ In a letter of 15 April 1783 to Washington, Hamilton remarked that "the usual practice of nations" was to release all prisoners upon "the ratification of the preliminary treaty." He advised Washington, in view of the "great diversity of Opinion in Congress," without communicating "our doubts to the British, to extract their sense of the matter from them" (Syrett and Cooke, *Papers of Hamilton*, III, 325–26). For a further quotation from this letter, see JM Notes, 16 Apr. 1783, n. 1.

11 For additions to the "varity" mentioned in JM's notes for this day, see Burnett, *Letters*, VII, 138, 141, n. 3, 149; Wharton, *Revol. Dipl. Corr.*, VI, 386–87; JM to Randolph, 15 Apr.; JM to Jefferson, 22 Apr. 1783.

From Thomas Jefferson

RC (LC: Madison Papers). Docketed by JM, "Tho. Jefferson Apl. 14. 1783." Alongside this docket JM also wrote "April." Using a new cipher which JM and Jefferson evidently had devised while they were together in Philadelphia, Jefferson encoded the words which are here italicized. This cipher will be designated hereafter as "JM-Jefferson Code No. 2."

SUSQUEHANNA[1] Apr. 14. 1783.

DEAR SIR

Meeting at our quarters with a mr. Levi[2] going to Philadelphia and having no other employment, I write by him just to say that all is well, and that having made our stages regularly & in time we hope to make better way than mr. Nash did.[3] the Carolina letter bearer is here also.[4] we pass one another two or three times a day. I never saw mr. Ingles[5] to speak to him about my books. will you be so obliging as to make my acknowlegements to him for his undertaking & to ask him to send them to Richmond to the care of James Buchanan.[6] be pleased to make my compliments affectionately to the gentlemen & ladies. *I desire them to Miss Kit[t]y particularly[7] Do you know that the ra[il]lery you sometimes experienced from our family[8] strengthened by my own observation gave me hopes there was some foundation for it I wished it to be so as it would give me a neighbour[9] whose worth I rate high [,] and as I know it will render you happier than you can possibly[10] be in a singl[e] state I often made it the subject of conversation [,] more [,] exhortation with her and was able to convince my[self] that she possessed every sentiment in your favor which you could wish But of this no more without your leave*

I am with much affection Dr. Sir Your sincere friend

TH: JEFFERSON

1 Jefferson seems to have been writing from an inn at the "lower ferry" which crossed the Susquehanna River (Jefferson to JM, 31 Jan. 1783, and n. 3). See also JM to Randolph, 8 Apr. 1783, and n. 9.

2 Unidentified, but the surname was that of several well-known merchants and lawyers at Philadelphia in 1783 (*Pa. Archives*, 3d ser., XVI, 449, 470, 475, 494; *Pa.*

Mag. Hist. and Biog., V [1881], 391; XVI [1892], 163; XLVI [1922], 284; Edwin Wolf, 2d, and Maxwell Whiteman, *The History of the Jews in Philadelphia from Colonial Times to the Age of Jackson* [Philadelphia, 1957], pp. 57–145 *passim*).

[3] Jefferson to JM, 14 Feb. 1783, 2d letter, and n. 46.

[4] Almost certainly the "Mr. Sitgreaves" who, on his way to North Carolina, had offered to carry to Richmond the letter of 10 April from the Virginia delegates to Governor Harrison (*q.v.*, and n. 1) and a letter of the same date from JM to Randolph (*q.v.*).

[5] Samuel Inglis of Inglis and Company of Philadelphia (*Papers of Madison*, V, 150, n. 16; JM to Ambler, 12 Apr. 1783, n. 2; *Pa. Mag. Hist. and Biog.,* V [1881], 335–39; XXVII [1903], 253; XXXVIII [1914], 384; LV [1931], 318; LXI [1937], 66, 396).

[6] For many years before his death in October 1787, James Buchanan was a prominent merchant-shipowner and proprietor of real estate in Richmond. Besides having the Virginia state government and Jefferson among his patrons, he was influential from 1779 until his death in arranging for the temporary quarters of the state officials in Richmond and in determining the sites and supervising the erection of the Capitol and other permanent public buildings in that town (Hening, *Statutes,* X, 317–20, 450; XII, 280–81; *JCSV,* III, 207, 433–34, 591; McIlwaine, *Official Letters,* II, 88, 316, and n. 236; Boyd, *Papers of Jefferson,* III, 18, 19 n.; VI, 127, 195, 321, 538; VII to IX *passim*; XI, 330, 333).

[7] Jefferson to JM, 31 Jan., and nn. 11–12; JM to Jefferson, 18 Feb., and n. 1; 22 Apr. 1783.

[8] That is, the residents of Mrs. Mary House's boarding house.

[9] The air distance from Monticello to Montpelier is about twenty-five miles.

[10] Jefferson used the cipher 1071, meaning "possible."

From Edmund Pendleton

Tr (LC: Force Transcripts). In the left margin at the top of the transcription, Peter Force's clerk wrote "MSS McGuire's." See *Papers of Madison*, I, xxii, xxiii. Addressed to "The Honbl. James Madison Esq Philadelphia." A passage, also taken from the original letter but occasionally varying in spelling, punctuation, and capitalization from the present text, is in Stan. V. Henkels Catalogue No. 694 (1892), p. 92.

VIRGA. April 14th 1783

DEAR SIR

Yr favr of the 25th past,[1] confirm'd what I expected to be the case that Congress in the first Moment of Peace, would turn their thoughts to such great Arrangements, as are necessary to realise the blessings of that important event,[2] and should they adopt measures as comprehensive & liberal as our situation requires, I can't doubt but they will be ratified by the several Members of the Union, who, now at leisure to reflect calmly & seriously without the sword suspended o'er their heads, will surely see the utility and indeed necessity of mutual concessions & good offices to preserve the fœdral strength & give it dignity amongst Nations: the adage so often mentioned in the commencement of the dispute, "united we stand, divided we fall," will be found no less true in Peace than in War.[3] An honourable and permanent provision for paying our debts foreign & domestic, seems amongst the foremost & most Important subject for consideration, and in order to that, the Ascertainment of the whole debt, the Quota of each state, and the Past Accounts of each; on view of which, certain & unchangeable funds should be provided for Paying the Annual Interest & certain proportions of the Principal, so as to sink the whole in a reasonable time. The fixing the value of domestic Loans, and the Rate of Redemption of the Continental paper yet in circulation, are also necessary steps preparatory to the fixing our debt wch will occasion some difficulty.[4] I think our Elections, as far as I have hitherto heard of them, have generally been in favr of the best men. Mr Gilchrist and Colo John Taylor are ours; the County seem'd more than Ordinarily anxious for the old Gentln to prove to the Assembly they did not think him within their resolutions agt Tory Members.[5]

I am happy to hear that the Army are appeased, and hope they will meet with no disappointment in the funds promised them, since I should be sorry to part with them in ill humour, after the merit they have acquired. [6]

I am told 22/6 cwt on James River & 30/ on Rappa hath been offered & refused for our tobo. I believe the one party knows not what to offer, nor the other what to ask, at present.[7] My Complts to Mr Jones. I miss'd his Letter by last Post.[8] I am with perfect respect & Esteem Dr Sr

Yr very Affe & obt Servt

EDMD PENDLETON

[1] Not found, but the contents of that letter may have resembled those of the letter which JM wrote to Randolph on 25 March 1783 (q.v.).

[2] JM Notes, 4 Apr. 1783, and hdn., and nn. 9, 10.

[3] The idea that union makes for strength is at least as old as the writings of Vergil and Plutarch, but John Dickinson in the following couplet of "The Liberty Song" (1768) may have been the first to state the matter epigrammatically:

Then join in hand brave Americans all,
By uniting we stand, by dividing we fall.

This general truth was embodied in Article III of the Articles of Confederation (*JCC*, IX, 908). The aphorism, in the exact form quoted by Pendleton, became the motto of Kentucky upon her admission to the Union on 1 June 1792.

[4] In these two sentences Pendleton mentioned most of the principal issues comprising the general problems of (1) determining with justice to each of the four classifications of creditors (foreign governments and bankers, state governments, civilians, and soldiers) the specie total of the Confederation debt; (2) deciding upon sources of revenue so varied in nature that together they would bear equitably upon

all the states; (3) devising effective methods of collecting the revenue without unduly encroaching upon the sovereignty of each state; and (4) providing sufficient annual income to restore public credit by paying at least the interest, overdue and to become due, on the debt. Although it obviously is impracticable to cite all the references to these issues in JM's notes, correspondence, and other papers, see for examples the index of the present volume under (1) Continental Congress, actions on or discussion of: army memorial and pay, debt of U. S., lack of money, requisitioning money, settling accounts with states or individuals, valuation of land in states, (2) Impost amendment, (3) Money, (4) Sectionalism and states' rights, (5) Taxes.

[5] Pendleton to JM, 31 Mar. 1783, and n. 8. The "old Gentln" was Robert Gilchrist. For the "resolutions agt Tory Members," see *Papers of Madison*, V, 454; 455, n. 8.

[6] JM Notes, 7 Apr. See also JM Notes, 13 Jan., and nn. 11, 21; 24 Jan., and nn. 20, 32, 39; 25 Jan., and nn. 8, 11, 12; 28 Jan., and n. 45; 4 Feb., and nn. 10, 11; 18 Feb., and nn. 3, 5; 20 Feb., and nn. 17–20; 25 Feb., and nn. 1, 2; 27 Feb.; 28 Feb.; 10 Mar.; 17 Mar., and nn. 1, 2; 25 Mar., and n. 6; JM to Randolph, 13 Feb.; 25 Feb. 1783.

[7] Virginia planters evidently were expecting the sales value per hundredweight ("cwt") to rise as compared with what it had been not long before (Harrison to Delegates, 31 Jan.; JM to Randolph, 11 Feb., n. 3; Pendleton to JM, 17 and 24 Feb., n. 3). Writing to Theodorick Bland on 8 April 1783 from Prince William County, Va., Arthur Lee commented: "The expectation of peace has had little apparent effect here as yet. There is so little money in this part of the state at least, that little tobacco is purchased, and no higher price than 20 shillings offered" (Charles Campbell, ed., *The Bland Papers: Being a Selection from the Manuscripts of Colonel Theodorick Bland, Jr., of Prince George County, Virginia* [2 vols.; Petersburg, Va., 1840–43], II, 108). See also *Papers of Madison*, V, 44; 45, n. 10; 71, n. 15; 202–3.

[8] Joseph Jones's letter, if any, would have been written on or about 3 April 1783. See *Papers of Madison*, V, 157; 158, nn. 6, 8; 192; 194, n. 2; 241, n. 3.

Notes on Debates

MS (LC: Madison Papers). For a description of the manuscript of Notes on Debates, see *Papers of Madison*, V, 231–34.

Teusday April 15.

The ratification of the Treaty & discharge of prisoners again agitated.[1] For the result in a unanimous ratification see secret Journal of the day; the urgency of the majority producing an acquiescence of most of the opponents to the measure.[2]

[1] JM Notes, 14 Apr. 1783, and nn. 1–3, 7, 9, 10.

[2] On 15 April Alexander Hamilton introduced two resolutions. During the ensuing debate their contents were considerably amended and regrouped into three resolutions before Congress adopted them. As passed, the first resolution provided that the preliminary articles of peace "be ratified, and that a ratification in due form be sent to our Ministers Plenipotentiary at the Court of Versailles, to be exchanged if an exchange shall be necessary." The second resolution directed Robert Morris, agent of marine, to have "all the naval prisoners" freed. The third resolution di-

rected Benjamin Lincoln, secretary at war, to make proper arrangements, "in conjunction with" Washington, "for setting at liberty all land prisoners," and instructed Washington "to make the proper arrangements" with General Sir Guy Carleton for taking "possession of the posts in the United States" and recovering all American-owned "negroes and other property" still held by the British (*JCC*, XXIV, 241–43). See also JM Notes, 16 Apr. 1783.

Following the adoption of these three resolutions, Congress agreed to a "form of the ratification" comprising four parts: (1) a preamble devoted principally to summarizing the credentials of the American peace commissioners empowering them to conclude and sign the preliminary articles; (2) the full text of these articles including the secret article; (3) the act ratifying "the said articles, and every part, article and clause thereof"; and (4) an attestation to the authenticity of the document as evidenced by the seal affixed and President Boudinot's signature (*JCC*, XXIV, 243–51).

This "form" was adopted by Congress without a recorded vote. Hence it is not clear whether JM remained opposed to the ratification or voted with the majority. Although as entered in the journal, the act of ratification clearly embraced the secret article, the American peace commissioners were informed by Livingston in his dispatch of 21 April: "You will observe that the ratification does not extend to the separate article. The treaty between Spain and Great Britain renders it unnecessary, and Congress not caring to express any sentiment upon that subject" (Wharton, *Revol. Dipl. Corr.*, VI, 386–87). Exercising the option mentioned in the first paragraph of this footnote, Adams, Franklin, and Jay exchanged ratifications of the provisional articles on 13 August 1783 with the representative of King George III (*ibid.*, VI, 556–57, 633, 645–46).

Virginia Delegates to Benjamin Harrison

Letter not found.

EDITORIAL NOTE

15 April 1783. After Congress had ratified the provisional articles of peace with Great Britain (JM Notes, 15 Apr. 1783, and n. 2), JM and Theodorick Bland, on behalf of all the Virginia delegates, apparently sent a brief letter, now missing, to Governor Harrison, informing him of the ratification (Anderson Galleries [New York] Catalogue, No. 1581 [2–3 May 1921], item 34).

From the Reverend James Madison

RC (LC: Madison Papers). Cover missing. Docketed, "Rev. J. Madison (Wmsburg.) to J M. Jr. Apl. 15. 1783."

April 15. 1783.

DEAR COL.

By a Letter from Mr. Jefferson 31. March.[1] he has the Expression, speaking of Peace, "tho there can scarcely be a Doubt." I hope by this

Time you have official Accts of its Certainty: for tho' no one indeed can scarcely doubt, yet every one wants the fullest Confirmation.[2] I am sorry to find that he will not probably go to Europe as a Resident, from what he says, tho' the Conclusion is rather indirect.[3] But it is certain we shall want Men of Abilities on this Side the Atlantic as well as the other. I wished to mention to you, that it is generally expected a Convention for the Purpose of reforming our [State][4] Constitution will be proposed to the People, as soon as the assembly meets.[5] Your Stay at Congress must be nearly at an End.[6] Suppose therefore you return in Time for this Business.

I have written by this Post to Mr. J. If he be returned, I must beg the Favr of you to take Charge of the Letter for him.[7] Dr. McC. is here, & begs to be affy. remembered[8]

Yrs sincerely

JM

Do you not intend to get the Encyclopedia Methodique.[9] I hope we shall import it by the first oppy. It must be in itself a compleat scientific Library.

[1] Not found.

[2] JM Notes, 10 Apr., and n. 2; Delegates to Harrison, 10 Apr. 1783, and n. 8.

[3] JM Notes, 1 Apr., n. 13. Unofficial but well-authenticated news of the signing of preliminary articles of peace by Great Britain with France and Spain was current in Philadelphia by 31 March. Writing that day to the Reverend James Madison, Jefferson probably anticipated the resolution of Congress on 1 April canceling his mission to Paris as a peace commissioner.

[4] The bracketed word appears to have been interlineated at a later date by someone now unknown.

[5] The Virginia General Assembly at the May 1783 session did not undertake to fulfill this expectation. See JM to Randolph, 8 Apr., and n. 10; Jefferson to JM, 7 May 1783 (LC: Madison Papers; Boyd, *Papers of Jefferson*, VI, 266).

[6] Article V of the Articles of Confederation stipulated that "no person shall be capable of being a delegate for more than three years in any term of six years" (*JCC*, XIX, 215). Having been thrice re-elected by the Virginia General Assembly, with each annual term expiring on the first Monday in November, JM at about the end of October 1783 would become ineligible to serve in Congress until three years from that time had elapsed (*Papers of Madison*, II, 40; III, 161; IV, 336; 358, n. 5; 365; 367, n. 8). Even though the Articles of Confederation, which had become effective on 1 March 1781, appeared to permit JM, if reappointed for "a fraction of a year" by the Virginia General Assembly, to serve in Congress until 29 February 1784, he soon concluded that an extension of term would not accord with his "private conveniency" (Boyd, *Papers of Jefferson*, VI, 270–71).

[7] Not found.

[8] Dr. James McClurg (*Papers of Madison*, V, 201, n. 5; Randolph to JM, 22 Feb. 1783, and n. 9).

[9] Report on Books, 23 Jan. 1783, entry No. 1.

To Edmund Randolph

RC (LC: Madison Papers). Cover missing. Docketed by Randolph, "J. Madison. April 15th. 1783."

PHILADA. Apl. 15. 1783.

MY DEAR SIR

My letter by a private hand who left this place a few days ago together with late public letters will have fully apprized you of the decisive events which have taken place in favor of peace.[1] The paper inclosed will amuse you with the bickerings in the British parliament on that subject.[2]

Genl. Carlton is very importunate for an immediate execution of the provisional articles on the part of Congress in the two points of liberating the prisoners, and recommending restitution to the Loyalists. On his part he has set the example in the first point, but says nothing of executing the other important conditions which are in our favor.[3] This proposition has led Congs. into a critical discussion of the import of the provl. articles, in which the opinions are almost as numerous as the articles themselves. Some think that the instrument was converted by the signature of preliminary articles between F. & G. B. into the Treaty of peace, of which a ratification in America is alluded to in the 6. art:[4] others think that it was conditioned no otherwise on terms of peace between those powers, than that such an agreement rendered it a lawful & necessary foundation for a *Treaty*[5] of peace between the U.S. & G. B. Some again suppose that the provl. arts need no ratification from Congs. but that they ought to wait for the Treaty to be grounded on them. Others suppose that a ratification is essential, or at least proper. The latter description again are divided, some proposing to ratify them as articles still contingent   others to ratify them as having taken effect in consequence of the preliminary articles between G. B. & F. This variety & contrariety of interpretations arise in great measure from the obscurity & even contrariety of the articles themselves.[6]

Mr. Jefferson left us on saturday last & will probably be with you by the time this gets to hand.[7]

I am Dr Sir &c &c.

J. M.

[1] Delegates to Harrison, 1 Apr.; 10 Apr., and n. 1; JM to Randolph, 8 Apr. 1783, and hdn.

² Probably the *Pennsylvania Packet* of 15 April. See Delegates to Harrison, 10 Apr. 1783, and n. 10.

³ JM Notes, 31 Mar., and n. 5; 10 Apr.; 12 Apr., and n. 8; 15 Apr., and n. 2; JM to Randolph, 1 Apr. Replying on 9 April 1783 to a letter from General Sir Guy Carleton, Washington stated that as soon as he received "Instructions from the Sovereign power of the United States," he would "rejoice" in doing everything he could to carry "into compleat Execution, that Article of the Treaty which respects the Restitution of all prisoners of War" (Fitzpatrick, *Writings of Washington,* XXVI, 307–8).

The "other important considerations," favorable to Americans, are in Article VII. It implicitly stipulates the return to their owners of Negro slaves in British possession, and explicitly provides for the restoration to states and private individuals of "all archives, records, deeds and papers" in the hands of British officers (*JCC,* XXIV, 249–50).

⁴ For the signing of the preliminary articles of peace between Great Britain and France on 20 January, see JM Notes, 13 Feb. and n. 10; 12–15 Mar., n. 6; 18 Mar., and n. 14; 24 Mar.; 31 Mar., n. 6; 10 Apr., and n. 2; JM to Jefferson, 18 Feb., and n. 2; Delegates to Harrison, 12 Mar., and n. 18; 18 Mar., n. 4; JM to Randolph, 25 Mar. 1783, and n. 5. The "6. art" was that of the preliminary articles of peace between Great Britain and the United States (JM Notes, 11 Apr. 1783, n. 3).

⁵ Underlined by JM.

⁶ JM probably wrote this letter before Congress' "unanimous ratification" of the preliminary articles on 15 April (JM Notes, 15 Apr. 1783, and n. 2). Many years later he or someone at his bidding placed a bracket at the close of the paragraph to signify that it and the preceding paragraphs should be included in the first comprehensive edition of his papers. See Madison, *Papers* (Gilpin ed.), I, 525–26.

⁷ JM to Randolph, 8 Apr., and n. 12; Jefferson to JM, 14 Apr. 1783.

Notes on Debates

MS (LC: Madison Papers). For a description of the manuscript of Notes on Debates, see *Papers of Madison,* V, 231–34.

Wednesday April 16th.

Mr. Hamilton acknowledged that he began to view the *obligation* of the provl. Treaty in a different light and in consequence wished to vary the direction to the Commander in cheif from a positive to a preparatory one as his motion on the Journal states.¹

¹ The italicizing of "obligation" is in lieu of JM's underlining of the word. In the second of his two resolutions introduced on 15 April, Alexander Hamilton had proposed that Washington "be directed to enter into the necessary arrangements" for a mutual release of prisoners of war and delivery by the British of posts still occupied by them in the United States. On that day Congress largely embodied this recommendation in its third resolution, although substituting the word "proper" for "necessary." Giving more thought to the matter, and perhaps above all to the significance of the fact that the number of prisoners of war held by the Americans

far exceeded those held by the British, Hamilton remarked in a letter to Washington on 15 April: "I doubt the expedience of a total restoration of prisoners 'till they are willing to fix the epochs at which they take leave of us. It will add considerably to their strength, and accidents though improbable may happen" (Syrett and Cooke, *Papers of Hamilton*, III, 326). That is, Washington, by speedily releasing the prisoners, would sacrifice one of his strongest bargaining points in securing a rapid departure of the British armed forces from the United States.

In line with this reconsideration, Hamilton on 16 April apparently retrieved the manuscript of the two resolutions he had introduced on the preceding day and wrote "preparatory" above a canceled "the necessary" in his second resolution (*JCC*, XXIV, 242). His motion, however, could not have been to so amend that resolution, but rather to substitute "preparatory" for "the proper" in the last of the three resolutions adopted by Congress on 15 April as an approximate concurrence with what he had recommended on that day. See JM Notes, 15 April 1783, and n. 2. Congress rejected Hamilton's motion by a tie vote (*JCC*, XXIV, 252).

The quotation from Hamilton's letter of 15 April to Washington, given above, is a sufficient answer to the charge by John C. Hamilton that his father had again been aspersed by JM in the notes for 16 April. According to the son, Alexander Hamilton's letters of late May and early June 1783 demonstrate his desire for "the immediate execution of the provisional articles." On this score John C. Hamilton was accurate, but he apparently failed to realize that the general situation, both in reality and as viewed by his father, had changed by then (John C. Hamilton, *History of the Republic*, II, 530–38, 534 n.). See also Syrett and Cooke, *Papers of Hamilton*, III, 367–72.

Amendment to Report on Restoring Public Credit

MS (NA: PCC, No. 26, fol. 419). In JM's hand. Docketed by him, "Report of Committee to which was recommitted the 10. clause in the Report relative to the establishmt. of funds &c April 11. 1783 Read Entd. April 17. 1783. On the question to admit the clause to which this is proposed as an addition, into the report on finance States called Virg, ay all the rest no."

EDITORIAL NOTE

Prior to 17 April 1783 this suggested amendment is not mentioned in Charles Thomson's committee book, in the journal of Congress, in JM's notes on debates, or, except for the docket quoted above, in any other contemporary source known to the editors. For this reason it seems more appropriate to use the date on which the proposal was debated than that on which it was read to Congress and apparently tabled for six days.

To avoid duplication, JM's copy of the amendment, which he included in his notes on debates for 17 April, will be omitted. Disregarding minor differences in abbreviations, capitalization, and punctuation, seven footnotes of the present item record the contrasts in phraseology between the two versions.

[17 April 1783]

The Come. to whom was recomd. the 10th. clause of the Report on Revenue &c,[1] report the following addition thereto: "And to the end that convenient provision may be made for determining in all such cases, how far the expences may have been reasonable, as well with respect to the object thereof as to the means for accomplishing it, thirteen Commissrs. namely one out of each State, shall be appointed by Congress any seven or more[2] of whom (having first taken an oath for the faithful & impartial exercise of their appointment)[3] who shall concur in the same opinion, shall be empowered to determine finally, on the reasonableness of all claims for expences incurred by particular States as aforesaid. And that[4] such determinations may be expedited as much as possible, instructions shall be given to the Commissrs. for adjusting accounts between the U. S. and individual States,[5] to examine all such claims and report to Congress such of them as shall be supported by satisfactory proofs, distinguishing in their reports the objects and measures as to[6] which the expences shall have been incurred; provided that no balances which may[7] become due to any State in consequence of this regulation or of the Resolutions of the   day of   [8] shall be deducted out of the preceding revenues; but shall be discharged out of[9] separate requisitions to be made on the States for that purpose.[10]

---

[1] In his notes for 17 April (*q.v.*), JM stated that he was reporting "with the *permission* of the Come on Revenue." Almost certainly he was delivering a minority report. The committee, consisting of Nathaniel Gorham, chairman, Alexander Hamilton, JM, Thomas FitzSimons, and John Rutledge, had been appointed on 21 February (JM Notes, 21 Feb. 1783, and n. 28). These men were all present in Congress when a vote on another issue was recorded on 17 April (*JCC*, XXIV, 255). Assuming that they were also present when the unrecorded vote was taken on JM's proposed amendment, and bearing in mind that only "Cont." and "Virga" voted "ay," Gorham, Hamilton, and FitzSimons must have voted "no," because the number of delegates present to represent their respective states was two each. Although Rutledge's vote is indeterminable, for he was one of three delegates present from South Carolina, his previous states'-rights pronouncements on the subject of public credit strongly suggest that he also opposed the amendment (JM Notes, 9–10 Jan., and n. 8; 14 Jan.; 29 Jan.; 11 Feb. 1783, and n. 10).

The eleventh paragraph of the original report of the committee on 6 March had become "the 10th" as a result of amendments adopted by Congress subsequent to that date (Report on Restoring Public Credit, 6 Mar. 1783, and n. 16). The "10th. clause" or paragraph had been recommitted ("recomd") on 27 March, along with James Wilson's proposal that before being merged with the Confederation debt, any state's expenses not authorized by Congress should "be limited to such as had been incurred in a *necessary defence;* and of which the object in each case sd. be approved by Congress" (JM Notes, 27 Mar. 1783, and nn. 10, 12, 14–16, 18, 19).

[2] In JM's Notes for 17 April, "or more" is omitted.

[3] JM replaced this word with "trust" in his notes for 17 April.

[4] This word is preceded by "in order" in JM's notes for 17 April.

[5] From "instructions" to "States," the corresponding passage in JM's notes for 17 April reads, "the Commissrs. now in appointment for adjusting accts. between the U. S. and individual States, shall be instructed." By an ordinance of 20 February 1782, Congress had provided for the appointment of these commissioners (*JCC*, XXII, 84–86; *Papers of Madison*, IV, 55; 56, n. 6; 71; 72, nn. 1–3; 332; 333, n. 2; V, 322; 323, n. 5; JM Notes, 5–6 Feb.; 10 Feb. 1783, and n. 14).

[6] JM wrote "in" instead of "as to" in his notes for 17 April.

[7] In JM's notes for 17 April, the passage from "may" through "of" is changed to "be found due under."

[8] The resolution of 1 April 1783 (*JCC*, XXIV, 223–24; JM Notes, 1 Apr. 1783, and n. 11).

[9] Instead of "out of," JM wrote "by" in his notes for 17 April.

[10] For the debate on JM's proposal, see JM Notes, 17 Apr. 1783.

Notes on Debates

MS (LC: Madison Papers). For a description of the manuscript of Notes on Debates, see *Papers of Madison*, V, 231–34.

Thursday April 17th.

Mr. Madison with the *permission*[1] of the Come. on Revenue, reported the following clause to be added to the 10 paragraph in the first report viz [2]

. . . .

In support of this proposition it was argued that in a general provision for public debts and public tranquility,[3] satisfactory measures ought to be taken on a point wch. many of the States had so much at heart,[4] & which they wd. not separate from the other matters proposed by Congress:[5] that the nature of the business was unfit for the decision of Congs. who brought with them the spirit of advocates rather than of Judges,[6] and besides required more time than could be spared for it.

On the opposite side some contended that the accts. between U. S. & particular States sd. not be made in any manner to encumber those between the former and private persons.[7] Others thought that Congs. could not delegate to Comrs. a power of allowing claims for which the Confedon. reqd. nine States.[8] Others were unwilling to open so wide a door for claims on the Common Treasury.[9]

On the question Masts. divided Cont. ay. R. Id. no. N.Y. no N.J. no. Pa. no. Maryd. no. Va. ay. N.C. no S.C. no.[10]

[1] The italics signify that JM underlined this word.

[2] For the text of "the following clause," see Amendment to Report on Public Credit, 17 Apr. 1783, and ed. n.

[3] The connection between maintaining "public tranquility" and providing for "public debts" had been frequently emphasized. See JM Notes, 13 Jan., and nn. 17, 21; 27 Jan., and n. 27; 28 Jan., and n. 34; 29 Jan.; 19 Feb., and n. 12; 20 Feb., and nn. 17, 18; 21 Feb., and n. 16; 26 Feb.; 17 Mar., and n. 12; 7 Apr.; JM to Randolph, 22 Jan., and n. 8; 13 Feb., and n. 6; 25 Feb.; 4 Mar., n. 5; 25 Mar.; 8 Apr. 1783, and n. 6.

[4] The "point" was to induce the Confederation to assume their "reasonable" war expenses, even though they had been incurred without authorization by Congress. Besides the references to this matter cited in Amendment to Report on Public Credit, 17 Apr. 1783, and nn. 1, 5, and 8, see JM Notes, 28 Jan., and n. 19; 8 Feb., and n. 3; 11 Feb., and n. 2; 19 Feb., and n. 6; 26 Feb., and nn. 37, 38, 40, 43; 8 Apr., n. 15; Report on Restoring Public Credit, 6 Mar., and n. 16; Amendment to Report on Restoring Public Credit, 28 Mar.; Harrison to Delegates, 7 Feb.; JM to Randolph, 25 Feb.; 11 Mar. 1783.

[5] The "other matters" included import duties, cession of western lands, evaluating the land of each state as a basis for allocating financial quotas, and military pensions. See, for example, JM Notes, 14 Jan., and n. 6; 29 Jan.; 30 Jan., and n. 2; 20 Feb., n. 14; 26 Feb., and nn. 38, 40, 43; 20 Mar., and n. 5; 27 Mar., and nn. 11, 14; 9 Apr., and n. 4; Report on Restoring Public Credit, 6 Mar.; JM to Randolph, 11 Mar.; 8 Apr. 1783, and n. 6.

[6] Heretofore, this argument had been chiefly advanced to oppose having each state evaluate its own land as a basis for a determination by Congress of equitable ratios in requisitioning the states for funds. See JM Notes, 9–10 Jan.; 14 Jan, and n. 7; 31 Jan., and n. 17; 11 Feb.; JM to Randolph, 25 Feb. 1783.

[7] Among "private persons" would be holders of continental currency, loan-office certificates, and receipts for supplies taken by military personnel, as well as unpaid soldiers, and Dutch bankers entitled to overdue interest on their loans to Congress. See, for example, *Papers of Madison*, V, 473; 474, n. 8; Randolph to JM, 3 Jan., and n. 12; JM to Randolph, 22 Jan., n. 8; JM Notes, 13 Jan., and n. 5; 27 Jan., and nn. 11, 13; 29 Jan., and nn. 14, 15; 30 Jan., and nn. 2, 6; 4 Feb., n. 16; 26 Feb.; 11 Mar., n. 7; 8 Apr. 1783, and nn. 16, 17.

[8] JM Notes, 9–10 Jan. 1783, and n. 9. Article IX of the Articles of Confederation forbade Congress, "unless nine states assent," to "ascertain the sums and expences necessary for the defence and welfare of the united states, or any of them, nor emit bills, nor borrow money on the credit of the united states, nor appropriate money" (*JCC*, XIX, 220).

[9] JM Notes, 27 Mar. 1783.

[10] Delaware and Georgia were unrepresented in Congress, and only one delegate was in attendance from New Hampshire.

Notes on Debates

MS (LC: Madison Papers). For a description of the manuscript of Notes on Debates, see *Papers of Madison*, V, 231–34. The italicized words signify those which JM underlined.

Friday April 18.

Application was made from the Council of Pa. for determination of Congs. as to the effect of the acts terminating hostilities, on Acts to be inforced during the war. Congs. declined giving any opinion.[1]

The motion of Mr. Bland for striking out recommendation to States which had agreed to cede territory to revise & *compleat* their Cessions raised a long debate.[2] In favor of the motion it was urged by Mr. Rutlidge that the proposed Cession of Va. ought to be previously considered & disallowed; that otherwise a renewal of the recomendation wd. be offensive; that it was possible the Cession might be accepted in which case the renewal wd. be improper. Virga. he observed alone could be alluded to as having complied in part only.[3]

Mr. Wilson went largely into the subject. He said *If the investigation of right* was to be considered, the U. S. ought rather to make cessions to individual States then receive Cessions from them, the extent of the Territory ceded by the Treaty being larger than all the States put together; that when the claims of the states come to be limited on principles of right, the Alleghany Mountains would appear to be the true boundary: this could be established without difficulty before any Court, or the Tribunal of the World. He thought however policy reqd. that such a boundary sd. be established as wd. give to the Atlantic States access to the Western Waters.[4] *If accomodation* was the object, the clause ought by no means to be struck out. The Cession of Virga. could never be accepted because it guaranteed to her the country as far as the Ohio, which never belonged to Virga. [here he was called to order by Mr Jones].[5] The question he sd. must be decided. The indecision of Congs. had been hurtful to the interests of U. S. If compliance of Va. was to be sought she ought to be urged to comply fully.

For the vote in the affirmative, with exception of Virga. & S. Carol: see Journal.[6]

The plan of Revenue was then passed as it had been amended; all the states present concurring except R. I. wch. was in the Negative & N. Y. wch. was divided Mr Floyd ay & Mr. Hamilton no.[7]

---

[1] JM to Randolph, 10 Apr., and n. 5. On 12 April Thomas FitzSimons, a merchant of Philadelphia and a delegate from Pennsylvania in Congress, asked President John Dickinson and the Supreme Executive Council "whether vessels or goods coming into this State from Great Britain, or any of her ports or Colonies, can be admitted to entry at the Custom house" (*Colonial Records of Pa.*, XIII, 555). Although couched in economic terms, the question implicitly posed the constitutional issue of the effect, if any, of the proclamation of Congress of 11 April "Declaring the cessation

of arms, as well by sea as by land" on the statute of Pennsylvania banning trade by sea with the British.

As soon as Congress on 15 April ratified the preliminary terms of peace and President Dickinson in Council issued a proclamation the next day "strictly" to "charge and command" Pennsylvanians "to forbear all acts of hostility, either by sea or land, against his Britannic Majesty or his subjects," the naval officer of the port of Philadelphia inquired how he should respond to applications "to enter vessels from New York." Uncertain of what his response should be, Dickinson in Council requested the Pennsylvania delegates to submit the naval officer's letter to Congress. On 18 April 1783 Alexander Hamilton, chairman, Oliver Ellsworth, and James Wilson were named as a committee to recommend a reply. Beside the entry in his committee book, Charles Thomson wrote "Report verbal," but it was submitted in writing on 22 April (*ibid.*, XIII, 559–61; NA: PCC, No. 20, II, 151–52; No. 69, fols. 445–46; No. 186, fol. 195; JCC, XXIV, 238–40). Congress appears to have agreed with the "opinion" of the committee that "it is inexpedient for Congress to come to any formal decision on the subject of that letter" (JCC, XXIV, 267). Four days later a merchant vessel from New York City apparently unloaded her cargo in Philadelphia without interference (*Pa. Packet*, 29 Apr.). See also Randolph to JM, 26 Apr. 1783, n. 6.

2 JM interlineated the words from "for" through "Cessions" long after he first drafted his notes. The ninth paragraph of the original report of the committee on restoring public credit was under debate. This paragraph, which urged states to offer Congress their titles to land west of the Appalachian Mountains, closed with the words: "and to the states which may have passed acts complying with the said resolutions" of 6 September and 10 October 1780 "in part only, to revise and complete such compliances" (Report on Restoring Public Credit, 6 Mar., and n. 14; JCC, XXIV, 172). Theodorick Bland, seconded by John Rutledge, moved to delete this quoted passage (JCC, XXIV, 256). See also Delegates to Harrison, 29 Apr. 1783, and n. 3.

3 JM Notes, 9 Apr. 1783, and nn. 2, 4, 6–11. On 2 January 1781 the Virginia General Assembly had offered to relinquish to the United States jurisdiction and title to her western lands, with the exception of the district of Kentucky and of a limited acreage potentially needed as bounty lands for her troops; and provided that "all purchases and deeds" from Indians and "royal grants" to private persons "inconsistent with the chartered rights, laws and customs of Virginia" be declared invalid (*JHDV*, Oct. 1780, p. 80). Virginia's offer, contrary to John Rutledge's statement, was a compliance with the resolution of Congress of 6 September 1780, which had asked the "landed" states only to make "a liberal surrender of a portion of their territorial claims" (JCC, XVII, 806–7). As late as 20 June 1783, JM would correct a misstatement that "Congress had declared the Cession of Virginia to be a partial one" (JCC, XXV, 973).

Rutledge also overlooked or ignored the terms of Connecticut's offer of cession. On 12 October 1780 she had proposed to relinquish to the United States her title to all her trans-Appalachian lands but withheld political jurisdiction over them (*Papers of Madison*, IV, 32; 35, n. 8). This offer seems to have been compliance "in part only," for the resolution of Congress of 10 October 1780, with its reference to forming "distinct republican states" almost certainly implied that prior to statehood Congress could govern the ceded area as well as dispose of its land (NA: PCC, No. 66, II, 178–79; JCC, XVIII, 915; XIX, 99).

4 James Wilson assumed as a self-evident truth that the title of the United States to the territory between the Appalachian Mountains and the Mississippi River, conferred by Great Britain in the preliminary treaty of peace in consequence of a large sacrifice of "blood and treasure" by the American people, superseded the titles held

by six of the states to portions of that vast area. Hence, although he may not have explicitly advocated that it be equally divided by Congress among the thirteen sovereign states, he evidently believed that to do so would be more in accord with "the principles of right" than would be an acknowledgment by Congress of the claims of the "landed" states to the west. Wilson apparently did not explain how he could give the four New England "Atlantic States," not to mention New Jersey, Delaware, and Maryland, "access to the Western Waters" without traversing the sovereign state of New York or his own commonwealth of Pennsylvania.

⁵ The brackets were inserted by JM. The twenty-fourth and twenty-fifth rules of procedure, adopted by Congress on 4 May 1781, may have justified Joseph Jones in calling Wilson to order for conduct inconsistent "with the utmost decency and decorum" (*JCC*, XX, 481). Whether President Elias Boudinot's ruling or a majority of the delegates sustained Jones's objection remains unknown, but Wilson's concluding remarks were evidently less controversial.

⁶ Many years later JM interlineated all the words following "vote" and preceding "see." The vote was on the question whether the passage, which the Bland-Rutledge motion sought to cancel, should be retained. All delegates except the four from Virginia and two of the three from South Carolina voted "ay" (*JCC*, XXIV, 256–57).

⁷ The handwriting suggests that JM squeezed this paragraph, long after 1783, into the narrow blank space originally separating his notes for 18 April from those for 21 April. Of the twenty-nine delegates present in Congress, all voted for the amended report on restoring credit except Phillips White, who alone represented New Hampshire, Stephen Higginson of Massachusetts, David Howell and John Collins of Rhode Island, and Alexander Hamilton of New York (*JCC*, XXIV, 257–61). For the opposing explanations of their votes by Hamilton, on the one hand, and by the Rhode Island delegates, on the other hand, see Burnett, *Letters*, VII, 147–48; Syrett and Cooke, *Papers of Hamilton*, III, 354–56; JM Notes, 1 Apr. 1783, n. 9. See also Delegates to Harrison, 22 Apr., and n. 4; Address to the States, 25 Apr. 1783, and ed. n.

The state-by-state requisitions, which JM had included in his notes on the session of 4 April (*q.v.*), were considerably revised before Congress adopted them two weeks later as part of the plan for restoring public credit (*JCC*, XXIV, 259).

From Jacquelin Ambler

RC (LC: Madison Papers). Cover missing. Docketed by JM, "Apr. 19. 1783."

RICHMOND 19. April 1783

DEAR SIR

I have not the pleasure of a line from you by the last Mail. The return of Peace I doubt not spreads Joy & Gladness through out America. I sincerely congratulate you on this happy event.

I send another Bill of five hundred pounds Virga. Curry. which the Gentlemen of the Delegation will be pleased to divide as they think proper, transmitting the Vouchers necessary for my justification.¹ I am Dear Sir with great regard Yr. affect Servt

J. AMBLER

¹ The bill of exchange was drawn by David Ross, the former commercial agent of Virginia, on John Ross, a merchant-shipowner of Philadelphia. When the post-rider from Virginia reached that city, most probably on 28 April, JM was about to leave for New Jersey and did not return until the evening of 2 May. On 1 May Theodorick Bland had been able to cash the bill, even though it was drawn in JM's favor. On 6 May JM signed a voucher acknowledging that he had received from Bland $332 15/90 in Pennsylvania currency (£100 Virginia currency) as his share of the bill of exchange for £500 (*Papers of Madison*, III, 60, n. 8; V, 204, n. 1; Bland's and JM's vouchers dated 6 May, MSS in Va. State Library; JM to Jefferson, 6 May 1783, in Boyd, *Papers of Jefferson*, VI, 264–65).

Benjamin Harrison to Virginia Delegates

FC (Virginia State Library). In the hand of Thomas Meriwether. Addressed to "Virginia Delegates in Congress."

RICHMOND April 19th. 1783.

GENTLEMEN

I received your favor by the last Post.¹ It appears to me astonishing that Nathan should give you so much trouble, when he must know his Debt can be paid no where but at this Place[;] this his Agent² has been told, and that there are no funds as yet establish'd for that Purpose; I shall lay the Award of the Arbitrators before the next Assembly, who will no doubt provide for the Payments.³ You must consult your own Prudence in the Affair of Pollock,⁴ the Assembly have refer'd it to you to take proper Security,⁵ and it will probably behove you to be cautious, as I have additional reasons (lately received) to those I formerly had for thinking he has been at least the most imprudent Man in the World;⁶ great Part of his demand is for Bills taken up by him after the receipt of a Letter from Col: Todd from the Illinois a Copy of which I have forbiding him to Pay them and informing him they were drawn by Adventurers who had no right to draw and who were procuring Money in that way for their Private Purposes.⁷

I am waiting for a Public Express with official Accounts of the Confirmation of Peace. your Proclamation is arrived by a Private Hand but of that I can take no official Notice.⁸ I am with respect

Gentlemen Yrs: &c.

B. H.

¹ Delegates to Harrison, *ca*. 8 Apr. 1783, ed. n. See also Harrison to Delegates, 4 Mar. 1783, and the citations in n. 6.
² Thomas Smith (d. 1813) of Henrico County, who in 1779 had been the agent to

settle the account of Virginia with the United States (*JHDV*, Oct. 1781, pp. 47, 56–57). After his death an inventory disclosed that a number of clients were indebted to his estate while others were credited in full (Henrico County Court Records, Will Book 4, p. 335, MS in Va. State Library). See also McIlwaine, *Official Letters*, II, 256–57; *Cal. of Va. State Papers*, III, 370; *Papers of Madison*, V, 229, n. 6.

³ In his message of 5 May to the Virginia General Assembly Harrison enclosed the "determination of an arbitration, had in Philadelphia, on the part of the State, with a Mr. Nathan." The governor commented that Virginia probably was "now bound to pay" the award, although he thought it too large. On 21 June the House of Delegates rejected a committee's recommendation that Nathan be paid all that he was still owed with 6 per cent interest since 8 June 1780 (*JHDV*, May 1783, pp. 72–75). On 24 and 25 June 1783 the Virginia General Assembly, upon being informed that "some circumstances" relevant to the issue had been unknown to the arbitrators, resolved to submit the issue and the award for review by two new arbitrators—one of whom should be named by the governor of Maryland and the other by Nathan (*ibid.*, May 1783, pp. 81–82, 84).

Among the "circumstances" was probably the belated arrival in Philadelphia of an important document adverse to Nathan's claim (Delegates to Harrison, 4 Feb.; 4 Mar.; Harrison to Delegates, 15 Feb.; 21 Feb. 1783). Another of the "circumstances" may have been the papers enclosed with Harrison's message of 25 June 1783 to the General Assembly, revealing "Abuses" connected with purchases made in the West by Virginia officials there. From some of these transactions, the claims of Nathan, as well as of Oliver Pollock, had arisen (Executive Letter Book, 1783–1786, p. 162, MS in Va. State Library; *JHDV*, May 1783, p. 73). See also nn. 4–6, below; Boyd, *Papers of Jefferson*, VI, 321–24 n.

⁴ The state of Virginia owed Oliver Pollock much money for military supplies purchased from him by General George Rogers Clark and other military officers of the state in the district of Kentucky and the Illinois country. The exact amount due Pollock was controversial, not only because his invoices seemed sometimes to list prices in depreciated currency and sometimes in specie, but also because goods chargeable to Congress were not always differentiated from those bought for Virginia. See *Papers of Madison*, I, 277, n. 7; III, 98; 99, n. 1; 256, and n. 6; 344, n. 2; IV, 349, and n. 5; 377–78; 378, n. 5; 402; V, 208, n. 5; 282; 287, n. 19; 455, n. 10. The report on 26 March of a committee of Congress, to which a memorial and statement of account from Pollock on 24 February 1783 had been submitted, illustrates the complications caused by these ambiguities and also by Virginia's making use of three of his shipments, even though they were "for account of the United States" (NA: PCC, No. 50, fols. 297–304, 389–91; *JCC*, XXIV, 149, n. 1, 234–38, 237, n. 1, 266, 318, 323).

⁵ On 27 December 1782 the Virginia House of Delegates agreed to reimburse Pollock with $30,000 in three annual installments, "and the balance in certificates, payable in four years from the date thereof: *Provided*, that the issuing of certificates for one half of the amount of the said accounts, be postponed until the said Oliver Pollock finds such sufficient security as may be approved of by the delegates representing this State in Congress, for the indemnification of the States from any demands for the bills drawn by him on Penette, De Costa, Freres and Company." The Senate concurred the next day (*JHDV*, Oct. 1782, pp. 83–84, 88). The governor may have enclosed a copy of this resolution to the delegates in his letter of 4 Jan. 1783 (*q.v.*, and n. 5).

Harrison understood that Pollock would deposit as "sufficient security" with the Virginia delegates in Congress his written authorizations from Governor Thomas Jefferson in 1779 and 1780 to draw bills of exchange on Penet, d'Acosta Frères et Cie of Nantes (Boyd, *Papers of Jefferson*, III, 158–60, 274, 320). By means of these bills, Pollock had expected to procure funds for reimbursing Bernardo de Gálvez, the governor of Spanish Louisiana, who, with Jefferson's endorsement, had advanced Pollock some of the money used by him to pay for Virginia's military supplies (*ibid.*, III, 167–69, 482–83; VI, 356; *Papers of Madison*, I, 218, n. 6; 277, n. 7). Being in dire financial straits, partly because of bills unpaid by Virginia for goods shipped to her from France, the Penet Company was unable to honor Pollock's bills of exchange. Consequently, in the spring of 1783, although her treasury was almost empty, Virginia found herself pressed simultaneously for cash by Simon Nathan, by representatives of the bankrupt Penet Company, by the virtually bankrupt Pollock, and by Gálvez (McIlwaine, *Official Letters*, III, 103, 105, 108, 110; *JCSV*, III, 427, 462, 484, 506; *Cal. of Va. State Papers* I, 347; III, 153; Lynch to JM, 15 Feb., n. 4; Livingston to Delegates, 15 Mar., and n. 1; Harrison to Delegates, 29 Mar., and nn. 2–8, 10–12, 14; Delegates to Gálvez, 4 May 1783, MS in Archivo General de Indias, Seville).

Probably from information contained in the now missing letter of *ca.* 8 April from the delegates in Congress to him, Harrison stated in his message of 5 May 1783 to the Virginia General Assembly that Pollock was willing to deposit with the delegates enough of the certificates issued to him, in accordance with the Assembly's resolution of 27–28 December 1782, to secure Virginia against the protested bills of exchange drawn by him on the Penet Company. See Delegates to Harrison, 8 Apr. 1783, ed. n. Shortly after sending this message, but before 12 May, when a quorum first assembled in the House of Delegates, Harrison received the delegates' letter of 29 April 1783 (*q.v.*) stating that Pollock refused to give "any security for the present."

[6] By the phrase "at least," Harrison suggested his suspicion, expressed as early as January 1782, that Pollock's business dealings with Virginia had been characterized by fraud as well as by extreme imprudence (McIlwaine, *Official Letters*, III, 138, 139, 260–61, 320–22; and citations in n. 4, above). In a letter written in 1782 to George Rogers Clark, Pollock admitted that, from his "desire of serving a country I loved" and his overconfidence in her "Gratitude and Justice," he had acted "Unprudently" (James Alton James, *The Life of George Rogers Clark* [Chicago, 1928], pp. 293–94).

Although the source of the "additional reasons" has not been definitely identified, it probably was a letter of 9 March 1783, "lately received" by Harrison from the Virginia commissioners to settle western accounts (James Alton James, ed., *George Rogers Clark Papers, 1781–1784* [Springfield, Ill., 1924], pp. 215–17; *Cal. of Va. State Papers*, III, 433, 436, 441–44, 452–54; Harrison to Clark, 3 Mar.; 9 Apr.; to Mr. d'Acosta, 13 Mar.; to the commissioners to settle western accounts, 8 Apr. 1783, all in Executive Letter Book, 1783–1786, pp. 60, 66–67, 91, 95–96, MS in Va. State Library). For the commissioners, see *Papers of Madison*, IV, 378, n. 5; V, 229, nn. 4, 5.

[7] The letter at issue from Colonel John Todd to Oliver Pollock has not been found, although Harrison submitted a copy of it to the Virginia General Assembly on 5 May 1783. On the same day he also seems to have sent to the Assembly copies of Todd's letters of 1 and 2 July 1779 to John Page, lieutenant governor of Virginia, telling what he (Todd) had written to Pollock in New Orleans (James A. James, ed., *George Rogers Clark Papers, 1781–1784*, p. 321; *Cal of Va. State Papers*, I, 326). Todd's letter, to which Harrison referred, was written either between 12 May 1779, when he became head of the civil government of the country of Illinois, and 1 and 2 July, or between then and about 15 November of that year, when he returned from Kaskaskia to the district of Kentucky (Clarence Walworth Alvord, ed., *Kaskaskia Records, 1778–1790* [Springfield, Ill., 1909], pp. 80–85, 131, n. 1, 133, and n. 1).

Since Pollock sent military supplies by batteaux up the Mississippi and Ohio rivers to Illinois, Kentucky, and Ohio country ports without always knowing whether his consignee was the United States or Virginia, and without always making clear whether his invoices cited prices in specie or in depreciated paper currency, the following quotation from his letter of 30 September 1779 to the commercial committee of Congress may signify that by then he had received the letter in question from Todd: "I never meant or expected you would pay them in Silver, and if the Holders [of my bills of exchange] have made their Demands for that Specie, they know they have done wrong . . . [Hereafter] . . . I shall give prices in Paper Currency, you allowing me the Exchange customary at the time of presenting said Bills" (NA: PCC, No. 50, fols. 115–18). For Todd, see *Papers of Madison,* I, 275; 277, n. 4; IV, 427, n. 3; 446.

Sharing Harrison's opinion that Pollock's accounts needed to be scrutinized more thoroughly, the Virginia General Assembly on 25 June resolved that, "until further orders," no more warrants should be issued in favor of Pollock, and no further payments should be made on warrants already issued to him or to his agent, Daniel Clark (*JHDV,* May 1783, pp. 83, 85). See also *JHDV,* Oct. 1783, pp. 40–41, 47.

Among the "Adventurers," Harrison surely would have included Captain Philip Barbour (d. 1797), Daniel Clark (d. 1799), Captain Robert George (1756–1837), John Henderson (1737–1787), Lieutenant Colonel John Montgomery (*ca.* 1742–1794), Daniel Murray (d. 1784), and possibly Todd himself (*Papers of Madison,* I, 276; 277, nn. 3, 11; III, 99, n. 1; 106, n. 15; 256, and n. 6; 342–44; 344–47, nn.; IV, 18; 377; 378, nn. 5, 7; *Cal. of Va. State Papers,* I, 460; *JCSV,* II, 362–65; James Alton James, ed., *George Rogers Clark Papers, 1771–1781* [Springfield, Ill., 1912], pp. 496–98; *ibid., 1781–1784, passim;* Clarence W. Alvord, *Kaskaskia Records,* pp. 130–32, 149–50, 197–98, 333–34; James Alton James, *Oliver Pollock: The Life and Times of an Unknown Patriot* [New York, 1937], pp. 350–54).

[8] Delegates to Harrison, 10 Apr., and n. 1; JM Notes, 11 Apr., and n. 1. Although an express bearing the official copy of Congress' proclamation declaring the cessation of hostilities arrived in Richmond during the night of 18–19 April, Harrison evidently had not seen the proclamation before writing the present letter. On Monday, 21 April, the governor issued his own proclamation, enjoining Virginians "to pay due obedience to the said proclamation of Congress" (*JCSV,* III, 246–48; *Va. Gazette,* 19, 26 Apr. 1783). On Thursday, by Harrison's order, "the proclamation of Congress for a cessation of hostilities was read at the courthouse and several other publick places" in Richmond "by the city Serjeant, attended by the Constables" (*Va. Gazette, and Weekly Advertiser,* 26 Apr. 1783).

Notes on Debates

MS (LC: Madison Papers). For a description of the manuscript of Notes on Debates, see *Papers of Madison,* V, 231–34.

Monday. April 21.

The Motion was made by Mr. Hamilton 2ded by Mr. Madison to annex to the plan of the 18th. instant the part omitted relating to expences incurred by individual States,[1] on the question, N. York, Pena. & Virga. alone were in the affirmative, Cont. & Georgia not present.[2]

Teusday Apr. 22. see Journal[3]

1 The report of the Committee on Public Credit, drafted by JM and submitted on 6 March, was frequently debated and considerably revised before Congress adopted it on 18 April (Report on Restoring Public Credit, 6 Mar., and nn. 15, 16; JM Notes, 6 Mar.; 7 Mar., and ed. n.; 18 Apr. 1783, and n. 7). On 27 March Congress unanimously rejected the ninth (the original tenth) paragraph of the report relating to "equitable exceptions and abatements" being granted in financial settlements with states which, as a result of "invasions" by the enemy, had become delinquent in paying congressional requisitions. On the same day the tenth (the original eleventh) paragraph of the report, providing for an assumption by the United States of "reasonable expences" incurred by states without prior sanction of Congress but made necessary by war within their borders, was recommitted (JM Notes, 27 Mar. 1783, and nn. 11, 12, 14–16, 18, 19).

JM had tried unsuccessfully on 27 March to have Congress accept a proposal of a tenor similar to that of the excised ninth paragraph, and on 17 April a revised version of the tenth paragraph (JM Notes, 27 Mar.; Amendment to Report on Public Credit, 17 Apr., ed. n., and nn. 1, 5; JM Notes, 17 Apr. 1783, and nn. 3–8, 10). In the present session JM obviously joined Hamilton in another attempt to "revive" the tenth paragraph, even though Congress had already adopted the plan for restoring public credit.

2 Neither the motion nor the tallied vote was entered in the journal. New Hampshire as well as Connecticut had only one delegate in Congress and hence could not cast an effective vote. Georgia was not represented. See JM Notes, 7 Apr. 1783, n. 4.

3 Among other proceedings on the 22 April, Congress took action on six private claims for compensation, including the defeat of a motion to pay Oliver Pollock an annual salary of $2,000 for five years' service as a commercial agent. Congress also appointed a committee, Samuel Osgood, chairman, and JM one of the other four members, to confer with Robert Morris "relative to his continuance" as superintendent of finance (JCC, XXIV, 265–68; Harrison to Delegates, 19 Apr. 1783, n. 4). See also JM Notes, 18 Apr., n. 1; 23–24 Apr. 1783, n. 3.

Virginia Delegates to Benjamin Harrison

RC (Virginia State Library). In hand of Theodorick Bland, except for JM's signature. Cover franked by Bland and addressed to "His Excelly. Benjn. Harrison Esqr. Govr. of Virginia." Docketed by Thomas Meriwether, "Lr. from the Delegs. in Congress. April 22d. 1783."

PHILADA. April 22d 1783

SR.

Your two Favors of April 5th & 12th[1] came both to hand by yesterdays Post. little Interesting has happend Since our last, except that Congress have agreed to a Modification of the Recommendation to the States, for Vesting in Congress a revenue adequate to the funding the Public Debt, which being limited in its duration, and divested of some other exceptionable conditions, containd in the former requisition, We anxiously hope will for the Public good, and our National Honor & Credit be speedily and generally complied with by the States.[2] A Frigate (the Active) arrived last night from France, at Chester. her dispatches are not yet come up. We hope in our next to Inform your Excelly. of their Contents.[3] We shall endeavor to procure your Excelly. a Copy of the recommendation above mentiond, but if disappointed in this, we expect you will soon receive it officially from Congress.[4] The Comr. in Chief and the Secy. at War have orders to make arrangements with Sr. Guy Carleton for receiving possession of the Posts occupied by the British in the United States, and for delivering up the land Prisoners in our possession. the Naval ones on both Sides are already set at Liberty.[5] We are sorry to add that late advices from New York inform us that no steps are taken there which Indicate a Speedy evacuation of that Place.[6] we are with perfect respect

Yr. Excellys. most obedt. Sevts.

J. MADISON JR
THEOK. BLAND

P. S. Since the above Sr. G: Carleton has written to Congress, to request some person or persons may be sent to N. York to take possession of the Negroes & Publick property in conformity to the 7th article of the Preliminary Articles[7]

---

[1] *Q.v.* Governor Harrison's letter of 5 April has not been found.

[2] JM's Notes, 18 Apr. 1783, and n. 7. The "former requisition" was the proposed 5 per cent impost amendment to the Articles of Confederation, which Rhode Island had refused and Georgia had neglected to ratify. In contrast with the intention of Congress to continue that suggested levy indefinitely and to control its administration, the customs duties in the new plan for restoring public credit were to be limited in duration to a maximum of twenty-five years and collected by state- rather than Congress-appointed officers. The new plan also sought to assure a more prompt and complete payment by the states of the annual requisitions of Congress, by assuring them that the financial quotas would be "equalized from time to time," would be allocated on the basis of comparative populations as soon as the states ratified an amendment of the Articles of Confederation to that effect, and would be accounted for yearly in an itemized statement of the income and outgo (*JCC*, XIX, 112–13, 217; XXIV, 257–61; *Papers of Madison*, V, 291, n. 9; 416, n. 3; 478, n. 2; JM Notes, 24 Jan., n. 20; 27 Jan., n. 12; 28 Jan. 1783, n. 19).

[3] The *Pennsylvania Packet* on 24 April announced that after a voyage of thirty-eight days from Rochefort-sur-Mer the French frigate "Active" had reached Chester on the Delaware River, about fifteen miles below Philadelphia, on the morning of 22 April, and that the fast sailer "George Washington" had arrived from Lorient the next day. In their letter of 29 April to Governor Harrison (*q.v.*), the delegates omitted mention of dispatches, possibly because, as the *Packet* had commented on the twenty-fourth, they contained no important news not already known.

Charles Thomson's record of correspondence suggests that the "Active" probably brought to the Chevalier de La Luzerne a dispatch of 27 February from the Comte de Vergennes relating to the ratification of the preliminary treaty of peace between Great Britain, France and Spain, and to the steps being taken to conclude a definitive treaty. Having received a copy of this dispatch from La Luzerne, Robert R. Livingston submitted it to Congress on 23 April (NA: PCC, No. 185, III, 62). The dispatches from William Carmichael, chargé d'affaires at Madrid, Charles G. F. Dumas, nominally chargé d'affaires at The Hague, and Lafayette apparently arrived on the "George Washington" and were laid before Congress on 25 April 1783. See NA: PCC, No. 185, III, 63; Wharton, *Revol. Dipl. Corr.*, V, 710–11, 783–85; VI, 184–87, 215–18, 256–57, 259–61, 268–71.

4 On 18 April Congress appointed JM, chairman, Oliver Ellsworth, and Alexander Hamilton, a committee to prepare an address to accompany the copy of "the recommendation" to be sent to the executive of each state (NA: PCC, No. 186, fol. 95). For the address, drafted by JM, see Address to the States, 25 April 1783. On 9 May Elias Boudinot, president of Congress, forwarded with his circular letter to the executive of each state a printed copy of "the recommendation" and the address (Burnett, *Letters*, VII, 160–61; Harrison to the House of Delegates, 22 May 1783, Executive Letter Book, 1783–1786, p. 133, MSS in Va. State Library).

5 In the first of these two sentences, Bland summarized a resolution adopted by Congress on 15 April (*JCC*, XXIV, 242–43). For "Naval" prisoners of war, see *Papers of Madison*, V, 41; 67, n. 3; 85; 106, n. 9; 257, n. 18; Ambler to JM, 8 Feb., n. 3; Delegates to Harrison, 12 Mar. 1783, n. 14; Burnett, *Letters*, VI, 565, n. 2. See also Fitzpatrick, *Writings of Washington*, XXVI, 340–41.

6 In a letter of 18 April, received three days later by Boudinot, Washington remarked that he was "totally ignorant of the designs of the Enemy in New York, who, from all I am able to collect, are making no shew of an early Evacuation of that City" (Fitzpatrick, *Writings of Washington*, XXVI, 331; *JCC*, XXIV, 265, first n. 1). See also *Papers of Madison*, V, 103, n. 7.

7 For this "article of the Preliminary Articles" of peace between the United States and Great Britain, 30 November 1782, see *JCC*, XXIV, 249–50; *Papers of Madison*, V, 111–12; 112, nn. 1, 11; Delegates to Harrison, 12 Mar. 1783, and n. 14. Upon receiving from Livingston the letter of 14 April to him from General Sir Guy Carleton, Congress on 22 April appointed Alexander Hamilton, chairman, John Rutledge, and Nathaniel Gorham, a committee to suggest a reply. Later the same day Congress adopted the committee's report recommending the appointment of three commissioners who, with their British counterparts, should "inspect and superintend all embarckations" for the purpose of reporting to Carleton "every infraction of the letter or spirit" of the seventh article. On 24 April Congress decided that Washington should "take such measures" to make its resolutions effective, "as to him shall seem expedient" (NA: PCC, No. 25, II, 209; No. 185, III, 62; No. 186, fol. 96; *JCC*, XXIV, 274, and n. 1).

As early as 15 April Carleton had published the text of the seventh article, warned all shipmasters "at their peril" and all troops under his command to comply strictly with the article, and stated that three British officers and two Americans, then in New York City, would "superintend all embarkations" (*Pa. Packet*, 24 Apr. 1783; Fitzpatrick, *Writings of Washington*, XXVI, 302–3, 364–65).

To Thomas Jefferson

RC (LC: Papers of Madison). Jefferson docketed the letter by writing "Madison Jas" above the date line. Using the JM-Jefferson Code N. 2, JM encoded the words that are italicized.

PHILADA. Apl. 22. 1783.

DEAR SIR

Your favor of the 14. inst:[1] written on the Susquehanna with the several letters inclosed were safely delivered to me. I did not fail to present as you desired your particular compliments to *Miss K*[2] *Your inference on that subject was not groundless Before you left us I had sufficiently*[3] *ascertained her sentiments Since your departure*[4] *the affair has been pursued Most preliminary arrangements although definitive will be postponed*[5] *untill the end of the year in congress*[6] *At some period of the intervail I shall probably make a visite to Virginia The interest which your friendship takes on this occasion in my happiness is a pleasing proof that the disposetions which I feel are reciprocal*[7]

The report on funds &c. passed Congress on Saturday last with the dissent of R. Island and the division of N. York only. The latter vote was lost by the rigid adherence of Mr. Hamilton to a plan which he supposed more perfect.[8] The clause providing for unauthorized expenditures, could not be reinstated, and consequently no attempt was made to link all the parts of the act inseparably together.[9] As it now stands it has I fear no bait for Virga. which is not particularly interested either in the object or mode of the revenues recommended, nor in the territorial cessions, nor in the change of the constitutional rule of dividing the public burdens.[10] A respect for justice, good faith & national honor is the only consideration which can obtain her compliance.[11]

We have recd. no intelligence from abroad which deserves to be noted, since your departure.[12] The interval between the preliminary & definitive Treaties has produced several nice & interesting questions. One is whether laws prohibiting commerce with British Ports during the war, have expired with the cessation of Hostilities.[13] A similar one is whether the soldiers enlisted for the war are entitled to a discharge. At least half of the army under Genl. Washington are under this description and are urgent for such a construction of their engagements.[14] A third question is whether the preliminary treaty between F. & G. B. has given such effect to the provisional articles between the latter & the U. S. as to

481

require an execution of the stipulations in the 6 & 7 artics. or whether a definitive Treaty only can produce this effect.[15]

The system for foreign affairs is not yet digested: and I apprehend will be long on the anvil, unless the actual return of our Ministers from Europe should stimulate Congs. on the subject.[16]

I am charged with many compliments from the whole family for yourself & Miss Patsy,[17] which you will accept with an assurance of sincere friendship from

    Yr Obt. & Hble Servt.

J. MADISON JR.

[1] *Q.v.* What letters Jefferson had inclosed to JM are not known.

[2] Catherine Floyd. See Jefferson to JM, 14 Apr. 1783, and the citations in n. 7.

[3] In encoding "ent," JM wrote 146, but the correct cipher was 1046.

[4] On 12 April (JM to Randolph, 15 Apr. 1783).

[5] For "ne," JM erroneously used the cipher 1096 rather than 1090.

[6] The congressional year began annually on the first Monday in November (*JCC*, XIX, 215).

[7] Many years later, after recovering the letter from Jefferson, JM heavily canceled the encoded portion of this paragraph and wrote "Undecypherable" in the left margin. Irving Brant was the first to penetrate the cancellation and decode the "Buried Cipher." For a facsimile of the first page of the letter and a sequential list of the ciphers used by JM, see Brant, *Madison*, II, opp. p. 225. See also JM Notes, 25–26 Apr. 1783, n. 2, for further evidence of his courtship.

[8] JM Notes, 18 Apr. 1783, and n. 7.

[9] JM Notes, 7 Mar., and n. 2; 21–22 Apr. 1783, and n. 1. Having been given by JM an annotated, printed copy of the committee report of 6 March on restoring public credit, Jefferson would recognize the "clause" to which JM referred. See Annotations on Report on Public Credit, 26 Mar. 1783.

[10] During the debates on the report, Congress had rejected the provisions for "abatements" in overdue quotas from delinquent states and for an assumption by Congress of the unauthorized war expenses of states which had been invaded by the enemy. Both of these provisions would have greatly helped Virginia. Although denied these concessions, she was urged in the report to make a more generous offer of her western lands to the United States and, along with the other states, to ratify amendments to the Articles of Confederation which would increase the purchase price of some of her imports and the amount of the annual financial quotas which would be allocated to her by Congress (*JCC*, XXIV, 257–61; Amendment to Report on Public Credit, 17 Apr., and n. 1; JM Notes, 17 Apr., and nn. 4–6; 18 Apr., and nn. 2–4, 6; 21–22 Apr., and n. 1; Delegates to Harrison, 22 Apr. 1783, and n. 2).

[11] This "consideration" of "justice" and "good faith" to the foreign and domestic creditors of the United States, and hence of its "national honor," had impelled the Virginia delegates to vote unanimously for the adoption of the report, even though economically it included "no bait for Virga." (*JCC*, XXIV, 261; Pendleton to JM, 14 Apr., and n. 4; Delegates to Harrison, 22 Apr. 1783).

[12] Delegates to Harrison, 22 Apr. 1783, and n. 3.

[13] JM Notes, 14 Apr., and n. 3; 18 Apr. 1783, and n. 1.

[14] JM's sentence mildly reflects Washington's great concern about this matter, as expressed to President Elias Boudinot in a letter of 18 April, read in Congress three days later and referred to a committee of which Samuel Osgood was chairman and

JM one of the other four members. The "Temper of part of the Army," Washington reported, had been greatly exacerbated by the "slow and dilatory manner in which the Intelligence of peace" had reached the troops, causing those who had "engaged *for the War*" to expect "a speedy Discharge" and to suspect that Congress had withheld the news in order to retain them "beyond the Term of their Engagements." For this reason and because Congress had given him no instructions regarding "the discharge of this Part of the Army," Washington feared that it could not be long "restrained from Acts of Excess." He urged Congress to make "the most speedy Arrangements for the War men," by sending immediately "to Camp" a committee "with plenary powers" (Fitzpatrick, *Writings of Washington*, XXVI, 330–34; *JCC*, XXIV, 264–65, n. 1, 269–70; JM Notes, 7 Apr.; 23–24 Apr. 1783).

[15] JM Notes, 15 Apr., and n. 2; 16 Apr., and n. 1; JM to Randolph, 15 Apr. 1783, and n. 3.

[16] JM to Randolph, 11 Feb., and n. 7; 12 Mar., and nn. 12, 13; JM Notes, 1 Apr. and nn. 13–15; 4 Apr., and nn. 9, 10; 12 Apr., and n. 7. See also JM Notes, 15 May 1783, in LC: Madison Papers; Syrett and Cooke, *Papers of Hamilton*, III, 351–53.

[17] Jefferson to JM, 31 Jan., and nn. 28, 29; JM to Jefferson, 11 Feb. 1783, and n. 16.

To Edmund Randolph

RC (LC: Madison Papers). Unsigned and lacks a complimentary close. Cover franked by JM and addressed to "Edmund Randolph Esqr. Richmond." Docketed by Randolph, "J. Madison. April 22. 1783."

PHILADA. Apl. 22. 1783.

MY DEAR SIR

The mail of yesterday like the preceding one brought no letter from you.[1]

I just understand that a Frigate from France is at Chester, but what intelligence she brings & particularly whether she brings a definitive peace is unknown[2] Several interesting questions are raised on the Preliminary Treaty. First whether laws prohibiting British Commerce & which were to be in force during the war are repealed or not?[3] Another of a similar nature is whether the enlistments for the war are to be terminated by the latter or former Treaty? half the army under Genl. Washington is computed to be interested in this question.[4]

The Report for establishing a Revenue &c. passed Congs. on Saturday. It has been defalcated of several clauses which were material, and which would have touched in particular the supposed interest of Virga.[5] Mr. Jefferson carried with him a copy of the plan as originally reported, and as it stood when he left us. It has undergone no material variation from the latter stage of it.[6]

[1] Randolph to JM, 26 Apr. 1783. JM inadvertently wrote "broungt" instead of "brought."

[2] Delegates to Harrison, 22 Apr. 1783, and n. 3.

[3] JM to Jefferson, 22 Apr. 1783, and citations in n. 13.

[4] *Ibid.*, and n. 14.

[5] *Ibid.*, and nn. 10–11.

[6] Annotations on Report on Public Credit, 26 Mar., and ed. n., and n. 4; Amendment to Report on Public Credit, 17 Apr., and ed. n.; JM Notes, 17 Apr.; 18 Apr., and nn. 2–4, 6, 7; 21–22 Apr., and n. 1; JM to Jefferson, 22 Apr. 1783, n. 9.

From George Washington

RC (Princeton University Library: Andre deCoppet Collection of American Historical Autographs). Cover missing. In the hand of Washington and addressed by him to "The Honble Mr. Maddison." Docketed by JM, "G. Washington Newburg. April 22. 1783." Variations between the draft of this letter (LC: Washington Papers) and the recipient's copy are noted in nn. 2 and 3, below.

EDITORIAL NOTE

Except for a brief note of referral written about three years earlier (*Papers of Madison*, II, 13), this letter and the reply by JM on 29 April (*q.v.*) mark the beginning of the correspondence between him and Washington. The next exchange also was initiated by Washington on 12 June 1784, addressing to JM a plea on behalf of Thomas Paine (Fitzpatrick, *Writings of Washington*, XXVII, 420–21). Thereafter until the close of 1796, Washington and JM communicated frequently with each other, both orally and in writing.

SIR,   NEWBURGH 22d. April 1783

Major McHenry, formerly an Assistant Secretary to me, & afterwards Aid de Camp to the Marqs. de la Fayette, informs me, that, Congress are about to appoint official Secretaries for their Ministers abroad; & expresses a wish to go in that character to the Court of Versailles—or London.[1]

Justice, if I could divest myself of the inclination to serve this Gentleman, would compel me to represent him as a Man of Letters & abilities,—of great integrity, sobriety & prudence. In a word, a Man of strict honor; possessing all those good qualities (without a bad one that I am acquainted with) necessary to fit him for such an office. He would, I am persuaded, render the Minister with whom he might be connected, very happy in the appointment, as he is of an amiable & obliging temper. His property too lyes in this Country.[2]

I have now to entreat your excuse for the freedom of this recommendation; a desire to serve a man who has followed my fortunes, and shared in my perplexities, has prompted me to it; but these considerations alone, would not induce me to recommend a person for an office whom I did not believe was fully competent to discharge all the duties required of him.[3]

I have the honor to be Sir, Yr Most Obedt. & Hble Ser[vt.]

GO. WASHINGTON

[1] James McHenry (1753–1816), a native of Ireland educated in Dublin, emigrated to America in 1771. After studying medicine with Dr. Benjamin Rush, he joined the army as a surgeon in the autumn of 1775. Captured by the British in Fort Washington, near New York City, on 16 November 1776, he was exchanged on 5 March 1778 and briefly resumed his medical service. From 15 May 1778 until August 1780 he was assistant military secretary at the headquarters of the main army. There he gained Washington's high esteem and Hamilton's warm friendship. In the autumn he joined Lafayette as a volunteer aide-de-camp, an assignment which he skillfully fulfilled until, following his election to the Senate of Maryland, he resigned his commission in grade of major on 3 December 1781, about three weeks before Lafayette sailed for France.

In January 1782 McHenry began a five years' tenure as a senator in the Maryland General Assembly. Writing to Washington from Philadelphia on 15 April 1783, he expressed a wish to be "official secretary to our mission or minister at Paris or London" and suggested that "Mr. Maddison from your State has weight in Congress and could promote such an appointment" (LC: Washington Papers; Bernard C. Steiner, *The Life and Correspondence of James McHenry, Secretary of War under Washington and Adams* [Cleveland, 1907], pp. 40, 48, 50–51; Syrett and Cooke, *Papers of Hamilton*, III, 127–30). In support of McHenry's hope, Washington wrote the present letter to JM and also a similar one to Robert R. Livingston, secretary for foreign affairs (Fitzpatrick, *Writings of Washington*, XXVI, 349, n. 85, 357).

On 11 June 1783, before JM retired from Congress, McHenry joined that body as a delegate from Maryland and served until 12 Dec. 1785 (*JCC*, XXIV, 389, XXV, 812; Burnett, *Letters*, VIII, lxxxvi). He was also a member of the Constitutional Convention of 1787 and of the Maryland convention which ratified the Constitution. He is principally remembered as the staunchly Federalist secretary of war from 29 January 1796 to 13 May 1800.

[2] In Washington's retained copy, the last two sentences of this paragraph read: "He would, I am persuaded, render the Minister to whom he should be appointed Secretary, very happy in such a connection; as he is of an amiable temper, very obliging, & of polished manners. His Interest too lyes in this Country."

[3] In Washington's retained copy, the passage after "has prompted me to it" reads, "but I never have, nor never will, from these considerations alone recommend a person to an Office of trust who I am not morally certain is fully competent to the duties of it." Washington docketed the retained copy "To The Honble. Mr. Maddison 22d. April 1783   A Similar Letter was written to Mr. Livingston Secretary of F: affairs."

Notes on Debates

MS (LC: Madison Papers). For a description of the manuscript of Notes on Debates, see *Papers of Madison*, V, 231–34.

Wednesday April 23.

The resolution permitting the soldiers to retain their arms was passed at the recommendation of Genl. Washington   see letter in the files.[1]

The resolution for granting furloughs or discharges was a compromise between those who wished to get rid of the expence of keeping the men in the field, and those, who thought it impolitic to disband the army whilst the British remained in the U. S.[2]

Apl. 24. see Journal [3]

[1] In a letter of 18 April to President Elias Boudinot, Washington mentioned "an Idea which has been hinted to me, and which has affected my Mind very forcibly." He urged that the troops who had "engaged for the War" be given "at the Discharge" the "Arms and Accoutrements" which had been the "constant companions of their Toils and Dangers." Besides being "an honorable Testimonial from Congress," he continued, these "Badges of Bravery and military Merit," used to establish "our National Independence and Glory," would be "preserved with sacred Care" by the veterans and "handed down" to their "posterity" (Fitzpatrick, *Writings of Washington*, XXVI, 332–33).

[2] This "resolution," together with the one adopting Washington's suggestion concerning "Arms and Accoutrements," comprised the three opening paragraphs of a committee report drafted mainly by Samuel Osgood and in small measure by Alexander Hamilton. Congress adopted the committee's suggestion that, although duration-of-war enlistments did "not expire until the ratification of the definitive treaty of peace," Washington should be authorized, "if circumstances shall require it, to grant furloughs or discharges" to soldiers of that status, "as he may judge most expedient" (*JCC*, XXIV, 269–70). This "compromise" reflected not only the divergence of opinions mentioned by JM, but also the ominous discontent, mentioned by Washington in his letter of 18 April, of duration-of-war troops, who believed that the news of the preliminary treaty of peace warranted their release from further service (JM to Jefferson, 22 Apr., n. 14). For the continuance of British armed forces in New York City and its neighborhood, see Delegates to Harrison, 22 Apr. 1783, and n. 6.

[3] On 24 April, besides adopting a resolution already mentioned (Delegates to Harrison, 22 Apr. 1783, and n. 7), Congress resolved: "That the Secretary at War and the Superintendant of finance, take immediate measures for removing the lines of Virginia, Maryland and Pensylvania, [together with the corps of artillery and cavalry] now under the command of Major General Greene, to such places within their respective states as they shall think proper." JM was one of the twenty-three delegates who voted in favor of the resolution. The three South Carolina delegates, together with Theodorick Bland and John Francis Mercer of Virginia, voted "no" (*JCC*, XXIV, 275–76).

During a conference on the morning of 24 April, JM and the four other members of a committee, Samuel Osgood, chairman, persuaded Robert Morris, superintendent of finance, to delay the effective date of his resignation if essential "for the Purpose of Compleating such Payment to the Army as may be agreed on as necessary to disband them with their own Consent" (Syrett and Cooke, *Papers of Hamilton*, III, 341, and nn. 2, 4, 342, and nn. 1, 3; *JCC*, XXIV, 283–85). In a letter of 23 April Richard Peters, a member of the committee, succinctly characterized the problem: "The Difficulty which heretofore oppress'd us was how to raise an Army. The one which now embarrasses is how to dissolve it. Every thing Congress can do for the Satisfaction of our deserving Soldiers will be done. But an empty Purse is a Bar to the Execution of the best Intentions" (Burnett, *Letters*, VII, 150). See also JM Notes, 4–5 Mar., n. 11; 22 Mar. 1783, n. 2.

Report on Address to the States by Congress

MS (NA: PCC, No. 24, fols. 335–46). Entirely in JM's hand except for insertions, mentioned in footnotes, 5, 23, 25, and 41, by George Bond, deputy secretary of Congress.

EDITORIAL NOTE

On 18 April, after adopting the plan for restoring public credit, Congress appointed a committee, JM chairman, Oliver Ellsworth, and Alexander Hamilton, to prepare an address to the states (NA: PCC, No. 186, fol. 95). Congress expected to print the address and the plan, and have President Elias Boudinot enclose copies in his circular letter to the executive of each state (JM Notes, 18 Apr., n. 7; Delegates to Harrison, 22 Apr. 1783, and n. 4; *JCC*, XXV, 986).

Although JM disagreed with several recommendations in the plan and regretted that several others had been rejected, he had voted for it as being the most satisfactory compromise which could be reached among the divergent sectional interests within the Confederation and the rival groups of creditors of Congress (Report on Restoring Public Credit, 6 Mar., n. 1; JM Notes, 18 Apr., n. 7; JM to Jefferson, 22 Apr. 1783, and nn. 10, 11). For this reason and because his aim in the address was to persuade every state legislature to approve the plan, JM naturally minimized its shortcomings and emphasized its virtues, along with the difficulties attending its adoption by Congress and the need of the states to ratify it for the sake of justice, national honor, and the continuance of the Confederation (JM to Randolph, 22 Jan., and n. 8; 25 Feb.; JM Notes, 21 Feb. 1783, and n. 16).

Nine years later, when JM and Hamilton were at odds on matters of fiscal policy, Hamilton chose to assume, although his memory could hardly have been so unreliable, that the address to the states demonstrated JM's approval of all recommendations in the plan of 1783, and hence his inconsistency in opposing the somewhat similar proposals of Hamilton during the first administration of President Washington. In a letter of 26 May 1792 to Edward Carrington, Hamilton remarked that "the evidence of Mr. Madisons sentiments at one period is to be found in the address of Congress of April 26th 1783, which was planned by him in conformity to his own ideas and without any previous suggestions from the Committee and with his hearty coopera- tion in every part of the business" (Syrett and Cooke, *Papers of Hamilton,* XI, 427). See also JM Notes, 20 Feb. 1783, n. 6; and n. 35, below.

[25 April 1783][1]

The Come. appd. to prepare an address to the States, on the subject of the recommendations of the 18th. instant, submit the following[2]

Address to the States by the United States in Congress Assembled

April 26. 1783[3]

The prospect which has for some time existed, and which is now hap- pily realized, of a successful termination of the war, together with the critical exigences of public affairs have made it the duty of Congress to review and provide for the debts which the war has left upon the U. S. and to look forward to the means of obviating dangers which may inter- rupt the harmony and tranquility of the Confederacy. The result of their mature and solemn deliberations on these great objects is contained in their several recommendations of the 18th. instant herewith trans- mitted.[4] Although these recommendations speak themselves the prin- ciples on which they are founded, as well as the ends which they pro- pose, it will not be improper to enter into a few explanations and re- marks, in order to place in a stronger view the necessity of complying with them.

The first measure recommended is effectual provision for the debts of the U. S. The amount of these debts as far as they can now be ascer- tained is 42000375 Dollars, as will appear by the Schedule No 1.[5] To dis- charge the principal of this aggregate debt at once or in any short period is, evidently, not within the compass of our resources,[6] *and even if it could be accomplished, both the true interest and the ease of the com- munity would require that*[7] the debt itself should be left to a course of gradual extinguishment, and certain funds be provided for paying in the mean time the annual interest. The amount of the annual interest, as will appear by the paper last referred to, is computed to be 2415956 Dollars. Funds therefore which will certainly and punctually produce this annual sum at least, must be provided.

In devising these funds Congress did not overlook the mode of supply- ing the common Treasury provided by the articles of confederation. But

after the most respectful consideration of that mode, they were con-
strained to regard it as inadequate and inapplicable to the form into
which the public debt must be thrown. The delays and uncertainties incident to a revenue to be established and collected from time to time by
thirteen independent authorities, is at first view irreconcileable with the
punctuality essential in the discharge of the interest of a national debt.
Our own experience, after making every allowance for transient impediments, has been a sufficient illustration of this truth.[8] Some departure
therefore in the recommendations of Congress from the fœderal constitution, was unavoidable; but it will be found to be as small as could be
reconciled with the object in view, and to be supported besides by solid
considerations of interest and sound policy.[9]

The fund which first presented itself on this, as it did on a former
occasion, was a tax on imports. The reasons which recommended this
branch of revenue, have heretofore been stated in an act of which a copy
No. 2 is now forwarded, and need not be here repeated.[10] It will suffice
to recapitulate, that taxes on consumption are always least burdensome,
because they are least felt, and are borne too by those who are both willing and able to pay them; that of all taxes on consumption, those on
foreign commerce are most compatible with the genius and policy of
free States;[11] that from the relative positions of some of the more commercial States, it will be impossible to bring this essential resource into
use without a concerted uniformity; that this uniformity cannot be concerted through any channel so properly as through congress,[12] nor for
any purpose so aptly as for paying the debts of a Revolution, from
which an unbounded freedom has accrued to commerce.[13]

In renewing this proposition to the States we have not been unmindful
of the objections which heretofore frustrated the unanimous adoption
of it. We have limited the duration of the revenue to the term of 25.
years: and we have left to the States themselves the appointment of the
officers who are to collect it. If the strict maxims of national credit alone
were to be consulted, the revenue ought manifestly to be co-existent
with the object of it; and the collection placed in every respect under
that authority which is to dispense the former, and is responsible for the
latter.[14] These relaxations will we trust, be regarded on one hand as the
effect of a disposition in Congs. to attend at all times to the sentiments of
those whom they serve; and on the other hand as a proof of their anxious
desire that provision may be made in some way or other for an honorable and just fulfilment of the engagements which they have formed.

To render this fund as productive as possible and at the same time to narrow the room for collusions and frauds, it has been judged an improvement of the plan, to recommend a liberal duty on such articles as are most susceptible of a tax according to their quantity and are of most equal and general consumption; leaving all other articles, as heretofore proposed, to be taxed according to their value.[15]

The amount of this fund is computed to be 915956 Dollars. The estimates on which the computation is made, are detailed in paper No. 3. accuracy in the first essay on so complex & fluctuating a subject is not to be expected.[16] It is presumed to be as near the truth as the defect of proper materials would admit.

The residue of the computed interest is 1500000 Dollars, and is referred to the States to be provided for by such funds as they may judge most convenient.[17] Here again the strict maxims of public credit gave way to the desire of Congress to conform to the sentiments of their constituents. It ought not to be omitted however with respect to this portion of the revenue, that the mode in which it is to be supplied, varies so little from that pointed out in the articles of confederation, and the variations are so conducive to the great object proposed, that a ready and unqualified compliance on the part of the States may be the more justly expected. In fixing the quotas of this sum Congs. as may be well imagined, were guided by very imperfect lights and some Inequalities may consequently have ensued. These however can be but temporary, and as far as they may exist at all, will be redressed by a retrospective adjustment, as soon as a constitutional rule can be applied.[18]

The necessity of making the two foregoing provisions one indivisible and irrevocable act is apparent. Without the first quality, partial provision only might be made where complete provision is essential; nay as some States might prefer & adopt one of the funds only, and the other States the other fund only, it might happen that no provision at all would be made: Without the second, a single State out of the thirteen might at any time involve the nation in bankruptcy, the mere practicability of which would be a fatal bar to the establishment of national credit.[19] Instead of enlarging on these topics, two observations are submitted to the justice and wisdom of the Legislatures. First: The present Creditors[,] or rather the domestic part of them, having either made their loans for a period which has expired, or having become creditors in the first instance involuntarily, are entitled on the clear principles of justice & good faith, to demand the principal of their credits, instead of accepting the annual interest. It is necessary, therefore, as the principal

490

can not be paid to them on demand, that the interest should be so effectually and satisfactorily secured, as to enable them if they incline, to transfer their stock at its full value.[20] Secondly: if the funds be so firmly constituted as to inspire a thorough & universal confidence, may[21] it not be hoped, that the capital of the domestic debt which bears the high interest of 6 perCt., may be cancelled by other loans obtained at a more moderate interest? The saving by such an operation would be a clear one and might be a considerable one.[22] As a proof of the necessity of substantial funds for the support of our credit abroad we refer to paper No 4[23]

Thus much for the interest of the national debt: For the discharge of the principal within the term limited, we rely on the natural increase of the revenue from Commerce, on requisitions to be made from time to time for that purpose, as circumstances may dictate, and on the prospects of vacant territory. If these resources should prove inadequate, it will be necessary, at the expiration of 25 years to continue the funds now recommended or to establish such others as may then be found more convenient.[24]

With a view to the resource last mentioned, as well as to obviate disagreeable controversies, and confusions, Congress have included in their present recommendations, a renewal of those of the 6th day of Septr. and of the 10th. day of October 1780. In both those respects a liberal and final accomodation of all interfering claims of vacant territory, is an object which cannot be pressed with too much solicitude.[25]

The last object recommended is a constitutional change of the rule, by which a partition of the common burdens is to be made. The expediency and even necessity of such a change has been sufficiently enforced by the local injustice and discontents[26] which have proceeded from valuations of the soil in every State where the experiment has been made. But how infinitely must these evils be increased, on a comparison of such valuations among the states themselves! On whatever side indeed this rule be surveyed, the execution of it must be attended with the most serious difficulties. If the valuations be referred to the authorities of the several States, a general satisfaction is not to be hoped for: If they be executed by officers of the U. S. traversing the Country for that purpose, besides the inequalities against which this mode would be no security, the expence would be both enormous and obnoxious: If the mode taken in the act of the 17 day of feby last which was deemed on the whole least objectionable, be adhered to, still the insufficiency of the data to the purpose to which they are to be applied, must greatly impair, if not utterly destroy all confidence in the accuracy of the result; not to mention that as far as the result can be at all a just one, it will be indebted for the advantage to the principle on which the rule proposed to be substituted is founded. This rule altho' not free from objections, is liable to fewer than any other that could be devised. The only material difficulty which attended it in the deliberations of Congress, was to fix the proper difference between the labor and industry of free inhabitants, and of all other inhabitants. The ratio ultimately agreed on was the effect of mutual concessions, and if it should be supposed not to correspond precisely with the fact, no doubt ought to be entertained that an equal spirit of accomodation among the several Legislatures, will prevail against little inequalities which may be calculated on one side or on the other. But notwithstanding the confidence of Congress as to the success of this proposition, it is their duty to recollect that the event may possibly disappoint them, and to request that measures may still be pursued for obtaining & transmitting the information called for in the act of 17 feby. last, which in such event will be essential.[27]

The plan thus communicated and explained by Congress must now receive its fate from their Constituents. All the objects comprized in it are conceived to be of great importance to the happiness of this confederated republic, are necessary to render the fruits of the Revolution, a full reward for the blood, the toils, the cares and the calamities which have purchased it. But the object of which the necessity will be peculiarly felt, and which it is peculiarly the duty of Congress to inculcate, is the provision recommended for the national debt. Altho' this debt is greater than could have been wished, it is still less on the whole than could have been expected, and when referred to the cause in which it has been incurred, and compared with the burdens which wars of ambition and of vain glory have entailed on other nations, ought to be borne not only with cheerfulness but with pride. But the magnitude of the debt makes no part of the question. It is sufficient that the debt has been fairly contracted and that justice & good faith[28] demand that it should be fully discharged. Congress had no option but between different modes of discharging it. The same option is the only one that can exist with the States. The mode which has after long & elaborate discussion been preferred, is, we are persuaded, the least objectionable of any that would have been equal to the purpose. Under this persuasion, we call upon the justice & plighted faith of the several States to give it its proper effect, to reflect on the consequences of rejecting it, and to remember that Congress will not be answerable for them.[29]

492

If other motives than that of justice could be requisite on this occasion, no nation could ever feel stronger. For to whom are the debts to be paid?

To an Ally, in the first place, who to the exertion of his arms in support of our cause, has added the succours of his Treasure; who to his important loans has added liberal donations; and whose loans themselves carry the impression of his magninimity and friendship. For more exact information on this point we refer to paper No. 5[30]

To individuals in a foreign country in the next place who were the first to give so precious a token of their confidence in our justice, and of their friendship for our cause; and who are members of a republic which was second in espousing our rank among nations. For the claims and expectations of this class of Creditors we refer to paper No. 6[31]

Another class of Creditors is that illustrious & patriotic band of fellow Citizens, whose blood and whose bravery have defended the liberties of their Country, who have patiently borne, among other distresses the privation of their stipends, whilst the distresses of their Country disabled it from bestowing them; and who even now ask for no more than such a portion of their dues as will enable them to retire from the field of victory & glory into the bosom of peace & private citizenship, and for such effectual security for the residue of their claims as their Country is now unquestionably able to provide.[32] For a full view of their sentiments and wishes on this subject we transmit the paper No. 7. and as a fresh & lively instance of their superiority to every species of seduction from the paths of virtue & of honor, we add the paper No. 8[33]

The remaining class of Creditors[34] is composed partly of such of our fellow Citizens as originally lent to the public the use of their funds, or have since manifested most confidence in their Country by receiving transfers from the lenders; and partly of those whose property has been either advanced or assumed for the public service. To discriminate the merits of these several descriptions of creditors would be a task equally unnecessary & invidious. If the voice of humanity plead more loudly in favor of some than of others; the voice of policy, no less than of justice pleads in favor of all. A wise nation will never permit those who relieve the wants of their Country, or who rely most on its faith, its firmness and its resources, when either of them is distrusted, to suffer by the event.[35]

Let it be remembered finally that it has ever been the pride and boast of America, that the rights for which she contended were the rights of human nature.[36] By the blessing of the Author of these rights on the means exerted for their defence, they have prevailed against all opposition and form the basis of thirteen independant States.[37] No instance has heretofore occurred, nor can any instance be expected hereafter to occur, in which the unadulterated forms of Republican Government can pretend to so fair an opportunity of justifying themselves by their fruits. In this view the Citizens of the U. S. are responsible for the greatest trust ever confided to a Political Society. If justice, good faith, honor, gratitude & all the other Qualities which enoble the character of a nation, and fulfil the ends of Government, be the fruits of our establishments, the cause of liberty will acquire a dignity and lustre, which it has never yet enjoyed; and an example will be set which can not but have the most favorable influence on the rights of mankind.[38] If on the other side, our Governments should be unfortunately blotted with the reverse of these cardinal and essential Virtues,[39] the great cause which we have engaged to vindicate, will be dishonored & betrayed; the last & fairest experiment in favor of the rights of human nature will be turned against them; and their patrons & friends exposed to be insulted & silenced by the votaries[40] of Tyranny and Usurpation.

By order of the United States in Congress assembled[41]

[1] This is the date when JM, on behalf of the committee, submitted the address to Congress (NA: PCC, No. 17, fol. 264; No. 186, fol. 95). The journal of 26 April records that the committee "reported a draught, which being read and amended, was agreed to" (JCC, XXIV, 277). Although both the manuscript of the address and its text in the journal contain changes of words and expressions, the alterations made by JM before he submitted the report and the amendments of it made in Congress can be seldom differentiated (JCC, XXIV, 277–83). See also nn. 2, 3, 7, 8, 13, 18, 21, 26–29, 34, 37–40, below.

[2] This statement no doubt prefaced the report as submitted but was canceled in the manuscript, probably after Congress adopted the report.

[3] On this date, entered in JM's hand, the address was adopted by a unanimous vote of the delegates present in Congress (JM Notes, 25–26 Apr. 1783).

[4] JCC, XXIV, 257–61.

[5] This, and the seven other papers mentioned in the present address, appear sequentially in JCC, XXIV, 285–311. Hereafter in the address, the number of each "paper" was inserted by George Bond. For other estimates of debt, see JM Notes, 13 Jan., n. 5; 27 Jan., n. 13; 29 Jan., and n. 15; 20 Feb., and n. 9; 8 Apr. 1783, and nn.; Randolph to JM, 15 Jan. 1783, n. 13.

[6] JM Notes, 19 Feb. 1783, n. 7.

[7] The underlining of the passage, here italicized, was later canceled, but probably not before the submission of the manuscript to Congress. The words "both the true interest and" were also deleted either by JM or as the result of an amendment by Congress. To pay the debt quickly was impossible, not only because the tax yield from the "resources" would be insufficient; but also because, among other reasons, the total of the "unliquidated" obligations was unknown, the balance of debits and credits between Congress and each state government was undetermined, the interest-bearing certificates, which had not yet matured, would be surrendered only at a

premium, and some of those "bonds," including the loan-office certificates, were a part of the capital of the Bank of North America and of other private companies (*Papers of Madison*, IV, 18–19; 20, nn. 6, 7; JM Notes, 27 Jan., n. 13; 28 Jan., and nn. 9, 19; 8 Feb., n. 3; 19 Feb., n. 7; 20 Feb., nn. 6, 7; 27 Feb.; 11 Mar., and nn. 7, 9; Report on Restoring Public Credit, 6 Mar. 1783, n. 7; E. James Ferguson, *Power of the Purse*, pp. 123–24, 130, n. 18, 136–38; Clarence L. Ver Steeg, *Robert Morris*, pp. 66–67, 87, 116–17, 178–79).

8 See, for example, JM Notes, 9–10 Jan., n. 3; 24 Jan., n. 20; 27 Jan., and n. 12; 28 Jan.; 31 Jan., and nn. 2, 11; 7 Feb., and n. 9; 11 Feb., n. 2; 17 Feb., and n. 3; Memo. on Revenue Plan, 6 Mar. 1783, ed. n.; *JCC*, XXIV, 173–74. In the last preceding sentence, "of which the principal cannot be discharged" is canceled immediately after "debt," and also "so large," originally written above "which."

9 *JCC*, XXIV, 257–58, 259–60; JM Notes, 26 Feb., and n. 44; Report on Restoring Public Credit, 6 Mar. 1783, and n. 8.

10 "Paper No. II," to be a part of the appendix of the present address, is a copy of the reply, drafted almost entirely by Alexander Hamilton and adopted by Congress on 16 December 1782, to the refusal of the Rhode Island General Assembly to ratify the proposed impost amendment to the Articles of Confederation (Syrett and Cooke, *Papers of Hamilton*, III, 213–23; *Papers of Madison*, V, 407, and n. 1; 416, n. 3; JM Notes, 19 Feb., and n. 4; 18 Mar. 1783; *JCC*, XXIII, 798–810; XXIV, 286).

11 Besides providing revenue, tariffs on imports would promote home industries and national self-sufficiency, thus lessening an economic reliance upon foreign powers which might threaten the independence of the United States.

12 JM Notes, 28 Jan., and nn. 12, 28, 29; 29 Jan., and nn. 28, 33, 34, 38; 19 Feb., and n. 3; 21 Feb.; 26 Feb.; JM to Randolph, 25 Feb. 1783, and n. 16.

13 JM Notes, 12 Apr. 1783, and n. 5. The "unbounded freedom" was somewhat of an exaggeration. Although the winning of independence had rid the states of the restrictions imposed by the British navigation acts, the same victory would end their accustomed use of trade routes within the British empire, under the protection of the British navy. Immediately preceding "from which," JM canceled "from which the right of free."

14 *JCC*, XXIV, 258. See also Report on Restoring Public Credit, 6 Mar., and n. 10; JM Notes, 12 Feb., and nn. 5, 6, 8, 14, 15; 18 Feb.; 19 Feb., and n. 3; 20 Feb.; 21 Feb., and n. 10; 11 Mar., and n. 11; 20 Mar., and nn. 5, 8; 21 Mar., and n. 1; 27 Mar., and nn. 4, 5, 27 Mar. 1783, and n. 7.

15 JM Notes, 27 Feb., and nn. 8–10; 28 Feb.; 11 Mar., and nn. 3, 9; 18 Mar. 1783, and nn. 8, 10; *JCC*, XXIV, 257–58.

16 *JCC*, XXIV, 286–87; JM Notes, 29 Jan. 1783, and n. 20.

17 JM Notes, 4 Apr., and nn. 1–8; 7 Apr., and n. 1; 18 Apr. 1783; *JCC*, XXIV, 258–59.

18 The words following "lights" in the immediately preceding sentence were an interlineated substitution by JM for a canceled "may consequently have fallen into some injustices." Article VIII of the Articles of Confederation required Congress to allocate its state-by-state financial requisitions in accord with comparative valuations of land (*JCC*, XIX, 217). Frequent debates over the "mode" of making this "constitutional rule" effective had demonstrated its impracticability. For this reason, although few states could furnish reliable census data, Congress continued to apportion quotas on estimated population figures, even after the inauguration of the government under the Articles of Confederation on 1 March 1781 (*Papers of Madison*, IV, 55; 56, nn. 5, 6; 77, n. 9; 122; 123, n. 3; V, 294; 295, n. 12; 351, n. 21). The present plan included a proposed amendment to make the "rule" conform with the practice (JM Notes, 9–10 Jan., and n. 2; 14 Jan., and nn. 6, 7; 27 Jan.; 31 Jan.; 11 Feb., and n. 2; 17 Feb., and nn. 1, 3; Report on Restoring Public Credit, 6 Mar. 1783; *JCC*, XXIV, 259–60).

If this amendment was ratified and each state enumerated its population, the quotas listed in the plan, to be paid as quickly as possible, would probably have been in some instances too large and in others, too small. Although JM confined his mention of "retrospective adjustment" to this expectation, he also could have referred to the probable need of a similar settlement after the debits and credits for war expenses were balanced between each state and Congress (JM Notes, 7 Jan., n. 1; 27 Jan., n. 27; 28 Jan., and n. 19; 5–6 Feb., and n. 9; 7 Feb.; 8 Feb., and nn. 3, 4; 10 Feb., n. 14; 17 Feb., nn. 1, 4; 20 Feb. 1783, n. 9).

[19] JM pointed out that the "provisions" in the plan for import duties and for allocating quotas on the basis of population, being indispensable to the restoration of public credit, must both be ratified by every state. To agree to one and reject the other would cause the entire plan to fail.

[20] For example, purchasers of loan certificates in 1776 had been assured by Congress that they would be repaid in three years. Congress had been unable to honor this pledge or even, beginning in 1782, to meet the annual interest due on the loans. Among the involuntary creditors were those who had been obliged by officials of Congress to furnish military supplies in return for interest-bearing promises to pay, sometimes stipulating a definite date of redemption in cash. With Congress far in arrears by 1783 and without any ready source of income, these paper evidences of debt had greatly depreciated in terms of their exchange value for goods and services. They obviously would regain much of their worth if Congress could pay the defaulted interest (JCC, V, 845–46; E. James Ferguson, *Power of the Purse*, chap. iv, *passim;* also pp. 179–85, 221–22; *Papers of Madison*, V, 294, n. 1; 380, n. 11; JM Notes, 7 Jan., n. 1; 27 Jan., nn. 13, 14; 29 Jan., and n. 14; 30 Jan., nn. 4, 6; 20 Feb., and nn. 6, 7; 26 Feb. 1783).

[21] Between "confidence" and "may," JM wrote and canceled "abroad as well as at home."

[22] For this funding, or re-funding, proposal, see *Papers of Madison*, V, 377–78; 378, n. 5; JM Notes, 24 Jan., n. 20; 29 Jan., n. 14; 11 Mar., and n. 7; Randolph to JM, 15 Mar. 1783, n. 4.

[23] This sentence is in the hand of George Bond. Paper "No 4" comprises an extract of Benjamin Franklin's letter of 23 December 1782 to Robert Morris, and a translated copy of the entire letter from the Chevalier de La Luzerne on 15 March 1783 to Morris (JCC, XXIV, 287–90). See also JM Notes, 12–15 Mar., n. 7; 19 Mar. 1783, and n. 11.

[24] The "term limited" for the duration of the revenue-producing measures in the plan was "25 years" (Report on Restoring Public Credit, 6 Mar.; JM Notes, 11 Mar. 1783; JCC, XXIV, 278). For the expected "increase of foreign commerce," see JM to Randolph, 11 Feb., and n. 11; JM Notes, 13 Feb.; 12 Apr., and n. 5; Lynch to JM, 15 Feb. 1783. For the "vacant territory" west of the Appalachian Mountains as a potential source of congressional revenue, see JM Notes, 14 Jan., nn. 6, 9; 29 Jan.; 30 Jan., n. 2; 26 Feb.; 27 Mar., and nn. 11, 14, 20; 18 Apr. 1783, and nn. 2, 4.

[25] Report on Restoring Public Credit, 6 Mar. 1783, and n. 14; JM Notes, 9 Apr., and nn. 2, 6–9, 11; 18 Apr., and nn. 2, 3–5; JM to Jefferson, 22 Apr. 1783, and n. 10. In spaces left by JM, George Bond inserted "6th," "Septr," "10th," and "October."

[26] Between "and" and "discontents," JM wrote and canceled "complaints."

[27] JM interlineated the words between "request that" and "the information." See JM to Randolph, 4 Feb. and citations in n. 7; 18 Feb. and citations in n. 3; 11 Mar.; JM to Jefferson, 11 Feb. and citations in nn. 8, 9; JM Notes, 14 Feb., and n. 7; 26 Feb.; 27 Mar., and nn. 4, 20, 21, 25, 27; 28 Mar., and n. 2; 1 Apr., and nn. 10, 11; 4 Apr.; 7 Apr., and nn. 1, 2; Report on Restoring Public Credit, 6 Mar.; Amendment to Report on Public Credit, 27 Mar., and nn. 3, 6; 28 Mar. 1783, and ed. n., and nn. 1, 2. For the act of 17 February 1783, requiring that Congress be informed by each

state of "the number of its inhabitants, distinguishing white from black," and of the amount of privately owned land, together with separate lists of the number of "dwelling houses" and "other buildings," see *JCC*, XXIV, 135–37; JM Notes, 17 Feb. 1783, and nn. 1, 3, 4.

28 The word "good" was interlineated above a canceled "the public" between "&" and "faith."

29 JM canceled "laborious" between "&" and "elaborate," and "entreat and conjure the several" between "we" and "call." He interlineated "justice and plighted faith of the."

30 For the military and financial aid of France, see indexes of *Papers of Madison*, Vols. II–V, under Army, French; France: alliance of with U. S., economic relations with U.S., finances of Congress and; Navy, French; also JM Notes, 1 Jan., and n. 2; 3 Jan., and n. 4; 9–10 Jan., and nn. 12, 14; 13 Jan.; 24 Jan., n. 18; 25 Jan., and n. 1; 27 Jan., n. 13; 29 Jan., n. 15; 30 Jan., and n. 4; 14 Feb.; 19 Mar., and nn. 24, 37, 38; 24 Mar.; 26 Mar., and nn. 4, 6; 8 Apr. 1783, and nn. 3, 17. Paper "No 5" is a copy of the contract of 16 July 1782 between the Comte de Vergennes on behalf of King Louis XVI, and Benjamin Franklin, on behalf of Congress, ratified by Congress on 22 January 1783 (*JCC*, XXIV, 50–64).

31 Immediately preceding "rank," JM wrote and canceled "national." For the recognition by the Netherlands of the independence of the United States, and for the loan of money by Dutch bankers to Congress, see *Papers of Madison*, IV, 391–92; 393, nn. 4, 10; 422, n. 30; 431, n. 6; V, 123, n. 3; 126–27; 131; 132, n. 2; 158, n. 7; 450, n. 5; 451, n. 14. Paper "No. 6" is a copy of the "contract entered into by the honble. J. Adams in behalf of the United States with sundries for a loan of 5 million of florins" (*JCC*, XIV, 290). See also *JCC*, XXIV, 61, 103, 285–86; Wharton, *Revol. Dipl. Corr.*, V, 594–95, 665; Clarence L. Ver Steeg, *Robert Morris*, p. 137.

32 *Papers of Madison*, V, 159; 162, nn. 15, 16; 213–14; 216, n. 21; 227, n. 12; 473; 474, n. 8; JM Notes, 18 Feb., and the citations in nn. 3, 5; 19 Feb., and nn. 11, 12, 16, 19; 20 Feb., and nn. 17–20; 17 Mar., and nn. 1, 2, and citations in n. 3; 20 Mar., and n. 4; 22 Mar., and nn. 1–3; 7 Apr.; 8 Apr.; 23–24 Apr. 1783, and nn.

33 Paper "No. 7" is a copy of the "memorial from the officers of the army," dated "December, 1782." Paper "No. 8" comprises copies of Washington's letters of 12 and 18 March 1783, and of their enclosures. These enclosures are (1) three anonymous papers circulated at West Point—one requesting a meeting of officers to consider how to obtain a "redress of grievances," and two addressing the officers and emphasizing why they should be discontented; (2) Washington's orders of 11 March summoning officers to assemble on 15 March; (3) Washington's speech at that meeting, together with its other proceedings, including a resolution, adopted unanimously, expressing "abhorrence" and rejecting "with disdain, the infamous propositions contained in a late anonymous address to the officers"; and (4) three extracts "from a representation made by the Commander in Chief to a Committee of Congress at the army, 29th January, 1778," and "of a letter from general Washington to Congress, dated Passaick Falls, 11th October, 1780" (*JCC*, XXIV, 290–311).

34 Between "of" and "Creditors," JM interlineated and canceled "public."

35 JM's contention in this paragraph that considerations of both "policy" and "justice" argued against discriminating between those creditors who "originally lent to the public the use of their funds" and those, including speculators, who as JM euphemistically wrote, received "transfers from the lenders," enabled Hamilton in 1792 to charge JM with inconsistency. See ed. n., above. See also JM Notes, 18 Feb., and nn. 7, 8; 19 Feb.; 20 Feb., and nn. 6, 7; 21 Feb.; JM to Randolph, 25 Feb. 1783, and n. 15.

36 The preamble of the Declaration of Independence is, of course, the most obvious example of this emphasis.

37 The phrase "at this time" was canceled between "form" and "the."

[38] Instead of "Qualities" and "but," JM at first wrote "virtues" and "fail to," respectively. His stress upon the opportunity enjoyed by Americans to create and justify "unadulterated forms of Republican Government" and thereby to render world-wide service to "the cause of liberty" reflected what later would be called "the doctrine of America's mission," embodied in many writings during and after the Revolution. See, for example, *JCC*, II, 77, 129, 140–41, 153, 212–13, 217; IV, 134, 141; VIII, 399, 401–2; XI, 474, 480–81. Thomas Paine depicted a similar prospect in the final (13th) number of his *The American Crisis*, dated 19 April 1783, but he also had done so, although less emphatically, in earlier numbers of that series and in *Common Sense*, originally published anonymously on 10 January 1776 (Philip S. Foner, ed., *The Complete Writings of Thomas Paine* [2 vols.; New York, 1945], I, 17, 30–31, 41, 46, 54, 105, 118, 123, 193, 230–35).

[39] JM wrote "Virtues" above a canceled "qualities."

[40] JM deleted the word "Sycophants" and wrote "votaries" above it.

[41] This line, in the hand of George Bond, probably was written after Congress adopted the address on 26 April (JM Notes, 25–26 Apr.; JM to Randolph, 29 Apr. 1783, and n. 4).

Notes on Debates

MS (LC: Madison Papers). For a description of the manuscript of Notes on Debates, see *Papers of Madison*, V, 231–34.

Friday 25. Apl.

Saturday april 26.

* Address to States passed nem: con: It was drawn up by Mr. Madison: The address to Rd. Isd. referred to as No. 2. had been drawn up by Mr. Hamilton. [1]

The writer of these notes absent till Monday May. 5th.[2]

---

* Added to appendix from Chap. 3. laws U. S. 1815.

[1] The journal for 25 April suggests that Congress took no important action on that day. See Address to States, 25 Apr. 1783, and nn. 1, 3, 41.

[2] William Floyd and his daughters, including Catherine, to whom JM was engaged, left Philadelphia on 29 April. JM accompanied them as far as New Brunswick, N.J., where the daughters may have remained while Floyd proceeded to Elizabethtown in the hope of continuing from there to his home on British-occupied Long Island, N.Y. Although JM arrived back in Philadelphia on Friday, 2 May, he next attended Congress on Monday, 5 May, for there was no session on the intervening two days (Jefferson to JM, 31 Jan. 1783, n. 28; *JCC*, XXIV, 329; Boyd, *Papers of Jefferson*, VI, 264–65, 333; Brant, *Madison*, II, 285; Hugh Hastings and J. A. Holden, eds., *Public Papers of George Clinton*, VIII, 139).

In his footnote JM refers to the copy of the "Address" published in *Laws of the United States of America, from the 4th of March, 1789, to the 4th of March, 1815, including the Constitution of the United States, the Old Act of Confederation, Treaties, and many other Valuable Ordinances and Documents; with Copious Notes and References, arranged and published under authority of an act of Congress*

(5 vols.; Washington, 1815), I, chap. iii, pp. 32–37. Although JM obviously could not have added the citation before 1815, he must have written it before 1830, for his handwriting is neither unusually small nor quavery. He evidently was engaged in preparing his papers for publication and had included the "Address" in an "appendix." See Madison, *Papers* (Gilpin ed.), appendix, pp. vi–xi.

From Edmund Randolph

RC (LC: Madison Papers). Unsigned but in Randolph's hand. Cover addressed by him to "The honble James Madison jr. esq of congress Philadelphia." Docketed by JM, "Apl. 26. 1783."

RICHMOND April 26. 1783.

MY DEAR FRIEND

For four weeks past I have been so hurried by the general court, that I have not had leisure to write a page, irrelative to law.[1] Indeed the calmness of our times cuts off almost every thing worthy of communication.

Our assembly will be composed of good men in general. Mr. Thomson Mason, Colo. Nicholas, Colo. J. Taylor, Gen: Lawson, Mr. Wm. Nelson and several others who have either never been elected, or not lately, will take their seats.[2] From the conversation of Mr. Jefferson I should hope for his return to the legislature; and it is certain, that Mr. Edw: Carter will disqualify himself in order to introduce him.[3] The circulation of the proceedings of the army, has demonstrated the necessity of consigning to congress a fund, independent of the breath of individual states: and many of those, who at first were vehement, are reconciled to the expedient.[4]

But satisfaction is by no means generally diffused, with regard to the stipulations concerning confiscated property, in the provisional articles.[5] Indeed some, who conceive, that Virginia has not fully parted from the power of peace and war to congress, are inclined, (as if our legislature were omnipotent) to move at the next session for a repeal of those stipulations. Such a measure as this will surely immortalize the understanding of the mover.[6] It is probable, that the late proclamation of congress has excited a jealousy of their *high powers*, and pointed out the propriety of wresting from them some of their constitutional authority. I have more than once endeavoured to conceive the author of this singular composition: and I hope my conjectures are not right, when I suppose that it came from the pen of the s—cr—y of fo—gn aff—rs.[7]

The delinquencies of the sheriffs are very great, in the business of collecting. Motions have been made against them this court for about 70,000 £. A great sum in a little revenue: But the excuses, which they have made, argue the poverty of the country. They have distrained, they say, but cannot sell for ¼ of the value of the thing taken, even in produce.[8] The courthouse of papers of Lunenburgh has been burnt, partly to prevent the obtaining of those documents, which are necessary to execute the tax.[9]

Mr. Pendleton came to town last night, to enter upon his duty as a chancellor.[10]

[1] Randolph had not written to JM since 29 March 1783 (*q.v.*). The General Court was Virginia's "principal court of judicature." Its spring term opened in Richmond on 1 April, and Attorney General Randolph necessarily attended its sessions (*JHDV*, Oct. 1777, p. 136; Oct. 1781, p. 74; Hening, *Statutes*, IX, 401–19; X, 455).

[2] Thomson Mason (1733–1785), younger brother of George Mason, was an English-trained lawyer who before the Revolution had distinguished himself as a constitutional polemicist. He represented Stafford County in the House of Burgesses in 1758–1761, 1765–1772, and Loudoun County in 1772–1774. He was a member of the House of Delegates for Loudoun County in 1777–1778, for Elizabeth City County in 1779, and for Stafford County in 1783.

For George Nicholas of Albemarle County, see Randolph to JM, 29 Mar. 1783, n. 6; for John Taylor of Caroline County, *Papers of Madison*, III, 37, n. 16; Pendleton to JM, 31 Mar., n. 8; 14 Apr. 1783; for Robert Lawson of Prince Edward County, *Papers of Madison*, II, 170, n. 7.

William Nelson (*ca.* 1759–1813) of James City County served in the House of Delegates only during the two sessions of 1783. In 1791 he was appointed a judge of the General Court of Virginia and continued in that office until his death (William Brockenbrough, *Virginia Cases, or Decisions of the General Court of Virginia* . . . [Richmond, 1826], II, xi; *Enquirer* [Richmond], 16 and 23 Mar. 1813; *Virginia Patriot* [Richmond], 23 Mar. 1813).

[3] JM to Randolph, 8 Apr. 1783, and n. 10. Edward Carter (1733–1792) of Albemarle County was a member of the House of Burgesses, 1765–1768, and a delegate in the General Assembly, 1783–1785 and 1787–1788 (Swem and Williams, *Register*, pp. 17, 19, 26; George Selden Wallace, *The Carters of Blenheim; A Genealogy of Edward and Sarah Champe Carter of "Blenheim," Albemarle County, Virginia* [Richmond, 1955], pp. 1–2).

[4] JM Notes, 20 Feb., and nn. 17, 18, 20; 17 Mar., and nn. 1, 2; JM to Randolph, 25 Feb.; 4 Mar., and n. 5; 18 Mar.; to Jefferson, 22 Apr. 1783, and n. 14. On 5 May Governor Harrison included with a message to the House of Delegates a copy of Washington's letter of 19 March 1783, giving "an alarming Account of the discontents of the Army" (Executive Letter Book, 1783–1786, p. 109, MS in Va. State Library; Fitzpatrick, *Writings of Washington*, XXVI, 239–41).

[5] JM Notes, 12–15 Mar. and citations in n. 2; 20 Mar.; 14 Apr., and n. 3; Delegates to Harrison, 12 Mar., and n. 12; Pendleton to JM, 31 Mar. 1783.

[6] In the May 1783 session the Virginia House of Delegates neither repealed the statutes providing for the confiscation of real estate owned by the enemy nor

adopted resolutions instructing the delegates in Congress to seek a repeal of the "stipulations concerning confiscated property" in the preliminary articles of peace. See *Papers of Madison*, V, 409–10.

⁷ For Robert R. Livingston, secretary for foreign affairs, and his "singular composition," see JM Notes, 11 Apr. 1783, and n. 4.

⁸ The journal of the House of Delegates during the May 1783 session of the Virginia General Assembly emphatically supports Randolph's comments. See also the *Virginia Gazette* of 26 April and 3 May 1783 for notices of sale of many acres of privately owned land to satisfy taxes unpaid by its owners.

Sheriffs, being frequently unable to collect taxes from impoverished families, to sell property distrained for non-payment of taxes, or to dispose of "commutables," such as tobacco or hemp, received in partial satisfaction of taxes, were by statute subjected to suit by the state for non-fulfillment of their obligations. On 28 June the General Assembly enacted a statute for "the Relief of Sheriffs," which admitted that, due to "difficulties unforeseen," they could not "comply with the letter of the law" and hence, until 1 August 1783, they should be immune from suit or enforcement of a court's judgment for dereliction of duty in collecting taxes for 1782 (*JHDV*, May 1783, pp. 7, 8, 11, 12, 20, 24, 27, 44, 46, 52, 58, 63, 64, 70, 82, 83, 98, 99; Hening, *Statutes*, XI, 189–91). Recognizing the "distressed state" of many Virginians, as illustrated by the letters of sheriffs and petitions from delinquent taxpayers, the General Assembly on 4 June adopted a law assuring them that they would not be sued until 20 November 1783 (*JHDV*, May 1783, pp. 6, 11, 14, 20, 21, 25, 29, 34, 42, 65, 66, 68, 78; Hening, *Statutes*, XI, 194).

⁹ Although the courthouse of Lunenburg was burned (*Va. Gazette*, 31 May 1783), the county's records for this period are mostly extant, possibly because the clerk had kept them in his home.

¹⁰ Edmund Pendleton, one of two surviving administrators of the estate of John Robinson, who died in 1766, had arrived in Richmond hoping to collect the money owed to Robinson's heirs. On the day after Pendleton arrived in town, both newspapers carried advertisements entreating all who were indebted to the estate "to discharge their respective balances without delay" (*Va. Gazette*, 26 Apr. 1793; *Virginia Gazette, and Weekly Advertiser*, 26 Apr. 1783, supplement). See also David J. Mays, ed., *Letters and Papers of Edmund Pendleton*, II, 443; *Papers of Madison*, IV, 227, n. 4.

Virginia Delegates to Benjamin Harrison

RC (Virginia State Library). In the hand of Theodorick Bland, except for the signatures of Arthur Lee and John Francis Mercer. Cover franked and addressed by Bland to "His Excelly. Benjn: Harrison Esqr. Govr. of Virginia." Docketed, "Lr. from the Deleg: in Congress, April 29th. 1783." The absence of JM's signature, even though he apparently was in Philadelphia on 29 April when he wrote to Jefferson and Washington (*qq.v.*), may reflect his preoccupation with other matters requiring attention before his departure from the city on that day with the family of William Floyd. See JM Notes, 25–26 Apr. 1783, and n. 2.

PHILADELPHIA April 29th. 1783

SR.

By yesterdays post we were Honord with Yr. Excellencys favor of the 19th Inst. We have informed Mr. Nathan of its contents, so far as they related to him. Mr. Pollock has declined offering any security for the present, as he expects the returnd Bills themselves, which he says will be the best Vouchers in his power to give.[1] We doubt not your having received, before this, the official information of the Cessation of Hostilities & the Proclamation Issued by Congress.[2]

Nothing Material has happend Since our last, except that it has been moved in Congress, by us, in order to sound the present disposition viz "that the United States in Congress assembled will and they do hereby accept the Cession of Territory made to them in the act of the Legislature of the Commonwealth of Virginia bearing date the   day of   on the Terms and stipulations therein mentiond, except so much thereof as stipulates that the U. S. in Congress assembled shall guarantee to the said Commonwealth the remaining Territory containd within the Bounds therein described"[3] It was committed and has produced a report of the Committe viz that the report of the former committe on the Cessions be taken up and Considerd; that report Yr. Excellency has been heretofore informd, has been repeatedly considerd and as often laid aside,[4] nor shd. we have now taken any steps to call it into view, but that we considerd it as our duty to produce if possible some decisive determination on a matter so important to the welfare of our state, and of such consequence to the U States in General.[5]

The report has not yet been taken up, on the recommendation of the Comme., but we expect will in a few days, when we shall inform Yr. Excellency of its fate[6]   we are respectfully Sr.

Yr. Excellys most obedt. Svts

THEOK: BLAND JR.
JOHN F. MERCER
A LEE

[1] Harrison to Delegates, 19 Apr. 1783, and nn. 1–7.

[2] *Ibid.*, and n. 8; Randolph to JM, 26 Apr. 1783.

[3] JM Notes, 9 Apr. 1783, and nn. 2–11; 18 Apr. 1783, and nn. 2–6. Except for unimportant differences in capitalization, punctuation, and abbreviation, Bland correctly quoted his motion of 23 April (NA: PCC, No. 30, fol. 579; JCC, XXIV, 271–72). In the offer of cession of 2 January 1781, the Virginia General Assembly listed the following among the provisos to which Congress must agree if it accepted the grant: "That all the remaining territory of Virginia, included between the

Atlantic Ocean and the southeast side of the river Ohio, and the Maryland, Pennsylvania and North Carolina boundary lines dividing them from Virginia, shall be guaranteed to the Commonwealth of Virginia by the said United States" (*JHDV*, Oct. 1780, p. 80; *Papers of Madison*, II, 72–77; 300, and n. 2; 301, n. 3). Of these boundary controversies, the ones with Pennsylvania and Maryland had been mostly adjusted, even though many Virginians who found that they had settled outside their native state continued to be unhappy, and the jurisdictional division of Chesapeake Bay between Virginia and Maryland was still unclear. The southwestern boundaries of Virginia had not been precisely defined, but Virginia and North Carolina were not sharply in conflict over that issue (*Papers of Madison*, II, 53, n. 3; III, 14, n. 17; 138, n. 7; 313, n. 2; IV, 38, n. 3; 52, n. 2; 118, n. 3; 126, n. 1; 154; 155; 184, n. 2; 187, n. 1; 215, n. 2; 268, n. 27; 287, n. 27; 341, n. 5; V, 115–16; 119, n. 19; 276–77; 277, nn. 4, 5, 8, 9; *JHDV*, May 1783, p. 90).

4 John Rutledge, chairman of the committee, reported on 25 April: "The Comee to whom was refr'd a Motion of Mr. Bland, of the 23 April, report, That, in their opinion, it will be proper for Congress to proceed to a Determination on the report of 3d. Novr. 1781 respecting the Cession from the State of Virginia, & that a decision upon the sd. Motion be *postponed*, until that report shall be taken into consideration" (NA: PCC, No. 30, fol. 577; No. 186, fol. 97). See n. 6, below.

The report on 3 November 1781, drafted by Elias Boudinot, chairman, on behalf "of the former committee on the Cessions," occasioned much inconclusive debate at that time but was not spread on the journal of Congress until 1 May 1782 (*JCC*, XXI, 1098, and n. 2; XXII, 225–32, 240–41; *Papers of Madison*, III, 294; 295, and n. 6; 304, and n. 1; 305, n. 2; IV, 157–59; 198, n. 6; 206, n. 2; 219–20; 221, n. 11). During the next eleven months, although the problem of the western lands was vigorously discussed several times in Congress, the Boudinot report apparently had not been revived. See, for example, *JCC*, XXII, 423, 604; *Papers of Madison*, V, 115–16; 117, n. 9; 201, n. 9; 292, n. 19; JM Notes, 9 Apr., and n. 2; 18 Apr. 1783.

5 The delegates probably hoped that Congress would reach a "decisive determination" upon the subject of Bland's motion in time for the result to be laid before the Virginia General Assembly during its session of May 1783.

6 The report of the Rutledge committee was not "taken up" and accepted by Congress until 4 June (*JCC*, XXIV, 381). The Virginia General Assembly, although informed on 19 June 1783 by Governor Harrison of this action, adjourned nine days later after instructing its delegates to seek Congress' consent to a larger reservation northwest of the Ohio River for bounty lands to allot to Virginia veterans than was withheld in the offer of cession (Executive Letter Book, 1783–1786, p. 157, MS in Va. State Library; *JHDV*, May 1783, pp. 90, 93; NA: PCC, No. 75, fols. 386 87).

To Edmund Randolph

RC (LC: Madison Papers). Unsigned but in JM's hand. Cover missing. Letter docketed by Randolph, "James Madison. (of Congress). April: 29. 1783."

PHILADA. Apl. 29. 1783

MY DEAR SIR

Yesterday's post was the third that has arrived successively without a line from you.[1]

The Definitive Treaty it is said is to be remitted to the two Imperial Courts for their approbation, before the last hand will be put to it. This will be mere compliment however, and as the parties have settled their contests without their intermediation there can be no pretext if there were a disposition to meddle.[2] It appears from English Gazettes that Shelburne has been so pressed by the unpopularity of some of the terms of peace, that he cd. not prevent a vote of the House of Commons declaring them to be disadvantageous & dishonorable. The consequence prognosticated is another change of the Administration in favor of North's & Fox's parties, who have made a common cause agst. Shelburne.[3]

The propositions relative to the National debt, with an address enforcing it & referring to sundry documents &c is completed and will soon be forwarded to the Legislatures.[4] Mr. Jefferson will have given you the general views of Congress on this subject.[5]

[1] Randolph to JM, 26 Apr. 1783, and n. 1.

[2] For the efforts of the Tsarina Catherine the Great of Russia and Emperor Joseph II of Austria to mediate between Great Britain and her enemies, see *Papers of Madison*, II, 56, n. 3; 165; 167, n. 3; IV, 5; 174–76, nn. 6, 12; 180–81; V, 235; 313, n. 1, 467; 469, n. 9.

JM probably derived his information concerning the referral of the treaty to these sovereigns from the *Pennsylvania Packet* of 24 April. This newspaper noted that an unidentified writer, in a letter dated 2 March in Paris, had stated: "The definitive treaty is in great forwardness, and there appears nothing in the way of its speedy conclusion. The belligerent powers have communicated it to the courts of Vienna and Petersburg, as mediators, and now await their answer." In a letter written in Paris on 28 March 1783 to Benjamin Vaughan, John Jay commented ironically upon a report that Great Britain and France had asked the "two Imperial Courts to send mediatorial ambassadors" to Paris to witness "the execution of the definitive treaties" (Wharton, *Revol. Dipl. Corr.*, VI, 349–50). For Vaughan, see comment by Jefferson, 25 Jan. 1783, n. 1.

[3] Delegates to Harrison, 10 Apr. 1783, and n. 10. On 24 February, three days after the House of Commons by a vote of 207 to 190 adopted "*Resolutions of Censure on the Terms of the Peace*," the Earl of Shelburne resigned as prime minister. Efforts to form a new ministry were unsuccessful until 1 April 1783, when William Henry Cavendish Bentinck, third Duke of Portland, became first lord of the treasury and head of a coalition "Government," comprising adherents of Charles James Fox and Lord North. In this new ministry North was home secretary and Fox, foreign secretary (*Hansard's Parliamentary Debates*, XXIII, cols. 498–571, esp. 571; A. W. Ward, C. W. Prothero, Stanley Leathes, eds., *Cambridge Modern History* [13 vols.; Cambridge, England, 1902–12], VI, 463–64). The *Pennsylvania Packet* of 24 April reported an unconfirmed rumor that Shelburne and other members of his ministry had "intimated to the king their resolution of resigning." The next day Congress received a letter addressed to Robert R. Livingston, secretary for foreign affairs, by Lafayette from Bordeaux on 2 March 1783, stating that news of North's replacing Shelburne as prime minister had greeted him in that French port. "But," Lafayette

added, "I can not give it as certain" (NA: PCC, No. 185, III, 63; Wharton, *Revol. Dipl. Corr.*, VI, 269–70). See also Delegates to Harrison, 22 Apr. 1783, n. 3.

⁴ Address to States, 25 Apr. 1783, ed. n., and nn. 5, 10, 23, 30, 31, 33.

⁵ JM to Randolph, 22 Apr. 1783, and citations in n. 6.

To George Washington

RC (LC: Washington Papers). Addressed to "His Excellency General Washington." Cover missing. A draft of this letter, varying from recipient's copy only in abbreviations, capitalization, and punctuation, is in LC: Madison Papers.

PHILADA. Apr. 29. 1783.

SIR

I have been honored with Your Excellency's favor of the 22d. inst: bearing testimony to the merits & talents of Mr. McHenry.[1] The character which I had preconceived of this Gentleman was precisely that which your representation has confirmed. As Congress have not yet fixed the peace establishment for their foreign affairs and will not probably fill up vacancies unless there be some critical urgency, until such an Establishment be made, it is uncertain when an opportunity will present itself, of taking into consideration the wishes & merits of Mr. McHenry.[2] Should my stay here be protracted till that happens, which I do not at present expect,[3] I shall feel an additional pleasure in promoting the public interest from my knowledge that I at the same time fulfill both your Excellency's public judgment & private inclination.

I have the honor to be with perfect respect & sincere regard yr. Excelly's Obt. & hble Servt.

J. MADISON JR.

[1] *Q.v.*, and n. 1.

[2] JM Notes, 4 Apr., and n. 10. On 12 June 1783, the day after James McHenry entered Congress as a delegate from Maryland, Congress gave a general answer to what "the peace establishment for their foreign affairs" would be by unanimously adopting a committee report, drafted by JM, which declared in part that "the true interest of these States requires that they shd. be as little as possible entangled in the politics and controversies of European Nations" (NA: PCC, No. 79, III, 255; JM Notes, 12 June 1783 [LC: Madison Papers]; *JCC*, XXIV, 389, 392–94; Boyd, *Papers of Jefferson*, VI, 276).

[3] Rev. James Madison to JM, 15 Apr. 1783, and n. 6.

INDEX

NOTE: Persons are identified on pages cited below in boldface type. Identifications made in earlier volumes are noted immediately after the person's name.

Madison, James, Jr.—*Continued*
  career—*Continued*
    papers edited by, 5 n. 4, 22 n. 1, 26
    n. 2, 53 n. 1, 151 n. 21, 157 n. 3, 222
    n. 11, 233 n. 1, 242 n. 1, 268 n. 13,
    354, 392 n. 1, 441 n. 10, 466 n. 6,
    472 n. 2, 482 n. 7, 498 n. 2; place of
    residence in Philadelphia, 28 n. 25,
    64, 234, 268 n. 13, 460 n. 8; "Que-
    ries" sent Ambler by, 210–11 and
    n. 1; tenure in Congress of, 464 and
    n. 6, 505
  views of: J. Adams, 53 n. 1, 221, 355,
    365, 376–77; army demobilization
    and discontent, 31, 230, 232–33,
    272, 286, 308, 348, 355–56, 375, 392,
    486 n. 3, 493; army officers' me-
    morial and pensions, 19 n. 3, 20–21,
    22, 34, 39, 55–56, 145–46, 148–49,
    157, 223, 250, 284 n. 4, 298, 301 n. 2;
    Articles of Confederation, 270–71,
    275 n. 6, 312; assumption of state
    debts by Congress, 290, 294 n. 17,
    310, 313, 400, 401–2, 406, 440, 477,
    478 n. 1, 482 n. 10; Barbé-Marbois,
    51 n. 8, 158, 222 n. 5, 383; coercing
    a state, 230, 265, 270–71, 275 n. 8,
    312; commerce of U.S. and Va.,
    291, 311, 356, 489, 490–91; Con-
    gress, legislative or executive in
    nature, 252 n. 14, 270–73, 274 n. 4;
    consular convention, 5 and n. 3,
    15–16; convention to amend Ar-
    ticles of Confederation, 426 n. 9;
    conventions called for by a few
    states only, 425; Dana, 452, 453
    n. 2; date of end of hostilities, 449–
    50; domestic tranquility required
    for Union, 258 n. 4, 287, 290, 293
    n. 15, 296 n. 42, 327, 392, 402, 429–
    30, 430 n. 3, 469, 470 n. 3, 487, 494;
    Dyer, 371 n. 4, 377 n. 3; English
    constitutional doctrine, 271; finan-
    cial issues in general, 12 n. 1, 22,
    24–25, 31, 34 n. 17, 55–56, 143–47,
    148–49 and n. 3, 153 nn. 33, 42, 156,
    166 nn. 7, 8, 174, 193, 195–96, 197
    n. 12, 250, 258 n. 4, 260, 262 n. 7,
    265, 270–73, 285, 290, 298, 308, 309–
    11, 311–14 and n. 1, 326–27, 348,
    356, 370, 374 n. 4, 392, 429–30, 439,
    440, 469, 488–94, 504; foreign af-
    fairs, France, 24–25, 31, 56 n. 8, 130
    n. 1, 221, 230, 348, 355, 363–65, 368
    n. 36, 369 n. 37, 392, 493; foreign
    affairs, Great Britain, 4, 31, 194,
    355–56 and n. 10, 430, 504; foreign
    affairs, Netherlands, Spain, Swe-
    den, 157, 158, 355, 364–65, 493;
    Franklin, 340–41, 355, 380, 430, 431
    n. 5; A. Hamilton, 35, 36, 37 n. 4,
    38 n. 9, 126 nn. 17, 18, 128 n. 39,
    143, 149 and n. 3, 153 n. 43, 158,
    175 n. 17, 217 n. 6, 276 n. 16, 425,
    456, 477, 481, 487–88, 497 n. 35; im-
    post amendment and tariffs, 22,
    55–56, 140 n. 18, 146–47, 149, 156,
    193, 256, 260, 262 n. 8, 264 n. 23,
    272, 311, 326, 374 n. 4, 407 n. 2, 429–
    30, 489, 496 n. 19; instructions from
    state legislature, 35, 147, 152 n. 32,
    274 n. 4, 383–84, 385 n. 14; isola-
    tionism, 223, 272, 287, 365, 452–53,
    495 n. 11, 505 (*see also* Continental
    Congress, actions on isolationism);
    Jay, 3 n. 2, 355; Jefferson, 4, 22, 41,
    64–65, 132, 156, 177, 194, 200 n. 10,
    207, 220, 223, 232, 242, 254–55, 257,
    309–10, 356, 373 n. 4, 397 n. 4, 440,
    459, 481, 482 n. 9, 504; La Luzerne,
    51 n. 8, 222 n. 5; H. Laurens, 355,
    356 n. 10; A. Lee, 157 n. 6, 286, 430;
    Livingston, 223, 450, 451 n. 4; loan-
    office certificates, 291, 292; loans
    in Europe, 31, 56 n. 8, 260, 272,
    392, 493; Loyalists and other Brit-
    ish subjects, 22, 47, 48 n. 11, 288
    and n. 1, 289, 465; McHenry, 505;
    Mercer, 256, 257 n. 2, 258 n. 4,
    285, 286–87, 288 n. 1, 289, 299 n. 4,
    308; military operations, 4, 223,
    288; R. Morris, 120, 305, 308, 326,
    348, 356, 409, 410 n. 2, 411, 439, 486
    n. 3; nationalism and states' rights,
    36–37, 55, 144–45, 146, 147, 151
    nn. 10, 23, 152 nn. 27, 28, 230, 270–
    72, 274 n. 4, 275 n. 8, 276 n. 16, 277
    n. 28, 285, 286–87, 314 n. 1, 326,
    429–30, 487, 489; new members of
    Congress, 16; newspapers, 4, 156,
    157 n. 4, 218 and n. 1; peace nego-
    tiations, 3 n. 2, 4, 22, 31, 49, 165 n. 3,
    194, 221, 224, 229, 230, 232, 242,
    254–55 and n. 2, 257, 286, 308, 326,
    327 n. 3, 328–29, 340, 348, 355, 363–
    65, 368 n. 28, 385 n. 11, 430, 481–82,

Peace treaties, definitive, 245 n. 3, 307, 315 n. 14, 331 n. 6, 332 nn. 8, 9, 333–34, 365, 394, 395, 439, 440 n. 2, 447, 452, 457, 458 n. 3, 465, 480 n. 3, 481, 486 n. 2, 504 and n. 2

Peace treaty, preliminary: between Great Britain and France, 206 n. 13, 231 n. 10, 243, 244 n. 2, 253 and n. 3, 254, 255 n. 2, 257, 308 n. 4, 331 n. 4, 333, 335, 338 nn. 16–18, 340, 351, 354 n. 4, 355, 356 n. 7, 360, 376, 382, 385 n. 1, 387, 388 nn. 2, 4, 389 and n. 2, 390, 391 n. 4, 394, 416, 418 n. 10, 422 n. 6, 440, 441 n. 4, 445, 446 n. 2, 447, 449–50, 450 and n. 3, 451 n. 4, 456–57, 464 n. 3, 465, 466 n. 4, 480 n. 3, 481–82, 504 and n. 3; between Great Britain and the Netherlands, 245 n. 3, 255 n. 2, 308 n. 4, 335, 338 n. 18, 340, 352 n. 14, 388 n. 4, 389, 447, 448 n. 9; between Great Britain and Spain, 4, 9, 50 n. 6, 165 n. 3, 206 n. 13, 238, 243, 244 n. 2, 245 n. 3, 253 and n. 3, 255 n. 2, 328, 331 nn. 4, 6, 335, 338 nn. 16, 18, 340, 352 n. 14, 355, 356 n. 7, 360, 361, 372 n. 2, 376, 383, 385 n. 1, 387, 388 n. 4, 389 and n. 2, 391 n. 4, 395 n. 2, 422 n. 6, 440, 441 n. 4, 445, 446 n. 2, 447, 449, 450, 451 nn. 3, 4, 457, 463 n. 2, 464 n. 3, 480 n. 3, 504 and n. 3; between Great Britain and the United States, 220 n. 4, 231 n. 10, 232 n. 3, 237, 241 and n. 2, 243, 244 and n. 2, 249 n. 3, 254, 268 n. 11, 277, 278 n. 4, 281, 286, 327 n. 6, 330 n. 1, 331 n. 6, 333 n. 13, 333–36 and nn. 7–9, 337 nn. 10–14, 340, 341 nn. 4, 5, 356, 357 n. 17, 360, 361, 362, 365, 369 n. 44, 370, 375, 378 n. 14, 379, 380, 382, 387, 388 nn. 3, 4, 391 n. 4, 392 n. 5, 422, 430, 435, 439–40 and n. 2, 442–43, 444 nn. 2, 6, 445, 447, 450 n. 3, 456, 458 n. 3, 462 n. 2, 466 n. 4, 472 n. 4, 479, 480 n. 7, 481–82, 483, 486 n. 2, 499, 500 n. 6, 504 and n. 3; see also Continental Congress, actions on preliminary articles of peace, preliminary treaty's "separate article"

Pendleton, Edmund (see II, 67 n. 1), 12 n. 1, 248, 249 n. 3, 343–45 and nn. 1, 8, 12, 346 nn. 13, 15, 422–23 and nn. 2, 7, 8, 424 nn. 9, 11, 460–61 and nn. 3, 4, 500, 501 n. 10

Penet, d'Acosta Frères et Cie, 244 n. 4, 342 and n. 1, 353, 412–13 and n. 3, 414 nn. 5–7, 11, 12, 415 n. 14, 475 n. 5

Penet, J. Pierre (see I, 294 n. 2), 342 n. 1, 353

Pennsylvania: boundaries of Md., Va. and, 133–34, 156, 245, 246 n. 7, 373 n. 4, 445 n. 8, 502 n. 3; boundary of Conn. and, 3 and n. 1, 6, 7 n. 5, 21; British prisoners of war in, 123 n. 1, 124 n. 12, 125 nn. 15–17, 229, 231 nn. 3, 4, 8, 265, 267 n. 10, 268 nn. 11, 12, 286; constitution, 118, 124 n. 9; creditors of Congress and, 251 and n. 3, 262 n. 6, 263 n. 20, 264, 267 n. 7, 273, 291, 292, 295 n. 35, 310; currency, 183 n. 2, 211 n. 3, 268 n. 11, 474 n. 1; delegates in Congress, 157 n. 9, 187, 198, 210 n. 4, 213, 216, 226, 227 n. 15, 251, 258, 259, 261, 264 n. 23, 323, 330, 370, 374 n. 4, 404 n. 25, 407, 408 and n. 2, 411 n. 7, 420, 437, 469, 472 n. 1, 477 (see also FitzSimons; Mifflin; Montgomery, Joseph; Peters; Wilson); government, 117–19, 123 nn. 1–5, 124 nn. 6, 9, 10, 14, 125 nn. 15, 17, 126 n. 20, 133–34, 138 n. 6, 142, 145, 148, 151 n. 23, 168 n. 21, 170, 187, 189 n. 6, 230, 231 n. 8, 263 n. 14, 265, 267 nn. 7, 10, 268 nn. 11, 12, 286, 370, 433, 434 n. 10, 471 and n. 1; history of, 101; impost amendment and, 291; Indians and, 110–11, 433, 434 n. 10; laws, 109; map of, 76; population, 432; requisitions of Congress and, 30 n. 8, 119, 291, 432, 434 n. 5; separatist movement in, 133–34, 138 n. 6, 156, 157 n. 9; taxes and, 152 n. 29, 161, 168 n. 21, 198, 199 n. 10, 260, 263 n. 14, 291; troops, 41 n. 8, 123 n. 2, 125 n. 14, 145, 270 n. 20, 486 n. 3; Vermont and, 156; western lands and, 291, 443, 472 n. 4; mention of, 4 n. 1, 251, 345 n. 8

Pennsylvania Gazette, 27 n. 4, 326, 441 nn. 3, 4

Pennsylvania Journal, 308 n. 4, 326, 333 n. 13, 339 n. 22, 354 n. 4, 391 n. 3, 450 n. 2

Pennsylvania Packet, 11 n. 16, 40 n. 1, 42 n. 2, 218 n. 1, 231 n. 10, 232 n. 3, 238 n. 6, 255 n. 2, 292 n. 1, 306 n. 7, 308 n. 4, 326, 333 n. 13, 339 n. 22, 354 n. 4

10, 11, 250, 252 n. 9, 259, 260–61, 262 n. 11, 305 n. 4, 408, 452, 472 n. 2, 473 n. 6; mention of, 43 n. 3, 48 nn. 1, 10

views of: funds for Congress, 147–48, 159, 274, 277 n. 28, 357, 365 n. 2, 404 n. 14, 468 n. 1; imposts, 162, 249, 250, 259, 298; Jefferson's mission to France, 233; Loyalists' property, 47; military issues, 43 n. 3, 129, 249, 259, 348, 420; peace negotiations and treaty, 359, 360, 363, 376, 383, 385 n. 13, 420; piracies and felonies at sea, 189 n. 6; requisitions, 24, 27 n. 8, 35, 36, 126 n. 17, 142, 170, 173, 175 nn. 11, 17, 188, 197 n. 9, 199 n. 6, 210 n. 4, 213, 215, 216, 217 nn. 7, 10, 297 n. 44, 401, 407, 408, 427 n. 11; supplies for prisoners of war, 117–19, 123 n. 2, 125 n. 15, 229–30, 267 n. 10, 268 n. 11; treaties of commerce, 452; Va. tobacco for merchants-capitulant, 213, 214 n. 7; western lands, 471, 472 nn. 2, 3, 503 n. 4

St. Croix River, 334, 336 n. 7, 340
St. John, Canada, 443 n. 1
St. Kitts, 220 n. 4, 241 n. 2
St. Lawrence River, 334, 336 n. 8, 340
St. Lucia, 388 n. 4, 389
St. Marys River, NW. Terr., 334, 340, 389
St. Petersburg, 427 n. 14, 452, 504 n. 2
St. Pierre, 60 n. 10, 388 n. 4
St. Thomas, 219, 220 n. 4
St. Vincent, 387, 388 n. 4
Salaries; see Prices, salaries, or fees
Salem, N.J., 169 n. 34
Salmon, Thomas, 73, 75
Salomon, Haym (see IV, 108 n. 2), 326 n. 4
Salt, 160, 161, 167 nn. 17, 18, 193, 298–99, 311, 350; see also Taxes, salt, tariffs and drawbacks
Samuel Inglis and Company, 379 n. 2, 455 n. 2, 459, 460 n. 5
Santo Domingo, 114, 335
Saratoga, N.Y., 138 n. 4
Satchell, William, Sr., 183 and nn. 6, 7, 211
Savage, Thomas Lyttleton, 13, 241 n. 1
Savannah, Ga., 106, 107, 436 n. 4
Scotland, 75, 82, 93, 165 n. 3, 275 n. 10

Sectionalism, 36, 38 n. 9, 159, 161, 163, 190 n. 13, 201, 207, 208 n. 3, 217 n. 4, 247, 248 n. 3, 249–50, 260, 264–65, 269 n. 14, 272, 273, 282–83, 284 n. 4, 286–87, 288 n. 16, 289–90, 291–92, 296 n. 40, 297 n. 44, 297–99, 314 n. 1, 315 n. 14, 351, 352 n. 11, 408 n. 2, 424–25
Senegal, 387, 388 n. 4
Sever, William, 404 n. 15
Shakespeare, William, 378 n. 10
Shattuck, William, 339 n. 22
Shelburne, William Petty, Earl of, 9, 10 n. 14, 132 n. 1, 200, 328, 329, 331 n. 4, 354 n. 4, 355, 357 n. 17, 366 n. 9, 367 n. 12, 382, 416, 418 n. 11, 449 n. 10, 504 and n. 3
Ship money, 272, 273, 276 n. 18
Shippen, Alice Lee (Mrs. William), 41 n. 8
Shippen, William, Jr., 41 and **n. 8**
Short, William (see III, 270 n. 2), 416, 417 n. 6
Sidney (Sydney), Algernon, 85
Silhouette, Étienne de, 100
Simmons, Francis, 233 n. 3
Simons, Maurice (see I, 229 n. 2), 184, 185 n. 6
Sitgreaves, John, 446, **448 n. 1,** 449, 460 n. 4
Slaves: British take, 48 n. 1, 209 n. 12, 296 n. 40, 337 n. 14, 344, 458 n. 3, 463 n. 2, 466 n. 3, 479, 480 n. 7; military service of, 153 n. 35; requisitions or tax apportionments and, 35, 153 nn. 35, 42, 190, 199 n. 7, 215, 216 n. 2, 256, 292, 297 n. 44, 311, 313–14, 316 nn. 19, 20, 402, 405 n. 27, 406, 407 n. 4, 407–8 and n. 2, 409 nn. 3, 5, 425, 427 n. 10, 433 n. 2, 435 and n. 2, 440, 492, 496 n. 27; mention of, 138 n. 6, 184, 185 n. 5, 229 n. 2, 288 n. 16, 414 n. 10
Smith, Adam, 86
Smith, Israel, 133, **138 n. 4**
Smith, Thomas, 474 n. 2
South America, 114–15, 396 n. 6
South Carolina: commerce of, 169 n. 33, 292; delegates in Congress, 24, 27 n. 8, 47, 129–30, 198, 210 n. 4, 213, 216, 217 n. 9, 226, 250, 259, 261, 306 n. 4, 323, 368 n. 36, 374 n. 4, 400, 407, 408 and n. 2, 427 n. 15, 437, 444 n. 2, 468 n. 1, 469, 471, 473 n. 6, 486 n. 3 (see also Gervais; Izard; Mathews; Ram-

The Papers of James Madison

DESIGNED BY JOHN B. GOETZ
COMPOSED BY THE UNIVERSITY OF CHICAGO PRESS
IN LINOTYPE JANSON WITH DISPLAY LINES IN
MONOTYPE JANSON AND CASLON OLD STYLE
PRINTED BY THE UNIVERSITY OF CHICAGO PRESS
ON WARREN'S UNIVERSITY TEXT, A PAPER WATERMARKED
WITH JAMES MADISON'S SIGNATURE AND MADE EXPRESSLY
FOR THE VOLUMES OF THIS SET
PLATES PRINTED BY MERIDEN GRAVURE COMPANY
BOUND BY A. C. ENGDAHL IN COLUMBIA BAYSIDE LINEN
AND STAMPED IN GENUINE GOLD